Bevis Hillier, like John Betjeman, went to Magdalen College, Oxford, where he read Modern History and in 1961 was awarded the Gladstone Memorial Prize. He then joined the editorial staff of *The Times*, subsequently edited *The Connoisseur* and *The Times Saturday Review*, and became Associate Editor of the *Los Angeles Times* colour magazine. He has written several books on art and design, including the earliest book on *Art Deco* (1968). John Betjeman, whom he knew for many years, authorised him to write this biography. Apart from his wide use of the printed and archive sources he also talked to Betjeman's friends and contemporaries, many of whom have since died. When researching this book he received a Leverhulme Fellowship and a Huntingdon Library Fellowship.

Bids to be the standard biography.'

'Bevis Hillier approaches his poet, John Betjeman, with all the energy and concentration of a true enthusiast. His first volume *Young Betjeman* which takes us to the poet's marriage in 1933, not only tells us everything that is important, inspiring and ridiculous about Betjeman but also gives a wide cross-section of the people he knew and loved (or hated) and the places he loved.'

'An attractive, affectionate portrait.'

'This book shows that Bevis Hillier was a natural choice as Betjeman's official biographer. It is impossible to imagine anyone having been more enthusiastic, sympathetic and industrious. He has produced a book which all Betjeman's admirers will find essential reading.'

'Bevis Hillier provides hours of sheer enchantment with this biography ... there is a giggle in almost every chapter ... Bevis Hillier has caught his subject beautifully.'

'Bevis Hillier knew Betjeman well and this superbly written and re-searched biography was authorised by Betjeman himself, but there is no whitewash and a colourful picture emerges of an eccentric and vulnerable young man long before he became a national uncle.'

'*Young Betjeman* is a well-wrought biography, deeply researched and ebulliently written ... Volume two of the biography will be awaited impatiently.'

'Hillier has discharged his biographical duties with an enthusiasm that would have delighted Betjeman. It is a virtuoso feat of gossip, and vividly evokes the world as seen by Betjeman.'

YOUNG BETJEMAN

BEVIS HILLIER

CARDÍNAL

A CARDINAL BOOK

First published by John Murray (Publishers) Ltd 1988
Published in Cardinal by Sphere Books Ltd 1989
1 3 5 7 9 10 8 6 4 2

Printed and bound in Great Britain by
Richard Clay Ltd, Bungay, Suffolk

Sphere Books Ltd
A Division of
Macdonald & Co. (Publishers) Ltd
66/73 Shoe Lane, London EC4P 4AB
A member of Maxwell Pergamon Publishing Corporation plc

To my dear sister Mary and her family –
Nigel, Amy and Oliver Thompson.

CONTENTS

LIST OF ILLUSTRATIONS

PLATES

LINE ILLUSTRATIONS

ACKNOWLEDGEMENTS

Plates: 1, 2, 3, 4, 6, 7, 8, 9, 14, 17, John Betjeman Archive; 5, 11, Miss Mary
Bouman; 10, *Telegraph*, Padstow; 12, Mrs Kenneth Crookshank; 13, BBC
Hulton Picture Library; 15, the late Wilfrid Blunt; 16, 21, the late John Bowle;
18 and p.86, John Piper; 19, Alan Pryce-Jones; 20, Oxford University Press;
22, Lady Fergusson of Kilkerran; 23, the late Lionel Perry; 24, David Synnott;
25, 34, the Earl and Countess of Longford; 26, Camera Press; 27, G.R.
Barcley-Smith; 28, 35, 36, the late Mrs Christopher Sykes; 29, Lady Mary
Dunn; 30, the Hon. Mrs Derek Jackson; 31, the late Christine, Countess of
Longford; 32, Mr Thomas Pakenham; 33, Joan Eyres Monsell; 37, 39, 40, 42,
Penelope Betjeman Archive; 38, Lady Harrod; 41, Author's Collection;
p.294, McPherson Library, University of Victoria, British Columbia.

ACKNOWLEDGEMENTS

My first and greatest debts of gratitude are to John Betjeman, for authorizing this book and recording some recollections for it, and to Penelope Betjeman, for giving all possible help and encouragement until her death in 1986; and I make grateful acknowledgement to their Estates.

I am deeply indebted to Mr Alan Bell, Librarian of Rhodes House, Oxford, for the time he has given unstintingly to reading the chapters and commenting on them. Ms Margaret Allen also made valuable suggestions for emendations and cuts. The major task of copy-editing was most admirably carried out by Ms Jan Dalley. And the book owes much to the tenacious and trustworthy research of Miss Doris Baum and of my mother, Mary Hillier.

The book's publisher, Mr John G. Murray, has shown an exemplary patience during the years it has taken to research and write the volume. He gave wise and tactful counsel both before and after it was delivered. I thank him and the staff at John Murray for their careful work, and Mr Douglas Matthews, Librarian of the London Library, for the excellent index.

My father, Jack Hillier, has read the text at all stages and has often urged on me the restraint which I did not inherit from him. Mr Anthony Hobson, Mr Derek Hudson (who also supplied recollections) and Dr Nicholas Orme kindly read certain chapters and offered advice which I took.

The late Professor J.E. Bowle gave particularly generous help with the Marlborough and Oxford chapters and allowed me to quote from his unpublished memoirs. Mrs Vera Moule (*née* Spencer-Clarke), besides remembering her friendship with Betjeman, permitted me to quote from the poems he wrote her. Mr Duncan Andrews of New York gave me the fullest access to his remarkable collection of Betjemaniana.

Without fellowships from the Leverhulme Trust and the Huntington Library of San Marino, California, and a loan from Barclay's Bank (thanks to the imaginative policy of Mr Christopher Norman-Butler and Mr Robert Moore) I could not have completed the book. I am also grateful to my employers on the *Los Angeles Times* – Mr Tom Johnson, Mr William F. Thomas, Mrs Jean Sharley Taylor and Mr Wallace Guenther – for their sympathetic interest in the book's progress during the last four years.

I wish to thank the librarians and staff of the British Library; the Bodleian Library, Oxford; the National Library of Scotland, Edinburgh; the McPherson Library of the University of Victoria, British Columbia, Canada; the Huntington Library; and the Marion E. Wade Center, Wheaton College, Illinois. Staff of these libraries who have done most to make my work lighter and more enjoyable are named below, in what is intended as a comprehensive list of people who have given me help:

Sir Harold Acton; the late Sir John Addis; Mr Kingsley Amis; Mr Mark Amory; Mr Clive Aslet; Mr Eric Asprey; Mr Philip Asprey; Mr and Mrs Kalidas Banerji; Mr G.R. Barcley-Smith; Mrs Alan Bell (who kindly read the proofs); Mr and Mrs Julian Berry; Mr Dietrich Bertz; Mr Jerry Bick; Lady Rachel Billington; Miss Rose Billington; the Countess of Birkenhead; Mrs Michael Birkin; Lady Caroline Blackwood; the late Noël Blakiston; the late Anthony Blunt; the late Wilfrid Blunt; Miss Mary Bouman; Mr J.B. Brown; Mr Arthur Byron; Mr Humphrey Carpenter; the late Lord David Cecil; Mrs Hugh Cecil; Mr Winston Churchill, MP; the late Lord Clark; Mr George Clive; Lady Mary Clive; Lady Silvia Combe; Mr Peter Conrad; the late Lady Diana Cooper; Mrs Theodore Crombie; Mrs Kenneth Crookshank; Mrs Margaret Darlington; the late Villiers David; Mr Frank Delaney; the headmaster and secretary of the Dragon School, Oxford; Mr Albert Dubery; the Marquess and Marchioness of Dufferin and Ava; Lady Mary Dunn; Mr Humphrey Ellis; Lady Elton; Mr Adam Fergusson; Lady Fergusson of Kilkerran; Mr John Fernald; the late Peter Fleetwood-Hesketh; Mr Mario Galang; Mr Simon Garwood; the Hon. Mrs M. Geddes; Mr Howard Gerwing; the late A.R. Gidney; Mr Martin Gilbert; Mr R.C. Giles; Mr Anton Gill; Mr Mark Girouard; the late John Gloag; Dr George Gomez; Mr Chandra Gopal; Mrs Gwynnydd Gosling and the Highgate Literary and Scientific Institution; the late Lt. Col. Andrew Graham; Mr Maurice Green; Miss Ti Green; Mr Graham Greene; the late Joyce Grenfell; Father Bede Griffiths, OSB; Mr John Gross; Mrs Valerie Grove; Mr John Guest; Mr and Mrs Martin Haldane; Mr Dean W. Halliwell; Mr Iain Hamilton;

Mr William Hammond; the late P.J.R. Harding; the late Sir Roy Harrod; Lady Harrod; Lady Selina Hastings; Mrs Joan Hechle; the late Martin Higham; Mr Derek Hill; Mr John Hilton; Miss Sue Hodson; Miss Hilary Holland; Sir Jasper Hollom; Mr Vincent Hollom; Mr Richard Holmes; Mr Michael Holroyd; Mr Aaron Howard; Mr Philip Howard; Mr Derek Hudson; the Imperial War Museum; the Rev. Prebendary Gerard Irvine; the Hon. Mrs Pamela Jackson; the late Edward James; Mr Simon Jenkins; Mr Stephen Jessel; Mr George Jones; Mr and Mrs Girish Karnad; Mr John Keay; the late Lord Kinross; Mr John Sandall Knight; Mr Michael Knight; Mr Andrew Knox; Ms Virginia V. Kolb; Mrs Joan Kunzer; Miss Sharon Kusinoki; Mrs Marie-Jaqueline Lancaster; the late Sir Osbert Lancaster; Mr James Lees-Milne; the Hon. Mrs Patrick Leigh Fermor; Mr Anthony Lejeune; the late Christine, Countess of Longford; the Earl and Countess of Longford; Miss Winifred Macdonald; Mr Ruari McLean; the President and Fellows of Magdalen College, Oxford; the late Sir Lancelot Mallalieu; the late Sir William Mallalieu; Mr and Mrs Philip Mansergh; the Master and Librarian of Marlborough College; the Rev. Canon Paul Miller; Mr and Mrs Hugh Marsden Morgan; Mr and Mrs Walter Moule; Lord Moyne; Mr and Mrs John Mummery; the late Gerald Murray; Mr Alan Nightingale; Mr James Orr; Mr and Mrs Thomas Pakenham; Mr Michael Parkinson; the late Lionel Perry; Dr William Peterson; Mr Christopher Petter; Mr and Mrs John Piper; Sir Anthony Plowman; the Horace Plunkett Foundation, Oxford; Mr Anthony Powell and Lady Violet Powell; Mr Alan Pryce-Jones; Mr David Pryce-Jones; Mr Peter Quennell; Dr Robert Ravicz; the late Lord Redcliffe-Maud; Mr James Reeve; Mr Kenric Rice; Sir James Richards; Mrs Nancy Richardson; Mrs Fergus Rogers; Dr A.L. Rowse; Mr Hilary Rubinstein and A.P. Watt; Miss Joan Ryan (whose help at Victoria went 'far beyond the call of duty'); Dr and Mrs Charles Rycroft; Mrs Robert Sackville-West; Miss Anne Scott-James; Major Bruce Shand; Mr Leslie Sherwood (who read the typescript with great care); Mr Martyn Skinner; Mr David Soltau; Mr Neil Somerville and the BBC Written Archives Centre, Caversham; Mr John Sparrow; Dr and Mrs Richard Squires; Miss Jaci Stephen; Mrs Elizabeth Stevens and Curtis Brown; Sir Roy Strong; Sir John Summerson; Mr A.G. Swift; Dr George Swift; the late Christopher Sykes and the late Mrs Christopher Sykes; Mr David Synnott; the late Pierce Synnott; Mrs Michael Tait; Sir

George Tapps-Gervis-Meyrick; Mr A.J.P. Taylor; Mr Erreg Thami; Miss Brenda Thompson; Mrs Mari Meredyth Thompson; Mr F.P. Threadgill; Miss Elizabeth Tollinton; Mr Ion Trewin; Mr Edward Walton; the late Sir Ellis Waterhouse; Miss Sarah Waters; Mr Auberon Waugh; Senator Trevor West; the late Eric Walter White; the Countess of Wicklow; Sir Angus Wilson; Mrs Ann Wolff; Mrs Oliver Woods; and the late Douglas Woodruff.

PREFACE

Lord David Cecil's biography of Max Beerbohm contains the despairing sentence: 'Even less happened to Max in 1927 than in 1926.' No such phrase could be applied to John Betjeman. Admittedly, his was not a life of tumultuous action. He defended the Goths from the Vandals, but he killed no one, sacked no cities. Yet his life never stagnated. He was in love; he was embattled against the 'developers'; he was sunk in melancholy; he was making himself conspicuous. He attracted friends and made it his business to know people whom he thought worth knowing; so his biography inevitably becomes a 'John Betjeman and His Circle', if not a 'Life and Times'.

This book is not a 'critical biography'. That seems to me a bastard art-form, one which yokes two disciplines that do not belong together – historical narrative and literary criticism. However, the works which influence a poet *are* part of his life, and in Chapters 5 and 16 I have tried to show what, in Betjeman's case, those works were, and to suggest at what stages he may have encountered them. Obviously, a writer's own works are also part of his life; in Chapter 17, 'Steps to *Mount Zion*', I have surveyed and quoted from Betjeman's writings up to 31 December 1933, without attempting a comprehensive bibliography such as Dr William Peterson of the University of Maryland is now preparing.

The end of 1933 is the cut-off point of the volume, which covers Betjeman's life from his birth to his marriage. In rare instances I have trespassed beyond that date-limit, to round off a particular epoch. For example, 'Archie Rev', the chapter about Betjeman's work on the staff of *The Architectural Review*, looks ahead to his storming out of the job in 1935. Some reference is made, necessarily, to the growth of his interest in architecture, in Victoriana and the conservation of old buildings; but this will have a chapter to itself in Volume II, as will his radio and television broadcasting and his articles in *The Listener*.

A few further aspects of the book need explanation. After this preface, I refer to Betjeman throughout as 'John', except where the nearby mention of another John (John Bowle or John Sparrow, for example) might cause ambiguity. I do not do so to boast, by implication, of my friendship with Betjeman, but for the sake of greater simplicity and intimacy. I refer to the sixth Earl of Longford, on occasion, as 'Edward Longford' or 'Edward', and to his wife as 'Christine Longford' or 'Christine', because reference to 'Lord Longford' or 'Lady Longford' would be likely to suggest to most readers the present Earl and Countess. In the chapter on Oxford I write of the two university magazines as 'the *Cherwell*' and 'the *Isis*'. In my time at Oxford they were known simply as '*Cherwell*' and '*Isis*', and they are still known as such, but John Betjeman and his contemporaries all used the definite article in the titles, and I have retained this usage, except in the notes.

I have already done much of the research for Volume II. In the course of it, I spent a weekend with John and Myfanwy Piper. They did not meet Betjeman until 1937, but they lent me a document of some importance for this first volume. It was the typescript of a long poem which Betjeman had sent them in 1941 – the beginning of a verse autobiography then half-facetiously called 'The Epic'. Part of it, about his early experiences in Cornwall, Betjeman published (with some changes) as 'North Coast Recollections' in *Selected Poems* (1948). Much of the remainder was incorporated – again with revisions – into *Summoned by Bells* (1960). But some passages of 'The Epic' were never published, and I have quoted from them.

All sources are given in the notes, but a full bibliography will appear at the end of the second and final volume. In the meantime, those who would prefer a deck-chair book on Betjeman – a short Life they could read on holiday while acquiring a sun-tan – should be advised that two such books have been published: Derek Stanford's *John Betjeman* (1961) and Patrick Taylor-Martin's *John Betjeman: His Life and Work* (1983). Neither book weighs more than an avocado pear; and Taylor-Martin's has been reissued in paperback. Both authors have assembled the landmark facts of the poet's life. For those who find the written word itself too taxing, my own *John Betjeman: A Life in Pictures* (1984) tells the story in photographs and drawings, with the minimum of intrusive verbiage.

Taylor-Martin modestly begins his book: 'This is not the last word on John Betjeman.' My book will not be the last word, either, but I have set out to create a more fully-fleshed portrait. At the same time, I am not an admirer of the vacuum-cleaner school of biography. It has also been called the Nennian method, after the medieval Welsh historian Nennius. '*Coacervavi*,' he coolly admitted, '*omne quod inveni*' – 'I have made a heap of all that I have found.' Yet in one sense I feel kinship with Nennius, and with his predecessor, Bede: we are not only biographers; we are, willy-nilly, 'sources', too, chroniclers with direct access to some of the people in our chronicles. I have had advantages which no future biographer of Betjeman can have: friendship and long talks with him and his wife Penelope, and interviews with many of his friends and associates.

John Betjeman authorized this biography in 1976, in a letter to me and in a formal agreement with the publisher, John G. Murray. 'Authorized' does not mean 'bowdlerized' or 'censored' (though in one case I have given two brothers pseudonyms to save them embarrassment). Those readers who still think of Betjeman as 'a teddy-bear to the nation' may find that the book is not a portrait of *their* John Betjeman – the rumpled, genial figure so familiar from the television screen. A woman who had been a friend of his for over forty years wrote to me in 1976, on learning I was to write his life: 'People who think him cuddly are going to be surprised when they find out that he could be prickly.'

Betjeman created his own myth through his writings and his television stardom. The myth was nearer reality than most myths are: in general, he was as nice as he seemed. There may be some for whom the revealing of any flaw in him will seem the desecration of a national monument; but I have no training as a hagiographer. I have tried only to discover the truth and to tell it. For myself, I can say of my subject what his contemporary A.J.P. Taylor wrote in the preface to a Life of Betjeman's sometime employer Lord Beaverbrook: 'I loved the man.'

1

FAMILY

The Tulip I. From Dutch line I descend:
So exquisite and of so pure a strain . . .

Lucien (Chardon) de Rubempré,
'The Tulip', in Balzac, *Illusions Perdues*,
1837–43

In August 1934, a few days before his twenty-eighth birthday, John Betjeman went to the New Gallery cinema in London for a private viewing of the Gaumont-British film *Little Friend*. He had been film critic of the *Evening Standard* for seven months. The film, directed by Berthold Viertel, starred the fourteen-year-old schoolgirl Nova Pilbeam.

John was impressed by the 'horrifyingly unsentimental' movie. 'I'm not sure that *Little Friend* isn't the best English film I have ever seen,' he wrote.[1] He tended to be liberal with such compliments. Within hours, he knew, the quotable encomium would appear on the New Gallery's billboards, artfully cut – ' "The best English film I have ever seen" – JOHN BETJEMAN, *Evening Standard*.' Perhaps those who had bullied him at school, those who (unlike him) had taken degrees at Oxford or those who had snubbed him when he courted their daughters, would pass by and see what an arbiter he had become.

But there was another reason for John's commendation of *Little Friend*. Its story rang disturbingly true to him, reviving memories of his own childhood.

Do you remember [he wrote] what it was like to dread the dentist's drill? Do you remember, as a child, being frightened by the villain in the pantomime? Being irritated by your nurse? Hating your

1

cousins? Being made to eat when you felt sick? Being made to 'lie down' when you wanted to get up and kick things?

And do you remember, worst of all, waking from a dream to hear, in the next room, your parents quarrelling?

That is how *Little Friend* will open when it first greets you at the New Gallery on Sunday. A little girl (Nova Pilbeam) wakes up after a nightmare to hear an acrid argument going on between her father and her mother.

The parents protest that nothing is wrong. But their daughter is too clever, as all children are, and too sensitive, as all children are too.[2]

The rows between John's parents, Ernest and Bess Betjemann, reverberate in his poetry.[3] 'They quarrelled all the time,' said Joan Kunzer (*née* Larkworthy), who knew the family from 1910.[4] In a passage of an early version of *Summoned by Bells* (1960), omitted from the published poem, John – speaking in the person of his father – suggested that relations between his parents had worsened after a second child had died at birth:

> And how house-proud and how baby-proud was she
> When first we knew the next was on the way.
> But oh! how still and ugly stood the pram,
> Disused and blocking up the little hall,
> How shut the tidy drawers of baby clothes
> When the child came, and choked a bit and died
> To leave us only with our one to love.
> Then it was 'us', now it is 'she and I'
> For I am deaf and she is someone else.[5]

One of the things Ernest and Bess quarrelled about was their surname. John's great-grandfather, a London cabinet-maker, spelt his name 'George Betjeman', in stylish copperplate, on the cover of his 'work-book' and in the printed heading of his business invoices. But John's grandfather and father both spelt their names with two 'n's' – Betjemann. The double 'n' suggested German origins. A single 'n', John's mother thought, looked Dutch; and she assured him that his ancestors had come from Holland.

When German products were popular, in the late nineteenth century, it was almost an advantage for the family firm, G. Betjemann

& Sons, cabinet-makers, to have a name that looked Teutonic.[6] But during the First World War, when the Battenbergs changed their name to Mountbatten and German traders' windows were shattered, a double 'n' became a liability. Ernest, however, continued to spell his name Betjemann until the end of his life, and his son's birth certificate was in the name of John Betjemann.

When John was seven, on the eve of the Great War, a neighbour in Highgate provoked an embarrassment about his name which he never quite lost:

> . . . it was the mother there who first
> Made me aware of insecurity
> When war began: 'Your name is German, John' –
> But I had always thought that it was Dutch . . .[7]

At Highgate Junior School, which John attended from September 1915 to March 1917, two boys danced round him shouting

> Betjeman's a German spy –
> Shoot him down and let him die:
> Betjeman's a German spy,
> A German spy, a German spy.[8]

This was not just a friendly tease to be taken in good part, 'sportingly'. How harmful such a taunt could be was suggested by the victimization of Harold Reichardt, a dark-haired, round-faced boy who was at Highgate Junior School with John. 'The poor boy lived a very ostracized existence . . . once the 1914–18 war had started,' their contemporary Robert Hurd remembered, 'as he was son of a German father.'[9] John's parents had lived in Highbury long enough to discredit the *canard* that he was German; but during the war his mother decided to drop the second 'n' from the surname. As he grew older he saw no reason why he, too, should not revert to the spelling favoured by his great-grandfather. At the age of sixteen, when he wrote his name on the inside cover of Lord Alfred Douglas's *Collected Poems* in a handwriting that was never so artlessly clear again, he dropped the final 'n'. In a letter of 1927 (when John was twenty-one) his father wrote to him: 'I see you sign as a "one enner". Very cowardly!'[10] But in 1933, for legality's sake, John signed the marriage register 'John Betjemann'.

Interviewed by James Fox in 1976, he at last felt able to talk about the dilemma of the 'n's' without inhibition:

> I've never talked about these things before. I was always rather ashamed of it all, you see, having a name with two 'n's' which was carefully dropped by my mother during the 1914 war because I was thought to be German. I have a terrible guilt about not having any right to be in this country. My father insisted on keeping the two 'n's'. It's been an awful nuisance. Now I'm rather pleased when I see it with two.[11]

The argument between John's parents was carried beyond the grave. When Ernest died in 1934 the tablet to his memory designed by Frederick Etchells for St Enodoc's Church in Cornwall bore the name Ernest Edward Betjemann. When his wife died in 1952, the slab of Delabole slate marking her grave in St Enodoc churchyard (also designed by Etchells) was engraved 'Mabel Bessie Betjeman.'

To the end of his life, John insisted that his ancestors were Dutch and that the founder of the cabinet-making business had come from Holland in the late eighteenth century.[12] Dutchmen had been emigrating to England for centuries, to escape religious persecution and to find work. But it is much more likely that John's family was of German origin. The name is German.[13] A tradition in the family, which after 1914 they did their best to forget, suggested that John's great-great-grandfather, George Betjemann (who spelt his name thus), was born in Bremen in 1764. There, according to John's kinswoman Rebecca Excelsior ('Celsie') Merrick, he was 'a sugar refiner and sat in the German Parliament'.[14] A search of the Bremen and Hamburg archives has failed to confirm this. But George Betjemann was described as a 'sugar baker' on two marriage certificates – his own on his marriage to a London girl, Eleanor Smith, in 1797,[15] and that recording the marriage of his daughter Rebecca (Celsie's mother) to John Merrick, a London cabinet-maker, in 1846.[16] In 1953 John Betjeman wrote a jocular note to David Bateman, who thought that his family and John's might be related: 'What records I have of my family say they were sugar refiners, but I think they were sugar bakers but liked to be refined about it.'[17]

The record of George Betjemann's death, in the register of St Botolph, Aldersgate Street, London, shows that he was forty-nine when he died in 1813, which suggests a birth-date tallying with that given by Celsie Merrick. It is possible that he was born near

Bremen,[18] that he was in the sugar trade in Germany[19] and that he emigrated to England at some date before his marriage to Eleanor Smith in 1797. The couple lived in Aldersgate Street. This family connexion may account for John's special interest in that street; in his poem 'Monody on the Death of Aldersgate Street Station' he evoked the City's past:

> Then would the years fall off and Thames run slowly;
>> Out into marshy meadow-land flowed the Fleet;
> And the walled-in City of London, smelly and holy,
>> Had a tinkling mass house in every cavernous street.

If not 'cavernous', Aldersgate Street still had some pretensions in George Betjemann's time. Six years after his death, it was described by an American tourist, Washington Irving: 'There are also, in Aldersgate Street, certain remains of what were once spacious and lordly family mansions, but which have in latter days been sub-divided into several tenements. Here may often be found the relics of antiquated finery, in great rumbling time-stained apartments, with fretted ceilings, gilded cornices and enormous marble fire-places.'[20] These houses still had an almost rural setting. Celsie Merrick records that George Betjemann's widow Eleanor ran a dairy in Aldersgate Street, surrounded by fields where the cows were grazed. Celsie's mother (born Rebecca Betjemann in 1812) could remember Eleanor 'in the early dark dawn, standing at her [?chest of] drawers reading the old Bible by the light of a candle before starting the men and women off to the cows'.[21]

John Merrick, husband of Rebecca Betjemann, was the son of William Merrick who had a cabinet-making business in Red Lion Square, London. John Betjeman's great-grandfather, George Betjeman (1798–1887), who was learning the same trade, used to visit the workshops. He fell in love with William Merrick's daughter Mary Anne and married her at St Giles, Cripplegate, on 16 July 1830. So the Betjeman(n) and Merrick families were doubly linked. The link fascinated John.

Celsie Merrick told John that her grandfather, William Merrick, was the younger of two boys born at Bodorgan, Anglesey, Wales – a mansion 'with large grounds round it, great iron pales topped with the Prince of Wales feathers'.[22] (Bodorgan was the seat of the Meyrick family, pronounced 'Merrick'.[23]) Celsie claimed that the two boys had been spirited off to London by guardians named Fuller and done out of their rightful inheritance.[24] The penny-dreadful story was unprovable; but a Gothic scandal, skulduggery, a fortune lost and the possibility of being descended from land-owning stock were just the skeletons a poet of John's temperament might like to find in his cupboard. He continued to take an interest in the Tapps-Gervis-Meyrick family who had succeeded to the allegedly misappropriated property, and mentioned them in *First and Last Loves* (1952).[25]

According to Celsie Merrick, 'my grandfather, William Merrick, who lived in Northampton Square, was a churchwarden of St George's, Clerkenwell, and always placed a sovereign in the collection.'[26] There is no St George's, Clerkenwell; but there was a Church of St George-the-Martyr, Holborn, and at that church William *Meyrick* was a gentleman of the vestry (one step above church-warden) from 1825 to 1836.[27] That he spelt his name in this way lends some faint support to Celsie's Bodorgan story. William died intestate in 1836, leaving £7000, which was divided among his children. One of them, Mary Anne Betjeman, was dead by then, but she had four children: John's grandfather John, George, Polly and Harriott Lucy. Part of the money was invested in the cabinet-making business which their father, George Betjeman, had established at 6 Upper Ashby Street. (The street joins Northampton Square and Goswell Road – the 'Goswell Street' where Dickens's Mr Pickwick lived.) By the time John Betjemann married, in 1870, the firm had moved to Pentonville Road, where it remained until the liquidation of the company in 1945.

John Betjemann (1835–93), who is mentioned in John's poem 'City', married Hannah Thompson, daughter of Edward John Thompson, a watch material maker, and his wife Jessica (*née* Roberts). Like the Betjemanns, the Thompsons were north London people of the lower middle class. But members of both families had accomplishments some way beyond the do-it-yourself enter-tainment of the average Victorian home. John's Thompson grand-mother wrote gushing verse,[28] and the Betjemann family included Cousin Stanley who belonged to a touring opera company.[29] A Cousin Henry (Betjemann) designed the Betjemann Patent Bedstead Lock.

The best-known member of the family, before John himself became famous through his poetry and his television appearances, was the violinist, conductor and composer Gilbert H. Betjemann (1840–1921), Musician-in-Ordinary to Queen Victoria and King Edward VII. He composed a cantata, 'Song of the Western Men',[30] but he was better known as a conductor of Beecham-like panache. John told Michael Parkinson, in a television interview of 1977: 'Gilbert Betjemann introduced Wagner to Glasgow. They just laughed at it. So he rapped with his baton on the rail and said, "Are you going to listen to this music or are you not? Because if you're not, I shall go home and enjoy a whisky toddy." '[31] John's grandfather, John Betjemann, was a cousin of Gilbert, and as a child John was taken to meet the old musician and his wife, the singer Rose Daffone, in Hillmarton Road, Camden Town, London.[32]

John Betjemann and his wife Hannah had two sons. The elder, John George, was considered a wastrel.[33] So it was left to Ernest, the younger son, to take over the family business as the 'third generation'.

Ernest Betjemann was the kind of man every Victorian headmaster's speech, every boys'-magazine, was calculated to produce. When Sarah Bernhardt was asked to fill in 'The quality I most admire in men' in an Edwardian 'Confessions' album, she wrote (not, perhaps, without her tongue in her cheek), 'Uprightness'. Ernest Betjemann was upright. With his sanguine complexion and military bearing, he looked as if he exercised with Indian clubs each morning. He was a cricketer, a footballer, an enthusiastic fisherman and a good shot – the epitome of *mens sana in corpore sano*.

Born in 1872, he was educated at Highbury Park School, at the City of London School and in Switzerland. He entered the family firm in 1899, when the main product was the Betjemann patent tantalus, a metal apparatus for locking away decanters of drink from the servants. In 1976 John wrote to a correspondent who owned an example originally sold by Orr & Sons, Madras: 'The tantalus with an *en garde* lock was invented I believe by my grandfather,[34] who died of the things he was locking up from the public, e.g. brandy, whisky and gin which were, presumably, in those square cut-glass decanters made in Birmingham for the firm.'[35] John described his grandfather's death (1893) in 'The Epic', the prototype of *Summoned by Bells* which he sent John and Myfanwy Piper in 1941; but the passage did not appear in the published version. Ernest Betjemann is speaking:

> ... The smell of sawdust, Bradshaw at the lathe,
> Pettit and Pettit's son and all the men[36]
> I trained to make me what I am today
> An artist-craftsman-manufacturer.
> My brother Jack, my sisters' morning room
> And photographs and portraits of the past
> And those decanters which had brought us down
> And Islington and Highbury and larks
> And sprees at Collinses when I could hear,
> Laugh with Dan Leno,[37] join in Coborn's[38] song,
> 'The Man who Broke the Bank . . .' and mount again
> The knife board omnibus and hear the wheels
> Go silent over straw in Upper Street.
> Jack Spuling, Tommy Godfrey, oyster bars,
> Returning squiffy in the family brougham
> And William's 'Master Ernest, something's up!
> They've left the gas on full inside the 'all.'
> And there was father dead upstairs at last
> And the decanters shining on the side.[39]

The tantalus remained part of Betjemann's manufacture until, towards the outbreak of the Second World War, it became harder to obtain servants than to stop them pilfering the drink. The factory also continued making the goods that George Betjeman had been producing in the 1820s: cabinets, dressing-tables and writing-desks.

In 1902 Ernest married Mabel Bessie Dawson, daughter of James Dawson, a maker of artificial flowers, and his wife Alice (*née* Daniel). In spite of slightly protruding teeth, 'Bess' was considered attractive. A friend who knew her before her marriage described her as 'such a pretty girl, always so gay, clever and amusing'.[40] Both bride and groom had grown up in Highbury, and they were married there at St Saviour's, Aberdeen Park:

> Great red church of my parents, cruciform crossing they knew –
> Over these same encaustics they and their parents trod
> Bound through a red-brick transept for a once familiar pew
> Where the organ set them singing and the sermon let them
>   nod . . .[41]

Perhaps because he felt *dépaysé* in lower Highgate, John half-adopted the Highbury of his parents and grandparents as his homeland, at the same time somewhat exaggerating his parents' social standing there:

These were the streets my parents knew when they loved and
won –
The brougham that crunched the gravel, the laurel-girt paths
that wind,
Geranium-beds for the lawn, Venetian blinds for the sun,
A separate tradesman's entrance, straw in the mews behind,
Just in the four-mile radius where hackney carriages run,
Solid Italianate houses for the solid commercial mind.

These were the streets they knew; and I, by descent, belong
To these tall neglected houses divided into flats.
Only the church remains, where carriages used to throng
And my mother stepped out in flounces and my father stepped
out in spats
To shadowy stained-glass matins or gas-lit evensong
And back in a country quiet with doffing of chimney hats.[42]

John's father was the son of a cabinet-maker; his mother, the daughter of a maker of artificial flowers. And the family was not exclusively High Church. In a letter of 1976 to the poet and journalist Terence O'Neil, John wrote:

My father and his brothers were baptized in Islington Parish Church although other members of the family supported Union Chapel in Compton Terrace. It's still the nicest bit of London up there on that hill. The greatest London novel, *We, the Accused* by Ernest Raymond (1935), pervades the whole district for me with a sense of doom and intending murder and autumn mists in Clissold Park. North of the Thames for me, though I prefer Southwark as a diocese.[43]

2

HIGHGATE

John Betjeman yesterday celebrated the sale of 65,000 copies of his collected poems by taking his publisher, Mr Jock Murray, for a ride.

It was on his favourite electric railway, the line which runs from Broad Street – what he once described as 'that smooth, useless, beautiful journey to Richmond' ...

There is ... a memorable succession of gaslit stations, ghostly and decayed, with sad formal gardens and fretwork edges to their roofs. It was within 200 yards of one of them – Gospel Oak – that Mr Betjeman was born.

Daily Telegraph, 9 December 1959

Ernest and Bess Betjemann's first home after their marriage was 52 Parliament Hill Mansions in north-west London. John, their only child to survive, was born there on 28 August 1906, and christened by the assistant curate of St Anne's, Highgate Rise, on 25 November. After his birth, his mother sent out beribboned cards to her acquaintance. The cards with their fine engraving and pretty bows (blue for a boy) were a *de luxe* trimming characteristic of Bess Betjemann. Like the woman in John's poem 'How to Get On in Society', she liked to have things 'daintily served'.

Parliament Hill Mansions is the kind of building which John was unjustly accused of liking when he began to champion Victorian architecture. It is an undistinguished terracotta block with railed-off balconies, just off the Highgate Road. Clevedon Mansions, just opposite, with octagonal towers and extravagant cast ironwork, interested him more. Lissenden Mansions, also close by, he recalled in his poem 'N.W.5 and N.6':

> Red cliffs arise. And up them service lifts
> Soar with the groceries to silver heights.

Lissenden Mansions. And my memory sifts
Lilies from lily-like electric lights
And Irish stew smells from the smell of prams
And roar of seas from roar of London trams.

He would have preferred to spend his early years in one of the Georgian houses of Grove Terrace, which runs parallel to Parliament Hill Mansions on the other side of the Highgate Road.

He did not mention Parliament Hill Mansions when he took Valerie Jenkins of the *Evening Standard* on a tour of the 'haunts of his childhood' in 1974.[1] But he rhapsodized then and also in *Summoned by Bells* over 31 West Hill, a more attractive villa to which his parents moved when he was still an infant.

Deeply I loved thee, 31 West Hill! . . .
Here from my eyrie, as the sun went down,
I heard the old North London puff and shunt,
Glad that I did not live in Gospel Oak.[2]

Gospel Oak is just where John *did* live in his earliest years. Parliament Hill Mansions was about as close to Gospel Oak station as it was possible to be. Behind the Mansions was Parliament Hill itself, where Guy Fawkes's confederates waited for the destruction of Parliament on 5 November 1605. Parliament Hill Fields, on which John wrote a poem, are two hundred and seventy acres of heathland which until 1884 belonged to Lord Mansfield, who also owned the great Adam house Kenwood nearby. In that year, through an initiative of the philanthropist Octavia Hill, the Fields were bought for the public for £300,000. There small boys flew kites (as they still do); and there John was moved, as a child, by the sight of children 'carrying down/Sheaves of drooping dandelions to the courts of Kentish town'.[3]

John gives one vignette of life in Parliament Hill Mansions in *Summoned by Bells* – not early in the poem, as one might expect, but as a 'flashback' to contrast with Ernest Betjemann's unwelcome arrival in Cornwall when John was a disaffected teenager:

That early flat, electrically lit,
Red silk and leather in the dining-room,
Beads round the drawing-room electrolier . . .

Singing in bed, to make the youngster laugh,
Tosti's 'Goodbye', Lord Henry's 'Echo Song' –
And windy walks on Sunday to the Heath,
While dogs were barking round the White Stone Pond.[4]

Bess Betjemann did not intend the family to stay in the Mansions for long. Socially aspiring, she wanted to move up the hill into more genteel Highgate. Marriage to Ernest had dampened her down, but she remained spirited, someone who liked having fun. Her cousin Queenie Avril recalled her as 'a vivid and vital person . . . when I was a gauche young girl and Bess an elegant, lovely and witty young married woman'.[5] Ernest was overbearing but Bess had a mind of her own; before the First World War she was a suffragette and attended Emmeline Pankhurst's meetings. As late as the 1940s John still thought her sharp enough to précis novels for him when he was reviewing books for the *Daily Herald*.[6] But, though she was bright and good-hearted,[7] Bess was a little snobbish and silly.[8] John wrote:

I feared my father, loved my mother more,
And just because of this would criticize,
In my own mind, the artless things she said.[9]

She used the exaggerated language of the society flapper – 'ghastly', 'simply maddening', 'simply charming', 'fearfully common', 'a perfect beast', 'a dream of comfort', 'thrilled to death'.[10] John enjoyed her wit and gaiety,[11] but too often in his childhood she was away from home, pursuing her social life. Mary Bouman, who as a child knew John and his parents, thought John was 'left on his own far too often – rather as Winston Churchill was neglected by Lady Randolph Churchill'.[12]

If Bess Betjemann was like Lady Randolph, then Hannah Wallis had the place in John's life that Mrs Everest had in Churchill's: the comforting, ever-benevolent nanny who was always there when he needed her. ('Perhaps it is the only disinterested affection in the world,' Churchill wrote of the nanny's love for her charge.[13]) Hannah Wallis lived with her daughter in Dongola Road, Philip Lane, Tottenham. 'She was an old-fashioned person, small and dumpy,' John remembered, 'and she wore a black bonnet when we used to take the train to Philip Lane station and walk to . . . Dongola

Road.'[14] She listened for hours while John read poetry to her: Bess was fond of recounting how she came home once and found John reading poetry aloud outside the lavatory door 'behind which the old girl had locked herself'.[15] Hannah played draughts with him and always let him win. He teased her and she laughed. 'I exceeded the bounds of decency and decorum and she didn't mind.'[16] She was never angry or fussed. Hannah's imperturbable goodwill even survived a 'fatal Christmas Day' which John evoked in a Christmas broadcast of 1947:

> I woke up early. Heavy on my feet were the presents of my relations, presents of sympathy for an only child. I don't remember what they were. But one of them I do remember. It was one of those pieces of frosted glass in a wooden frame and behind the glass a picture in outline which one was supposed to trace on the glass with a pencil. 'To Master John with love from Hannah Wallis.' I stood up on my bed among the brown paper of the opened parcels. I stood up. I stepped a step. Crack! I had smashed the frosted glass of her present.
>
> Hannah Wallis, you who are now undoubtedly in Heaven,[17] you know now, don't you, that I did not do that on purpose? I remember thinking then that she might think I had smashed it because I did not think it a good enough present and that it looked too cheap among the more expensive ones of my relations. But, as a matter of fact, it was just what I wanted. And now I had smashed it. I remember putting it on a shelf over my bed between some books so as to hide the accident. Guiltily I went down to breakfast.
>
> 'Did you like the slate? It was just what you wanted, wasn't it? The biggest I could get!' Poor people were poor in those days and she must have saved up for it.
>
> 'Oh yes, and thank you very much. It was lovely.' Oh, the guilt, the shame! I did not dare, for fear of hurting her feelings whom I loved so much, – I did not dare to tell her I had smashed it. Yet that evening when my room had been tidied and the presents put away, I found the broken glass and frame put in my waste-paper basket. She must have found it out. But we neither of us ever mentioned it again. I think that cracked glass was the first crack in my heart, the first time I lost ignorance and the first time I realised the overwhelmingly unpleasant things of the world.[18]

John described himself, in *Summoned by Bells*, as 'an only child, deliciously apart';[19] but he was often pitifully lonely. He treated his teddy bear, Archibald, as a surrogate brother. The loneliness was tinged with an irrational feeling of guilt: he learned about the child who had died, and who might have been so much more to his father's liking than he was.[20] Because of his lack of brothers and sisters, John had no readily accessible standard with which to compare his own behaviour. Was it normal, he wondered, to lock a small girl in the lavatory and to wait outside until she cried?[21] (He played this trick on Hannah Wallis's granddaughter, Hilda.[22]) Did other small boys have a strong desire, as he did, to smash the faces of china dolls?[23]

> Being an only child [he said in a radio talk of 1950] I didn't compare notes. I preferred my own company to that of other children always. I preferred electric trains and maps of the Underground railways to people any day. I believed inanimate objects could feel and think. . . . I felt very sorry for horse chestnuts if they were left on the road. I picked them up and took them home. A rubber ball I had gave me a lot of trouble. It had a hole in it, but I thought it would be offended if I threw it away. I kissed it goodnight every night so that it should not be offended. If you are a psycho-analyst listening you can probably explain all this.[24]

Before delivering the talk, John altered 'rubber ball' and 'had a hole in it' to 'wooden train' and 'was badly smashed' – perhaps feeling that the first version might give the analysts too intimate a hold on his psyche.

Hannah Wallis was prepared to put up with all John's eccentricities; but his Calvinist nursemaid, Maud, the dark angel of his childhood, was not. Her sadistic treatment of him is described in *Summoned by Bells*; and she instilled in him a dread of eternal damnation, as he recalled in 'N.W.5 and N.6'. Her frightening prophecies gave him nightmares, including 'a clear vision of the Devil':

> I used to go up in a black lift made of wood. We would arrive at the top where it was blindingly white and I would be in this little wooden lift one side of which was open and showed that we were floating on a limitless white sea. But I was not alone in the lift. Oh no! There rose up from the corner a tall thin-faced man with ram's horns springing out of his forehead. He was the Devil. His horns were outlined black against the sky. He was coming nearer. There was no escape.[25]

In 'N.W.5 and N.6' John suggests that the indoctrination by Maud took place in 1911. This date cannot be relied on with much confidence, as John was rhyming it with 'Heaven'; 1910 and 1912 would not serve. But the 1950 radio talk confirms that the words which made such an impression on him were spoken after the Betjemanns moved to West Hill, Highgate.

Lying in bed of a late summer evening I remember hearing the bells ring out from St Anne's Highgate Rise – the church where I was christened ... Maud, the nurse, was looking out of the open window. Crossed in love, I suppose, and for once fairly gentle with me. I remember asking her if I should go to Heaven. 'You will, but I won't,' she said. I remember recognizing even then that she spoke from her heart about herself. I did not recognize this, at the time, as any sign of grace in Maud.[26]

Moving to 31 West Hill was, literally and metaphorically, going up in the world. The villa is about a mile uphill from Parliament Hill Mansions. It is outwardly little changed, in spite of a fire caused by an arsonist in 1975 when Iain Hamilton, a former editor of *The Spectator*, owned the house.[27] After the fire, John wrote to Hamilton, offering him, by way of consolation, any piece of his own furniture that Hamilton would like to choose. In his letter he recalled red squirrels leaping among the hornbeams on the Holly Lodge estate on the other side of West Hill, which could be seen from the windows of No. 31 when he was a child.[28] The Baroness Burdett-Coutts – Dickens's friend – who had owned Holly Lodge, died in the year of John's birth, and her mansion was soon afterwards demolished. In 1864 she had built a Gothic village for her servants; it had a sinister fascination for John. ('And Holly Village with its prickly roofs/Against the sky were terrifying shapes.'[29]) Flocks of sheep were driven up and down West Hill.[30] The scene was almost sylvan, but one could hear, beyond the trains at Gospel Oak, 'the low growl of London'.[31]

Though Highgate stood in a wilderness of suburbs, it had the air of a Middlesex village – and still has, even if the old shops with wooden canopies over the pavement have been painted up and converted into 'galleries'. The publication of *Summoned by Bells* in 1960 drew recollections from people who remembered Highgate in John's childhood. Marjorie Bond, who had lived on North Hill 'and always wanted to move up to the Village', remembered

'Ballard the milk people with churns and always a smell of sour milk,
Lake the butcher with awful carcases dripping gore into basins,
Atkins the pork butcher, where – if you were brave – you could see
the pigs killed, Lipscombe where my brother had his hair cut, up
steep steps, oh, and do you remember the Coxheads' shop in
Southwood Lane, Miss Kate and Miss Jennie and large hoops always
outside, [and] Ann's in High Street where we bought fireworks if our
1d a week [pocket-money] ran to any . . . ?'[32] Robert Hurd, formerly
of Jackson's Lane, wondered whether John used to be taken, after
walks in Highgate Cemetery, to have a glass of milk and a sponge
cake at the Express Dairy corner shop in South Grove. 'I remember
the large open earthenware bowl of milk, so insanitary by modern
standards, and the pewter ladle with which Miss Davies (who had
piled-up black hair Edwardian style, this was in 1910 or so) put the
milk into a tumbler. I really only took the milk because it was the one
certain way of being allowed by my rather strict nurse to enjoy the
crisp sugar coating on sponge cakes.'[33] Anne Lee Michell, who had
been John's neighbour at 26 West Hill, recalled Mrs Gay, 'the green-
groceress in High Street . . . Very suave to customers: "I'll send them
down immediate, Mrs Garnett. Let me see, 10 lbs potatoes, sprouts
and caulies" – (*sotto voce*, to offspring:) "GET OUT you little devil
or I'll pop your eyeballs." '[34]

When John was nostalgic about the Highgate he had known in
the reign of Edward VII, he liked to claim that 'At that hill's foot did
London then begin,/With yellow horse-trams clopping past the
planes . . .'[35] The horse-drawn trams were succeeded by electric
trams, and to these, also, John had a lifelong attachment.[36] His
poem 'Parliament Hill Fields' has far more to say about trams than
about fields. It begins with a piece of Turneresque scene-painting,
all sunset and smoke:

Rumbling under blackened girders, Midland, bound for
                                                    Cricklewood,
Puffed its sulphur to the sunset where the Land of Laundries
                                                    stood.

Rumble under, thunder over, train and tram alternate go,
Shake the floor and smudge the ledger, Charrington, Sells Dale
                                                    and Co.,

Nuts and nuggets in the window, trucks along the line below.[37]

The steep road from Gospel Oak to Highgate Village was like a graph of rising social status. Parliament Hill Mansions; Brookfield Mansions (still flats, but more impressive); 31 West Hill (semi-detached); then soaring to the Georgian grandeur of 82 West Hill, home of John's friend Peggy Purey-Cust, and finally to the Parnassian heights of the Grove, where Coleridge had lodged. On his Highgate Revisited jaunt with Valerie Jenkins in 1974, John insisted on making a detour across West Hill into Holly Terrace, where his governess, Miss Cray, had lived. He was delighted to find the haven unspoilt – still a private road with glades of flowering elder, ivy, beech, limes and sycamores. 'Isn't it paradise?' he exclaimed. 'It's Keats and Leigh Hunt. Untouched Georgian railings, and gas lamps straight from Stevenson's "Lamplighter" ... This gives you the Highgate that I knew: no combustion engines!'[38] That was a romantic exaggeration: elsewhere, John wrote that West Hill was so steep that the motor-car drivers of his childhood did not dare attempt it.[39]

The Betjemanns' stucco villa was about half-way up the social graph: the ideal vantage-point for gaining a nice sense of English social distinctions. Snobbery is a branch of applied sociology, and in this discipline John proved instinctually adept. Comparisons were to be made even among immediate neighbours. John early realized that

> we were a lower, lesser world
> Than that remote one of the carriage folk
> Who left their cedars and brown garden walls
> In care of servants.[40]

But he could also tell

> That we were slightly richer than my friends
> The family next door: we owned a brougham
> And they would envy us our holidays.[41]

The family next door were the Boumans, whose children were, for a while, like a brother and sisters to John. Jan Bouman, the father, was a Dutch journalist, who worked for the Press Association of America in London, Paris, Berlin and The Hague.[42] His wife Ethelwynne came of Scottish and Cumbrian parents, border folk in

Northumbria. They had three children: Bill (b. 1907), Mary (b. 1908) and Betty (b. 1909). Mary Bouman recalled John as 'a rather sad little boy'.[43] Tears poured down his face when he could not do his sums in the nursery: 'he found them extraordinarily difficult'. But he was capable, too, of impishness. 'We haven't any paste,' Mary observed when they were cutting out pictures for their scrap books. 'Oh, that doesn't matter,' he said. 'We'll stick them in with marmalade.'[44]

The Bouman children did not go to Byron House, John's first school. But Bill Bouman, a year younger than John, was his best friend and companion, a handsome and popular child, even though a severe attack of scarlet fever had, in Mary's words, 'left something missing'. John used to take Bill out on to Parliament Hill Fields and say 'We will write poetry.' John would sit on a seat on top of one of the two small hills above Highgate Ponds and wait for inspiration, pencil and paper on his knees. 'What [Bill] did I can't remember,' John later said, 'except that I made him bring pencil and paper too.'[45] 'John is out with Bill,' Ethelwynne Bouman wrote to her husband (then in Holland) in January 1916. 'They walk to Golders Hill Park every morning.'[46]

It seems likely that John engaged in some sexual experiments with Bill Bouman; that Bess Betjemann discovered them and warned John to cool the friendship; and that John later made the incident the subject of his poem 'Narcissus', published in 1966. The poem describes how the poet-narrator would go for walks with his friend 'Bobby'

> And when we just did nothing we were good
> But when we touched each other we were bad.

The poet's mother said they were 'unwholesome' in their play.

> And then she said I was her precious child,
> And once there was a man called Oscar Wilde.

The narrator is easily identified as John: a delicate only child with a father in trade, a suffragette mother, and a teddy-bear to cling to when in trouble. 'Bobby' (Billy) lives near the poet and has sisters. In a radio talk of 1950 John said: 'Bill was, my mother told me, "easily led". Perhaps this was why I liked him so much.'[47]

Ethelwynne Bouman, a serenely beautiful and sweet-natured woman, encouraged John's interest in poetry. After he had taken part in a radio programme in 1956 she wrote (at eighty-three) to remind him how, when he was about seven or eight, 'you . . . used to come into our nursery, your face bright with the joy and music of words, [and] you used to recite to me your latest discovery, amongst them [Allan] Cunningham's[48] "A wet sheet and a flowing sea" & even some of Meredith's poems . . .'[49] John replied: 'I remember you very well at West Hill & your talking about George Macdonald[50] and Scotch poetry. Those poems you mention came from "Lyra Heroica" which Miss Finlay Peacock (still alive) gave to me – the Cunningham & the "Head of Bran" by George Meredith.'[51]

In 1916, when John was ten, Jan Bouman was posted abroad and his family joined him. 'I did not realize at the time,' Mary Bouman said, 'how utterly desolating that was for John. It meant that he lost his "second mother" and his brother and sisters.'[52] John himself said in 1950: 'I think the saddest moment of my life, as numbing as any subsequent loss, was the time when Bill, Mary and Betty left the district . . . The pavements outside our houses on West Hill, the Heath, our little gardens seemed empty for ever.'[53]

In 1922 the Boumans returned to London. In April Bill Bouman wrote to his father, who was in Paris for the Peace Conference: 'I got such a nice surprise one day. It was the day after we had broken up at school and mother came to take us for a walk. I went out of the schoolroom to put on my boots and who should I see but John Betjeman standing next to mother. My breath was taken away when I saw him. We had a nice walk together on the Heath. John is the same old John as when we left [in 1916], as jolly as ever.'[54] He described a visit he and John had made to the British Museum, where they saw Indian masks, spear-heads, arrowheads and bronze instruments. 'John was very interested and afterwards we had tea at Lyons, such a jolly tea with bath buns, etc.'[55]

The Betjemanns' other neighbours on West Hill included Arthur Hayden, author of *Chats on Old China*;[56] the chauffeur to the Suffragan Bishop of Islington; and Mr Lightfoot who 'would walk down to Highgate Ponds every day with a springy step and a towel round his shoulders and then dive from the topmost board. Even to save my life I couldn't do it,' John told Valerie Jenkins.[57] Further down were the Bunneys, whose name made Mary Bouman and

John giggle. John saw old Mrs Bunney being carried out in her coffin: ' "What would Miss Emily want with a box/So long and narrow, without any locks?" – Remember De La Mare?' John reminded Miss Jenkins.[58]

At the top of the hill lived John's 'first and purest love', Peggy Purey-Cust, daughter of Admiral Sir Herbert Purey-Cust. Satchel on back, he used to hurry up West Hill to catch her as she walked to school, accompanied by her nanny.[59] She had fair hair, ice-blue eyes, long pale lashes, freckles and a turned-up nose – 'all my loves since then/Have had a look of Peggy Purey-Cust.'[60] It was in her Georgian home that John experienced the first social snub of his life. Having been invited to tea once ('It seemed a palace after 31'[61]) he was never asked again. After the tea he called on Peggy many times, but was always told she was out, away or unwell. When she was sick, he took her 'House of the Sleeping Winds,/My favourite book with whirling art-nouveau/And Walter Crane-ish colour plates'[62] to cheer her up; but it was merely taken in to her.

> Weeks passed and passed . . . and then it was returned.
> O gone for ever, Peggy Purey-Cust![63]

Another, more brutal, social slight also rankled with John into adult life. Eventually he 'wrote it out of his system' as his growing reputation gave him confidence. 'False Security', written after 1954, apparently exorcized the memory of a children's party in The Grove, Highgate:

> Can I forget my delight at the conjuring show?
> And wasn't I proud that I was the last to go?
> Too overexcited and pleased with myself to know
> That the words I heard my hostess's mother employ
> To a guest departing, would ever diminish my joy,
> I WONDER WHERE JULIA FOUND THAT STRANGE, RATHER
>   COMMON LITTLE BOY?[64]

John was at least able to walk with Peggy Purey-Cust, under the limes of The Grove, to his first school, Byron House in Hampstead Lane. (The building has since been demolished.) The school had been set up in 1885 and was run on the Montessori system.[65] There were two headmistresses, the Misses Legge. The elder, in her thirties, was the more businesslike. She was known as 'Miss Catherine'. The younger, Miss Florence, was 'artistic' and painted dewy water-colours. Miss Catherine was tall, statuesque and formidable. Miss Florence was short, twittering and kindly.

Mary Chubb, who was at Byron House with John, spoke warmly of Miss Catherine in a BBC radio talk of 1953: 'I think she was probably the finest person I've ever known.'[66] She remembered her quick, incisive voice and the sensitive mouth which could break into a flashing smile when a child's remark upset her usual gravity. One day Miss Catherine told her class that the world became colder the further north one went. A small boy who lived up the North Road agreed. 'Yes, Miss Catherine, you're right: it's much colder in our house than it is here.' More than anything else, Mary Chubb recalled, Miss Catherine 'passionately wanted every one of us to be good'. Montessorians thought children were more likely to be good when they were happy, and more likely to be happy when they were interested in their work. A large part of the curriculum was handi-craft, 'blob-work, weaving, carpentry and art'. Subjects were first approached through practical examples: geometry through folding and cutting up paper of different colours; geography and history through building models; nature-study through walks and the col-lection of leaves and wild flowers for pressing.

Mary Chubb met John on her first day at Byron House:

> I remember arriving at the school very clearly, although I was only five and it's getting on for fifty years ago; the feeling of panic as I clung to my mother's hand in a rather dark little cloakroom full of shoe lockers and the smell of galoshes. My mother helped me with shoelaces because my fingers had suddenly gone cold and clumsy. Miss Garnett [the kindergarten mistress], a tall lady in a green skirt swishing down to the floor, led me through into the big room beyond. My insides stopped churning. Anyone's qualms would have disappeared in that room. One or two other ladies were stand-ing by a blazing fire. There was an open piano in one corner. The sun poured in at a great window . . . There were big vases round the room holding branches of chestnut with their sticky buds just bursting open . . . There were pictures everywhere . . .
>
> Miss Garnett put me down at a low table in company with several other solemn fledglings. We were given cards with black letters on them, and shown how to put them side by side to make words. A little boy in a bright blue smock, brooding eyes beneath a dark

fringe, began to fit his cards carefully together – a poet of our day was picking up his craftsman's tools for the first time. By the time elevenses appeared – a mug of milk and a biscuit – we were blissfully happy, and most of us could have told you how to spell cat and dog . . .[67]

Photographs of John at this period confirm Mary Chubb's description of him. With his darkening hair, big brown eyes and waxy complexion, he looked less English than Mediterranean – perhaps the soulful child on a 'His First Communion' postcard from Italy or France. On Sundays, his mother dressed him like an expensive doll, in a white coatee and white, buttoned shoes.

John's earliest poems belong to his Byron House days. Miss Brenda Thompson, who was in his class in 1914, remembered that one day they were asked to write some verse:

I wrote some lines about bunnies in the snow – John and I were seated side by side and he looked to see what I had written.

He said, 'Oh I like that, did you really make it up yourself?' and I replied that I had read it in a Christmas annual. Had it been any other child in the class I feel sure I would have said indignantly, 'Of course I did' but with John the stark truth was right, and safe, he would not 'split' because he would understand . . .[68]

Brenda Thompson also remembered that when she and another small girl were comparing the lengths of their hair in the playground at Byron House, John, who was present, suddenly exclaimed with great emphasis: 'I'm going to have long hair when I grow up and be a poet.'

In 1964, Miss D.G. Doubleday, who had taught John at Byron House, wrote to him that she remembered him 'as a small eager boy entering the kindergarten room from the cloakroom, with much determination, thrusting his way through rows of children assembled for register, declaring urgently that he could not take his place until he had shown his poems to Miss Catherine.'[69] There was already in John's character an element of the exhibitionism that shy people sometimes assume to mask or conquer their shyness. Winifred Macdonald, another of his contemporaries at the school, remembered his proclaiming, at a school picnic: 'I had nineteen helpings of pudding yesterday!' The other children were impressed by this, but Miss Griffin, the teacher in charge, replied: 'All I can say, John, is that you are a very greedy little boy!'[70]

School began at 9 a.m. Many of the children arrived carrying mulberry leaves for their silkworms, which were kept in the kindergarten room with hyacinths, tadpoles, stick-insects and beans sprouting on blotting-paper under bell-jars. (One of the first things the children made in the carpentry class was an insect box with a sliding glass front.) The hymns in morning assembly included the Harrow School Song, 'Forty Years On' – 'such a strange thing for little children to sing,' said John's contemporary Nancy Richardson (*née* Walker), '– it always puzzled me so much to know what "the tramp of the twenty-two men"* was.'[71] After two lessons there was a mid-morning break. In the playground the games were still 'French versus English': Germany was not yet regarded as England's enemy. All the children had garden plots to attend. In 1911 they grew red, white and blue flowers as the Coronation of George V drew near. Some also planted 'G.R.' in mustard-and-cress. Miss Florence advised them that if they sowed the 'G' in mustard and the 'R' in cress, the 'G' had to be planted three days earlier, because mustard took that much longer to surface.[72]

On chilly mornings, Miss Florence would race all over the school, in and out of every classroom, holding a long-handled shovel full of burning tar, which gave off a heavy blue smoke, supposed to ward off colds. 'The door would shoot open, Miss Florence would rush round the room, and then vanish as suddenly, leaving behind the blue trail swaying up and down as we waved it about and sniffed up the spicy fragrance,' Mary Chubb recalled.[73] Then the children would settle down to the morning's work: perhaps a geography lesson with a model of a desert oasis in the classroom sandtray – brown paper palm trees, wooden camels and Bedouin round a looking-glass pool. Other models illustrated history lessons. John's class made a 'Parthenon' from cotton-reels, glued together and sandpapered into columns.

---

* 'Forty Years On', the Harrow School Song composed by E. E. Bowen (1836–1901), includes the lines:

> Follow up! Follow up! Follow up! Follow up! Follow up!
> Till the field ring again and again,
> With the tramp of the twenty-two men,
> Follow up!

The Misses Legge had a brother who had been at Harrow, which may explain the choice of song.

The school play was sometimes historical, too. *Hereward the Wake* was performed in eight parts, with a different Hereward in each scene. The parents, overflowing kindergarten chairs, tried gallantly to follow the plot – 'a tricky business when Hereward might be a thin, red-headed boy at one moment and a plump little fair girl the next'.[74] An adaptation of Christina Rossetti's *The Months* gave more legitimate scope for a large cast: the twelve principals who played the months (who included Peggy Purey-Cust) were accompanied by snowflakes, bees, autumn leaves and other seasonal attendants. John made his debut as a robin. *A Midsummer Night's Dream* was the most ambitious production. The part of Titania was taken by Joan Harben, whose brother Philip, also with John at Byron House, became a 'television personality' in the 1950s, as the bearded 'television cook'. (The Harbens' parents, Hubert Harben and Mary Jerrold, were both actors; and Joan was to play the lugubrious Mona Lotte with Tommy Handley in the Second World War ITMA ['It's That Man Again'] radio show.) John would have been a 'natural' for Puck, but the part went to a girl, Margaret Upcott (now Darlington).[75]

John always recalled his days at Byron House as an idyllic time, marred by one act of gratuitous violence, which he could neither understand nor forgive. He described the attack, though disguising the location, in his poem 'Original Sin on the Sussex Coast' (first published in *Time and Tide*, 8 December 1951) and in *Summoned by Bells*; but probably the most reliable account of the incident is the one he gave in a radio talk of 1950:

> I recollect Jack Drayton [Jack Shakespeare], a dissenting minister's son. He asked me to tea. He was very nice to me. He showed off at tea and made me laugh. Then he grew thick with Willie Dunlop [Willie Buchanan], a fat little boy who even when he was seven looked like the beefy business man he probably now is. Together they waited for me after school one afternoon.
>
> 'You come down Fitzroy Avenue,' they said. I did. But they seemed a bit strange.
>
> 'Stand here,' said Drayton and stood me against a wall. 'You're not to speak to us, see?'
>
> 'Yes.'
>
> 'Promise.'
>
> 'Yes.'
>
> 'Punch him, Willie.' Willie punched. It winded me a bit. I started

to blub. They ran away. I had no idea why they suddenly turned nasty. I don't know to this day. Perhaps one of their parents had said, 'You're not to know that horrid little Betjeman boy.'

That happened going home from a kindergarten – Byron House, Highgate. It was an enlightened, happy place. Jack and Willie were its only blots.[76]

When John went on to Highgate Junior School, he found that 'this detestable couple' had got there first. (They were the boys who danced round him shouting 'Betjeman's a German spy.'[77]) To gain admission to Highgate Junior, John had to attend for interview, accompanied by his father, in the headmaster's study, 'where, somewhere in a corner, there were canes'.[78] The interview was not a success. John was asked how many half-crowns there were in a pound. He sat answering nothing; his father, who was deaf, smiled indulgently.

> The gold clock ticked; the waiting furniture
> 'Shone like a colour plate by H.M. Brock . . .[79]
> No answer – and the great headmaster frown'd;
> But let me in to Highgate Junior School.[80]

John entered the school in September 1915 and stayed for five terms, leaving in March 1917.[81] Recalling that period of the First World War in *Summoned by Bells*, he remembered Alfred Leete's poster of Kitchener pointing an imperious finger, with the slogan 'Your Country Needs YOU!'; the large sepia gravures of Allied generals given away with Brooke Bond tea; a neighbour's son killed at Ypres.[82] (Peggy Purey-Cust's elder brother, a midshipman, was also killed, in the Battle of Jutland.)

During the war, there were air-raid warnings, usually at night, though one daylight raid was made in 1917. Sir Anthony Plowman, a fellow-pupil of John's at the school, recalls it: 'The whole school was taken into the school field and made to lie flat on the grass while we watched the German 'planes flying over London. Later we picked up shrapnel from the field.'[83] He remembers John's 'reciting verses of his own composition in the playground, surrounded by a ring of small boys . . .' Sir Anthony remembers some of the verses, too:

On dark nights when the lights are put out
That is the time when the Zepps are about.

They frighten the people and do so much harm
And set the whole place in a state of alarm.

We shoot them at times and then they come down
But not once in a while do they fall on the town.

* * *

So we must shoot them all and bring them to the ground
So that bits of Zeppelin may easily be found.[84]

Another of John's early poems, transcribed by him at fifteen in a fair-copy book, is headed 'An Air Raid Dec. 16 Written during one'. This may be fact or self-dramatization; but the eight-stanza poem suggests that John had either direct experience of an air-raid or a first-hand account of one. The poem begins:

I

When I was having tea
  Approaching six o'clock
I suddenly heard quite a bang
  It gave me quite a shock.

2

'What was that?' I said,
  While trembling were my hands,
'Only rumbling lorries
  Or the milkman's cans.'

3

'There it goes again:
  I think it is a raid;
Let us seek some shelter
  For I am much afraid.'

4

Then I shouted loud,
  'Fly to the funk-hole, quick!
It is safer there
  For the walls are thick . . .'[85]

In a book of 1948, John wrote that Highgate School had been 'a rough place' during his time there.[86] 'I hated that school,' he told his contemporary, Harold Langley.[87] There were bullies among both boys and masters. Two boys wheedled John off his route home and down Swain's Lane. John knew from the tone of their voices that it was a trap, but submitted with the resignation of a predestined sacrificial victim. 'I can't think why I went with them,' he said in 1950. 'I think it was a deep-seated terror of having to fight if I didn't go with them.'[88] They threw him down, pulled off his shorts and ran away.

> And, as I struggled up, I saw grey brick,
> The cemetery railings and the tombs.[89]

When Frank Delaney interviewed him for his *Betjeman Country* (1983), John was still revolving his persecutors' names in a 'frightened couplet', like some primitive chant to ward off evil spirits – 'Robson and Ibbotson/Ibbotson and Robson'.[90] (Lancelot Ibbotson became general manager of the Southern Region, British Railways.)

John loathed the headmaster of Highgate Junior School, E.H. Kelly. In *Summoned by Bells* he recalled

> how Kelly stood us in a ring:
> 'Three sevens, then add eight, and take away
> Twelve; what's the answer?' Hesitation then
> Meant shaking by the shoulders till we cried.[91]

He remembered the shakings again on his Highgate tour with Valerie Jenkins – 'and you would be held down at the foot of this slope, so that boys could take a running jump at your bottom.'[92] Was he exaggerating? Sir Anthony Plowman thinks so: 'Kelly was no Wackford Squeers in my experience and I was in his form for at least a year ... I asked my younger brother (who entered H.J.S. after I had gone to the Upper School) what his opinion of Kelly was. His immediate reply was "He was a very kind man, strict but kind." I myself never suffered at his hand.' Plowman added: 'J.B. was a rather tender plant in those days.'[93]

But Harold Langley recalled Kelly's brutality in a poem he wrote for John in 1954 titled 'At Highgate Prep. in 1917'. ('I think Kelly ought to have been put in prison,' John wrote in his letter of thanks.[94]) The publication of *Summoned by Bells* prompted further memories of the headmaster's cruelty. N.C. Selway recalled that he had once been given 'twelve of the best' by him. 'I was beaten . . . with a boy called Allwork. His father came to our house late that night to persuade my father to go to the police about it. I was got out of bed and examined, but my father was a strict man and would have no interference with discipline. In these days [1960] there would be questions in the House!'[95] And Robert Hurd wrote to John:

> Heavens! I'll never forget Kelly at the Junior School. I was very frightened of him at the age of nine and remember being hauled up in front of the whole school and accused of writing and drawing obscenities on the street wall *of my own home in Jackson's Lane* [Hurd's italics] and threatened with the usual thrashing. Being completely innocent (to the point of not beginning to understand the obscenities) I eventually escaped physical punishment, but was regarded as a confirmed liar for a long time.[96]

The only thing John could find to say for Kelly was that he stopped the throwing of steel-pointed darts dipped in ink. 'One stuck in my head and raised a lump.'[97]

A master who did not bully John was T.S. Eliot, known as 'the American master',[98] who taught at Highgate Junior for the three terms of 1916. John wrote in a symposium on Eliot:

> Some of the cleverer boys from Muswell Hill[99] . . . knew he was a poet. How? I have often wondered, for I cannot imagine him telling them or anyone. . . Anyhow, they persuaded me to lend (or did I present it to him?) a manuscript called *The Best Poems of Betjeman*. I had forgotten the incident until he reminded me of it, in as kind a way as possible, in the early 'thirties. I record this now purely out of self-advertisement, because I think I must be the only contributor to this book [the symposium on Eliot] of my age who knew him so long ago.[100]

John was never sure about Eliot's reaction to *The Best Poems of Betjeman* (the title is abridged to *The Best of Betjeman* in *Summoned by Bells*, presumably for the sake of the metre):

> That dear good man, with Prufrock in his head
> And Sweeney waiting to be agonized,

I wonder what he thought? He never says
When now we meet, across the port and cheese.
He looks the same as then, long, lean and pale,
Still with the slow deliberating speech
And enigmatic answers. At the time
A boy called Jelly said: 'He thinks they're bad' –
But he himself is still too kind to say.[101]

John not only 'knew as soon as I could read and write/That I must be a poet';[102] he was sure he was going to be a famous poet, whose early literary development would be of interest to posterity. *The Best Poems of Betjeman* has not survived: perhaps he did give it to Eliot. But in the Betjeman Archive of the University of Victoria, British Columbia, are two notebooks with covers and title pages elaborately lettered by John. One, with a cover design mimicking that of a slim 1890s volume published by Elkin Mathews and John Lane, is entitled, in a small box in the top right-hand corner,

BILGE

BY JB

and is dated February 1922, when John was fifteen and at Marlborough College. It contains a fair copy of his poems up to that date. The other book is larger. Its title, in the bulging lettering of Mabel Lucie Attwell, is *Versatile Verse*. In it John again copied out the poems, recording the date at which each was written. The latest was written at fifteen.

Three poems in *Versatile Verse* – 'The Fairies', 'The Silent Pool' and 'The St Enodock Ghost' – were written at the age of eight, though John later confessed that he falsified the date of 'The Fairies' to make it appear that he was seven 'when these weak stanzas were written'.[103] 'The Fairies', which is printed in *Summoned by Bells*, was inspired, John indicated, by William Allingham's 'Up the Airy Mountain'.

Characteristics of the later Betjeman show up in these novice exercises. 'The St Enodock Ghost' foreshadows the ghost of Captain Webb from Dawley in John's poem 'A Shropshire Lad', which came 'dripping along in a bathing dress/To the Saturday evening meeting'. It begins:

In St Enodock Church one dreary night,
    Came a figure that no one knew,
It was tall, and thin, and dressed in white
    'And its body you could see through'.

It walked into the village street
    And slowly pranced along,
Making no sound with its bony feet,
    Moaning no ghostly song . . .[104]

'Our Local Station: By a villager', written at eleven, shows an early talent for assuming other voices and accents for comic effect:

I

Our local station be most fine –
    A splendid sight it be
It's on the local railway line
    From Muddleton-on-Sea.

2

We 'ave a little waitin' room
    (The vicar gave the mats)
But the fast express from Muddlecombe
    Keeps shakin' up the rats . . .

5

We 'ave a little garden too
    With plants all fresh and green
And a thing you puts a penny through
    Wot's called a slot machine . . .[105]

The notebooks can be compared to a scientist's record of failed experiments. False scansion, lame rhymes, maudlin sentiment and over-ripe lyricism mar most of the verses; those which are redeemed, are usually redeemed by humour.

For a poet who relied so heavily on past models, Highgate was an apt place in which to grow up. Marvell and Coleridge had lived there; Hopkins was educated there. Alaric Watts, Christina Rossetti and Judge Rayne, the 'Ragged School Rhymester', are buried there. A.E. Housman did not write *A Shropshire Lad* in a room overlooking the coloured counties; he wrote it in a Highgate villa.

In Hampstead, a bracing walk away, were the houses of Keats and Leigh Hunt, little changed since the nineteenth century. When John tripped off to the Heath with pencil and writing-pad 'to await inspiration from the sky', he looked across the scene Constable had painted when he lived in Hampstead. Wordsworth and Crabbe had enjoyed the same view, as Wordsworth recalled in 'Extempore Effusion upon the Death of James Hogg':

> Our haughty life is crowned with darkness,
> Like London with its own black wreath,
> On which with thee, O Crabbe, forth-looking
> I gazed from Hampstead's breezy heath.

John may have remembered Wordsworth's lines, as well as his own childhood, when he wrote in his late poem 'Meditation on a Constable Picture':

> Go back in your mind to that Middlesex height
> Whence Constable painted the breeze and the light
> As down out of Hampstead descended the chaise
> To the wide-spreading valley, half-hidden in haze . . .

The most direct effect of the poetic tradition in Highgate on John's work was the story of the minor poet Ebenezer Jones. He, too, had had his early schooling in Highgate, at the boarding-school of the Rev. John Bickerdike at the foot of Highgate Hill. In an 1879 reissue of Jones's poems *Studies of Sensation and Event*, his brother Sumner recalled a school incident. A lurcher dog had strayed into the classroom. A sadistic usher had lifted the dog high above his head at the top of a flight of stairs 'with the evident intention – and we had known him to do similar things – of hurling the poor creature to the bottom'.

'YOU SHALL NOT!' rang through the room, as little Ebby, so exclaiming at the top of his voice, rushed with kindling face to the spot from among all the boys – some of them twice his age.

But even while the words passed his lips, the heavy fall was heard, and the sound seemed to travel through his listening form and face, as, with a strange look of anguish in one so young, he stood still, threw up his arms, and burst into an uncontrollable passion of tears.

With a coarse laugh at this, the usher led him back by his ear to the form; and there he sat, long after his sobbing had subsided, like one dazed and stunned.

John quoted this passage as preface to his poem based on this incident, which was published in *Old Lights for New Chancels* (1940). Using the phrase 'You Shall Not!' as a dramatic refrain, he rendered the story into triads, in pastiche of Jones's poetic style.

Highgate seems to echo with the cries of schoolmasters' victims: Ebenezer Jones at Bickerdike's school; Edmund Yates, Gerard Manley Hopkins, Marcus Clarke and W.W. Skeat under Dr Dyne at Highgate School; John and his friends under Mr Kelly at Highgate Junior. No doubt John worked off some of his pent-up loathing of Kelly in the Ebenezer Jones poem, the one brutal Highgate usher standing in for the other. In 1950 he summarized what he had learnt at Highgate Junior School. 'I learned how to get round people, how to lie, how to show off just enough to attract attention but not so much as to attract unwelcome attention, how to bribe bullies with sweets (four ounces a penny in those days) – and I learned my first lessons in mistrusting my fellow beings.'[106]

3

THE DRAGON SCHOOL

[I remember] intense home-sickness when I first went to boarding school, where there was a smell of bat oil and stale biscuits and everyone shouting: 'Quis?' 'Ego.' 'Anyone seen my ruler?' 'Anyone seen my pencil case?' 'Shut up!' 'Betjeman, you'll get unpopular if you go on like this.' Then I seem to have directed all my wits to making myself popular, siding with the majority, telling lies to get out of awkward situations.

John Betjeman, 'Christmas Nostalgia', BBC radio talk,
25 December 1947

John's release from the terrors of Highgate Junior School came through his parents' friendship with A.E. ('Hum') Lynam and his wife May, who had a cottage called Cliff Bank in Trebetherick, the Cornish resort where the Betjemanns spent their holidays. 'Hum' was senior master, and was soon to be headmaster, of the Dragon School, Oxford – also known as 'Lynam's' and 'the O.P.S.' (Oxford Preparatory School). The Lynams' children, Joc and Audrey, were among John's childhood friends. John recalled:

I first knew Hum when I was about six or seven in Cornwall. Once, when my parents were away, I was sent to stay with him, while Joc was still at Rugby and Audrey was at the Baby School, at Cliff Bank. I was the most frightful nuisance, always drawing attention to myself and taking offence when not sufficiently noticed. I realized this at the time and I realize it now. I was at an extremely badly run Junior School of Highgate School and a day boy there. Hum must have realized this predicament. Anyhow I know that through letters and conversation with my parents, he got me to Lynam's.[1]

John arrived at the Dragon School in May 1917 and left in July 1920.

The main school buildings, at the junction of Bardwell Road and

Charlbury Road, had been designed by Hum's father, Charles Lynam – 'a Staffordshire antiquary, a disciple of Norman Shaw, a church restorer and a long way ahead of his time,' John wrote. 'When most architects were still building in revived Gothic or French Renaissance for institutional buildings, Charles Lynam designed the Dragon School buildings in a severely practical manner which yet fits in with the red brick part of North Oxford . . .'[2]

The nucleus of the buildings was the Old Hall, a traditional school hall flanked by five classrooms each side, with high sash windows and a pitched roof. At one end of the hall were two further classrooms separated by a partition. One was for 'Modern', the 'thicks'' classroom, presided over by 'Pug' Wallace. The thicks, even if stupid, were often popular. At the other end of the hall was a platform and a piano. Here the daily prayers were held, after physical training. A hymn would be sung, with J.B. ('Bruno') Brown thumping out a piano accompaniment: a favourite was 'O Son of Man, our hero strong and te-en-der' to the tune of the Londonderry Air. If Hum Lynam found boys fighting he would drag them on to the platform and either beat them with an umbrella or make them kiss. After prayers the boys dispersed to their classrooms.[3]

The desks were rickety, much carved and grooved; the floors, of worn pitch-pine, with knots and nailheads in relief. In the hall the pictures varied from classical to Pre-Raphaelite, with a Burne-Jones damozel above the piano. A portrait of John Smyth VC in army uniform was prominent, with an account of how he had won the medal in 1915. The school had a whole holiday ('VC Day') on the anniversary of his winning it. Off the hall was an octagonal building with a pointed roof, topped by a weathercock shaped like the Dragon crest, which figured in the rah-rah school song:

> *p.* But a weathercock glistens on high
> And upon it a dragon is seated
> And the words on that tin
> Mean 'Go in and Win!'
> *ff.* And the dragon is rarely defeated.
> For the dragon above
> Is the dragon we love
> And so to the Dragon we sing.

The octagonal building 'looked a bit like the Bishop's Kitchen at Glastonbury', a former pupil recalled,[4] but was in fact an evil-smelling lavatory. Beneath the hall were changing-rooms, redolent of sweat and gym-shoes. At the far end was the Plunge – three foot deep and icy-cold.

In the playground was the carpentry shop. If a boy was naughty or idle, Bruno Brown would send him to the woodwork master for 'something to beat you with'. The boy was likely to return bearing a twelve-foot plank and grinning widely. The most popular manufacture of the carpentry shop was wooden boats, hollowed out with a brace and bit: drill too deep, and you had a hole. John was not an expert boat-builder. In the school museum, above the carpentry shop, the star exhibit was an elephant's foot wastepaper basket. New boys were taken up to have their heads forced into the vile-smelling foot.

A covered playground was used for indoor football. Beyond it, the playing fields ran down to the River Cherwell by way of a steep bank, soon to be crowned by a granite war memorial cross designed by Charles Lynam in 'Celtic Twilight' style. The boys learnt swimming in the Cherwell in a belt attached by a rope to a pole. Eventually most of them were able to dispense with the belt and 'swim the river': once across the Cherwell and back, accompanied by the PT instructor, Mr Purnell, a Boer War veteran with battle scars, who was known inevitably as 'Colonel Purnell'.

Junior boys boarded in Stradlings and Charlbury houses, and the Vassall brothers, G.C. ('Cheese') and Archer, great-uncles of the spy,[5] also took a few boarders. The two main boarding houses were School House and Gunga Din. John was in Gunga Din, presided over by Gerald ('Tortoise') Haynes, who earned his nickname both on Lewis Carroll principles ('because he taught us') and because he looked like a tortoise. John's near-contemporary J.P.W. Mallalieu[6] thought Haynes 'glaringly unattractive-looking'.[7] Lanky, with a small head and protruding, bloodshot eyes, Haynes wore baggy grey flannels and a patched brown sports jacket. An expiring Gold Flake cigarette was usually attached to his lower lip. He applied board compasses to the bottom of any boy who failed to prepare his Latin exercises. 'Once, during a prolonged fit of coughing, he swallowed a still smouldering Gold Flake and lost his voice for a fortnight; but he continued to teach effectively with board compasses alone.'[8]

Tortoise Haynes also used more conventional methods of punishment. In *Summoned by Bells*, John described how he was beaten by him:

> A gym-shoe in his hand, he stood about
> Waiting for misdemeanours – then he'd pounce:
> 'Who's talking here?' The dormitory quailed.
> 'Who's talking?' Then, though innocent myself,
> A schoolboy hero to the dorm at last,
> Bravely I answered, 'Please, sir, it was me.'
> 'All right. Bend over.' A resounding three
> From the strong gym-shoe brought a gulp of pain.
> 'I liked the way you took that beating, John.
> Reckon yourself henceforth a gentleman.'[9]

When John arrived at the Dragon School, Hum's elder brother, Charles Cotterill ('Skipper') Lynam was still headmaster. John remembered 'the dramatic moment at a prize-giving when Skipper threw off his gown and Hum assumed it'.[10] John recalled Skipper as having 'red tie, blue shirt, unpressed clothes and flowing grey hair and low, gruff voice' and later realized that he had been 'an early radical with High Church leanings and, strongly and without any pose, unconventional'.[11] J.P.W. ('Per') Mallalieu, on his first evening at the school in 1916, thought Skipper looked like a retired pirate, because he was 'so relaxed and jolly, and because a parrot was nibbling at his ear . . . When I saw him again, early next morning, he was wearing only a towel and was racing three of his senior boys along a passage to the cold plunge.'[12] Skipper had a weathered, seaman's face; he spent most of his holidays sailing Blue Dragon IV, a twelve-ton yawl, among the Scottish islands or across the North Sea.

He believed in the virtue of learning Latin and Greek. He also believed in corporal punishment, for 'slackness in school work' even more than for lies or theft. But he was kind to John. 'When I first arrived, like most boys I was miserably homesick and in tears for days. I remember him walking up and down with me along the pavement outside the Lodge with his arm on my shoulder and telling me not to cry and how in some inexplicable way his sympathy brought comfort.'[13] John also recalled the happier times when 'on Sunday nights in the winter in the boys' room he would stand in front of the fire and the lights were put out and he would tell us Monty James ghost stories as though they had happened to himself. I do not think I have ever since in my life been so thrilled by the spoken word.'[14]

Hum Lynam, so called because he hummed while doing the rounds of the dormitories to give the boys the chance of *not* being caught out of bed, also gave readings, from *Moonfleet* by John Meade Falkner. On winter evenings he strolled round the School House corridors playing snatches of arias on a violin.[15] Hum could be testy or sarcastic; but, like Skipper, he was kind to John.

Hum was like a father to me [John recalled]. One always knew one could go to him if up the spout, although one never did. There was the feeling that he was there as a protection against injustice. He taught me how to speak in public and how to recite. 'Hands behind your back. Eyes on the clock. Stand at the front of the stage. Now speak up.' Hum's preoccupation with religion and the school services, I realise now, greatly affected me. Here was this great, but never remote and always kind man, interested in religion. There must be something in it. Preoccupation with it since, for which I am especially grateful, must be due to Hum and always, of course, one was part of his family in holidays in Cornwall, Joc and Audrey, the Adams family and the Walshams, all of whom were at the school.[16]

John thought that he learned most from Hum Lynam when he managed to squeeze in next to the master at school luncheons and ply him with questions about poetry. 'I remember him talking of Swinburne to me one day and recommending "Les Noyades" which was, to say the least, a liberal piece of advice to a private schoolboy. But he knew I would love the sound of the words and miss their meaning . . .'[17]

Dragon School boys were allowed a freedom which seemed extraordinary to boys at other comparable schools of the time. They did not have to wear Eton suits on Sundays and walk in a crocodile, as did the pupils of the slightly older and snootier Summerfields, higher up the Cherwell. Summerfields boys thought of Dragon boys as 'oiks' (non-gentlemen) because they drank lemonade straight from the bottle.[18] Tony Bushell, the actor, who was at Magdalen College School, recalled that at a cricket match with the Dragon School, Hum Lynam said to their terrifying head-master, 'When are you going to get rid of these things?' – tapping Bushell on his Eton collar.[19]

One of Skipper's most enlightened acts was the admission of girls to the school. Naomi Haldane (now Mitchison) had been a pupil as well as her brother J.B.S. Haldane, the scientist. Among John's contemporaries was Biddy Walsham, who, like the Lynam children, lived in North Oxford and holidayed in Cornwall. She was the daughter of a baronet, Sir John Walsham, and the granddaughter of an admiral, John Warren, and her brother, (Sir) John, also became an admiral. John knew her both at school and in Cornwall, and fell in love with her. In 1976, when *Betjemania*, a revue in which some of John's poems were set to music, was running at Southwark, Audrey Lynam wrote to John that she thought Gay Soper, in the show, was like Biddy Walsham. She added: 'I can see Biddy in our garden at 85 Banbury Road [Oxford] with John [Walsham] beside her, very solemn and his shorts too long . . . Biddy was the girl that you all admired and I thought her grown-up and marvellous.'[20]

John replied:

You're quite right; now I come to think of it, Gay Soper was very Biddy, one of my first stirrings of heterosexual passion or indeed any sex passion. I was bound to have been there at 85 Banbury Road. I was at all those parties with Biddy and John including his grandmother's (Mrs Warren) at 8 Winchester Road [Oxford] when we had fireworks in the garden . . . Biddy married a very nice fella called Crookshank and had handsome children . . . She was adorable and kind and still is.[21]

John's love for Biddy Walsham was at its height when he was in his late teens in Cornwall, though Mrs Crookshank says he did not reveal it to her at the time.[22]

'Dragons', as the pupils were called, knew few people outside the English middle class. The future socialist Per Mallalieu only realized another world existed when he was taken down a tin-mine in Cornwall owned by the father of one of his school-friends; a year later, the slump struck, the mine was flooded, and Hum Lynam organized a collection for the tin-miners thrown out of work.[23] But the First World War did impinge on Oxford slightly. Mallalieu remembered wounded officers at Somerville College, officer cadets learning semaphore in the Parks, pilots learning to fly on Port Meadow, Australian soldiers kissing girls in punts on the Cher. In *Summoned by Bells* John recalled how Skipper would announce, before the morning hymn, 'the latest names of those who'd lost their lives/For King and Country and the Dragon School'.

> Sometimes his gruff old voice was full of tears
> When a particular favourite had been killed.
> Then we would hear the nickname of the boy,
> 'Pongo' or 'Podge', and how he'd played 3Q
> For Oxford and, if only he had lived,
> He might have played for England – which he did,
> But in a grimmer game against the Hun.[24]

The boys would look solemn at this: they knew there would be no extra holiday that day. They 'did their bit' for the war effort, knitting shapeless string gloves for men in mine-sweepers, sticking Allied flags along the Somme on the map, and, 'for no reason that I ever heard,' Mallalieu wrote, delivering bags of horse chestnuts to the Great Western Railway station '– we pretended to ourselves that they were needed to make explosives.'[25]

The boys were also made to learn John Oxenham's[26] patriotic lines

> What can a little chap do
> For his country and for you?

'He can boil his head in the stew,' John and his friends would add. Trenches and guns meant less than 'bicycles and gangs/And marzipan and what there was for prep'.[27]

When Skipper Lynam had become headmaster in 1887 there were fifty day-boys and no boarders. By 1916, the year before John arrived, Skipper was defending himself against the charge that the school was overcrowded, with one hundred and forty-three pupils, about half of them boarders.[28] Six years later this number had nearly doubled. However, classes remained small. The curriculum was heavily classical. About half the teaching periods were devoted to Latin and Greek. The book-case one climbed to booby-trap a skylight in Upper I classroom was full of Kennedy's *Shorter Latin Primer* – the title altered by time-honoured custom to 'Shortbread Eating Primer' – with its gender rhymes:

> Many nouns in -*is* we find
> to the masculine assigned:
> *amnis, axis, caulis, collis,*
> *clunis, crinis, fascis, follis* . . .

There, too, were the Latin grammar books of Hillard and Botting and North and Hillard, which John recalled when describing the school's routine:

> And, in the morning, cornflakes, bread and tea,
> Cook's Farm Eggs and a spoon of marmalade,
> Which heralded the North and Hillard hours
> Of Latin composition . . .[29]

French was well taught by Tortoise Haynes, whose pupils could ever afterwards distinguish between the French for fish and poison, cousin and cushion, hair and horse. The amount of 'prep' – up to two hours – depended on age and form. It included much memorizing of poetry, particularly of Tennyson's 'Ulysses' and 'Morte d'Arthur'. John learnt a lot of poetry by heart and won a prize for recitation. A near-contemporary at the school, Arthur Lanham, wrote to him in 1976 to recall John's winning the prize in 1920. 'I still have a vivid memory of you on the stage in the Big School room declaiming your piece.'[30] Replying, John wrote: 'I think I recited James Hogg's "Skylark".'[31]

John was also noticed at this time by one of the masters, Bruno Brown. In 1976, living in retirement in Oxford, Brown wrote:

I knew him as a sensitive and far from typical Prep School boy, and little, if at all, interested in games of any sort. However not many boys of thirteen went about with a volume of Charles Dibdin's poems – the author of 'Tom Bowling' – in their pockets, or had already become fascinated by architecture. . . For this last, Gerald ('Tortoise') Haynes was the great influence: John himself never forgot this, and later dedicated a book to him. (Haynes died in 1944.)

I was a Scot in origin, and at the end of term sing-song (it would be the Easter term of 1920) sang a song in broad Scots, 'A lum hat wantin' a croon'. This apparently struck John, for from then onwards for the next fifty years he affected what he imagined was a Scots accent when we met, and wrote letters in a hybrid Anglo-Scots

dialect – full of 'Macs', 'toons', 'och ayes', 'ye' (for you) and so on.
He called this extraordinary language 'Skitch'.

John's great friend among the boys was, like him, a rather
unusual type in a Prep School – Ronnie Wright. He later became a
Roman Catholic priest. I think he died in 1969.[32]

Another friend was Hugh Gaitskell, the future leader of the
Labour Party, whom John was to meet again at Oxford University.
Gaitskell was five months older than John: the school roll for Christmas Term, 1918, showed that H. Gaitskell of form VIa was aged 12
years 8 months, while J. Betjemann of form Va was aged 12 years 3
months. Gaitskell's parents refused to let him invite John to their
home in Onslow Gardens, London, because John's father was 'in
trade'. But the two boys sometimes met in London. When Alan
Wood wrote an article on Gaitskell for *Picture Post* in 1951, John
told him that he remembered seeing Gaitskell 'in the holidays, at
the age of twelve, walking about London impeccably dressed with a
bowler hat and a stick'. He added that at the time Gaitskell was
'mild and friendly and very correct'.[33] Himself at least emotionally
a conservative, John was teasingly implying that Gaitskell, the
socialist, had been brought up as a toff. Gaitskell disputed the story
about the bowler hat, and riposted that 'by Betjeman's standards,
then and since, almost anyone else but Betjeman would have been
described as "very correct".'[34]

John was also on generally friendly terms with another future
Labour politician, Per Mallalieu. 'This morning we had a very short
service it lasted about three minutes and it had no sermon,' Mallalieu wrote to his mother in 1917. 'Then we went for a walk. I went
with a boy called Jhon Betchiman and we told Ghost stories to each
other which passed the time very well.'[35] But Mallalieu appears in
Summoned by Bells as 'Percival Mandeville, the perfect boy . . ./
Upright and honourable, good at games . . .' who challenged John
to a fight behind the bicycle shed. John got out of the fight by lying,
'My mater's very ill.'

> No need for more –
> His arm around my shoulder comforting:
> 'All right, old chap. Of course I understand.'[36]

Mallalieu did not mention this episode in his autobiography, but he did recall John and Ronald Wright as 'two of the odder boys during my time in a far from even school':

> Betjeman first achieved notice when his father sent him an unusually sophisticated stationary steam engine which inspired me to some pyrotechnical mis-spellings. 'Betgiman's engin was going to-night,' I wrote to my mother, 'and it has go a lovely pump that pumps in water whill the thing is going.' The 'engin' drove a variety of tools including a miniature circular saw on which H.K. Hardy tried to cut his finger nails, spending a week in bandages after. . .
>
> Betjeman, too, got himself in bandages. He had been intoning some chant to himself in one of the classrooms and marking the beat by pulling and releasing the rope which opened and shut a glass skylight. They spent about a week in the Sick Room picking bits of glass out of his head. This was a serious matter for the rest of us because no one was allowed to play with his 'engin' until he returned which, eventually, he did, looking like a Sikh.
>
> Thereafter Wright and Betjeman specialized in eccentricity. They drew plans for taking over the State of San Marino and keeping it as a pet, they had visiting cards printed for 'Ronald Wright and John Betjeman, Crumpen House, New South Wales' and on Saturday nights they entertained with ribaldish music hall songs – words as amended by Betjeman, music as hammered out on the Boys' Room piano by Wright. They also went in for elaborate hoaxes. Once I received a letter on expensive notepaper with a letterhead gravely printed 'The West London Lunatic Asylum' and signed by a physician. The perfectly typed text told me, with regret, that two school friends of mine, Ronald Wright and John Betjeman, had just been admitted to the asylum babbling about somebody called 'P.M.M.P.' 'Having,' wrote the doctor, 'discovered that the correct name is Mallalieu, I thought best to let you know the nature of their illness which is that they imagine themselves to be tea cups and we have to provide large saucers for them to sit in.'[37]

John found himself in competition with both Gaitskell and Mallalieu at the end of Easter Term 1919, when one of the parents, Mr Fitch, established a Speech Prize, open to the whole school. The entrants had to speak for five minutes, proposing or replying to the toast of 'The British Navy' or 'The British Army'. The result was: *1st* P. Mallalieu, *2nd* H. Gaitskell, *3rd* J. Betjemann, *4th* J. Brunyate. Mallalieu remembered nothing of this contest – not even entering it – but he vividly remembered the 1920 competition. He had been preparing his speech, recommending Asquith as Liberal candidate, all term, trying out each section on the dormitory until he knew the whole thing by heart. In the competition, he spoke with confidence and fluency and was sure he had won, 'though Betjeman came up with some strong stuff about the merits of ancient over modern buildings'.[38] But the last speaker, John Basil Williams (whose father had been a candidate in the 1910 General Election) made a speech in favour of Home Rule for Ireland which was hesitant and diffident, but thoughtful and 'compelling'. 'I never again shouted from a platform,' Mallalieu wrote.[39] The judges awarded a tie between Williams and Mallalieu, and placed John third.

John also performed alongside Gaitskell and Mallalieu in the school plays. His first appearance was as Ruth in Bruno Brown's production of Gilbert and Sullivan's *The Pirates of Penzance* in 1918. Reviewing it in the school magazine, R.E.C.W. wrote: 'A pleasing buxom wench was Ruth who scored a great success in the part of "Maid of all work". Always perfectly self-possessed she enunciated her lines with a clearness which even in that company was remarkable.'[40] Per Mallalieu played 'Edith, one of General Stanley's daughters', and Gaitskell was in the Chorus of Police.

In 1920, John took two parts in the school play, *Henry V*: Charles VI of France and the Earl of Cambridge. Frank Sidgwick wrote of Wylie's Henry:

> It was a gallant performance, and I don't think anyone else could have been cast for the part. Except, perhaps, Betjemann. Having beheld him manufacture, out of two small parts, the Earl of Cambridge and the King of France, two separate, distinct and perfect gems of character-acting, I am not prepared to say that he could not have acted, with equal insight and genius, Henry the Fifth, Fourth, Sixth and Eighth, or Othello, Falstaff, Imogen, Caliban, Hamlet, Juliet's Nurse or Lance *and* his dog Crab. I can't give him higher praise than by saying that he ought to play Bottom; but if next year he is cast for the part of Biondello in *The Taming of the Shrew*, who I believe has little to do except eat an apple, I will again break all engagements to come and see him do it.[41]

The *Oxford Times* critic was equally enthusiastic: 'The cleverest actor of all was John Betjemann – he played the mad old King of France in such a way that, instead of being completely minor, it became one of the most impressive parts in the whole play. There was remarkable genius in this performance.'[42] Rosa Filippi, a professional West End actress, also reviewed John favourably, though she thought 'he should not . . . use a tremolo in his voice.'[43]

John's acting success was to be repeated at Marlborough and Oxford, and gives the clue to his later mastery as a television performer. Acting ability – the ability to put oneself in somebody else's shoes – also helped him to understand people of the past, especially the Victorians. And the Victorian poets he read and learned by heart at the Dragon School intensified his feeling for the Victorian age: its heroic, impossible ideals; its pervasive religiosity and lugubrious doubts; the matrix of its hierarchical society. They introduced him to its cruelties, prudery, codes of honour, freaks of humour, passions and self-delusions, its angularities of vision, its generous and wizened souls. In the architecture of North Oxford he read the same themes – the same social hierarchy, from mustard brick terrace to marble mansion; the same angularities and freaks in gable and campanile, the same religiosity in the Ruskinian Gothic of stained-glass windows, arches and madonnas in niches. A lusciously Pre-Raphaelite religious aesthetic is given expression in a short prose piece by him published by the school magazine, *The Draconian*, in October 1921 (more than a year after he had left the school):

> The sun was sinking in an almost cloudless sky, as the old man, with his head reverently bowed, passed up the sombre nave of the lofty cathedral. Before him in all its magnificence stood the high altar, the candles already lit for evening service. He turned and faced the west window, through which the parting rays of the sun were shining. Seen from the choir, the colours melted into each other like clouds gathering in the sky . . .

Though he was alive to the beauties of the ancient Oxford of 'dreaming spires', John from the first found that he responded more to the Gothic Revival buildings of North Oxford. 'Malarial spot! Which people call medeeval, though it's not': he enjoyed Belloc's lines, which expressed something of his own less than reverent attitude towards the Oxford that tourists come to see. The crumbling grey stone of old Oxford, 'whispering from her towers the last enchantments of the Middle Age,' as Matthew Arnold had written, had less enchantment for John than the gaudy geometric brick of St Barnabas or Butterfield's Keble. The contrast was as of a living language set against a dead one.

North Oxford had come into being in the mid-nineteenth century when dons were at last allowed to marry. John, who had only to see the outside of a building to visualize the inhabitants, was always aware of the dons and their wives in the academic ghetto of North Oxford. In his poem 'Oxford: Sudden Illness at the Bus-stop' he described a don's wife waiting at a bus stop outside her North Oxford house, a rose pinned to her evening velvet.

> From that wide bedroom with its two branched lighting
> Over her looking-glass, up or down,
> When sugar was short and the world was fighting
> She first appeared in that velvet gown.

That was precisely when John himself first lived in North Oxford – the latter years of the First World War. He is more commonly regarded as an escapist than as a brutal realist, but after all the idyllic poems about Oxford, John's verses for the first time showed the squalid reality of university life – ill-paid dons, suburban gardens, petty gossip, tinned peas, toothbrushes airing on the window-sill.[44] North Oxford also figures in the two 'Myfanwy' poems which recall his undergraduate years, and in 'On an Old-Fashioned Water-Colour of Oxford' ('Bound for the Banbury Road in time for tea'). His strongest evocation of the district is in 'May-Day Song for North Oxford', based on 'Annie Laurie', one of the unison songs he would have sung at the Dragon School:

> Belbroughton Road is bonny, and pinkly bursts the spray
> Of prunus and forsythia across the public way . . .

John wrote three accounts of his days at Lynam's: one in *Summoned by Bells* (1960), another in an introduction to *Victorian and Edwardian Oxford from Old Photographs* (edited by himself and David Vaisey, 1971) and the third in *My Oxford* (1977), a symposium of essays edited by Ann Thwaite. All three suggest that he gained more from looking at Oxford and the surrounding limestone villages than from his education at the Dragon School. The instrument of liberation was the bicycle.

> Take me, my Centaur bike, down Linton Road,
> Gliding by newly planted almond trees

> Where the young dons with wives in tussore clad
> Were building in the morning of their lives
> Houses for future Dragons . . .[45]

Because the bicycle was a means to an end – visiting churches – John mastered it as he mastered no other sport. 'Most of us could bicycle with our hands in our pockets, slowly zigzagging past the railed-in gardens where tamarisk and forsythia grew; or we would lean against the cream-coloured lamp-posts with their terra-cotta coloured gas-lamps which were placed at infrequent intervals down all the leafy North Oxford roads.'[46]

The Dragon School was in 'the redbrick Anglo-Jackson[47] part of North Oxford, which only burst into full beauty when the hawthorn and pink may was in flower'.[48] But John preferred the inner North Oxford – Crick Road, Norham Gardens, Norham Road, and 'the magic, winding Canterbury Road, the cottages and stables by North Parade, and those ecclesiastical-looking houses gathered round the northerly spire of St Philip and St James ("Phil-Jim")'[49] – which he found 'more haunting and more daunting'.[50]

> Show me thy road, Crick, in the early spring:
> Laurel and privet and laburnum ropes
> And gabled-gothic houses gathered round
> Thy mothering spire, St Philip and St James.
> Here by the low brick semi-private walls
> Bicycling past a trotting butcher's cart,
> I glimpsed behind lace curtains, silver hair
> Of sundry old Professors. Here were friends
> Of Ruskin, Newman, Pattison and Froude
> Among their books and plants and photographs
> In comfortable twilight. But for me,
> Less academic, red-brick Chalfont Road
> Meant great-aunt Wilkins, tea and buttered toast.[51]

Great-aunt Wilkins was Elizabeth, wife of John R. Wilkins, architect and surveyor of Oxford. They lived at 4 Chalfont Road. Wilkins was architect to one of the breweries and 'did some nice little public houses in a free, Tudor style'.[52] He also restored the Clarendon Building and supervised the construction of a house for Professor Dicey, professor of Law, on the corner of Bardwell and

Banbury Roads on behalf of Colonel Edis, another architect. But 'as he wasn't Sir Thomas Jackson or one of the architects who had been to the University',[53] John once heard him referred to as a 'townee'. (The 'town and gown' hostility which had led to bloodshed in the Middle Ages was still a divisive force in Oxford life.)

Like West Hill, Highgate, North Oxford could be graded, geographically, in terms of class distinctions:

It mattered a lot in those days in hawthorn-scented North Oxford [John wrote] to which house in Norham Road, Crick Road or even as far out as Rawlinson Road, you were invited. Widows of Heads of Houses were Queens of North Oxford society. Polstead Road and Chalfont Road where I would go to tea, were slightly beyond the pale, and Summertown, except of course for Summerfields School, was out of the question. No one visited Cowley Road, except to hear plainsong in Bodley's beautiful church built for the Cowley Fathers, otherwise East Oxford was associated with commerce and those real bulwarks of the University, the college servants. To go to Jericho, now becoming fashionable as a residential place, was then to go slumming, though that was always permitted because it was 'good work'. The services at St Barnabas, with their ritual and incense, were a rival attraction to the Cowley Fathers.[54]

Dragons were free to bicycle into the city and look at colleges and churches. John usually went with Ronald Wright, who was the son of 'a barrister of Tractarian opinions and . . . a mother who had recently been converted to Rome'.[55]

Ronald Hughes Wright, come with me once again
Bicycling off to churches in the town . . .[56]

The two boys noticed the liturgical differences of the churches. John's favourite was St Peter-le-Bailey, always empty and always open. He preferred it to 'the arid Norman revival of St Andrew's church, which was also very evangelical'.[57] The explorations usually ended in the Roman Catholic church of St Aloysius, 'where in a side chapel,' John wrote, 'there was a relic of the True Cross, surrounded by candles, polished brass and jewels, which seemed to me very sacred and alarming, as, indeed, did the whole church, with its apse of coloured saints and its smell of incense and many *dévoués* crossing themselves and looking back at us while on their knees'.[58] But Ronald Wright, who found the doctrine and worship at the school 'far too fundamental',[59] asked to be allowed to attend Mass at St Aloysius' Church. He placed himself under instruction and was received into the Roman Catholic Church at the age of twelve.

Other Dragons collected butterflies or postage stamps; John collected churches. At an age when his friends were excited by Red Admirals or Penny Blacks, he was absorbed by the mystique of church-viewing, which had its own argot:

> Can words express the unexampled thrill
> I first enjoyed in Norm., E.E. and Dec.?[60]
> Norm., crude and round and strong and primitive,
> E.E., so lofty, pointed, fine and pure,
> And Dec. the high perfection of it all,
> Flowingly curvilinear, from which
> The Perp.[61] showed such a 'lamentable decline'.[62]

With Tortoise Haynes, there were bicycle excursions to the village churches near Oxford. Haynes would fix up his huge plate camera and photograph font or pulpit with 'pale grey slides/Of tympana, scratch dials and Norfolk screens'.[63] Haynes had a passion for Norman architecture. 'From him,' John wrote, 'I learned to think that Norman was the only style that mattered, and that Iffley Church was far the most interesting building in Oxford or its vicinity.'[64] There were also orchid-hunts in the Wytham Woods, rounders at Oxey mead and belly-flops from punts near Godstow. John was soon to break free from many of Haynes's prejudices, but he remembered him always as a great, natural teacher: 'He was the giver: ours it was to take.'[65] In 1952 John dedicated *First and Last Loves* to the memory of Haynes, 'who first opened my eyes to architecture'.

While John was at the Dragon School, his parents moved to 53 Church Street, Chelsea, a Georgian box almost opposite the mansion where Charles Kingsley had lived. He missed Hannah Wallis, who was given her *congé*. He missed the familiar scenery of Highgate, the hawthorns, the sheep-tracks and the mulch of trodden leaves in autumn. In a part of Chelsea served only by bus, he longed for the Highgate trams, the North London trains and the Underground to Kentish Town. But there was one big compensation: Ronald Wright also lived in Chelsea.

Together the boys explored London – its churches and its suburbs, as far out as the Metroland of 'beechy Bucks'. To mystify other passengers, they sometimes talked 'Loud gibberish in angry argument,/Pretending to be foreign'.[66] On his own, John visited the second-hand bookshops of the Essex Road and the Farringdon Road bookstalls. He bought poetry books, books on churches and Edward Lear's *Views of the Ionian Isles*, the flyleaf inscribed by the artist. He enjoyed the smell of old books, their polished bindings and the armorial bookplates of obscure country squires. Book-collecting was one of the few enthusiasms in which his father encouraged him. He slipped him half-a-crown and said: 'If you must buy books, buy the best.'[67] He also gave him George Godwin's *The Churches of London*, which he inscribed: 'To my dear boy in the hope that his appreciation of all that is beautiful will never fade.'[68]

The move from Highgate to Chelsea was an uprooting and intensified John's loneliness at home. His mother's smart new friends assured her that the Chelsea home was 'simply sweet' as they deposited their wraps and settled down to a game of bridge;[69] but during the school holidays John escaped from the 'poky, dark and cramped' house as often as he could. On Sunday evenings he attended Evening Prayer in different City churches.

> A hidden organist sent reedy notes
> To flute around the plasterwork. I stood,
> And from the sea of pews a single head
> With cherries nodding on a black straw hat
> Rose in a neighbouring pew. The caretaker?
> Or the sole resident parishioner?[70]

Guilt, not just antiquarian interest or religious fervour, drew John to these bleak services. His mother's querulous, self-pitying refrain ran through his mind: 'When I am dead, you will be sorry, John.'[71] He prayed that she would live.

Bess may have neglected John in his early childhood, but now that he was at the Dragon School and away from home more often than she, her love for him became oppressive. The character who represents her in his Oxford playlet 'The Artsenkrafts' tells her son: 'You know I love you more than anything else in the world'[72] and when he complains of the way his room is constantly tidied up, she bursts into tears 'with very loud sobs'. John writhed under this smothering, blackmailing love. What he felt for Bess in return was strong enough to put him in danger of being a 'mother's boy'. He could not repress it, but did his best to mask it: 'The love that waited underneath,/I kept in check.'[73]

4

FATHER AND SON

And when he could not hear me speak
He smiled and looked so wise
That now I do not like to think
Of maggots in his eyes.

John Betjeman, 'On a Portrait of a Deaf Man', 1940

Ernest Betjemann was overjoyed when his first-born was a son. His ambition to perpetuate the Betjemann dynasty was as ardent as Henry VIII's to secure the Tudor succession. Like Henry VIII, he was blessed with a son wise beyond his years, a prodigy with the pen – but a boy unhandy with a gun, a milksop who cut no figure in the trials of physical prowess in which his father excelled. And like Henry VIII, Ernest intended to make sure that his son was fit to succeed him when the time came.

During the First World War, the luxury goods trade languished.[1] G. Betjemann & Sons made Sopwith propellers and shell cases at as patriotic a cost to the Government as they could afford. In the 1920s business picked up wonderfully. Ernest realized earlier than most traditional manufacturers that some concession must be made to the popular new Art Deco style, then known as 'Jazz Modern' or *moderne*; but by refusing to sacrifice the quality of materials or workmanship, he achieved an upper-middle-class compromise which suited Asprey's, Harrods and the maharajah market. Eric Asprey of the Bond Street store said: 'Ernest Betjemann was far the best of the manufacturers supplying Asprey's. Everything was of immaculate quality.'[2] Apprenticeships at Betjemann's were long and rigorous. All timber used was left outside the Pentonville Road factory to weather for two years, and was then brought in under a gantry to weather again, so that it would be perfectly seasoned. Upstairs in the factory were stocks of the best veneers that could be found: walnut, satinwood, thuyawood, macassar, ebony.

There were sumptuous commissions for individual clients. Through Asprey, the firm obtained a big order to refurnish the house of Captain Woolf Barnato, the racing driver, near Gatwick. (Because of a fault in the electrical wiring, the house was burnt out shortly before completion.[3]) In *Summoned by Bells* John wrote of goods made in his father's factory 'To shine in Asprey's show-rooms under glass,/A Maharajah's eyeful.'[4] The scornful phrase may be an allusion to what became the great *chanson de geste* of Betjemann factory lore. F.P. Threadgill, who joined the firm in 1924, recalled:

> During the Round Table Conference on India held in London in November 1930, the Indian princes were put up in various hotels. The Maharajah of Patiala was in the Haymarket Hotel. Through Asprey's we were given the commission to make five huge teak trunks, one for each of his five wives. Each trunk was fully fitted with solid silver washing and bathing utensils – bowls, wash-basins, hand-basins, soap-boxes, soap-dishes, toothbrush holders. The bottles for pouring hot water had spouts with tigers' heads. We had to work overtime on it, it was a terrific job.[5]

William Hammond, who worked on the commission, remembered that the toilet set contained 'goesunders – you know, goes under the bed – in eighth-inch silver'. He added: 'The Union at that time allowed no bonuses of any kind. But when that job was completed, Mr Ernest asked us all to leave a registered envelope at the office and we all received a cheque according to our standing in the factory from ten bob for the shop-boy upwards.'[6]

The union-flouting gesture was characteristic of Ernest Betjemann. He ran his business on paternalistic lines, but he accepted the welfare responsibilities of being an employer as well as the profits. When George Jones fell ill with nephritis (kidney disease) in 1918 after serving only two years of his apprenticeship, Betjemann paid for him to stay in the London Hospital for fourteen weeks.[7] Betjemann allowed three of the apprentices at a time to go to the Norfolk Broads and stay on his three-berth yacht, moored at Coltishall. 'It was called "Queen of the Broads",' remembered Albert Dubery, another of the apprentices. 'Mr Ernest had it made partly in the works, from finest Honduras mahogany.'[8] John also used to stay on the yacht, with his father, in the untroubled times before they quarrelled.[9] Recalling those holidays in his 1945 poem 'East Anglian Bathe', John described spartan swims in Horsey Mere, not far from Coltishall:

> On high, the clouds with mighty adumbration
>   Sailed over us to seaward fast and clear
> And jellyfish in quivering isolation
>   Lay silted in the dry sand of the breeze
> And we, along the table-land of beach blown
>   Went gooseflesh from our shoulders to our knees . . .

Ernest provided the funds to set up company football and cricket teams, which played other firms' teams in Regent's Park and on Clapham Common. 'Old Mr Betjemann used to come over and have a look at us, but not Mr John,' George Jones said.[10] But sometimes John went on the firm's annual outings, to Southend, Hastings, Margate or Wormley by the River Lea. Ernest would travel down in his car with the managing director, Horace Andrew, while the men went in solid-tyre charabancs from the Carrimore Motor Service. When young, John travelled with the men. The first stop was a pub. Shortly after arrival at the seaside or river, lunch was held in a big restaurant and speeches were made by Ernest Betjemann and Horace Andrew.

After lunch, Ernest would drive off with Andrew and the men were left to their high jinks. Some of the jinks were very high indeed. Bill Hammond remembers that on an outing to Wormley, two of the workmen, Joe Pettit and Dick Gatwards, became very drunk and fell asleep under the trees. 'The rest of the boys danced round them and covered them with leaves. Unfortunately another one, Clifford, who was also the worse for wear, struck a match and set fire to the leaves. It then became urgent to rescue those two.'[11] John had left with his father by that Lupercalian stage, but this was the outing of which he wrote in his poem 'Essex', referring to 'Epping Forest glades[12] where we/Had beanfeasts with my father's firm':

> At huge and convoluted pubs
> They used to set us down from brakes

In that half-land of football clubs
Which London near the Forest makes.

Ernest Betjemann had one great handicap as an employer: his deafness. You could only speak to him through his 'trumpet', which had a black Moorish silk tube and an ebony mouthpiece. 'If he didn't agree with you,' Albert Dubery said, 'he would snatch the trumpet away.'[13] Brave spirits had been known to seize it back. Bill Hammond recalled: 'On one occasion I had a bookcase to do with only two boards of Austrian wainscot oak to use. Mr Ernest came along and said that two panels didn't match and should do. He flung it up the shop, and wouldn't listen to me. So I ran after him, and grabbed hold of the trumpet. Then I put all the boards together and I proved to him that I couldn't get two matching panels out of the boards. And without being too humble, he agreed I'd done the best I could.'[14] Ernest's deafness exacerbated his rows with John. Sometimes he misunderstood what John said, and bridled; John's pert replies seemed the more insolent when bellowed into the speaking-tube.

Because of the deafness, Percy Threadgill had to bid for Ernest at Sotheby's and other auctions. Ernest was an enthusiastic antique collector. He would bring his finds into the factory to be copied or incorporated into a new piece of furniture. It was his interest in eighteenth-century antiques that gave him the idea of reviving shagreen work, which was made not from sharkskin, as is commonly believed, but from Japanese sting-ray skin. The 'shagreen skins' were dyed green, pink or blue, and the fashion set by Ernest Betjemann became the rage in London for a while. When he went down to Cornwall on holiday, he collected stones on the beach and later had them cut up in the factory to inspect the grain. A pink stone with a white vein, which he called 'Rosita', was used to decorate ladies' dressing-mirrors.

Ernest's taste was not impeccable. Percy Threadgill remembered that 'He designed a coffee-set in china, called "Reynard the Fox".[15] The handle of the coffee-pot was in the form of a hunting-crop with the thong wound round the base. On the side was Reynard in semi-relief with his brush curled round his bottom. Each of the cups had the hunting-crop handle and the whole set was on a figured walnut tray with chromium-plated horseshoe handles.'[16] The coffee-set sold well at Asprey's.

Ernest's changing fortunes were indicated by his house-moves from Gospel Oak to West Hill to Church Street, Chelsea, and by the standard of his successive motor-cars. In 1974, W. Boddy, who had been editor of *Motor Sport* for forty years, wrote: 'John Betjeman cannot have liked the motor-car very much and I often wonder what he used for travelling about this changing land and looking at old churches . . .'[17] In a reply, John wrote:

> The first motor-car my father had was a Rover Landaulette and it would only just get up West Hill, Highgate, where we lived. It would take him to his factory in Islington and to his golf club in Barnet. The driver was the ex-coachman, a wonderful man, not mechanically minded, called William Allwright. I wish he were alive now. He used to hiss as he cleaned the Rover.[18] Then my father, when we moved to Chelsea, bought an Arrol-Johnston from a man named Dorson Kay-Bunn who had a motor showroom in Putney. Our chauffeur was called John and he knew about cars and studied my father who, being deaf, could never drive a car. After that we sank to an Essex Saloon.[19]

Like many other manufacturers of luxury goods, Betjemann's suffered from the 1929 Crash: this probably explains why Ernest 'sank to an Essex Saloon'. Percy Threadgill remembered that in the early 1930s the men accepted a ten per cent cut in wages, and that the factory was put on short time – no Saturday working, and finishing at four o'clock each day.[20] But luckily the firm's palmy days coincided with John's years at Oxford and the setbacks of his early career, so his father was able to bolster his bank-balance when he got into scrapes such as bouncing cheques or a fine for speeding; though Ernest was far from being a fondly indulgent father, and financial first-aid was invariably accompanied by a lecture.

The conflicts started when John was at the Dragon School. The first two surviving letters from Ernest to his son show something of the relationship between them during and just after the First World War. With both letters Ernest enclosed pocket-money. The first, from 53 Church Street, Chelsea, is dated 16 June 1917:

> Dear Boy,
>   Enclosed is £10, hope it sees you through. Mother comes to London Saturday and the operation is on Tuesday.
>   Macmanus[21] says I *must* lie up for a week, more or less, and rest, Mother doesn't know this, so I shall be glad to see you home after

the Exams, and help me out with the numbers of little things to be seen to.[22]

The second letter, of 1 May 1919, suggests that John had offended his father and was now repentant or feigning repentance:

My dear Boy,

I send you 5/- don't waste it – it's not easy to earn.

No, old chap, I would much rather not go to China until you can come with me, so will try to put it off until then.

Have a shot at getting a poem in the 'Draconian' this term.

So pleased you have decided not to be a second-rate chap. – Had a lovely ride home. We did it easily in the day, and came through Camelford and round by Brown Willie and Rough Tor [in Cornwall], it is *most desolate*, and miles away from Camelford – it is more dreary far than Salisbury Plain or Dartmoor.

All well at home,

Thomas can almost beg.

Your affectionate

Daddy.[23]

Until Ernest Betjemann began to realize that John had no intention of entering the family business, relations between them were generally cordial.

My dear deaf father, how I loved him then
Before the years of our estrangement came!
The long calm walks on twilit evenings
Through Highgate New Town to the cinema:
The expeditions by North London trains
To dim forgotten stations, wooden shacks
On oil-lit flimsy platforms among fields
As yet unbuilt-on, deep in Middlesex . . .
We'd stand in dark antique shops while he talked,
Holding his deaf-appliance to his ear,
Lifting the ugly mouthpiece with a smile
Towards the flattered shopman . . .[24]

The walks with his father had one by-effect on John that was lasting. On Michael Parkinson's television show in 1973, John said he thought he had developed his eye for architecture because his father, being deaf, had especially developed his eyesight and would always point things out.[25] In his response to architecture, John did not disappoint Ernest; but he was unresponsive where an enthusiastic interest would have given most pleasure – on visits to the Betjemann factory in Pentonville Road. Ernest was showing off the works to his son, but he was also showing off his son to the works:

> Most of all
> I think my father loved me when we went
> In early-morning pipe-smoke on the tram
> Down to the Angel, visiting the Works.
> 'Fourth generation – yes, this is the boy.'[26]

When John revisited his childhood haunts with Valerie Jenkins in 1974, they drove to the old factory in Pentonville Road, 'passing through Pooter-land, ponderous Victorian Holloway, trying to imagine where Mr Pooter's Brickfield Terrace might be'.[27] Miss Jenkins recorded:

Nowadays the works are the premises of the Medici Society, publishers of the Medici prints, and makers of greeting cards.[28] We walked in to be surrounded by Old Master cards in unfolded piles. Traces of the old firm remain: a door engraved in florid style, 'Counting House', and the parlour with its old fireplace, where there would always be biscuits in a barrel.

Once, as a child, exploring upstairs, John Betjeman discovered a dusty drawing-room, completely furnished, where great-grandfather had lived above his work, before moving up to sylvan Highbury.[29]

But Master John, the heir-apparent, was not enthralled. As a small boy he amused himself in a desultory way, pretending to be an electric train over the silversmith's uneven floor – 'First stop the silver-plating shop (no time/To watch the locksmiths' and engravers' work)'[30] – or pretending to work with old Buckland as he electroplated, dropping 'dull bits of metal into frothing tanks' and bringing them out 'all gold or silver bright'.[31] The words John chooses to describe the factory processes, in *Summoned by Bells*, suggest the resistance and distaste he felt at the time: the 'whining saws' of the cabinet-makers' shop; the 'scream of tortured wood'; the 'blackened plank/Under the cruel plane'; the 'reeking swabs' of the French polishers. Like someone in an interminable discordant concert looking forward to smoked salmon and champagne in the interval, he waited eagerly for lunch-time, which 'brought me hopes of ginger-beer'.[32] But to obtain that he had to wait for his father, who was among his clerks in the counting-house and greeted him absently with the saintly smile of the deaf. So John was left to his own devices: hours of tedium in the upper rooms – 'One full of ticking clocks, one full of books'.[33]

Ernest also tried to interest his son in the history of Betjemann's by showing him early documents relating to the firm.

> With joy he showed me old George Betjeman's book.
> (He was a one-'n' man before the craze
> For all things German tacked another 'n'):
> 'December eighteen-seven. Twelve and six –
> For helping brother William with his desk.'
> Uninteresting then it seemed to me,
> Uninteresting still.[34]

As John grew older, his father began to prepare him for his succession in more practical ways. But John was no more adept at carpentry under Ernest's instruction than when making model boats at the Dragon School. ' "Not *that* way, boy! When will you ever learn" –/I dug the chisel deep into my hand.'[35] He proved an equal duffer in shooting lessons, forgetting to release the safety-catch when his father shouted at him to shoot a rabbit.

John's most humiliating shooting recollection was of Hertfordshire, in his poem of that title: trudging with his 'knickerbockered sire' in a syndicated shoot at Buntingford, he fired by mistake into the ground.[36] On the drive home in the Rover Landaulette, through Welwyn, Hatfield and Potter's Bar, he had to suffer his father's recriminations. 'How many times must I explain/ The way a boy should hold a gun?' More often the sport was in the neighbourhood of Mundford in Norfolk, where Ernest rented a shoot of some eight hundred acres. His best friend and shooting companion was Philip Asprey, who had entered the family business in Bond Street at the age of twenty-five after army service in France from 1914. It was politic for Ernest to get on well with a member of the family who sold so many of Betjemann's goods; but from the moment of their first meeting in 1919, when Asprey was still 'working his way up from the bottom' under the exacting surveillance of old Dewey, the stockroom keeper at Asprey's, a friendship developed between the two men. They were temperamentally alike – diligent and scrupulous in business, and happiest when out in the open with gun, rod or golf-club. Sometimes Philip Asprey and his brother Eric stayed at the Rock Hotel, Cornwall, to join Ernest in golf on the St Enodoc links. After one of these holidays, Eric Asprey gave John a lift back to London in his snub-nosed Bentley. He remembered John, who was still a schoolboy, leaning over the dashboard and shouting: 'Faster! Faster!'[37]

Ernest introduced Philip Asprey to shooting, persuading him to buy a £20 gun from Vaughan in the Strand. On Thursday nights Asprey would drive Ernest to Mundford, where they took over the King's Arms. Asprey later acquired a shoot of three hundred acres next to Ernest's and borrowed his keeper, Jones, to look after it. 'Ernest Betjemann was a crack shot,' said Asprey. 'But because he was stone deaf, and couldn't have any idea where the birds were coming from, he had Jones walk behind him to tap him on the shoulder and point. We used to bring back a tremendous amount of birds – partridge, pheasant or duck – and those would be distributed among the staffs of Asprey's and Betjemann's.'[38] Eric Asprey also came up sometimes, and more rarely John would make up the party, a reluctant and erratic shot. After the shoots there were post-mortems and jollity at the King's Arms. In that company John must have felt as out of place as Horace Walpole was when he was dragooned into one of the Rabelaisian carouses of his father, the Prime Minister, at Houghton, also in Norfolk.

John could not share his father's interests, but Ernest made at least some attempt to humour John in his. As the letter of 1919 shows, he gave him some encouragement in his verse-writing. However, there was a certain forced jocularity to the encouragement which undermined the kind intention:

> 'And how's our budding bard? Let what you write
> Be funny, John, and be original.'[39]

The jollying-along approach might well embarrass, rather as teasing questions as to 'Who's your little lady-friend, then?' can infect with an adult unease the kind of childhood romance that John wrote about in 'Indoor Games Near Newbury' and *Summoned by Bells*. When John and his father visited the Tate Gallery and John was enraptured by Frank Bramley's painting 'The Hopeless Dawn',

Ernest suggested he should translate the picture into verse, and gave him the inspiring opening

> Through the humble cottage window
> Streams the early dawn.

John completed the rhyme

> O'er the tossing bay of Findow
> In the mournful morn.

But a hunt through a gazetteer showed that there was no such place as Findow ... 'and the poem died'.[40] John's choice of Bramley's painting may have had psychological significance: in 'The Hopeless Dawn' a young wife and an old mother gaze out to sea (an angry sea which reminded John of the waves 'in splendid thunder over Greenaway'), knowing that the man of the house is lost and will not return. Wishful thinking?

With both father and son, love was overlaid by resentment and resentment hardened into antagonism. The mutual hostility had causes deeper than John's lack of interest in carpentry or shooting pheasants. It was the inevitable counterpart to his excessive emotional dependence on his mother. Six years after Ernest's death in 1934, John wrote a poem about him – 'On the Portrait of a Deaf Man' – that has an almost vindictive quality. He dwells on his father's fate with a morbid relish that recalls the gloating mortification of the flesh in medieval German paintings of martyrdom:

> He would have liked to say good-bye,
> Shake hands with many friends,
> In Highgate now his finger-bones
> Stick through his finger-ends.

Compare these lines with the exalted *In Memoriam* tone of John's 1945 threnody on Basil, Marquess of Dufferin and Ava, whom he loved.

Later, when remorse had set in, John recalled in his poem 'Norfolk' the happy times he had spent on his father's yacht on the Norfolk Broads, and wondered when and how the rift had grown so deep between them:

FATHER AND SON

How did the Devil come? When first attack?
These Norfolk lanes recall lost innocence,
The years fall off and find me walking back
Dragging a stick along the wooden fence
Down this same path where, forty years ago,
My father strolled beside me, calm and slow.

5

EARLY INFLUENCES

Of course, like all precocious children, I was derivative without realizing it. Only healthy, normal children not afraid to be themselves are truly original.

John Betjeman, 'Childhood Days: or Old Friends and Young Bullies',
BBC radio talk, 16 July 1950

Mr Betjeman's borrowings may have enriched him: they have not made him what he is.

Derek Stanford, *John Betjeman*, 1961

That T.S. Eliot taught the ten-year-old Betjeman was a bizarre coincidence which could only have been matched if Verlaine, during his stint as a private schoolmaster in England (an episode mortalized in one of Max Beerbohm's caricatures), had taught the infant Henry Newbolt. But unlike the master-pupil relationship which had developed between Richard Watson Dixon and Gerard Manley Hopkins in Highgate School seventy years before, the encounter between Eliot and John at Highgate Junior School was not fruitful in the younger man's work. Indeed, Lord David Cecil has pointed out that at Oxford John led a reaction against the pervasive influence of Eliot. 'You have no idea,' Lord David said, 'how original it was for John to be writing in the style of Tennyson and other Victorians when his friends were all pastiching Eliot.'[1]

John's natural stance would have been anti-Eliot; but because he had known and liked him at an early age, and Eliot had been absorbed into the Betjeman automythology, John continued to feel sympathy for him and to give him as much benefit of his doubts as he could. This was made easier by their like thinking on religion. '[Eliot's] soul's journey,' John wrote in 1948, 'travels in the same carriage as mine, the dear old rumbling Church of England which is high, low and broad all at once. I know that we are both "high" and object to certain weaknesses of the system, and that we both regard the Church of England, despite these weaknesses, as *the* Catholic Church of this country.'[2]

As for the poetry, John dwelt not on the differences between Eliot's vision and technique and his own, but on those fragments in which he could find welcome similarities. He liked Eliot's topographical exactitude. John could identify with Eliot when the older poet wrote of 'the wind that sweeps the gloomy hills of London/ Hampstead and Clerkenwell, Camden and Putney/Highgate, Primrose Hill and Ludgate . . .'[3] These places were of John's own world – and that of Mr Pooter.

John wrote that people must not be misled by the solemnity of Eliot's poetry and criticism, and his serious face, into thinking him an unhumorous person. 'Allow one doomed for ever to be thought a "funny man" to say that Eliot is extremely funny. He has a slow deep humour, subtle and allusive, the sort of humour that appreciates that immortal book *The Diary of a Nobody*.'[4] John also emphasized Eliot's 'exquisite ear for rhythm'. He remembered an old poet of the Nineties complaining to him that Eliot's poetry did not scan. (That was before the publication in 1939 of Eliot's *Old Possum's Book of Practical Cats*, whose metrical ingenuity John thought 'a combination of Gilbert and A.A. Milne'.) But John argued that 'Eliot has rhythms of his own. Each line he writes is a scanning line that could not possibly be mistaken for prose . . . And each line sets off the rhythm of the line that follows it.'[5] The passage of Eliot that John quoted with most approval was one he might almost have written himself:

> O City, city, I can sometimes hear
> Beside a public bar in Lower Thames Street,
> The pleasant whining of a mandoline
> And a clatter and a chatter from within
> Where fishmen lounge at noon: where the walls
> Of Magnus Martyr hold
> Inexplicable splendour of Ionian white and gold.[6]

The liberties taken in this passage are not much more adventurous than those of Hilaire Belloc's 'Tarantella', a poem it resembles, even down to the similarity of Belloc's 'And the hammer at the door and the din' to Eliot's 'And a clatter and a chatter from within' and the understood *obbligato* of guitar in Belloc's poem, mandoline in Eliot's. John's appraisal is that of an appreciative fellow-craftsman: 'The sudden contrast of the public bar, all dactyls and short *a* sounds, with the caesurae and spondees of those rolling lines which describe the cool still City church across the road need no conventional forms. They are a pattern in themselves.'[7]

The poets John read at Highgate Junior School included Henry Wadsworth Longfellow, Thomas Campbell and Edgar Allan Poe.[8] His affectionate derision of Longfellow is made clear in two 1930s poems about Dumbleton Hall,[9] in 'A Literary Discovery' (1952) and in his later poem 'Longfellow's Visit to Venice' ('To be read in a quiet New England accent'). He enjoyed 'Hiawatha's Photographing', Lewis Carroll's parody of Longfellow's 'Hiawatha', and could recite it from memory when in party mood.

Like Longfellow's 'Wreck of the Hesperus', Campbell's 'The Soldier's Dream' – a poem John enjoyed at school[10] – was a stock piece in schoolboy anthologies of the time. It begins:

> Our bugles sang truce, for the night-cloud had lower'd,
> And the sentinel stars set their watch in the sky;
> And thousands had sunk on the ground overpower'd,
> The weary to sleep, and the wounded to die.

When John used this kind of metre, he was imitating Thomas Moore rather than Campbell (as in *Sir John Piers*, John's 1937 pamphlet of Irish poems). But one of his poems, 'Senex' (1940), may owe at least its title to Campbell, whose 'Senex's Soliloquy on his Youthful Idol' expresses an old man's striving to remain platonic, faced with the beauty of a young girl:

> Platonic friendship at your years,
> Says Conscience, should content ye:
> Nay, name not fondness to the years
> The darling's scarcely twenty.

John's 'Senex' has the same kind of reproachful conscience:

O would I could subdue the flesh
Which sadly troubles me!
And then perhaps could view the flesh
As though I never knew the flesh
And merry misery.

To see the golden hiking girl
With wind about her hair,
The tennis-playing, biking girl
The wholly-to-my-liking girl,
To see and not to care.

(The verse style here is that of W.S. Gilbert, which John first encountered in the Gilbert and Sullivan operas produced by 'Bruno' Brown at the Dragon School.)

Campbell was himself old when he wrote his poem, while John was in his early thirties. Campbell's Senex is evidently going to allow himself some licence, and will not try too hard to be platonic. John's Senex indulges in an agony of self-repression:

At sundown on my tricycle
  I tour the Borough's edge,
And icy as an icicle
See bicycle by bicycle
  Stacked waiting in the hedge.

Get down from me! I thunder there
  You spaniels! Shut your jaws!
Your teeth are stuffed with underwear,
Suspenders torn asunder there
  And buttocks in your paws!

Oh whip the dogs away my Lord,
  They make me ill with lust.
Bend bare knees down to pray, my Lord,
Teach sulky lips to say, my Lord,
  That flaxen hair is dust.

In a letter of 1946 to Randolph Churchill, who had asked for elucidation, John explained the images of spaniels and bicycles:

As to *Senex*. Spaniels are symbolic. I hate them as they fawn on me and try to attract one's attention by false affection when one does not really want to have them slobbering over one.

'bicycle by bicycle' suggests lustful thoughts – underwear, suspenders and buttocks, of people half-undressed behind some hedge or haystack near the bicycles, and spaniels present the thoughts to me. I mean the thoughts come like spaniels to attract me with their false glamour or shall we say? un-lasting glamour.[11]

One of the merits claimed for Eliot's verse is that he does not deliver his message to us on a plate: by deliberate obscurantism he forces the reader to prise out the meaning from a welter of symbolism and sophisticated allusion; and it is further claimed that this very act of teasing out the meaning makes its final exposure more rewarding, like the capitulation of a lover who has 'played hard to get'. This was not a theory of poetry to which John subscribed. He did not see poetry as an elaborate crossword puzzle in which the poet provided the clues and the reader struggled for the answers. But the letter to Churchill shows that he was capable of symbolism, allusion and enigmatic concentration of meaning. Indeed, John's thought-sequence, as glossed by him for Churchill, is so idiosyncratic as to be undecodeable except to spaniel-haters – a rare breed.

If John's title 'Senex' may have been suggested by one of Campbell's, another of Campbell's titles, 'Lines on the View from St Leonard's', might have been composed by John. The poem has some affinity with John's poem 'Greenaway'. It reveals a similar delight in shingle and wild headlands. But the two poems differ in the same way as the two 'Senex' poems. Again, Campbell's is an optimistic, almost Panglossian voice. To him the 'green savannahs' of the sea are a beneficent element:

> The Spirit of the Universe in thee
> Is visible; thou hast in thee the life –
> The eternal, graceful and majestic life
> Of nature, and the natural human heart
> Is therefore bound to thee with holy love.

To John (in 'Greenaway'), the sea, however seductively beautiful and wild, is a source of potential terror:

> But in a dream the other night
> I saw this coastline from the sea

And felt the breakers plunging white
Their weight of waters over me.

John belonged to the generation which abandoned the optimism of the Victorians and ceased to believe in happy endings. When, at the end of 'Greenaway', he asked to what dreadful jaws the sea would drag him, he was voicing the same kind of fear as Eliot had expressed, ten years earlier, in 'The Dry Salvages'.

Though John was seen by Lord David Cecil and others as the heresiarch against Eliotism, his world-view had far more in common with Eliot's than with Campbell's. Two world wars, which the two high churchmen had shared, and Campbell had not, saw to that. Campbell celebrates the consolidation of his world; Eliot and John are constantly aware of the disintegration of theirs. The difference between Eliot and John is that, confronted by this disintegration, John takes refuge in 'arrested development', dwelling on the former joys that war has disrupted or dispelled, paradise lost; while Eliot (in 'Four Quartets') believes that

We cannot revive old factions
We cannot restore old policies
Or follow an antique drum . . .
. . . to make an end is to make a beginning.
The end is where we start from . . .

The two poets represent, to adopt an image of Eliot's, the live nettle and the dead nettle which flourish in the same hedgerow: detachment and attachment, history as freedom, and history as servitude.

Intellectually, John could be radical, but emotionally he was conservative. The antidote to his permanent sense of insecurity was an accretion of experiences and characters, built into a personal mythology. He reinterpreted his friends and enemies as *dramatis personae* in the masque of his life, and with such consistency that he not only believed in them himself, but was able to impose his version on other people. Least real, and therefore (as in a religion) *most* real and central to the cosmography, was Archibald, his teddy bear:

I used to wait for hours to see him move,
Convinced that he could breathe.[12]

The loneliness John suffered was intensified by his father's deafness and his mother's uncerebral garrulity. In Archibald he found solace when he had been spanked by his 'hateful nurse', Maud, for being late for dinner. 'One dreadful day' Archibald was hidden from him as a punishment:

> Sometimes the desolation of that loss
> Comes back to me and I must go upstairs
> To see him in the sawdust, so to speak,
> Safe and returned to his idolator.[13]

Archibald was taken up to Oxford, and was later immortalized as the teddy bear of Lord Sebastian Flyte in Evelyn Waugh's *Brideshead Revisited*. He also became the hero of John's fable *Archibald and the Strict Baptists*. Once, when John and his wife Penelope had a quarrel in their house at Wantage, Penelope dangled Archibald over a well and threatened to throw him down; John's distress was acute.[14]

'Arrested development' might seem too strong a phrase for John's dependence on the *penates* and remembered fragments of his past. It was hardly on a Proustian scale, and it did not prevent his having a 'normal' sex-life. But the same aspect of his character is shown by his fascination with his childhood romances. The freckled face of the Admiral's daughter 'So haunted me that all my loves since then/Have had a look of Peggy Purey-Cust'.[15] When *Time and Tide* set a competition to write a poem in John's manner, he wrote (but did not dare to submit) 'Indoor Games near Newbury' about 'that early intense love one feels at a children's party':

> Love that lay too deep for kissing –
> 'Where *is* Wendy? Wendy's missing!'
> Love so pure it *had* to end,
> Love so strong that I was frighten'd
> When you gripped my fingers tight and
> Hugging, whispered 'I'm your friend'.

Here there is a close parallel with another of the poets John read at Highgate Junior School – Edgar Allan Poe, who had died so interestingly of dissipation ('And what is dissipation, please, Miss Long?'[16]). In 'Annabel Lee', Poe wrote:

I was a child and *she* was a child,
In this kingdom by the sea;
But we loved with a love that was more than love –
I and my Annabel Lee.

For the moon never beams without bringing me dreams
Of the beautiful Annabel Lee,
And the stars never rise but I feel the bright eyes
Of the beautiful Annabel Lee;

And so, all the night-tide, I lie down by the side
Of my darling – my darling – my life and my bride,
In the sepulchre there by the sea,
In her tomb by the sounding sea.

Compare that ending with the cosily sensual last stanza of 'Indoor Games near Newbury':

Good-bye Wendy! Send the fairies, pinewood elf and larch tree
                                               gnome,
   Spingle-spangled stars are peeping
   At the lush Lagonda creeping
Down the winding ways of tarmac to the leaded lights of home.
   There, among the silver birches,
   All the bells of all the churches
Sounded in the bath-waste running out into the frosty air.
   Wendy speeded my undressing,
   Wendy is the sheet's caressing
   Wendy bending gives a blessing,
Holds me as I drift to dreamland, safe inside my slumberwear.

Both passages, even down to the mention of stars (symbols of un-attainability) and dreams (the only means of attaining the unattainable) convey an impression of a platonic love more intense and more rewarding than carnal love; Poe disguises this theme with morbidity, Betjeman with comedy.

Many of John's early influences must have been imbibed from the poetry he read and often learned by heart at the Dragon School. Although *The Dragon Book of Verse*, compiled by W.A.C. ('Whack') Wilkinson and N.H. Wilkinson, was not published until 1935, it contained several of the poems learnt by John and his contemporaries fifteen to eighteen years before. The first poem in the book is William Allingham's 'Up the Airy Mountain', a poem with which John may have been familiar before he went to Lynam's, as he mentions it as inspiration of an early verse he wrote in Highgate:

> When the moors are pink with heather
> When the sky's as blue as the sea,
> Marching all together
> Come fairy folk so wee.[17]

The Wilkinsons' anthology contained three poems from Lewis Carroll's *Alice* books. The opening stanza of one of these poems, 'You are old, Father William' ('And yet you incessantly stand on your head. . .') may have influenced the first verse of John's early poem 'An Eighteenth-Century Calvinistic Hymn' ('And if I but take to my Couch/I incessantly Vomit and Bleed'); though the main inspiration of the poem, as John made clear to Mark Ogilvie-Grant when he sent him the poem to illustrate, was a hymn-book compiled by a dissenting minister in the early nineteenth century and used by the Particular Baptists.[18] More generally, John's whimsical, eccentric, Church of England humour resembles Lewis Carroll's. ' "Yes, rub some soap upon your feet!" ' at the beginning of John's 1932 poem 'A Hike on the Downs' has a nonsense-appeal akin to that of ' "I must sugar my hair" ' in Carroll's ''Tis the Voice of the Lobster'.

The Wilkinsons included one poem by a writer with whom John had perhaps more in common than with any other Victorian, Charles Stuart Calverley. This again was less a case of direct influence than of a similar cast of mind in two men of different centuries. At the end of Calverley's 'Waiting', the only verse of his in the Dragon book, are two stanzas which collapse in Betjemanian bathos:

> 'Hush! Hark! I see a towering form!
> From the dim distance slowly roll'd
> It rocks like lilies in a storm,
> And O, its hues are green and gold.

> 'It comes, it comes! Ah rest is sweet
> And there is rest, my babe, for us!'
> She ceased, as at her very feet
> Stopp'd the St John's Wood omnibus.

Calverley and John were alike in their mischievousness – the arrested-development naughtiness that lasts into adult life, perhaps as a reaction to the curbing of high spirits by too authoritarian an upbringing. In a biographical notice of Calverley which prefaced the *Complete Works* published in 1901, Sir Walter Sendall, Governor of British Guiana, commented that Calverley 'vexed the souls of dons' at Oxford.[19] (Calverley was sent down from Balliol for 'an exuberance of animal spirits'.[20]) John too vexed the souls of dons at Oxford – particularly the soul of C.S. Lewis – and like Calverley he left Oxford without a degree; though, unlike Calverley, he did not proceed to a brilliant classical career and academic honours at Cambridge. Calverley shared Poe's and John's sentimental nostalgia for childhood sweethearts. The serenade to Julia Goodchild in Calverley's 'Visions' is like John's to Peggy Purey-Cust in *Summoned by Bells* –

Miss Goodchild! – Julia Goodchild! – how graciously you smiled
Upon my childish passion once, yourself a fair-haired child:
When I was (no doubt) profiting by Dr Crabb's instruction,
And sent those streaky lollipops home for your fairy suction!

The poem includes stars (stanza ii) and a dream (stanza ix). Calverley again apostrophized a childhood girlfriend in his 'First Love':

O my earliest love, still unforgotten,
With your downcast eyes of dreamy blue!
Never, somehow, could I seem to cotton
To another as I did to you!

Calverley and John have much else in common. John's mockery of snobs who set store by petty social triumphs ('I know the Inskips very well indeed'[21]) is matched by Calverley's verses on the man who pocketed cherry-stones from a pie eaten by the Prince of Wales:

My Cherrystones! I prize them,
No tongue can tell how much!
Each lady caller eyes them,
And madly longs to touch.

Like Disraeli in *Sybil*, Calverley and John both pined for what they pictured as the benevolent system of feudalism. John said that when he first went to Ireland in the 1920s 'I saw things very much in the terms of Mrs Alexander's hymn "All things bright and beautiful" – "The rich man in his castle,/The poor man at his gate,/He made them high and lowly/And ordered their estate." '[22] The system had been destroyed by electoral reform and by education for the masses. The two poets lamented the passing of the old order in verses which had both themes and rhymes in common. Calverley wrote, in 'Charades':

> Ere yet 'knowledge for the million'
> Came out 'neatly bound in boards';
> When like Care upon a pillion
> Matrons rode behind their lords:
> Rarely, save to hear the Rector,
> Forth did younger ladies roam;
> Making pies, and brewing nectar
> From the gooseberry-trees at home . . .

John wrote, in 'The Dear Old Village':

> Along the village street the sunset strikes
> On young men tuning up their motor-bikes,
> And country girls with lips and nails vermilion
> Wait, nylon-legged, to straddle on the pillion.
> Off to the roadhouse and the Tudor Bar
> And then the Sunday-opened cinema.
> While to the church's iron-studded door
> Go two old ladies and a child of four.
> This is the age of progress. Let us meet
> The new progressives of the village street.

John had first used the vermilion/pillion rhyme in a cheeky squib on 'Hum' Lynam and his wife May which he contributed to the September 1920 issue of *The Draconian*:

> Hum and May went out one day
> On a motor-bike painted vermillion [*sic*]
> Hum was the nut of the latest cut
> And May was the girl on the pillion.

The model for this was not Calverley but the nursery rhyme 'Jack and Jill'. Another nursery rhyme inspired John's 'Ode to a Puppy (By His Mistress)', published in *The Draconian* of April 1920, which began:

> Oh! puppy dear, I sadly fear
>   Your waistcoat's at the wash,
> Your cutlet, too, is soaked right through
>   With all your lemon squash.

Here the debt was to the rhyme usually ascribed to the New England writer Eliza Follen (1787–1860), of which the third line is so close to John's first:

> Three little kittens they lost their mittens,
>   And they began to cry,
> Oh, mother dear, we sadly fear
>   That we have lost our mittens.

The April 1920 issue of *The Draconian* contained a second poem by 'J. Betjemann, age 13', titled 'Dawn':

> Ever ting-a-linging my bedroom clock is ringing,
>   Ringing, ringing,
> As the sun breaks in the east;
>   And, stretching with a yawn,
>   I curse the lovely dawn,
> And wait in moody silence till the bedroom clock has
>   ceased.
>
> I've read the poet's rhymes about early morning
>   chimes
>   At awful times;
> And the sun through window panes;
>   The little birds twitting
>   And the big ones flitting
> But poets *never* write about the dawning when it
>   rains.

This is an early example of John's pitting the unlovely truth against soupy poeticism, humour against sentimentality. The two opening lines suggest an echo of Alfred Noyes's 'The Highwayman':

> And the highwayman came riding –
> Riding – riding . . .

Noyes's poem, that staple of anthologies for schoolboys, was probably the direct source of this trick of style in John's verse, though the convention had been common in the Scottish ballad for centuries, as in

> The cattie sits in the kiln-ring,
> Spinning, spinning;
> And by came a little wee mousie,
> Rinning, rinning.

Only one of John's contributions to *The Draconian* has seen the light of day since the 1920s: 'Summer Poem' (September 1920), which was first reprinted in *The Wind and the Rain, an Easter Book* (1962). It begins:

> Whatever will rhyme with the Summer?
> There is only 'plumber' and 'drummer':
> Why! the cleverest bard
> Would find it quite hard
> To concoct with the Summer – a plumber!
>
> My mind's getting glummer and glummer.
> Hooray! *there's* a word besides drummer;
> Oh, I *will* think of some
> Ere the prep's end has come,
> But the rimes will get rummer and rummer . . .

This poem shows John experimenting with rhyme – teaching himself by trial and error the techniques of an art in which no formal tuition was to be had. The limerick metre is a natural one for a schoolboy to have chosen; but there are some mature touches, such as the easy conversational tone of 'Would find it quite hard' in the first stanza. At the same time, John was not going to succumb to the Colloquial Fallacy of modern poetry – the belief that poetry must at all costs preserve what Hopkins called 'the rhythm of common speech'. John was (and remained) equally taken by the idea of a special language reserved for poetry: this was in line with his High Church leanings and his reverence for the old, tried forms; while the striving for colloquialism smacked of freethinking, of extempore preaching replacing ritual, and impertinent new texts ousting the Authorized Version. In *Summoned by Bells* he wrote of his earliest compositions: ' "O'er" and "ere" and "e'en"/Were words I liked to use.'[23] 'Summer Poem' has an 'ere' and (in the third stanza) a 'showeth'.

Much of John's later verse *is* cast in the rhythms of everyday speech (and in religion he was at times drawn to Nonconformity as well as to Anglo-Catholicism) but even in quite late poems a condiment dash of archaism is often added, as, for example, in 'Lines written to Martyn Skinner before his Departure from Oxfordshire in Search of Quiet – 1961':

> ... For there the leafy avenues
> Of lime and chestnut mix'd
> Do widely wind, by art designed,
> The costly houses 'twixt.

Such lines as these probably owed as much to hymns as to the prescribed poets. 'The costly houses 'twixt' resembles 'The quiet waters by' in the hymn version of Psalm XXIII, 'The Lord is my Shepherd'.

'Bruno' Brown recalled that John carried round a copy of Charles Dibdin's poems at the Dragon School.[24] Besides the mournful and moving cadences of Dibdin's 'Tom Bowling', which may have been sung to the poet's own music as well as read, John would have read the jolly jack-tar drinking songs. The shanty rhythms of Dibdin, and sometimes a close approximation to his sense, are often found in John's verse. In Dibdin's 'Jack in his Element' a self-satisfied sailor preens himself ('Bold Jack the sailor here I come,/Pray how d'ye like my nib?') and boasts of his women and his welcome in every port:

> I've a spanking wife at Portsmouth Gates,
> A pigmy at Goree,
> An orange-tawny up the Straits,

A black at St Lucie:
Thus, whatsoever course I take,
I leads a jovial life,
In every mess I find a friend,
In every port a wife.

John's equally complacent young businessman, in 'Executive', also preens himself, and boasts of his material comforts and of his welcome in every drive-in restaurant:

I am a young executive. No cuffs than mine are cleaner;
I have a Slimline briefcase and I use the firm's Cortina.
In every roadside hostelry from here to Burgess Hill
The *maîtres d'hôtel* all know me well and let me sign the bill.

Both Dibdin's poem and John's could be sung to the air of 'The Girl I Left Behind Me' or that of 'Sweet Lass of Richmond Hill'. And both men wrote poems about Margate, though Dibdin's Margate of watermen, gunnels and oyster-smacks and John's 1940 Margate of putting-courses and *thés dansants* have only ozone in common.

Not all the poetry John read as a child was, to use Herbert Lomas's phrase, 'under-vitaminized fodder'.[25] Coleridge was represented in the Dragon anthology by 'Kubla Khan' and 'The Ancient Mariner', and there are affinities with Coleridge (not necessarily echoes of him) in John's poetry: for example, in the recurrence of a sense of guilt in 'N.W.5 and N.6':

'World without end.' What fearsome words to pray.

'World without end.' It was not what she'ld do
That frightened me so much as did her fear
And guilt at endlessness. I caught them too,
Hating to think of sphere succeeding sphere
Into eternity and God's dread will.
I caught her terror then. I have it still.

The same kind of resurgence of guilt and terror is described in 'The Ancient Mariner': 'Since then, at an uncertain hour,/That agony returns . . .' (Again, compare that with John's recurring anguish at the hiding away of Archibald in his childhood: 'Sometimes the desolation of that loss/Comes back to me . . .'[26])

Wordsworth's *Prelude* is the ultimate model for *Summoned by Bells*, though it was probably a long autobiographical poem of 1940 by John's old Oxford tutor, J.M. Thompson, that gave John the idea of writing his own early life in verse. Shadows of Wordsworth's Lakeland fall on others of John's poems, such as 'North Coast Recollections', originally part of 'The Epic':

<blockquote>

Black

Rises Bray Hill and, Stepper-wards, the sun
Sends Bray Hill's phantom stretching to the church.
</blockquote>

But Tennyson was the prime influence John absorbed in child-hood. The scene-setting lines in Tennyson's 'The Princess', such as 'Myriads of rivulets hurrying thro' the lawn,/The moan of doves in immemorial elms' were still having their effect in '14 November, 1973', a poem on Princess Anne's wedding ('Hundreds of birds in the air/And millions of leaves on the pavement'), but they were already embedded in John's poetic consciousness by the time he wrote 'Pot Pourri from a Surrey Garden' (published 1940) ('Miles of pram in the wind and Pam in the gorse track,/Coco-nut smell of the broom . . .') and 'Bristol' (published 1945) ('And an undersong to branches dripping into pools and wells/Out of multitudes of elm trees over leagues of hills and dells . . .'). John delighted in Tennyson's sensuous imagery and his decorative use of euphonious stones (*Tennyson*: 'Nor winks the gold fin in the porphyry font';[27] *Betjeman*: 'In topaz and beryl, the sun dies away.'[28]) The lulling rhythms of 'The Lady of Shalott' are used to comic purpose in 'Indoor Games near Newbury':

<blockquote>

Rich the makes of motor whirring,
Past the pine-plantation purring
 Come up, Hupmobile, Delage!
Short the way your chauffeurs travel,
Crunching over private gravel
 Each from out his warm garáge.
</blockquote>

Tennyson was considered suitable for gentlemen in the making because he celebrated the ideals of medieval chivalry in the *Morte d'Arthur.* (The lascivious interpretation of the legend in Aubrey Beardsley's illustrations to Malory might have had less appeal to the Dragon School anthologists.) The robust Browning, with his thoroughly acceptable attitudes respecting England in April or poetic leaders who left their disciples for handfuls of silver, was equally in favour. John adopted his dialectical method in 'The Arrest of Oscar Wilde at the Cadogan Hotel', 'A Hike on the Downs', 'Bristol and Clifton', 'Hunter Trials', 'How to Get On in Society', 'Narcissus', 'Reproof Deserved' and – most successfully of all – in 'Shattered Image', a portrayal of cynicism on a level with that of Bishop Blougram, Mr Sludge the Medium or the double-crossing aldermen in *The Pied Piper of Hamelin.*

When John draws on the work of great poets, such as Coleridge, Wordsworth, Tennyson or Browning, the result is usually a half-mocking pastiche. It is less like Mozart developing the manner of Haydn, or Beethoven revolutionizing the techniques of Mozart, than Tchaikovsky having fun in Mozartian vein in his fourth Serenade and his Variations on a Rococo Theme. John could not rival the visions of Wordsworth or the despair of Coleridge; but he could and did match the moods of three poets who described and gently satirized the everyday – William Cowper, George Crabbe and Winthrop Mackworth Praed. He paid tribute to all three: to Cowper, in 'Olney Hymns'; to Crabbe, in 'The Electrification of Lambourne End', a poem published in *The Architectural Review* in 1933; to Praed, in 'Winthrop Mackworth Redivivus'. And when he wanted to deplore what was happening to 'The Dear Old Village' and to 'The Village Inn' in the twentieth century, the satirical style of these poets, quiet and lethal, was the weapon he chose.

In 1939, John reviewed a biography of Praed by Derek Hudson. ('I had always imagined Praed against the background of a new chaste stucco mansion of the 1820s, with a Doric lodge, a copper-beech, a winding avenue and the warm Devon sunlight and large arboreta associated with that county. I had imagined him at a ball in the Assembly Rooms transfixing all female hearts with his handsome appearance and willowy figure. Mr Hudson has proved my suppositions correct.'[29]) John liked Praed's detail: Hudson's biography, he wrote, was 'as finished as a poem by Praed'. But where the two poets most resemble each other is in their nostalgia for Old England.

Praed, 'An Every-day Character: "Quince"':

> Near a small village in the West,
>   Where very many worthy people
> Eat, drink, play whist, and do their best
>   To guard from evil Church and Steeple,
> There stood, – alas! it stands no more! –
>   A tenement of brick and plaster,
> Of which, for forty years and four
>   My good friend Quince was Lord and Master.

Betjeman, 'The Dear Old Village':

> See that square house, late Georgian and smart,
> Two fields away it proudly stands apart,
> Dutch barn and concrete cow-sheds have replaced
> The old thatched roofs which once the yard disgraced.

Because John was certain, from an early age, that his destiny was to be a poet, he began learning his craft before most of his contemporaries. This precocity did not, as might have been expected, put him ahead of them. Beginning so early, he gave himself, in effect, the training of a Victorian poet. The models available to him were nearly all pre-twentieth century. It must have been a shock, when he arrived at Oxford University, to find that his contemporaries were infatuated with Eliot and that they were experimenting enthusiastically with *vers libre*. It was like training for the cavalry as a cadet and then growing into a world of nuclear warfare – only to find that one's old cavalry instructor had become the foremost expert in atom-splitting.

6

CORNWALL

... the long express from Waterloo
That takes us down to Cornwall. Tea-time shows
The small fields waiting, every blackthorn hedge
Straining inland before the south-west gale.
The emptying train, wind in the ventilators,
Puffs out of Egloskerry to Tresméer
Through minty meadows, under bearded trees
And hills upon whose sides the clinging farms
Hold Bible Christians. Can it really be
That this same carriage came from Waterloo?
On Wadebridge station what a breath of sea
Scented the Camel valley! Cornish air,
Soft Cornish rains, and silence after steam ...

John Betjeman, *Summoned by Bells*, 1960

Every summer, the Betjemann family took a London and South Western train down to Cornwall. You could get to Wadebridge by the Great Western Railway, by way of Plymouth and Bodmin, but the Betjemanns preferred the L & SW's longest run, along the edge of Dartmoor, through Halwill Junction and over the Tamar into Cornwall just before Launceston.

Devon woods gave place to long sweeps of barren moorland. Beyond Otterham station the downs dropped away, giving a tantalizing flash of distant sea. At Camelford the rugged lines of Rough Tor and Brown Willy on the Cornish moors rose on the left; at Delabole the line ran close to the slate quarries. The landscape became greener as the train drew parallel with the Allen River, which joins the River Camel and passes near Egloshayle Church standing by the waterside.

It was a fifteenth-century vicar of Egloshayle who built the great seventeen-arched bridge at Wadebridge. John would crane out of the window to see it as the train snaked into Wadebridge station. Beyond was a straggling Nonconformist landscape, studded with Methodist chapels. At Wadebridge, the Betjemanns alighted. As the train steamed on to its terminus below the Metropole Hotel in Padstow, a brake hired from Derry's, the Wadebridge carriers, took the family to Trebetherick. When the brake neared the village and the carriage lamp caught the pennywort and fennel in the hedgerow, John would wonder whether Mr Rosevear, the bad-tempered local schoolmaster, had built himself a house,[1] and whether there had been another wreck on Doom Bar, the lethal sandbar across the Camel Estuary between St Enodoc and Stepper Point. Later he would be lulled to sleep by the sound of the Atlantic rollers down in Daymer Bay.

The Betjemanns' first lodgings were in a boarding-house called The Haven. Another regular guest there was the palaeontologist (Sir) Arthur Keith, who was bamboozled by the Piltdown skull forgery in 1912.[2] Keith came down to play golf with Gordon Larkworthy, who owned The Haven. Larkworthy's daughter Joan (now Mrs Kunzer) first met John in 1910, when he was four and she was five. 'I can remember to this day the arrival of the Betjemanns,' she recalled.

> I was frightfully quizzy to know who was coming – peering about. The first one I saw was Bess Betjemann. She always bustled about tremendously: John used to walk exactly like her, rather fast. And then this little thing – I can see him now – coming in in a white suit, little anxious face, big eyes. I'm not sure how many times they stayed at The Haven; but Ernie Betjemann took Linkside when John was about seven or eight. The bit that always makes me feel quite ill in *Summoned by Bells* – that awful red fly that got burnt[3] – that was in Linkside . . . I often used to stay with the Betjemanns there, and then they built a house, Undertown.[4] By that time Ernie Betjemann had bought nearly all the land in Trebetherick. He stipulated that all the houses built had to be white.[5]

As a small boy, John did what other small boys do at the seaside: paddled, built dams and sandcastles, climbed cliffs and collected shells. He knew where to find cowrie shells – 'on the tide line where there are little pieces of coal which must be of the same specific gravity'.[6] At about ten years old he was allowed out on the rocks to fish for prawns and crabs. When he and the other holidaying children had been down in Cornwall for a week or two, 'the soles of our feet had got so hard that we could walk over mussels quite easily in order to get a better view into some secret pool'.[7] The rock pools were 'full of colour, much more colour than autumn woods'.[8] On many stretches of the coast, the waves were considered dangerous and unfit for bathing; the fashion for surfing did not reach Cornwall until just before the Second World War.

Treasure hunts were organized for John and the neighbours' children in the afternoons, followed by splits and cream under the old apple trees of the Oakleys'[9] garden, where the winners received their prizes. Once John won, 'but that was an unfortunate affair': Mrs Betjemann had set the clues and John, the host, knew how her mind was likely to work. One prize he gained legitimately was a *Daily Mail* award for sandcastle-building: Biddy Walsham (now Mrs Kenneth Crookshank) has a photograph of him with the winning entry, many-turreted and moated, a very *Neuschwanstein* of a sandcastle.

Joan Kunzer said that, though nervous, John forced himself to take a leading part in deeds of daring.

> We went round in such a gang [she remembered] – there must have been fourteen or fifteen of us. We used to do the most appalling things, and it was always John who would volunteer. There was one awful occasion; we had this terrific scheme, we all went out at dead of night, and it was decided that one of the party was to go into St Enodoc's Church[10] and pull the bell. Well, who volunteers? John. And I have never seen . . . when he came out, I can see his face now, he was so petrified – white and trembling. But he'd *done* it, you see.[11]

Another time, John said he would like to spend a night on the top of Rough Tor. Joan's brother Tom Larkworthy agreed to go with him. They arranged that at midnight they would flash a lantern from the top of the hill as a signal to Joan. 'As it was some twenty miles away I could never have seen it,' she said. 'But they *did* it. And, poor John, his description of when he woke up in the morning: "I thought I was in Hell," he said. Apparently there was some wild thing, a ram or something, with horns, bending over him. And my brother Tom said, "I have *never* seen anyone look so frightened. John just took to his heels." '[12]

At times, John's nerve failed him. Joan Kunzer recalled:

We used to have ghastly cricket matches – we were all terribly hearty. Poor John, there weren't enough children one year, and he had to be in one of the teams. And I've never forgotten, we were all sitting round waiting and a figure appeared in rather funny kind of cricketing clothes and he was walking in a very stiff, painful way. So I asked what on earth was the matter. He said: 'I'm covered in newspapers. I'm afraid of being hurt.' He had newspapers rolled round his arms, newspapers rolled round his legs, newspapers padding his chest and stomach, newspapers stuffed down his trousers. He looked like the Michelin Man.[13]

In spite of his lack of *esprit de corps*, John was popular with the other Trebetherick children, because he knew how to make them laugh. Probably his unorthodox cricket pads were worn as much for comic effect as for protection. And he was already writing funny verse. Joan Kunzer remembered:

There were two . . . well, we thought of them as old ladies; I suppose they were in their thirties – the Miss Pouldens. (Miss Rhoda Poulden is mentioned in one of John's poems.[14]) Their father was an admiral; they were frightfully grand and very prim. We saw they were sitting on the beach one day. I said, 'Good afternoon' or something like that. John never said a word; but when we walked away, he just started, and I can remember it now; it was:

> In a rum-diddle, dum-diddle, dum-dum hat,
> Round as a pancake, squashed and flat
> Sat the rotary Rhoda Poulden.

She *was* very fat. He made it up as we stood there.[15]

That was the day John persuaded the Misses Poulden to enter the caves in Mundy Cove, near Trebetherick. To the children's smothered amusement, Miss Rhoda commented: 'What very unpleasant *effluvia!*'[16]

In *Summoned by Bells*, John recalls how he took part in organized sports against Joan Larkworthy and Joc and Audrey Lynam, 'Hum' Lynam's children. Joan and he once decided to be 'non-cooperative' and refused to be organized in heats. When at last they were made to, and had to race out to the low-tide line and back again, 'A chocolate biscuit was the only prize.'[17] John got the giggles and was sent home to bed; Joan laughed more discreetly, and escaped.

John did not enjoy organized games or organized anything. He was still, essentially, a solitary. (In some senses he remained one. However gregarious he became in later life – partly in reaction against the loneliness of his childhood – he always needed a bolt-hole, a place to which he could escape and where he could be quiet.) He liked to get away from the other children, on foot or by bicycle. At first, wild flowers were his main interest. He learned about them from Gerald Haynes, from books, and from his father, who was glad to encourage him in any pursuit which took him into the open air.

The flora of north Cornwall were as varied as the terrain of salt-marshes, foreshores, sand-dunes and slacks, cliffs, rocks and 'hedges', as the Cornish call banks of upturned slates.[18] At Tre-gligga, near Tregardock (the subject of a Betjeman poem), was hare's-foot trefoil, its feathery, purple flowers unlike those of any of the other trefoils. On the steep path from Port Isaac were yellow and white bedstraw and great hemlock. Phalanxes of hemp-agrimony, hemlock, burdock and foxgloves stood on the cliffs around. Mallow, poppies, briar rose and traveller's joy spread with wilderness abandon through the ghost village of Port Quin. Patches of willow-herb, thyme and giant mullein added to the hazards of the St Enodoc golf course. Golden samphire, with its fleshy leaves, covered the summit of the quartz dyke which runs across the peninsula at the northern end of Mother Ivy's Bay, and on Trevose Head was greenweed, *genista tinctoria*.

The names of plants gave John the same kind of pleasure as the terminology of church architecture: a sense of being initiated into an exclusive mystery with its own enchanting shibboleths. He rolled the names voluptuously round his palate: purslane, Babington's orache, marram, ivy broomrape, autumn squill, rupture-wort, rock samphire, Hottentot fig. Some of the names turned up in his poetry. In *Summoned by Bells* he wrote of the bladder-wrack and iris at Daymer Bay, tamarisks and pink convol-vulus further inland, toadflax and periwinkles in the belt of elm sur-rounding Padstow. Thrift and bladder-wrack are mentioned in 'Trebetherick'; lady's finger, thyme, ragwort, sea-pink, bent-grass and 'bright varieties of saxifrage' in 'Sunday Afternoon Service in St Enodoc Church, Cornwall'; veined sea-campion, gorse, kidney-vetch and squills in 'Cornish Cliffs'.[19]

John went flower-hunting in Cornwall as he went church-hunting. His quarry might be a cinquefoil flower or a quatrefoil window. As he grew older and his interest in people became predominant, architecture came to mean more to him than flowers. Buildings were the spoors of human beings. Flowers were only interesting insofar as they were chosen by people for their gardens, houses or costume. Flowers can symbolize, as in the dahlias blackening in the forest which represent death at the end of 'The Heart of Thomas Hardy'. But no *Zeitgeist* inhabits them, as it inhabits architecture.

As John reached adolescence, church architecture became his overriding enthusiasm. The local church of St Enodoc could be easily reached on foot. It was no architectural masterpiece, but it had a romantic history. St Enodoc or Caradoc was a Welshman ('What faith was his, that dim, that Cornish saint,/Small rushlight of a long-forgotten church'[20]). The church had been built in 1430 on the site of the saint's cell. For several generations, the little building, with its bent spire like a crooked witch's-hat, was almost overwhelmed with sand, and was known locally as 'Sinkininney Church'. In the early nineteenth century the church was so deeply buried in sand that, to secure its privileges, a clergyman had to be lowered through a skylight once a year to hold a 'service'. In 1863 the church was dug out and restored. Sabine Baring-Gould makes this digging-out a central episode in his novel *In the Roar of the Sea* (1892), which John read as a child.

St Enodoc's Church was approached across the golf links, probably the main attraction of the area to John's father. John described the approach in 'Sunday Afternoon Service in St Enodoc Church, Cornwall': as he and his friends walk to church, the 'tinny tenor' of the bells rings out. ('Do you know why the bells of S. Enodoc are so sweet?' asks Mr Scantlebray in *In the Roar of the Sea*. 'Because, so folks say, melted into them are ingots of Peruvian silver, from a ship wrecked on Doom Bar.')

The interior of the church was nothing to write home about. It had 'a humble and West Country look'.

> Oh 'drastic restoration' of the guide!
> Oh three-light window by a Plymouth firm!
> Absurd, truncated screen! oh sticky pews!
> Embroidered altar-cloth! untended lamps!

St Enodoc by John Piper

But because, like Archibald the teddy bear, or T.S. Eliot, the non-descript little church was part of his childhood experience, John was prepared to suspend his critical powers for it.

> So soaked in worship you are loved too well
> For that dispassionate and critic stare
> That I would use beyond the parish bounds
> Biking in high-banked lanes from tower to tower
> On sunny, antiquarian afternoons.

John bicycled as far afield as Blisland, at least fifteen miles from Trebetherick. The church, dedicated to St Protus and St Hyacinth, but known locally as 'St Pratt's', was 'the first really beautiful work of man which my boyhood vividly remembers,' John later wrote. It answered, he felt, Sir Ninian Comper's demand that 'a church should bring you to your knees when first you enter it'.[21] (Some early Comper – the Molesworth family tombs – was to be seen in Little Petherick Church near Wadebridge.) John was freeing himself from prejudice about the age of architectural features. To him, the glory of Blisland Church was the red, green and gold screen designed by F. C. Eden in 1897. Gerald Haynes's insistence on the supremacy of the Norman style was now forgotten or scorned. 'What do dates and style matter in Blisland Church?'

John asked in *First and Last Loves*. 'There is Norman work in it and there is fifteenth- and sixteenth-century work and there is sensitive and beautiful modern work. But chiefly it is a living church whose beauty makes you gasp . . .' And he was learning to record architecture in his own language, not that of architectural textbooks or guidebooks. Who but he would have thought of describing the sixteenth- or seventeenth-century gable ends of the house near Blisland Church as curling round 'like Swiss rolls'?[22] The teatime simile is funny, memorable and exact.

Nearer Trebetherick was the parish of St Endellion, which contained not only the church of St Endelienta, but the 'steep, sunless' fishing harbour of Port Isaac and the deserted harbour of Port Quin, of which all the men had been drowned, in the village boat, within living memory. 'The sea,' John wrote, 'seems to be licking its chops and thirsting for more lives . . .' Not much further up the coast was Morwenstowe, where the poetic and Tractarian vicar R.S. Hawker, much admired by John, had had the vicarage chimney stacks built as miniature church towers, expressions of his 'Gothic fancy'. In the church (St Morwenna) Hawker was the first in the world to introduce the custom of Harvest Festival. John enjoyed the 'harvest festival of the sea' at Port Isaac, when the small Victorian church was hung with lobster pots and dressed with crabs and seaweed.

Padstow, the main town of the area, was visited by rail or ferry rather than by bicycle. The railway journey, which finished with 'the utter endness of the end of the line at Padstow – 260 miles of it from London', was to John 'the most beautiful train journey I know . . . See it on a fine evening at high tide with golden light on the low hills, the heron-haunted mud coves flooded over, the sudden thunder as we cross the bridge over Little Petherick creek . . .'[23] But the approach to Padstow John preferred – 'the one I have made ever since' I was a child'[24] – was by ferry from the other side of the estuary. The ferry was run by an old man called Matt England who had gold earrings: 'he was a real old smuggler,' Joan Kunzer thought. At first he had a dinghy, but later, with the profits of ferrying or smuggling, he bought a motor-boat. John relished the ferry ride most 'in a bit of a sea' with a stiff breeze against an incoming tide. 'We would dip our hands in the water and pretend to feel seasick with each heave of the boat and then the town would spread out before us, its slate roofs climbing up the hillside from the wooden wharves of the harbour till they reached the old church tower . . .'[25]

For John, shopping in Padstow was excitingly different from trailing behind his mother at Daniel's or the Bon Marché in Kentish Town. On the slippery quay was a marine store, its window gleaming with lanterns, brass and ships' compasses. From the Misses Quintrell, fancy stationers, he bought dialect tales in verse published by Netherton and Worth of Truro, and model lighthouses of serpentine. Miss Tonkin's boot shop in the square was cool and dark; it had gone by the time John published *First and Last Loves* (1952), although 'her house with its ferns in the window and lace curtains, its lush, enclosed front and back gardens, still stands.'[26] John would also wander up by fern-fringed lanes to the elm-circled church – the church of St Petroc, 'Servant of God and son of a Welsh king', who had crossed the sea from Ireland in a coracle and had landed at Trebetherick. In the church were monuments to the Prideaux and Prideaux-Brune families of Place, carved with their arms and their crest, which John also noticed on the lead rain-water heads of the E-shaped manor house – to which he never gained admittance.

Sometimes John and his parents would return from Padstow 'on a fine, still evening, laden with the week's shopping, and see that familiar view lessen away from the ferry boat while the Padstow Bells, always well rung, would pour their music across the water, reminding me of Parson Hawker's lines –

> Come to thy God in time!
> Thus saith their pealing chime
> Youth, Manhood, Old Age past!
> Come to thy God at last!'[27]

Ernest and Bess took John to see the ancient May Day festival of the hobby horse (or ''obby 'oss') at Padstow, in which a circular 'horse' covered with a black tarpaulin was jogged round the town, followed by the townsfolk singing a pagan hymn. Today it is a lusty and flourishing rite and a tourist attraction; but in John's childhood the people of Padstow did not trouble to make much of a show of it. John's imagination was caught by the ritual, which he was to see re-enacted many times. 'It is as genuine and unselfconscious,' he later wrote, 'as the Morris Dancing at Bampton-in-the-Bush,

Oxfordshire, and not even broadcasting it to an influx of tourists will take the strange and secret character from the ceremonies connected with it.'[28] He added: 'I knew someone who was next to a Padstow man in the trenches in the 1914 war. On the night before May Day, the Padstow man became so excited he couldn't keep still. The old 'obby 'oss was mounting in his blood and his mates had to hold him back from jumping over the top and dancing about in No-man's land.'[29]

The Padstow 'obby 'oss, about 1838

The 'obby 'oss festival was a rare instance of something John and his father could enjoy together. (Edwardian-style music-hall entertainment would have been another, but Ernest was deaf by the time John could enjoy it.) In golf, too, there was an element of ceremony – the ritual with mashie and niblick – and on the St Enodoc links John wore the prescribed dress: flat cap, jazzy pullovers, plus-fours, clocked stockings and mahogany-coloured brogues. It is clear that the beauty of the links' setting gave him more pleasure than the game,[30] though at times he found an almost hearty exhilaration in some unexpected deftness of his.[31] He never became an expert golfer: in his 1973 television film *Metroland* he gave a hilarious exhibition of duff play at Moor Park, collapsing afterwards into his most convulsive, soundless laugh. But the limited proficiency he did gain was a golden asset when he went to Marlborough College. It enabled him to beg off hated team games to play golf on the downs.

MARLBOROUGH

Luxuriating backwards in the bath,
I swish the warmer water round my legs
Towards my shoulders, and the waves of heat
Bring those five years of Marlborough through to me,
In comfortable retrospect: 'Thank God
I'll never have to go through those again.'
As with my toes I reach towards the tap
And turn it to a trickle, stealing warm
About my tender person, comes a voice,
An inner voice that calls, 'Be fair! be fair!
It was not quite as awful as you think.'

John Betjeman, *Summoned by Bells*, 1960

John came to Marlborough College in September 1920, just after his fourteenth birthday. He was slim and below the average height, with a sallow complexion, large, questing eyes – saved from femininity by the satyric slant of his eyebrows – and full lips which he twisted downwards when smiling, so as not to expose his buck teeth. A contemporary, Arthur Byron, remembered John's distinctive hair – 'long, straight, jet-black . . . almost Chinese in effect.'[1]

The college was less than a century old when John arrived there. It had been founded in 1843 for the sons of Church of England clergymen. In John's time there were servants at the school whose memories went back almost to the foundation, including Green the college lamplighter, known as 'Bloater Bill', and Emma Higgins of 'C' House wardrobe who retired in 1923 after 62 years' service. (A tribute to her in the school magazine recorded that when increasing age and girth stopped her climbing the wardrobe ladder, she developed an unerring aim in throwing the boys' socks into their lockers.)

'C' House was an early eighteenth-century inn building, part of the original nucleus of the school. But all new boys went into one of the houses reserved for first-year boys: about 94 into 'A' House, a prison-like economy building designed in the 1840s by Edward Blore; and about 35 each into The Priory or Upcot, whose inmates were known as 'S.O.B.s'. The initials did not have the American connotation, but meant 'small outhouse boarders'. John was assigned to Upcot in the Bath Road, a house like a small Victorian rectory. The housemaster was Clement Carter, a Fellow of the Royal Geographical Society and joint author of *The Marlborough Country*. The portrait-painter Derek Hill, who was in Upcot come years after John, said of Carter: 'He was not very human. He was the sort of master who, if you complained of bullying, would punish you for being a "sneak".'[2]

The 'new bug' at Marlborough had to learn in his first few weeks – on pain of beatings – the school slang. Grey trousers were 'barnes'. The cushion-cum-bag in which he carried his books was a 'kish' (pronounced kīsh).[3] It had to be carried under the left arm, with only a quarter of the cushion sticking out in front. A characteristic word in the Marlborough argot was 'coxy'. Suggestive of 'cocksure' and 'coxcomb', it had roughly the same meaning as the slang word 'uppity'. Third-termers were given powers of punishment to curb the coxy. They could make offenders 'turf down basement' – walk down a long flight of stone steps and up again, as many as ten times.[4]

More slang and etiquette had to be learned by experience and by heart at mealtimes. A milk-jug was a 'tolly'. The poet Louis Mac-Neice, a near-contemporary of John's at the school, got little to eat at his first few meals because he did not understand the custom of 'rushing': as soon as you entered hall you were expected to stick a fork in your patty and a spoon in your porridge, otherwise anyone could 'rush' (appropriate) them.[5]

'The food,' recalled John's friend John Bowle, 'was atrocious.'[6] The only hot meal of the day was lunch in hall, where tepid and greasy joints were carved by whichever master was at the end of one's table, a course followed by suet rolls and treacle or 'spotted dog', known as 'College bolly'.[7] In the evening a high tea of bread, margarine and jam was served. Those who could afford to, supplemented the diet at the tuck shop. A contemporary of John's wrote to him in 1967: 'Do you remember Mr James Duck's little daughter at the Tuck Shop when the so-called "Honour System" was practised and one admitted to having eaten "One sausage roll and two cream puffs" – whereupon this wretched little girl with a strident voice that rang across the shop would scream, "Naaow, Dad, he 'et two sausage rolls, one pork pie and three puffs." '[8]

Slang, having dogged the new boy all day, pursued him to bed. He had to know that the scarlet counterpanes covering the beds in his dormitory were 'College redders'. With the blue wash-basins – one for each boy, on a long washing-stand – they gave the only colour to the cheerless room, with its bare boards and iron bedsteads. At about a quarter to nine each night the dormitories 'started to fill with shrieking boys, who continued shrieking till 9.15, when a bell rang and they knelt down (rather out of breath) to pray.'[9] At 9.30 'lights out' was sounded. 'The captains of dormitory then lined up, looking very pink and clean, in their pyjamas, to say good-night to the housemaster . . .'[10]

Dormitory entertainments included two tortures: 'bum-shaving' (two boys in pyjamas or less bent down and the prefect made a swift vertical cut with his cane between them) and 'hot-potting' (toothmugs filled with flaming paper were clapped on the victims' buttocks where, when the oxygen was used up, suction held them in place.)[11] John devised his own entertainments. In 1967 his contemporary Charles D'Costa[12] wrote to him:

> I wonder if you remember those evenings after lights out in the dormitory when you used to imitate Dr Norwood [the Master of Marlborough] riding up the hill on his bicycle and being spoken to by God and telling God what Marlborough stood for?
>
> I well remember one particular beating from which you saved me when I was assigned to clean the Captain of the Dormitory's shoes. If my memory serves me right, his name was Sinclair and he was a very tall boy. Quite frankly, I had never cleaned shoes before in my life and all I did was to clean the fronts and not the backs. You pleaded with him that he shouldn't beat me on the grounds that I was a good soldier in as much as I never looked behind![13]

At the end of a boy's first year, there was much fearful speculation about which senior house he would be assigned to. Whichever it was, gloating older boys would assure him that it contained the most fiendish masters and prefects in the school. John would have liked to be in 'C' House, the old Castle Inn building with its panelled rooms and great oak staircase. Instead he was put in 'B2', one of the graceless 1840s buildings by Edward Blore. The furnishings inside were – and are – spartan: iron beds in an austere room, and a big communal showerbath opposite a row of lavatories with no doors. L.E. Upcott, who had joined the staff in 1875 when Dean Farrar was Master, and left in 1911, wrote: '. . . even at the end of my career an R.E. [Royal Engineers] Colonel, bringing his boy to the College, after a round of inspection, said to me bluntly: "I should not pass your domestic arrangements for Army barracks." '[14]

'Marlborough really was the most awful barbarous place,' said John Bowle, 'and it was extraordinary that people were willing to pay large sums to subject their children to it.'[15] But he conceded that the school had some good masters, and an exceptional headmaster in Cyril Norwood.

Norwood [Bowle said in 1976] has been blackguarded by Maurice Bowra by the phrase that he 'looked like an Edwardian policeman':[16] and John Sparrow in a broadcast dismissed Norwood by just quoting that, as though Norwood was a most ghastly kind of tyrant. But this isn't true at all. Norwood was in fact, under a terrifying exterior, a man of, I'd say, something like genius. He certainly had a very great impact on all of us, including John. He had a wonderful voice and his sermons I can still remember, and John will still give an imitation of Norwood, a parody of one of his sermons. He was a formidable man out for efficiency, with a certain moral purpose without cant in it. Underneath his forbidding exterior, Norwood concealed a great sense of humour and great perceptiveness about character.[17]

Norwood was a headmaster in the Dr Arnold tradition. The college had had a double dose of Arnoldism in the nineteenth century. The Rev. George Cotton, who was Master from 1852 to 1858, had been on Arnold's staff at Rugby and is immortalized in *Tom Brown's Schooldays* as the 'grave young master' admired by Tom and his friends. His successor, the Rev. G.G. Bradley, had been a Rugby housemaster.

Arnoldism meant a gruelling study of the classics as a 'discipline' and a preparation for life; sport, to keep busy hands for which the Devil might otherwise find work; the prefectorial system (control of the boys by the boys); and religion, to provide an ethical system for life and in many cases a livelihood as muscular Christian clergy. This prescription was still in force when John joined the school.

'The only part of the curriculum that was taken seriously,' John Bowle recalled, 'was classics. If you weren't good at Greek and Latin, you were regarded as almost expendable.'[18] Beverley Nichols, who was at the school just before John, wrote that Greek was taught at Marlborough 'as though it were not merely dead but as though it had never lived at all.'[19] John's natural antipathy to the classics, a subject which required a learning by rote of irregular verbs and participles before any literary glories could be discerned, was aggravated by his dislike of the masters who taught the subject. Bowle recalled in 1976:

John was put through the normal grind of the classical curriculum. He went into the Classical Fifth which was in the charge of a pedantic old gentleman called Emery – quite a benevolent old boy but a complete pedant. Then he went on to the Lower Sixth where he was taken by a man called A.R. Gidney.

Gidney was an Oxford man, with a very icy kind of mind, and a very cutting, sarcastic tongue, and he really lashed John with his sarcastic tongue – cut him up horribly for inaccuracies in grammar; and John has never really forgiven that, you know. He simply hates 'Gidders' still.[20]

John sustained his vendetta against Gidney for over fifty years. In March 1958, when asked to contribute to a series called 'John Bull's Schooldays' in *The Spectator*, he took the opportunity to write a vitriolic open letter to Gidney, disguising him as 'Dear Mr Atkins'.[21] It drew a witty riposte in the next issue, signed 'Benjamin Atkins' and thus possibly by Gidney, but more probably a spoof by one of John's contemporaries:

Sir, – Betjeman! Name seems familiar. Let me see – eighty, ninety years ago? Yes, I've placed him. A pestiferous little fellow, if ever there was one. One thing I remember clearly. Never an essay came from Betjeman's pen but he inveighed against the school bell-tower, calling it a 'Puginistic horror' and 'a preposterous neo-Gothic pimple'. Do you blame me for shouting in exasperation: 'Betjeman, you're showing off!'? And when the offending tower was removed (not, I hasten to explain, at Betjeman's insistence, but as part of a rebuilding plan) he had the effrontery to form a School Preservation Society which issued leaflets abusing anyone who dared to 'tamper with our aesthetic heritage', or some such phrase. He's absolutely right in one thing. He *was* a masochist! He wanted me to pull his ears and I flatly refused . . .[22]

John's *Spectator* attack on Gidney drew a protest from George White of St Columba's College, Rathfarnham, Dublin, who had also been taught by Gidney at Marlborough:

I remember that you used to imitate him calling you 'decadent'! . . . But if this was Gidney I think you are unfair in calling him sarcastic: I never saw any sign of cruelty in him at all and I knew him pretty well . . . I hope you will not mind my saying that, whether he was Gidney or not, my chief feeling when I finished reading your open letter was distress that you, being what I believe you to be, should after so many years retain such bitter feelings about anyone.[23]

Perhaps as a result of White's letter, John was remorseful enough to make a pilgrimage to Marlborough to apologize to his old teacher. But the late Gerald Murray, archivist of Marlborough College, said that John was unwelcome at the school for some years after the episode. And John's repentance did not last long. In December 1958 he told a *Daily Mail* interviewer: 'I was bullied and crushed by a master, and it is immensely gratifying to me to know that the hidebound old prig is still alive and perhaps occasionally reading my name.'[24] In *A Nip in the Air* (1974) he published the poem 'Greek Orthodox' which begins:

> What did I see when first I went to Greece?
> Shades of the Sixth across the Peloponnese.
> Though clear the clean-cut Doric temple shone
> Still droned the voice of Mr Gidney on;
> 'That ὅτι? Can we take its meaning here
> Wholly as interrogative?'

John's unassuaged hostility to Gidney is also shown in his 1970s letters to Gerald Murray. *1 April 1971*: 'How splendid R.A. Butler is about [Charles] Sorley in the current *Marlburian*. Sorley was so associated with Gidney in my mind that he never got a chance with Yours ever, John Betjeman.'[25] *26 January 1976*: 'I've not yet recovered from Gidney who they tell me is still alive, didn't they say so at lunch?'[26]

Gidney continued to live in Marlborough until his death in 1978. With his short-cropped white hair and erect bearing, he seemed an affable 'Mr Chips' figure, but it was clear that he had little time for John Betjeman. 'He was in no way distinguished,' he said. 'The only thing I remember about him is that at the beginning of one term, when the form list was being passed round, he said to me: "Please, sir, I can't remember whether my surname is spelt with one 'n' or two." He was posing as usual, you see. So I said: "Make up your mind and let me know when you've decided." The class laughed and seemed to think that was the right reply – which showed what they thought of *him*.'[27]

In *Summoned by Bells*, John listed what to him were the main horrors of life at Marlborough:

> The dread of beatings! Dread of being late!
> And, greatest dread of all, the dread of games![28]

The school's reputation in games outweighed its reputation in anything else. The official school history was full of Marlburian legends, such as E.E. Kewley, 'famous for his dribbling powers' and F.H. Fox, 'considered by many to be the finest half-back ever turned out by Marlborough'.[29] John was uninterested in rugby or cricket; and he did not find 'exhilarating' (as did Louis MacNeice) the gruelling runs over the downs with a time limit out and back and a caning if you were late either way.[30] One of the few sports that John and his equally games-hating friend John Bowle enjoyed was swimming. Bowle competed for the Brooke Swimming Cup but was defeated by the captain of his house. 'I'm so glad,' he commented in his diary. 'I rather admire the animal physically.'[31] James Robertson Justice, the future film actor, also took part in the diving competition. 'James has an amazing backwards somersault dive which is hugely applauded,' Bowle wrote. 'It is very bad for him. He is temporarily a little popular in his frightful house.'[32] Another future film star, James Mason, was also remembered by John and Bowle in connexion with the swimming-pool: he was flung in, dressed in his dinner-jacket, for 'coxiness'.[33]

When John arrived at Marlborough, Cyril Norwood had been Master for three years. But three years had not been enough to remedy the harm done by the administration of his predecessor, the Rev. St John Wynne Willson, for whom the prefectorial system had been a way of shrugging off his own responsibilities rather than developing those of the boys. A pernicious pecking order ran from the Senior Prefect, usually a prize athlete who was *ex officio* editor of the school magazine, down through Upper School Captains, minor 'bloods' and juniors to the persecuted fags. MacNeice's and John's descriptions of the institution called Upper School, in *The Strings are False* and *Summoned by Bells*, are so nearly identical in content that the latter might have been a rendering into verse of the former. Yet neither can have seen what the other wrote before putting pen to paper: MacNeice's manuscript was finished by 1941 (when he handed it to E.R. Dodds for safe-keeping) and was not published until 1965, five years after *Summoned by Bells* appeared. MacNeice wrote:

> When a boy first entered a senior house such as mine he spent most of his day in a building called Upper School. It had been built about 1850 and, though enormously large, hardly seemed like a building at all. It was just a great tract of empty air, cold as the air outside but smelling of stables, enclosed by four thin walls and a distant roof. One half of the floor was covered with desks and benches, the other half was empty; there were only two doors and two fires. These were coal fires and radiated heat for not more than two or three yards. One was called Big Fire and reserved for less than twenty boys who were the oligarchy; the other fire, Little Fire, was open to the rest of us who numbered about a hundred. To be elected to Big Fire was a great honour but could only be hoped for by athletes or boys so stupid that they remained in Upper School longer than the normal span.[34]

John wrote:

> There was a building known as Upper School
> (Abolished now, thank God, and all its ways),
> An eighteen-fifty warehouse smelling strong
> Of bat-oil, biscuits, sweat and rotten fruit. . .
> Great were the ranks and privileges there:
> Four captains ruled, selected for their brawn
> And skill at games; and how we reverenced them!
> Twelve friends they chose as brawny as themselves.

'Big Fire' we called them; lording it they sat
In huge armchairs beside the warming flames
Or played at indoor hockey in the space
Reserved for them. The rest of us would sit
Crowded on benches round another grate.[35]

There is also a striking similarity between MacNeice's and John's descriptions of the captains, who arrived slapping the desks with their canes and made the juniors scavenge for apple-cores and paper darts.[36] The captains would throw blank cartridges into the fireplaces, which exploded and blew live coals on to the boys' desks.[37]

The most dreaded disgrace in Upper School was a 'basketing'. A chosen victim ('Perhaps he sported coloured socks too soon,/ Perhaps he smarmed his hair with scented oil'[38]) was stripped of most of his clothing, smeared with ink, treacle or paint, then hoisted in one of the two big waste-paper baskets. MacNeice describes this ceremony as 'a perfect exhibition of mass sadism' and adds, 'The masters considered this a fine old tradition, and any boy who was basketed was under a cloud for the future. Because the boys have an innate sense of justice, anyone they basket must be really undesirable. Government of the mob, by the mob, and for the mob.'[39] John makes the same point in *Summoned by Bells*:

'By the boys, *for* the boys. The boys know best.
With that rough justice decent schoolboys know.'
And at the end of term the victim left –
Never to wear an Old Marlburian tie.[40]

John gave a more detailed and highly dramatized account of the ordeal-by-basket in his contribution to *Little Innocents* (1932), a book of childhood reminiscences edited by his Oxford friend Alan Pryce-Jones. Here, as in *Summoned by Bells*, he recalls how someone told him that he was next for the basket, and how as a result he crept about for three terms afterwards, keeping his books down in a basement where boots were cleaned.[41] Over the years, the story lost nothing in the telling. Lady Longford remembers how 'When John came to stay at Pakenham Hall in 1930 – Evelyn Waugh was there as well and mentions John in his diary – John kept us in fits with stories of going up in the basket at Marlborough. It made your flesh creep in the shadowy great hall at Pakenham. I remember John's saying how when the boy was hoist up in the basket, they threw "darts of sharp pen-knibs" at him.'[42] From merely being lifted on to a table in *Little Innocents*, the wretched victim was 'strung . . . up among the beams' in *Summoned by Bells*.[43] John himself became so identified with the story that some of his contemporaries firmly believed eventually that he had been basketed: his schoolfellow T.C. Worsley states in his autobiography *Flannelled Fool* that 'He [John Betjeman], like many others, paid the supreme penalty of the "basket".'[44] This was denied by John Bowle, who said: 'You mustn't think of John as having been a miserable, persecuted creature at Marlborough: he has always been popular wherever he's been, always had plenty of friends.'[45] And Anthony Blunt (the art historian and spy, who was John's contemporary at Marlborough) explained in 1977: 'He had this marvellous sense of humour, and when the toughs tried to be bloody, he simply laughed in their face: and, as you know, when John Betjeman laughs, it's quite something. They were absolutely routed. In his last year he had a study right down the other end from mine, the narrow court between Upper School and the Museum block – and one would suddenly hear this great hiccough of laughter, very very infectious.'[46]

The school was divided into battle-lines of aesthetes against hearties. The antagonism between them had been a part of Marlborough life for at least half a century, and successive Masters had vainly tried to reconcile the two sides.[47] The masters as well as the boys were divided into two camps on this issue. The old guard, led by Gidney and by the fanatical T.C.G.S. Sandford, housemaster of Bowle's house, faced the younger generation appointed by Norwood as a 'leaven'. Among the latter was Oswald Flecker, a younger brother of James Elroy Flecker, author of the begemmed, exotic play *Hassan*.

Bowle was impressed by Oswald Flecker: 'He was my first experience of the impact of a really brilliant Jewish mind on myself,' he said.[48] John's memory of Flecker was cooler. When, in 1954, *The Spectator* invited him to review the reviewers of his latest collection of poems, *A Few Late Chrysanthemums*, John wrote:

I have come to dread all but unstinted praise or friendly or constructive criticism from people who write poetry themselves.

Perhaps an experience I had when a boy of about fifteen at school may partly account for this morbid fear. I was in a set taught by Mr H.L.O. Flecker, the present headmaster of Christ's Hospital, a brother of the poet, and I showed him a poem I had written about a City church. It was very bad and, for motives no doubt kindly meant, he read out my verses to the set of boys, making fun of each line as he went along. Most boys who write verse must have had similar ragging, if not from masters at least from contemporaries.

But most boys who write poetry do not intend to be poets all their lives. That had always been my intention.

John found much more sympathetic Christopher Hughes, the art master, who took the boys on sketching expeditions into the Wiltshire countryside and gave them old-fashioned instruction in the art of water-colour.[49] John's favourite venue for sketching was Ramsbury Manor, a late seventeenth-century mansion in a landscaped park. 'No words can express my longing to get inside this house,' John later wrote. '. . . What the Louvre was to Anthony Blunt and the Parthenon to the boring master [Gidney] who taught us Greek, Ramsbury Manor was to me. I think the mystery of its winding drive gave me a respect for the system of hereditary landowning which I have never shaken off.'[50]

Christopher Hughes was modern enough to ridicule Landseer – causing John, by natural contrariness, to become fascinated by Victorian art. But Hughes disapproved of Blunt and Ellis Waterhouse (the future art historian), who were full of Cézanne and 'significant form', and Hughes crossed swords with a master, Clifford Canning, who abetted them. In 1925 Blunt, Betjeman, Bowle, Mac-Neice and MacNeice's friend John Hilton wanted to start an Art Society. Blunt asked Canning if he would be president. Canning agreed. But when Hughes heard of this, he said, 'If there's going to be an Art Society, then I, as art master, must be president.'[51] The ever-devious mind of Blunt soon thought of a way round this obstacle. He persuaded the others to dissolve the Art Society and to found a new club called, with calculated insolence, the Anonymous Society. He again asked Canning to be president, but Canning said, 'Sorry. Hughes has made such a stink about this that I can't take it on now.'[52] Another master, George Turner, became president of the Anonymous Society instead, and meetings took place in his rooms. Blunt recalled: 'I read the first paper, which was an astonishingly dull piece on Titian – highly respectable. And then

John read one on Victorian art: that was extremely amusing, the real Betj. gaiety, and of course highly intelligent. It was done rather as a joke kind of thing. I think that was the only paper he read to the Anonymous Society.'[53]

In March 1924 John Hilton wrote in his diary: 'There's a new college paper coming out for the first time next Saturday called the "Heretick". It is a very high-brow sort of thing I believe. Blunt's got a lot to do with it. He says it is meant to form a focus for the literary talent in the school.'[54] John Bowle's diary suggests that Matthew Wordsworth (son of the Bishop of Salisbury) was the prime mover of the new magazine: 'Wordsworth is starting a paper. Tonight Betj., Wordsworth, myself, Philip Harding, Ben Bonas and Sam Soames had a tremendous talk in W's study. The project is superb. Wordsworth has a very large study [in 'B' House] with a fine wall and well furnished. They all call each other by amazing nicknames and are greatly happy.'[55]

The Heretick was a snook-cocking attack on the athletic faction. It aimed (Anthony Blunt later wrote) 'to express our disapproval of the Establishment generally, of the more out-of-date and pedantic masters, of all forms of organized sport, of the Officers' Training Corps and of all the other features that we hated in school life, not so much the physical discomforts – they were almost taken for granted – but, you might say, the intellectual discomforts of the school.'[56]

On St Valentine's Day 1924, Bowle had his first idea for the cover design which he, as the best artist of the group, had been assigned. It was to be 'a Betjemanesque spirit tormenting a "bourgeois" under a tree; mound, Chapel, R. Football goal etc.' By early March the paper was far enough advanced for Bowle to note: 'I am too dissatisfied with the cover I have designed to publish it, so I have to design another by Saturday when we meet again.' John Betjeman was now suggesting 'an athlete trampling on an aesthete in a welter of footballs' but 'he spent the afternoon playing golf,' Bowle recorded, and could contribute no more to the final editorial meeting as he was in the Classical Fifth and had 'to cope with a deluge of impositions'. Bowle prophetically suggested: 'At the present pace the paper will probably be suppressed. There is an undercurrent of attack on athleticism and Sandfordism and my part in it is pretty violent. It should sell very well indeed.'[57]

At last on 29 March *The Heretick* appeared. (The title had been suggested by Christopher Hughes, the spelling by Bowle.) Before Hall, it was sold from a classroom. 'Court alive with the orange covers on black suits,' Bowle wrote in his diary. 'A strange silence in Hall, everyone reading it.'[58] It was John Betjeman's first experience of the power of the pen.

Bowle's final cover design showed a scowling 'tough' with a hockey stick, seated on a mound in front of rugby posts, while fauns (perhaps 'Betjemanesque') played pipes and taunted him from the branches of a tree. Under the picture was the magazine's motto: 'Upon Philistia will I Triumph.' John's contributions were a 'Prodigies' Song', a satire on the classical scholars among the boys; a short story entitled 'Death'; and an account of 'Dinner of Old Marlburian Centipede Farmers in Unyamwazi, S.A.'

The reaction of the school's ruling athletes to the new magazine was no less gratifying for being predictable. It was rumoured that the 'bloods' were going to attack the editors after the end-of-term concert. John Bowle was so alarmed by the threat of vengeance that he obtained a 'squailer' from a boy in College – a stick about a foot long with a lump of lead on the end, traditionally used to kill squirrels in Savernake Forest. Armed with it, he made his way back from his house after the concert, unmolested.[59]

On the last Sunday of term, Dr Norwood preached a sermon and quoted the magazine's motto. If, he said, it meant 'overcoming the Philistine in all of us', it was a good thing; if it was 'an expression of intellectual snobbery', it was *not* a good thing.[60] He took a tolerant stance and reproved the extremists of both camps. The second issue, published in June 1924, contained a poem initialled 'J.B.' in a manner already recognizably 'Betjemanesque':

YE OLDE COTTAGE
(QUITE NEAR A TOWN)

The happy haunt of typists, common, pert,
'We're in the country now!' they say, and wear
Tweed clothes, and let the wind disturb their hair.
And carry ash sticks. 'Don't be silly, Gert!
Afraid of cows?' 'Oh Elsie, mind my skirt,
It will get muddy.' 'Oh, just look! down there
A factory. . .' 'O dearest, how they dare
To ruin all the country with their dirt!'

And Gert and Elsie's cottage – 'just too sweet'
With rustic furniture, no bath, no drains,
But still it is *so* countrified. A friend
Can sleep upon the sofa. And they eat
Off pottery (hand-painted). Oh! the pains
And saving for their game of let's pretend!

The Heretick was suppressed after this issue because it contained an article by Anthony Blunt on the Wildean theme that there can be no morality in art. Norwood was reluctant to close down the magazine: he, too, opposed the excessive athletic bias of the school. But Blunt's article was thought to be so shocking that a parent wrote to Norwood and threatened to remove his boy from the school if the magazine were not suppressed. It is likely that *The Heretick* made a small but direct contribution to John's later poetry before it went. At the end of the magazine was an advertisement section. One of the advertisements was for 'The Parade Toilet Saloon, Marlborough: First-Class Toilet Requisites and Walking-Sticks'. Archard, the college barber, also advertised 'Toilet Requisites' on the inside back cover. The genteel, ambiguous phrase may have remained in John's mind, to surface in his poem 'How to Get On in Society':

> Are the requisites all in the toilet?
> The frills round the cutlets can wait
> Till the girl has replenished the cruets
> And switched on the logs in the grate.

John also contributed to the official school magazine, *The Marlburian*. Most of the verse contributions were under real or pseudonymous initials, and it is sometimes difficult to determine which are by John. 'Ode to a Char-à-Banc' (17 November 1921) cannot be ascribed to him with absolute confidence, though the opening ('O "Charabang", thou breath of Tooting's being...') and the mention of Margate as well as Tooting, are strong circumstantial evidence: both places were to recur in Betjeman poems.

The first *Marlburian* poem certainly by John appeared in the issue of 26 March 1923. A pastiche of Thomas Moore's 'The Minstrel Boy', it was aimed at the classics as taught by old Mr Emery, the Fifth Form master, two of whose favourite phrases, 'You little owl!' and 'You won't get on!' were mocked.

THE SCHOLAR

The Classical boy to his Fifth has gone,
In the chairs at the top you'll find him,
Pondering over his Xenophon,
For which the Lord designed him.

You little owl! quoth the master stern
Who out of the window starest,
When will the difference you discern
Between the present and aorist?

The Scholar gazed with a look of alarm
And he murmured the wrong translation
But a volume of Vergil under his arm
Gave him classical consolation.

'For two long terms have I taught this form
But it brings my proud soul under.
You won't get on,' did the master storm
In a classical clap of thunder.

Anti-Science.

By this time there was a feeling among the senior boys that John, only a third-year boy, was getting above himself, or 'coxy'. Ellis Waterhouse, a daunting Marlborough intellectual but also a rebel who was never made a prefect, decided to take him gently down a peg. He composed a satire of John's more yearning manner and published it in *The Marlburian* over the reversed initials 'B.J.' His other motive in doing this, he recalled, was to mystify his friend George Abell (later Sir George, First Civil Service Commissioner) who as Senior Prefect was then editor of *The Marlburian*.[61] Waterhouse and Abell alternated as head of the Classical Sixth and enjoyed scoring off each other. Waterhouse's 'Betjeman' poem appeared in the issue of 19 June 1923:

THE RESULT OF A SURFEIT OF SWINBURNE: OR WAS IT THE MARLBURIAN?

Where is that beauty of old named Cytherean,
That loveliness that men called Erycine,
White marble features of the form divine:

> Where too is he for whom men raised the Paean,
>   Who built on sea-washed Delos' isle his shrine
> Towered over by his own dark Cynthian hill:
>   Or she, his sister, Leto's moonbrowed child? . . .

John was quick to retaliate. As a reader of *The Marlburian* since 1920, he knew that Waterhouse himself had been responsible for some archaic and derivative effusions, including 'A Lost City' in the issue of 23 June 1921 –

> Oh beauty, buried in a tangled tomb
> Of tree and grass and many-coloured flower,
> How long hast lain thus hidden in Time's womb? . . .

So in his reply (12 July 1923) he reprimanded Waterhouse for his hypocrisy in attacking John for a fault of which he himself had been guilty; and he beat Waterhouse at his own game by making his reply an acrostic of 'WATERHOUSE, E.K.':

LINES INSPIRED BY REVERSED INITIALS

> Who art thou, second Calverley,[62] who hast
>   Aspired in nonsense uninspired by skill
> To crush extravagance, which once was cast
>   E'en from thy mighty pen, no doubt at will,
> Revealing youth? As nonsense was the theme
>   Happy you were to write of, for the gaze
> Of mocking intellectuals, or the dream,
>   Unwittingly Swinburnian faults displays.
> Spare me! thou slaughterer in bombastic verse;
>   England hath need of thee for more – why waste
> Elaborate genius on a rhymster worse,
>   Knowing we both have written in poor taste?

If Waterhouse's parody was intended to shame John out of his silvery style, it was unsuccessful. *The Marlburian* of 1 November 1923 contained John's 'Moonlight in Kensington Gardens' –

> In the Gardens above City murmurs
>   Come silver pipings over lawns so pale,

Stolen from the babblings of small waters
Wrung from the breast of the red Nightingale. . .

But the comical Betjeman reappears in 'A.D. 1980' (5 March 1924),
predicting that the earth will be lit night and day by Osram's Never-
wane and that people will live on 'Pill-food'; and in 'Ode to a Dead
Valve' (31 March 1924), which, like Horace Smith's 'Address to
the Mummy in Belzoni's Exhibition' (1819), apostrophizes something now defunct but once glowingly alive –

It was not many moons ago
That men did praise thee, but
Thou art no longer any use
Thy filament's gone fut.

A sixteen-stanza ballad called 'Revenge' was published on 26 June
1924, its beginning set in the Stone Age –

When England was a marshy land
By gentle breezes often fanned,
And when the sun shone every day,
The bronchtosauri [*sic*] used to play.

They'd gambol in the oozy mud
They'd go to sleep, or chew the cud,
Or else, if hungry, off they'd trot
And eat a cave boy in his cot.

In the issue of 23 October 1924 appeared a long unsigned poem,
'The Song of a Cold Wind', which was later published over John's
name in Volume V of *Public School Verse* (1925), an annual
anthology edited by Martin Gilkes, Richard Hughes and P.H.B.
Lyon. This poem shows John on his best poetic behaviour, courting
the judges with the robust Georgian lines and Chesterbelloc echoes
that they might think desirable from a public schoolboy:

The song of the wind in the telegraph wires,
The breathing wind of the downs,
The wind that whistles through twenty shires
Of red-roofed country towns.

'By river water splashing
I whirl the creaking mills,
As their great flat sails come crashing,
I fly . . . and my laughter shrills
Up to the reach at Horning,
Over the windy Bure,
As I leap from the arms of the morning,
Fresh and bitter and pure . . .'

The Marlburian of 18 December 1924 contained the first of John's poems about Cornwall, which he defensively entitled 'A Sentimental Poem':

For the last time the light on the tamarisk bushes
Swinging and swaying with glittering drops of rain;
For the last time the wrinkled ferryman pushes
From Padstow quay again . . .

John was almost certainly the author of 'Diogenes Up-to-Date' (18 February 1925) about a woman who sets up house in a tub, calling it 'Kruschen' – after Kruschen liver salts. As the tub is in the middle of the road, a huge traffic jam piles up, and John's description of it suggests his love of motor-car names, brand names, place names and social distinctions, and his hatred of profiteers. 'Tips for Travellers' (28 May 1925) includes two words which alone are almost enough to stamp the work as John's: 'Bakerloo' and 'vestibule'. The traveller is advised:

When travelling to Timbuctoo
Don't set out on the Bakerloo.

And he is warned that

You will discover many a rule
On ceiling, wall and vestibule.

Later John was to write a poem on the Baker Street station buffet ('The Metropolitan Railway'), and his 'How to Get On in Society' contains the lines

It's ever so close in the lounge, dear,
But the vestibule's comfy for tea . . .

The Marlburian also reveals something of John's other school activities. A report of an exhibition of drawings and paintings (12 July 1923) records that 'J. Betjeman exhibited a water-colour painting of a sea-shore. His technique is a bit rough and unfinished, but, stepping back from the picture, it certainly struck one very favourably indeed.'

In 'Scenes from Shakespeare', acted in the gymnasium on 15 December 1923, John played Olivia's maid, Maria, in an extract from Twelfth Night ('Betjemann was a very intriguing Maria') and Puck in an extract from A Midsummer Night's Dream. Among his friends in the same production were John Bowle as Philostrate, Neville Greene as Demetrius and Philip Harding as Quince. The plays were produced by Charles Boughey and Oswald Flecker.

Bowle, who had just heard that he had won the Brackenbury Scholarship at Balliol College, Oxford (John had accompanied him to the post office to send a telegram to his parents), wrote of a rehearsal of Twelfth Night: 'Betj acts as Maria in a black skirt and yellow top, and a dairy maid cap. Mr Flecker makes love to him as Sir Toby Belch and Chilton overacts hopelessly as Sir Andrew Aguecheek. But it will do.'[63]

John's first recorded speech in the School Debating Society was on 30 May 1924, supporting the motion proposed by Bowle 'That in the opinion of this House, progress is a figment of man's imagination'. The Marlburian reported: 'Mr Betjemann, eloquently recalling the exhibition of 1851 with scorn, lamented the fact that then, as now, comfort was mistaken for progress. Progress is not control over nature, it is control over self. He railed against the "advantages" science has brought, liquorice, anchovy paste, Wembley [the British Empire Exhibition of 1924 at Wembley] and the Daily Mirror. If this is progress we can only look forward to "an eternity of yellow ochre".'

John again rose to speak on 10 October 1924, to the motion 'That morality is incompatible with success in politics'. A.R. Gidney spoke against the motion, and it was therefore almost inevitable that John would speak for it, especially with the anti-morality philosophy he was accepting from Oscar Wilde through Anthony Blunt. The Marlburian commented: 'Mr Betjemann enunciated Theorem 22, and, by a dexterous application of "politics to parallel straight lines", produced a quite astonishing metaphor. After repeating a quotation in French, Latin and English, Mr Betjemann inconsequently mentioned Richlieu [sic], Walpole, George III, the Empire, Gladstone, and Mr Baldwin in defence of immorality. Party government is immoral, federal government more so. Therefore politics are immoral. Hence successful politicians are immoral. Morality in politics stands in much the same position as rice puddings in childhood. Mr Betjemann ended abruptly; he was amusing but somewhat disjointed in his arguments.'

The Marlburian also records the first of John's many conservation campaigns. The issue of 18 February 1925 contained this letter from him to the editor:

Dear Sir,

   The College is not devoid of architectural curiosities, and it possesses one which was the culmination of polite elegance in the eighteenth century. This is the historical grotto in the Mound,[64] built by Lady Hertford and referred to by Stephen Duck, the 'thresher poet' of Queen Caroline's court, in the following lines:

> . . . Within the Basis of the verdant Hill,
> A beauteous Grot confesses HERTFORD's Skill;
> Who, with her lovely Nymphs, adorns the Place;
> Gives every polished Stone its proper Grace;
> Now varies rustic Moss about the Cell;
> Now fits the shining Pearl, or purple Shell;
> CALYPSO thus, attended with her Train,
> With rural Palaces adorns the Plain . . .

It is rather a desecration to use such a rare rural establishment as a storehouse for College Potatoes. The 'ruins' in the wilderness have been removed, and the upper grotto has been allowed to tumble to pieces by the absurd proselyte of Mr Ruskin. The one remaining relic can still be saved. Surely we have advanced enough now not to condemn a thing because it is 'artificial'?

   Yours faithfully,

     ALEXANDER POPE.

The Mound in which Lady Hertford's grotto was set had one particularly romantic association: it was supposed to contain the bones of Merlin. The town's motto, added to its coat of arms by a herald of James I, was *Ubi nunc sapientis ossa Merlini?* (Where now are the bones of the wizard Merlin?) – a reference to the affectation of the day by which the town's name was spelt Merlinsbarrow. In cold fact, it is far from likely that either town or mound had any connection with Merlin, and the 'marl' part of the name may merely mean 'rich soil'. But the legend was well enough known for John to enlist it as propaganda in his campaign. He contributed to *The Marlburian* of 11 March 1925 a short story headed 'Where Now are the Bones of Merlin?'

> 'Ubi nunc sapientis ossa Merlini' – the words caught my eye on the arms of Marlborough Town portrayed in a piece of Goss China modelled like a lighthouse on a rock, an article whose usefulness was as dubious as its art. Thanks to this little ornament, I paused when turning the leaves of a book in the Adderley Library [the school library] that evening upon seeing for the second time in the same day the words 'ossa Merlini'.
>
> The book I was studying was 'The Autobiography of Prince Metternich', volume two, published in the eminently worthy, if somewhat uninspiring style of about eighteen hundred and sixty. It seemed strange to me that Merlin's bones should have anything to do with the statesman . . .

The tale develops as an M.R. James ghost story. On the same page of the Metternich book as the 'ossa Merlini' reference, is an illustration of 'a portion of a wall containing two niches . . . set with shells and pieces of pointed stone'. It persuades John to take another look at the grotto on the Marlborough Mound. 'As usual, the floor was littered with potatoes and old brooms and it was some time before I could clear away the rubbish in front of the inside wall.' A ring, apparently of stone, shines in the dark 'with the irridescence [*sic*] of a butterfly's wings'. John grasps it. 'As I did so, an odour of dry laurel bushes and dusty ivy leaves filled the grotto and I heard a voice say "Ladyship" and stop abruptly.' A vision 'of the whole Mound shining, of circles of stretched-out bodies winding round and round in tiers up to the stars . . . a realization of terrible stillness as in a room where they have drawn the blinds on Death . . .' makes him charge out of the grotto.

The letter and story herald John's tactics in future conservation battles: his use of ridicule to goad the authorities into taking action, and his tenacity in returning to the charge. He renewed the attack in

The Marlburian of 25 May 1925: 'In all the debris only one building remained intact, and this was the grotto. But it has not been repaired – so the College lost a fitting monument as the crowd eagerly groped for potatoes strewn about the floor.' That John's campaign to save the grotto was successful, we learn from a letter signed 'G.R. Otto' in *The Marlburian* of 25 October 1925.

This victory was not his only success in his last year at school. On 28 March 1925 he took part in *The Grand Cham's Diamond* by Allan Monkhouse. *The Marlburian* of 28 May reported: 'Betjemann, whose acting was masterly throughout, made a most realistic Mrs Perkins, and carried the whole weight of the play on his shoulders.' On Prize Day he took the part of Lady Teazle in *The School for Scandal*, which was repeated before an audience from Marlborough town on 7 July. (*The Marlburian* of 24 July commented that 'Betjemann's rendering of his part was the best of the evening.')

One of John's paintings was in an exhibition held during Prize Day weekend. His choice of subject was characteristic: 'The chapel by Betjemann recalls effectively the atmosphere of the last century,' the *Marlburian* critic judged. John also carried off the Furneaux English Verse Prize. In his Prize Day speech, Dr Norwood said: 'There has, I think, been equal advance in *The Marlburian*, where the poetry, if I may venture to offer an opinion, is distinctly in advance of the prose – a rare thing. I have been struck by the freshness and originality of two or three pieces in the past year, and rejoiced that the sacred fire has not been quenched by the Philistinism so-called of the public school.' This no doubt drew a laugh by complimenting John and at the same time teasing him and his allies about the cover motto of *The Heretick*.

John was also active in the school's Literary Society. His friend Philip Harding, as secretary of the society, recorded in the minutes on 2 December 1923 that 'a visitor, Mr Betjeman, read a paper on Early Victorian Art and Literature . . . an extremely amusing and enlightening paper which he very aptly illustrated by passing round examples to prove to what artistic depths the Victorians had debased themselves. He also read us several amusing poems for "Young Ladies".' Harding described John as a 'visitor' because John had not yet been elected to the society. He was elected, with Louis MacNeice and Graham Shepard (son of the book illustrator E.H. Shepard), in September 1924.

John and MacNeice regarded each other with mutual wariness, and never became close friends. MacNeice recalled John in his memoirs, *The Strings are False*:

Down the passage from Graham [Shepard]'s study was a door with an inscription above it:

> *Here thou, Great Anna, whom three realms obey,*
> *Dost sometimes counsel take and sometimes tea*[65]

– and inside sat John Betjeman writing nonsense on his typewriter or polishing his leather books with boot-polish. John Betjeman at that time looked like a will-o'-the-wisp with Latin blood in it. His face was the colour of peasoup and his eyes were soupy too and his mouth was always twisting sideways in a mocking smile and he had a slight twist in his speech which added a tang to his mimicries, syncopating the original just as a slightly rippling sheet of water jazzes the things reflected in it. He was a brilliant mimic but also a mine of useless information and a triumphant misfit. I felt ill at ease with him, not understanding his passion for minor poetry and misbegotten ornament . . .[66]

A letter of 1930 from John to his Oxford friend Patrick Balfour shows his dislike of MacNeice, only a few years after they had been together at Marlborough (and at Oxford):

I have not read it yet, but I believe the new School book called 'Out of Step' by Derek Walker Smith (Gollancz) is really by Louis Mac-Neice – that fucking little Oxford aesthete who lives near Belfast. If so it will be about Marlborough and about me – for I remember someone telling me that MacNeice had written a school story which contained a description of me. Please expose him [in the gossip column Balfour was then writing for the *Daily Sketch*] so that he gets lynched – unless it is a Good Book – but I expect, if it is by this creature, it will be a sexless, complaining affair.[67]

MacNeice's oxymoron 'triumphant misfit' is probably a fair description of John at Marlborough. John seemed almost to have *chosen* the rôle of misfit – and it was a rôle that suited him. A friendlier observer among his Marlborough contemporaries, Arthur Byron, remembered him as 'the boy who always had to be different from the others'.[68] His hair was suspiciously long, at a time when 'short back and sides' was the rule. To other boys, letter-writing was a penance, 'but John seemed to revel in it and he impressed us all by having large, expensive deep blue writing paper and over-sized envelopes which nearly matched the blue 2½d stamps. In 1924 postage was reduced to 2d, but John went on using the blue stamps instead of the orange 2d which aesthetically clashed with his envelopes.' John was unique, too, in his method of evading team games:

> 'May I half change?' This question, to a house prefect in charge of games, was how a junior boy would ask if he could change his school jacket for a blazer, be excused the compulsory games which he hated, and go off to the Marlborough Downs to play golf. He was the only boy in the house who brought his golf clubs to school. Others had sets at home, but they either enjoyed games, tolerated them or lacked the moral courage to do the same as John Betjeman. John's request was seldom refused.[69]

John's failure to conform did not make him universally unpopular. Chief among his friends in 'B' House was Philip Harding, who entered the school with him in September 1920 and remained a friend until Harding's death in 1972. Harding was born in Dorset, and he introduced John to that county one vacation: the two made a tour of the towns and villages which resulted in John's early poem 'Dorset'.[70] The poem makes play with Dorset place-names, includ-ing Shroton, the seat of Harding's mother's family, Ryves. It was probably as a compliment to Harding that John included Shroton, which otherwise would not have earned its place in competition with the mellifluous quaintness of Rime Intrinsica, Fontmell Magna, Sturminster Newton, Melbury Bubb, Bingham's Mel-combe, Iwerne Minster and Plush.

Because John Betjeman and John Bowle were in different houses, they did not meet until both were quite senior in the school. 'I never knew John until I was about sixteen and he was fifteen plus,' Bowle said. 'We met through the art room and we used to spend hours there, drawing and painting. John would improve the occasion by reading poetry aloud to me from *The Oxford Book of English Verse*: he educated me a great deal in those days.'[71] On a winter's day in 1923, Bowle spent an afternoon with John in the art room. 'He roused me out of my stupor by reading Austin Dobson aloud,' Bowle wrote in his diary. Another afternoon, 'Betj and I spent what is usually [Officers' Training Corps] parade time in Adderley [Library] over the *London Mercury*, where we found a superb article on "Hymns Happy and Unhappy".[72] In early December Bowle recorded his admiration for the paper John had read the Literary Society on Victorian minor poets and artists. 'His descriptive passages on Victorian Christmases are particularly good and unselfconscious – the "cosy" church and the snow flakes and the broken pillars over the graves ... His intimate knowledge of London helps him very much. I am tremendously pleased that he has shown himself so clever, besides being so charming.'[73]

John and Bowle also met in 'extra mathematics' classes given by John's housemaster, the Rev. Cornwell Robertson, known as 'the Vicar'. Bowle wrote to his mother on 12 May 1924:

> I have just come back from 'private tu' [tutorial] in maths with Robertson and Betj: it is the most grotesque P.T. set in the world. He is a frightful old man with a muddled mind ... It is so desperately difficult not to laugh. Especially when B. is made to read aloud: 'If a bucket going down a well X feet deep, having a rope Y inches across takes 5 minutes to fill at the bottom and leaks 1 dram every foot ascended, what is the cost of the rope?'[74]

Through Bowle, John met the blond giant Arthur Elton, who was in the same house as Bowle (Preshute) under the games fiend T.C.G.S. Sandford. Though no good at games, Elton 'was so large that he was left alone'.[75] The heir to a baronetcy, he lived at Clevedon Court in Somerset, to which the body of Tennyson's Arthur Hallam had been brought for burial in 1833. John visited the house in Sir Ambrose Elton's old Ford and admired the 'Eltonware' made by his friend's grandfather, which had a glaze like gilded sun-cracked mud. In later years John wrote affectionately of Clevedon in *First and Last Loves* (1952) and campaigned to save its clock-tower, covered in Eltonware tiles, and its pier, 'delicate as a Japanese print'.[76]

Bowle was one of the few of John's Marlborough friends who were invited to visit him at his parents' home in Chelsea. Two of Bowle's uncles had sent him cheques for winning the Brackenbury Scholarship at Balliol. He used the money to go to London and from the Berners Hotel off Oxford Street called the next morning at 53 Church Street, Chelsea. He thought it elegant and snug – 'small Queen Anne, twisting oak staircase, good furniture and original drawings by Victorian artists. Also saw quite good pictures by Mr Betjemann ...'[77] The two boys set out to explore City churches on an open-topped bus; at Westminster they took a tram along the Embankment to St Paul's and the City. They visited the Monument and the Wren and Hawksmoor churches around it. Bowle returned to Salisbury that evening by one of the non-stop steam trains of the Southern Railway.

On 14 February 1924 Bowle confided to his diary: 'Betj inserted a rhymed valentine into M . . . 's hymn book. There was an immediate and blushing reaction.'[78] In later years John and his friends were candid about the prevalence of homosexual behaviour at Marlborough in their day. In 1973 John wrote to Kingsley Amis, whose new novel *The Riverside Murders* had been reviewed in *The Times* that morning:*

Dear Kingers,

A bloody good review I thought . . . I enjoyed every word of the book including the extremely complicated end, but top for me is the chapter called 'Moments of Delight'. I think it would be very nice if you were to write a school story. No one has done it properly for years. What is so wonderful about your writing about Peter Furneaux, old boy, is that you've entered completely into the unshockable practical mind of Peter and his friend, Reg. That's the way to do it. It's the way Dean Farrar did it in *Eric* and in *St Winifred's*.[79] If you just substitute what really happened, which was quick, practical sex, for drinking whisky, you have got the guilt- and doom-ridden life that I lived as a boarder in the early 1920s . . .[80]

Anthony Blunt's recollection was that 'There was not much "quick, practical sex", but there were many romantic friendships. John was wildly in love at one stage with a boy in my house [C3] and once asked me to deliver a note to him: but I annoyed him considerably by delivering it too *publicly*.'[81] John Bowle said: 'There were various boys that John found attractive and made a great fuss about. He would come up to you and say, "Ooh, isn't he lovely!" One was a boy called Neville Greene, to whom John applied a line

---

* The novel was reviewed by Myrna Blumberg, who wrote: 'Peter Furneaux, of Riverside Villas, near Croydon, is 14, keen on Wodehouse and *The Wizard of Oz*. It is the 1930s, Geraldo's Band days, and though he feels enslaved by hypocritical prohibitions he frees himself of some. "I masturbate and I've done things with other boys and I've *thought* of all sorts of things . . ." he tells his neighbour Mrs Trevelyan while they spend an afternoon in her bed.'

by Lord Alfred Douglas – "Wet green eyes, like a full chalk stream".'[82]

John was not only reading and quoting Lord Alfred Douglas at Marlborough. Ernest Betjemann was scandalized to discover that his son was also corresponding with the former lover of Oscar Wilde.

When I was at Marlborough [John recalled] I discovered that Oscar Wilde was someone one ought not to mention; so naturally he had great attraction for me. And I borrowed from one of the masters a volume containing *Lady Windermere's Fan*. The master seemed rather reluctant to lend it to me – he had a whole set of Oscar in that lovely Methuen edition. Then I discovered that Lord Alfred Douglas was actually still alive. So I wrote to him from Marlborough. He was only too pleased to reply and asked me for a photograph. So I went round to the school's photographers, Roberts, and had myself taken, sideways-on and looking, I hoped, rather like the portrait of Rupert Brooke in that Sidgwick and Jackson edition – of Rupert Brooke with an open shirt – and sent it to him, and it brought a reply at once. He was in Belgium at the time; he was living there with his mother as he had libelled Winston Churchill in some speech he had made, which was published in Aberdeen.[83] He said that Winston Churchill had published a false report of the Battle of Jutland in order to satisfy the Jews. He was madly anti-Semitic. That I didn't know about at the time. He wrote me long letters about Shakespeare. Well, then I bought some of Bosie's [Douglas's] poems. I said how beautiful his poems were, as indeed I thought they were . . .

Bosie in those days went I think fifty times to *The Immortal Hour*, words by Fiona McLeod (real name was Sharp),[84] music by Rutland Boughton. He thought that was the best thing that had happened in England since Shakespeare. He wrote all about it in his letters to me. These letters arrived from Belgium about once a week while I was on holiday in Cornwall. My mother noticed them and must have steamed them open, because one day Nancy Wright, the sister of my friend Ronnie Wright, a fair-haired girl – very pretty but I never thought of sex in those days either with my own or the opposite sex – was invited to stay; and in a rather marked way my mother and Nancy Wright left the room at luncheon and my father took me for a walk up a lane.

You know that he was deaf and could only speak through a speaking tube. And if he didn't want to hear you, he would roll it up and put it in his pocket and he couldn't lip-read very well. His sister, my aunt, wrote a rather good book on lip-reading, which I think is still the text-book on lip-reading: her mother, my grandmother, was deaf too. He said: 'You've been having letters from Lord Alfred Douglas.' I couldn't deny it. 'Do you know what that man is?' I said: 'No.' 'He's a bugger. Do you know what buggers are? Buggers are two men who work themselves up into such a state of mutual admiration that one puts his piss-pipe up the other one's arse. What do you think of that?' And of course I felt absolutely sick, and shattered. And then I thought of this beautiful sonneteer, going to *The Immortal Hour* and writing all those lovely sonnets:

> I have been profligate of happiness
> And reckless of the world's hostility,
> The blessed part has not been given to me
> Gladly to suffer fools. I do confess
> I have enticed and merited distress,
> By this, that I have never bowed the knee
> Before the shrine of wise Hypocrisy,
> Nor worn self-righteous anger like a dress.[85]

My father said: 'You're not to write another letter to that man.' And I didn't. And more and more letters came – 'If I don't hear from you again, I shan't write.' My father did not let me see the further letters that arrived. He put them in his safe. After my father's death I gave them to a biographer of Bosie – Evan Morgan, or it may have been a man called Colson.[86] They weren't very interesting.[87]

In *Summoned by Bells* John described his romantic feelings for boys at Marlborough. In the Victorian chapel the Old Marlburian Bishop of London, Dr Winnington Ingram, preached a sermon on Purity – 'When all I worshipped were the athletes, ranged/In the pews opposite,' John wrote.[88] And in his last term at the school, in 1925, John to his surprise was asked to go into town by 'a noisy boy,/One of a gang so mad on motor-cars/That I, the aesthete, hardly noticed him'.[89] Back in college, after the trip into town, they found they had time for a bicycle ride in the summer sun. They rode to Silbury. At the top of Hackpen Hill John's new friend 'sat among the harebells in his shorts,/Hugging his knees till I caught up with him'.[90] Pushing back a lock of hair that kept falling on his face, the boy asked 'Why do you always go about with Black [ie Greene]?'[91]

> Here was love
> Too deep for words or touch. The golden downs
> Looked over elm tops islanded in mist,
> And short grass twinkled with blue butterflies.
> Henceforward Marlborough shone.[92]

The new friend was Donovan Chance, of Compton Kinver, Stour-bridge. In the 1930s he opened a garage, Friary Motors (agents for Lagonda and Chevrolet) at Old Windsor, Berkshire, and in 1937 he answered a query from John about his Ford.

John almost enjoyed his last two years at Marlborough. He was too puckish and too hopeless at games to be made a prefect; but he was a recognized school 'character'. His near-contemporary G.K. White has written:

> John Betjeman has made a good deal of literary capital out of the miseries which he says he endured at Marlborough. He may well have been genuinely unhappy in his early years there – he was a couple of years senior to me – but I know that for the last two years at school, when we were members of the same house, he was on top of the world. My mental picture of him is of one always laughing, giving and getting endless amusement. Having given Norwood the appropriate name of 'God', he produced for us this surprising line of blank verse, 'I saw God on a bicycle today'. And he had a rather cruel tongue: he said of two brothers, without ensuring that neither could hear him, 'It is lucky that the two _____ s are such friends of each other, for otherwise neither of them would have any friend at all.'[93]

With Anthony Blunt and Louis MacNeice, John joined in a 'cult of childhood' intended to enrage the hearties. Blunt and MacNeice provocatively bounced enormous rubber balls at each other across the rounders pitch, and were chased off. John bowled a hoop through the school court, wearing a green feather behind his ear.[94]

In spite of this flaunted 'bolshiness', John was given a most unlikely official honour: he was made a cadet second lieutenant in the Officers' Training Corps. (The highest rank a schoolboy could attain was cadet lieutenant.) He later wrote:

> I find it difficult to decide whether I disliked compulsory games or 'voluntary' Corps more. The Corps had these advantages over cricket: it did not last so long and was less dangerous. Certainly the

most awful days were those when there was a Corps parade first and then games afterwards.

I was lucky in my Corps career. Early in it, I decided to join the Signal section in order to avoid carrying a heavy rifle. By sheer long service I rose to the rank of 2nd lieutenant and thus had higher rank than any captains or prefects in my house.[95]

The OTC uniforms still included puttees – long, khaki tapes wound round the legs – which had not yet been superseded by canvas gaiters with buckles. John's puttees always came undone. The place just after him on parade was coveted because his neighbour would appear relatively immaculate.[96] G.K. White recalled the eccentric figure John cut as a subaltern:

> On one memorable day the whole Marlborough battalion of about six hundred paraded before marching off to a field day. We stood at ease. The commanding officer, a master who had spent the war in the Grenadier Guards and had a terrific presence and voice, called out: 'The Battalion will move to the right in columns of fours in the following order – Signallers, A Company, Band, B Company, C Company!' We waited in silence. Then Betjeman's voice rang out, clear and cultured and unmilitary: 'Signallers! Signallers – Halt!'[97]

John had one sweet triumph to set against this fiasco. 'At camp, which I could not avoid,' he wrote, 'the head of my house tried to have the tents commanded by house ranks, so that I was put under one of my own lance-corporals. But the C.O. overruled him on my appeal. That was my only success of any note at Marlborough.'[98]

It is not easy to assess how unhappy John was at the college. Clearly, he enjoyed dramatizing his tribulations there; but the evidence of his contemporaries, too, suggests an institution closer to a concentration camp than a school. 'Even now,' one of them wrote to him in 1960, 'I tend to wake screaming in the night at the thought of an impending flogging from Sandy[99] or Canning for having gone down three places in form during the week. Has such treatment made men of us?'[100] An Anthony Blunt might decide: 'If this represents the establishment, I shall conspire to destroy the establishment.' (That is the theme of Julian Mitchell's 1982 play *Another Country*.) John's response to the ordeal was to adapt rather than rebel. He used his burgeoning charm and wit to make things easier for himself, while storing up hatred of those he took to be his chief tormentors. A desire to *épater* sometimes triumphed, but he did not want to make himself so noticeable that he would be put in the basket. As he moved up the school, his schoolfellows became more sophisticated and were better able to appreciate his quiddities, so that the sixth form was a comparatively happy time for him. But he leaves us in no doubt that he was unhappier at Marlborough than he thought he had any right to be. Along with the bullying and the beatings, the poor food and the cold, lack of privacy was one of his main grievances. He liked Bodley and Garner's 1880s chapel, not just because it was Victorian Gothic and decorated with sensuous Pre-Raphaelite murals by Roddam Spencer-Stanhope, but because it was 'The only place where I could be alone'.[101] In a BBC radio broadcast of 1954, John said that the first tune he remembered deeply loving was the Welsh hymn tune '*Hyfrydol*'.

> It has happy associations for me because I first heard it at school in chapel. This happiness was not because I was particularly happy at school, but because chapel services, though not religious moments to me, were yet moments of peace and security. No one could get at you in chapel, no one could beat you or bully you there. You couldn't possibly do any school work in chapel, and even if you didn't join in the singing, which I was always too nervous to do, you could pretend you were singing by opening and shutting your mouth, and thus avoid committing the crime of being out of the ordinary. '*Hyfrydol*'! I see the rows of gas-lit faces at Sunday Evensong. I feel warm inside me a mountain of buttered toast and also I remember those early stirrings of poetry and impressions of Welsh hills, lonely farms, slate chapels, Celtic saints, Hallelujahs, Evangelicals, Celtic knots, all tied up together which this hymn brings back to me.[102]

THE SECRET GLORY

Bang! Boom! His big fists set the cups a-dance,
The willow-pattern shivered on the shelves,
His coat-sleeve swept an ash-tray to the floor . . .
'Just down for breakfast, sir? You're good enough
To honour us by coming down at ten!
Don't fidget, boy. Attention when I speak! . . .'

John Betjeman, *Summoned by Bells*, 1960

As John reached adolescence and failed to develop into the kind of
son and heir that his father wanted, he was subjected to Ernest's
bullying tantrums during the Cornish holidays. From his mid-
teens, he was glad to escape from these outbursts and from his
mother's hypochondriac prattle. Once again, his bicycle was the
instrument of freedom. One summer afternoon, when he was
fifteen or sixteen, he pedalled off to the parish of St Ervan. It was to
be a day of Damascus-road revelation.

The revelation came at tea-time, the equinox of John's day.[1] He
was coasting along, past lichened stones and buddleia, when he
heard the note of a bell from the combe below. Following the
sound, he came upon the half-ruined church of St Ervan. A heavy
bell hung from an elm tree by the churchyard gate, and by it stood
the bearded rector, a gong stick in one hand, a book in the other. He
invited John to Evensong and then to a cup of tea in the damp,
ramshackle rectory where, evidently, he lived alone. The rector was
Wilfred Johnson, minister of St Ervan's for forty years (1915–55).[2]

John was not impressed by the church: 'There wasn't much to
see, there wasn't much/The *Little Guide* could say about the
church./Holy and small and heavily restored';[3] though if he had

had time to look carefully, he might have noticed a seventeenth-century wall-tablet to a kinsman of John Keats. But the gaunt bachelor priest made on him an impression he never forgot.

> He talked of poetry and Cornish saints;
> He kept an apiary and a cow;
> He asked me which church service I liked best –
> I told him Evensong . . . 'And I suppose
> You think religion's mostly singing hymns
> And feeling warm and comfortable inside?'
> And he was right: most certainly I did.
> 'Borrow this book and come to tea again.'
> With Arthur Machen's *Secret Glory* stuffed
> Into my blazer pocket, up the hill
> On to St Merryn, down to Padstow Quay
> In time for the last ferry back to Rock,
> I bicycled – and found Trebetherick
> A worldly contrast with my afternoon.[4]

'When John came back to Marlborough the next term,' John Bowle recalled, 'he was full of *The Secret Glory*.'[5] By modern standards the book seems blowsily overwritten, and too didactic, like a Bernard Shaw preface run out of control; but it appealed to John powerfully on two fronts. It was suffused with a poetic romanticism, a passionate nostalgia for the old saints, grail-quests, holy wells and holy bells of Celtic Wales, which chimed in perfectly with his interest in primitive Cornish saints and in his own supposedly Welsh ancestry. (By beguiling coincidence, Machen had given his hero the surname Meyrick.) But even more appealing to John than the mystical raptures was the satire that Machen levelled at the British public school system, from which John, when he first read the novel, was suffering in much the same way as Ambrose Meyrick. Everything John most loathed about Marlborough was savagely guyed – the discipline, the team games, the emphasis on classicism. Machen also satirized the hypocrisy about sex in the near-monastic society of the public schools: 'Suppose . . . a whole society organized on the strict official understanding that . . . breakfast, lunch, dinner and supper are orgies only used by the most wicked and degraded wretches . . . In such a world, I think, you would discover some very striking irregularities in diet.'[6]

When John first read those words, he was already familiar with the 'quick, practical sex' of the Marlborough dormitories.[7] His early relations with girls were slower and less practical. Biddy Walsham and her brother John (whose parents were usually in China) grew up in Trebetherick with the Adams boys, Ralph, Vasey and Alastair, who lived with their aunt, Elsie MacCorkindale, as their mother had gone off with a young naval officer called Geoffrey Bligh. Miss MacCorkindale shared a house, 'Torquil', with the Walshams' aunt, Ursula Warren. The house was full of Chinese souvenirs, because Elsie MacCorkindale (Mrs Adams's sister) had also been out in China. Of all the adults in Trebetherick, she was the only one, John felt, who took him at his estimate of himself –

> Aunt Elsie, aunt of normal Scottish boys,
> Adopted aunt of lone abnormal me . . .[8]

He plucked up his courage and asked if he might borrow her Talbot-Darracq motor-car to take Biddy to a dance.

> The eucalyptus shivered in the drive,
> The stars were out above the garage roof,
> Night-scented stock and white tobacco plant
> Gave way to petrol scent and came again.
> A rival, changing gear along the lane,
> Alone disturbed the wide September night.
> 'Come in, John, and I'll tell you why you can't.'
> And there, among the water-colours, screens,
> Thick carpets, Whistler books and porcelain,
> There, in that more-than-summer residence,
> She would explain that I was still a boy.
>   'Was still a boy?' Then what, by God, was this –
> This tender, humble, unrequited love
> For Biddy Walsham?[9]

In his fantasy of driving Biddy to the dance, John pictured himself braking, switching off the headlights. And if his hand should accidentally touch hers, perhaps the love in him 'would race along to her/On the electron principle? . . .'[10] No-nonsense Scottish Miss MacCorkindale told him it would be more sensible to walk.

That particular dance was held in the bungalow of Kathleen

Stokes, the sister of Bess Betjemann's Trebetherick friend Nell Oakley.[11] Mrs Stokes's late husband had been a judge in India, and the bungalow was decorated with Benares brass. Many Trebetherick residents had been in India or China. Others were retired school-masters: Trebetherick was known as 'Beaks' Corner'. These 'foreigners', and the local folk, appear in John's poems. No other English poet has so freely introduced his acquaintance into his verse under their own names. A musical parallel would be the *Enigma Variations* of Sir Edward Elgar, who said: 'I have in the variations sketched portraits of my friends . . . in each variation I have looked at the theme through the personality (as it were) of another Johnny.' John has similarly preserved in his poetry several 'Johnnies' of whom posterity would otherwise know nothing: the Ransomes and their mower; Ethel Harden, Bess Betjemann's bridge friend; Mr Rosevear; Kathleen Stokes and her sealyhams; surly Tom Blake with the collection plate; and Anne Channel, a local *salonnière*.

Joan Kunzer said of Anne Channel: 'She was very daring. We were almost not allowed to speak to her. She was a great friend of some people called De Paula who were friends of the Betjemanns, and I think she came down to Cornwall through them. John always liked her very much. She was about forty and used to run after all the young men. She had a bungalow on the way to Polzeath, they used to sit there surrounding her like a male harem – these *boys*. I thought she was horrible, of course! But John liked to go to her because he said she was so funny – and I think she probably was.'[12] In his poem 'Old Friends' John wrote:

> Where is Anne Channel who loved this place the best,
> With her tense blue eyes and her shopping-bag falling apart,
> And her racy gossip and nineteen-twenty zest,
> And that warmth of heart?

Anne Channel (as 'Miss Pansy Wavery') and Ethel Harden (as 'Mrs Sibyl Larden') both became characters in a novel about Cornwall which John began in the late 1920s or early 1930s but never finished.[13] The aborted book was first entitled *St Mattock* (ie St Enodoc), later *St Ivy* and finally *St Zennock*. It was flagrantly a *roman à clef*. If it had ever been completed and published, John would have been *persona non grata* in Trebetherick, as E.F. Benson was in Rye after his 'Lucia' stories were issued.

1 G. Stanley Betjemann as Count Almaviva, photographed in Leamington Spa, the setting of an early Betjeman poem. He was one of several of John's kinsmen with histrionic and musical talents. Gilbert Betjemann, violinist and Musician-in-Ordinary to Queen Victoria, was his brother. Stanley emigrated to the United States in the 1880s.

2 John's great-grandfather, Edward John Thompson, a London watch-material maker. Thompson's daughter Hannah married John's grandfather John Betjemann (1835–93).

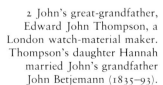

3 John's mother, Mabel Bessie Betjemann, *née* Dawson (1878–1952).

4 (*below*) John's father, Ernest Betjemann (1872–1934).

5. West Hill, Highgate, in 1910 when John was four. The
Betjemanns lived at No. 31.

6 As an only child with few friends, John made a confidant and companion of his teddy bear Archibald, who survived into patched old age. Evelyn Waugh pirated him for Lord Sebastian's teddy in *Brideshead Revisited*.

8 (*opposite*) Ernest Betjemann was considered the Chippendale of his day. In the 1920s, G. Betjemann & Sons (founded 1820) became prosperous by making cocktail cabinets and dressing-tables for Asprey's. Ernest hoped John would join the firm as 'the fourth generation', but John showed no interest in cabinet-making.

7 Even as a small child, John showed the dramatic talent which was later so evident in his television programmes.

G. BETJEMANN
& SONS
Ltd. (Founded A.D. 1820.)

36, PENTONVILLE RD.,
LONDON, N.1.

North 2092. BETJEMANN, London.

9 John and his mother: a studio photograph taken in Kentish
Town Road, London, about 1910.

10 Port Isaac, Cornwall, in 1906. 'Then you see it all, huddled
in a steep valley, a cover at the end of a combe, roofs and
roofs, tumbling down either steep hillside in a race for shelter
from the south-west gales . . . Port Isaac is Polperro without
the self-consciousness, St Ives without the artists.' (*First and
Last Loves*, 1952).

11 Ethelwynne Bouman, the Betjemanns' next-door neighbour on West Hill, was a 'second mother' to John. Her son Billy, John's childhood friend, was almost certainly the 'Bobby' of John's poem 'Narcissus'.

St Zennock begins with high-pitched farce – the theft of Mrs Larden's birdbath, which is later hurled through the window of the bridge room at the Dormy House. (There was a Dormy House in Trebetherick, a club run by the Bannerman family.) But John soon loses his grip on the plot as he anatomizes the social grouping in 'Zennabay' (Trebetherick), and the last surviving part-chapter, headed 'Cow Parsley on the Altar', is a severely argued treatise on the purchase and re-sale of advowsons.

John's analysis of the social groups of 'Zennabay' was more than half in earnest. Trebetherick *was* full of snobbish cliques: in ironic reference to the attitudes then prevailing, Biddy Crookshank said of Nell Oakley's husband: 'Oh, he was one of the unmentionable jute boys! Tea was all right, coffee was *pukka* – but never jute!'[14] As usual, John was worried about his own social standing. A 'foreigner' from beyond the Tamar: well, that was all right, the poshest of the English visitors were 'foreigners' too. But his family were not in 'the County set'. Ernest Betjemann ended up, as Joan Kunzer said, by buying up most of Trebetherick; but to the Raj families and old China Hands in the bungalows, he was 'in trade', and a cabinet-maker from Clerkenwell ranked even lower than a Calcutta 'jute boy'.

Still, John felt more at home in north Cornwall than in north London, and a named house in a remote county was a 'better address' than a numbered villa in an unfashionable London street. Not that Trebetherick was 'smart'. The village was remote from the tourist-trap part of Cornwall. It had none of the prettified charm of St Ives, with its colony of be-smocked artists and studio potters, or Fowey, home of Sir Arthur Quiller-Couch ('Q'), or Falmouth, where Henry Tuke – 'the Boucher of the Boy Scouts', as John later called him – painted his naked boys.[15] It was too northerly to qualify as part of the 'Cornish Riviera'. Even today – though John in a late poem, 'Delectable Duchy', abominated its 'cara' parks and potato crisp wrappings – the Padstow region is off the tourist beat.

That the area was not popular or well-known or typical of Cornwall commended it to John. With Coventry Patmore, he was always disposed 'to love the lovely that are not beloved'. Byways interested him more than highways, minor poets more than major. Because no 'Q' or Lamorna Birch[16] had commemorated the Padstow district, sung or painted its charms, John was free to make it his own. 'Some think of the furthest among places as Spitzbergen or Honolulu. But give me Padstow,' he wrote in *First and Last Loves*, dramatizing the remoteness of his chosen domain.[17]

Rather as Hilaire Belloc, the doggedly English Frenchman, adopted Sussex as his preserve, stumping over the South Downs and composing odes to ale and windmills, John, with his foreign name and ancestry, made his family honorary citizens of north Cornwall. When his father died he had a stone tablet designed for the south wall of St Enodoc's nave. On the plaque was no mention of Highbury or Clerkenwell or Gospel Oak: it was 'Sacred to the memory of Ernest Edward Betjemann of Undertown in this Parish.' When his mother died, John had her buried under the north boundary wall of St Enodoc's churchyard under a slab of Delabole slate. And in a rainswept ceremony of 1984, John too was buried there, under a stone carved with Gothic letters.

9

OXFORD

Balkan Sobranies in a wooden box,
The college arms upon the lid; Tokay
And sherry in the cupboard; on the shelves
The University Statutes bound in blue,
Crome Yellow, Prancing Nigger, Blunden, Keats.
My walls were painted Bursar's apple-green;
My wide-sashed windows looked across the grass
To tower and hall and lines of pinnacles.
The wind among the elms, the echoing stairs,
The quarters, chimed across the quiet quad
From Magdalen tower and neighbouring turret-clocks,
Gave eighteenth-century splendour to my state.
Privacy after years of public school;
Dignity after years of none at all —
First college rooms, a kingdom of my own . . .

John Betjeman, *Summoned by Bells*, 1960

Magdalen College, Oxford, to which John went in the Michaelmas
Term of 1925, was not the most academically distinguished of the
colleges: Balliol had not lost the intellectual supremacy which
Benjamin Jowett had wrested for it from Newman's Oriel in the
nineteenth century. Neither was it the most aristocratic: Christ
Church was even more familiar with the clamour Evelyn Waugh
described in *Decline and Fall* — 'the sound of the English county
families baying for broken glass'. But by common consent Magdalen was and is the most beautiful of the colleges. 'Balliol was my
mother, All Souls was my lawful and loving wife, and Magdalen my
very beautiful mistress,' said Cosmo Gordon Lang, a former Dean

of Divinity at Magdalen, in a phrase thought *risqué* for an Archbishop of Canterbury.

Magdalen stands at the edge of the old city on the bank of the
River Cherwell. It is one of the largest colleges, a congeries of archi-
tectural showpieces: William of Waynflete's slender tower of perfect proportion, from which the choristers sing their half-pagan
anthem on May morning; echoing medieval cloisters guarded by
grotesque gargoyles, some lewdly embracing; dark corners such as
Kitchen Quad or Chaplain's Quad which gives a glimpse into the
Senior Common Room; St John's Quad with its open-air pulpit;
Pugin's Grammar Hall, picturesquely decrepit; the honey-coloured
New Buildings (1703), colonnaded, festooned with wistaria in
summer, and overlooking the deer park. The park furnishes
venison for college feasts, tableaux for tourists' cameras and a
natural setting for productions of *A Midsummer Night's Dream*.
John remembered how he and his friends used to feed the deer with
sugar-lumps soaked in port.[1] His rooms did not overlook the park,
but were on the sunnier side of New Buildings with a view of Cloisters and the tower; so he was spared the noise of rutting and of
antler-clashes as the stags battled for their mates. The beauties and
comforts of Magdalen encouraged lotus-eating and languid self-
indulgence. The college emblem, the Waynflete lily, symbolized, it
was said, the habits of many of the undergraduates: they toiled not,
neither did they spin.

Herbert Warren, who was President of Magdalen when John
arrived at the college, was born at the beginning of the Crimean
War. A legendary snob, he had the arms of De Warenne, to which
he was not remotely entitled, set in stained glass in the Founder's
Tower. When introducing his wife, he would say, 'Meet Lady
Warren, the daughter of Sir Benjamin Brodie, Bart.' He was only
thirty-one when he became President in 1885. He set out to change
the character of the college. 'Magdalen had been too much identified with aestheticism, peacocks' feathers and blue china,' he told
the *Isis* in 1929. 'I had been taught at Clifton and by Plato that the
cult of the Muses and the Arts to which I was devoted, should be
tempered by politics and athletics. I encouraged the devotees of
these.' In 1911 he was elected Professor of Poetry. Just before the
First World War, his career reached its glorious zenith: the Prince
of Wales was sent to Magdalen as a 'commoner'. Warren might
then have murmured a *Nunc Dimittis* – 'Lord, now lettest Thou

Thy servant depart in peace, . . . For mine eyes have seen thy Salvation' – but he stayed on until 1929.

John owed his admission to Magdalen almost entirely to Warren's personal intervention. He did not go up with a scholarship, as Evelyn Waugh had to Hertford College three years before, or with an exhibition, like his Marlborough friend Philip Harding, also at Hertford. Like the Prince of Wales he was to be a commoner, maintained at his father's expense. He may have done well in the Magdalen entrance examination paper which he sat in April 1925. The printed question-paper, which survives in the Betjeman Archive at the University of Victoria, shows that he put a mark against (and presumably answered) question 8: 'Can "skyscrapers" or railway stations be made beautiful? If so, how?' – a question he was to devote much of the rest of his life to answering. Other questions on this imaginatively conceived paper were: 'What kind of services do you think should be rewarded in the Birthday Honours list?'; 'What reasons are there for thinking that life may exist in some of the planets? If it could be proved to exist, what difference would it make to us?'; and 'Should "faith-healing" be encouraged?' John put an exclamation-mark in the margin against this last question.

He was still expected to pass 'Responsions', an elementary test in mathematics and Latin. He had failed the examination twice by May 1925, and it began to look as though he would have to abandon thoughts of Oxford and enter his father's business. Ernest Betjemann wrote to him on 13 May (John was in Trebetherick) that President Warren, on being asked if John might have another try, had replied that John's case would be considered 'but he is not sanguine of the result'. Ernest added: 'I do not share your easy optimism: there is no special reason why Magdalen or anywhere else should want you or break rules for you.'[2]

But at that date the President of Magdalen had the power to admit anybody he liked to the college. (The privilege was later docked to a statutory fourteen places, and has since been abolished.) Warren fancied himself as a poet, and John seems to have made a good impression by sending him some of his Marlborough verses. By August 1925 it had been arranged that he would come up to Magdalen as a commoner in the next term, and Ernest Betjemann was consulting Warren as to the preliminary reading John ought to do before October. Warren advised that John should obtain *Longinus on the Sublime*, edited by Professor Rhys Roberts, 'and read it slowly'. Also, if he had not read them, he should read Matthew Arnold's *Essays in Criticism* (both series), his *Collected Essays on Poetry* and his *Lectures on Translating Homer*. Warren added a postscript: 'Does he know Matthew Arnold's Poems? It might be suitable to read "Tristan & Iseult" at Trebetherick.'[3]

Ernest bought John this diet of texts and told him to send the President a (now lost) sonnet which had won him a Marlborough prize, and two other poems. Warren replied to John on 21 August:

Dear Mr Betjemann,

I am glad to have your poem. I am much interested in it. I shouldn't have called it a 'typical' Prize Poem at all and I have written one and read a great many in my time. I think the Marlborough authorities must have been open-minded and discerning to give it the Prize. I am not sure that I follow all the meaning, but it has a great deal that is original and individual in observation and expression. I like the second octet especially . . .

Do you care for Milton? You ought to for you seem to me to have the perception that poetry should be *artistic* as well as philosophic, if also philosophic as well as artistic . . .

Yours sincerely,

Herbert Warren.

There is another vol of Matthew Arnold very suitable to Cornwall. His volume on Celtic literature.[4]

John went up to Magdalen on 8 October 1925. Michaelmas Term began the next day. Ernest was proud of him; but while he was glad to finance John in an education he himself had never enjoyed, he could not miss the chance of delivering some Polonius-like injunctions. On 16 October he wrote enclosing £50. He hoped John was keeping accounts, as agreed: these were to be sent on the first of each month to the Pentonville Road works, not to home – perhaps to avoid worrying Bess Betjemann with John's excesses. 'I know you will not be extravagant,' Ernest wrote, 'because you realise it is all a sacrifice for your Mother and me.' He added: 'So glad you are happy, am sure that you will enjoy every moment. Be slow in choosing your friends.'[5]

It was the Oxford of plus fours, verandah suits, violet hair cream, batik or Charvet silk ties and open sports cars; shingled hair and slave bangles for the rare fashionable 'undergraduettes'. Bryan

Guinness (now Lord Moyne), who preceded John as editor of the *Cherwell* and became one of his best friends, wrote of 'the gramophonic, cinematographic life of the Oxford set'.[6] Most of the gramophones had trumpets, and the records were of the Black Bottom, 'Chili Bom Bom', 'Happy Days Are Here Again' and 'Squeeze Up, Lady Letty'. Oxford was near enough London for visits to West End nightclubs, theatres and cinemas, by car or by train – returning on the so-called 'Flying Fornicator' – or staying overnight with a bribe to one's 'scout' (college servant) not to inform the authorities. Sophie Tucker was at the Kit-Kat. Rudolph Valentino could be seen at the Marble Arch Pavilion. John went to see *The Immortal Hour*, Lord Alfred Douglas's favourite play, at the Haymarket Theatre, and Melville Gideon in *The Co-Optimists*.[7] At the Super Cinema in Oxford, haunted by John's Magdalen friend Henry Yorke (the novelist 'Henry Green'), Mary Pickford was the 'star attraction'.[8]

In spite of the new jazzy tempo of life for the Bright Young People, some formalities were preserved. Evening dress was still *de rigueur* for dinner. For daytime wear, the extravagantly wide 'Oxford bags' had until recently been the fashion, and some of the more exhibitionist undergraduates still sported them. In one college, it was reported, the servants had orders 'to ignore undergraduates thus attired'.[9] In an article of 1958, 'The Silver Age of Aesthetes', John wrote:

I came up to the University just as 'Oxford Bags' were going out. I doubt if they had ever come in with the grand sets in which I aspired to move. The year must have been 1925 when still the tales of Harold Acton, Brian Howard and Cyril Connolly lingered and the few aesthetes of that generation who had not been sent down, were staying on for a final year. Most aesthetes belonged to the Liberal Club, to which no Liberals were ever admitted but which was supported, we believed, out of the pocket of Lloyd George. No aesthete was political and the Union was only used for a wash and brush up – whether one was a member or not. Of course I was an aesthete and never played any game for my college and never discovered, nor have yet discovered, where the playing fields of my college were.

The world for me and for many undergraduates was divided into aesthetes and hearties. These divisions overrode all social and college distinctions. True there was one college, Brasenose, which was entirely hearty and dangerous for an aesthete to enter wearing the usual badges of his party – a shantung silk tie, lavender trousers, orange, red or saxe blue shirt. A friend of mine, Michael Dugdale, always entered it limping as he thought the hearties would be too sporting to attack a fellow athlete. Otherwise one's college did not matter and one very much despised the sub-men who tried to whip up college spirit. It was too much like school.[10]

Magdalen was predominantly a college of hearties. President Warren had been only too successful in de-aestheticizing it. Martyn Skinner, John's exact contemporary at Magdalen, said: 'I can't remember a single night when there wasn't a drunken party and somebody breaking glass. It was riotous. The idea was that you could do what you wanted within college, within reason, provided you didn't do it outside. You couldn't be drunk in the streets, but you could be drunk in college. One man got so tight that he smashed up his *own* rooms without realizing they were his.'[11]

John had no wish to antagonize the athletes. He followed the same strategy as at Marlborough, turning himself into a joke figure whom they would laugh at rather than persecute. Humphrey Ellis, the future literary editor of *Punch*, who came up to Magdalen the year after John, recalled: 'One day I noticed a figure in extraordinary clothes standing just inside the door of the porter's lodge. I asked somebody who it was, and he said, "Oh, that's John Betjeman, waiting to be hissed by the athletes." '[12] In a footnote to his handwritten letter, Ellis emphasized: 'Hissed, not kissed.'

John entitled his 1958 article 'The Silver Age of Aesthetes' to distinguish his undergraduate days from those of the preceding Golden Age of Aesthetes – the age of Harold Acton, Brian Howard and Robert Byron, who had been at Eton together. Also of the 'Golden Age' were Evelyn Waugh, John Sutro, Christopher Hollis and Douglas Woodruff, who had enjoyed such *réclame* at Oxford that they could hardly bear to leave it. They returned at weekends to add their lustre to parties and salons. John eventually met them all, through Philip Harding's older brother Archie, who was a friend at Keble College of Waugh's cousin Claud Cockburn; through such dons as Maurice Bowra and 'Colonel' Kolkhorst; casually at the 'George' restaurant; and in the Christ Church rooms of Harold Acton's younger brother, William.

But in the Michaelmas Term of 1925 he was only just acclimatizing himself to life in Oxford. It was intoxicating to be free at last of the oppressive authority of home and school, but there were new difficulties to cope with – such as living within his income, which meant the income his father chose to allow him. Ernest Betjemann was to pay all John's college bills ('Batells' as they were and are archaically called), including a levy for 'argent', use of the college's fine silver. (One of the silver beer mugs was engraved with an inscription commemorating the poet Ambrose 'Namby Pamby' Philips, 1675–1749). Ernest had also agreed that in the first term – the most expensive time for an undergraduate – he would pay for clothes and accessories up to £18. Perhaps to propitiate him, John's first clothes list ('I need . . .') included a golfing cap and golf shoes.[13] As promised, John sent his father monthly accounts of his expenditure. In the early months Ernest expressed himself satisfied with the returns, but found other topics for a good-humoured grouse. Writing from the Junior Constitutional Club, Piccadilly, on 7 November 1925, he complained: 'In your last letter you spelt "of" "off", in fact it seems to go from bad to worse, and if you don't improve your degree will be B.S. (bad speller).'[14]

By John's third term, Ernest was beginning to warn him about over-spending. He wrote on 13 May 1926: 'I enclose you a cheque for £5, try to keep the provisions and drink bill down a bit, there is a steady upward progress. I don't mean to say at all that you are extravagant.'[15] The reason John's food and drink bill had risen is that he had ceased to take his meals in College Hall after his first term. 'Only sub-men ate in hall,' he later explained.[16] A pleasant but more expensive alternative to eating in hall was to have meals brought over from the kitchens by one's scout. The richer under-graduates often held breakfast, lunch or dinner parties in their rooms, ordering from the chef and butler in advance. The *Cherwell* of 7 November 1925 reported that 'old Jynes' (Gynes), steward of the Magdalen Junior Common Room, had acquired for his college one of the finest cellars in England. Nineteen twenty-one was the best year for hock in half a century and Magdalen was plentifully stocked with the different varieties, including Johannisberger, which by 1925 it was impossible to obtain on the Continent. Tokay from the Imperial Palace of Austria-Hungary – the wine mentioned by John in *Summoned by Bells* – was also on sale.

Another alternative to eating in hall was to go to St George's Café-and-Restaurant – 'the George' – at the junction of the Corn-market and George Street, 'where there was a band consisting of three ladies, and where punkahs, suspended from the ceiling, swayed to and fro, dispelling the smoke of the Egyptian and Balkan cigarettes. Mr Ehrsam, the perfect Swiss hotelier, and his wife kept order, and knew how much credit to allow us.'[17] The George was a domain of aesthetes, including the revenants who could call in there without a special invitation from anybody. The aesthetes who dined at the George were known as 'the Georgeoisie'. John Fernald (another Old Marlburian) recalled that one of their favourite jokes was to discomfit a hearty by staring at him in silence and then, on a pre-arranged signal, bursting into a chorus of guffaws.[18]

There was one public controversy of 1925 on which all aesthetes had to take sides. On 19 May the Prime Minister, Stanley Baldwin, had unveiled Jacob Epstein's 'Rima' in Kensington Gardens with a visible shudder. The bas-relief tablet was a memorial to the naturalist W.H. Hudson, who had died in 1924. Epstein, already notorious for his tomb of Oscar Wilde (1912) in the Père Lachaise cemetery, Paris, had carved the goddess Rima in crude Art Deco style with flaring hair and an earth-mother bosom. 'Take this horror out of the Park!' was the *Daily Mail* headline after the unveiling. One MP called Rima 'the terrible female with paralysis of the hands'; another said she was 'the bad dream of the Bolshevist in art'. A letter signed by, among others, Sir Arthur Conan Doyle and Hilaire Belloc, demanding that the sculpture be removed from the Park, was published in the *Morning Post*. Another letter, signed by G.B. Shaw, Arnold Bennett, Ramsay MacDonald and Augustus John, demanded that the sculpture be kept. The Oxford aesthetes were divided on the issue, between those, such as Tom Driberg, who favoured anything *avant-garde* in art, and those, including John, to whom the tablet seemed crude and ugly. The Balliol wit Denis Kincaid made ironic reference to this feeling in a clerihew about John Bowle and another Balliol man, Wyndham Ketton-Cremer (the future historian), on whom Bowle had a passionate 'crush':

> John Edward Bowle
> Had a superflux of soul.
> He was more beautiful than Rima
> But not as beautiful as Ketton-Cremer.[19]

In his first term John was also experiencing the gentle constraints of the Oxford tutorial system. Unlike 'redbrick' universities, which tend to count heads at lectures, the Oxford academic system puts a flattering and not always justified reliance on the undergraduates' will to learn and sense of responsibility. Attending lectures is encouraged, but optional; only the weekly tutorial, *tête-à-tête* with one's tutor, is obligatory.

C.S. Lewis was John's tutor in English language and literature. One might have expected that these two men – both poets, both Christian apologists – would have been compatible. But though John had already been Summoned by Bells, Lewis had not yet been Surprised by Joy. (It was not until 1929, the year after John left Oxford, that Lewis gave in to his inner spiritual urgings, 'admitted that God is God', knelt on his Magdalen carpet and prayed, 'perhaps that night the most dejected and reluctant convert in all England'.[20]) Their love of English literature, too, might have led to some rapport; but Lewis preferred the oldest gnarled roots of the language, John its most luxuriant Victorian blossoming. The lover of bleak Norse legend and Tolkienesque hobgoblins could not understand the lover of cosy suburbs and garden gnomes. No Underground line connected Middle Earth with Metroland.

In 1925 Lewis was a pugnacious atheist, while John was flirting with Anglo-Catholicism, a persuasion unlikely to appeal to someone who had been brought up by Ulster Protestants. Lord David Cecil, who liked Lewis, said: 'It's one of those great comedy ideas, that John Betjeman should have been Jack Lewis's pupil. The very idea of believing in the Church but at the same time making fun of it, would have been distasteful to him. It was too bewildering, this odd little boy making jokes about the things he [John] claimed to think sacred, and yet with tears in his eyes at a hymn. It was rather shocking to Jack Lewis.'[21]

Lewis's mind was analytic; John's was intuitive, addicted to fantasy and flippant posturing. Lewis favoured the big guns of English literature – Shakespeare, Spenser, Milton. John's taste was for the minor figures – Frederick Locker-Lampson, T.E. Brown, Lord de Tabley. John's thesis that Lord Alfred Douglas was greater than Shakespeare did not strike Lewis as an entertaining conceit or as the starting-point for an enjoyable exercise in critical debate: he thought it merely perverse and exasperating – another of Betjeman's silly stratagems for wasting tutorial time. He was not amused when John turned up for his tutorial in carpet slippers. On 27 May 1926 Lewis wrote in his diary:

Betjeman and [Deric] Valentin came for Old English. Betjeman appeared in a pair of eccentric bedroom slippers and said he hoped I didn't mind them as he had a blister. He seemed so pleased with himself that I couldn't help saying that I should mind them very much myself but that I had no objection to *his* wearing them – a view which I believe surprised him. Both had been very idle over the O.E. and I told them it wouldn't do.[22]

He was again incensed with John on 19 January 1927: 'While in College, I was rung up on the telephone by Betjeman speaking from Moreton-in-Marsh,[23] to say that he hadn't been able to read the Old English, as he was suspected for measles and forbidden to read a book. Probably a lie, but what can one do?'[24] John confirms these suspicions in *Summoned by Bells*:

> I cut tutorials with wild excuse,
> For life was luncheons, luncheons, all the way.[25]

He found Old English an arid subject; and even when Lewis discussed nineteenth-century poetry, there was little common ground. John recalled: 'He ruined Coleridge's "Kubla Khan" for me by wondering whether the pants in the line "As if this earth in fast thick pants were breathing" were woollen or fur.' Lord David Cecil said: 'Jack Lewis had a loud voice and asked John difficult questions which he couldn't answer. John did awfully good imitations of being taught by Lewis. "What's wrong with you, Betjeman, is that you've no *starl*. No sense of *starl*." '[26]

John made one game attempt to lure Lewis into his world, but it was a failure. In his diary for 24 January 1927 Lewis describes how John invited him to a party in his lodgings, then in St Aldate's – 'a very beautiful panelled room looking across to the side of the House [Christ Church]'.

I found myself pitchforked into a galaxy of super-undergraduates, including [John] Sparrow of the Nonesuch Press and an absolutely silent and astonishingly ugly person called McNiece [*sic*], of whom Betjeman said afterwards, 'He doesn't say much, but he's a great poet.' It reminded me of the man in Boswell 'who was always thinking of Locke and Newton'. The conversation was chiefly about lace curtains, arts and crafts (which they all dislike), china ornaments, silver versus earthen teapots, architecture, and the strange habits of 'hearties'. The best thing was Betjeman's very curious collection of books. Came away with him and back to college to pull him along through Wulfstan until dinner time.[27]

John's other tutor in Magdalen was the Rev. J.M. Thompson, whose friendly interest in him was an antidote to Lewis's spikiness – a dock-leaf, as it were, growing beside the nettle. He prepared John for the History Previous examination, the equivalent of the modern 'Prelims'. 'Thompie', as he was affectionately known to his Magdalen pupils, was about fifty when John was first taught by him; but he lived to see John reach the same age. He was the only laudatory referee John could find for the scholastic agents Gabbitas-Thring when he applied for a preparatory school job in 1928. On a list of pet hates drawn up in the same year, John included 'All Magdalen dons except J.M. Thompson'.[28] From the start, he liked and respected this 'shy, kind, amusing man'.[29]

Thompson, too, was a poet. His fluent *My Apologia* (1940), a long verse autobiography printed for private circulation, was probably a more immediate inspiration of John's 'The Epic', part of which became *Summoned by Bells*, than Wordsworth's *Prelude*. John enjoyed Thompson's reminiscences of Oxford in the late nineteenth century, when he had met the Christ Church don C.L. Dodgson (Lewis Carroll). Thompson had become Dean of Divinity at Magdalen in 1906. As John was obsessed with religious differences in 1925, Thompson had a special fascination for him, because in 1911 he had caused a furore by denying the existence of miracles in his book *Miracles in the New Testament*. The Bishop of Winchester, Visitor of Magdalen, had withdrawn Thompson's licence to exercise a cure of souls in the college. However, Thompson was so popular with his Magdalen colleagues that he was at once re-elected to his tutorial Fellowship. During the First World War – unacceptable as an army chaplain – he taught at Eton. When he returned to Oxford after the war he turned his hand to a new trade.

> Finding the changing fashion of the Schools
> Called for new tutoring, I changed my tools,
> Unyoked my mind from theologic mystery,
> And hitched it to the sober car of history.[30]

Thompson was a vivid and sympathetic tutor. Another of his

former pupils recalled that he could summon to mind episodes of the French Revolution 'as effortlessly and colourfully as though he had been talking of his own childhood'. He added: 'Thompson had the charming habit of reading your essays to you. When you became aware that you had written something peculiarly silly, he would pause for a moment, produce a brilliant defence of your point of view, say "Ah yes, I see what you mean" and go on to the next point.'[31] This technique was flattering and beguiling to John: it was as though C.S. Lewis had read out John's theory that Lord Alfred Douglas was greater than Shakespeare and had then devoted ten minutes to an entrancing defence of it, as tongue-in-cheek as John's original nonsense.

Martyn Skinner liked Thompson too, but was less impressed by him than John was. 'Thompie was a clergyman but he had lost his faith – had suddenly seen the dark! As our tutor, he was very easily deceived . . . We had the art of filleting a book; and Thompie thought we were very erudite – he said so at Collections [the tutor's end-of-term report to the President of Magdalen]. We were not erudite at all, we were just con-men. He was a nice chap – urbane, kindly – but he was no damn' good as a tutor. He didn't teach one anything.'[32] John wrote to Skinner in 1960: 'Lewis was my undoing at Magdalen as well as my own temperament. Thompie was a rock of goodness and I loved him.'[33] Thompson's widow Mari Meredyth, interviewed in Oxford in her mid-nineties, recalled that John used to come most Sundays to their house in Chadlington Road, North Oxford, for tea and talk, often about religion. John would leave when summoned to evensong by the bells of St Barnabas, Oxford ('St Barnard's, Octopus', as he called the church) –

> Good Lord, as the angelus floats down the road,
> Byzantine St Barnabas, be Thine Abode.[34]

In his article 'The Silver Age of Aesthetes', John wrote: 'I went to one lecture when I was at Oxford. That was in my first term, given by T.S.R. Boase, known as "the popular dean of Hertford", on *Gesta Francorum*.'[35] This was an ironic in-joke: Boase was anything but popular with John and his friends. Like Maurice Bowra he was one of the generation of young dons who had fought in the First World War. He had lost an eye and won the Military Cross. But he was not the tough character that this war record might suggest. He was silkily charming and a touch effete: Bowra called him 'a man of large public virtues and small private parts'.[36]

John's surviving lecture-notes show that in fact he attended more than one of Boase's lectures. That he was not engrossed by them is suggested by marginal notes to the unknown person sitting next to him:

> I love you, yes, I think I do.
> Oh God! that such a thing is true.[37]

And below: 'His name is Prentice. He was at school with Ronald Wright and me. He Scottish – very. Broad accent and pince-nez.' And then: 'Try writing your notes in blank verse – it makes things more interesting.' At this point John began converting the lecture into verse as Boase spoke:

> . . . Seems to dislike ALEXIS and the Greeks
> We must be on our guard against all this.
> The other leaders are conventional
> In their descriptions. And alone are praised
> Friends Boamund and Tancred. Adjectives
> Quite uncomplimentary have been put in
> – For instance in the Norman manuscript
> When Robert's name occurs – of Normandy.
> No criticism otherwise is made
> Of any leaders save but once and that
> I could not put on paper – I forgot
> Because of this blank verse. The author was
> Quite loyal and unthinking, so it seems.
> The author puts to Boamund some thoughts
> Which are too good for him and that he knows.
>
> The subject matter of the *Gesta* now
> *The hermit Peter* is considered first.[38]

Few poets can have attempted this exercise – high-speed versifying, aiming at a moving target. At the top of the next page, John wrote: 'I was not thinking – brain stupefied'; and, a few pages later: 'Is your watch right?'

John's greatest friends among the dons were Boase's enemy

Maurice Bowra, Dean of Wadham, and Bowra's enemy 'Colonel' George Kolkhorst, a University lecturer in Spanish. Bowra and Kolkhorst were a kind of contrapuntal Chorus to his life. Only accredited aesthetes were welcome at Kolkhorst's, but Bowra liked to be accepted as 'one of the boys' by the Wadham rowing eight. Kolkhorst giggled; Bowra guffawed. In modern slang, Kolkhorst was 'camp' and Bowra was 'butch'.

Lord Clark wrote that Bowra was 'without question, the strongest influence in my life'.[39] 'You made us what we were,' wrote John Sparrow in a valedictory ode.[40] And John Betjeman was

> certain then,
> As now, that Maurice Bowra's company
> Taught me far more than all my tutors did.[41]

It may seem surprising that John should have been so susceptible to Bowra's influence, since in significant ways the Dean of Wadham resembled C.S. Lewis. The two dons were born in the same year, 1898; both served in the Great War and both took double Firsts in classics. Bowra too had a booming voice. 'The noise was invariably colossal,' Osbert Lancaster wrote, 'for our host was never one who hesitated . . . to exploit his great reserves of lung-power to gain a conversational advantage.'[42] Kenneth Clark was reminded of Yeats's lines, 'Trumpet and kettledrum, and the outrageous cannon'.[43] And, like Lewis again, Bowra favoured the big guns of literature. 'At the back of his mind,' Clark wrote, 'were Homer, Pindar, Aeschylus, Dante, Pushkin, Tolstoy, Camoens and St Paul, all read in the originals.'

It was quite possible that John would be frightened by this formidable person, and that Bowra would be added to the growing list of his bogeymen. Why did that not happen? First, although Bowra held an establishment job (the Dean of Wadham would be asked to serve on committees and would have his letters published in *The Times*), he was in some respects an anti-establishment figure. In *Summoned by Bells* John speaks of his 'grand contempt for pedants, traitors and pretentiousness'.[44] This attitude had been formed in the war. Bowra had detested army 'bull' and had been impressed by some ribald Australian officers who had refused to submit to pointless rules.[45]

Second, vulnerability in others always appealed to John; and, beneath his super-confident exterior, Bowra was vulnerable. He was worried about his appearance. Anthony Powell thought him 'noticeably small, this lack of stature emphasized by a massive head and tiny feet'.[46] A.L. Rowse remembered Bowra's appearing in court on behalf of a Wadham undergraduate who had been found *in flagrante* with a mechanic on the Oxford Canal bank. ' "Stand up, Mr Bowra," said the judge. "I am standing up," said Maurice. Everybody laughed – and Maurice was terrified of being laughed at.'[47]

But what most won John over was that Bowra warmly appreciated *him*. The second Lord Birkenhead recalled in 1958: 'Many years ago, when I was an undergraduate at Oxford, Sir Maurice Bowra remarked to me of John Betjeman, who was then writing such verses as "The 'Varsity Students' Rag" and other juvenilia: "Betjeman has a mind of extraordinary originality; there is no one else remotely like him." '[48] This remark, which was doubtless intended to get back to John, doubtless did. And though Bowra may have preferred the 'big stuff'[49] of literature, he was wise enough to accept John on his own terms. At their first meeting they discussed minor Victorian poets, as Bowra recalled in his memoirs:

> He was slight and not very tall, and had a wonderfully expressive and mobile face, which changed from moment to moment, and a certain elfin quality. The first time I met him he talked fluently about half-forgotten authors of the nineteenth century – Sir Henry Taylor, Ebenezer Elliott, Philip James Bailey, and Sir Lewis Morris, but this was not done for effect. He was fascinated by the Victorian Age and was already exploring its bypaths.[50]

'This was not done for effect.' Bowra did not fall into Lewis's disparaging assumption that John's enthusiasm for the minor poets was just a pose. He might challenge John's views – he challenged all his friends' views. But he also encouraged him, taught him not to be embarrassed by his own personality, but to trade on it. At the Bowra salon John also learned 'how not to be a bore':

> And merciless was his remark that touched
> The tender spot if one were showing off.[51]

John became the chief clown in the Bowra circus. 'I thought of him as an entertainer,' Lord David Cecil said, 'an extraordinary entertainer. He would do marvellous turns – sudden parodies, imitations of a radio play, anything – and it all came out spontaneously.' But what struck him most about John was 'his saying he loved a thing, and laughing at it. I mean, it wasn't just a kindly smile at what he loved. He would say: "I love that building, it's so ugly." '[52] Elizabeth Longford thinks this was something else John took from Maurice Bowra, who 'had this famous saying of some girl: "I like her, she smells." '[53] When a few years later Elizabeth's brother-in-law, Edward Longford, and John performed religious charades in Ireland, dressed in tablecloths as bishop and priest, 'one knew, even in those early days, that John was deadly serious about religion at the same time as laughing at it.'[54] Bowra also influenced John's taste in poetry by his enthusiasm for Yeats and Hardy, who were both still living. Bowra made Yeats almost as popular in the Oxford of the 1920s as Swinburne had been in the 1860s when young men had linked arms and had marched through cloisters chanting the choruses from 'Atalanta in Calydon'.

In Bowra's salon, John made friends who were not only congenial, but influential. Kenneth Clark is a good example. But for the relaxed atmosphere of Bowra's parties, and Bowra's propaganda on John's behalf, John might never have become a friend of this aloof man. Clark was one of the powerful figures who made sure that John's talents were not wasted during the Second World War, despite his being turned down by a medical board as unfit for any service. Later, Clark was also useful to John as chairman of the Independent Television Authority. Freddy Furneaux (later the second Lord Birkenhead) introduced one of the collections of John's poetry. John Sparrow became Warden of All Souls and wrote the introduction to another. Bowra himself pulled strings to obtain John a job on *The Architectural Review* in 1930.

Some of the undergraduates in Bowra's circle also attended the salon of 'Colonel' George Kolkhorst at 12.30 on Sunday afternoons. Those who did were in danger of being regarded as 'double spies' by both dons; and some remained strictly loyal to only one – for example, Kenneth Clark was a committed Bowra man, and no mention of Kolkhorst is found in his memoirs. At first, Kolkhorst was known as G'ug (the apostrophe, indicated by a little yawn, was supposed to imply deference). But Denis Kincaid and John invested him with a mythical colonelcy in the Portuguese Medical Corps –

A 'Colonel' Kolkhorst Sunday salon by Osbert Lancaster. Kolkhorst is in the centre of the top right-hand window. John is second from the left in the adjoining window.

because he looked wonderfully unlike a colonel. His rooms were at 38 Beaumont Street, near the Ashmolean Museum. In the sitting-room where he received, there were suits of Japanese armour in which, Osbert Lancaster alleged, 'whole families of mice had made their homes';[55] oriental figures under glass domes; fly-blown *kakemonos*; copies of *The Yellow Book*; a collection of novels of school life; and a photograph of Walter Pater on which Lancaster had scrawled 'Alma Pater'.[56]

The Colonel was a tall, stooping, pampered-looking man. He wore an eye-glass on a black moiré ribbon and hung a lump of sugar round his neck 'to sweeten conversation'.[57] His close friend Toby Struth, described by Lancaster as 'a very dim member of the Exeter [College] Senior Common Room'[58] and nicknamed ''Strewth!', was usually present at the Sunday salon. Kolkhorst received his guests beside a table on which were a tray of glasses and two decanters, one of sherry and one of very sticky marsala. Those who were in his good books were handed a glass of sherry; those who had in some way offended were given marsala. Too apprecia-tive a reference to Bowra was a sure way to earn marsala.[59]

Like Bowra, Kolkhorst had a clear memory of his first meeting with John. In 1956 he wrote to him: 'So you have reached your 50th birthday! Just the other day you were 20, and Paul Wilson[60] brought in a dark young man (an *ephebe* {Socratic all right}) with flashing black eyes and a marked strain of the satirical and a faked-up love of Schopenhauer.'[61] And in 1957 he wrote:

> I often think of you and your clever, vivid face. What a big influence – and gusto – you were in one's life. . . Do you remember when you were an undergraduate and were taken up by Paul Wilson and spent the memorable day at Gloucester with Dotty [Lord Clonmore] and me – returning via Cheltenham and reciting A.E. Housman? I remember *your* infancy as well as Paul's [ie the infancy of John's son, Paul Betjeman].[62]

There was an almost ritual order to events at the Beaumont Street Sunday salons. After a few glasses of sherry or marsala, the junket-ings began. At a given signal those present would form a circle round the Colonel and sway from side to side, chanting 'The Colonel's drunk! The Colonel's drunk! The room's going round!' As the pace hotted up, everybody joined in what was regarded as the 'school song', to the tune of 'John Peel':

D'ye ken Kolkhorst in his art-full parlour,
Handing out the drinks at his Sunday morning gala?
Some get sherry and some Marsala —
With his arts and his crafts in the morning!

O and Toby's there in his dirty woollen scarf,
With his acolytes and overcoat and sycophantic laugh.
He only gets Marsala and he's puzzled by the chaff
Of the High Church nancies in the corner.

Another Beaumont Street chant was composed by Colin Gill,
later Rector of St Magnus-the-Martyr, City of London:

G'uggery G'uggery Nunc,
Your room is all cluttered with junk:
Candles, bamboonery,
Plush and saloonery —
Please pack it up in a trunk.[63]

The Colonel might be outraged by these antics and expel one of the
malefactors, usually Alan Pryce-Jones (who turned up in a bathing-
dress one day) or John. If in more mellow mood, he could be persuaded to move into the back room and sing 'Questa o quella' from
Rigoletto in 'a very juicy tenor' to his own accompaniment on the
harmonium.[64] After one party, Kolkhorst climbed with Robert
Byron, Billy Clonmore and some other undergraduates to the top of
St Mary Magdalen's tower in the Cornmarket, where they sang
hymns and began spitting on the people below. 'The Proctors were
called,' John wrote, 'and waited at the bottom of the tower for the
delinquents to descend, which they eventually did, headed by the
Colonel in his white suit. As a graduate of the university and
lecturer in Spanish, he was immune from punishment, but the
others were fined.'[65] This kind of irresponsibility appealed to John.
Maurice Bowra, with all his irreverence for the establishment,
would never have behaved in that way.

According to Osbert Lancaster, Kolkhorst's 'very existence was
denied by the Dean of Wadham, who held that he was nothing but
an intellectual concept thought up by Betjeman.'[66] As contributor
to and later editor of the Cherwell, John constantly referred to
Kolkhorst. These lines appeared in the issue of 10 December 1927:

> Mr Betjeman
> Went to fetch a man
> From Waring and Gillow
> Who certainly *will* show
> The celebrated Mr Kolkhorst
> how he can
> Describe his famous Furniture to
> Almost any man.

On 4 February 1928 a prose lampoon by John was published in the *Cherwell*. 'CAN WE PUT NEW FRETWORK INTO OLD OXFORD: A Plea for Beautification by Wilhelmina Hand-Stitch':

> ... an archaeologist has seen in one of the passages in that charming old part of Balliol which faces St Gyles [*sic*] a rival prophecy to that of the passage in the great pyramid. By a complicated series of measurements, he has discovered that it prophesies a wave of barbarism in taste from 1928 to 1950, during which old buildings will be destroyed wholesale, and such atrocious acts will be perpetrated as are at present being done in Peckwater Quad, where by their 'cleaning', as they call it, they are making this charming old spot look for all the world like Selfridge's stores ...
>
> How can we stop all this renovation and barbarism? The beauties of the old world are now confined to a few strongholds – the Olde Oake Tea Roomes, Balliole College, the Moorish, & Constantia Lady Kolkhorst's charming old rooms in Beaumont Street ...

The last reference made to Kolkhorst in the *Cherwell* was a Beaumont Street witticism of Osbert Lancaster's, quoted in the issue of 8 December 1928: 'The Colonels and the Queens depart.'

John's first friendships in Oxford were made, not in the Bowra and Kolkhorst salons, but in his own college. Magdalen was so large and various that one did not need to venture into the wider university to find agreeable company. One of the first people John met there was Martyn Skinner, who, like Joseph Addison and Oscar Wilde before him, was a Demy (the Magdalen word for a scholar, since scholars had originally received half a Fellow's emolument.)

Martyn Skinner was the son of Sir Sydney Skinner, chairman of Barker's, the Kensington store, and had been at Berkhamsted with Graham Greene and later at Clifton. John and Skinner arrived in

Oxford as freshmen on the same day. In 1979 Skinner recalled their first meeting:

> I met John about the first week. I became friendly with Hugh Waterman, who had been at Marlborough with him; and John chiefly remembered him, I think, because of his name, which was Hugh Nurle Nunnerley Waterman. As you know, John is fascinated by names. I got to know Hugh, and a few people came in to see him. Among them was Betjeman; and I thought, 'What a fascinating chap that looks!' I was very taken with his face, and I thought, 'I'd like to get to know him,' but I didn't get to know him well at Oxford, because he went on his social round and I was exploring the countryside.[67]

At Oxford, Skinner 'went native'. With a small group of friends, he lived a kind of Scholar Gypsy life, in which the gypsy element considerably outweighed the scholarship. He was what would later be called a dropout. John shared his reaction against public school, his love of the countryside and his cavalier attitude to the Oxford syllabus. In later life the two became good friends, and in 1961 John addressed a poem to Skinner, which was published in *High and Low* (1966), but in his undergraduate days John did not want to drop out of Oxford society. He wanted to be at its spinning centre.

His best friend at Magdalen was Lionel Perry, who had an entrée to some of the sets John was most eager to join. Perry, who had come up to Magdalen the year before John, was rich, handsome and witty. From his blonde hair and unfading suntan, he was known as 'the Golden Boy'. His father, Fred Perry (known as 'Peter', perhaps to distinguish him from the tennis player) was a Fellow of All Souls and had been a leading member of Lord Milner's 'Kindergarten' in the Transvaal. Lionel Perry's year of seniority enabled him to introduce John to some of the previous Oxford generation who belonged to the Golden Age of Aesthetes. In the later part of 1926 Perry shared rooms with John at 142 Walton Street, Oxford.

> Of course he was terrified of the landlady [Perry recalled]. John had this great capacity for making his phobias and guilts very enjoyable conversation for a lot of other people. At Magdalen, his great fear was the head porter, he didn't like going through the Lodge alone. 'I daren't go through it. That man hates me.'
> When we shared rooms we never had any bad words; but John

and I both disliked being out of college, and got back into college. John wasn't a bit rich, and his rooms were done up pretty grimly. There were plenty of architectural, ecclesiastical and poetry books, though. His favourite poets at the time were Tennyson, Cowper, Crabbe and John Newton – 'Abounding Grace'. We went round churches, borrowing a car sometimes from a splendid man with a fur coat called Billy Price.[68]

Henry Yorke, who came up to Magdalen with John in 1925, had his first novel, *Blindness*, published in 1926 under the pseudonym Henry Green. He had begun it at Eton, where he was secretary of the Eton Society of Arts. He collected Victoriana and was interested in Gothic architecture and the writings of William Beckford; and he and John were further drawn together by their common loathing of C.S. Lewis, who was Yorke's tutor also. Yorke did not finish his course at Oxford, partly because he was so 'irritated and bored' by Lewis,[69] and partly because he wanted to work in his father's Birmingham factory to get copy for another novel.

A Magdalen incident related by Yorke in his memoirs, *Pack My Bag* (1940), may have inspired one of John's more exhibitionist pranks. Yorke describes how one evening he was hurrying through the college cloisters with a bottle of Eno's Fruit Salts to 'the one friend I had in College'[70] (possibly John himself). A drunken member of the college rowing eight lurched up to him, seized the bottle and, thinking the contents were drink, poured them down his throat. He fell on his back and 'began silverly frothing'.[71] Contributing to a television programme to mark John's seventieth birthday in 1976, John Sparrow recalled how, as an undergraduate, John had lain down on the pavement of the High and had frothed at the mouth as if in a fit. When a crowd of concerned people had gathered round, John had stood up and nonchalantly walked away: the effect had been achieved by a mouthful of fruit salts. It is likely that he got the idea for this escapade from Yorke's recounting the Magdalen Cloisters incident.

Another Etonian who became a friend of John's arrived at Magdalen in 1927: Alan Pryce-Jones, the future editor of the *Times Literary Supplement*. Pryce-Jones was a freshman and John a third-year swell when the two first met. Pryce-Jones recalled: 'I was wearing a dressing-gown on my way to the very remote bathroom which one had in those days, about half a mile from one's room in college;

and John thought it such a curious dressing-gown – it was kind of cape-shaped – that he suddenly said, "What are you doing wearing that extraordinary garment?" and we made friends from that point.' John drove him to see churches – 'In those days the eighteenth century was his great interest, not the nineteenth.'[72] The first church Pryce-Jones was driven to see, in the open Morris Cowley John by then owned, was St Katherine's, Chiselhampton (1762), on which John was to write a poem in 1952.

Alan Pryce-Jones's father was a colonel at the Duke of York's Headquarters, Chelsea, not far down the Kings Road from John in Church Street. So the two undergraduates were able to meet often in the vacations and got to know each other's families. Pryce-Jones's mother Vere took a particular liking to John and asked him to look after her son at Oxford. Osbert Lancaster said it was like asking Satan to chaperone Sin, but a more apt parallel is Lady Marchmain's asking Charles Ryder to watch over Lord Sebastian, in *Brideshead Revisited*. A letter Vere Pryce-Jones wrote John in 1927 has exactly the Lady Marchmain tone, flattering and con-spiratorial:

> May I regard you as a real Friend – and ask you to try to keep a rather stern and kindly eye upon Alan at Oxford? I do worship him so, and *know* he could make something Great and Good out of his life if only he does not fritter it away . . . He is so terribly 'casual' – and would have missed all three Hervey Prizes [at Eton], by simply not taking the trouble to write down his poems, if we had not driven him at the point of the bayonet . . .[73]

Again in the same year she wrote to John: 'I think it says much for Alan's sterling character, that he would rather be with you than with anyone else, – and you have opened up a new vista and interest for him, by making him so keen about architecture.'[74] The sterling character did not prevail long against the temptations of Oxford: in 1928 Pryce-Jones was 'rusticated' for various misdeeds, and his father would not allow him to return.[75] 'The dear boy *has* been stupid!' Vere Pryce-Jones wrote to John.[76] Pryce-Jones obtained a job as assistant editor of *The London Mercury*, and soon persuaded the editor, John Squire, to publish work by John.

Lionel Perry introduced John to Lord Clonmore, son of the seventh Earl of Wicklow: the Perrys and the Wicklows had known each other from far back in Ireland. 'Billy' Clonmore was an ordinand at St Stephen's House in Norham Road, North Oxford. John Bowle said that he 'looked exactly like the Mad Hatter: he *was* the Mad Hatter.'[77] Waugh wrote that 'his extravagances were refined by a slightly antiquated habit of speech and infused by a Christian piety that was unique among us . . .'[78] John shared Waugh's view of Clonmore's piety: when Clonmore (by now Earl of Wicklow) died in 1978, John wrote to Lionel Perry: 'You must have been through agony, as Crax [pet name for Wicklow] was a saint, the only *certain* one I knew. Saints don't die . . . He is with me now as I write to you. Perhaps he is keeping me legible.'[79]

Clonmore was the first real live lord to be numbered among John's friends. He was amusedly aware of this aspect of his appeal to John, and he both teased him about it and encouraged him in his not too vicious kind of snobbery. For years afterwards they sent each other newspaper cuttings and anecdotes about obscure peers. John's interest in this subject led to his 1933 *Evening Standard* article 'Peers without Tears', which persuaded Lord Beaverbrook to employ him as the paper's film critic.

Through Clonmore, John met Robert Byron, who had been in Clonmore's house at Eton. John's and Byron's undergraduate days overlapped by only one term but Byron was one of the most frequent revenants. He was killed in 1941 when the ship taking him to Egypt as a newspaper Special Correspondent was torpedoed, so his youthful image remained clear in his Oxford contemporaries' minds and was not overlaid by the palimpsest of an older self. He looked remarkably like Queen Victoria, and he made full use of the resemblance whenever he went to fancy-dress parties. He was a master of spoken and written invective. In his company, Brian Howard wrote, one felt 'like an empty electric battery which has suddenly and mysteriously become recharged'.[80] Probably nobody among the friends John made at Oxford so profoundly influenced his taste and prose style; it was through Byron, too, that John met his future wife.

A friend of Byron's, and like him a survivor of the Golden Age of Aesthetes, was John ('the Widow') Lloyd, whom Lionel Perry described as 'small, with sparkling black eyes . . . infinitely vivacious, infinitely malicious'.[81] Lloyd knew John less well at Oxford than in later years, when Lloyd composed a pasquinade on him in Gilbertian measure ('I am the very model of a perfect Betjemanian,/ I know all the London churches, from R.C. to Sandemanian . . .'[82]).

In this, he suggests that he was introduced to John at one of Kolkhorst's 'Sundays'. Both Clonmore and 'the Widow' were decidedly of Kolkhorst's côterie rather than Bowra's.

Another regular at Beaumont Street and friend of Lionel Perry was Graham Eyres-Monsell, also one of the 'Georgeoisie' and a giver of memorable parties. He and his beautiful sister Joan – now Mrs Patrick Leigh Fermor – were children of the First Lord of the Admiralty, 'Bobby' (Sir Bolton, later Lord) Monsell. The Eyres-Monsells' family home was Dumbleton Hall, Evesham. John visited them there and wrote two poems about the house. One, in the mock Longfellow style later used in 'Longfellow's Visit to Venice', begins:

Not so far from Evesham's city on a woody hillside green
Stands an ancient stonebuilt mansion – nothing modern to be seen,
Not a farmhouse, not a homestead, only trees on either hand
Billowing like heaps of cushions on the sofa of the land . . .[83]

The other is a nonsense-poem in which Alan Pryce-Jones (known as 'Boggins') and Sir Bolton Eyres-Monsell both figure:

Dumbleton, Dumbleton, the ruin by the lake,
  Where Boggins and Sir Bolton fought a duel for thy sake;
Dumbleton, Dumbleton, the Gothic arch that leads
  Thro' the silver vestibule to where Sir Bolton feeds.
The groaning of the golden plate,
The sickly social shame;
Oh heirs of Dumbleton! The Monsell in thy name![84]

Lionel Perry had known John Dugdale since the age of thirteen: they had been at school together. It was through his introduction to Dugdale by Perry that John came to stay in his first great English house, for John Dugdale lived at Sezincote, a mansion in Indian style. Its domes, minarets and multifoil arches of golden Stanway stone rise like a mirage from the Gloucestershire countryside between Stow-on-the-Wold and Moreton-in-Marsh, about twenty miles from Oxford. It was designed for a 'nabob', Sir Charles Cockerell, in about 1805, by his brother, the architect Samuel Pepys Cockerell. The main block has a great onion dome of turquoise oxydized copper. The Cockerells appreciated the surface enrichment of Moghul architecture, and the intricate fretting they ordered was carved with skill by Cotswold masons. Humphrey Repton had laid out the fine water-gardens, which are fed by a natural spring. To John, it was all magical:

> The bridge, the waterfall, the Temple Pool —
> And there they burst on us, the onion domes,
> *Chajjahs* and *chattris* made of amber stone:
> 'Home of the Oaks', exotic Sezincote!
> Stately and strange it stood, the Nabob's house,
> Indian without and coolest Greek within . . .[85]

Though John was fascinated by the architecture and the landscape vistas, he was still more interested in the new experience of staying in a great English mansion:

> First steps in learning how to be a guest,
> First wood-smoke-scented luxury of life
> In the large ambience of a country house.[86]

Sezincote became a second home (or a third, if one counts Oxford) to John and his friends. John Dugdale's grandfather had bought the house in the 1880s. Dugdale's father, Colonel Arthur Dugdale, was a farmer and a Conservative. His mother, Ethel Dugdale, was an ardent socialist. In *Summoned by Bells* John describes a lunch at Sezincote at which Clement Attlee, the Labour politician and future Prime Minister, was a fellow guest:

> The Colonel's eyes looked out towards the hills,
> While at the other end our hostess heard
> Political and undergraduate chat.
> 'Oh, Ethel,' loudly Colonel Dugdale's voice
> Boomed sudden down the table, 'that manure —
> I've had it shifted to the strawberry-beds.'
> 'Yes, Arthur . . . Major Attlee, as you said,
> Seventeen million of the poor Chinese
> Eat less than half a calory a week?'[87]

John became very fond of the Dugdales, especially Ethel Dugdale, 'mother of us all', who, in her Edwardian-style dresses, looked like a Sargent portrait. From her he received the intelligent sympathy that his own mother had never been able to offer in the abundance he needed. Ethel became his 'Sweet confidante in every tale of woe'; he gabbled away to her as she pruned shrubs as exotic as the house.

John Dugdale shared his mother's political views. He later became a Labour MP and Parliamentary Private Secretary to Attlee. At Oxford, he was already a member of the Labour Club and a friend of Hugh Gaitskell. Lionel Perry was also among Gaitskell's friends in this group of socialites with some kind of a social conscience. John and Gaitskell had not seen each other since they had left the Dragon School (Gaitskell had gone on to Winchester College). They met again at Maurice Bowra's dinner parties. Gaitskell, John later recalled, still looked exactly the same as he had done at the Dragon School, 'with curly hair and the habit of suddenly blushing'.[88] He was more of an aesthete than a hearty, though he never dressed as one. John detected the influence of Winchester in his way of making words markedly disyllabic: 'chapel'; 'li-ttle'. Gaitskell was easy company and full of jokes, and 'had no objection to a drop of drink'.[89] John did not think of him as politically-minded, though he noted that, in this pre-Slump Oxford when many undergraduates still had big allowances from their fathers and did not bother about degrees, Gaitskell (who was by no means poor) lived on two shillings a day, ate at fish-and-chip shops, and took a First.

It was during the General Strike of 1926 that John became aware of Gaitskell as someone more than the usual Oxford aesthete. The Strike impinged on the university as few other public events did. Only the most cloistered of dons or the most butterfly-brained of undergraduates could ignore it. Some undergraduates became strike-breakers. Henry Yorke unloaded bananas at Avonmouth.[90] Geoffrey Grigson unloaded apples at Hull docks.[91] Anthony Powell joined the emergency Civil Commission housed in Reading Gaol, where he was shown Oscar Wilde's cell, the 'foul and dark latrine'.[92] Emlyn Williams, who as grandson of a collier and son of a stoker was an unlikely strike-breaker, helped unload pigs and crates of cheese at Hay's Wharf, London.[93]

To other undergraduates, the Strike was a 'lark', perhaps the chance to realize boyhood dreams of driving a train. Ernest Betjemann wrote to John on 13 May 1926: 'Times have been stirring in London, the tubes and buses have been better run by the boys than by the pros.' He told John some of the facetious slogans on the buses: 'I have no pane now, Mother dear'; 'The Flapper's Rest'; and 'Travel the Easy Way, the Drage Way'.[94]

A much smaller group of undergraduates gave help to the strikers. Bede Griffiths, who was with John at Magdalen, offered to sell the *Daily Worker* in the streets.[95] Cecil Day Lewis was one of the drivers maintaining liaison between the strikers and the Trades Union Congress in London.[96] Tom Driberg, who had joined the Communist Party during his last year at Lancing, distributed literature from CP headquarters in Covent Garden. He was arrested and interrogated at Scotland Yard.[97] Wystan Auden, from no very serious motive but, as he himself said, 'out of sheer contrariness', decided to support the strikers; for a few days he too drove a car for the Trades Union Congress in London. Once, after driving R.H. Tawney home, he decided to visit a cousin who lived nearby. When it emerged, at lunch, that he was working for the strikers, he was thrown out of the house by his cousin's husband: Auden was amazed that anyone took the strike so seriously.[98]

John might easily have become a strike-breaker. Nothing could have been more tempting to him than the prospect of driving a train or a bus. (He achieved both ambitions in the 1960s and 70s.) But Gaitskell and John Dugdale persuaded him to help the strikers. Gaitskell and Lionel Perry took him to meet G.D.H. Cole and his wife Margaret in Holywell. John was pleased to find that the left-wing Reader in Economics was not just a politico, but something of an aesthete too, a connoisseur of antique glass. With Gaitskell and Perry, John was sent to Didcot in Dugdale's Morris, to take messages for the National Union of Railwaymen. 'I do not recall their having any messages for us to take,' John wrote. 'The gesture, however, was made.' But John lacked any real commitment to the Strike. 'To Hugh and John,' he wrote, 'the General Strike was not the lark it was to me. It was a righteous cause.'[99]

At that time, John was working for Bryan Guinness on the *Cherwell*, which in the absence of the national papers had assumed a new importance as an instrument of propaganda. Guinness, on duty as a special constable in London, felt that his co-editor, Charles Plumb, was taking an anti-government line in his absence. Guinness telephoned the *Cherwell* owner, Harold Sissons, 'in a frenzy as though the destiny of the nation depended on the exact balance of views in our undergraduate weekly'.[100] The *Cherwell*'s

'Emergency Strike Number' of 8 May contained an impartial mix of conflicting viewpoints: 'Why the Strike?' by G.D.H. Cole; 'The Coal Problem' by Edward Hulton, the future press baron; and 'The British Fascists and the Strike' by the Acting Officer Commanding British Fascists, Oxford University District. The rival magazine, the *Isis*, published an inflammatory article by Martyn Skinner suggesting that the miners' leader, A.J. Cook, should be debagged to see if he wore purple underpants.[101]

By this date (mid-1926), John had still written no signed article or poem for either the *Isis* or the *Cherwell*. His first contribution appeared in the *Isis* at the beginning of his second year at Oxford, on 27 October 1926 – an article entitled 'Our Lovely Lodging Houses'. ('Let us open that yellow "grained oak" front door whose upper panels of stained glass foretell what may be ecclesiastical within. The clouds of Irish stew make the room more impenetrable and the elaborate bamboo umbrella stand more emphatic than ever. Clutching the rather greasy knob of the pitch pine banisters we ascend to the front room ... The interspace of the windows contains a lithograph of Our Lord on one of the mountains around Palestine.')

On 3 November 1926 John contributed his first verse to the *Isis*, a quatrain on 'Arts and Crafts':

> Orange and black, orange and black,
> And the sitting-room blue and yellow,
> All made out of an army shack
> By a handy-andy fellow.

John included the 'handy-andy' poem in *Mount Zion* (1931), but excluded it from later selections and collections of his poems, perhaps because by the time they appeared he had revised his opinion of the Arts and Crafts movement, under the influence of C.R. Ashbee and C.F.A. Voysey.[102] The immediate occasion of the 'handy-andy' verse was the Arts and Crafts show (including Ruskin pottery) which had been held at the Oxford Town Hall in October 1926. But John's constant mocking references to Arts and Crafts while he was at Oxford were in reaction to Ernest's boast that everything was 'done by hand' at the Betjemann factory.

From January 1927 John contributed architectural notes to the *Cherwell*. The issue of 29 January noted that 'A VERY BEAUTI-

FUL NINETEENTH-CENTURY SHOP FRONT in the Corn-market that used to belong to Hookham's has been destroyed in the march of commercialism round Oxford and a probably more useful creation in the Tuscan style has taken its place.' The same issue carried a photograph of the Norman west doorway of St Ebbe's Church which (the caption claimed) 'contains beautiful beakhead moulding'. The issue of 5 February contrasted the 'Edwardo-Victorian baroque' of Cousins Thomas, Chemists, Banbury Road, with the seventeenth-century baroque of Grey-friars, Paradise Street, St Ebbe's. John was learning that odious comparisons are often the most effective form of criticism. In the issue of 12 February he illustrated the Gothic Revival porch of 5 Norham Gardens, North Oxford. This was the kind of building he was later famous for championing, but in 1927 he wrote:

> I have found that for which I have long been searching – the worst and most senseless building in Oxford. It is an unobtrusive house in Norham Gardens of the usual lack of proportions and taste typical of North Oxford, but possessed of one feature – the porch – which sets it on a pinnacle of badness alone. Shut your eyes and you forget its shape, since it has none . . . It is an uncomfortable reflection that there existed an architect, who thought it out.

He opposed to it the Greek Revival porch of the Wesleyan School (the Old Chapel) hidden away in New Inn Hall Street in the heart of Oxford.

John's rising status in the *Cherwell* hierarchy was marked by his writing a leader (5 March 1927) headed 'Are We Gentlemen?' On 18 March, 'School Song', a Latin poem by W.P.R. Mawdsley, scholar of New College, was published, with a very loose transla-tion by 'Bishop Betjeman' in adroit Byronic rhymes:

> Give to all our masters suaveness,
> Grant our monitors to rave less . . .

John succeeded Bryan Guinness as editor of the *Cherwell* in May 1927. The change of regime was marked by an immediate stepping-up of the paper's architectural content. 'Go and look at the back quad of the Examination Schools,' the issue of 14 May advised readers. 'It will all count towards your period of purgatory. Its architecture is in the Neo-State-Public-Baths style.' In the same issue, John wrote on 'Saxon Remains in Oxford'. A typical Betjeman exercise followed a week later: speculation about a room's occupant from its contents –

> Rooms in Oxford so frequently betray their owners. How well we know those little reproductions of a Lionel Edwards[103] that once hung in the study at school and have the additional advantage of sentiment; how well, too, we know the bookcase with nothing but the Law of Torts, cake-crumbs and a tobacco-jar with a college crest upon its shelves; the ukelele slung across a sofa whose back is black with Anzora Violet . . .[104] Now and then a man gives himself away by some slight touch. Is he the sort of man who keeps his drink outside on a shelf? Or if it is in a cupboard, is that cupboard locked? These are indications of character.

A more serious editorial by John on 4 June ('DOWN WITH THE UNIVERSITIES! THE NEW MOVEMENT') contained this characteristic sentence, harbinger of so many attacks on insensitive development in the future: 'Unkind materialism which is evident enough in Oxford City with Woolworth's and the tentacles of the Oxford super-man dragging down the houses at one end of the Broad to make an arcade, and the reddening of that monstrosity by the Cadena, has not (God be praised!) yet got a complete hold on the University.'

On 11 June, John revived his old joke of mocking the Arts and Crafts movement:

A NEW ARTE AND CRAFTE INNE

is to be run by the *Cherwelle* in the Hygh Streete. It will be next to the King's Arms, and will be called 'The Prince's Legges'. The walls and celing will be decorated with Oake Beames, liquid (teae) will be drunke from newe-olde Portlande-Cemente Pottes, and there will be tables of Rosewoode. The attendants will be gentlewomenne, and will wear aprons of yellowe checke canvasse, to tone with tableclothes and panelles of the same coloure.

He was still on the same tack a week later:

> . . . This is an age of batik-work, of fret-work, of leather-work, of stencilling and design. The CHERWELL has always championed these causes and now, ably headed by Miss Charitye Handweaver, it is entering another phase of craft rescue-work, destined in the end to unqualified success. The whole staff of the CHERWELL asks its

readers to co-operate in a fascinating scheme for leaving Oxford and modern life and joining a community for the worship of the crafts and for the ideal of craftsmanship.

Miss O. Keble has already given a piece of land on one of the higher crests of Boar's Hill, beside Matthew Arnold's signal elm, where it is hoped that undergraduates may become, as it were, stationary Scholar Gipsies. Mr Kipling has written a poem from Bateman's, Burwash, Sussex, to celebrate the founding of the settlement; it begins thus:—

> There's an oldy worldy housy
> With an oldy worldy name
> Where my ties are all handwoven
> And my knickers are the same.

Shortly after John's editorship ended, the *Cherwell* published 'A 'Varsity Student's Rag', one of the juvenilia which were to have a permanent place in his *Collected Poems*. The announcement read: 'A 'VARSITY STUDENT'S RAG is the first of a series to be written by Mr Betjeman which will be ultimately comprehended in a new " 'Varsity Students' Song-Book". These are primarily intended to be sung as curtain-raisers for "shows" on Boat-Race night, but may also be used as "wines" and "cyders".'[105] Unfortunately, this ambitious plan — if plan it was — came to nothing. But 'A 'Varsity Student's Rag' remains (under a slightly altered title) as an enjoyable skit on the rowdy hearties whose idea of fun was a 'rag' at Monico's (Delmonico's), the Troc (Trocadero) or the Grill Room at the Cri (the Criterion Theatre Restaurant), followed by the excitement of smashing up somebody's rooms:

> And then we smash'd up ev'rything, and what was the funniest
> part
> We smashed some rotten old pictures which were priceless works
> of art.

Another Betjeman poem appeared in the issue of 18 February 1928. A parody of a Metaphysical poem, it was reprinted in *Mount Zion* but was not retained in the *Collected Poems*:

(MS found by Mr Betjeman and attributed by him to Donne)

> The bluish eyeballs of my love
> Are so enormous grown
> The muscles, which the pupils move,
> Won't twist 'em round alone.
>
> But lo! They hold an alien course:
> I must myself outshine:
> They yield to the magnetic force
> Of other stars than mine.

John may also have been responsible for 'Up and Down: A Social Causerie by Sir John Matterhorn' which appeared on 25 February. It began: 'Travelling up in the train from my College Gaude,[106] my eye was caught by a young fellow who told me his name was Watkins-West, who said he could put me on to some jolly fellows who were going to have a "blind" up at Oxford that night.' This refers back to 'A 'Varsity Student's Rag'; and the piece goes on to mention several friends of John's – Kolkhorst, Patrick Balfour, R.D. Girouard (father of John's godson, Mark Girouard), Bryan Guinness, Julian Hall and Gavin Henderson (later Lord Faringdon), all carousing at the George.

On 24 October 1928 one of the best of John's early poems appeared in the *Isis* under the title 'To the Blessed St Aubin'. (It appears in his *Collected Poems* as 'Hymn' and is based on S.J. Stone's hymn 'The Church's One Foundation'.) He had already sent a copy to his father, who replied: 'Thank you so much for the "Restoration" poem. I think it splendid and have sent copies to Mrs Atkinson and Father Deakin (of St Augustine's, Queen's Gate).'[107] As the last line of the poem, John had written: 'He has renewed the roof.' In returning the typescript, Ernest arrowed 'renewed' and commented: 'Probably unnecessary.' John accepted this technical advice and altered the word to 'restored' in later versions. After the poem was reprinted in *Ghastly Good Taste* (1933), he was forced to make another change. The original third stanza began:

> Church Furnishing! Church Furnishing!
> Come, Mowbray, swell the praise!

Mowbray's, the church furnishers, objected to the use of their name in this context, and John altered the second line to the weaker

Sing art and crafty praise!

The *Cherwell* files show John's growing notoriety as an Oxford figure. The first mention of him is on 13 February 1926 in a review by S.P.B. Mais of the Oxford University Dramatic Society's *Henry IV* Part II: 'J. Betjemann (Magdalen) is to be congratulated on his face. There was true comedy in his Wart as well as in his porter.' John proudly showed this comment to Colonel Kolkhorst, who said *he* liked port and water too – a neat Spoonerism. By the summer term of 1926, John was well established in the Oxford University Dramatic Society (OUDS), to which his introduction was probably through his Marlborough friend John Fernald (the future head of the Royal Academy of Dramatic Art, London), though he may also have been talent-spotted by the Olympian Gyles Isham, a Magdalen Demy who had been an admired under-graduate Hamlet. To Emlyn Williams, already a figure of some importance in the OUDS, the club seemed that year 'less inhibited, more whimsical, and hadn't people got less tall, more my size? . . . They all looked more like promoted schoolfellows than OUDS members.'[108] He remembered especially 'a bouncing fresh-faced head boy biting a pipe called J.B. Fernald . . . and a zany wiseacre with a protruding tooth: a fourth-former by the difficult name of Betjeman'. Williams recalled that another member of the club was unwise enough to disclose that his mother had given him a long mirror so that he could practise gestures in front of it. ' "How thoughtful of her, Percy dear," said John B., "obscene ones?" '[109]

In 1926 J.B. Fagan came up to Oxford to produce *A Midsummer Night's Dream*. Two years earlier, he had staged the Gyles Isham *Hamlet* there, with a future Lord Chancellor, Gerald Gardiner, as Horatio, Patrick Balfour as Osric and John Sutro as First Grave-digger. In the 1924–25 season he had put on *The Cherry Orchard* with Gielgud as Trofimov. For his *Midsummer Night's Dream*, Fagan chose John Betjeman as Starveling, John Maud (later Lord Redcliffe-Maud) as Bottom, Ben Bonas (who had been at Marl-borough with John) as Egeus and David Talbot Rice (the future pro-fessor and authority on Byzantine art) as stage manager. The president of the OUDS was Denys Buckley (now Lord Justice

Buckley) and John Fernald was general manager. All of them appeared with Fagan in a photograph of a rehearsal in Magdalen Grove published in the *Cherwell* on 12 June 1926. The same issue included some pen-portraits of 'Personalities in the OUDS', including: '*J. Betjemann* – quite a little comedian ... He is the club naughty little boy. He could be a poet if he took the trouble.'

A producer more exotic than Fagan came to Oxford in 1927 – his friend the Russian Theodore Komisarjewsky, who had designed costumes for some of Fagan's productions. The *Cherwell* reported on 9 January 1927: '*King Lear* is being produced by Mr Komissarjewsky for the OUDS. He says that it is not to be produced in the manner of Moscow. The scenery will be negligible and the play acted only on raised platforms. A gold background will, when lighted, have the effect of white sky. The lighting will show the emotions in each scene.'

For this production, John was cast as the Fool – a plum part. But two weeks before he was due to appear in the role, he was expelled from the OUDS in disgrace, as Osbert Lancaster recalled:

It so happened that the *Cherwell*, the less reputable but by far the livelier of the two undergraduate magazines, was at that time edited by John Betjeman, who published a cod photograph, with a ribald caption, of the OUDS rehearsing.[110] The club, which in those days took itself very seriously, was furious and both Denys Buckley, the president, and Harman Grisewood, who was playing Lear, insisted on the poet's immediate expulsion. Unluckily this resolute but rather hastily considered move involved a major reshuffle of the cast less than a fortnight before the first night, for Betjeman was playing the Fool, a major role which now had to be taken over by John Fernald, who relinquished the part of the Duke of Cornwall to Peter Fleming, until then only the Duke of Cornwall's servant, to enact whom I was now promoted from the anonymous ranks of Goneril's drunken knights.[111]

Colonel Kolkhorst tittered that 'For playing the fool, John has been prevented from playing the Fool.'[112] John was quite unrepentant over the incident. In the *Cherwell* of 26 February he published an apology as impudent as the original spoof: 'WE MUST APOLOGISE to the OUDS for the unfortunate misprint that appeared under the photograph of our office dramatic society the initials of which are O.O.D.S., which were naturally supposed by the printers to stand for a better known dramatic institution, and altered accordingly.' After this piece of calculated cheek, John was soon back on good terms with the ruffled officers of the OUDS. The *Cherwell* reported on 21 May 1927 that 'John Betjeman gave an amusing lunch-party on Tuesday, at which some of the guests were Bryan Guinness, Denys Buckley, and erudite young John Sparrow.' The same issue contained another reference to him as 'Bishop Betjeman'. In an account of Ascot published on 25 June the *Cherwell* noted that 'exotic-looking John Betjeman had to stay at home with Mr Sissons, but Maurice Green [the future editor of the *Daily Telegraph*] managed to be there.'

John was in the news again for his acting on 7 December when the *Isis* critic wrote: 'Mr Betjeman made a great success of Galsworthy's hero, *The Little Man* who (as the author takes vast pains to assert) because he is not of pure British descent, does his duty quite naturally and very inarticulately (rather like an educated *Kipps*).'

John's religious tendencies continued to be a subject of interest. The *Cherwell*'s editorial of 11 February 1928 observed:

A new paper called *Protest* has been launched upon us. It is the organ, we understand, of Oxford Anglo-Catholicism. Where would Oxford be without ritualism? The picture of undergraduate life of romantic fiction would be incomplete without the cultured enthusiast hurrying Romeward. On Saturday, Mr Betjeman delivered a spirited harangue from a balcony in the High Street which was listened to by several taxi-drivers in supine astonishment.

John's emergence as an undergraduate religious leader surprised those of his friends who remembered him at Marlborough. Though baptized and brought up in the Church of England, he had 'suddenly decided' at Marlborough that he was an atheist, and had refused to be confirmed.[113] Was this part of a rebellion against his parents? Was he influenced by humanist friends such as Anthony Blunt? Or was it just another example of John's inclination to *épater* and be different? Most probably, in a setting where authority seemed to him malign, he was learning to challenge all received opinions. ('Honest doubt' continued to assail him for the rest of his life.[114]) At Marlborough, religion seemed to him 'hymn singing and feeling good and not being immoral and always having a high moral tone and [being] really rather priggish'.[115] But then he met Father Johnson in Cornwall and was given Machen's *The Secret Glory* 'which [John told Derek Stanford] suddenly showed me there were the Sacraments, and then I became very interested in ritual and I was first, I suppose, brought to belief by my eyes and ears and nose. The smell of incense, and sight of candles, High Church services, they attracted me and I liked them.'[116]

Ritualism led naturally in the direction of Anglo-Catholicism, and Oxford was the fountainhead of Anglo-Catholicism. The Oxford Movement had begun in the 1830s as an attempt to reassert the authority of the church. An appeal to historical precedent was accompanied by a new interest in the Middle Ages and their architecture, resulting in the Gothic Revival style in which North Oxford was so rich. (A prime example was the pinnacled and crocketed Martyrs' Memorial of 1841 – 'Maggers Memoggers' in 1920s slang.) The Oxford Movement had split into two main factions: those who 'went over to Rome', and those who, while ritualistic, remained within the Church of England, which they considered an integral part of the Catholic Church. The converts included J.H. Newman and Gerard Manley Hopkins; John Keble and Edward Pusey were leaders of the rival party. In John's Oxford there were living links with the Oxford Movement and other religious controversies of Victorian England. Osbert Lancaster had as one of his tutors Canon A.J. Carlyle, the last surviving friend of the 'Christian socialist' F.D. Maurice.[117] John met V.S.S. ('Stuckey') Coles, author of the hymn 'We pray Thee, Heavenly Father', who had been a friend of Hopkins at Balliol in the 1860s and had recently retired as Principal of Pusey House, the centre of Anglo-Catholicism.[118]

When John first came to Oxford, he worshipped at St Peter-le-Bailey, the church he had liked best when a boy at the Dragon School. But soon he began to attend High Mass at Pusey House:

> Those were the days when that divine baroque
> Transformed our English altars and our ways.
> Fiddle-back chasuble in mid-Lent pink
> Scandalized Rome and Protestants alike:
> 'Why do you try to ape the Holy See?'
> 'Why do you sojourn in a half-way house?' ...
> I learned at Pusey House the Catholic faith.
> Friends of those days, now patient parish priests,[119]

By worldly standards you have not 'got on'
Who knelt with me as Oxford sunlight streamed
On some colonial bishop's broidered cope.[120]

The 'Travers baroque'[121] and the colonial bishops reappear in John's poem 'Anglo-Catholic Congresses' in which, forty years on, he recalled 'the waking days/When Faith was taught and fanned to a golden blaze'. It was Billy Clonmore who persuaded John, in July 1927, to attend the Third Anglo-Catholic Congress whose subject was The Holy Eucharist.

'Stuckey' Coles was succeeded as Principal of Pusey House by Darwell Stone, white-bearded, donnish and unworldly. When mention was made in Stone's presence of the Dolly Sisters – vaudeville artists of the time – he said he was not familiar with any nuns of that name.[122] John's closest friends on the staff were Maurice Child, a flamboyant figure who largely masterminded the Congresses, and Freddy Hood, who abetted John in mixing reverence with humour. In a characteristic note to John, Hood wrote: 'If you can possibly come to a meeting of the NICENE at Mansfield SCR [Senior Common Room] tonight . . . at 8.15. Wheeler Robinson on "The Marriage of Cana and its Significance in Theology". It will be frightfully funny – I want you to come and take part in the discussion "speaking as an Irvingite I should like to suggest. . ." Do try ever so hard.'[123] (John was not an Irvingite, but at Oxford and later he was sympathetically interested in the Irvingite or Catholic Apostolic Church, a nineteenth-century foundation.[124]) John attended the Pusey House Retreat for University Men in March 1928, and on 13 October of the same year F.L. Cross wrote to him from Pusey House: 'Fr [Miles] Sargent has suggested to me that you might be able and willing to serve [at the altar during services] here this term.'[125]

The portrayals of John in the *Cherwell* suggest that his reputation in Oxford was mainly as an Anglo-Catholic, an architectural expert, a socialite, a journalist, an actor and a practical joker. At that time he was not widely regarded as a poet, still less as a good poet. The kind of poetry admired in Oxford was the luxuriant style of the Sitwells, tangled with the deliberate obscurities of Eliot and the literary surrealism of Gertrude Stein. (Both Sitwell and Stein made dramatic appearances in Oxford, like demon queens). There was less appreciation of John's revamped hymns and music-hall ditties, or the Nordic austerities of W.H. Auden, then an undergraduate at Christ Church. The *Isis* review of *Oxford Poetry*, a book published by Blackwell in 1926, had sneered: 'Through about seventy lines Mr Auden continues to show his inability to appreciate the meaning of words ...'[126] Other poets who, though published in the *Cherwell*, had to wait a little longer for literary acclaim included C. Day Lewis, Louis MacNeice and Stephen Spender; Charles Plumb, Martyn Skinner and Geoffrey Tillotson were also represented in the magazine. The stars among the undergraduate poets of the time were Harold Acton, Peter Quennell, Eric Walter White and Tom Driberg.

John recalled that Harold Acton 'was never seen inside the college [Christ Church] in my day. He was a frequenter of restaurants and his own lodgings were somewhere in the High.'[127] They knew each other quite well. Sir Harold Acton remembered John as he was when he first met him:

> Since I was born in Italy and mainly brought up there he might have conceivably regarded me as a 'sewer'; on the contrary we became friends at first sight. He looked as if he had tumbled out of bed and dressed in a hurry, necktie askew and shoe-laces undone, while a school bell seemed to be tinkling in the distance. A boy scout out of uniform, with Ruskin as his Baden-Powell. His surname sounded less English than mine, yet I only had to be with him to feel certain that I was in the green heart of an Anglia besprinkled with placid church belfries. He is a genius of the *genius loci*, either pastoral or suburban.[128]

Peter Quennell's and John's Oxford careers overlapped for only ten days, because on 18 October 1925 Quennell was sent down for the offence, unusual for an Oxford undergraduate of that time, of having sexual relations with a woman in Maidenhead. But he continued to be published and reviewed in the university magazines. Though only a year older than John, he had arrived at Oxford in 1923, with the reputation of being a Marvellous Boy. At fifteen he had had some pieces published in *Public School Verse*, the yearly anthology which published John's 'Song of a Cold Wind'. He was taken up by Edith Sitwell and Edward Marsh and qualified as the last and far the youngest of the Georgian Poets by his inclusion in the final *Georgian Poetry* volume. The climax to this precocity had been the publication in 1922 of a book of his verse illustrated by himself with Beardsleyesque vignettes.

John heard all about Quennell from Eric Walter White who was at Balliol with Quennell in the academic year 1924–25 and hero-worshipped him. White, too, had contributed to *Public School Verse* – the 1923–24 volume which included 'Wood in Rain' by W.H. Arden (*sic*) of Gresham's School, Holt. He had been at Clifton with Martyn Skinner. By the time White arrived at Oxford he had made himself an expert on R.L. Stevenson and begun forming an outstanding collection of modern first editions of poetry. Both Harold Acton and Tom Driberg courted him for the Sitwell faction and helped to make him known among the Oxford literati. The first time White met John was at the George just after the Easter vacation of 1927. John had been down to Cornwall and was giving an enthusiastic account of the north Cornish beaches. White knew that part of the country too; his uncle had married into a Cornish family from Crackington Haven. He introduced himself.[129]

John was fascinated by White's multiple names. Why did he use all three? White explained that he had been told of another Eric White, an American writer on jazz. He had chosen to use his middle name to avoid confusion, though he was beginning to regret what looked like affectation. (The *Oxford University Review* of 3 March 1927 called him Alec Bloater Blight.) When John became editor of the *Cherwell* he published avant-garde poems by White, who was already a contributor.[130] And he himself contributed a nonsense-rhyme about White to the issue of 18 June 1927.[131]

By 1927 the best-known undergraduate poet in Oxford was Tom Driberg. He stage-managed the appearance of Edith Sitwell in June of that year, introducing her and – always the opportunist – tacking on to the end of the programme a composition of his own, 'Cottage Squalor'. Another of his works had appeared in the *Cherwell* of 14 May, which was then under John's editorship:

SPRING CAROL

The latterday compendium
has burst a half, has burst a half,
And winter's deep has come to equal
the supervision of the first.

Destitute, destitute of caramel.
White water comes to take its place.
The fountain burns spasmodically

and (quick, quick Kamchatka swells and streams
                              (quick grace and face
dying dying dying down
'Calm and Free' (*Wordsworth*)
                  quite abstract

Despite giving it space in the magazine, John was not taken in by this high-falutin' gibberish. On 21 May he published a parody of 'Spring Carol', which indeed he may have written:

Mr DRIBERG's NEXT POEM?

An aard-vark, Aaron's-beard aback:
Abacus Abaddon, abaft abandon
Abase, abask.

A, ab, absque, coram, de:
Y, yaffil, yapp:
Zeppelin, zouave, zygote:

Destitute, destitute of meaning –
The Concise Oxford Dictionary comes to take its place:
The beginning and the end –
Between A and Z
          quite obviously %.

But many Oxford intellectuals accepted Driberg at his own estimate of himself. Geoffrey Grigson was taken round to see him in his rooms at Christ Church. 'The black hair, the white face, the nervous insolence, the elegant tailoring – Stendhal might have seen him and modelled upon the sight a young priest, machiavellian and subfuscly burning with ambition. . . No one else, so far as I know, reached the flesh-pots of the *Daily Express* by way of the bare sustenance of *Prufrock* and *The Waste Land*.'[132]

As the first 'William Hickey' of the *Daily Express*, Driberg was able to help publicize the career of the young Betjeman. Later, he had a more valuable role in John's life. When John wanted an opinion or a revision of his poetry, it was to Driberg (and John Sparrow) that he turned. In that capacity Driberg served him well: he was a better editor of other people's poetry than of his own.

Driberg's most famous exploit at Oxford – it was reported in the

Sunday Times as well as in the *Cherwell* – was glancingly mentioned by John in *Summoned by Bells*:

> What *was* my own? Large parts of it were jest.
>   Recall the music room in Hollywell,
> The nice North Oxford audience, velvet-dress'd,
>   Waiting a treat whose title promised well:
>
> HOMAGE TO BEETHOVEN the posters show
>   'Words: Thomas Driberg. Music: Archie Browne'.
> Good wives of Heads of Houses, do you know
>   For what it is you've given your half-crown?[133]

If the dons' wives were expecting a piano recital, they were rudely disabused. Just what they were in for, John described more fully in *Parson's Pleasure* in 1958:

> It was called 'Homage to Beethoven' and so a nice collection of old ladies from North Oxford in silk shawls was present. The music, which had typewriters in it, was by Archie Gwynne Brown. The words were by Tom Driberg.

> > If I forget thee, Sion, Sion,
> > May all my members lose their skill,

> one section began, ending with lines something like these:

> > . . . a naked phallus beckons,
> > In blushing starkness from the hill

> and so on until the climax which was the flushing of a lavatory situated just behind the stage.[134]

As John won acceptance by the 'smart set', he did not lose touch with his Marlborough friends – Philip Harding at Hertford, Ben Bonas at Worcester or John Bowle at Balliol. The lustre of Bowle's Brackenbury Scholarship was wearing thin: he was having too good a time. The reckoning came in 1927, when he sat his Finals. Billy Clonmore wrote to John Betjeman on 16 August: 'John Edward got a Third. I hear he nearly got himself ploughed as at the Viva he was asked a question which he thought irrelevant and unfair and answered: "I am not an encyclopaedia." '[135] The Bowle debacle was still a topic in the *Cherwell* more than a year later. This rhyme (probably by John) was printed on 27 October 1928:

> John Bowle
> Will not barter his soul . . .
> He said that Kant
> Reminded him of his aunt
> So he got several thirds and no second
> And is not reckoned
> Good enough to be a don
> Which he is so keen upon.

It was true that Bowle was eager to claw his way back into academe. In this he eventually had some limited success. He became a history master at Westminster School. Maurice Bowra, though he dubbed him (*pace* Fitzgerald's *Rubáiyát*) 'that inverted Bowle we call the sky',[136] obtained him a temporary teaching post at Wadham College. After retiring from an academic posting in Bruges, Bowle was given dining rights in Balliol Senior Common Room. But he continued to feel a sense of brilliance spurned. His string of grievances became a running joke among his friends: he *would* have taken a First and become a leading don if it had not been for his unsympathetic father, his bad sight, his sexual lusts, and the too lavish hospitality of Ben Bonas. John rehearsed all Bowle's complaints in a long, malicious poem for private circulation – a lament for innocence lost and genius wasted.[137] John may have been competing with Bowra, who had composed a derisive ballad on Bowle,[138] but also, perhaps, he may have been working out the jealousy he had felt at Marlborough when Bowle was regarded as a scholar with a distinguished future and he himself was thought a clown with some eccentric talents, a 'misfit'. At Oxford and for the rest of his life, Bowle pontificated as to who in his opinion had a 'first-rate' or 'first-class' brain, never omitting himself from the roll. In two poems, 'A Hike on the Downs' and 'Mortality', John applied a phrase of this kind to somebody he detested – respectively, C.S. Lewis and Lord Bridges, the 'senior civil servant' whose first-class brains John ungrievingly (and with some anatomical licence) pictured as 'sweetbread on the road' after an imagined car-crash.

*   *   *

At Oxford John met the men who were to be his best friends until their, or his death – an inner circle of intimates to which only a few later friends (John and Myfanwy Piper among them) were added. Other Oxford friends, less close, drifted in and out of his life like the subsidiary characters in Anthony Powell's *A Dance to the Music of Time*. Indeed, Powell – who was at Balliol with Bowle – was one such friend. He remembers meeting John only once at Oxford, when they talked about bamboo furniture.[139] The Balliol generation then drawing to an end included Cyril Connolly, grappling ineffectually with the enemies of his promise; Graham Greene, whose now forgotten poetry, published in the *Cherwell* in John's first term, may have influenced John; Patrick Balfour, Lord Kinross's son and heir, one of John's greatest friends; and Pierce Synnott, with whom Bowra and John stayed in Ireland in 1926. Synnott was a dandy and wore cloth-of-gold waistcoats. F.F. ('Sligger') Urquhart, the Dean of Balliol, called him 'a gilded popinjay',[140] but Synnott confounded him by taking a First and went into the Admiralty.

Michael Dugdale had also come up to Balliol with Synnott and Peter Quennell in 1923. A raffish figure (not to be confused with John Dugdale of Sezincote, who was no relation) he is mentioned in *Summoned by Bells* as one of John's companions. Bowle thought he was 'a bad influence' on John: he was an exaggerated aesthete who, in the slang of the day, 'willowed about'.[141] He had been admitted to Balliol because of 'Sligger' Urquhart's friendship with his mother, Blanche ('Baffy') Balfour, who wrote a biography of her uncle, the Prime Minister. During the vacations, John visited the Dugdales at their London home in Roland Gardens.[142]

The Balliol undergraduates of John's own vintage included the very rich Villiers David, who was seldom out of the *Cherwell* gossip column. ('Mr David's chief hobby is playing the pianola stripped to the waist, his favourite tune being "Red, red Robin" which, when an organist, he played as a voluntary in Holy Trinity.'[143]) David worked with John on the *Cherwell* and later became editor. Like John he shamelessly used the paper for self-promotion.

Osbert Lancaster came up to Lincoln College in October 1926 and quickly became a friend of John's, possibly through the Old Marlburian Graham Shepard, also at Lincoln. Their shared interest in the Victorians must have been immediately apparent, for Ernest Betjemann wrote to John on 19 October 1926: 'I cordially agree with you and Osbert. I was born in 1872 and the Victorians were unpleasant as a rule, due no doubt to the fact that prosperity had greatly increased and many quite well-to-do people were ignorant, vulgar and hypocritical. But let's not bother our heads about them, there is so much in the present world pulsating with thrills.'[144] Lancaster, who for fifty years was to contribute a 'pocket cartoon' to the *Daily Express*, was already an accomplished cartoonist, and in 1927 he drew a series of cartoons for the *Isis* called 'Little Known Gems of Victorian Art'. These included 'The Prince Consort personally superintending the planning of sanitary offices in the Neo-Gothic style for the sailors' home of rest at Portland Bill – School of Winterhalter' (19 October) and 'Sir Muddibum being given a sword by the Ladye of the Ford at the gnarled tree-stump – Dante Gabriel Holman Madox Jones' (9 November).

At New College, with Hugh Gaitskell and Frank Pakenham, was John Sparrow 'with his cowlick lock of hair/And schoolboy looks',[145] who was to remain one of John's closest friends. Together John and Sparrow edited a magazine called *Oxford Outlook*, to which John contributed (under the pseudonym 'Archibald Dixon') a playlet, 'The Artsenkrafts', satirizing his parents. Richard Crossman, the butt of John's early poem 'The Wykehamist', was also at New College. So was Hamish St Clair-Erskine, son of the Earl of Rosslyn, a socialite with whom John often stayed at the Rosslyns' home in Sussex. Lionel Perry introduced John to a New College man who did not take to him – Roger de Candolle.

John was puzzled by foreigners [Perry said]. My friend Roger de Candolle came from Geneva, and he was one of the few people I knew who never particularly cared for John. Roger was a strict Calvinist: he explained to me that so strict is the Geneva thing that they are not supposed to take any pleasure from the eyes. Well, John was slightly shy of him and insisted, for some reason, on speaking to him in very bad French. And as Roger was completely bilingual, that didn't go down with him very well. He also disapproved of some of John's riskier jokes.[146]

New College was about on a par with Magdalen in the snob-ranking of the Oxford colleges, but *the* college of the smart set was Christ Church. It contained a few poor scholarship boys, including the Cornishman A.L. Rowse and the Welshman Emlyn Williams. But here too were Lord Dunglass (later Sir Alec Douglas-Home and

Prime Minister), Quintin Hogg (later Lord Hailsham and Lord Chancellor), the Earl of Rosse, Lord Weymouth (now Marquess of Bath), the Earl of Cardigan, the Earl of Dumfries, Lord Stavordale and the fabulously rich Edward James.

If self-interest had been the motive for John's social climbing, Edward James would have been his best catch. There was probably nobody, throughout his life, who gave him more valuable help when it was most needed – a debt acknowledged in *Summoned by Bells*. Edward James was the son of Mr and Mrs Willie James of West Dean Park, Sussex. King Edward VII was his godfather. His father was of American parentage and his fortune came from copper mines and railways. James may be best known to posterity from the back view of his brilliantined head – in Magritte's portrait of him, *La Reproduction Interdite*. He was to be a leading patron of the surrealists, especially of Magritte and Dali. Already in the mid-1920s his rooms at Oxford showed something of the eccentric creativity which was manifested in later life in the Gaudí-like concrete towers which he designed and built in the Mexican jungle. The most striking of his four rooms was the drawing-room. In *Summoned by Bells* John remembers the ceiling as black, but James said it was purple.[147] An Oxford decorator stencilled for him round the cornice an inscription in gold on silver: ARS LONGA VITA BREVIS SED VITA LONGA SI SCIAS UTI, which James translated as: 'Art is long, life is short, but you can make life seem longer if you know how to use it.' There John enjoyed breakfasts of champagne and Virginia ham, swung a censer around to banish the breakfast smells with incense-smoke,

> And talked of Eliot and Wilde
> And Sachie's *Southern Baroque Art*,
> While all the time our darling child,
>   The poem we had learned by heart
> (And wrote last night) must be recited,
> Whether or not it were invited.[148]

These heady sessions gave James the admiration for John's poetry which caused him to publish John's first poetry collection, *Mount Zion*, in 1931.

James had a clear memory of John at Oxford:

I noticed two things, neither of them very kind. One was that his teeth were sort of greenish – slightly prominent, and not a good colour. He giggled a lot, so the teeth showed a lot. And, as I am very conscious of aesthetic things – I like people to have good looks – I realized very quickly that I was enormously drawn to Betjeman *in spite* of his looks, by his charm and his vitality. And I began to think: 'It's funny, that you should like this fellow, who is not very pretty.'[149]

John persuaded James to put money into the ailing *Cherwell*. The printer was owed a lot of money; James agreed to pay off this debt and, at the beginning of Michaelmas Term 1927, he succeeded John as editor. By nature quarrelsome and easily bored, James held the job for less than a month before 'retiring', but during his brief tenure he published John's 'A 'Varsity Student's Rag' and created a new cover for the magazine, imitating the design of Grinling Gibbons's carving in Queen's College. 'In each circle I put some word that showed what we intended to cover – "HUMOUR", "IMAGIN-ATION", "POETRY", and so on. After that we had no trouble at all. We had an awful lot of people contributing, including Christopher Sykes and Lord Birkenhead, he was then Freddy Furneaux.'[150]

James was distantly related to Christopher Sykes, but little love was lost between them. Sykes's impression was that James's pro-tégés often suffered more than they benefited from his patronage:

He had that meanness which very rich men have. He counted every penny and he suspected people of sponging. I dare say John saw the red light. A trick James had was taking up people who were not well off and giving them a nice, jolly time, taking them out in society. And then they'd say, 'Well, I haven't got the right clothes, I've not got a tail coat,' 'Oh, go and get it on *me*.' And then he'd suspect them of overstepping the bounds, and he would suddenly turn on them and demand repayment of all the money he had spent on them. He tried to do that to Dali, but Dali saw the danger, as John may have done.[151]

Sykes had a low opinion of James's contributions to the *Cherwell*. In 1927 he wrote to John:

Dear Betjeman,
   I came here specifically to talk shop about that damned paper. James has written an article which passes belief, it's so bad and he wants to publish all my worst pictures and Villiers David has sent in

some infuriatingly silly ideas – so my Napoleon's brain has just evolved a most enormous idea – let us leave little James to talk about [Harman] Grisewood's 'resonant forehead' if he wants to, but let us write a weekly supplement that will just shatter the rest of the damned paper and finally will eat it up with little James and ugly Villiers – come up to Oxford *immediately* and talk it over – it's all a question of time fuck you.

Xtopher.[152]

Sykes had more respect for John than for Edward James and Villiers David, but even so he regarded him as a bizarre eccentric. 'I remember one thing that was odd about him. When he passed a building he admired, he used to clap.'[153]

Through Edward James, John also met Basil, Marquess of Dufferin and Ava, who followed John Bowle as a Brackenbury Scholar of Balliol. Dufferin had been with James not only at Eton but earlier, at his 'prison-like' private school, Lockers Park. 'I was told to look after him, because he was a year and a half younger than I,' James recalled, '– but he was so much more intelligent and alive than I was that it ended by him looking after me.'[154] At Oxford, Dufferin might have been an understudy for the Duke of Dorset, the nonpareil undergraduate of Max Beerbohm's *Zuleika Dobson*. Randolph Churchill later wrote: 'Basil Dufferin was the most lovable man I met at Oxford. His liquid spaniel eyes and his beautiful, charming manner, commanded affection. He was the most brilliant of all my contemporaries at Oxford. An undue addiction to drink blighted what might have been a fine political career.'[155] To Edward James, Dufferin seemed 'very Irish':

He had this round Irish nose, like a sort of Paddy caricature; beautiful brown eyes, very very alive and deep and large; very quiet and reserved, beautiful manners. And I was in love with him. And John was, too. And I suppose we both told him we were. Anyway, he asked us both over to Clandeboye [the Dufferins' family home in northern Ireland].[156]

Elizabeth Longford also remembered John's attachment to Basil Dufferin: 'John made fun of everything he liked: that was his line. It was he who christened Basil "Little Bloody"; he was always known as "Little Bloody". John adored him, and Basil was brilliantly clever, not little at all, very well grown, extremely handsome, very athletic – but this was John's way of expressing his affection, to give him this funny nickname.'[157] John's mock-Metaphysical poem 'The bluish eyeballs of my love . . .' was a tribute to Dufferin's *beaux yeux*. When Dufferin was killed in Burma at the end of the Second World War, John was middle-aged and the father of two children; yet something of the romantic exaltation of the Oxford friendship survives in his threnody on 'my kind, heavy-lidded companion', written in Oxford where John was working in 1945:

> Stop, oh many bells, stop
>   pouring on roses and creeper
> Your unremembering peal . . .[158]

Two friends made John slightly ashamed of chasing the lords and Croesuses of the smart set. One was Randolph Churchill, who, with his Blenheim Palace connexion, was 'smart' enough himself to feel no need of social climbing. Writing of him in 1969, in a letter to Kay Halle who was planning a biographical symposium on Churchill, John could not remember whether he had met him in the rooms of his cousin Johnnie Churchill at Pembroke College ('a favourite college of mine, because it was so retiring') or in Edward James's rooms. 'Johnnie had painted the walls of his room in the front quad at Pembroke with classical perspectives, and I certainly saw these in Randolph's company. I wonder if they survive in Pembroke today.' John thought the meeting had more probably taken place in James's rooms:

So far as Randolph had a set of friends in those days, I suppose it would be with the members of Canterbury Quad in Christ Church, who consisted chiefly of Edward James, Christopher Sykes and Lord Dumfries. To me, an outsider from Magdalen, these people were the height of fashion, and suddenly with Randolph I realized that my standards were barmy. Randolph was not in the least bit the snob I was. He took them on their own merits, and he took me on mine, which were in those days poetry. He encouraged me to read the stuff out loud at dinner parties, and he insisted on my reading satires I had written, when I was quite sure that the other people round the table did not want to hear them at all. Any table that he was at Randolph dominated. That was how I got a hearing for my verses.[159]

John took Churchill to one of Colonel Kolkhorst's Sundays. Churchill was amazed when suddenly, in the middle of a company of forty or fifty people, John stamped loudly on the floor and sang 'D'ye ken Kolkhorst in his artful parlour . . .' to the tune of 'John Peel'. ('The refrain was taken up by all the company . . . I was naively astounded by the suave equanimity with which Colonel Kolkhorst received this eccentric outburst.'[160])

The other friend who gave John qualms about his tuft-hunting was W.H. Auden, who came up to Christ Church at the same time as John arrived at Magdalen. Auden was 'not in the least interested in the grand friends I had made in the House'.[161] This 'tall, milky-skinned and coltish' undergraduate impressed John by his knowledge of poetry. Like John he had already read Ebenezer Elliott and Philip Bourke Marston 'and other poets whom I regarded as my special province'; he dismissed the Sitwells in a sentence and 'really admired the boring Anglo-Saxon poets like Beowulf whom we had read in the English School'. Auden belonged to no clique. He was not a member of the 'Georgeoisie'. He did not join the OUDS. But he was a friend of John Bryson and Nevill Coghill '– real dons [John wrote] who read Anglo-Saxon, Gutnish, Finnish and probably Swedish and Faroese as easily as I read the gossip column of the *Cherwell* . . .' Alone among John's Oxford friends, it seemed, he 'reverenced his father'.[162]

John and Auden had much in common besides writing poetry. They both loved railways and canals and Bradshaw's timetables. Auden, too, was drawn to the Church of England, and enjoyed visiting churches. He was interested in the social life of the Victorians and lent John a book with coloured illustrations of soil-pipes and domestic privies for the working classes. (Characteristically, John lost this, and was still being pestered for its return after he had gone down from Oxford.) It was Auden who encouraged John to go to the Isle of Man, a place both came to love. Above all, Auden liked poetry. He chanted it aloud after tea. The two appreciated each other's poems (Auden later anthologized John's for publication in the United States, and said there were many he wished he had written). Together they discovered unknown poets. They stumbled on the work of the Rev. E.E. Bradford, DD, 'whose lyrics, innocent and touching about the love of "lads", as boys were so often called by scout-masters in those days, used to bring us uncontrollable mirth:

Once a schoolboy newly come,
  Timid, frail and friendless,
Feared to face a footer scrum
  Oh! The taunts were endless.

Suddenly he drew apart
  Soon they heard him crying.
With a penknife in his heart
  Home they brought him dying.'[163]

Bradford was a paedophile poet and novelist: his novels were
eagerly collected by Colonel Kolkhorst and a line from one of them,
Boyhood ('a novel in verse') was adapted by John as the first line of
his poem 'A Shropshire Lad'. John later visited Dr Bradford;[164] and
with Auden he went to hear another paedophile, the Rev. S.E.
Cottam, MA (author of *Cameos of Boyhood*) preach at his Sung
Mass at Wootton, under Boar's Hill.

He and Bradford [John recalled] had been Anglo-Catholics together
as undergraduates at Oxford. Later Bradford went Modernist and
their friendship cooled, for Cottam remained Anglo. I remember
Bradford telling me that he was at work on a poem about the love of
a Modernist boy for an Anglo-Catholic boy, in which the Modernist of course triumphed. I don't think there were more than about
four people at Cottam's 11 o'clock when Wystan Auden and I went,
but there were two boys acting as servers, and one of them hummed
while Cottam intoned the Gospel, and Cottam suddenly stopped in
the middle of the Gospel and said 'Will the boy or boys who is or are
humming kindly refrain?' I can't remember what he preached
about, but I remember that his eyes rolled round like those of someone with persecution mania. He had a great objection to Sir Arthur
Evans [the archaeologist, owner of a neighbouring estate] on moral
grounds. He was a little man, like Dr Bradford, and clean-
shaven.[165]

In his *W.H. Auden: The Life of a Poet* (1979), Charles Osborne
suggested that John and Auden had slept together at Oxford and that
they were discovered in bed by Auden's scout, who had to be bribed
£5 to keep quiet about it. This passage appeared in the American
edition, published by Harcourt Brace Jovanovich, but John's law-
yers secured its removal from the English edition published by Eyre
Methuen. Auden himself often described the incident, according to

his brother Dr John Auden, adding the punchline: 'It wasn't worth the £5.'[166] Was the story true? John denied it but it is an indication of the Oxford sexual mores at that time.

When the Rev. J.M. Thompson, in his 1925 lectures on European History, came to the delicate question of Frederick the Great's adolescent relationship with the fellow military student whose execution he was forced by his father to watch, his comment was housemasterly and reassuring: 'We know something of this type, at school, and in the Varsity. We call it a "phase" – it is often no more: and we have methods of our own for dealing with it.'[167] For once, Thompson's historical sense failed him. If he had looked about him he would have been bound to conclude that Oxford was full of men for whom homosexuality was no passing phase, but a permanent condition. A don's life had always had attractions for homosexuals – a life of monastic seclusion with a constantly renewed supply of young men. And it is no exaggeration to say that the majority of John's undergraduate friends at Oxford were homosexual; among them Brian Howard, Patrick Balfour, Robert Byron, John Bowle, Lionel Perry, Michael Dugdale, Gyles Isham, Hamish St Clair-Erskine, Mark Ogilvie-Grant, Edward James and of course Tom Driberg, who made a career of his homosexuality to which his political activities were secondary. (The historian A.J.P. Taylor recalled that Driberg tried to pick up the waiter at his, Taylor's, twenty-first birthday party.[168]) Some were discreet; others were flamboyant queens, such as Alec Clifton-Taylor described in his poem 'A Lofty Ideal' (*Isis*, 16 May 1928) about an aesthete whose burning ambition was to win a Blue for bézique:

> He came up to Oxford an infant adult,
> And was pledged to the latest aesthetical cult,
> His waistcoat was seen
> To be soft apple-green
> And he painted his finger-nails ultramarine.
> His pyjamas were purple with bobbles of black,
> And some verse by the Sitwells was seen on his back:
> But the charms of the aesthetes, the charms of his clique,
> Were small when compared to the charms of bézique!

Maurice Bowra later wrote that 'Women at Oxford were kept

almost in purdah, and association with them earned the disapproval of the young and the darkest suspicions of the old.'[169] Brian Howard claimed 'I've only ever seen one passable undergraduette and *she* looked like a boy scout.'[170] Neither man could be called susceptible to the opposite sex; but Osbert Lancaster, who was, confirms that interest in women in the Oxford of the late 1920s was generally slight. 'Women played a very small part in our lives. There were, it is true, the women's colleges but their inhabitants were for the most part unknown and unregarded and their entertainment, which took the form of morning coffee at the Super, was left by right-thinking men to the scruffier members of the dimmer colleges.'[171] There were exceptions: Elizabeth Harman (now Countess of Longford),[172] Margaret Lane (now Countess of Huntingdon) and the actress Margaret Rawlings, then known as 'Gloria'. The Oxford women asserted themselves in 1926 by founding a magazine called *Fritillary* after the graceful flowers in Magdalen Meadows. The men undergraduates were soon calling it 'Fritters'. Their overall attitude to women can be judged by the rare jokes about girls in the *Cherwell*. 'Answers to Correspondents' in the issue of 5 November 1927 included: 'N.G. No, the undergraduette you mention, who satisfied the examiners, was not doing History Finals, but Biology Preliminary.' More explicitly homosexual jokes went the rounds: 'Would you rather stroke your college boat or your college cox?'

Of course not all male undergraduates were rouged epicenes or uninterested in girls. 'A very ordinary female' wrote indignantly to the *Isis* ('Felt in the Dark', 8 February 1928) to protest at the increase of what she called 'jellyfish' in Oxford – men who went to the cinema alone and showed 'persistent and nauseating attentions to whatever female happens to be sitting next to them . . . the pressing shoulder, the twisting leg, the caressing hand of one of the loathsome species . . .' But the general tenor of undergraduate sex-life was homophile. A.J.P. Taylor (John's exact contemporary) brought a historian's objectivity to the subject when he discussed it in his volume of the *Oxford History of England*: 'The strange one-sexed system of education at public schools and universities had always run to homosexuality. In Victorian times this, though gross, had been sentimental and ostensibly innocent. At the *fin de siècle* it had been consciously wicked. Now [in the 1920s] it was neither innocent nor wicked. It was merely, for a brief period, normal.'[173]

It is in the light of that statement, by a heterosexual who if anything was unsympathetic to homosexuals,[174] that John's alleged night with Auden should be considered. There is other evidence that he was homosexually inclined at this period. John Bowle said that at Oxford John frequently slept with an Old Marlburian Balliol undergraduate of John's year, David Dent (who took a First in Jurisprudence, married in 1930 and died in 1933). Lionel Perry remembered that John 'had a crush' on Hugh Gaitskell. 'He would say to him, "Hugh, may I stroke your bottom?" And Hugh would say, "Oh, I suppose so, if you *must*." '[175]

John's name was also linked, as the gossip writers say, with the names of other Oxford contemporaries. The long erotic poems he wrote at this time were about schoolboys. John Bowle said that one of the poems was called 'Bags in Dorm'. Another, titled 'Going back to Bradfield', was a fantasy about John's sitting opposite a boy on a train and noticing from his luggage labels that he was bound for Bradfield School. In the poem 'John seduces the boy into going in his car to Reading – then off into the woods where an indecency takes place'. Bowle described both poems as 'very indecent and very vivid'.[176]

But there were already signs that John's inclinations were not exclusively homosexual. In February 1926 he attended a party given by an Old Marlburian friend in Cambridge. After the party, the friend wrote to him from Trumpington Street: 'You may be interested to hear that the δαρκ γιρλ [dark girl] at θε 43 [the 43] with whom I δανσεδ [danced] and with whom you were decidedly τακεν [taken], has been shot out of the above haunt for having an ιτχινγ δισεασε [itching disease] and is now in Cambridge giving δανσινγ λεσσονσ [dancing lessons]. And of course lots of other things.'[177] Another Old Marlburian friend who had been at the same party wrote: 'Dear Benjy . . . I thought that sooner or later you would go completely mad and get mixed up with some *girl* or other . . .'[178]

For a time John courted a waitress from the George restaurant. He took her round churches with him, but gave her up when she performed dance steps in the aisle of Gloucester Cathedral.[179] 'He remembers her still,' wrote Michael Davie in a 1972 profile of John; '– "Olive Sparks. Eton crop. Very nice." '[180] Another romance was evidently flagging when John wrote to Pierce Synnott, in September 1927: 'My girl has broken my heart – she sent me some hideous etchings in the picturesque style for my birthday – I put them in the waste paper basket at once.'[181]

In later life John's tastes were predominantly heterosexual, but he liked to speculate about the 'percentage' of homosexuality in people's psychological make-up, including his own. He commented on a well-known Conservative politician: 'I never realized what percent he was until I saw him pouring tea.'[182] His own 'percentage' probably remained above the average, but Alan Pryce-Jones thought that John's occasional professions of homosexuality should not be taken too literally:

> I think he has moments of considerable revulsion when he would like to be free from everything: I mean, his absurd emphasis on his queerness, in conversation, really has no foundation or literal meaning, I would think. It's a kind of protest against being dominated by anybody. He likes to feel he might do anything. . . He has got this curious wish for some kind of totally anarchic freedom, an imaginary world. It's not something he has ever done much about. I mean, he had crushes on people at Oxford, like the late Lord Dufferin, but it had no meaning, it was never intended to be translated into any form of action. He liked snapping his fingers at the world at that time.[183]

Certainly John enjoyed snapping his fingers at authority, then and later. (It was this natural propensity that put such zestful animus into his battles with planning committees and 'developers'.) He annoyed the Oxford librarians by not returning books; fell foul of the President of the Magdalen Junior Common Room by not paying his JCR account; was expelled from the OUDS for the irreverent spoof photograph; and continued to drive his car into Oxford after he moved out to lodgings in Headington village, though forbidden to do so by the Senior Proctor.

It was at the beginning of Michaelmas Term 1927 that John moved out to The Beeches, Sandfield Road, Headington. The village was an enclave of rural Oxfordshire life (Cecil Sharp, the recorder of English folk music, learned the traditions of morris dancing from an old inhabitant, William Kimber) and the optimistic idea was that in this peaceful setting John would be able to buckle down to his studies, making rare visits to Oxford. The plan did not work. He was by now too enmeshed in Oxford society to become a rustic hermit. By January 1928 he had so often failed

'Divvers' – the Divinity examination all undergraduates then had to sit – that there was talk, at Magdalen, of sending him down. Sir Herbert Warren decided he should be given another chance, but wrote sternly to Ernest, who in turn wrote sternly to John on 22 January:

> I was on the point of replying to Sir Herbert Warren but have not done so. I have re-read his letters through and commend to you the following: 'Another year here, he must justify it by working *really* well and beginning at *once*. The Long Vacation is a very important period.'
>
> *also*
>
> 'Of course if you are to give him this great opportunity he must really set himself to work and forgo some of the pleasurable cultivation of his taste which up to now he has been allowed.'
>
> No doubt the above reads amusingly, it probably would have been so to me at your age but you are getting rather near the time when a man only gets his chance once.
>
> I was glad to hear you arrived safely – what a beastly day it was – but deplore that you should have considered it necessary to send the glad news by 'phone trunk calls (2); it seems to me that a postcard (1d) instead of 2/- would have served the purpose.[184]

On 2 February he wrote again: 'How are you getting on? and did you pass your "divvers" or "divers" or whatever it is, silence I am afraid denotes that the topic is one best avoided.'[185] He was right: John had failed yet again. This time the college authorities decided that he must be 'rusticated' for a term – temporarily sent down from Oxford to concentrate on his work away from the distractions of parties and acting and undergraduate journalism. He could return in October for one last try.

Maurice Bowra had a theory about John's repeated failure in 'Divvers'. As the examination was 'dishonourably easy', and as no undergraduate was more obsessively interested in religion than John, it followed that 'unconsciously he wished to fail . . . He had no wish to take his finals, for which he had done very little work, and found instinctively a way out.'[186]

On being rusticated, John took himself, as had Evelyn Waugh (and Paul Pennyfeather of *Decline and Fall*) before him, to the scholastic agents Gabbitas-Thring of Sackville Street, London. They were quite prepared to find a job for him even though he had no degree and was uninterested in team sports. But there proved to be a difficulty. John was asked for written testimonials from the President of his college, from the headmaster of his school and from his tutor. When he applied to C.S. Lewis for a testimonial, Lewis told him that he could not say anything in his favour academically. All he could say was that John was 'kindhearted and cheerful'.[187] On the strength of this, John was turned down by the first three schools to which Gabbitas-Thring introduced him. In some desperation, the agency began sending him the details of jobs abroad, including a post to teach English in Krakow, Poland, for 7,600 Polish *zlotys* (about £176) a year.[188] At this point John decided to ditch Lewis's testimonial and to ask for one from his old friend, the Rev. J.M. Thompson – who warmly recommended him. John was soon offered a post as a master at Thorpe House preparatory school, Oval Way, Gerrard's Cross. The salary was £30 a term.

John wrote to Lewis to tell him what was happening and to ask whether he might have his permission to complete the three years at Oxford necessary to qualify for a degree. He took occasion to complain about the testimonial which had lost him three 'decentish' jobs. Lewis now sent him a letter which made John his enemy for life:

Dear Betjemann,
You must write to the Secretary of the Tutorial Board at once, telling him your position, and asking to be allowed to take a pass degree. . .

As to my being "a stone", I take it we understand each other very well. You called the tune of irony from the first time you met me, and I have never heard you speak of any serious subject without a snigger. It would, therefore, be odd if you expected to find gushing fountains of emotional sympathy flowing from me whenever you chose to *change* the tune. You can't have it both ways, and I am sure that a man of your shrewdness does not really demand that I should keep "sob-stuff" (is that the right word in your vocabulary?) permanently on tap in order to qualify me for appearing alternately as butt and as fairy godfather in your comedy. But you are quite mistaken if you attribute any animosity to me, and, if I am consulted, I shall certainly advise any measures that are necessary in order to enable you to get a degree.

Yours v. sincerely
C.S. Lewis.[189]

John kept up the vendetta with Lewis in his published works. The opening salvo was fired in *Ghastly Good Taste* (1933): 'Finally, the author is indebted to Mr C.S. Lewis . . . whose jolly personality and encouragement to the author in his youth have remained an unfading memory for the author's declining years.' In the foreword to *Continual Dew* (1937) he again expressed indebtedness to Lewis, 'for the footnote on p. 256'. (There was no p. 256.) In 'A Hike on the Downs', a poem in the same book, he sniped:

> Objectively, our Common Room
> Is like a small Athenian State –
> Except for Lewis: he's all right
> But do you think he's *quite* first-rate?

And in 'May-Day Song for North Oxford' (*New Bats in Old Belfries*, 1945):

> Oh! well-bound Wells and Bridges! Oh! earnest ethical search
> For the wide high-table λογος of St C.S. Lewis's Church.

The *Ghastly Good Taste* acknowledgement was left in the 1970 reprint, to pursue Lewis beyond the tomb.

From the 1950s onwards, John received letters from disciples of C.S. Lewis (who had almost as large a following as Tolkien, especially in America) saying, 'I have heard that you do not like C.S. Lewis. Could you please explain why?' John declined these invitations as politely as he declined the several invitations to speak in Slough, the town whose destruction by 'friendly bombs' he had willed in a much-quoted poem. But a comprehensive answer to the question exists in the Betjeman Archive of the University of Victoria, British Columbia. It is an eight-page letter which John wrote to Lewis in a cold fury of recrimination on 13 December 1939. Osbert Lancaster had a story that at the time of John's rustication 'Lewis told John, "You may think I'm being hard on you now; but you will be grateful to me by the time you are forty." John waited until his fortieth birthday and then sat down and wrote Lewis the stinker of a lifetime.'[190] This may be *ben trovato*, like several of Lancaster's best stories; it is probably a reference, accurate in substance but not in chronology, to the 1939 letter.

With the letter, in the Victoria archive, is an envelope addressed to Lewis at Magdalen College, which has been ripped open. It is possible that John, having purged his feelings towards Lewis by 'writing them out', decided that the letter was too savage to send; or it may be that he wanted to make a fair or revised copy. Whether sent or not, the letter shows how, more than ten years after John was Lewis's pupil, the bitterness he had felt towards him at Oxford was still fermenting. Addressed from Garrard's Farm, Uffington, Berkshire (John's home in 1939), the letter begins:

> Dear Mr Lewis,
>   Since I have just expunged from the proofs of the preface of a new book of poems of mine which Murray is publishing [*Old Lights for New Chancels*], a long and unprovoked attack on you, I wonder whether you will forgive my going into some detail with you personally over the reasons for my attitude? . . .
>
> You were kind enough to say in a letter to me of about 1½ years ago that you had always regarded ours as a purely literary battle. I must say that it may have become that now, but it started on my side as a rather malicious personal battle. I think it only fair to explain why.[191]

John reiterated his complaint that Lewis's damning testimonials had lost him three jobs 'in the inevitable prep-school mastering to which all unsuccessful undergraduates of my type are reduced' (when 'my father had quite rightly washed his hands of me').

> Naturally [John continued] I was inflamed against you and thought, with the impulsiveness of a young man, that you had done it out of malice from the easy security of an Oxford Senior Common Room. The tragedy of it was heightened by the fact that I have always had a great love for English literature – and none for philology – and that it was my ambition to become a don and read English literature to the accompaniment of lovely surroundings. I thought of you as reading philology in surroundings which you did not appreciate. I visualized that white unlived-in room of yours in New Buildings, with the tobacco jars and fixture cards from Philosophy clubs and the green loose covers on the furniture which always depressed me. And when I was working in various far more repulsive surroundings in suburban and Industrial England, I often thought of those rooms and envied you . . .

More rancorous paragraphs followed, on Lewis's alleged mockery of Tennyson; on his preference of Hopkins's 'Wreck of the

Deutschland', which John admitted he did not understand, to Hopkins's 'Epithalamium'; on Lewis's insensitivity to architectural beauty; and on his lack of sympathy for John in the 1920s. John hoped that 'when one of the Betjeman type comes to you now for tutorials', Lewis would send him to somebody else, such as John Bryson or Nevill Coghill. He apologised for being 'unpardonably rude' in the letter, which, he admitted, 'reads like a heart-to-hearter from someone who has just joined the Oxford Movement'. But there was one last gripe. 'When I went in for the English group [in the Pass School examination at Oxford], I had a viva [*viva voce* or oral examination] from Mr Bret Smith [*sic*]. My answers on 18th and 19th cent: writers were not, I suspect, bad, and Mr B.S. asked me at the viva, "Why are you not in for the Honours School?" You were at the same table with him.' John concluded by saying he could now put his letter into the post and sleep contented, 'for I still sometimes wake up angry in the night and think of the mess I made at Oxford'.[192]

John's fame as an Oxford 'character' was never greater than after his inglorious departure. On 17 March 1928 the *Cherwell* published his poem 'Home Thoughts from Exile', which began:

> When I picture the scenes of my prime
> In a little North Hinksey abode,
> I can fancy the warm summer-time
> Still breathes o'er Divinity Road:
> I can hear Holy Trinity bells
> That entranced me in Gasworks Lane
> Where I swotted in spite of the gas and the smells
> From a pungent and neighbouring drain.
>
> I remember the jolly suppers
> The tripes and the kippers and all,
> I remember my first year's cuppers;*
> I'd have died for St Ernest's Hall;
> I remember the boats like coffins
> When we rowed St Stephen's and won;
> And I think of those gorgeous spreads in Boffin's
> Whenever I look at a bun . . .

* Cuppers: inter-collegiate drama competition with a silver cup as a prize.

On 5 May the following appeared:

IN MEMORIAM
JOHN BETJEMAN, MARLBOROUGH AND MAGDALEN,
DEPARTED SUDDENLY, MARCH 1928

There was a young man who the minute he
Attempted it, failed in Divinity.
    Magdalen Coll. didn't care
    Being quite unaware
Of the name of 'that aesthete from Trinity'.

Beneath the limerick appeared this announcement: 'Mr Betjeman has left Oxford. He tells us that he is temporarily a schoolmaster at Oval Way, Gerrard's Cross.' At Thorpe House, a purpose-built school next door to All Saints' Church, John's pupils included Austin Reed of the Regent Street tailors, John Dege, the future Savile Row tailor, Richard Meyjes, later a photographer for *Country Life*, and G.R. Barcley-Smith, who became landlord of the Tiger's Head Inn, Rampisham, Dorset. 'John Betjeman was well-liked by the boys,' Barcley-Smith recalled. 'Decent bloke. Bit of a joker.'[193] John kept up a correspondence with Barcley-Smith at his public school, addressing him as 'Dear Ugly Face'. He also corresponded with another Thorpe House pupil, A.H. Windrum, who went on to Wykeham House, 'a rotten little hole at Worthing'.[194] In August 1928 John asked him to send some photographs of himself. In September, Windrum wrote to John: 'Dear Benjy, If you call me "Faceache" I'll call you Benjy. I would like Nobby [Ernest Noble, headmaster of the school] to hear what you said about Thorpe House(!). Even though you are not an artist you are jolly good at sketching. Mother says she is glad you NOTICED MY SNUB NOSE! . . .'[195]

On 17 May 1928, John wrote to John Bowle:

My dear John Edward,
                I am surrounded by nineteen shrieking boys; I am settling quarrels and starting new ones. One blasted little brute is asking me a question now and I am ignoring him. Another is sulking because I have made him sit down. It is impossible to write coherently because I have continually to get up and go into the changing room to stop the bullying; wait a moment – oh God. The

boys all got wet from cricket to-day & after we had changed their socks, I was left in charge of them while they were in the confined space within doors. How I loathe them all.

The week after next, thank God, is my time off.

The boys will keep coming and looking at this letter. I shall have to go for a walk with them soon. Oh Lord – one of them is crying because the others have tied him up with rope . . .[196]

John's friends rallied round to alleviate his exile with amusing letters and occasional visits. The most entertaining letters came from Edward James. In reply to a letter with which John had sent one of his pupils' essays, James wrote, on 31 May: 'This "sucking up" to you on the part of your pupils, which is so evident in the essay, is highly distasteful. But you must admit that to set "An Essay on Schoolmasters" was asking for trouble . . . Furneaux has asked to be allowed to put the essay in *Oxford University Review*.'[197] (Another subject John set as 'prep' was 'My Father's Ghost' – a subject which may have had the same 'wish-fulfilment' appeal to him as Bramley's painting 'The Hopeless Dawn' perhaps had for him in childhood.)

In the same letter, James described a Christ Church party held by George Harwood:

All the buggers were of course dressed as women. I had tried hard to collect enough 'hearties' to break it up and put the guests in Mercury [the ornamental pond at Christ Church, with a figure of Mercury], but all I was able to gather was a few weedy cricketers who would have been too much in a minority to frighten even Harwood. They stood about Tom Quad with expressions of disgusted disapproval, while shrill hermaphrodite laughter was wafted with the odour of sherbet and face-powder from the gaily lighted windows of the 'green parlour' . . . I hope to be able to motor over within the next ten days with Little 'Bloody' Deprava to see you at Oval Way . . .

In 'Home Thoughts from Exile', the last poem he wrote for the *Cherwell* as an undergraduate, John chose 'St Ernest's Hall' as the name for an Oxford College. Relations with his father were becoming increasingly strained. Alan Pryce-Jones observed the tensions at 52 Church Street, where he was occasionally invited to dinner in the vacations. 'A lot of John's troubles,' he said in 1976, 'arose from the great hostility he felt towards his parents when he was young.'

He really couldn't bear his father. Or his mother. One of the things he used to do was fearful jokes at the expense of his father. John knew that his father was deaf, but he used to make one play the piano to his father. And I can see his poor old father – not only did he have an ear trumpet, he had a mysterious object with a tube, with an acoustic device on the end, which you put on the piano keys, and it sort of danced; and when one played a piece he would try to hear, politely, poor old gentleman, and John would stand behind, making appalling faces at one, in order to make one laugh.[198]

His parents were always known to John as Ernie and Bess, never as Father and Mother, and he was extremely contemptuous of his father in those days . . . and very contemptuous of his mother, who he thought was a very stupid and tiresome woman; she was, as a matter of fact. They were a pretty constraining couple, because old Mr Betjemann couldn't bear John's not going into the family business, and Mrs Betjemann was a nice cottage-loaf of a lady. They did not at all care for John's activities, and he did not care for theirs . . . Also, it has to be said, he is rather snobbish, and he didn't think they were very grand – and they weren't. They had pretty things and quite a lot of taste, the father especially. The house in Church Street was delightful – pretty eighteenth-century panelled house – but it wasn't somehow what John wanted. He felt that they were sort of 'people from Highgate' – rather as Evelyn Waugh felt about his parents in Golders Green.[199]

John put all his resentful feelings about his parents into 'The Artsenkrafts', the short play he contributed to *Oxford Outlook* in 1927. The dramatic sketch is flimsily plotted. Mrs Artsenkraft (Bess Betjemann) chats querulously to the maid; Mr Jim (John) arrives and tells his mother about an 'awful business'; the dog, Sambo, which he was taking for a walk, has been run over by a bus. Then Mr Artsenkraft (Ernest) comes home from the works, and we are held in suspense: when will the news of the dog's death be broken? It never is; by the end of the play, Jim has still not summoned up the courage to confess. Whether the accident occurred in reality, or whether it is an example of John's wishful thinking, is not known; but much of the playlet's dialogue has the ring of authenticity.

Jim, described in the stage directions as 'anaemic-looking and repressed', is clearly a self-portrait. 'His complexion is unhealthy. He looks unhappy. He speaks in a precise manner which distinguishes him from the rest of the household. He has literary tendencies.' Mr Artsenkraft is 'a fat person with sensual lips and a hard face. His suiting is very neat and in the true business-man[200] style. He wears a hard white collar . . . Mr A. is stone deaf.' The setting is the drawing-room of the Betjemanns' Chelsea house, furnished with 'one or two good things arranged with no regard for period', with an 'orange "Nell Gwynn" candle in the silver Georgian candlestick on the table'.

When Mr Artsenkraft comes in, he tells Jim to 'cut along and get me a whisky and soda', then remarks to his wife:

> The boy doesn't look up to much. He's as yellow as a guinea. I can't think why he doesn't take more exercise instead of mooning about round churches all day. I've paid his subscription at Combe Hill and he can have the car to play golf if he likes. When I was his age I was always making something in the workshop or going out with other fellows to play cricket or sail model yachts; why, it's all he'll do to take Sambo for a walk. I've had enough of it, Mary. I've spent thousands to send him to a decent school, and this is all I get for it. Anything that interests him . . . well and good; but as far as anybody else is concerned he is superciliously indifferent. I can't help thinking I was quite wrong in sending him to Oxford . . .

When Jim returns, he is told to 'brace yer shoulders back!' and to 'cut up stairs and brush your hair properly. Don't come down here looking like an inferior workman.' Jim shouts into the speaking-tube: 'I'm not going to be treated like a child of two.' And the two men snarl insults at each other until the play ends with Jim's taking 'a feeble blow at Mr. A's bloated stomach'.[201]

No doubt John exaggerated the friction with his father. If it had been as extreme as 'The Artsenkrafts' suggests, it is unlikely that Ernest would have written to him, as he did, in March 1928: 'I hope, old man, in the coming vac, that you won't go away to study, you can work as well or better in your own room at home. I have never been alone for a very long time, and it is decidedly dull to have my small (but expensive) family continually residing anywhere but under the parental roof provided for them, verily a sign of the restless spirit of the age . . .'[202] But there was further cause for reproach two months later. On 14 May the Westminster Bank, Oxford, wrote to tell Ernest that John had drawn a cheque for £5 payable to the St George Café, which the bank was not going to honour. 'I am rather surprised,' the manager wrote, 'in view of the fact that I wrote and asked him not to draw any further cheques, that he should have done this. Should you wish me to pay this if you telephone me tomorrow morning I should be able to protect the cheque.'[203] Ernest wrote to John, 'I hope you realize the danger you are running into, this sort of thing is not far removed from fraud.'[204] On 20 May he further wrote to him at Thorpe House that he had agreed to be responsible for John's overdraft of about £83 at the Oxford bank. He added: 'I view you as one who is likely to have trouble because of a want of resolution to say NO to the luxury of enjoying the present moment, and some inability also to say NO to the specious pleader, of whom I am sure Oxford has its full share.'[205] But, to soften the admonition, he wrote that two things had pleased him: John's getting the Thorpe House job, and his decision to sell his car, for which Ernest had obtained £40. On 22 June he wrote again to say that he was meeting his cousin Arthur at Dieppe the next day 'and we shall fish in the lovely Normandy trout streams together until Monday'.[206] He signed with his initials and the three-ball sign of a pawnbroker: Ernest was not without a sense of humour.

In July 1928 John went to stay with Philip Harding in Dorset. One result of this holiday was John's poem 'Dorset'. Another result was a fine for speeding. On 27 September Ernest wrote to him: 'Why on earth didn't you let me know you had been fined £4 at Blandford on July the 28th and allowed four days in which to pay? I've just had to settle with the police who were on the point of issuing a warrant of arrest. It's too bad of you not to face facts and humbug me so.'[207] But this chicken had not come home to roost by 29 July when Ernest wrote from St Enodoc View, Trebetherick, that he was very pleased John had made a success of the schoolmastering. Ernest was in skittish holiday mood: 'I find that small limpet shells with bright yellow tips stuck over the face, give the most horrible effect of skin eruptions . . .'[208]

In October 1928 John returned to Oxford for what was to be his last term. As C.S. Lewis had suggested, he had written to the secretary of the Tutorial Board of Magdalen, stating his 'position'. The secretary, G.C. Lee, had replied that he would put his application to take a Pass degree before the Board at its next meeting. He could not say what view the Board would take of the application, but personally hoped it was a favourable one. He would consult Mr Lewis as to what chance John had of getting a class in the English School,

1929. (Predictably, Lewis's answer was 'none'.) Lee reminded John that the Pass School involved three subjects, one of which must be a language, 'presumably in your case Latin or French'.[209] It was always a mistake to presume anything in John's case. When permission to read the Pass School came through, he chose as his language, with maximum perversity, Welsh. Osbert Lancaster suggests in his memoirs that John's failure in this subject was 'partially compensated for by the knowledge that in order to gratify this strange ambition Magdalen had been put to all the trouble and expense of importing a don from Aberystwyth twice a week, first-class.'[210] In view of the fact that Jesus College was packed with Welsh-speaking dons, this seems a tall story; but John did study Welsh for a short time. In *Ghastly Good Taste* he quoted the Welsh translation of a psalm.

Magdalen might not be enthusiastic about receiving back its prodigal son, but the staff of the *Cherwell* were delighted. They regained a contributor, a subject for the gossip column, and a victim for the caricaturists. A full-page cartoon of him, wrongly dressed in a scholar's gown and with his usual lopsided smile, appeared on 27 October.

John Betjeman, Esquire.

The issue of 17 November, which announced the engagement of Bryan Guinness and Diana Mitford, included in its Sayings of the Week, '"Tinkerty-Tonk" – Mr John Betjeman'. This masher's *au revoir* remained a favourite ending to his letters.

On 1 December he contributed a *jeu d'esprit* to *The University News*, a short-lived undergraduate magazine. It was a special 'Divvers Number'. For it John designed cut-out cuffs to be fitted over one's own during the examination – an Old Testament cuff and a New Testament cuff. The Old Testament cuff listed the Kings of Judah:

XIV	AMAZIAH	(good)
	AZARIAH	(a leper)
XV	JOTHAM	
XVI	AHAZ	(a lot about him)
XVIII	HEZEKIAH	(2 chapters, ever so good)
XXI	MANASSEH AMON	(naughty)
XXII	JOSIAH	(good)

The printed instructions read: 'Don't be facetious. It never pays and costs a pound a time. Remember JOHN BETJEMAN.'

The New Testament cuff recommended absurd mnemonics for remembering the missionary journeys, such as 'So Paul Pottered About Inspiring Luke to Do the Acts' (Salamis, Paphos, Perga, Antioch, Iconium, Lystra, Derbe, Attalia). And John warned candidates: 'Don't confuse the Pool of Siloam with the Well of Loneliness. They were different places.' Other spoof questions included: 'Where is Rugby mentioned in the Bible?' Answer: 'And he made them heel in the name of the Lord.' The issue concluded with a poem into which John put all his repugnance for the pettifogging examination which had caused his downfall:

> Matthew, Mark, Luke and John
> Bless the bed that I lie on
> Let not sleep steal all the facts
> I have crammed about the Acts.
>
> Peter, Paul and Ananias,
> Patron Saint of cheats and liars,
> Help me thro' my Viva. God's
> Own grace I need for Mods.

I can't remember – Jezebel
Uzziah, Jehu, Japhet – Hell!
Og, Ur, Ai, Habbakuk –
What's that? Yes, I did say muck.

May four Angels bless my bed,
Two for the foot and two for the head,
And me for the middle. Stay thy shivers!
I'm working all tonight for divvers.

The *Cherwell* of 8 December reported that John had produced, for the Magdalen College Dramatic Society, A.P. Herbert's *Two Gentlemen of Soho*: 'There were elements of brilliance in Mr Betjeman's production of the play.' The printed programme with its border of Magdalen lilies, which survives in the Victoria collection, shows that Humphrey Ellis, the future literary editor of *Punch*, played a waiter; Donald McLachlan, first editor of the *Sunday Telegraph*, was Sneak, a private detective; the music was arranged and conducted by Edward Croft-Murray, the future Keeper of Prints and Drawings at the British Museum; and 'pictures in the will' were by Oliver van Oss, the future headmaster of Charterhouse.

At the end of that Michaelmas Term of 1928, John was sent down from Oxford for good. It was obvious to everybody by then that he was not going to pass 'divvers'. He was still of interest to Oxford undergraduates after he left. On 26 January 1929 his 'School Song' was reprinted in the *Cherwell*. The same issue asked 'DO YOU KNOW – that Maurice Green is Vice-President of the New Poetry Society and John Betjeman has applied for the Roman Catholic chaplaincy of it?' A parody of a parish magazine – that of St Cherwell in All Innocence – appeared on 18 May. It contained a caricature by Osbert Lancaster of John as 'Bishop Betjeman' in a stained-glass window design: 'This handsome window has been specially designed to the order of the Earl of Ava, Bishop Betjeman's life-long friend.' (There was a half-prophetic irony in this, for in the event it was John who supervised the commissioning of a memorial to Dufferin in 1945, at the request of Dufferin's widow.) A paragraph of explanation followed: 'Another popular priest who was with us until recently, Fr. John Betjeman, who afterwards became Bishop of North Oxford, and who died last year as a result of a nasty complaint, has left behind him a collection of writings entitled "Squeaks from a Clerical Pen". Some of which we hope to publish shortly.' In a feature headed 'Sensations of the Vacation' in the *Cherwell* of 19 October, No. X was 'HAGIOLOGY: Bishop Betjeman'.

'A 'Varsity Student's Rag' was reprinted on 23 November. The poem's phrases were evidently part of normal conversational currency in Oxford by then; the editor of the *Cherwell* must have assumed that most of his readers would pick up the allusions in the issue of 25 January 1930, which described Villiers David's bringing his friend 'Bishop Betjy' to the annual rugby football match between Oxford and Cambridge: 'He was a real sport, too, despite being in Holy Orders. We went into Leicester Square where he yelled "Cheeriosky" to all the passers-by. Then we shouted "Varsity"... Then we drove to all the fashionable restaurants in London from the "Troc" to the Regent Palace and from the Regent Palace to the "Cri"...'

The 'Bishop Betjeman' joke was still current five months later. On 7 June this paragraph appeared in the *Cherwell*: 'The Right Reverend Bishop Betjeman conducted a confirmation service at All Gugs, Beaumont Street, last Sunday. The candidates were mostly girls from St Ruth's School for orphaned gentlewomen, and the service was fully choral. A person who gave his name as Hobhouse[211] was ejected for making a disturbance in the chancel. It appeared that he was protesting against the misuse of the prayer-book.' The issue of 21 June, which announced the engagement of Basil Dufferin to Maureen Guinness, also recorded: 'After last Sunday's supper, a few old boys gave a short entertainment at the St George Memorial Hall. Amongst them was *Betjeman, ma.*, whose impersonations proved as popular as ever.' On 18 October 'A 'Varsity Student's Rag' was reprinted for the third time, for the benefit of a new set of freshmen. 'Sir John Matterhorn's Social Causerie' for 8 November reported: 'With Osbert Lancaster to the George. I saw that pretty Miss Harman with my young friend Jack Betjeman...' And on 29 November: 'A very large romp indeed was organized for us over the week-end by the indefatigable Mr [Hamish St Clair-] Erskine, the hospitable Earl of Jersey, Lord Donegall, who provided a band, and many others ... It was nice to welcome back amongst us the old boys Messrs Sutro, Betjeman and Driberg...' The last reference to

John in the *Cherwell* was in the issue of 31 January 1931: 'BETJEMAN: This past master was also in evidence last Saturday.' By then, John had been gone from Oxford for more than two years and had held four jobs.

10

THE STATELY HOMES
OF IRELAND

'Yours was the first country house in which I stayed . . . & since then
how many pairs of linen sheets have received my pampered limbs in
what fine mansions . . .'

John Betjeman to Pierce Synnott, 1972, in reply to a Latin panegyric which
Synnott had sent him on his becoming Poet Laureate

John met Pierce Synnott (usually called 'Piers') in Maurice Bowra's
rooms at Wadham College. Bowra was in love with Synnott and
sent him love-letters and poems bad enough to suggest genuine
emotion rather than a classical attitude.[1] It was cattily rumoured
that Bowra used his influence with the examiners to obtain Synnott
his somewhat unexpected First.

Bowra's advances were repelled. 'Take it away,' he was told
when he put his arm round Synnott's shoulder.[2] But Synnott had
been Patrick Balfour's lover; he was admired by Cyril Connolly;[3]
and he had confided in Balfour his own infatuation with a Balliol
Boat Club oarsman: 'I have a terrible love for him, a quite hopeless
one. He is . . . a Christian saint and rather like Marcus Aurelius.'[4]

Bowra and John were invited to Synnott's Irish home, Furness,
Naas, County Kildare, in June 1926. Synnott owned the house, as
his father had died in 1920. Furness had been built about 1740,
probably to the design of Francis Bindon. The drawing-room ceiling was of delicate plasterwork, with a central medallion of
Minerva attending a kneeling hero.[5] In the grounds were a half-
ruined monastic church, an eighteenth-century 'ice house', or
primitive refrigerator, and yew trees from which rebels were said to
have been hanged in the rising of 1798.

The Irish poet Katharine Tynan (Mrs Hinkson) and her daughter Pamela were also guests in the house when John and Bowra arrived. Katharine Tynan had met Gerard Manley Hopkins[6] and was a friend of Yeats, who as a young man had frequented her father's house, Whitehall, Clondalkin, near Dublin. 'Do you know a queer poetess called Katharine Tynan?' Synnott wrote to F.F. ('Sligger') Urquhart, the Dean of Balliol. 'She is staying in the house, + daughter, recites poetry, chiefly Celtic, all day in a wheazy [sic] twilight voice . . . a kind of bath of sentiment. But rather a dear. Mr Bowra is visiting Furness, Naas, also Betjeman whom I think you know. We examine Irish country houses and antiquities most of the time.'[7] One of the houses they visited was Russborough at Blessington, County Wicklow, a Palladian mansion of about 1748 considered by some 'the most beautiful house in Ireland'.[8]

At Furness, Katharine Tynan was on the *qui vive* for ghosts; and of course she spotted one. John, Bowra and Synnott were bidden to chase it. She wrote a newspaper report of the adventure, dated 11 August 1926:

> It is a small monastic church. The walls of the church stand and the gables with their windows, but the roof is open to the sky. There are graves under your feet, and the slab of a vault with an iron ring in it, and all around lie ancient stone fonts and vessels overturned in the rank grass . . . Looking from the window one heavenly night over the heavenly landscape, two or three of us saw the figure of a man standing just within the shadow of the woods. He was gone quicker than any natural man could go.
>
> The boys from Oxford, sitting up late, were called, and started a half-burlesque, half-serious man-hunt. It was not so long ago that such an apparition would have been ominous. They carried the burlesque pursuit right up to the yews. Further they did not go. They said they were held back.[9]

The three Oxford men drove to the restored sixth-century round tower and 'St Kevin's Kitchen' at Glendalough ('Betjers's archaeological knowledge of great use,' Synnott wrote to Billy Clonmore[10]) and on to Shelton Abbey. Clonmore himself was in London, but they were shown round his home by the butler, Atride. John was entranced.

Ireland seemed to me Charles Lever and aquatints come true [he recalled in 1976]. I thought it was the most perfect place on earth.

Really what I liked was the Ireland of the Ascendancy, and I liked particularly people who'd gone rather to seed . . . The entrance to Shelton Abbey was the *dream* of the Gothic Revival, and all I could wish. It was by [Sir Richard] Morrison. You went in under a Gothick arch into a large hall, Gothick, lit with enamelled stained glass, purplish and amber-green, and that was called the Prayer Hall. Then there were rooms to left and right. I'd never seen such luxury and splendour – rolling parkland down to the river at Woodenbridge, the Meeting of the Waters. It was paradise.[11]

Synnott wrote to Billy Clonmore about the visit. Atride had been kind to them, though 'the boom of his voice was somewhat oppressive at first'. The house had been thoroughly examined – 'even your once nursery' – to the consternation of a gaggle of housemaids. Synnott could not understand why Clonmore did not live there always. 'It seems incredibly lovely. Complete tropical vegetation, climate like Italy, perfect Gothic effects in the garden . . .'[12]

Synnott had begun his letter in a 'vile temper', as he and John had walked half round Dublin looking for Mrs Synnott and her sister. Further, Ernest Betjemann had just telegraphed his arrival in Ireland, 'and is tearing the son to Galway to hold his [fishing] line while he jokes with Ranjitsinghi [the Indian cricketer, who had bought the 30,000 acre Ballynahinch estate]. Selfish and incongruous pursuits. He must be the vilest man ever lived, v. rich, gives his son nothing, forbids him to read poetry, kicks his wife, brings mistresses into the house,[13] spends all on keeping shoots and fishing, makes his son go with him, makes scenes in public, and spends his spare time in persecuting people. . .'[14] Synnott added: 'You must meet Betjers; a pet. Funny, learned, quite unmoral. Magnificent with the Synnott family; a perfect foil to Maurice, in case the latter gets too hard for the tribe of women.'[15] In retelling the tale of woe to Patrick Balfour, Synnott described how Ernest Betjemann had lost his temper in a Dublin hotel, throwing his cap across the lounge. 'Horrible scene: I was feeling sick, like sudden death.'[16] Synnott's first-hand witness and shocked reaction corroborate John's allegations about Ernest, which might otherwise be taken for vindictive over-dramatization.

Synnott told Clonmore that Katharine Tynan was introducing John and himself to 'all the Irish intelligentsia', though they had trooped off without her to tea with 'A.E.' (Russell) – 'full of budding poets and budded politicians, talking really vividly about ruling their country; of course they are doing it.' Yeats had made a dramatic entrance, 'divinely clothed . . . He talked very passionately, holding the floor the whole time about the Lane pictures,[17] and was very polite to us.'[18]

When John left Naas to join his father, he travelled to Galway with Yeats. 'I cannot divulge all our conversation now,' he tantalizingly told Synnott.[19] He met his father and they went to the Ranjitsinghi estate at Ballynahinch. John felt 'unwanted' there. He fished in the heat, 'with my blood being drained by enormous flies and poison being put in its place by still larger ones . . .'[20] He claimed to have got sunstroke and to have arrived in Dublin, on his way back with his father, with a temperature of 101. Ernest Betjemann insisted on John's crossing with him that night. 'This I did suffering agony and vomiting the whole way.'[21] But now John was better and was exploring Greek Revival churches in London. He also went to the Tate Gallery, with Bowra and John Sutro, to see the Lane pictures whose loss Yeats had lamented in Dublin.[22]

John and Bowra again arrived in Ireland on 31 December, to spend the first two weeks of 1927 with Clonmore at Shelton Abbey. Bowra wrote to Patrick Balfour on 11 January: 'It has been very agreeable here. A foul man called Maryon Wilson[23] came for a week-end. He is the real snake in Billy's grass. They talked about copes, albs and birettas . . . But for him Billy would not dream of becoming a priest.'[24] Never a passive onlooker, Bowra was already working out schemes to rescue Clonmore from Wilson's clutches.

In the same letter, Bowra reported: 'Betjeman is here in good form. He pretends to be in love with the Howard girl, Billy's cousin, a flaxen flapper with her bum swung very low and some large spots. There is also her brother here, but you probably know him.'[25] John was indeed taken with Clonmore's cousin Katharine Howard. Recalling that second visit to Shelton, he said: 'Katie played the piano, and her brother Cecil was there; and we sang "The Meeting of the Waters" by Thomas Moore, Maurice very loudly and out of tune –

> Sweet Vale of Avoca, how calm could I rest
> In thy bosom of shade, with the friends I love best.'[26]

Somebody who was not happy at the growing intimacy between

John and Clonmore and his family, was Harold Newcombe, whom the Earl of Wicklow had appointed as a 'social tutor' to his son. Newcombe had become a friend of Wicklow's when the two worked in the Censorship Office during the First World War. He usually lived in the Wicklows' small London house, looked after by a housekeeper; when Lord Wicklow was there, Newcombe moved out to his club. He was a nephew of Rhoda Broughton the novelist. Sir Delves Broughton (a leading figure in the Lord Erroll scandal in Kenya[27]) was his first cousin. The Broughtons owned property in Cheshire, and Newcombe used to take Clonmore there to instruct him in society manners. He also accompanied him to parties and on trips abroad. Lady Wicklow (widow of Billy Clonmore, later Wicklow) recalled:

> Mr Newcombe was for upholding the social proprieties of life ...
> He used to try to cure Billy of his friendship with John. He would say, 'That poor common little John Betjeman, he looks as if he'd been sent round with a brown paper parcel.' He didn't like John, but John seemed to like him – I suppose he never heard what Mr Newcombe said behind his back, spiteful old thing. John used to say, 'Oh, he's so *well-connected*, Mr Newcombe.' He was a sort of introduction for John. It was from Mr Newcombe that he learnt all those 'U' and 'Non-U' phrases that he put into the poem in Nancy Mitford's *Noblesse Oblige* ['How to Get On in Society']. Billy said that John had put in as many of Newcombe's 'don'ts' as possible. He said: 'Those are all the things that Newcombe used to correct *John* for saying.'[28]

Newcombe did not manage to deter Clonmore from his friendship with John, who was invited several times to Shelton. One of the things John and Clonmore had in common was a bad relationship with their fathers. In Clonmore's case, the relationship was strained almost to breaking-point when he became a Roman Catholic in 1932: his father disinherited him and allowed him to come home only in mid-week so that he would not be seen going to Mass with the servants on Sundays. But relations were already soured by Wicklow's open liaison with Lady Beatrice Wilkinson, wife of Sir Nevile Wilkinson, who was Norroy King of Arms and architect of the grandiose dolls' house known as 'Titania's Palace'. From filial as well as religious piety, Clonmore deeply disapproved of this affair, and the misogynistic Harold Newcombe called Lady

Beatrice Wilkinson 'the Policeman', describing her ungallantly as 'a tough woman with a black moustache'.[29]

Clonmore and John commiserated with each other over their fathers' *bêtises*. In September 1928 Clonmore wrote from Shelton: 'We are having a plague of wasps here, and Wicklow enjoys poisoning them very much, and takes the keeper with him to help him. He has killed over 45,000 and this new sport has outdone the fretwork and the rhododendrons.'[30] And in an undated letter, probably referring to John's term at Thorpe House preparatory school, he wrote: 'It is good to think you are now out of that swine Ernie's clutches for the next two months.'[31]

Clonmore invited John to Shelton again in August 1927, but Ernest Betjemann forbade him to go, claiming that he was ill and needed John to 'help around the house' in Chelsea. John wrote to Pierce Synnott from 53 Church Street on 7 August: 'It is hellish here. I lost my trunk – at least my suitcase was as good as taken from my hand – when travelling from Wilnecote to Bath, at New Street Birmingham station, the other day. Ernie proposed to make me a 21st birthday present of another suitcase back again; he was thwarted by the thing turning up from Bournemouth yesterday. I have to take the dog out at 8 o'clock for a ten minute walk EVERY BLOODY MORNING.'[32]

Some days John managed to escape from Ernest on church explorations. He told Synnott he had been to see 'a beautiful baroque church' at Edgware built by an eighteenth-century Duke of Chandos. 'It has high pews, an east end consisting of altar and Corinthian columns supporting a broken-ended pediment behind which is an apsidal end painted blue to imitate the sky and containing a dark Renaissance organ with great pipes which was used by Handel. The walls and ceiling and west end of the church are covered with very elaborate paintings in the Guido Reni manner but c. 1770. The best thing of its kind I've seen in England and at Edgware of all places among a lot of pseudo-Elizabethan bungalows.'[33] He had also (he later told Synnott) been to West Wycombe. If Russborough was 'nearly perfection', West Wycombe was 'the real perfection': 'There is a church on top of a hill (1760) where Bubb Dodington is buried, whose proportions, painted ceilings, plaster & furniture beat anything I saw at Syon House, Brentford.'[34]

On 1 October 1927 Maurice Bowra wrote to tell Synnott that

John was in a Pimlico, London, nursing home 'and seems to be ill. The doctors are cutting him about, and God knows if he will recover.'[35] Two days after receiving this alarmist report, Synnott heard from the invalid himself. John had had an operation on his nose, 'which was very painful'.[36] It had kept him away from Ernest Betjemann for ten days, but John was due to leave the hospital on 5 October and on the 8th, a Saturday, was going 'to spend a ghastly few days in Cornwall with my parents. Ernie has only got "pseudo" angina (although this can kill him, it is curable) but he also has structural disease of the heart. This means that he will die in about five years – just enough for him to wreck my life.'[37]

While in hospital, John had been reading Samuel Butler's *The Way of All Flesh*. As the book satirizes an authoritarian father, it might have been expected to appeal to him; but John was repelled by the humanist ideology of the book. 'To what purpose – other than the apparent side issue of the evils of family life – was it written?' he asked Synnott. 'He does away with Xtianity by very old fashioned methods & I cannot believe he thinks the shallow fatalism that he leaves is an adequate theory of existence. You probably know all about it, you old ugly, and you'll be able to tell me what is wrong and right with the book . . . Do you believe in the existence of a God? I want nice, definite, logical proofs you old dear.'[38] Perhaps persuaded by John's need to convalesce, Ernest agreed to his going to Shelton again in early November. Once more John flirted with Katharine Howard. On 14 November Clonmore wrote: 'Before you left I forgot to give you this Gothic Revival bookplate, which may please you. *Katie also* [Clonmore's italics] thought you might like it.'[39]

Northern Ireland, with its harsh, Calvinistic Protestantism, never appealed to John as much as the south. But he enjoyed visiting Clandeboye, Basil Dufferin's home in County Down. He first stayed there in August 1928, when Edward James was also of the party. After the comforts of Church Street, Chelsea – cosiness incarnate – the big house must have seemed dark and forbidding, like the sinister mansion depicted by Dufferin's kinsman, Sheridan Le Fanu, in *Uncle Silas*. Outwardly it was not a distinguished house. It had been superimposed by R.A. Woodgate in 1800 on a plain eighteenth-century block to which wings had been added.[40] But the entrance-hall had an Imperial splendour. It had changed little since the days of Dufferin's grandfather, the Viceroy of India. Harold Nicolson, who was burstingly proud of his family connection with the Dufferins (the Viceroy was his uncle), described the outer hall of Clandeboye in his book *Helen's Tower* (1937):

> The steps which led down to the front door were flanked by a double row of curling stones from Scotland and from Canada, some of which bore silver plaques commemorative of curling triumphs at Inverary or at Montreal. To the left of these unwieldy playthings stood an enormous block of Egyptian granite carved with the semblance of the cow-headed Hathor and bearing the ibis cartouche of Thutmosis I. Balanced upon this pink monolith was the stuffed and startled head of a rhinoceros ... The wall behind ... had been covered with wire netting on which were affixed dirks, daggers, cutlasses, pistols, lances, curling brooms, and a collection of ... fly-whisks ...'[41]

The inner hall was 'more deliberately baronial'. It was lit by a vast mock-Tudor window bearing the arms and the quarterings of the Blackwoods and their kinsmen the Hamiltons. 'There flamed the cap of maintenance and the scarlet crescent,' wrote Nicolson. 'There blazed the heraldic tiger ermine and the flags of Burmah charged with a peacock in its pride proper. There glittered the stars and collars of the Indian Empire, St Patrick and the Bath.'[42]

John's favourite room was the library, with its terracotta busts of Greek gods and goddesses, and its secret door covered by dummy book spines: *Our Mineral Resources* by Cole and Clay, MPs for Fermanagh and Kingston-on-Hull; *Antediluvian Man* by Adam, MP for Clackmannan; *Humorous Versicles* by the Rt. Hon. W.E. Gladstone; *Gull upon Quacks*; and *The Lost Poems of Sappho*.

John and Dufferin swam in the lake and walked through the Victorian park to Helen's Tower, a grey stone folly with pepper-pot turrets, which the Viceroy had dedicated in 1862 to his then still living mother, a granddaughter of the playwright Sheridan. Near the top of the tower was a room with Gothic woodwork and bronze tablets expressing the love between mother and son. Tennyson had contributed a poem, by no means one of his best:

> Helen's Tower, here I stand
> Dominant over sea and land
> Son's love built me and I hold
> Mother's love in lettered gold.

The rich Victoriana of Clandeboye (most of it still in place today) delighted John, but living there was far from luxurious. Nobody has described that experience better than Basil Dufferin's daughter, Lady Caroline Blackwood, in her novel *Great Granny Webster*, a *roman à clef* in which Clandeboye appears as 'Dunmartin Hall'. The smells of damp-infested libraries mingled with those of cow dung, potato cakes and paraffin. There was something badly wrong with the plumbing; '. . . it was considered a luxury if anyone managed to get a peat-brown trickle of a bath.'[43] Soggy strings hung from the ceiling to direct drips from the leaky roof into pots and pans and jam-jars. The food – often 'frizzled, unappetizing pheasants' – was usually stone-cold because it had to be carried by the butler from a dungeon-like kitchen in a different wing from the dining-room.[44]

As Max Beerbohm remarked of his old school, Charterhouse, Clandeboye was a place one was happier to have been at, than to be at. But several of John's poems – especially his poems about Ireland – show that he relished the desolation of neglected mansions and estates, perhaps as an antidote to the stifling suburban comfort he was used to. Decayed mansions could be delightful, provided one did not have to spend one's life in them. And against the creature discomforts of Clandeboye had to be set John's affection for Basil Dufferin and the cachet of staying in a great country house.

Frizzled pheasants and bad plumbing were not the only hazards at Clandeboye. There was also Basil's mother, Brenda, Marchioness of Dufferin and Ava, who was regarded as more than half-crazy by most of those who knew her. Edward James remembered her 'abject terror' of her servants[45] – a trait confirmed by her portrayal as 'Lady Dunmartin' in *Great Granny Webster*. She claimed to receive messages from the fairies. Elated and jabbering, she would announce that they had chosen her as their queen.[46] Her attitude to her son was unpredictable. She believed that he and his sister Veronica were demon substitutes for her real children, changelings left by evil fairies. At times she would glide into the room with bare feet and a silvery shawl, rush up to her son and embrace him. But these sudden displays of affection were 'more like an aggressive assault than something that one could feel very grateful for'.[47] Basil tried to keep out of her way. In the evenings, he would take Oxford friends to an attic where he had put a couple of chairs and a bamboo table. 'In this room, in which his mother was most unlikely to make one of her swooping fairy-magic appearances, he would get out a bottle of brandy and relax . . .'[48]

Basil could not shield John from Lady Dufferin entirely. As it turned out, that did not matter, because John and the Marchioness quickly made friends. John was used to humouring a mother who, though not mad, suffered from 'chronic nerves' and hypochondria. And he had a streak of zaniness to which the wilder eccentricity of Lady Dufferin could respond. He was quite equal to chatting with her about the Little Folk, just as he had discussed the 'fairy rings' of Ireland with Katharine Tynan. Had not his first poem been about 'fairy folk so wee'? Edward James thought that 'John made a great hit with Brenda Dufferin.'[49] And, according to one account, she may have recommended John for one of his early jobs.

Back in Cornwall in early September 1928, John described the Clandeboye visit to Billy Clonmore: 'Oh how peaceful were those first few days with "the most intelligent conversationalist for his age" – laughing at Edward James's poetry and getting the enormous eyes of Bloody [Dufferin] to roll round in my direction.'[50] John had been moved to compose some verse, which he sent Clonmore:

Lord Ava had enormous eyes
And head of a colossal size,
He rarely laughed and only spoke
To utter some stupendous joke
Which if it were not understood
Was anyhow considered good.
He was so very good at games
He'd even beaten Edward James
And others of the wealthy set
Who fill the pages of Debrett.[51]

'But,' John told Clonmore, 'the peace was rudely shattered by the arrival of two girls in that Classical library, one of them carrying a gramophone record – a new one to be tried. Then we all started to practice [sic] the Charleston. We moved the gramophone into the saloon where there was a parquet floor and tried there. I was miserable. Edward tried to get his own back (not without success) on Bloody & me because we had laughed at his poetry. But it was over in a little while when Edward departed. I found that by altering my plane of thought I could get on quite well with Veronica.' John ended his letter: 'I have got to go out with a lot of jolly girls now – oh God I wish I were dead.'

11

'H.P.'

'... being slightly off his head [he] has written the first chapter of a book of nine chapters no less than seventy-two times. He says the same thing over and over again and rarely completes one of his sentences which suits my style of thinking.'

John Betjeman to Patrick Balfour, 1929

In January 1929 John was appointed private secretary to the Irish politician Sir Horace Plunkett. A letter from Patrick Balfour to his mother, Lady Kinross, suggests that it was Basil Dufferin's mother who obtained him the job.[1] John's own recollection was that the post was procured for him by Plunkett's principal secretary and adviser, Gerald Heard,[2] and Plunkett's diaries confirm this.[3]

10 January 1929
Gerald has found a new secretary who will be able to do literary work. He found McKay [Plunkett's then secretary] quite ready to leave.

24 January 1929
Gerald brought Betchmann [*sic*], a young Oxonian who will take on McKay's job. He is extremely intelligent, knows nothing of my work but will step into McKay's shoes and work under Gerald. He has just graduated at Magdalen, Oxford, in Modern Literature, is working in the City for his father, was offered a job by the *Daily Express* but doesn't like it and will take on my job. He will come at end of next week.[4]

John seems to have been 'shooting a line' to Plunkett. He had not graduated in anything at Oxford, and it is unlikely he would have turned down a job on the *Daily Express* had it been offered. He was, in fact, desperate for a job. Since leaving Oxford, he had been 'knocking at editorial doors in Fleet Street in the hope of a journalistic opening',[5] with no success. His father had obtained him a post with Sedgwick, Collins & Company, marine insurance brokers in Gracechurch Street, City of London, but John found the work dispiriting. 'I just had to go about,' he told Derek Stanford, 'with a little leather wallet, get it signed and then drop into Mecca Cafés for coffee.'[6] So he jumped at the chance of working for Plunkett, who was the kind of aristocrat about whom he and Billy Clonmore enjoyed corresponding: son of the sixteenth Baron Dunsany, an admiral; uncle to the literary eighteenth Baron; cousin of Lord Fingall (and, some said, lover of Lady Fingall); cousin of the poet Emily Lawless, Lord Cloncurry's daughter; and formerly owner of the first motor-car brought to Ireland, a De Dion Bouton.[7]

Plunkett was seventy-five when John began working for him on 2 February 1929, and had only three years to live. John Bowle, who succeeded John as his secretary, described him as 'tall and thin with a little goatee beard: he looked rather like a Van Dyck portrait.'[8] Others noticed a strong resemblance between Plunkett and Sir Roger Casement.

Plunkett, who had been a delicate child, went out to Wyoming in the United States in 1879 to work on a ranch, in the hope that the fresh air would improve his health. He lived rough, rode across the high plains stripped to the waist, drank hard and once won a buggy and harness playing cards. He returned to Ireland, rich and healthy, in 1884. The cowboys had said he could not keep his mind on anything long enough to boil an egg, but he proved them wrong. He decided that the Irish peasants needed organizing, and for the rest of his life he pursued with monomaniac zeal his theory of Cooperative Creameries – the subject with which John was almost exclusively concerned during his service with Plunkett. When Plunkett began his life's work, the Irish peasants were recovering from the famine years and from the bad harvests of the 1880s. But because of improved steamship and railway transport and new preservation processes, crudely blended Irish butter was competing for the English market with excellent butter from Scandinavia. The answer was for the farmers to combine, bringing their produce to big centres where new mechanical cream separators were available, and from which it could be efficiently marketed in bulk.[9] Pessimists told Plunkett the plan was doomed. Irishmen, they said, could conspire but could not combine. By the time John became his secretary, the Cooperative Creameries scheme had been in existence for forty years, and Plunkett was still dissatisfied with its working.

He had early realized that he would only achieve wide currency and powerful backing for his ideas if he entered politics. He was elected for South Dublin in 1892. He called himself a Liberal-Unionist, but he lacked the taste and the guile for party politics, which he regarded as 'tomfoolery', 'shoddy makebelieves', 'silly and wicked'.[10] His life revolved round committees on butter standards, inquiries into irrigation schemes and sugar-beet factories, Empire Marketing Boards, Schools and Rural Economy, Agricultural Economics Research Institutes, Rural Community Councils, Congested Districts, the Allotments and Smallholders Organization Society and Cooperative Congresses. 'Horace Plunkett thinks that his mission in life is to beget leagues,' said the Ulsterman Edward Carson.[11] Plunkett was knighted in 1903 and had enough political clout at that time to obtain baronetcies and knighthoods for those who gave funds to aid the Cooperative cause.

Except for a few extreme republicans and extreme Unionists, most people who knew him agreed that Plunkett was sincere and disinterested. 'He is a good man,' wrote Lady Gregory,[12] '– one feels the presence of goodness in the room.'[13] When Erskine Childers[14] was about to be shot by the British in 1922 he told his wife: 'Horace's face has often appeared before me tonight, I hardly know why except that he has the heroic quality that you have, and he is so deeply connected – and in an inspiring way – with our first big push for Ireland.'[15] Yet there was something unsympathetic about the man. 'Plunkett was a puzzle,' wrote G.B. Shaw. 'He devoted his life to the service of his fellow creatures collectively, and personally he disliked them all.'[16]

Plunkett was, as he admitted to Shaw's wife, 'a born bore'.[17] He probably wrote more letters to the editor of *The Times* than any other politician of his generation. George Moore,[18] who thought that Plunkett 'had the courage of his platitudes'[19] recorded one of his stammering, tedious monologues: 'Er – er – er, the uneconomic man in his economic holding, er – er – er, is a danger to the State, and the economic man in his uneconomic holding, er – er – er, is probably a greater danger, and to relieve the producer of the cost of distribution is the object of the Cooperative movement.'[20] Plunkett's nephew, Lord Dunsany, satirized him as the self-important Charles Peever in his novel *The Story of Mona Sheehy*:

'It has come to my knowledge,' said Charles Peever. 'It has come to my knowledge.' And he liked the phrase so much, so much better it sounded than the mere words 'I have heard' that he repeated it yet again. . . He never said to anyone: 'I want to go to Ireland' or 'I am going to London' but always 'I have to go to such-and-such a place.' The difference may not seem to have been worth making; and yet he never spoke in any other way of his journeys and it left the impression of a conscientious man, serving other people while the rest of us go here and there for our own idle amusement.'[21]

Plunkett had a reputation for driving his assistants relentlessly: J.R. Campbell, who ran the agricultural side of the Irish Department of Agriculture and Technical Instruction, said: 'That man's a vampire. He sucks the blood out of you.'[22] Plunkett was also known as 'a good sacker',[23] and John was among the many who discovered the truth of that. By the time he met Plunkett, the statesman's failings were aggravated by age, illness and drug addiction. Nightly morphine had been prescribed after an attack of pneumonia in 1918 and an operation for cancer of the bladder in 1919; Plunkett was unable to give up the drug. It caused wild fluctuations in his mood. 'We never knew whether we would find him manic or depressive,' said John Bowle.[24]

In 1923, while Plunkett was on one of his 'dashes' to America, Irish republicans showed what they thought of him and his Cooperative Creameries by burning down his house, Kilteragh, at Foxrock, County Dublin.[25] After the fire, Plunkett did most of his writing at The Crest House, Weybridge, Surrey, and in a flat-cum-office at 105 Mount Street, London. The Crest House, which Lady Fingall had found for him,[26] had almost the same ground plan as Kilteragh. Only the views differed: Crystal Palace and Windsor Castle on a clear day, instead of Dublin Bay encircled by mountains. The house also lacked the revolving 'hutch' Plunkett had constructed on the roof of Kilteragh to enable him to sleep in the open air, summer or winter.[27] John was in both the Weybridge house and the London flat a lot; Plunkett did not stay in either for long, but travelled restlessly about England, preaching the gospel of Cooperation.

John's opinion of his new employer is made clear in a letter he wrote Patrick Balfour from the Beresford Hotel, Birchington-on-Sea, Kent, on 10 February 1929:

I am at the moment private secretary to Sir Horace Plunkett who in the early eighties was a big man in agricultural Cooperation. He is still more than keen on it and being slightly off his head has written the first chapter of a book of nine chapters no less than seventy-two times. He says the same thing over and over again and rarely completes one of his sentences which suits my style of thinking. The pay is fair and the food and travelling excellent. He is in bad health at the moment and this hotel is furnished in that Japanese style so popular with the wives of Anglo-Indian colonels who retire to Camberley.[28] There is a ballroom and an 'Oak and Pewter' room which is very pretty.

I was working in the City when Bryan [Guinness]'s wedding occurred and could not accept that invitation I was so proud to possess. If you hear of any article that needs to be written on architectural or obscure religious questions you might let me know as I am now reduced to turning an honest penny to pay off my bills at Oxford . . .

Tinkerty-tonk old boy. I shall be in London on Wednesday and up at least once a week from the Crest House, Weybridge, Surrey (Edwardian old-world) and I hope I shall see you . . .

Love and kisses,
John B.
p.s. I have got a new suit – it is black and very smart and natty.[29]

On the same day as John was writing this account of his master to Balfour, Plunkett was confiding his qualms about John to his diary:

10 February 1929
Tried to break in JB for my work. I think he will like it – only question is – can he stick to any definite work? His mind is most unsettled! This evening he went to Margate and worshipped at some strange sect – Countess of Huntingdon's Connection,[30] I think.[31]

There were few other respites from Plunkett's austere company in Birchington, though John played truant from Cooperative Creameries long enough to visit the grave of the Pre-Raphaelite poet and painter Dante Gabriel Rossetti in Birchington churchyard. He may have been alerted to its existence by Evelyn Waugh's biography of Rossetti (1928).[32]

Back in London, the daily routine was enlivened by visits from Plunkett's debonair principal secretary, Gerald Heard.[33] Then aged forty, Heard was a brilliant conversationalist and a mystic who was later to become a guru in California and a great influence on Aldous Huxley,[34] with whom he sampled mescalin and lysergic acid. He also impressed the young Auden, who dedicated to him his poem 'A Happy New Year' (1932), and believed him to be 'one of the few sane men in a world of mountebanks'.[35]

John Bowle was less impressed by Heard:

> His idea was to get as much money from Plunkett as he could and to do as little work for it as possible. So he supplied Plunkett with a succession of bright young male secretaries, few of whom lasted for more than three months. Always at first Plunkett thought he had found the ideal man for his great enterprises; but he soon became disenchanted with them – and they with him. The only real attraction of the job was that Plunkett had two Chryslers, one a saloon, the other open. When high on morphine he used to drive the saloon round London at breakneck speed. The secretaries were usually allowed to drive the open Chrysler.[36]

John found Heard's conversation too cerebral – 'Gerald Heard but not understood,' he quipped[37] – but he was influenced by him. Heard was a man-about-town, with an entrée to the kind of society John enjoyed: literary parties in Bloomsbury, the high tables of Oxford and Cambridge colleges and fraudulent seances. It was probably Heard who persuaded him to become a Quaker. Heard was not a Quaker himself, but he considered the Society of Friends 'the most promising force for spiritual regeneration within the Christian Church'.[38] John was already attending Quaker meetings in 1929; in 1931 he joined the Society of Friends in St Martin's Lane, London, and he did not formally resign until March 1937.

John remained a friend of Heard long after parting company with Plunkett. In July 1930 Evelyn Waugh noted in his diary: 'John Betjeman brought Gerald Heard to dinner who is said to be the cleverest man in the world. He was well informed about theology and spiritualism. Clearly an active and retentive mind. Personally unattractive.'[39] John would not have agreed with the last part of this assessment. In July 1935, reviewing John Grierson's and Stuart Legg's documentary film *BBC – The Voice of Britain* for the *Evening Standard*, he wrote: 'I think the finest face of [the prominent figures who appeared in the film] is that of the ascetic Gerald Heard, as dolichocephalic and haunting as Conrad Veidt.'[40]

Unfortunately, John did not have the same kind of rapport with

Plunkett as he had with Heard. Plunkett belonged to that minority of people who could not see the point of John because they were deficient in a sense of humour. Plunkett was a man of some wit. There was wisdom as well as wit in his remark that 'Anglo-Irish history is for Englishmen to remember, for Irishmen to forget.'[41] But when he attended a revue at the Hippodrome, it 'was to him no more than a tangle of costly absurdities, and he was puzzled at the general laughter. Had he no sense of humour, he wondered?'[42] The plaintive question reveals him as poles apart from John, the lover of music-halls, who wrote a maudlin valedictory ode to the Crazy Gang after their last performance in 1962.[43]

Plunkett was never content with the drafts his secretaries made of routine circulars and other papers: several revisions were always insisted on. One of his assistants said: 'Lord! that man would amend the Lord's Prayer!'[44] John, who prided himself on his prose, was prepared to have the odd split infinitive pecked out; but to have everything he wrote tampered with and revised was exasperating. Plunkett's diary records his initial high opinion and high hopes of John, and his swift disillusionment:

16 February 1929
With my new Secretary. Told him he must work for me 4 hours a day and I think he will . . .

17 February 1929
. . . I . . . had to fetch John Betjeman from his Meeting House of the Society of Friends at Esher. Four Quakers and he communed (mostly in silence). I have at any rate a good, honest, extremely clever secretary. His working in will be difficult.

18 February 1929
Had to spend today and tomorrow in the country. Working in JB is the thing that matters most. The whole trouble is that he cannot concentrate on anything. He reads a bit of agricultural cooperation stuff and then writes a poem or a story which comes much easier than my dull drab toil.[45]

By 1 March, John had what the doctor considered influenza and was 'very depressed'[46] On 2 March, Plunkett recorded: 'JB more depressed than ever and made me doubt his being able to stand the strain of my rough [draft] which he has not yet faced. I am helpless.' On 3 March Doctor Beare again had to be summoned for John 'who had diagnosed jaundice (rightly as it was found) and suspected cancer on the liver, the result of searching the Encyclopaedia on jaundice! He won't be fit, Beare says, for a fortnight for any serious work.'[47]

John arranged with John Bowle that he should stand in for him as Plunkett's secretary until he himself was well again. Bowle arrived at Mount Street on 5 March and Plunkett, who drove him down to The Crest House that day, wrote in his diary:

> He is no cleverer than the other JB but 2 years older and knows much more of life.
>
> Found the invalid much better. But he won't be able to work for another ten days.[48]

The next day Plunkett recorded:

> Well (?) again and tried to work. The two JBs were a strange contrast – both as clever as can be, the dilettante religious Dutch-Englishman and the Anglo-Saxon son of a corn merchant – gloomy, but now facing facts – between them I have all I want. But their careers not my end must be my main concern.[49]

Plunkett wrote to ask the Master of Balliol his opinion of Bowle, and was told that he 'was like Gibbon (minus the bad doings)', that he 'might have done better' at Oxford and that he would suit Plunkett's work.[50] On 10 March John Betjeman went off to Sezincote for a week of convalescence. On 12 March Bowle travelled to Manchester to be interviewed for a post on the *Manchester Guardian*. He did not get it; and on 16 March he agreed to stay with Plunkett for three months. John Betjeman was now summarily dismissed, and Plunkett even accused him of having deceitfully taken on the secretarial job, when ill, to obtain sick-pay. John, in turn, jumped to the conclusion that Bowle had ingratiated himself with Plunkett and had conspired to replace him permanently. Bowle indignantly denied this, and in a postscript to a letter which Plunkett sent John on 19 March 1929, Sir Horace wrote: 'I hope you will tell John Edward that you wronged him in suggesting that he had in any way been unfriendly to you. I never knew such scrupulous loyalty.'[51] But the episode led to a breach between the two friends, which was not repaired for several months. Probably the truth was that Bowle, who had far more interest in politics and social theories than John, impressed the old man more. At first Bowle, too, was Plunkett's blue-eyed boy. He enjoyed charging about in the open Chrysler and reading, in Mount Street, the works of Havelock Ellis which Gerald Heard had rescued from the Kilteragh fire.[52] But Plunkett was not sorry when Bowle left his service in May 1929. 'He is utterly incapable of any interest in life outside his own future,' he wrote.[53]

Ernest Betjemann was concerned to hear of the new turn in his son's fortunes. It was beginning to seem that John was unable to hold down a job, and that he was going to be a wastrel like Ernest's elder brother Jack. John's relations with his father had in any case reached a new low point during his service with Plunkett. As usual, his financial mismanagement was the *casus belli*, though the underlying causes of estrangement were deeper and more complex. On 16 February 1929 Ernest wrote to John from the Pentonville Road works:

My Dear Boy,
 I have your letter, my opinion of it is poor.
 You thank me, very properly, for paying the accounts, and express regrets for the worry these accounts cause me, as it is so often with you, you however grasp the wrong end.
 You are my son, the matter of the money is not the really most important point, and although I feel rather considerably your desertion, I would do a great deal more for you than pay out money.
 The point that worried me was that you undertook that the £8 a week was to settle everything including lodgings but excluding college bills; if you had not squared up with Landlady I have little doubt you omitted others.
 Now my boy, what I am sorry about and what worried me was you do not mention your breach but only suggest palliatives as a remedy and it was precisely in order that you should see these things in their proper light and realise their importance that I asked you to go to Sedgwick's for 3 months.
 Probably you and others consider that you have done much better by leaving them, I am not of that opinion. I accept your explanation about the Court business[54] – possibly you sent the money, without any reference to the number on the Summons and with a perfectly illegible signature, however I've paid it and enclose copy of my letter to the plaintiff's Solicitors (which they have acknowledged.)
 Newcastle,[55] never very lovely, must have been rather dull, however now you are back again in the 'Sunny South' life will be pleasanter.

We have several pivotal men away, in fact for the last 12 months illness amongst the others has given me a great deal of anxiety and work. The British Industries Exhibition is on. You ought to go.

I have a new Colour, a glaze just like Chinese jade, it is simply lovely, and I am sure will be a great success. Take Sir H. to see the Fair, go in at the Wood Lane Entrance to the Silversmiths' and Jewellers' Section.

I also have invented another Cocktail cabinet – it's so amusing.

Hope you are well, Mother didn't give a very good account of you in that respect.[56]

Ernest wrote to John again on 22 February:

Dear John,
Mother is very ill with pleurisy and bronchitis, it was impossible to put up Bowles [John Bowle], the night nurse has your room. [Dr] Macmanus says she requires every care and attention, no worry, speaks seriously of her condition . . .

She has not been well for some time, and I know how she has worried about you and your apparent carelessness. I ask you again to be very careful of her feelings in all things.

Sorry you find your work a bore. I consider you fortunate in obtaining what with board and lodging is the equivalent of £450 to £500 a year, and my advice to you is to stick to the work all you can and hold the position.

Why do you refer to Sir Horace as 'H.P.'? He has done much and such reference seems to me to be stupidly schoolboyish. I make the same comment on your addressing me as 'Ernie'. These, John, are *serious* times, serious for us, *very*, and a less flippant attitude more sensible . . .
Your affectionate Father,
Ernest Betjemann.[57]

This letter infuriated John. He sat down and wrote a passionately indignant reply. It was never sent, but remained among his private papers. Across the top he scrawled: 'What I ought to have said in reply.'

The Crest House,
St George's Hill,
Weybridge.

25 - 2 - 29

Dear Father,
I imagine it is your anxiety over mother that makes you

write me a letter like the one you wrote on Saturday. It seems rather caddish to try to put the blame on me because mother is ill. As far as I remember you said to me some weeks ago that you were going to send her to the South of France. Since you do not have to pay for the extravagance of a son I think you might have afforded it. I do not think I can forgive your inferences. You can hardly think I am not dreadfully worried about mother. What I should have expected from you would have been a letter telling me details about her illness and offering something to cheer us both up, in the way of a hopeful sentence. Instead you seem to be an alarmist.

It is odd, too, that while you insist on the 'seriousness' of the times, half your letter consists of condemnations of the most trivial points in my remarks to you. I will answer them.

In point of fact I do not really find my work a bore at all. You and I at one time laughed about the abstruseness of agricultural co-operation.

A knickname [sic] is an expression of affection and I am very fond of the old thing and perfectly content. It will be quite simple to refrain from calling you 'Ernie'.

I do not think that what is said or written matters, but what is felt. Often most 'serious' feelings are expressed in a joke. I very rarely talk about what I really feel.

I have got flu and am in bed with it so I cannot be up today.

Yours
John B.[58]

The news that John's illness had been diagnosed as jaundice brought a more sympathetic letter from Church Street, dated 8 March. Ernest was sorry that John was not yet well enough to go to Sezincote, where he had hoped he would be enjoying the spring sunshine by now. 'Somehow or other we don't seem to have hit upon how to keep you fit . . . Don't you think it would be a good plan to be what Mother would call "thoroughly overhauled" and then follow out instructions?'[59] John's mother was still in bed, 'rather white, but making progress, she will not get right until she can go away'.[60]

Then came the disturbing news that John had been dismissed. Ernest decided to visit Plunkett to find out for himself what had gone wrong. Plunkett wrote in his diary for 17 March 1929:

Ernest Betjemann, father of JB, came to confer with me about his son who ought never to have taken on my job, in order to hold it while sick, got John Bowle (who can do it) and must now leave. The father is 10 years my junior. He is a manufacturer in the luxuries which adorn the Bond Street shop windows. Lives a double life, finds his staff no longer willing to carry on without an understanding as to their future interest (which E.B. wants JB to inherit but JB can't and won't) and practically asked me to help him in his perplexities. A bounder of the worst kind! I must try to help the boy to get away from the father – but how?[61]

Plunkett seems to have convinced Ernest that John's dismissal was well merited. Ernest now refused to support John: he must 'learn to stand on his own two feet'. He may have hoped that economic necessity would eventually force John back into the family firm. As a temporary measure while looking for another job, John moved into a house at 28 Great Ormond Street, London, which Hugh Gaitskell was sharing with Lionel Perry. He wrote to Plunkett asking whether he could help get him into journalism. (Sir Horace had some experience of journalism: he had once owned the *Dublin Daily Express*.)

Plunkett replied from Weybridge on 19 March:

Dear J.B.,
        I was with Gerald Heard this morning and unfortunately left your letter with him, but I think I remember its contents. Your things will be taken to 28 Great Ormonde [*sic*] St tomorrow and you are to send me keys.

Regarding your future plans for work, of course I shall be glad to help in any way I can. I have made inquiries about journalism and, like every other career in this overcrowded country it seems to be extremely difficult to get into. The only people I know in that galere are Garvin and C.P. Scott. The former would have no regular work as he only runs a Weekly and the latter Bowle's experience [with the *Manchester Guardian*] shows it would be useless to approach. Beyond question the provincial press is the best to begin with and if you can get on the staff of the Portsmouth paper, you should certainly get a start there. I am convinced that, even if I had journalistic connections and influences, you would find that you would have to make a very big effort of your own to hold the initial job . . .

Casual journalism has the defect that one soon comes to the end of the real goods one has to offer and the pay to all who have not made a name is at a starvation rate. So I think you told me of the contributions you had sent to the lighter journals . . .[62]

Like so much that Sir Horace had to say, this was kindly meant, sententious and useless. As crime reporters say of the police, he offered 'every assistance short of actual help'. Whatever the possibilities in Portsmouth may have been, they evidently came to nothing. So John once more joined the queue of Oxford and Cambridge down-and-outs at the door of Gabbitas-Thring, scholastic agents. They again found him employment as a preparatory school master, this time at Heddon Court, Cockfosters, at East Barnet on the northern outskirts of London. He was returning to Hertfordshire, county of Lionel Edwards[63] skies and 'mildly undistinguished hills',[64] the scene of his boyhood humiliations in shooting.

12 (*above*) Some of the
childhood friends John
mentioned in his poem
'Trebetherick': *foreground*,
John Walsham; *back row, left
to right*, Alastair Adams,
Ralph Adams, Biddy Walsham

13 T. S. Eliot taught John at
Highgate Junior School in
1916. John showed him *The
Best Poems of Betjeman*.

14 John (*top centre*) at Marlborough.

15 Anthony Blunt, the future art historian and spy, at Marlborough.

16 John contributed to *The Heretick*, a Marlborough magazine founded as a rival to the official school magazine, *The Marlburian*. (John Bowle designed the anti-hearty cover.) *The Heretick* was banned after two issues when parents complained about an article by Anthony Blunt.

THE HERETICK

"UPON PHILISTIA WILL I TRIUMPH"

17 John about 1925, the year he went up to Magdalen.

18 The fifteenth-century tower of Magdalen College, Oxford, by the River Cherwell. John was at the college from 1925 to 1928.

19 John striking a Wildean pose in 1928.

20 Edward James, the publisher of John's first book, *Mount Zion* (1931): a portrait by Yevonde on the cover of James's book of poems *The Bones of My Hand* (Oxford University Press, 1938).

21 John Edward Bowle, historian. A friend of John's at Marlborough and Oxford, he shared rooms with him in London in 1930.

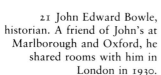

22 (*above left*) Lord Clonmore
(later Earl of Wicklow). 'He
looked exactly like the Mad
Hatter,' said John Bowle. 'He *was*
the Mad Hatter.' Evelyn Waugh
credited Clonmore with 'a
Christian piety that was unique
among us'.

23 (*above*) Lionel Perry came up
to Magdalen the year before John.
He introduced him to Lord
Clonmore and others who were to
be John's friends for life. In 1929
Perry shared a London flat with
Hugh Gaitskell and John.

24 (*left*) Pierce Synnott invited
John to his Irish mansion,
Furness, Naas, in 1926.

25 Maurice Bowra, Dean of Wadham College, Oxford, a pencil portrait by Henry Lamb, 1931. John believed that 'Maurice Bowra's company/Taught me far more than all my tutors did.'

26 W. H. Auden aged twenty-two, by Cecil Beaton.

27 John, in a Magdalen College blazer, as an assistant master at Thorpe House School, Gerrard's Cross, in 1928.

28 John at Little Compton, the home of Camilla Russell.

29 Lady Mary St Clair-Erskine (now Lady Mary Dunn). John proposed to her unsuccessfully in the winter of 1929–30.

30 (*above*) Pamela Mitford and her motor-car in Ludgershall. John, who was much attracted to her, called her 'Miss Pam', which was what the cowmen on Bryan Guinness's farm called her.

31 At Pakenham Hall in 1931: *left to right*, Lady Pansy Lamb, Maurice Bowra, Elizabeth Harman (now Lady Longford), John Betjeman, Henry Lamb, Evelyn Waugh, Christine Longford.

HEDDON COURT

You will remember these schooldays as the happiest time of your life.

Evelyn Waugh to John Betjeman, *c.* 1929

Gabbitas-Thring's record card shows that John worked at Heddon Court from April 1929 to July 1930.[1] His salary had risen from the £90 he earned at Thorpe House, to £180. To get the job, he had to pretend to be competent at cricket – as he recalled in his poem 'Cricket Master':

> 'The sort of man we want must be prepared
> To take our first eleven. Many boys
> From last year's team are with us. You will find
> Their bowling's pretty good and they are keen.'
> 'And so am I, Sir, very keen indeed.'
> Oh, where's mid-on? And what is silly point?
> Do six balls make an over? Help me, God!
> 'Of course you'll get some first-class cricket too:
> The MCC send down an A team here.'
> My bluff had worked . . .

In a BBC television interview with Michael Parkinson in 1973, John again described this period of his life, recalling how in desperation he bought a Letts' Schoolboy's Diary 'to mug up the names of places on the field'. He added: 'I was soon found out and given the worst team to coach: the best one went to another master.'[2]

Heddon Court was one of a cluster of moderately grand houses and estates in East Barnet. Among them was Trevor Park (formerly Church Hill House) from which Lady Arabella Stuart had made her escape in man's clothing in 1611. John was more interested in a later resident of Trevor Park, Letitia Elizabeth Landon, who had lived there with her uncle between 1809 and 1815. As 'L.E.L.' she had written poems about troubadours for the *Drawing Room Scrapbook*, and novels such as *Ethel Churchill* (1837) before her death by prussic acid in Cape Coast Castle, West Africa, in 1838.[3] A greater poet had lived in East Barnet Manor – James Thomson, author of *The Seasons*, who completed his 'Winter' there while serving as tutor to the second Earl of Haddington. Heddon Court was not least among the houses of East Barnet. The original building on the site had been called Mount Pleasant. In 1635 it was tenanted by Elias Ashmole, the antiquary, after whom the Ashmolean Museum in Oxford is named.[4] In the 1750s the house's name was changed to Belmont.

Heddon Court preparatory school was founded in Hampstead in the 1890s by Henry Frampton Stallard, an ex-Indian Army officer who looked like Lord Baden-Powell and was obsessively interested in scouting. The school had strong links with Westminster School, and at Heddon Court the Westminster system known as 'Substance and Shadow' was in force: a new boy was allotted a mentor-protector from among the older boys who, like medieval whipping-boys, took the punishments for the neophyte's misdeeds. Stallard's favoured method of punishment was feelingly described by the naturalist Gavin Maxwell, who was a pupil at Heddon Court just before John arrived there: 'We were caught fighting once, by the matron, and Mr Stallard beat us both with a No. 4 cricket bat on our bare buttocks, in his horrible pipe-smelling study . . .'[5]

In the 1920s the school moved out to Cockfosters; Belmont was greatly enlarged and renamed Heddon Court. Stallard retired in 1927 and the school was bought by a rich Old Etonian called John Humphrey Hope. He had been an usher (assistant master) at Eton. He also had a mysterious thespian past. Sir John Addis, a Heddon Court pupil who later became British Ambassador to China, recalled: 'Hope had on his desk a striking photograph of himself as the King in *Hamlet* – which he must have done very well! He was very keen on acting in the school, and did productions. With the wisdom of hindsight, there was clearly something a little odd about him, as he was immensely nervous on these dramatic occasions – he'd be *pouring* with sweat.'[6]

It was also disconcerting that Hope was a communist. David Soltau, a pupil of John's, remembered that 'After visits to Russia,

Hope would come back and say how marvellous the Communists were, which of course did not go down well with most of the parents.'[7] Under Hope's influence, John became a 'parlour pink'. 'Palme Dutt, Rust and Campbell were my new leaders. I bought *Das Kapital* by Marx in English translation, but could never get beyond the first two paragraphs. I subscribed to the *Worker's Weekly* and liked to be seen reading it in public transport.'[8] But how were these left-wing attitudes (or poses) to be reconciled with his Anglo-Catholicism? John thought he had found the answer in the teaching of Conrad Noel, the Red Vicar of Thaxted, 'with his lovely incense-laden, banner-hung, marigold-decorated church, with its folk-dancing and hand weaving, going hand-in-hand with joyous religion, in what was then unspoiled country'.[9] John's week-end visits to Noel's Thaxted reawakened his interest in medieval churches. 'This time I visited them not just for their architecture, but also for their churchmanship.'[10]

In spite of his radical politics, Hope did not change the regimen at Heddon Court much. He even continued the tradition of cricket-bat beatings.[11] Also at variance with his professed communism was the luxury in which he and his family lived. They occupied the fine Georgian house which was the core of the school buildings. 'The Hopes lived in great style,' David Soltau said, 'complete with a butler and full supporting staff.'[12] Paul Miller, a Betjeman pupil who became a Canon Resident and Precentor of Derby Cathedral, disliked Hope. 'Because he was an agnostic and freethinker, I think he felt I came from a frowsty Protestant background and reflected it.'[13] But Canon Miller too had pleasant memories of the Hopes' luxurious menage:

> When I read Osbert Sitwell's description of the neighbouring prep school he was at, Ludgrove, and the hateful headmaster and his sister, I thought, 'Well, Mrs Hope's drawing-room was lovely, it really was enchanting.' She did the flowers very well. There were good paintings, silver, china. On Saturdays, which was the day parents came, Mrs Hope received very lavishly. She would be dispensing tea and cream cakes and the assistant masters, including John Betjeman, would come and chat to the parents. The boys were only allowed one piece of cake, but the parents would smuggle out more for us.[14]

Like her husband, Mrs Hope was not a popular figure, though she was indulgent enough to let the boys chant 'Good-night, Mrs Soap!' when she toured the dormitories at bedtime. James Orr, a pupil of John's who became private secretary to Prince Philip, said, 'We didn't like her much. She had awful false teeth and used to go *"Awf, awf, awf"* – laughter without mirth, you know what I mean?'[15]

The Hopes had a daughter, Ann, who was four when John came to the school. Paul Miller remembered:

> John Betjeman hung round the Hopes' little girl, whom he used to call 'Ă – *ner* – *ner*' because I suppose at some time or another she had told him that was how she spelt her name. But he victimized that child. . . Ann developed a sort of defence, which was to intone various phrases, one of which was 'Silly Mister Bee!' He would go up to her curling his fingers like a tiger's claws and saying 'Ă – *ner* – *ner!*' And she would say: 'Silly Mister Bee!'[16]

Ann Hope (now Mrs Wolff) has no fond memories of John, on whom she based an unlikeable character in her 1985 novel about a prep-school, *The Grand Master Plan*.[17] She recalls:

> I first knew him when I was four years old, and learning to read. I was being taught by a governess at home (i.e. Heddon Court), and she had an advanced technique of teaching the alphabet, not A ae, B bee, C see, but phonetically. So when I first met John Betjeman on the stairs, and he asked me what my name was, I, having just learnt to spell my name, said proudly, 'ă – n – n.' He screamed with laughter and shouted out, 'hark to the trains they go ă – ner – ner.' I was much put out by this and went to my mother, and she said off-handedly that I should find something to say back to him. So when I next met him I shouted at him 'Hark to the bells they go Silly-Mr-Bee, Silly-Mr-Bee.' Thereafter we chanted these phrases at each other.[18] And these were not fun exchanges, we were both in vicious earnest.
>
> In my book I loosely base the character of the English master on him, and I imply that he, the master, was having a romantic relationship with my mother – that is, the character of my mother in the book. I thought this up while trying to explain to myself why John Betjeman picked on me in reality. He was merciless towards me. I do not forget his sideways grin, changing to a watery giggle, changing to a cackle of laughter, all delivered with a mocking sneer. All the time I knew him he gave the impression of someone who has

early looked closely at life and has profoundly despaired, and from then on he was filling in time until his death. He later mellowed, but at Heddon Court he seemed to be looking for a target on which to vent his unhappiness, e.g. me. His poems in *Mount Zion* [1931] are not the cute nostalgia which they later became, but a sick hatred of all the persons in them, a lashing-out coated in a Twenties-style jocularity.[19]

Mrs Wolff describes her father as 'pompous and correct . . . not a dedicated headmaster, but an educated man turning his hand to a profession'.[20] He does not sound a sympathetic character, but he and John were well-disposed towards each other. 'Hope got on very well, I thought, with Betjeman,' James Orr said. 'He realized Betjeman's ability, book-wise. They were invariably looking at books together walking up and down the passage. Hope hated Eton almost as much as John hated Marlborough. He told me he never went to the Eton-Harrow match because he met so many people he didn't want to meet.'[21] Vera Spencer-Clarke (now Mrs Moule), the gym mistress mentioned in 'Cricket Master', agreed:

'Huffy' Hope loved John. They saw eye to eye. I came across a letter of Huffy Hope's in which he says, 'I was in Hyde Park the other day, and I saw a lump of something, and I followed it for a while, and it moved, and so I prodded it with my stick, when it invited me to lunch' – never mentioning John's name, but obviously it was he, because John used to go round London in the shabbiest old clothes imaginable, getting copy.[22]

Kenric Rice, one of John's pupils, noted that 'John used to follow Hope some Sundays when Hope put on his filthy old mac and got on a soapbox at Hyde Park Corner to harangue the public about communism.'[23] In 1933 Hope and his wife were witnesses at John's wedding – three years after John had left the school and one year after Hope, with capitalist canniness, had sold the Heddon Court estate for building development.

John made a less favourable impression on Walter Summers who, though a much older man than Hope, was his junior partner in the school. Summers had been a pillar of the Stallard regime. He enjoyed organizing bloody boxing matches between the boys, and was given to uplifting aphorisms such as: 'The two R's are much more important than the three R's: Responsibility and Reliability.'[24] In 'Cricket Master', where Summers is called 'Winters', John describes his first meeting with him:

> I sought the common-room,
> Of last term's pipe-smoke faintly redolent.
> It waited empty with its worn arm-chairs
> For senior bums to mine, when in there came
> A fierce old eagle in whose piercing eye
> I saw that instant-registered dislike
> For all unhealthy aesthetes such as I.

Summers asked John and the other new master, Huxtable (whom John calls 'Barnstaple'), out for a practice in the nets. After John had failed dismally to stand up to a hail of balls from both men, he was left alone with Huxtable among the ash-trays of the common-room.

> He murmured in his soft West-country tones:
> 'D'you know what Winters told me, Betjeman?
> *He didn't think you'd ever held a bat.*'

Vera Moule thought that 'John was the bane of Summers's life, absolutely. When they were on duty on a Sunday, old Summers used to be in his sitting-room, which overlooked the courtyard. All the boys had to go through there. And suddenly, there would be a *tearing* crowd of boys going through, and he would go out and say: "Hrrrrumph! *Betjeman* on duty." '[25]

John 'got across' most of the other masters, too. They regarded him as a subversive influence, and in particular they were annoyed to hear that he mimicked them in front of the boys. Occasionally they took their revenge. The staff had their evening meal at a High Table, set apart from the boys, while the Hopes dined in their own quarters. 'And if John was beginning to be a bit much for some of the staff who didn't like him,' Vera Moule said, 'they would rap on the service-hatch, and when old Shipton the butler opened it, thinking they wanted the next course passed through, they would pick John up bodily and shove him through. Old Shipton, he used to get pretty mad.'[26]

Some echoes of the antagonism between John and the other staff are found in his letters of this time to Patrick Balfour.

9 December 1929: I was very rude to one of the mistresses today. There is rather a bust up.[27]

10 February 1930: I do apologise for the regrettable business of tonight. The truth of it is there has been rather a row with Godfrey and I am morally obliged to take preparation in order to keep my own end up. It is not so much a case of Perrin and Traill[28] as you would think but rather that he has turned out to be the only person able to take prep tonight and he is unwilling to do it. Blast his colossal ego . . .[29]

Vera Moule, John's main ally among the staff, shared his feelings about Godfrey. 'He was horrible – ill-mannered and gauche,' she said.[30] He was the one master she did not invite to her wedding; and when he asked her why, she replied, 'Because I didn't want you.' He had mortally offended her by suggesting that Stallard should have appointed an army sergeant to put the boys through physical jerks, not a gym mistress with fancy training in physiology, pathology and hygiene.

Vera was one of those dominant sports-girls to whom John was attracted. He was impressed when she threw to the ground the games master, Jack Malden, who had playfully gripped her wrist as she was about to take a cup of tea.[31] She, in turn, thought John fascinating. 'There was such a depth there. And he was very, very funny.' She had become engaged to another master, Walter Moule, in 1927, but in that year he had gone out to Maseru, Basutoland (now Lesotho), as a school inspector ('because it was impossible to get married on a prep school master's salary') and had advised his fiancée, 'Take off your ring and have a fling!' Vera took the limited advantage of this invitation that was intended, and she and John engaged in a delightful and innocent flirtation. He wrote her several poems, which she has preserved. In most of them he compares himself with the absent Walter Moule (whose surname is pronounced 'Mole', though John takes the poet's licence to rhyme it either with 'pole' or with 'pool'.) Vera had a photograph of Walter in her bedroom. 'When I went back one day, one of John had been put in its place. And he found one of me and put it up in his room. It was all a lot of nonsense.' Even so, she was secretly pleased to hear that John had asked the headmaster's wife 'whether there was any . . . er . . . *hope*'.[32]

The poem the Moules like best is a parody of Kipling. 'John just went off [Vera Moule recalled], said "I'm going to write you a poem," and came back with this in about ten minutes.' The ten-verse poem began:

KIPLING ON DIVORCE

Yus, she's a regular lady,
Yus, she's a regular sport
                    Chorus
    Oh gawd 'ow she'd look just lovely,
    Trippin' it into the court.

'Er in a smart divorce case,
'Im, were a blinking fool,
With pipe, and strong and silent,
By the name of Mister Moule.

He filed a petition agin her
For the time when he was away,
Keeping the old flag flyin'
In old Basuto Bay.

Lickin' the damned old niggers,
Showin' them 'ow we won
For England the name o' justice –
Shootin' them down with a gun.

'Eddication', 'e called it –
Well, blimey, I know his sort;
O gawd 'ow she looked just lovely,
Trippin' it into court.

Then there's the other feller –
A yeller-faced sort o' bloke
A thunderin' half-wit poet,
Who laughed at the judge's joke . . .[33]

Another of the poems was written when John picked off Vera's
desk a scrap of paper printed 'PLEASE SEND TO . . .' which somebody had cut off a bill to save paper. On the spot, John scrawled on
the sheet eight lines of verse.

PLEASE SEND TO Vera, by return of post,
A portrait of the man she loves the most;
Is he a fellow who, with pipe in hand,
Teaches the natives in Basutoland?
Is he a silent, strong-limbed sort of man,

Whose sportsmanship is thorough as his tan?
Was he at Lancing?[34] No, I am appalled
He's elegant, aesthetic too, and bald.[35]

'He wrote those lines as quickly as I've just read them,' said Vera Moule.

The next poem was written to Vera 'when John first started taking notice of me. He hadn't been in the place more than a few weeks'.

As I was walking through the park
I met Miss Vera Spencer-Clarke;
And since I am the sort of chap
Who's always smart in a mishap,
I said to her, with eyes aflame,
'Now have I met you? What's your name?'
She answered, elegant and proud,
'I do not like the common crowd.'
Not unrebuffed, I further said:
'Now are you yet in wedlock wed?'
What change suffused her noble brow;
She was no simple Vera now,
But like a man she swung her arms,
And masculine became her charms;
With heavy stride she forward strode
And threw my body on the road.
But still I'm praying for the soul
And body too, of Mr Moule.[36]

At breakfast, some of the staff sat with the headmaster (and sometimes the headmaster's wife) at High Table; the rest were strategically disposed at the boys' tables across the hall. The teachers sat at High Table one week, and on a boys' table the next. Vera Moule recalled:

If John Betjeman was down the room, he was always at the next table to me, whispering to the boys, 'Isn't she lovely!' I couldn't get on with the meals because of him. But if we were sitting at the High Table, old Shipton, the rather grand butler, would ask, 'What would you like for breakfast?' – and then John would start. He'd say, 'What would you like this morning? What style would you like today, Tennyson or a hymn tune?' And I would say, 'Not *now*, John, please.' But that did not stop him, and here is one of the poems he wrote off the cuff. It is signed 'Yours sincerely, A.C. Swinburne'.[37]

> Who is this, with her Spanish features,
>   Shown up bright by her dark brown hair?
> Lithe and lissom like God's good creatures
>   That float and flit in the noonday air.
>
> What is that which her frame is wearing?
>   Deepest navy and bluest serge
> Can she speak, for is she not sharing
>   With such as me an erotic urge?
>
> For I am humble, and do not wash much,
>   She is sturdy and does not too;
> She likes soft drinks and a lemon squash much,
>   More than a chap like me could do.
>
> Always healthy and quite in training,
>   What would she think of the debauchee?
> She much prefers (and I'm not complaining)
>   Mr Moule to a chap like me.
>
> Someone healthy, who's fond of reading,
>   And fond of sport, and keen and cool,
> From a public school and its high-class breeding,
>   Fair, square and upright Mr Moule.[38]

In that poem, Walter Moule is given the victory; but in the one which follows, John seems to be gaining ground, and Vera is made to say of him –

> He is decadent, I hate him:
>   I despise him, Heaven above,
> Help me, help me, now I wait him –
>   Irresistible is love.[39]

In the next poem, John seems even nearer to triumphing over his rival. 'This,' said Vera Moule, 'is what he had the cheek to send to my future father-in-law, who was in a nursing-home in London having an operation on his eyes.'

Come cease from all debating
 And vain poetic strife;
Miss Zeglio[40] is waiting
 With sharp and whetted knife
 To take away your life.

And Vera too deceiving
 The faithful heart she stole,
Forgetful of her grieving
 Is pouring out her soul
 No more to Walter Moule.

When gloom is round your thinking,
 And gauze is round your eyes,
Then there will be no winking
 But when they loose the ties,
 Oh what a sad surprise!

Poor Walter as he ponders
 A few salt tears will shed,
Where lone Basuto wanders
 Along her chalky bed:
 Miss Vera will have fled,
 And married me instead.[41]

What did her father-in-law think of that?

He loved it! My father-in-law used to write poems, and he was very keen to meet John, but he didn't meet him till this occasion. His eyes were bandaged by that time, and I took John to visit him. We had to go on the Inner Circle, and of course he had to have Archie the teddy-bear on his lap, with everybody staring. He used to bring him out of his little brief-case and sit him up on his lap and would talk to him: 'Now, Archie, you know where we are? We're in an Underground; some people call them "tubes". See that couple over there? They're looking at you. Behave!' And he'd go on like that throughout the journey, and although I enjoyed it I used to be acutely embarrassed. Well, the day we went to see my father-in-law at the Sir John Lister Nursing Home, we had to go on the Inner Circle; and John in a loud voice and cockney accent shouted 'EUSTON ROAD!'[42]

Vera made one journey with John which was still more embarrassing – the hair-raising ride in Huxtable's bull-nosed Morris which ended in the desecration of the school's holy-of-holies, the cricket pitch, as described in 'Cricket Master'. The true events of that evening, recounted by Vera, were somewhat different from those described in the poem. The three teachers did not drive straight back to the school from the Cock Inn at Cockfosters. First they drove on to Haringey greyhound stadium, where they spent half an hour and each won a pound – 'which, in those days, was something'.

So we got in the car, and chased up Piccadilly. And there we went into a pub, and John said, 'You'd better sit there,' and leaving me and Huxtable he went to the counter. He banged on the counter and decided what he wanted to drink, and didn't take any more notice of me or Huxtable. And then he listened to the conversation of some men at the side of him. I don't know what they were talking about, but he said in a rough voice, 'Well, my son's in a school, and they want 'im to learn Lat'n 'n' Greek. Now what's the use of Lat'n and Greek to a son of mine?' And they asked him, 'What do you do?' and he said 'I'm in *lino*.' So they carried on the conversation for quite a little while. Whether the men were taken in or not, I don't know. Screamingly funny. And when we came away from there, he tied a kipper on the front of the car, so that when the car started, we stank to high heaven.

Well, having reached Heddon Court rather late, we went up the stony drive and we zig-zagged across the cricket pitch, which had been prepared ready for this wonderful match – everybody telling Huxtable, '*Don't* go across there! *Don't* go across there!' But he did. He landed again on the stony drive, and decided to go *straight* for a brick wall that was higher than this room – the boundary of the peach garden. And John honestly thought that he was going into it, he was so drunk; and John yelled out: 'Remember you've got a lady in the car!' And Huxtable pulled up about two inches from the wall. But of course Huxtable got the sack, and then, as John says in the poem, he himself survived for three more terms.[43]

Vera Moule has a photograph of John on his knees, supposedly 'proposing' to her, and another on which he has written 'The accepted fact'. But she also has a photograph of him, unusually dapper in morning suit and tall hat, accompanying Mr and Mrs

Hope to her wedding (at which he made a speech) on 11 April 1931. Shortly after the marriage and the Moules' honeymoon in Torquay, he went to stay with them in their new home in St Luke's Avenue, Maidstone, Kent. The poetic badinage continued. They all went out to a pub one evening, and while they sat there, John took out some paper and wrote two poems. The first, headed 'A Funny Poem by Clever John Betjeman', ends:

> But now she cannot love me more
> With all the love of heretofore,
> Her Walter too must now regret
> The lithe Basuto's blackest jet,
> And passionate and warm and dark,
> And cling instead to Vera Clarke,
> Who too regrets, now love is cool,
> That she is Vera Spencer Moule.[44]

The second poem, headed 'Another Funny Poem by Clever John Betjeman', begins:

> Give me a tongue to praise without rebukes
> The avenue behind the new St Luke's;
> And let me see, behind the green-stained glass,
> Thy face, my Vera, curly-headed lass.[45]

In the poem, John plots to kill Walter Moule, to convince Vera that 'I was once a man':

> Then will I plunge, by passion rift apart,
> This knife into your Walter Riddel's heart.
> Then will we soon see, in the *Daily Sketch*,
> That you are Frances Vera Spencer-Betj.[46]

When Vera Moule went to see old Mr Stallard in Reigate after his retirement, she gave him an enthusiastic description of John. 'I'd love to have had that man on my staff!' he exclaimed but, as she later commented, 'Of course he wouldn't: Indian Army wouldn't have gone with John at all.'[47] Sir Jasper Hollom – a Betjeman pupil who later 'signed the banknotes' as Chief Cashier of the Bank of England – thought that 'Stallard would never conceivably have employed him for a moment: his concept of what it was proper to expose the youth of the nation to, was quite, quite different from Hope's.'[48] Certainly John burst on to the scene at Heddon Court as a new phenomenon. Hollom found that 'his general approach to life came as something which was quite remarkably fresh, and extraordinary, and hence liberating.'

> I mean, he had a developed sense of the absurd and a familiarity with living with the absurd – he almost cultivated the absurd as a household pet – that was totally alien to the Stallard regime which was *mens sana* and committed to the Boy Scout movement, with Baden-Powell as the guiding light. It was all very traditional, very forecastable, it was, I suppose one would have thought in those days, admirably set on tramlines. But with Betjeman, of course, the one thing you could be sure of was that nothing would run on established and expected lines.[49]

Sir John Addis was not himself taught by John, but his brother Richard was. Sir John recalled: 'Dick was immensely exhilarated by this unusual master, and told us stories about his English lessons. Sometimes John wouldn't be standing at his desk, or sitting in his chair, but he'd teach lying on the floor. And on other occasions the class would be dutifully waiting for Mr Betjeman to arrive, and instead of walking in through the door, he'd come in through the window.'[50] John's clothes also excited comment. 'He came down to breakfast in a yellow tie, which caused a great stir,' recalled Dr George Gomez, another pupil. 'And he had Oxford bags, which were new to us.'[51] Sir John Addis remembered: 'He had very long hair at the back, which we thought rather strange. One simply wouldn't notice that, now. But it was incredibly long for then.'[52]

Then there were the smart Oxford friends who visited John at weekends, such as Patrick Balfour, Edward James and the Marquess of Dufferin and Ava. Among them was Evelyn Waugh, who had also served his turn as a private schoolmaster, and told him, not entirely facetiously. 'You will remember these schooldays as the happiest time of your life.'[53] In a BBC recording that John made for Waugh's biographer Christopher Sykes, he told how he and Waugh had lunch together at a Barnet hotel where they drank 'a lot of very strong beer, and I was so drunk when I came back that I wasn't able to take the game of football, and the boys kindly took me up to my room and never said anything about it. That was the effect Evelyn had on my schoolmastering, the only one I remember. But he felt that just being a schoolmaster was rockingly funny, and I remember him telling me, when I was offered a job on *The Architectural Review*: "Don't take it. You'll never laugh as much as you do now." And he was quite right, of course.'[54]

The other staff were not just carping or being 'stuffy' when they complained of John's subversive influence. He *was* subversive. Sir Jasper Hollom was struck by the way in which John provided diversions for himself on a dull Sunday afternoon, 'when a lot of small boys had to be pushed out to take fresh air and exercise, and all they could do was admire the dripping rhododendron bushes'. John's approach was different from any other master's. 'Anybody else would have started with some degree of order; he started with the idea of introducing some degree of *dis*order – actually in a totally controlled way (though it wasn't visible as being controlled) which caught the imagination of the young, they had never found anything as amusing before in their lives.'[55]

One 'disorder' which got memorably out of hand is recalled by nearly all John's ex-pupils. He organized a riot, which centred on the 'bothie', a gardener's cottage in the angle between two walls, with one room upstairs and one down. No campaign more momentous had been fought in the area since the Battle of Barnet, 1471, when Warwick the Kingmaker was slain. Canon Paul Miller remembers:

> One Sunday afternoon Betjeman set off with his court, who were mostly sixth-form – including Oxley-Parker, perhaps [Alan] Nightingale – and they somehow got into the upstairs room of the bothie and were peering out of the window and making faces at people down below. And somebody started throwing acorns, conkers and finally apples, which Betjeman and his court threw back. Very soon the word got round that the bothie was under siege; so little boys came from every direction, and so it was Betjeman and his court versus the rest of the school. The battle 'escalated' and the pace became quite fast – I remember it really got quite exciting, because there were apples and other missiles flying through the air, and Betjeman was getting more and more excited. Some windows

were broken. At a certain point, the inevitable Mr Summers appeared, and Betjeman was led away. After that it was rumoured that somebody had seen him, through a window, in tears. And then it was rumoured that he had got the sack, and a hush fell over the school. But he had not been sacked. I would guess it was autumn 1929 that that happened.[56]

From a letter of David Soltau to his parents, we know that the battle took place in September 1929.[57] Summers referred to the sixth-form ringleaders, in Assembly, as 'the Six Cads'. They were made to stand outside the headmaster's door during every break. 'But Betjeman was *the* ringleader!' said George Gomez. 'Incredible, that in the hierarchy of Them and Us, he should be one of Us.'[58] John's good relations with Hope protected him from the fate of Huxtable. As Sir Jasper Hollom said, 'Disgrace came naturally to John Betjeman: there was a magnetic attraction between him and disgrace. But one always felt that he had a staunch ally in Hope, and so the risks weren't very great.'

Sir Jasper described another of John's Sunday afternoon ploys:

There was a long frontage on the road past Heddon Court, along which a certain amount of traffic and a few buses went. One of his ideas to keep small boys reasonably occupied and yet amused on a Sunday afternoon was to go out, conceal a quantity of small boys in the bushes, fling himself down in an artistic heap on the road as one who had been run over; wait till a bus came along, when everybody would climb out to rescue him, whereupon he leaped up and scampered away into the bushes, and a lot of jeering boys appeared to the discomfort of the would-be Samaritans. It was the sort of thing which immensely endeared him to the boys.[59]

The prank was also remembered by Robert Vernon Harcourt (Harcourt II), who told John, in a letter of 1959, 'The betting on the first car stopping or driving over you was about even, and many grubby peppermint creams changed hands when the result was known.'[60]

Vera was John's accomplice in one of his escapades. James Orr recalled:

It was the end of term, we were all round the swimming-pool – an awful ropey old pool in the garden – and John was walking along a passageway which had been erected by somebody for very little money, I should think, a sort of wooden track. And Vera Spencer-Clarke pushed him in. And as he fell he yelled: 'You brute!' but it looked very much a put-up job. He had on an even ropier sports coat and grey flannels than usual.[61]

The swimming-pool figured in a more heroic exploit of John's which David Soltau mentioned in a letter to his parents. The pool, which was about four feet deep, had duckboards at the bottom. One afternoon the boys were bathing when a boy called Bryans[62] jumped into the pool and got his foot jammed between the duckboards. Soltau reported: 'Mr Bejhiman [sic], iron crowbar in hand, dived in with his shirt on and levered up the board so that Bryans could get his foot out. Then Mr Bejhiman swam about the pool a little until a bathing dress was thrown out to him and then he came out while we all cheered.'[63]

John impressed the boys just as much inside the classroom as outside. Sir Jasper Hollom's elder brother Vincent (Hollom IV) wrote:

Memories of John Betjeman tend to remain clear while others become hazy, which is an indication of the intense impression he made, mainly in his teaching of English literature. The hitherto familiar and laborious hours of 'parsing' and grammar were transformed into the sounds and usage and rhythms of words conveyed with such inspiration that sparks of understanding seemed to be struck from every single and different boy in the classroom. Few, if any, were insulated from J.B.'s electrifying and entirely communicable vision of literature.

Most often his communication was by reading aloud which soon secured absolute attention. It was an unforgettable experience to hear him read Belloc's 'Tarantella', in places extremely fast, but with never a syllable indistinct. . . In his own classes there was no tendency to ragging: one's mental energy was all needed to keep up with J.B.'s easy intellectual lead.[64]

Alan Nightingale, too, found John an inspiring teacher:

He taught me English and history. Even in those days he was interested in Victorian architecture, London life and so on. I remember him quite vividly in a new approach to English and history in that he said, not, 'Was Henry IV a good king?' or 'What is the imperfect subjunctive passive of "to wish"?' He used to do what he has done more recently in his books, and say: 'Look at that row of houses there. Can you see anything there which you like, or don't like?' And of course at that age one takes things for granted, what one's told, what one's fed. And he was the first person who taught me to have a critical eye.[65]

John did not try to ingratiate himself with the boys by treating them as equals. On the contrary, he asserted his intellectual superiority with an exhibitionist relish. 'He never hesitated,' Paul Miller said. 'I mean, all respectable educationists are told that they must never mock the child's taste, but must draw it out; but he never hesitated to mock our enthusiasms for all they were worth.'[66] If the boys wanted to read an adventure book by G.A. Henty or Percy F. Westerman, they now had to do so in secret, as though the books were pornography. Instead, they expressed an enthusiasm, genuine or feigned, for Edith Sitwell or the other writers John approved of. Canon Miller added:

> He cut at the foundations of the establishment's regard for games, and this was obviously one of the things that Mr Summers hated. Our success at games simply plummeted. You see, John substituted one standard of snobbery for another. The old snobbery was for games, and the people who were good at them. The new snobbery was for literature and architecture and those who could appreciate them. It wasn't purely intellectual in the conventional sense, I don't think that would have worked. He made it all such fun, and so attractive, that we readily accepted his standards – about who was interesting and who was not. With just a few exceptions. There was a boy whom he persecuted, rather, called Messum. He used to call him 'Jack Dashaway', who was a character in a Percy F. Westerman novel. Messum was impervious to his charm. He typified the games-playing prep school boy.[67]

John's classroom was at one end of a series of three classrooms which could be turned into one by folding-screen walls. Canon Miller recalled that John used to get his class to recite poetry together – 'what is now called "choral speaking"'. Miller remembered John's 'conducting' Vachel Lindsay's 'Congo':

> Fat black bucks in a wine-barrel room,
> Barrel-house kings, with feet unstable,
> Sagged and reeled and pounded on the table,
> Pounded on the table,
> Beat an empty barrel with the handle of a broom,

Hard as they were able,
Boom, boom, BOOM . . .

'BLOOD' screamed the skull-faced, lean witch-doctors,
'Whirl ye the deadly voo-doo rattle . . .
Boomlay, boomlay, boomlay, BOOM.'[68]

John would be waving his arms about in a frenzy at the front and bringing the boys to a crescendo – 'boomlay, BOOM!' – and at that moment Mr Summers would come in: 'Mr Betjeman, *do* you mind?' and John would look crestfallen. In the end, he was given a classroom on its own, across a courtyard. 'Nobody had ever suggested to us that poetry was actually fun and enjoyable,' Miller said. 'I think Pope was beyond us – I'm sure he was. But John was obviously going through a Pope period and tried to make us enthusiastic about him too. I don't think any of us were; but because it was the thing to do, we pretended to like Pope. Edith Sitwell had just produced a book on Pope,[69] that is probably why Pope was such a passion of John's at that time.'[70]

As a result of the 'new snobbery', even the games-mad boys began to take an interest in poetry. John could be sharp with them if their interest lapsed or their attention waned. James Orr said:

When he was around, you couldn't take your eyes off him, he was a personality. He was tolerant of me although I wasn't academic, and still am not – I'm a most unread person. I was crazy about sport, I loved football and rugger and cricket. He was tolerant, except on one occasion. It was just midday, and he was in the middle of talking about Dr Johnson. He was a great Dr Johnson fan. And the school bell rang for the staff lunch. They had their lunch at 12.00 and we had ours at 1.00. And I looked at my watch. He was really very annoyed. He said something like: 'Orr, I know that lunch is much more important than Dr Johnson.' He was furious.[71]

John even got the sporting boys to *write* poetry. Vera Moule was astonished that 'the most athletic boys who were really cricket and rugger maniacs, boys who thought of nothing but games all day long, started writing poetry, which they got into the school magazine. Particularly a boy called Robert Hunter. He was quite extraordinary. The little poem he wrote in the magazine was only about six lines long, but it was amazing because normally he just kicked a football or was bowling or batting, and he was quite good in my gym too.'[72] Hunter continued to write poetry. In 1944, as a lieutenant in 'Q' Branch, Dunstable, Bedfordshire, he wrote to John to ask his advice about his poems ('I well remember how strict you were over rhymes!'[73]). Within a month John had persuaded J.R. Ackerley to publish some of Hunter's poems in *The Listener*, and, both during the war and later, as a master at Merchant Taylors' School, Hunter regularly contributed to literary magazines.

Another sportsman who began – and continued – to write poetry with John's encouragement was Roger E. Hende Roughton, a star fielder in cricket. By the time he committed suicide in Dublin during the war, at the age of twenty-four, he had edited *Contemporary Poetry and Prose*, appeared in the *Labour Monthly*, acted in films in Hollywood and London and, under another name, raced successful greyhounds in Dublin. An unorthodox strain had already begun to show in his character at Heddon Court, where he resigned his prefectship voluntarily, an unprecedented act. Roughton wrote to John from Uppingham when John's poem 'Westgate-on-Sea' was published in *The Architectural Review* of November 1930: 'Is that the poem you wrote, that you told me about when I showed you my Pseudo-Gothic churches? You said it was best to write in an ordinary metre when writing about ordinary things.'[74] John always remembered the opening line of a poem by another athlete, Robert Vernon Harcourt, 'The rain came down like a silver gown'; but Harcourt did not go on writing verse. 'Modern poetry, like most modern art,' he wrote to John years later, 'has left me miles behind, dancing with the daffodils.'[75]

John read prose aloud as well as poetry. 'He had a modulated, musical, quiet, sensitive voice,' said George Gomez. 'He used to read stories to us. One of them was a ghost story by Oscar Wilde, "The Canterville Ghost" – the ghost had chains on, but a couple of Americans who didn't believe in ghosts kept on taking the mickey out of him. We were all enraptured by John Betjeman, he was fascinating. I can hear his voice now.'[76] David Soltau remembered John's reading ghost stories by M.R. James – the same stories as had been read to John by 'Skipper' Lynam at the Dragon School. John may have underestimated the effect of blood-chilling stories on impressionable boys. His pupils became acutely ghost-conscious, and David Soltau remembered that on one occasion a deputation of boys plucked up the courage to report some ghostly footsteps to the headmaster. These turned out to be the nightwatchman, stoking the boiler.

Inevitably, humour was another method by which John gained the boys' attention. 'He once drew a wonderful castle on the blackboard,' James Orr recalled. 'And somebody came in late and asked, "What's that, sir?" And quick as lightning, Betjeman said, "It's the inside of a radiator." '[77] John encouraged the boys to be humorous, too. They could score marks for being funny. In a general knowledge test he asked: 'Which is the worst public school in England?' Knowing where he had been educated, all the boys, except one, wrote: 'Marlborough'. They were given one mark for that. But one boy answered: 'Monkton Combe'. 'And Betjeman was so amused, he gave him two marks,' James Orr remembered. 'I don't think anybody knew anything about Monkton Combe, it just sounded funny.'[78]

Even when he was not teaching, but was just grappling with the everyday hazards of school life, John put on an act which was literally something to write home about. David Soltau told his parents on 26 June 1929: 'I am writing this letter in No. 4, the second form classroom, while Mr Bejhiman [sic] is struggling with the blind which is broken and is knotting bits of string together and they have just broken now and he is very cross about it. He has just knocked himself on a piece of wood and is furios [sic] with it.'[79]

John's considerable skill as a draughtsman also came into play. When he arrived in the classroom – before anything else happened and without saying a word – he would draw on the blackboard a series of pictograms of certain boys. Kenric Rice, whom John called 'the famine child', was given a skull-like head with deep-sunk eyes. Terence Glancy was depicted as a kind of Hallowe'en pumpkin lantern, with triangles for eyes and nose, a wavy line for a mouth, and a coconut tuft of hair. Murrant was a fish. Stevenson was always drawn in profile, as he had a head like a sausage-balloon. 'When John put up the lists of results at the end of each fortnight,' Kenric Rice remembered, 'there were no names at all, just these signs. I was a skull and crossbones. Vilvandré was a house-fly.'[80]

Rice is the one Heddon Court boy who is mentioned in 'Cricket Master' ('Matron made/ A final survey of the boys' best clothes–/ Clean shirts. Clean collars. "Rice, your jacket's torn./ Bring it to me this instant." ') He was a particular protégé of John's, and there was more to his nickname than his slightly cadaverous appearance. He was born in Yokohama, Japan, where his father was chief accountant in the Hongkong and Shanghai Bank. (Rice senior had sat next to P.G. Wodehouse during the novelist's brief service with the bank.) Having survived the Yokohama earthquake of 1923, the Rice family went to Tientsin in China. When it was time for Kenric to go to a preparatory school, he had to be found a home in England: he could not return to China every holiday. None of his aunts and uncles would have him, so his father advertised him in the personal column of *The Times*. He was taken by a family called Bruce in Sussex – 'and they charged my parents a whacking great fee for doing it'. Kenric Rice remembers 'the agony of the day that my mother – she went to China after my father – saw me into Heddon Court. It was pretty miserable, aged seven, suddenly to be dumped. I can see her now, walking down Cat Hill, I watched her till she disappeared. She said: "Cheer up, don't worry: the same moon shines over Cockfosters as shines over Peking." I mean, *that*, aged seven! And I didn't see her again for ten years.' Rice hid under his bed for a whole day and the staff could not find him. 'That is why John always called me "the poor little famine child" – he thought I was an orphan, you see.'[81]

Realizing Rice's loneliness, John made something of a pet of him. During the morning tea break he got him to sing popular songs to the others in the corridor, including:

> You're the cream in my coffee,
> You're the salt in my stew;
> You will always be
> My necessity –
> I'd be lost without you.[82]

And at the end of term, John would see Rice safely across London from King's Cross to Victoria, telephone the Bruces to say 'Ken's on the 11.40 to Hailsham', and make sure he got into the right train. Kenric Rice never forgot John's kindness and sympathy. They remained friends: when John had a stroke in 1981, Rice was one of the few people invited to visit him in Sheffield Hospital, to which John had been rushed from Chatsworth, where he was staying. 'When I think of your childhood, so lonely and brave,' John wrote to him in the same year, 'I thank God for my pampered youth.'[83]

Paul Miller was another boy who had cause to be grateful for John's almost clairvoyant skill at finding out what was worrying people. Miller's main worry was the approaching End of the

World. His parents were Plymouth Brethren. They were not conventionally oppressive, like Edmund Gosse's Brethren father (though the only films Miller was ever allowed to see were nature films at the Regent Street Polytechnic, about eagles and otters). But the sect was oppressive, especially in its constant emphasis on the End of the World. 'I used to think that the End of the World was going to take place at any minute and that I should be caught out by it in some act of sin.'[84]

Miller knew he was not one of John's favourites. John did not draw a pictogram of him on the blackboard, as he did of Rice and Stevenson. But one half-holiday, the new young master stopped to talk with him. Canon Miller recalled:

> I was late back that summer term of 1929. I had had my adenoids and tonsils out, and was therefore three weeks late in coming back; so the first and most fascinating discovery was that there was this new assistant master. I worshipped from afar: I was fascinated by him. . . The custom was, on certain half-holidays, that you took a rug out into the garden and read. I wasn't good at making friends – a very solemn, priggish little boy. So I took my rug out on my own and laid it out among the azalea bushes. And John Betjeman walked by, and out of an impulse of kindness, I suppose, sat down on my rug and started to talk to me. And that was when he discovered that I had this Plymouth Brethren background. And his way of making a discovery of this sort was highly characteristic. There was no reticence at all – I mean, he screamed with delight, and waited on your every word. Well, this was terribly flattering, especially coming from somebody who I had already decided was quite fascinating. He represented a world that I had never had any contact with but had always suspected existed. And here he was being interested in me among the azaleas.[85]

Miller wrote to his parents and told them that the new master had been asking a lot of questions about the Brethren's 'Meetings'. They assumed, much to John's amusement, that he must be one of the Brethren himself, as he knew so much about the sect. They told Paul Miller to find out from Mr Betjeman where he was 'in Fellowship'. John continued to question Miller about the Brethren. 'He was always asking questions. It had a releasing effect on me. I hated my parents' religion, and by his talking about it and finding it, clearly, extremely amusing, I was able for the first time to begin to look at my religious background with a degree of objectivity – which was enormously beneficial.'[86] John lent Miller *Mary Lee* by Geoffrey Dennis, a satirical novel about a small girl brought up by Plymouth Brethren.[87] Miller took it home and it was confiscated. 'By that stage my parents had cottoned on, and Betjeman's influence was considered not to be good.'

Paul Miller was accepted on to the fringe of the Betjeman 'retinue'. He recalled:

When John Betjeman first came to Heddon Court, he must have lived in some room for assistant masters, but he made no imprint on it. But after he'd been with us for about a term, he was given better quarters in a small house which was the other side of the yard from the main school; and he then had all his books sent. They were glorious books, and he was most generous in allowing us to see them. I was one of the privileged few, though fairly low down on the list, and I was invited over to look at them. I remember that the only other boy on that occasion was one of the Geddes family – there were a lot of Geddeses at Heddon Court. I was completely fascinated, and John Betjeman was most helpful and imaginative in the way he showed us the books. We all forgot – he in particular, because it was his responsibility – the passage of time. And eventually, whether it was old Summers . . . anyway, there was a meal in progress, and that fearful knock at the door: 'Mr Betjeman, have you got Miller and Geddes?' And Betjeman looked around rather ostentatiously and said, 'Yes, I'm rather afraid that I have.' But I think that as we went into the dining-room we were on the whole pleased with ourselves, to be late in such company.[88]

As with Kenric Rice, the friendship was as lasting as the influence. Paul Miller went on to Haileybury, where he introduced John to Gerard Irvine, the beginning of another lifelong friendship. Miller's ordination in the Church of England after the war brought him closer to John, who sent playful congratulations after Miller became Canon Residentiary of Derby Cathedral in 1966.[89]

Paul Miller's father, a City of London clothing manufacturer who could afford to build a house on Hadley Common and send his son to an expensive private school (the fees were £52 a term) would have been considered 'comfortably off' by most people in 1929; but many of the boys came from far richer families. Their parents arrived in Rolls Royces and Bentleys. Alan Nightingale's family had the most coveted car, a 45 hp Renault with a cocktail cabinet in the back. The masters' cars – Mr Godfrey's Clyno, even Mr Hunter Blair's Hupmobile[90] – cut less of a dash.

Among the privileges bought for the boys by the fat fees their fathers paid was a special Heddon Court carriage on the train from London to New Barnet at the beginning of term, supervised by a master. John sometimes undertook this duty, and the experience may have prompted his attempt at a poem called 'School Train', of which only an opening fragment survives in one of his notebooks:

> Faces like boots and melons
> And older boots and melons standing near
> Split into smiles of cheerless bonhomie,
> The grins to hide the nearby starting tear.
> 'Five minutes more, Angus, and don't forget
> To change your stockings if your feet are wet.'
> That new boy there who still sustains the looks
> His mother had when she was young and sweet . . .[91]

Another task which sometimes fell to John was to supervise 'Lining Up'. As the boys finished breakfast they were caught as they came down the passage, usually by Vera, and told to line up opposite the lavatories. 'As a cubicle became free, so you went in,' Alan Nightingale recalled, '– but you couldn't get past. And John Betjeman was often on duty at Lining Up, as this lavatory parade was called, and would have to ask each boy, "Have you been?" A frequent reply was: "No, sir. Have *you*, sir?"'[92]

John contributed his skills of writing, acting and even make-up to the school plays and concerts. In December 1929 David Soltau wrote to his parents about *The London Wall Mystery*, a play presented by the sixth form. 'It was about a man who was very rich and who was stolen [ie kidnapped] by motor car bandits, and how he was recovered by his clerks and office boys.'[93] It is possible that John, with his brief City experience, helped write this drama. In a letter of January 1930 Jasper Hollom told Alan Nightingale of two plays in which John had been involved: 'On the last Saturday [of term] the sixth form actually acted a play in front of the masters, a most thrilling play, regular Edgar Wallace, written by Mrs Engleheart [wife of the music master]. It was a huge success. Mr Betjeman came and made us up awfully well. On the last day

Messrs. Betjeman, Hope and Godfrey acted an awfully [*word missing*] play.'[94] Perhaps it was of Mrs Engleheart's play that the verse critique appeared in the school magazine of which Sir Jasper Hollom remembers these lines:

> We wrote a play, a thrilling one,
> A shocker, yes, a shilling one –
> Presented it politely
> With Smith, who played Golightly . . .[95]

John was again entertaining the boys in March 1930, when David Soltau wrote to his parents:

> Last Wednesday was the prefects' supper . . . After the supper we went down to the gym where the masters sang songs. Mr Godfrey and Mr Betjeman sang a song about the forms and the boys in them. The verse for our form was this:

> > In Mr Godfrey's form room,
> > They are a comic lot:
> > De Havilland is off his head,
> > And who says Soltau's not?[96]

John may well have been responsible for this doggerel (and perhaps also for the verse critique of Mrs Engleheart's play).

John invited some of the boys to shows in London. He took Vincent Hollom to a film on the newly fashionable and shocking subject of lesbianism, *Mädchen in Uniform*, 'whose heroine victim,' Hollom recalled, 'haunted me almost unbearably (as perhaps he intended)'.[97] John gave John and Dick Addis lunch at the Café Royal and took them to see Nancy Price in Galsworthy's *The Silver Box*.[98] Sir John Addis said: 'He made out that this was rather dashing for a schoolmaster taking out schoolboys – that it ought to have been Shakespeare, not Galsworthy.'[99] Another time he went with them to Hatchard's bookshop in Piccadilly to buy them both a book. 'I forget what he gave Dick,' Sir John said, 'but he gave me, again after apparent hesitation that this, perhaps, was not quite right for a schoolmaster, *The Wild Party* by Joseph Moncure March. By a schoolmaster's standards, it *was* rather shocking. It really was about a wild party, with all sorts of goings-on.'[100]

In August 1929 John was invited to the Addises' holiday home in Scotland. John and Dick Addis again had lunch with him in London when he was working as an assistant editor on *The Architectural Review* in 1931. 'I would probably be sixteen or seventeen by then,' Sir John Addis thought. But soon after that an incident occurred which severed relations between John and the Addis brothers for ever. The boys had once more been invited to lunch at the Café Royal. They went by Underground, and were going up the escalator at Piccadilly at the right time for their appointment with John, when suddenly they saw him haring down the 'Down' escalator, two steps at a time. 'It was an agonizing moment, a nightmare vision,' Sir John Addis said. 'He did not recognize us and we were struck dumb and in a childish way didn't call out anything.' Whether John had forgotten their appointment, or had remembered another, they never learned. 'What was really wounding, was that he never followed it up with an explanation or apology. It was the end of the acquaintance. It was being dropped that hurt Dick.'[101]

Against such occasional lapses into insensitivity must be set John's notable kindness to Rice and Miller and the exhilaration of his teaching and of his irresponsibility as an alternative to the Stallardian code of self-control and team-spirit. As Vincent Hollom has suggested, John may have gained as much from his time at Heddon Court as his pupils:

Heddon Court was a short chapter in J.B.'s long life and numberless acquaintance. Even so, it was perhaps quite a formative experience for him also. Perhaps it was a surprise to him that his ideas could be so catching, so effective . . .

Youthful adulation would not intoxicate such a man: but surely it did stimulate, might nourish. His eyes used to light up with . . . was it pleasure? was it just amusement?[102]

ARCHIE REV

My own life is mixed up in architectural journalism and I should say that next to sewage disposal it is, to the outside public, one of the most seemingly uninteresting jobs to which man can be called.

John Betjeman, 'Architecture', *The London Mercury*, November 1933

James Lees-Milne, for thirty years architectural adviser to the National Trust, was a friend of John's from the early 1930s until John's death. (They went on holidays together when in their seventies.) They narrowly missed meeting at Magdalen, and met in 1931 through John's future wife Penelope Chetwode.

The traumatic event which turned Lees-Milne into a professional architectural conservationist happened during one of his summer terms at Oxford, when he was taken by friends to dine at Rousham, a mansion on the Cherwell between Oxford and Banbury. The Jacobean house had been redecorated in about 1740 by William Kent, who also designed the surrounding landscape, adding temples, follies, grottoes and sculpture.

The Cottrell-Dormers who owned Rousham had leased it to Maurice Hastings, described by Lees-Milne as 'a capricious alcoholic . . . rich, clever and slightly mad'.[1] The young visitor was horrified when Hastings lashed at family portraits by Kneller and Reynolds with a hunting crop, and was even more outraged when he fired a rifle at the private parts of the garden statues. Though Lees-Milne was 'numb with dismay', the other guests 'cheered and egged on our beastly host . . .'[2] They were mostly undergraduates, but among them was an Oxford don, 'a man of letters who was to become a clamorous champion of western ideologies'.[3]

The don was Maurice Bowra, who had met Hastings when both of them were undergraduates.[4] Hastings had gone to America, where he had married a young heiress.[5] They had settled in England, renting a succession of country houses. Alan Pryce-Jones recalled: 'Hastings wore a monocle, he drank, he was like Squire Mytton. He would put his hunter to the dining-room table, when it was fully charged with silver and crystal, and jump it. People used to hide from him at Rousham, because he was very violent: he'd take you on in boxing matches in the corridors, while his wife was sobbing upstairs and hiding under a bed.'[6]

When Hastings was shooting at the statues, with whoops of encouragement from the other guests, James Lees-Milne felt sick, 'as many people would feel sick if they watched from a train window an adult torturing a child, while they were powerless to intervene'.[7] Lees-Milne looked back on the episode as his Damascus Road vision. That evening he made a vow to devote his energies and abilities to preserving the country houses of England.

So, in a negative way, Maurice Hastings was responsible for setting Lees-Milne on the course of his life's work – rather as Captain Bligh helped to civilize the Pitcairn Islands. In a more positive way, he changed the direction of John's career, from prep school master to architectural journalist. With Bowra and Pryce-Jones frequently driving out to Rousham, it could be only a matter of time before John was taken there. In fact it was Bowra who made the introduction. The qualities which attracted John in Bowra he found reflected (if in a slightly distorting mirror) in the other Maurice; besides, a hedonistic eccentric, even one given to bouts of philistinism, would always have an appeal for him – far from diminished by wealth, good food and drink, and the setting of a historic house. For his part Hastings responded to John's charm, wit and bubbling enthusiasm for Kent's work, and was impressed by his knowledge of architecture. As usual, John marked a new friendship by bestowing a nickname. For every kind of good reason he called Hastings 'Malpractice' (a corruption of Malshanger, near Basingstoke, Hampshire, another of the houses Hastings rented). Evelyn Waugh pirated the name in the third impression of *Decline and Fall* (1928), as he was later to appropriate John's teddy bear for Lord Sebastian in *Brideshead Revisited*.

Malpractice was a son of Sir Percy Hastings, head of the company which owned *The Architectural Review*, and since 1928 his brother Hubert de Cronin Hastings had effectively been in control of the magazine. Like most of John's friends, Maurice Hastings thought it absurd that John's unique talents should be wasted in teaching small boys. Alan Pryce-Jones was present when Hastings decided to do something about it. He recalled:

> I was at Rousham with Maurice Bowra, Maurice Hastings and John Betjeman. John was still teaching at a private school. And I remember Maurice Bowra saying, 'There must be *something* that you can do.'
>
> 'No,' said Betjeman, 'not a thing. I can't teach, I can't get on with my father, if ever I earn two hundred a year I shall be extremely lucky. I'm absolutely sunk. There's no future of any kind for me.'
>
> 'Well, you could be a bellhop,' said Maurice Bowra rather unfeelingly.
>
> 'No I couldn't,' he said. 'I shall never forget seeing the maid at school come in and upset an enormous tureen of boiled potatoes on to the floor, pick them all up again and put them in the dish – no, I could never be a waiter.'
>
> And finally, we wondered if we could not find him a job on *The Architectural Review*.[8]

Maurice Hastings recommended John to his brother, who asked him for interview. John later suggested that de Cronin Hastings gave him the job because of his foreign name:[9] foreign architects were the only ones who counted in the *Review* at that time. John wrote some trial articles and on 1 October 1930[10] began work as assistant editor with a salary of £300 a year, in the handsome building which the company still occupies at 9 Queen Anne's Gate, London. This warren of eighteenth-century rooms was an improbable nerve-centre for the Modern Movement in Britain. Its narrow staircases were perpetually cluttered with builders' ladders and painters' buckets. ('Reconstruction as usual during business,' as Hugh Casson, an Architectural Press employee from 1935, quipped.[11]) Again marking affection by a nickname, John and his friends called the magazine 'the Archie Rev' – an abbreviation used by the printers.

The *Review* had been started in 1897 with a gold cover design by Charles Shannon. After a year it was bought by Professional and Trade Papers Ltd, a too ambitious company which failed in 1899 with debts of £70,000.[12] In 1900 a small syndicate headed by Lord Rothermere bought the properties out of bankruptcy and carried them on under the title Technical Journals Ltd (later renamed the

Architectural Press) of which Percy Hastings was the first managing director. In addition to *The Architectural Review*, the syndicate owned *The Architects' Journal, Specification* (an annual technical compilation) and three other magazines. An advisory committee of distinguished architects was appointed. Originally it included the architect Norman Shaw and four of his pupils. In the early years there were constant battles between the committee, who wanted to convey an architectural vision, and the management, who wanted to make profits. Two of the committee, Reginald Blomfield and John Belcher, stalked out when D.S. McColl, their choice for editor, was spurned in favour of Mervyn Macartney.

Hubert de Cronin Hastings took control, aged twenty-five, early in 1928. Like God, Sir Percy Hastings was sending his son to offer his creation the chance of a new beginning. When John joined the staff, de Cronin Hastings was known as 'Mr Hubert', but most of his friends called him 'de Cronin'. Hugh Casson, who met Hastings five years later, remembers him as of middle height, plumpish, balding and trimly moustached. '[He] had a vaguely military air spiced with some rakish mystery. The land agent perhaps of a renegade duke? The proprietor of a small and exclusive fishing hotel where poaching was not unknown? A major who had retired mysteriously early from the army in order to collect butterflies or to dissect the pyramids?'[13]

Those who worked for Hastings, whether on his staff like John, J.M. Richards and Casson, or as outside contributors, like John Piper and John Summerson, are agreed that he was a brilliant journalist but a difficult man. 'He was an admirable editor to learn from,' Richards wrote. 'His comments were incisive and he had a keen journalistic sense, insisting, for example, that the news value of a story must never be lost in the recital of the facts.'[14] It was news sense, Richards thought, rather than any profound philosophical convictions about architecture, which caused Hastings to espouse the Modern Movement. John Piper also thought the Modern Movement 'ill sorted with Hastings's normal aesthetic response',[15] but was full of admiration for the editorial lead he gave. It was Hastings who suggested the title 'Pleasing Decay' for an article by Piper on what Piper liked about buildings in relation to his art – 'why I liked the way ruins were *not* looked after in France better than I did the way they *were* looked after in England, where they were made too tidy'.[16]

But against Hastings's originality and pioneering creativeness had to be set the problems which his personality caused those who worked for him. John Summerson (speaking two years before Hastings's death) thought him 'extremely able, very witty – an original mind. I always met him with pleasure, but also with some slight apprehension, perhaps. Difficult of course. Difficult as hell. He was, and still is, a very withdrawn person, never mixes . . . They gave him the Gold Medal of the RIBA, to his great embarrassment, and he absolutely declined to receive it at a public meeting. They had a dinner party and just slipped it to him quietly.'[17]

'He had an obsessive dislike of seeing strangers,' Sir James Richards confirmed. 'He never saw anyone at all. The role of the assistant editor was to deal with every person because Hastings never admitted anyone to his room when he was there except members of his staff and one or two old friends.'[18] Although Hugh Casson worked at the *Review* every week after his initial interview with Hastings, he did not see him again for eighteen months, 'nor, for all I know, did many of my colleagues'.[19] Hastings's appearances at editorial meetings were 'wildly irregular: once a month for two months, and then utter silence – not even a telephone call – for three months, followed perhaps by a draft for a special issue, a pile of magnificent photographs, a sudden bouquet, or a sharp reprimand'.[20] The staff were left in no doubt of his wishes.

> In the phrase 'remote control' [Casson wrote], the adjective was as accurate as the noun. But even if we never saw him, we heard from him all right. From a hilltop farm buried deep in a Sussex wood, from a Rolls Royce caravan so heavy that the wire wheel spokes snapped like banjo strings, from a motorboat aground in a forgotten Shropshire canal . . . the bullets of criticism or ideas hailed down on Queen Anne's Gate in a target-hitting and often very personally painful fusillade . . .[21]

John, who enjoyed socializing as much as Hastings abhorred it, often had to represent him at public functions. In the postscript to a letter of March 1932 to E.J. ('Bobby') Carter, librarian of the RIBA, he wrote: 'de Cronin Hastings, with characteristic self-effacement, refuses to go to the R.I.B.A. dinner, so that I shall be obliged to go in his stead. I would be very much gratified if you would pull a string so that I sat near somebody interesting, instead of as is usually the case next to .... of *The Builder*; though a delightful man with a family at Upminster in Essex, he is inclined to pall after a few hours.'[22] The only good result of Hastings's refusal to meet 'new people' was that when Penelope Chetwode arrived in 1931 to offer Hastings an article on Indian temples, she was passed straight on to John.

Those who did get to see Hastings found his temper unpredictable. 'He hated being thwarted,' said Sir James Richards, who joined *The Architects' Journal* in 1933, succeeded John as assistant editor of the *Review* in 1935, and became the *Review*'s editor in 1937. 'He used to trot out ideas that he hoped you would follow. If you didn't follow them, he often went in for grumpy silence for a week. I had any number of brushes with him.'[23] Inevitably, John also had brushes with Hastings. There were only four years between them in age; they were both originals, and their originalities ran in opposite directions. But Hastings had the redeeming virtue which for John usually outweighed all faults: a highly developed sense of humour. It meant that he would put up with a lot of John's chaff, and he could not help laughing at his more outrageous pranks. 'He let John get away with murder,' said Piper.[24]

John jibbed at the petty rules imposed by the management. One was that bus tickets must be retained and stapled to expense sheets. John went to the bus station, obtained a sackful of used bus tickets, and tipped them over Hastings's desk.[25] Another time, John took an even longer lunch break than usual. It turned out that he had been busking outside a local cinema; when he had obtained enough money by singing music-hall songs, he used it to go into the film.[26] The only time one of John's escapades embarrassed Hastings was retailed to Richard Holmes[27] (who worked for Hastings some time after John) by the architect and Architectural Press journalist F.R.S. Yorke over a pub lunch. Holmes remembered:

F.R.S. Yorke (referred to by H. de C. as Ferdinand Reginald Sebastian – which I naturally assumed were his names, but they weren't) told me: 'Betjeman comes into the office one hot mid-July day with a very small suitcase. "Ah! You don't know what I've got in here!" Whereupon he changes in the office and appears in the very briefest of brief swimming trunks. While he is in this garb, Hastings senior comes into the office with an eminent visitor. Betjeman advances across the room, utmost nonchalance, to greet them. Thumbs down for Betjeman, I heard.'[28]

Hastings senior, Sir Percy Hastings, retired in 1933. 'The whole office was terrified of him,' Sir James Richards recalled. 'When he clambered out of his canary-yellow Rolls Royce and came into the office, everybody cowered. I assumed that de Cronin had inherited his rather tyrannical style from his father.'[29]

John was not intimidated by de Cronin Hastings. The friendship between the two is indicated by the nicknames they bandied. John called him 'Obscurity' (a reference to his shunning company) and Hastings called him 'Jaggers'.[30] The warmth of feeling also comes through in Hastings's letters to John, full of easy badinage. In 1938, for example, three years after John had left the *Review*'s staff, Hastings wrote to him:

> My dear Jaggers,
>   I quite forgot, when writing to you before, to tell you that Marx and I went together to Comper's church in Baker Street to make sure that you were mad. To our surprise – to our inexpressible surprise – we discovered it was absolutely lovely. Not everyone's cup of vodka, perhaps, but indubitably the work of an architect – with a remarkable feeling of space and clarity of planning; qualities which, you and I know so well, are practically non-existent to-day under whatever disguise the pseudo architect presents himself. I confess that I was much astonished and so too, strangely enough, was Marx who was immediately converted. You have scored again, brother.
>   Yours,
>   de Cronin.[31]

'Marx' was John's nickname for J.M. Richards. At first he had been called 'Gordon', after Gordon Richards the jockey, but John's nickname won the day. It was conferred, Richards remembers, after the two men had had a political argument, just before John left the *Review* in 1935. 'John was going through a rather extreme Anglo-Catholic right-wing phase; and I was going through a left-wing phase.'[32] When Richards sent John an office memorandum later that day, he addressed it to 'Ignatius Loyola'. John promptly addressed a reply to 'Karl Marx'. 'He continued to refer to me as Karl Marx long after I had stopped calling him Ignatius Loyola,' Richards said.

Richards's office at Queen Anne's Gate was just across the landing from John's, which John had persuaded the company to decorate for him with a William Morris wallpaper. Richards recalls in his memoirs:

> The appearance and the contents of the *Review* were enlivened by Betjeman's personal enthusiasms: for the Gothic Revival, for Victorian typefaces, for the Arts and Crafts movement. Office life in Queen Anne's Gate was enlivened too by his mercurial personality and his pose of disrespect for authority. He practised at that time an undergraduate style of exhibitionism which was tolerable because accompanied by wit and good humour. I remember, as an example of the kind of prank he took a pride in, his boasting to me one day that he had just come from the Geological Museum, then housed in a dusty, unvisited red-brick building in Piccadilly, by Pennethorne,[33] and had contributed an exhibit of his own. 'Do go and look,' he said. So I went, and there indeed beneath the glass of one of the show-cases, which someone had I suppose carelessly left unlocked, was a small brown object with a neatly lettered card reading 'Horse Chestnut picked up in Bushey Park. Donated by J. Betjeman Esquire.' I believe it remained unnoticed and undisturbed until the building was demolished in 1935 to make way for Simpson's store.[34]

Richards's account was written almost fifty years after John's practical joke, and may have lost something in the telling. 'Museum Piece', a Lamb-like essay contributed by Alan Pryce-Jones to the May 1933 issue of *The London Mercury* is probably more accurate, and *en passant* gives some glimpses of the flamboyant and erratic twenty-five-year-old Betjeman, to whom the essay is dedicated. In it, Pryce-Jones describes his introduction to the Geological Museum:

> To find such a museum in the heart of London was . . . an important discovery for me. When I say 'find' I mean 'be shown', for it was you, John, who did the finding, as so often before. This time, however, we did not drive in that car of yours which, from the recklessness of your driving and a certain dilapidation of the car itself, always made me feel like Boadicea charging the Romans. We took the 'bus. And into a strange quiet world, a world of apatite and aventurine into which, whenever the exterior world is too much for me, I never lose an opportunity of returning . . . There is a case of curite from Chinkolobwi, the land, supposedly, where the bong-tree grows; and there is the treasure which you found, John: the

section of cast-iron water pipe nearly choked with calcareous deposit from water derived from the Oolites and supplied to the City of Bath. The very name Oolite is dark and sinister. I should not wonder if the Oolites were at the bottom of many of our present troubles. If they will tamper with the Bath water supply they will stick at nothing . . .

And of course you, John, had an instantaneous vision of an Irish peer, elderly, dim and poor, plumbing his Galway bogs in search of a geological formation. It seemed a pity not to commemorate such efforts. Do you remember how we accordingly wrote out a laborious ticket, *Mount Prospect Bequest. Horse-Chestnut found at Mount Prospect and presented by Viscount Mount Prospect, 1892* (for you happened to have a horse-chestnut in your pocket), and how we found an empty case and exhibited it? That was seven months ago. Yesterday the Bequest was still there. The ticket is a little dusty, the chestnut has shrunk rather and become very dusty indeed. I took it out and cleaned it on my handkerchief and blew on the ticket.[35]

This contemporary account is inherently more plausible than Richards's of half a century later: John's first contribution to *The London Mercury*, in 1929, had been a short story about Lord Mount Prospect, and it would be natural for him to prolong the joke when in the company of Alan Pryce-Jones, who was the magazine's assistant editor.[36]

Though Hastings ran the *Review* when John joined the staff, the nominal editor was Christian Barman ('Barmy'), who left the magazine just before John in 1935 to become publicity officer of the London Passenger Board.[37] Richards described him as 'blond, bland, partly Swedish, really a conscientious editor but with very little impact outside. The kind of editor who doesn't really let other people go their own way, though he made a nice contrast to de Cronin Hastings in that he wasn't always shouting round the building and getting everybody in line, he just went on editing'.[38] The only other member of the *Review*'s staff, besides a couple of secretaries, was an older man, A.E. Doyle. Since John was far from well-organized, and besides spent much of his time out of the office talking to authors and architects or taking photographers round buildings, Doyle coped with the day-to-day paperwork. 'John called Doyle "A.E.D." and was very fond of him,' said Richards.[39]

Doyle took part in the monthly laying-out of the magazine. He had worked for Batsford's and had laid out A.E. Richardson's *Monumental Architecture in Great Britain and Ireland*. De Cronin Hastings supervised the lay-out himself when he was in the office.

> To watch him lay out an issue was a treat [John recalled]. 'Oh Mr Hubert!' A.E. Doyle would say in a shocked voice when Obscurity decided to give a full-page bled-off plate to a membrane of glass stretched between the elements of the framework of a block of flats in Paris by Ginsberg & Lubetkin, 1932. But in the block went – large and clear and full of contrast. Obscurity would take some lay-out paper and with a thick pencil make rough sketches of the photo-graph which AED and I would then have to scale down. Obscurity had such a good eye that he was always able to reduce a photograph in sketch form, and when I measured it up I found that his free-hand reduction was always right to an eighth of an inch.[40]

Surviving letters from Doyle to John, signed 'A.E.D.' accompanied by miniature self-caricatures with bowler hat, mous-tache and pipe, show the affectionate relationship between the two, mutual commiseration about their lot and an element of good-humoured conspiracy against de Cronin Hastings. In a letter of 27 September 1932, sent to Pakenham Hall, Ireland, where John was staying with the young Earl and Countess of Longford, Doyle wrote: 'I am so sorry you are having bad dreams about de Cronin – funnily enough I dreamt about *you* last night, but it wasn't a night-mare! But you had grey hair and I thought (in the dream) how frightfully old you were looking; the strain of working on the Archi-Rev was indeed getting you down!'[41]

John had less cordial relations with Mr Budd, the doorkeeper at Queen Anne's Gate, who was also a one-man sorting-office for all the post which arrived. When Patrick Balfour sent John a letter full of indecencies, John wrote to him: 'My dear Patrick, Many thanks for your captions which arrived nicely in time. Unfortunately the somewhat loose wording of your letter met the eye of Mr Budd, an ardent Evangelical in our correspondence department, and I have been told to tick you off for it . . . However it cheered up de Cronin Hastings a good bit, and God knows no one has ever heard of him.'[42]

The elderly Mr Budd sat in the outer office with a list of members of the staff. His job was to write down the hour and the minute at which each arrived in the morning and left in the evening, and the times when they left for lunch and returned from it. 'He was a kind of human time-clock,' said Richards, 'so John had constant rows with him: why hadn't John been in the office longer that day, and so on. John never regarded himself as bound by office hours or disciplines or conforming to normal customs. He came and went as he liked. And I always had the feeling when I went into his room that the particular thing he was scribbling hard at had nothing to do with *The Architectural Review*.'[43] Peter Quennell had a similar impression. Visiting John's office with some proofs, he found his chair unoccupied, though his desk was heaped with papers. 'Among them I saw a huge blotting-pad, evidently quite new, on which, using a sharp pencil and decorative Gothic script, he had inscribed the now familiar couplet:

> I sometimes think that I should like
> To be the saddle of a bike.'[44]

(The couplet, which Tom Driberg described as 'the shortest erotic poem in our language',[45] was allegedly written jointly with Auden and MacNeice.[46] Three poets, two lines – hardly a productivity record.)

In spite of his sidelines, John contributed many articles, and some poems, to the *Review* during his four years on the staff. His first contribution, written as a trial piece before he joined the magazine, was a critique of *The English Tradition of Education* by his old headmaster Dr Cyril Norwood, in the issue of December 1929. He largely resisted the temptation to vent his resentment on Marlborough, though he sourly recorded that 'in "Upper School", where corporate life among well over two hundred boys was pursued with a vengeance, the most fearful form of bullying known as "Upper School Basket" flourished even in Dr Norwood's time.' His main quarrel with Norwood was that the book said next to nothing about aesthetics and art education.

There is still a suspicion about art, hanging over from the 'nineties, which considers a lovely room slightly corrupt and consistent with an unstable character.

It is amusing to look at the consequences. How well we know those plum-coloured books whose inside covers were all advertisements for French grammars, whose pages fell out, whose backs were weak. How well we knew 'An Edition (Abridged) for Schools', some gracious unbending of a great publishing house, illustrated in an *art nouveau* style that would have disgraced 1903. How well, too, we knew the Parthenon, the late headmaster and other relics which hung dismally photographed on the classroom wall. How well we remember the writhing gas bracket, the cusped pitch-pine, the terra-cotta Queen Anne, the luscious stained-glass window. So well do we remember them that we fail to notice our own over-mantels and the ornamental brickwork over our own front doors. That much of our souls is shut.[47]

John's first major article for the *Review* was also contributed before he joined the staff: '1830-1930 – Still Going Strong' (May 1930), subtitled 'A Guide to the Recent History of Interior Decoration'. It is a virtuoso performance for a man of twenty-three. His treatment of the subject is swashbuckling and erratic, but he has a confident grasp of the way cycles of taste succeed each other. He gives high praise to Charles Rennie Mackintosh, but also to Le Corbusier. Here is a child of the insouciant 1920s doing his best to adapt to the committed 1930s, and trying to reconcile what he likes with what he is required to like.

Doctrinaire adherents of the Modern Movement later denounced John as having been a kind of Trojan Horse within the Modernist citadel. The barebones architect Maxwell Fry, for example, thought that 'The key to John Betjeman's character is that he's a journalist and a Fleet Street man – and a popularist – and vain. He was the enemy to Modernism. I knew he would draw a facetious veil over our earnestness and that at the end he would find himself in some other camp . . . as far as I was concerned, he was a bloody nuisance.'[48]

But the *Review*'s attitude to the Modern Movement was itself ambivalent. Hastings and Barman both professed to be for it. But, as John later pointed out, '*The Architectural Review* could not quite throw off classical town halls and civic centres partly because of the advertising revenue that came from makers of bronze doors, light fittings and from importers of marble and stone.'[49] The old conflict which had plagued Percy Hastings in the early years of the century – architectural vision versus commercial profits – was still vexing to his son. John and his colleagues were expected at least to pay lip-service to the Modern Movement. John later recalled:

The new policy of *The Architectural Review* – or Architectural

Revue as Baillie Scott[50] used to write it on his envelopes to me – was modern as opposed to *moderne*. We didn't like Cubism[51] but we liked what was pure and simple and Scandinavian like our nominal editor [Christian Barman]. Edward and Prudence Maufe, the Mansard Gallery at Heal's and Carter's Poole Pottery were ousting the neo-renaissance. Marble, bronze and gold were out, pastel shades were in. There had already been a Swedish number of the *Review* and Finland was leaping to the fore with the work of Alvar Aalto introduced by P. Morton Shand and J. Craven ('Plywood') Pritchard.[52]

Jack Pritchard had been sales director of Venesta, the plywood manufacturers, since 1925. In 1932 he commissioned the young architect Wells Coates to build, near Belsize Park Underground station, London, the advanced Lawn Road Flats – in the communal restaurant of which John's old schoolfellow from Byron House, Philip Harben, made some of his early experiments in cooking. John sent these lines about Pritchard to the furniture historian John Gloag:

> We're giving a little party –
> Not exactly lowbrow, not exactly arty.
> For us functional folk who like beauty stark
> And decorate our rooms with it in Belsize Park,
> To know Craven Pritchard is a pretty good scoop:
> He's the live-wire behind the Twentieth Century Group.[53]

P. Morton Shand, the other writer mentioned by John as a promoter of Aalto's work, was the most influential contributor to the *Review* during John's time there, and became a great friend of his. After an orthodox English education – Eton and King's College, Cambridge – he had gone on to the Sorbonne and Heidelberg and spoke both French and German fluently. Besides his keen and far-ranging interest in architecture, he was an expert on French wine and a student of pomology, cultivating varieties of apple that were no longer grown commercially and were in danger of becoming extinct. J.M. Richards, who thought him 'more responsible than anyone for the *Review*'s, and therefore for English architects', contact with modern Continental building', found him meticulously accurate, cynical, unhappy, always hard up (because of expensive divorces from several wives) and exceptionally good company.

'When his tall, balding figure sidled into the office . . . I could count on a rapid fire of challenging, at times malicious but always entertaining talk, punctuated by "What-what-what?", uttered between his perpetually ill-fitting false teeth.'[54]

Morton Shand spent much time in France, where he had inherited some financial interest in a silk business at Lyon. He travelled in Germany, Holland, Switzerland and Scandinavia. He was a friend of Gropius, Aalto and Le Corbusier. When he returned to England he would file stories on what he considered the most exciting new buildings, such as the new Rathaus at Rüstringen, Germany, or a kindergarten at Königrätz, Czechoslovakia. He was also an architectural historian. In a series of articles with the grandiloquent title 'Scenario for a Human Drama' (July 1934–March 1935), which John sub-edited, he pioneered the theory – also advanced with enthusiasm by Nikolaus Pevsner – that the Modern Movement was in clear descent from such Arts and Crafts men as C.R. Mackintosh and C.F.A. Voysey. This was a wonderful let-out for John, to whom Morton Shand expounded his theories some time before they appeared in print.[55] The theory which ingeniously and improbably linked the folksy tiles and gables of Voysey with the 'architectural nudism' of Le Corbusier and Gropius gave John *carte blanche* to forget what Osbert Lancaster called 'the Bauhaus balls' and to devote much of his time to tracking down the Victorian and Edwardian architects who were now to be acclaimed as 'pioneers', and whose work was far more congenial to John than sheets of vita-glass and ferro-concrete.

The greatest of the so-called pioneers, William Morris, whom John revered for his poetry[56] as well as his designs, had died in 1896; but his house, Kelmscott Manor – the 'Nowhere' of his book *News from Nowhere* – could still be visited, and there, John recorded in his article of 1930, 'his daughter, Miss May Morris, still weaves from her father's bold designs.' (John later negotiated unsuccessfully to live at Kelmscott, and at the Kelmscott sale of July 1939 he bid for such hallowed relics as Morris's French working blouse and his initialled silk handkerchief.[57])

Some of the Arts and Crafts men were still living. Voysey wrote a letter of protest against the modern format de Cronin Hastings had introduced into the *Review*. John recalled: ' "Every page must be a surprise," said H. de C. It was. Voysey's letter was in a large clear hand in brilliant blue ink on dark blue paper. A glance at his address, 73 St James's Street, sent me across St James's Park from Queen Anne's Gate to that little flat above Rumpelmayer's where Voysey lived in solitude.'⁵⁸ The architect was small, clean-shaven and bird-like. His jacket had no lapels, as he considered those 'non-functional survivals of eighteenth-century foppery'.⁵⁹ He wore a saxe-blue shirt and a blue tie in a gold ring. John found that Voysey did not regard himself as a pioneer of the Modern Movement. The son of an Anglican clergyman and a descendant of John Wesley, he disliked William Morris 'because he was an atheist'; had no time for the Glasgow architects Mackintosh and Walton, whom he called 'the spook school'; and thought the buildings appearing in the *Review* were hideous.⁶⁰

In October 1931 an exhibition of Voysey's drawings, designs for fabrics and furniture, was held under the auspices of *The Architectural Review* and B.T. Batsford, Ltd., at the latter's galleries in North Audley Street, London. To mark the opening, John contributed an article on Voysey to the *Review* that month, under a curiously laid-out headline in lettering designed by Voysey:

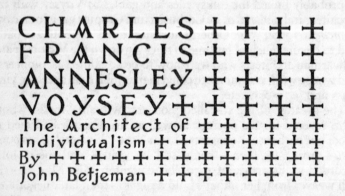

In the article, John gleefully suggested that 'Mr Voysey is as high a Tory as the old Duke of Wellington' (from whom, in addition to Wesley, Voysey was descended). In his book *Individuality* (1915) Voysey had deplored the foundation of architectural schools and the disappearance of the personal contact between architect and pupil. John quoted this reactionary blast from the book: 'It is the old trades union tendency to provide one dead level of mediocrity in order that the feeble may fare as well as the famous.' But to justify the inclusion of such a benighted theorist in the *Review*, John was obliged to emphasize Voysey's alleged status as a 'pioneer': 'Although we see many of his decorative details reproduced *ad nauseam* in tea shop, waiting room and monster furnishing store, the simplicity to which he – as much if not more than William Morris – leads us back from the complex and futile revivalism in which many architects still remain, has made itself felt at least on the Continent.'[61] The case for regarding Voysey as a pioneer of the Modern Movement was hardly strengthened by an article by him which prefaced John's, a panegyric of the Gothic which ended: 'When Gothic architecture ceased to be fashionable, away went that lovely quality so often to be seen in the old towns of Holland, where all the houses are different, though sympathetically respecting each other, like gentlemen. Now an angry rivalry, or a deadly dull uniformity, is the dominant feature of our street architecture.'[62] Neither was the case improved by a whimsical little foreword by Sir Edwin Lutyens which praised Voysey for creating an architecture 'with which you could laugh . . . the "hearted" shutters, the client's profile on a bracket, the absence of accepted forms . . .'[63]

Lutyens, John recalled in 1968, was the only classical architect he and his colleagues on the *Review* had been allowed to admire, though 'bankers' Georgian' was despised. An exception was made for Lutyens because in his youth he had been associated with the Arts and Crafts Movement. 'We all knew, of course, that the movement was laughably out of touch with the great machine age into which we were emerging but we realized that it was at least "sincere" and not copying Greek and Roman details. And anyhow Lutyens was a rebel. Hadn't he had a row with the RIBA?'[64] Christian Barman sent John round to Lutyens's office to obtain drawings and photographs for reproduction. Lutyens was 'as welcoming as he was fascinating'. With the aid of a pencil and a penny he showed John 'how to turn a moulding from half a pipe into a living curve, by just stopping it being a quarter or a half and making it between the two'.[65]

In 1931 John went to see M.H. Baillie Scott, another survivor of the older generation of architects, at his office in Bedford Row. He was not in, but John was cordially received by his partner Edgar

Beresford, who had become Baillie Scott's assistant in 1905. Baillie Scott was in the country. Did John want to illustrate some of their houses in the *Review*? No, that was not really why he had come. He wanted to look at the early work. The houses Baillie Scott was designing in 1931 seemed to John neo-Georgian, 'and though I did not say it, I would not have dared to show such a style of house to H. de C. Hastings'.[66] John must have made a favourable impression on Beresford, as he soon received an invitation from Baillie Scott to stay with him and his wife at their house, Ockhams, near Edenbridge, Kent. It was a Kentish farmhouse with an uneven tiled roof, brick chimney stacks, timbers and 'as far as I can remember, leaded windows but leaded, of course, in the right way, that is to say in oblong panes proportioned to the house'.[67] Inside were dark oak furniture, watercolours and chintzes, 'but the chief thing I remember was the presence of flowers everywhere in patterns, in vases and wherever you looked from the windows'.[68] Baillie Scott himself was a surprise.

> I had been used to architects looking like architects. There were two types in the thirties, the business man with a pin-striped suit and the addition either of an eyeglass or a little beard to show there was something artistic about him too, and there were the younger architects in hairy tweeds with knitted, woollen ties and bright shirts in primary colours. Baillie Scott was like neither type. He was an unassuming countryman and looked like Thomas Hardy but bigger.[69]

In his 'sleepy, laconic way with his melancholy expression, half-shut eyes and drooping moustache', Baillie Scott told John the events of his life with the kind of throwaway humour John enjoyed most. 'I went to the Isle of Man for a holiday,' he said. 'I was so seasick I couldn't face the journey back so I set up in practice there.'[70] John especially relished the story of Baillie Scott's visit to Darmstadt to decorate the Grand Duke's palace. 'He was met at the station by the royal carriage. Behind it was a wagonette with four horses for his luggage. This consisted of a single grip.'[71]

John wrote a strangely contorted review of Baillie Scott's and Beresford's book *Houses and Gardens* in the *Review* of May 1933. The two architects had not made it easy for him to claim them as 'pioneers': their text was largely 'reasoned invective against the architecture of concrete and steel'.[72] Adroitly, but with heavy irony, John exculpated them for these embarrassing views:

I doubt whether the authors, had they been born into this generation, would have taken up such an attitude. The courage which caused them to build in an original and refreshing manner in 1900 would have been the cause of their adoption of modern methods to-day . . . This generation has realized that by now there is no escape and that we must fall in with the machine, that the England of quiet lanes and elm-surrounded villages is finished, and that instead a new international civilization has grown up in Europe of urban peoples whose church is the office, whose fields are the cinema, whose lanes are arterial roads, and whose houses are mere dormitories in a block of flats.[73]

Charles Rennie Mackintosh, the *art nouveau* designer and architect whom John admired most, died in 1928, too early for John to meet him; but John was able to talk to Fra Newbery, who had taught Mackintosh at the Glasgow School of Art. And in 1933 he was just in time to meet Mackintosh's exact contemporary George Walton, who had worked with Mackintosh on Miss Cranston's Tea Rooms in Glasgow, which John had described affectionately in his 'Still Going Strong' article of May 1930.

In December 1933 John arrived without appointment at the Waltons' little flat in Greycoat Place, Chelsea. They had come to London as Walton wanted his young son Edward to go to Westminster School, and could not afford boarding fees. At risk to Walton's health, the family moved into a converted fireman's-flat. John had tracked him down from his previous addresses in Shepherd's Bush, London, and Hythe, Kent. Edward Walton recalled: 'Betjeman was very enthusiastic about my father's work, called him "Architect" and wanted to write about him. My mother was pleased at the attention and after Betjeman left said how nice it was for [Walton] to be recognized still . . .'[74]

On 7 December, George Walton became ill in the middle of the night. He was taken by ambulance to St John and St Elizabeth Hospital and died three days later. Unaware of this, John reappeared at the flat in a few days, bringing the text of an article on Walton for the architect to check and approve. 'On hearing the news of my father's death, he was stricken,' Edward Walton wrote. 'He left in great confusion.'[75] During the next few weeks, John took the family's affairs in hand. On 10 January he waited on H.V. Vincent at 10 Downing Street to explain why Walton's Civil List pension should be transferred to his widow,[76] and he persuaded the trustees of the

Architects' Benevolent Fund to pay Edward's school fees. Walton's death was recorded in *The Architectural Review* of January 1934, in the caption to a large illustration of the Regency-like White House, Shiplake, which he had designed in 1908. A short obituary, presumably written by John, was published in the same issue.[77]

Another of the older architects whom John was eager to meet was Ninian Comper, a hero to him since his childhood days in Cornwall when he had admired Comper's Molesworth Chapel in Little Petherick Church and had bicycled to Blisland, whose golden altars are among Comper's earliest work. He did meet Comper, and was a friend for the rest of the architect's long life (1864–1960) and an executor of his will. 'Comper I knew well,' he wrote to Canon Peter Bourne in 1975. 'He had a beard and always wore black pin-striped suits and talked in a rather lah-di-dah way about Aubrey Beardsley and rood screens and ciboria.'[78]

The three architects whose friendship and influence were most important to John, both in his *Architectural Review* days and later, were Frederick Etchells and H.S. Goodhart-Rendel (both born in 1887) and John Summerson (born 1904). John's other mentor was always known as 'P. Morton Shand', in full, but Etchells was called just 'Etchells', except in a couplet which John and his friends used to sing to the tune of 'The Volga Boatman':

> The sunset sheds a horizontal ray
> On Frederick Etchells, F.R.I.B.A.[79]

As a Vorticist Etchells had contributed, with Ezra Pound, to the first issue of Wyndham Lewis's magazine *Blast*. He had also worked in the Omega Workshops with Roger Fry. In 1927 he had given the Modern Movement in England the first of its gospels by translating Le Corbusier's *Vers Une Architecture*.[80] (Morton Shand provided the second in 1935 with his translation of Gropius.) Etchells designed one of the first[81] 'modern' buildings in Britain, the Crawford office block in Holborn, London (1929–31) – 'because,' John commented, 'poor old Welch of Welch and Landor could not get it finished properly'.[82] A feature on the Crawford building appeared in the *Review* of February 1931.

John became a wide-eyed disciple of Etchells. It was Etchells whose 'inspired monologues on architecture' first made him realize the difference between 'modern' and *'moderne'*.[83] *Moderne* (usually called Art Deco today) was virtually outlawed by the *Review*, although the Daimler Hire Garage in Herbrand Street, London, by Wallis, Gilbert & Partners, who were regarded as the most heinous offenders in 'façadist' *moderne*, was illustrated in the issue of November 1931. John's Oxford friend Michael Dugdale – then himself studying at the Architectural Association – contributed a verse satire on Wallis, Gilbert to the issue of July 1932. Titled 'Ornamentia Praecox', it was accompanied by a drawing by William Edmiston showing a jazzy factory in the 'Great South Road' by 'Jones, Smith & Family' (unmistakably intended as a take-off of the Hoover Factory in the Great West Road by Wallis, Gilbert & Partners). Three of the nine stanzas ran:

> Leave no space undecorated;
> Hide those ugly wheels and pipes.
> Cover them with noughts and crosses
> Mess them up with stars and stripes.
>
> Now for curves and now for colour,
> Swags and friezes, urns and jars.
> Now for little bits of faience,
> Now for giddy glazing bars.
>
> Whoops! Tra-la! let's all go crazy.
> Tirra-lirra! let's go gay.
> Sanity may come tomorrow,
> Ornament is in today.[84]

John was told that one of the partners of Wallis, Gilbert called at Queen Anne's Gate with a horsewhip, 'but he never found the ever-elusive H. de C.'[85]

After John's marriage in July 1933, he persuaded his father-in-law, Field-Marshal Sir Philip Chetwode, to employ Etchells as the architect of his new house at 40 Avenue Road, St John's Wood, London. 'You can see the feller's never built a gentleman's house,' barked the Field-Marshal. 'There's no brushin' room.'[86]

H.S. Goodhart-Rendel[87] had already been a regular contributor to *The Architectural Review* for years when John came on to the staff: for example, he had contributed two articles (January and February 1926) on Temple Moore, the architect mentioned by John in his poem 'Perp. Revival i' the North'. Goodhart-Rendel's most celebrated building of the 1930s, Hay's Wharf, London (the *Review* devoted eight pages to it in February 1932) has been claimed for the Modern Movement but really has far more in common with the *moderne* buildings of Wallis, Gilbert with its swaggering gilt letters, zig-zag window casements, marquetry lift doors and exterior reliefs by Frank Dobson. In his writings, Goodhart-Rendel made clear his distaste for the Modern Movement with a debonair facetiousness which outraged the more solemn ideologues. His detachment and wit seemed out of place in the committed 1930s, and Robert Furneaux Jordan has described him as 'an erudite flâneur'.[88] But of course his humour recommended him to John, who particularly enjoyed Goodhart-Rendel's comment to Osbert Lancaster after inspecting the Parthenon: 'Well! Not what you'd call an unqualified success, is it?'[89]

John Summerson was another subversive ostensibly within the Modern Movement. Like Betjeman, he was part of what Dr Gavin Stamp calls 'the MARS gang': the Modern Architectural Research Group, founded in 1933 by Wells Coates and P. Morton Shand. Summerson was even The Voice at the MARS Group Exhibition of 1938, booming slogans from a gramophone record.[90] But he had too subtle and dispassionate a mind to be altogether bowled over by what he later called 'the hurricane functionalists'. Even in 1938 he concluded that the only explanation of the wholesale loyalty of the Architectural Association school to Modernism was its 'poetic appeal; and the poet is the Ruskin of our age, Le Corbusier'.[91] In 1933, when he first met John, Summerson was still beguiled by that poetry. The two met in an exhibition of Alvar Aalto's work in Fortnum & Mason's attic gallery. Morton Shand had obtained Summerson a job as Aalto's secretary. In that capacity he met not only John, who came along as the *Review*'s representative, but the Hungarian photographer and designer László Moholy-Nagy, soon to become a friend of John's and illustrator of his book *An Oxford University Chest* (1938).[92] At that time Summerson was researching the life and architecture of John Nash, on whom he published a monograph in 1935.[93] A little later he became assistant editor of the *Architect and Building News*, but moonlighted by writing articles commissioned by John for *The Architectural Review*, under the nom-de-plume 'Coolmore' – by which John addressed him ever afterwards.[94]

Like Summerson, John's Oxford friend Michael Dugdale trained at the Architectural Association. Later he joined the avant-garde Russian architect Berthold Lubetkin in the Tecton partnership, whose best-known works were the gorilla house (1932) and penguin pool (1933) at London Zoo, and Highpoint Flats in Highgate (1935 and 1936-38). Apart from the expansive coverage given to Tecton buildings in the *Review*, John commissioned several articles by Dugdale and published three of his poems. But an unusually acid letter of 1931 from John to Dugdale suggests that Dugdale may have been talking out of turn and biting the hand which fed him:

My dear Michael,

I am told by various A.A. people that the Architectural Review is held in great contempt there. It therefore seems rather a waste of your time to send any articles up to it.

– Seriously, though, I think it rather disloyal of you to run it down since it has to circulate among architects for its advertisement revenue – and they are bloody enough God knows – moreover by broadcasting the fact that no one on the staff knows about architecture – a fact which is quite untrue and seems a little jealous – you do it infinite harm in the future. Had I been given the chance that you have had to learn architecture, I would have taken it, tho' had I known that it would lead to my building in the style of ex A.A. students and developing a character like that heterosexual sycophant F.R. Yerbury,[95] I should have desisted. You will probably do me a lot of harm. Please don't mention the paper at all, old boy, if you want 10/6

for the sake of

Your indignant and former friend,

J.B.[96]

Besides showing a certain jealousy of Dugdale on the part of the degreeless John, forced to earn his living by journalism, this letter prompts the question: how influential *was* the *Review* in the 1930s? John himself was in no doubt of the answer. 'If anyone asks me who invented modern architecture,' he wrote in 1974, 'I answer "Obscurity Hastings".'[97] John Summerson has described the *Review* as 'the Diaghilev of the English architectural stage'.[98] In the opinion of John Brandon-Jones, who was at the A.A. with Michael Dugdale, the influence of the *Review* was not only strong but pernicious:

I never understood why so many of my contemporaries were taken in by the International Style, even though every generation tends to revolt against the one before. But the style was taken up and sold by people who were not architects but critics, like H. de C. Hastings and Pevsner. For years they published it and nothing else, and they managed to sell it to intellectuals . . . Architects took it up when it became clear that you could not get a building into the *Review* unless it was in the style. It was a propaganda exercise, unparalleled since Burlington brought in the Palladian style.[99]

Brandon-Jones thought that much of the effectiveness of the *Review* as a propaganda instrument came not from the writing but from the artful photography. The buildings were always photographed when they were new and when the shadows and the background sky were right.[100]

As third-in-command at the *Review*, then, John could have been a figure of some power on the British architectural scene of the early 1930s. De Cronin Hastings might be 'tyrannical' when he descended on the magazine to deliver his edicts and reprimands, but his long absences and his Tibetan inaccessibility even when he was on the premises, gave his lieutenants considerable discretion – and opportunities for indiscretion. John was more interested in contributing history, comedy and poetry to the *Review* than in trying to affect the course of the Modern Movement. In a prophetic article, 'Dictating to the Railways' (September 1933) he discussed the future of the Euston Arch. 'For many years now there have been rumours about the reconstruction of Euston, the demolition of its great arch and its old booking hall, now known as the Great Hall.'[101] John further declared that 'a new Euston is not a matter to be decided by old gentlemen [the directors of the L.M.S.] in the mahogany confines of Hardwick's imposing Boardroom', and proposed that, if the arch had to go, it should at least be re-erected elsewhere.[102] He also wrote a caption to a full-page photograph of the arch taken by Maurice Beck:

GREECE OFF THE EUSTON ROAD

Hardwick's Doric arch at Euston is the supreme justification of the Greek Revival in England. It is so often said, in criticism of this building and its neighbour the Inwood's St Pancras Church, that Greek architecture looks wrong in England, that it is a style built for sunlight and strong shadows. The now blackened Craigleith stone of Euston Arch, even more than the brighter Portland stone of St Pancras Church, makes the Doric Order appropriate and native to the Metropolis. In this *Close Range* illustration we can see how the Order was made for London gloom. Euston Great Arch looms like the gateway of a gaol over the schoolboy, once in his hansom, now in his taxi-cab, going over those cobbles from London and back to school: its boding mass is a portent of troubles in Ireland to which the trains go daily from Euston: its magnificent proportions make the newspaper men and loungers who cluster round its base seem like ziczacs round a crocodile: its immobility has been the despair of the L.M.S., and if vandals ever pulled down this lovely piece of architecture, it would seem as though the British Constitution had collapsed, or the Army and Navy Stores had closed its doors . . .[103]

John's contributions on architectural history included an essay on Sezincote (May 1932). His reviews of such books as E. Jervoise's *The Ancient Bridges of the South of England* (1931), A.E. Richardson's *Georgian England* (1931), F.R. Yerbury's *Modern Dutch Buildings* (1932) and Noël Carrington's *Design in the Home* (1933) showed his learning, if not always the strictest impartiality: the despised Yerbury got short shrift. And John could not keep his mischief and vivacity in check for long. They constantly showed through, like a brocade waistcoat under a sub-fusc jacket. Imaginary societies were advertised. Spoof letters were published and received spoof answers. A caption to a deadpan photograph of Giles Gilbert Scott telephone boxes, in April 1934, read: 'A SEDAN CHAIR PARK? No – just a nice tidy corner of London's art centre – telephone boxes at the back of Burlington House'. A feature on Robert Lorimer (November 1931) was headlined 'The J.M. Barrie of Architecture'. An article by John on Wolf's Cove, Thirlwall Mere & District (January 1932), turned out to concern a miniature model village in the garden of Snowshill Manor, Gloucestershire, home of the architect Charles P. Wade, and John had named all the people in the village after his friends ('The Miller, George Kolkhorst, is old now, and young Toby, his son, is carrying on the business . . .'). Increasingly, the *Review* had a flavour of the *Cherwell* – cleverness and camp.

Many of the old *Cherwell* crowd were brought in by John as contributors. Robert Byron, Cyril Connolly, Christopher Hobhouse ('Hobvilla') and Peter Quennell were already writing for it when John arrived, and to them were added Michael Dugdale,

Clonmore, Evelyn Waugh (an article on the Spanish architect Antonio Gaudí in June 1930), Bryan Guinness, Alan Pryce-Jones, Ellis Waterhouse, John Bowle, Osbert Lancaster (whose 'Pelvis Bay' series was first published in the *Review*), Randolph Churchill, Patrick Balfour, John Sparrow, Norman Cameron, Louis Mac-Neice (a poem in June 1934) and W.H. Auden (a book review in July 1933). One old *Cherwell* hand who, as ever, brought trouble with him, was Brian Howard, the Oxford aesthete to whom Waugh applied Lady Caroline Lamb's description of Lord Byron: 'mad, bad and dangerous to know'. John commissioned Howard to review, in the November 1930 issue, *The London Promenade*, a book on contemporary London both written and illustrated by the young artist and art critic William Gaunt. The book had already been praised in the Press by the art historian R.H. Wilenski. Howard waspishly commented: 'The knell-like note ... of Mr Wilenski's approbation had rung out for me before I received this volume for review, and, not unnaturally, I was on my guard ... Whenever I read one of this gentleman's enthusiastic articles in the newspaper, hailing, in his madcap way, yet another world genius, I feel exactly as if I were some Dartmoor farmer who hears, resigned but resolute, the baleful drone of the prison siren. It means that one more unfortunate has got to be harried back into the obscurity from which he should never have been permitted to escape.'[104] This drew from Wilenski an indignant protest, published in the next issue, against the 'shameless confession of prejudice on the part of a reviewer in your important and responsible publication.'[105] Brian Howard's services were not requested again.

The *Review* published verses by John. In February 1930 it printed 'The Church's Restoration' (which had first appeared in the *Isis*) and in November 1930, 'Westgate on Sea'. (The first line of the last stanza read: 'For me in my Voisey [*sic*] arbour'; for subsequent publication in book form, John altered this to 'timber arbour', perhaps feeling that the general public could not be expected to understand the reference to an architect who was well-known to readers of the *Review*.) 'A Railway Prospect of a Provincial Town' appeared in the issue of May 1935.

Some of the verse John contributed to the *Review* was never reprinted. In October 1931, when the Leicester Galleries, London, held the first complete exhibition of Algernon Newton's paintings of sun-soaked stucco villas, John wrote a verse caption to three of the works – 'Hampstead Garden Suburb', 'Coloured Houses on the Regent's Canal' and 'Chepstow Villas, Bayswater':

> Those trees in awkward silence wait
> A new 'Desirable Estate'.
> In lines of scaffolding and tin
> They contemplate the growth of sin
> And yet the very sin creates
> Strange beauty from its new estates . . .[106]

To the special 'Electricity Issue' of November 1933 he contributed a long poem in heroic couplets titled 'The Electrification of Lambourne End – A Poem in the Manner of the Rev. George Crabbe'. It was preceded by 'An Apology for the Poem':

The poem, which starts in the next column and goes on for such a long time in the others, must not be taken as a declamation against the benefits of electricity. It serves to show the old-fashioned abuses of electricity. Within the last ten years electricity has made such vast strides that the old shams of mediaeval electric lanterns, mediaeval electric log fires, mediaeval electrically lit beams have passed away. This is an old-fashioned poem on an old-fashioned theme. Antiquarians will appreciate it as such; those who see in electricity a new and beautified life and landscape for England will understand its salutary message.[107]

The poem was exactly what John pretended it was not: a hymn of hate against electricity. It began:

> How ALBERT SPARKE has licences to sell
> Both beer and spirits in his new Hotel:
> How he, who once sold paltry pints of beer,
> Now profits in Martini shall appear.
> My muse shall show how small the changes are
> Which make a palm court of a public bar.
> How Albert's income rose from night to night,
> From fifty pounds to fifteen hundred quite
> Largely because of *the Electric Light*.[108]

The poem went on to describe how Albert Sparke had made his fortune by floodlighting his pub, 'The Tranter's Load', and picking out in electric bulbs 'This house is over seven centuries old.'

What matter if 'twas six whole centuries out,
When Albert Sparke knew what he was about?

The poem ends:

Who is that man with Old Harrovian tie,
Enliven'd footwear and commercial eye?
That pros'prous, gentlemanly business shark?
Why that, fond reader – that is Albert Sparke.
See what *Electric Light* with transport's aid
Has brought to him who understands his trade.
The signboard is repainted o'er the door:
Not 'Tranter's Load', but now 'La Nuit d'Amour'.[109]

Working for *The Architectural Review*, John found, was not all
fun – chatting with Edwardian architects or writing funny captions
and verse. Much of the day's routine seemed drudgery. 'I write and
I write and I write,' he complained in 1933, 'under different names
and in different styles, yet no one has heard of either me or my
pseudonyms. I must have written the word architecture more times
than there are people in England who can pronounce it
properly.'[110] We get a glimpse of his more run-of-the-mill work at
that time from a letter written to him in 1960 by Mr R. Morris. His
father had founded the Morris Singer Company ('not to be confused with motor cars or Singer sewing machines'), a firm which
carried out 'high class architectural metal work – bronze statuary –
stained glass windows, etc. etc.' In about 1930, Morris told John,
he had called at the *Review* with photographs of his own designs in
stained glass and leaded lights.

I was ushered into an impressive Editor or Assistant Editor's Office
which was furnished in the very latest mode of chromium plated
wonder that I had ever at that time seen. And at a super modern
desk and in a super modern chair sat a gentleman whose name was
Mr Betjeman. If this was you indeed, I must do you the justice to say
that you interviewed me with every gesture of sympathetic interest
and I presume controlled tolerance, tempered with kindness and
not spoiled by any flavour of patronage. You struck me as being a
real 'High Brow' but a pleasant one at that – although you deemed it
wise, and I now know you to have been right, to have nothing to do
with the wares I was offering at the time.[111]

'Controlled tolerance' is probably a fair description of John's attitude to life on the *Review*. The tolerance could not last for ever; the control snapped. When growing rewards from the *Evening Standard* and from editing county guides for Shell-Mex offered him a measure of independence, he jumped at the chance and left the *Review* abruptly.

J.M. Richards happened to be in de Cronin Hastings's room discussing an article when John burst in to give his resignation.

> He flung into the room [Richards recalled]. John had a way that perhaps impressed Hastings more than my polite way of knocking at the door, of just storming in when he wanted to. Anyway, he flung into the room and shouted: 'Well, if you're not going to pay me another £300 a year I'm leaving tomorrow.' And he did leave shortly after that. But I don't think that was the reason he left. De Cronin wasn't ungenerous, financially. John obviously wanted to leave and his temperament was of that kind which made him want to create a scene in order to excuse him. He had decided he had other fish to fry and didn't want to spend his life being a magazine editor – still less an assistant editor.[112]

In spite of his petulant flouncing-out, John remained on good terms with Hastings and continued to contribute to the *Review* for many years. But leaving the magazine released him from any further obligation to subscribe to the Modern Movement's philosophy of architecture. He no longer needed to claim that the Victorian and Edwardian architects and designers he admired were 'pioneers'. (He wrote of Mackintosh and Walton in *First and Last Loves*: 'They are wrongly, I think, heralded as pioneers of modern architecture. They now seem to me to belong to the *art nouveau* of the 1890s . . .'[113]) Neither did he need to pretend that steel pylons were an enhancement of the English landscape. To be fair to him, it was almost certainly he who in the *Review*'s 'Junius' column of September 1932 described the village of Woodstock, near Blenheim Palace, as 'like a poor fly caught in the meshes of a gigantic spider's web, except that the wires and pylons of the electric light company have none of the uncomplicated delicate art of the spider, but rather show the unpremeditated beastliness of the commercial mind at its most ruthless . . .'[114] But by October 1933 the *Review* was publishing, with a suitably romanticizing photograph of skeletal steel, Stephen Spender's poem 'The Pylons':

> ... But far above and far as sight endures
>   Like whips of anger
>   With lightning's danger
>   There runs the quick perspective of the future
>
>   This dwarfs our emerald country by its trek
>   So tall with prophecy ...'[115]

And John himself was probably responsible for an extended caption to a photograph in the same issue: 'these marching shapes of slender metal ... purposeful lines ... the possibility of a cleaner land where industry has already conquered the countryside, reasserting its colours as smoke is withdrawn and untainted sunlight returns.'[116]

In later years, pylons were to be among John's favourite bugbears. ('Encase your legs in nylons,/Bestride your hills with pylons,/O age without a soul.'[117]) In a lecture at the Royal Society of Arts in 1956 he delivered a furious attack on pylons, but when the lecture was printed, George Mansell wrote to him: '... and if memory does not belie me, I remember in 1932 at Painters Hall in the City of London a certain young enthusiast for functional beauty showing a lovely slide of a PYLON in all its austere (and functional) beauty!! I was a fellow lecturer at that same event. TEMPORA MVTANTVR NOS ET MVTAMVR IN ILLIS.'[118] John replied:

> I remember that slide of a pylon and I think I have still got it somewhere. Of course lecturing about it in that silly way does untold damage. A pylon in itself may be all right, but its setting is something in those days I did not regard. Pylons may look all right in large rolling landscape, but they look perfectly ghastly in quiet Cotswold country or among Essex elms. The same silly consideration of things caused the Royal Fine Art Commission, many years ago, to approve one kind of concrete lamp standard. Oh dear, one must be careful![119]

As his early imprudences reared up to haunt him, John's stance was somewhat like that of a 'good German', a Rommel who had worked for the Nazis without being tainted by their ideology. But when antagonism to the Modern Movement, led by Dr David Watkin and Dr Gavin Stamp, gained ground in the 1970s, he was sometimes made to seem more like an Albert Speer, denouncing the former masters whom he had served too well. Watkin and Stamp were both devoted to John, but they could not altogether exonerate him for suggesting, in *Ghastly Good Taste* (1933), that James Gibbs, who placed the classical Radcliffe Camera, Oxford, in the heart of a Gothic setting, 'would also have had the courage to build today as sincere an essay in modern materials in its place.'[120] Even more damning, in Watkin's view, was a passage in John's pamphlet *Antiquarian Prejudice* (1939) in which he attacked 1930s buildings for exemplifying 'the timidity miscalled "tradition" but really antiquarianism, which enslaves be-knighted architects' and urged architects to imitate the example of Soviet Russia in producing 'an honest plain structure of steel, glass and/or reinforced concrete.'[121] John was also taken to task for having been a member of the MARS Group. John Summerson, another unlikely MARS recruit, had at least shown proper contrition in 1959 by describing the Group's New Burlington Galleries exhibition of 1937–38 as 'plastered with captions and exhortations of the most vacuous pomposity (I wrote them and I know)'.[122]

A more surprising recantation than John's and Summerson's was that of P. Morton Shand. In 1958, two years before his death, he wrote John a letter from Saint-André-de-Sangonis, France, to which he had retreated because 'awful new buildings going up so rapidly drove me into a nervous frenzy . . . Finally my state of mind got so bad that I had to emigrate to here, where there are as good as no symptoms of the Twentieth-Century Way of Life, and all the villages have noble but crumbling little Romanesque churches – *no* Gothic, thank heavens, anywhere near here.'[123] Morton Shand had always teased John about his fondness for the Gothic, especially Victorian Gothic. The only reason he would wish to see Victorian buildings preserved, he told John in the same letter, 'is to prevent their sites being occupied by the unspeakable box-frame crudities now being erected everywhere, with universal admiration, as enlightened examples of "contemporary modern idiom" and "original clothing".' Morton Shand was prepared to shoulder some of the blame as a part-creator of this architectural Frankenstein.

I have frightful nightmares, and no wonder, for I am haunted by a gnawing sense of guilt in having, in however minor and obscure degree, helped to bring about, anyhow encouraged and praised, the embryo searchings that have now materialized into a monster neither of us could have foreseen: Contemporary Architecture (=

the piling up of gigantic children's toy bricks in utterly dehuman-
ized and meaningless forms), 'Art' and all that. It is no longer funny;
it is a frightening, all-invading menace.[124]

John marked this passage and later reprinted it as evidence that
Morton Shand had renounced what he had believed in the 1930s.

John's own recantation was as unequivocal as Mucius Scaevola's
or Cranmer's. Expressions of it are to be found in many of his
poems, articles and letters of protest in the Press. But perhaps the
most telling evidence of his *volte-face* is a letter which he wrote in
1943 to the man who had first led him up that shining path, Hubert
de Cronin Hastings.

My dear Obscurity,
          I have just bought, in Dublin, *Towards a New
Britain*, which I suspect you wrote. It both shocked and delighted me.
Delighted because it will help to make people think beyond the local
district council: because it was clear and full of instruction. Shocked
because it put up such a poor show for contemporary building. The
drawing on the cover for instance. Between you and me I'd rather live
in that pottery town where the chimneys are made of wine-bottles
and T-squares, than in that summer 'land labourer's cottage' with the
[Ernö] Goldfinger paving and sheets of glass looking over on to the
tall skyscrapers. And so would you. Why do we both live in
farmhouses and not at High Point? Oh my dear Obscurity, we *must*
make contemporary domestic architecture according to rules of proportion and with textures which will fit in with the buildings we have
got. Is there no map of buildings which are built up to, let us say,
1850? And of the better ones after that date? And of skylines? and
trees and prevalent materials and inbuilding? Is the flat roof essential
in the pre-fabricated house? . . . If you can show one decent domestic
unit – NOT A BLOCK OF FLATS – and not from Arizona or
Sweden: if you can show it in *use* and in action in the photograph and
if you can guarantee by imposing it on a photograph of a street of old
houses, that it is the sort of house you wouldn't mind living in with a
family or living opposite – then you will have done more than all your

book can do, for you will have appealed to the heart as well as the head. If bricks and stucco made this:–

which fitted in with mountains or marshes from 1800–1830, why don't we find its equivalent for the present time in England. I haven't seen it yet...

    Love from all to all,

John B.[125]

14

WITH THE BRIGHT YOUNG PEOPLE

How glad I am that I was bound apprentice
To Patrick's London of the 1920s.
Estranged from parents (as we all were then),
Let into Oxford and let out again,
Kind fortune led me, how I do not know,
To that Venetian flat-cum-studio
Where Patrick wrought his craft in Yeoman's Row.

John Betjeman, 'For Patrick, *aetat* LXX', 1974

Several of John's contemporaries hated their fathers almost to the point of parricide. John Bowle, Clonmore and Lionel Perry are well-documented examples. The trouble usually began over money. Today, most Oxford undergraduates are largely financed by state grants. But John and his friends were reliant on their fathers both for boarding and tuition fees and for 'spending-money'. In some cases, fathers got into financial difficulties and were unable to send their sons adequate funds. Other fathers were rich but miserly, 'tight'. 'He doesn't give you much of the oodle,' John remarked to Lionel Perry of Perry's millionaire father.[1] More often, in a snob-ridden Oxford where lavish living won kudos, the sons overspent and had to be bailed out of debt by their fathers.

After Oxford, there was sometimes a tussle over the sons' choice of career – or over their failing to find a career. Their taste in girlfriends could also be a source of conflict. And if, as was the case with many of John's friends, the son was homosexual, that could cause further hostility. To these young men, Patrick Balfour's studio-flat at 26A Yeoman's Row – 'the Yeo', as they called it – became on a modest scale what the Prince of Wales's Carlton House had been during George III's reign: a place of refuge and a headquarters of disaffection.

After Oxford, Balfour had been sent by his parents to learn French at the Sorbonne. He found that he preferred the Ritz. After blewing most of his money he returned to Scotland in 1926 and began serving an apprenticeship in journalism on the *Glasgow Herald*, supplementing his income by sending social tit-bits to the London papers, 'paragraphs about people I did not know.'[2] The gossip column was Balfour's natural vehicle. He moved to London and worked first for the *Weekly Dispatch*, then for the *Daily Sketch* as 'Mr Gossip,' and finally for 'The Londoner' column of the *Evening Standard*, where John was to be among his colleagues.

When 'Sligger' Urquhart heard that Balfour had left Glasgow for London, he said: 'That's that. He'll become a butterfly.'[3]

He was right [Balfour conceded]. I took a studio-flat in Bromptonia,[4] done up in Italianate style, and settled down to make enemies. The style was one that was already out of fashion with the discovery, by the ladies of Mayfair, of the decorative properties of whitewash ... I was nevertheless photographed in this studio for *Vogue*, seated at a refectory table with Mr Cyril Connolly, who shared the place with me until he found my snobbish way of life too distasteful and ... sensibly left for abroad to get married. In later years he once referred wittily to this period when 'we didn't know where the next meal was coming from, nor whom to ask to it'.[5]

In about June 1928 Connolly told Balfour that he ought to find somebody else to share the flat with him. 'I really can't afford it,' he wrote.[6] He left the Yeo in July, and by the end of the year was experiencing the 'irrecoverable intensity'[7] of life in 1920s Paris. His place in the Yeo was temporarily taken by George Schurhoff, a City man who had been at Oxford with Balfour and who gave him dubious advice on the stock market. He was a figure of fun to Balfour and John, who called him 'Shrufty' or 'The Sarcophagus'. Romney Summers, who had been a notorious aesthete at Oxford – he had held no fewer than six leaving-parties – also stayed in the house from time to time. But when John was dismissed by Sir Horace Plunkett in March 1929, Balfour offered him Connolly's old room.

If Connolly, who had a salary from the *New Statesman*,[8] could not afford the rent, how could John, now jobless? The answer seems to be that Balfour asked John to be his guest. That may explain a letter to Balfour from Bess Betjemann, dated 7 February (?1930) in which she tells him that 'Your great kindness to John leaves me under a sense of heavy obligation to you.'[9]

In March or April 1929 Balfour wrote to his mother, Lady Kinross:

> I have just been having John Betjeman to stay with me. He is the most delightful person, with such a quick brain and exquisite sense of humour ... He has a passion for things that are obscure: obscure peers, obscure suburbs, obscure religions. We trotted out last Sunday to Alexandra Park, in North London, & rowed upon the lake, & walked for miles through suburbs, & John knew every single Baptist & Methodist Chapel by name that we passed. He started a novel here, which I think will be frightfully good, about a boy who runs away from home because he is bullied, & is taken pity on & sent to live with a Baptist family & to a third-rate school in Chingford – & then becomes an assistant in a 'furnishing house' in Tottenham High-road, N.22, all full of fumed oak and linoleum. He has a marvellous insight into that kind of life, and writes in a good, crisp, direct style. Brenda Dufferin got him a job as secretary to Sir Horace Plunkett, & when he was ill he put a friend (so-called) into his place as a temporary substitute, and the friend made bad blood and undermined John & got the job for himself, & John is left penniless, cut off by his family because they swallowed the bad blood. Really some people are monsters.[10]

No draft of the novel seems to have survived, but the plot summarized by Balfour reflects John's state of mind at the time. Indeed, John may have been giving Balfour a broad hint in describing a hero who 'runs away from home because he is bullied, & is taken pity on . . .'

The Yeo was John's London base during the whole time he taught at Heddon Court. His favourite pupils were invited there for tea or lunch at weekends or in the holidays. Among them was Roger Roughton, who was still corresponding with Balfour by February 1932. (From Uppingham School: 'I saw Betjeman last holidays; I think his book [*Mount Zion*] is brilliant.'[11]) Two other pupils of John's, Marcus Sheldon (Sheldon IV) and his brother Stephen (Sheldon V),[12] also visited the Yeo. 'I am on tenterhooks,'

John wrote to Balfour in December 1929. 'Sheldon IV follows me about wherever I go. He likes to look at those large copies of the *Architectural Review* with me. He says he wants to ask me a question and somehow he doesn't know how to ask it. In a private way he told me that twice today. I wonder what the question can be?'[13] Marcus Sheldon wrote to Balfour in June 1930:

Dear Patrick,
            It was fun seeing you on Sunday with George [?Schurhoff]. Were those your sisters? One looked like you, but the other might have been anyone (I don't mean in the social scale). In the dining hall there is a ghastly side-board, the sort all garnished with curtains and corners. While taking tea on Monday, Mr Betjeman looked in the mirror in it and said, 'Good looking fellow, eh?' to Miss Taylor. The maids were all standing by, so the direct effect was that they burst into a shriek of hysterical laughter . . .
    Great excitement the other day, when I received a beautiful pear from Evelyn Waugh. Everyone was most envious, and I, proud.[14]

In October 1930 John sent Balfour a poem Marcus Sheldon had written about the R101 airship, which had passed over Heddon Court on its fatal last journey on 4 October. Almost twenty years later, Balfour (by now Lord Kinross) sent John a photograph of Marcus Sheldon which he had been given in 1929 or 1930. John replied: 'Very nice to see that picture of Sheldon IV again. IV for love, but V for fun I suspect, don't you?'[15]

John tended to exaggerate his homosexual leanings in his letters to Balfour, because he knew he was playing to a receptive gallery. Balfour was well-known as a boy-fancier. But other friends noticed John's burgeoning interest in girls after he left Oxford. Elizabeth Longford, who as Elizabeth Harman was a fellow-guest at Pakenham Hall, Ireland, in 1930, was surprised by the contrast with the aesthete she had known at university.

At Oxford [she recalled] I saw him mainly at parties, and I was under the clear impression that his friends were men. Though I went to parties where there were a few women, some up from London, John's friends were men, just as mine were. But in those days it was an almost homosexual society. When I saw him at Pakenham everything was different, because at Pakenham there were men and women. There was no kind of homosexual life at all. Therefore John was one of us, so to speak, he was in an ordinary situation, not in this special Oxford circle. I must say I was amazed at how sort of gallant he was. I remember going to a dance – one of those interminable Irish drives to some party forty miles away. And he was the life and soul of the party; he certainly flirted with every girl that he found himself with – to my amazement then, because this was *not* what I connected him with.[16]

Even in his letters to Balfour, John revealed some of his awakening interest in girls. In August 1929 he wrote from Trebetherick: 'I have discovered a rather beautiful girl here aged 13 and like a Shepperson[17] drawing and my sex becomes rampant. Blue slanting eyes and beautiful voice and figure.'[18] Earlier in the same year, when he was still with Plunkett at Birchington-on-Sea, he had written to Balfour: 'I am amazed at the beauty of Mary Erskine (Hamish's sister) and I love to contemplate the anger of Hamish if I were to elope with her.'[19] In the winter of 1929–30 John did his best to turn this fantasy into reality.

Hamish St Clair-Erskine, younger son of the Earl and Countess of Rosslyn, was a friend of John's at Oxford. John stayed with him eight or nine times at the Rosslyns' home, Hunger Hill, an eight-bedroomed mock-Tudor house at Coolham, Sussex. Erskine's younger sister, Lady Mary St Clair-Erskine (now Lady Mary Dunn) used to be turned out of her twin-bedded room to accommodate the party, which often included Alan Pryce-Jones and Tom Mitford. She was only fifteen in 1926, the year John first came to stay. 'I was horse-mad, so I was out hunting or exercising most of the time,' she recalled. 'But we all met for lunch or for sherry in the nursery, to keep out of the older people's way. And then we'd play charades (John was very inventive); probably go for a walk; sometimes go to a point-to-point.'[20] John introduced her to Victorian architecture. 'We drove to Reading and had a lovely jokey time. I never knew if he was pulling my leg as he showed me the most hideous red brick church you've ever seen, and I tried to think whether there was anything beautiful about it.'[21]

Lord Rosslyn, in one of his volumes of autobiography, described himself as 'a sere and yellow leaf' because he was twenty-five years older than his wife. He drank, betted 'on the tape', played bridge and occasionally went to his London club. 'He probably wondered whether John could be called a gentleman,' Lady Mary said. 'But I think my mother found him so funny that she became *un*-class-conscious.'[22] Lady Rosslyn had been an Edwardian beauty. Irish by birth and a 'rabid Catholic', she had been brought up in India without formal schooling, but she was 'getting her culture' from her close friend Robert Bruce Lockhart, the former diplomatist, who often stayed at Hunger Hill. Lord (Valentine) Castlerosse, the gossip columnist, was another frequent guest. Both men worked for Lord Beaverbrook, and it may have been one of them who drew to his attention an article by John in 1933 which persuaded Beaverbrook to appoint him film critic of the *Evening Standard*.

In 1929 Hamish Erskine was twenty. Though predominantly homosexual, he began that year what Harold Acton later called an 'indefinite flirtation'[23] with Nancy Mitford. It led to an engagement not finally broken off until 1933. Mary Erskine was eighteen in 1929 and John was not the only young man paying court to her. Sir Michael Duff[24] and Count John de Bendern[25] were both admirers. Daphne Fielding met her in 1929 at Vaynol Park, Duff's home in north Wales. 'She ... looked like a pretty and impertinent schoolgirl dressed up in her mother's clothes,' she wrote. 'She could get away with almost anything through her charm, and was always forgiven; and there was often plenty to forgive.'[26] Lady Mary's escapades were already legend. She had been whirled around 'like an Indian club' by a roller-skating apache dancer in a London cabaret; only by biting him had she been able to stop his gyrations. At Vaynol she accidentally drove Richard Sykes's[27] Rolls Royce into Michael Duff's Rolls Royce: the latter cannoned into the wrought-iron gates, 'which slowly toppled and crashed like the walls of Jericho.'[28] (Daphne Fielding thought that there was 'a certain chic' in an accident which involved two Rolls Royces.[29]) In further disgrace for breaking Duff's radio-gramophone, Lady Mary was whisked away from Vaynol in Count de Bendern's private aeroplane.

It was on this gossip-columnist's delight that John had set his sights. But Mary Erskine was not just the socialite flibbertigibbet that Daphne Fielding's memories suggest. She was combatively intelligent and corresponded with John about poetry and religion. He was suffering from doubts about the after-life, and was wondering whether to become a Roman Catholic, perhaps even a Roman Catholic priest. The first of these alleged ambitions may have been intended to recommend him to Lady Rosslyn; the second, to pique Lady Mary into rescuing him from a life of holy chastity. Lady Mary's response was at least vehement. 'My *dear* Betjeman,' she wrote, 'you oughtn't to be *allowed* to become a clergyman or pastor or whatever you *are* going to be. It was the P.S. in the margin about "God did not say the soul could not feel . . ." as regards Heaven etc. and the subject under discussion, that roused me to a remonstrance. *Must* I quote the *whole* Bible to you? – "Eye hath not seen, nor ear heard, *neither has it entered into the heart of man what things God hath prepared for him.*" – Now will you see my point?'[30] This undated letter came from Rome, to which city Lady Mary had been sent by her mother. She asked John for copies of 'Death in Leamington' and 'Westgate-on-Sea'.

John proposed to her in the winter of 1929–30 in his father's study in Church Street, Chelsea. 'It was lit entirely by stained glass,' Lady Mary recalled. 'John must have loved it. I was rather shocked – you know, there was a three-piece suite in violet brocade. And I was extremely flattered but said, "No thanks, I'd much rather have you as a friend." '[31] John remained her friend. In her copy of *Mount Zion* (1931), he wrote: 'Maria, good little thing, bought this. She is not only the only deep love of my life but she is the Angela Brazil[32] of my dreams.'[33] There follows a drawing of a hockey stick, a cricket bat, a tennis racquet, a skipping-rope, a lacrosse stick and cricket balls; and then: 'O hard – that husky voice – that simple schoolgirl. Don't get rid of your freckles.'

Lady Mary married Sir Philip Dunn in 1933. 'I was rather cross when I found out there was a real Miss Hunter Dunn,' she said, 'because I thought John's poem was based on me.'[34] In 1978, after sitting next to her daughter Serena in a box at the Royal Opera House, Covent Garden, John wrote to Lady Mary:

It was a marvellous experience for me suddenly to be transported to Hunger Hill, Coolham, and memories of Loughie [Lady Mary's half-brother, Lord Loughborough] and his father, who was Harry, and all those Tudor beams and David [Lady Mary's younger brother] reading MY MAGAZINE and Ham [Hamish] and Captain Pryce-Jones, as he then wasn't, getting ready for a dance, and the flip of cards and the splash of soda and the Sussex night outside and Harry Rosslyn finishing a whole bottle of port. A smell of Balkan Sobranie cigarettes and the leather thongs to the doors and the beams on the ceilings and the great capacious beds. Loveliest of all, you, with your freckles and smile and pleated skirt and boyish figure and ways. 'Our little spiritual tennis-ball,' as Osbert L[ancaster] used to call you. That marvellous photograph of you by Victor Rothschild[35] haunts my memory as it must have haunted that of your husband when he chose you from the high St Clairs as his wife.[36]

In July 1929 John again stayed with Billy Clonmore at Shelton Abbey. By late July he was in Cornwall. 'Ernie has built himself a most luxurious house here looking straight on to the villa of the local Baronet,' he told Balfour on 31 July.[37] He wrote to him again on 5 August, Bank Holiday Monday:

1,000 thanks for your letter. I have been very busy this morning avoiding a ghastly day of fishing and picnicking on Bodmin Moor. The arrival of a letter for me in the hubbub gave me an excuse to stay a long time in the lavatory and so avoid going. I have now the house to myself and can criticize to my heart's content the old-world floor and the older-world great [sic] and the crazypaving and bits of brass and pewter. This house is amazingly like [illegible] Hill . . . I wish to heaven it were more comfortable. Bess is infused with an idea that the maids have too much to do. We are almost reduced to making our own beds although I should have thought that three servants for three people was adequate.[38]

On 16 August, John travelled to Scotland to spend just over a week with his Heddon Court pupil Dick Addis and the boy's family. As the Addises' only permanent home was in London, they rented for two months every summer a large house, usually in Scotland. 'The sort of house no one would rent,' Sir John Addis recalled '– a large house but without good shooting or fishing.'[39] Between 1928 and 1931 the chosen house was Hartrigge, in the Border country near Jedburgh. A good example of Scottish Baronial in yellow sandstone (now demolished), it was the home of Lord Stratheden, who was serving with the army in Kenya. The Addis boys were encouraged to invite friends to stay. Dick Addis asked whether he might invite Mr Betjeman, and the request was granted. The normal Hartrigge house party was of twelve to twenty young people, most of them under the age of twenty.

We didn't shoot and we didn't fish, except in the most clumsy way [Sir John Addis said] but there were a great many climbing expeditions and picnics; and also, as we were tough and hardy, every day before lunch we liked to swim. The only place where you could swim near Hartrigge (apart from special excursions out to the

North Sea at Bamburgh) was the River Jed, which was absolutely *ice*-cold. We bicycled down, and beside a bridge we plunged into this icy water and swam upstream. I can remember John Betjeman coming with us and nobly plunging into the water too – and he turned the most extraordinary colour, sort of greyish, purplish blue. But he was the most enormous fun. He very quickly accommodated himself to this rather strange family, and I still remember the excitement of half a dozen or more of us sitting round, squatting on the floor, and him telling his anecdotes or talking in his amusing way – very much, then, taking off suburbia and all the standards that went with it.[40]

In the 1929 Hartrigge visitors' book John (giving Sezincote as his address) drew a fanciful half-timbered building which he labelled 'YE TUDOR CLOSE'.[41]

On 17 August John wrote to Patrick Balfour from Hartrigge:

My dear Patrick,
              I do dislike those uncompromising Scotch females who sit like vicious swans over their lunch on the Railway. The train was full of them from Pont Street with their powder put on rather badly and with an air of martyrdom when they were travelling third and felt that they ought to have been travelling first but could not afford it.[42] They all wore simply fearful hats and carried dogs about.
    We have family prayers here which last a good time and then a sung grace of two verses, we stand up to eat porridge so that by the time breakfast begins one is quite tired.
    Everywhere the peasants will point out boulders behind which Burns took down his trousers and ruins where Sir Walter Scott took down his sheep dog. I think I am being rather witty . . .[43]

One result of John's nine days at Hartrigge was a long friendship with the Addises' sister Margie, who married another of John's Heddon Court pupils, Alexander Geddes. She remembers that

John's hair was so unacceptably long that she offered to cut it for him with a pair of nail-scissors when they were about to visit some local grandees. 'I am afraid I was not a very expert hairdresser; and when we got to this family's house, the mother took me aside and said, "My dear, what is wrong with your friend Mr Betjeman? Has he got the *mange*?"'[44] Though John's friendship with the Addis boys was cut short by the incident at Piccadilly Underground station, his friendship with Margie Addis lasted to the end of his life.

Early in 1929 Pierce Synnott and John joined Patrick Balfour and his family at their holiday home on the Isle of Skye. On 16 September, back at Heddon Court, John wrote Lady Kinross a thank-you letter decorated with caricatures. 'It was so depressing,' he told her, 'to leave Skye & wait about two hours in Kyle of Lochalsh while men did nothing to the car, still in sight of the misty mountains, that my temper became very bad.'[45] He and Balfour had travelled on to the Kinrosses' Edinburgh home, 17 Heriot Row. It had been the home, for thirty years, of Robert Louis Stevenson; the gas-lamp in the street outside was that of which Stevenson had written in *A Child's Garden of Verses* –

> For we are very lucky, with a lamp before the door,
> And Leerie stops to light it, as he lights so many more.

John was shown watercolours painted by Lady Kinross – 'miracles of taste and technique,' he assured her. 'Gosh! I did enjoy myself in Skye,' he added. 'School is going to be so awful after it. There is a new games master from Malvern coming.'[46] Synnott had enjoyed the visit too. He wrote to Balfour on 25 September that he liked being on Skye 'and being with the lovely rich assorted Balfours again. The medicinal climate was very agreeable . . . and I even at the end became reconciled to the scenery – though Betjeman's Gothick interpretation was lamentable.'[47]

Although she had three marriageable daughters, Lady Kinross looked upon John with favour – a rarity among upper-class mothers. Knowing she was sympathetic, Balfour kept her well informed of John's plunges in fortune. On 29 October 1929 he reported:

John Betjeman has finally broken with his father, who assaulted him – hit him on the head six times and went for his hunting-crop.

John put up no resistance, judging it the most dignified and humiliating course to take – then got a letter from Ernie saying 'I am surprised I have received no word of apology for your violent attack upon me. I only regret I had no friend near me to give you the thrashing you deserved, and which you have been badly wanting these last two years. However, you will one day no doubt get laid out by someone whom you have insulted and derided; until then you will probably tread the perfect cad's path.' It is magnificent, isn't it?[48]

On 3 January 1930 he wrote to her again: 'John's father has cut him out of his will altogether. He gave him a long lecture on it, beginning, "My poor boy, for poor indeed I must now call you." '[49]

Balfour's accounts of Ernest's alleged behaviour provoke once again the question: how true were John's stories of ill-treatment by his father? Together, Balfour's two reports suggest Victorian melodrama garnished with Wildean humour. Indeed, John might have been re-enacting Lord Alfred Douglas's duels with the Marquess of Queensberry. Ernest's letters to John, though often nagging in tone, are usually good-natured and forgiving. Against this case for the defence, William Hammond's memory of Ernest's flinging wood across the workshop, and Synnott's report on the tantrum in the Dublin hotel, tell against John's father. And a gap, between February 1929 and June 1931, in the sequence of Ernest's letters that John preserved might indicate that the two were not on writing terms; or that the letters were so galling that John tore them up; or that in later years he regarded them as 'sensitive material' and destroyed them so they would not go to Victoria with his other papers.

Did Ernest use violence towards John? Did he write him the wrathful, Queensberry-like letter quoted by Balfour? Was he capable of the stinging jibe that Balfour also records? It would be plausible to assume that John was exaggerating, and that Ernest's fits of temper, as magnified by him, became a standing joke with him and his friends – part of his act, along with the spoof Shakespeare recitals and the horror-stories of basketing at Marlborough. But there are two kinds of exaggeration. Some people see the truth, but embellish it in the telling. Others perceive reality in a distorted way and relate that perception more or less faithfully. John never failed to exploit a good story for what it was worth, and sometimes for more, but he may well have been predisposed to misinterpret, adversely, whatever Ernest said or did. John seems to have been genuinely distressed by Ernest's conduct; but that does not necessarily mean that Ernest's conduct was as cruel as John thought it was, or said it was. The Balfour family did their best to cheer John up, inviting him to parties and dances. 'I did enjoy myself on St Andrew's night,' John wrote to Balfour on 9 December 1929. 'I should like to hear of her Ladyship's opinion of it. I was delighted to see her in that velvet coat. She is perfection. I often think of Rosemary [one of Balfour's sisters].'[50]

In late March 1930 John moved into a flat at 3 Middle Temple Lane sub-let to him by John Sparrow. He shared it with John Bowle, who was teaching history at Westminster School. Angus Wilson, the novelist, then a schoolboy at Westminster, was introduced to Lord Alfred Douglas at the house.[51] He also remembered John's coming to see a school play. 'John Bowle got very drunk; and John Betjeman stood on a table and said: "I say, you chaps aren't going to *peach* on John Edward, are you?" – in the manner of a Victorian public-school novel.'[52] The charwoman in Middle Temple Lane, Mrs Groves, also 'did for' Harold Nicolson in King's Bench Walk.[53] Mrs Groves characterized John's and Bowle's regimen as ''ock for breakfast, 'ock for dinner, 'ock for tea and 'ock for supper'.[54] She tried to keep the young men in order. ''Igh spirits I don't mind,' she told them, 'but 'ooliganism I won't 'ave.'[55]

In April John travelled to Germany with Billy Clonmore and the ever-vigilant Mr Newcombe. To some of John's friends, travel abroad was an escape from unhappiness at home. Not so to John. 'Isn't abroad *awful!*' he once said to Edward James;[56] and Sir Osbert Lancaster said, 'When John is abroad, he has to be surrounded by friends, like a rugby-football player who has lost his shorts.'[57] John wrote lugubriously to Patrick Balfour from the Königshof Grand Hotel Royal, Bonn:

It is useless to pretend that I enjoy myself abroad. The continual difficulty of overcoming a foreign language which the meanest children in the public gardens opposite can speak with fluency, the constant frustration of natural impulse through inability to communicate with the object of one's desires overcomes the spirit as much as it mortifies the flesh. For instance I have drunk tea in my life, but never have I wanted to drink it so much as in this town. It is obtainable but I do not know how to ask for it; it is waiting steaming hot, but I have not the courage to depend on my Hugo's Simplified Course.

I suppose the birds are appearing now outside the Yeo but here they are out already, indecently forward. If the Sarcophagus [Schurhoff] were here with his knowledge of German and you with yours of French we might scrape through comfortably. At the moment it is like being cold-shouldered at Harrogate. Dotty [Clonmore] is never out of the minster church and Mr Newcombe never out of his armchair. The overheating of the hotel is unendurable . . .

Do you remember how Victorian the evening light was on that road to Inverness last summer? Do you remember the rocks and the small conifers at the edge of brake and brae? This place is like that. Not unlike an oleograph. It is disfigured by festoons of electric wire. Across every field run several cables, up every hill a funicular railway. Nor is that all. Down every dusty road tread the wanderfögel or some such word. It is hardly necessary to describe them since they wear velvet and pepper pot hats. When the bells start thundering from the Romanesque churches and the sun sets behind the pinnacled forests, on the roads alongside the tramway lines march the wanderfögel with their arms locked, their hearts and their mouths open. They are going to walk across Germany for their Easter holidays in groups of ten . . .[58]

The three men travelled down the Rhine, looking at baroque palaces. In April they witnessed the Easter ceremonies of the Moravian settlement at Neuwied, near Koblenz.[59]

John was back in London by 26 May, when Evelyn Waugh, after watching Paul Robeson as Othello at the Savoy Theatre, met John at a supper-party given by Frank Pakenham in the Savoy Hotel.[60] Basil Dufferin and Maureen Guinness, who were to be married in July, were also among the guests. Waugh met John again in Oxford on 15 June, and travelled down to Sezincote with him and Frank Pakenham for 'a delightful weekend' on 21 June.[61] Waugh thought that the Regency style of Sezincote was 'like Brighton Pavilion only everything in Cotswold stone instead of plaster'.[62] The fountains were playing. The swans were belligerent. Colonel Dugdale's farming talk was as inconsequential as ever.[63]

It was at Sezincote that John met Camilla Russell, daughter of Sir John Russell, known as Russell Pasha in Cairo, where he was head of the police. Her home was in Ghezireh, Cairo, but when in England she stayed with her great-aunt Gertrude Harris at Little

Compton Manor, not far from Sezincote. Lady Harris's late husband, Sir Leverton Harris, had been Conservative MP for Stepney before the First World War. At the end of the war he had become Minister for Blockade, but his political career was ruined when his wife went to see her godson in prison. The godson was a German officer. 'That was the way people thought in those days,' Camilla Sykes (*née* Russell) explained. '*John Bull* got hold of the story, and Leverton had to resign.'[64]

Camilla Russell was staying at Little Compton Manor on Christmas Eve 1929 when the house was burnt down. She and her brother John (whom John Betjeman always called 'Wriothesley', his middle name) were taken in by Mrs Dugdale at Sezincote. As they drove up to the front door, they saw John with Ralph Radcliffe – a brother of Cyril, the future Lord Radcliffe – walking up the drive, returning from church. 'I thought John was very funny, very nice,' Camilla Sykes recalled, 'but I thought Ralph Radcliffe was the more handsome of the two. He later had many antique shops, one after the other.'[65]

Camilla's friendship with John developed into a light-hearted romance. They wrote each other long letters, often using rebuses. ('I love you' was rendered as an eye, a dove with an 'l' substituted for the 'd', and a yew tree.) On 6 August 1930 John wrote to her from *The Architectural Review*: 'The more I see you the deeper my devotion to you becomes.'[66] On 12 August he wrote: 'My hat I am cracked about you with those goo-goo eyes', and added that he had written to Lady Harris that it was essential for Camilla to remain in England, 'not to go to Cairo there to lie on dromedaries & divans & be scolded [by her mother].'[67]

They became unofficially engaged. John wrote to Patrick Balfour on 18 August:

> I ought to tell you that I proposed marriage to a jolly girl last week and got accepted. It has left me rather dippy. It occurred at two in the morning. Suddenly two arms were raised from the floor and put round me, for I was sitting in a chair in an old world Tudor manor house [Little Compton Manor, by now restored] and then I was accepted and I kissed first the tip of the nose and then the neck and then the forehead and we took off our shoes in order to go upstairs quietly and we turned off the lights and stood on the stone floor of the hall and suddenly the cool little hands were in mine and then a subtly unresisting body pressed against me and I kissed er [*sic*] full

THE ARCHITECTURAL REVIEW
9,Queen Anne's Gate,Westminster,S.W.1
PROPRIETORS
THE ARCHITECTURAL PRESS
LIMITED
TELEPHONE VICTORIA 6936

Extract of John Betjeman's rebus letter to Camilla Russell, 6 August 1931

My dear 'müller ['miller],
Alas! I cannot stay at Seizincote [Sezincote] this week end because a lot of sisters and relations are staying there, John [Dugdale] says. What an awful bore it is. I fear that as my holiday starts next week I shan't see you for ages. This is hell because the more I see you the deeper my devotion to you becomes . . .

on the lips for the first time. Since then there have been other kisses. Patrick don't say anything about it because the parents are certain to object and with my reputation it would be very trying if it got about.[68]

Balfour, whose profession was gossip, might just conceivably be relied upon to keep quiet, but others were already spreading the fascinating news. Alan Pryce-Jones wrote to Balfour on 7 August that 'Betj's hypochondria is much worse and . . . he is crazily in love with Camilla Russell.'[69] On 23 August John wrote to Camilla from Clandeboye: 'I find to my horror that John Sparrow knows I have fallen in love. But how? The Longfords & the Dugdales alone know the state of my affections & Maureen [Dufferin] guessed it to-day. They must be silenced. But if Sparrow knows the Dean knows & there's no silencing him . . .'[70] And indeed, Bowra already had the full story. 'Betjeman is said to be engaged to be married,' he wrote to Balfour on 23 August. 'She is called Camilla Russell, rather a crafty sort of tart, fond of practical jokes, water over the door, dogs in the bed, Eno's on the bacon. Very suitable for him so long as they don't marry.'[71] Bowra also lost no time in telling Evelyn Waugh. Camilla, meanwhile, had confided in Mrs Dugdale, who was 'much amused at the marrying idea,' Camilla reported to John.[72]

When Camilla's mother, Lady Russell, got wind of the engagement, she did not find the prospect so entertaining. She took Camilla off to a house called Catball, not far from Little Compton, and forbade her to see John. 'This sudden blow,' John wrote to Camilla, 'is no more than an incentive as far as I am concerned. Why the Ethel M. Dell are you not allowed to see who you like?'[73] He suggested that Camilla should pick some deadly nightshade in the garden and put it in her mother's tea.[74] In the couple's correspondence, the symbol for Lady Russell was a red nose – the nose which pried into their affairs. In his letters, John imitated Lady Russell's nagging: 'How many times have I told you not to leave your things about? Why the hell don't you take them up to your bedroom & put them away instead of cluttering up the space here? And haven't I told you not to write to that young man? Who are his people? Do you know him well? If so you have seen enough of him – at any rate, I have.'[75]

John spent his summer holiday of 1931 in Ireland, staying first with Basil Dufferin at Clandeboye, then with the young Earl and

Countess of Longford at Pakenham Hall.[76] He wrote to Camilla from Clandeboye on 23 August, describing a motor-race the house party had attended: 'Semi-conscious from a hideous journey with toughs in mackintoshes and old school scarves, I was whisked off to a prominent position on a grand stand to see a lot of small & noisy cars go down a rather boring piece of road. One of the drivers – a Sir Henry Birkin – was staying here so the talk has been motor cars only so far.'[77] It was, he told her, a very grand party – 'all the richest & most titled of the Guinnesses & Little Bloody & Veronica'.[78] He could not think why he had been asked. Three days later, having just left Clandeboye, he wrote: 'There were too many smart, bright young people to suit me.'[79]

John's exasperation with his fellow-guests at Clandeboye boiled over in a letter of 29 August (by which time he was in more congenial company at Pakenham):

My dear 'Milla,

     I feel obliged to write so soon on top of the other letter simply to complain of the hellish people staying at Clandeboye ... There was Seymour Berry about whom I may have complained to you in the past. He is the typical social success, – dear old Seymour so witty you know & so influential – the sort of chap it's well to keep in with, you know – the son of Lord Camrose. Oh! he's so epigrammatic that the whole table hangs on his words. Then there's dear old Buzzy – both he & Seymour have got six-litre Bentley's, topping little buses they can rev up & charge down in less than twenty minutes – splendid shock absorbers, too. Dear old Seymour – dear old Buzzy. I can't understand why little B[loody] surrounds himself with them.[80]

In his letter of 26 August, written on the express from Belfast to Cavan on the way from Clandeboye to Pakenham, John wrote: 'Poor darling, I hate to think of what an awful time you must be having . . . I should like to arrive at Catball in a super-charged, all spring sprocket, steam-valved, streamlined Mercedes & with a small piece of flannel charged with ether, asphyxiate our little friend (*Nose*) & watch you pack your paint brushes & lovely dresses, give you a terrific kiss on the lips & seal your eyes with 2 more kisses & take you away to a large & comfortable house in the Irish Free State . . .'[81] He advised her to be 'calmly and quietly rebellious' and not to wait until she was back in Egypt, to defy her mother.[82]

In the same letter, he gave her news of his teddy bear, Archibald. '[He] has accepted a call to the Congregational Church on Wanstead Flats where he has been doing the duty of lay reader for some years. He is also very keen on solo dancing.'[83] (This passage was accompanied by a caricature of Archibald in the pulpit and another of him dancing.) Later in the year, there was further news of Archibald's journey of the soul: 'Archibald has accepted the incumbency of Ram's Episcopal Chapel, Homerton, E.17. It is a proprietary chapel & in communion with a part of the Church of England. It has always been associated with the Evangelical party & he will have to wear a black gown in the pulpit as the surplice is considered ritualistic.'[84]

Camilla, a talented artist, was planning to study at the Slade School of Art, London, with her cousin Karen Harris (the future Mrs Osbert Lancaster). John commissioned her to design a cover for *Mount Zion*, but her drawings were not used, probably at the insistence of Edward James. She had seen page-proofs, but not the finished book, by the time she left for Egypt in October. By then, it is clear, John's passion for her was waning. 'Try to see me if you can before you leave,' he wrote negligently on 2 October.[85] He was going to Malshanger, Basingstoke, for the weekend 'to get tight with Maurice Bowra & Maurice Hastings . . .'[86] On 17 October he wrote:

> There's one consolation in being me & that is that I am not you. I don't think for a moment that you go through the emotional hell that I do when I see those enormous eyes so wide apart, but my God better hell than a brawling woman in the same house. I wish I were near to help you out with (*Nose*) . . . Don't forget to write to me even when I am a drunken memory which I probably will be when you get this letter.[87]

While Edward James was in America, John moved into 3 Culross Street, James's London house. He shared it with Randolph Churchill. 'You would certainly fall in love with him,' he wrote to Camilla '– long hair, succulent lips & wide blue eyes – jungen style so popular in our more fashionable resorts'.[88] He called Churchill 'the Mayfair Lady Killer'.[89] Sir Osbert Lancaster said: 'You'd go round to 3 Culross Street and John would be shrieking with laughter while Randolph was on the telephone to some cabinet minister whose wife happened to be in bed with Randolph at the time.'[90]

When Camilla was about to return to Cairo for the winter of 1931–32, a *bon voyage* party was held for her in the house; the bill was footed by Peter Watson, a new friend of John's who had inherited millions from his father's dairy business.[91] 'I went back to my parents in Cairo,' Camilla Sykes said, 'where I would be surrounded by very few girls and millions of young men. Betjeman wrote me a prayer, which was something like – "May God preserve me from cavalry officers and handsome Egyptians . . ."'[92]

On 23 October Camilla wrote to John from the P & O liner *SS Corfu*, then at Marseilles, asking whether he had fallen in love with 'Baby' Jungman, 'because I believe somebody else has . . .'[93] She almost certainly meant Evelyn Waugh, who in the early 1930s was in love with Teresa ('Baby') Jungman, one of the two daughters of Mrs Richard Guinness (formerly the wife of Nico Jungman). By 1 November Camilla was back in Cairo: 'It fills me with gloom to see the same deadly old people ambling round on the same deadly old horses . . .'[94] She had met 'a charming young Greek' but was not allowed to ask him to tea 'because he is half Indian by mistake & therefore a dark mahogany colour'.[95] She told John of an American girl who was thought to be a lesbian as she had spent the summer sharing her Cairo flat, at intervals, 'with various females equally extraordinary & mysterious as herself'.[96] John replied, on 22 November: 'I am so glad to hear there are Lesbians in Cairo. You might get into this set. That would do you in socially & you would have to be sent back before your time.'[97] He apologized for not having written to her for over a month. 'It is the result of neither overwork nor annoyance but mere epistophobia. I love you, duckie, just the same.'[98]

Back in August, when he was at Clandeboye, John had written to Camilla: 'I can't digest my food because in my plate I see your eyes & then when I look at a book I cannot concentrate because there they are again. You might blindfold yourself when I do see you or I shall go dippy.'[99] And in early September, when she had several times kissed the margin of a letter, leaving red lipstick impressions, he had written: 'How I loved the red marks on your letter. They were a stroke of genius. It was almost as though you had come into the room & we had a passionate embrace.'[100] But now, in late November, there was a tepidity to his endearments which suggested that his heart was no longer in the affair. 'Darling, do pawn your blasted [?engagement] ring & come to Culross Street. I shall make no demands for I think you are more in love with love than with me, but I will do anything to help you because that woman [Lady Russell] is BLOODY AWFUL & will be your downfall. She has no right to have children.'[101]

John had by now met Pamela Mitford and Penelope Chetwode, both of whom attracted him more than Camilla. And by early December, Camilla had met her future husband, in Cairo: 'A new man has arrived!!! Thrill!! he is Christopher Sykes, friend of Robert Byron's, perhaps you know him? he seems quite nice though he had that same disconcerting stammer as Li [Lionel Perry] – *and* he rolled his eyes upwards at the same time just the same as Li!'[102] But what really finished off the romance between John and Camilla was the discovery, by Russell Pasha, that John had sent her James Hanley's new novel *Boy*. Russell considered the picaresque life-at-sea book 'pornographic'. He forced Camilla to break off the engagement.[103] It is unlikely that he would have reacted so strongly if a marquess or an earl had sent her the book. 'Later on,' Camilla Sykes recalled, 'when John was becoming well-known, my mother said she would like to meet John again. But I refused to arrange it. I said, "You were poisonous to him when we were engaged. You can't just smile at him now and expect him to like you." '[104] The love affair fizzled out after the *Boy* episode. 'Partly because of opposition on all sides,' said Camilla, 'partly because I was very young and didn't know my own mind in those days, and I think John realized it. I was very frivolous – absolutely idiotic. I only thought about Paris clothes.'[105]

On 10 January 1932, Edward James returned to London and John had to move out of Culross Street. There he had shared with Randolph Churchill the excitements of the 27 October General Election in which the National Government had beaten Labour, with a big Conservative majority; and there the copies of *Mount Zion* had been delivered in November and stacked in the hallway. As a temporary expedient, John now stayed in Peter Watson's house in South Street, London, while Watson was in Switzerland. Watson came back in March and in early April John moved to Jordans, the Quaker settlement near Beaconsfield, Bucks., where William Penn is buried.

At weekends he went away, as often as he could, to friends' houses in the country. One of his favourite retreats in 1931 and 1932 was Biddesden House, near Andover, the Queen Anne home of his Oxford friend Bryan Guinness, who had married Diana Mitford in 1929. At Biddesden, John met Pamela Mitford, Diana's sister, who was twenty-three in 1931. She lived in a flint-and-brick cottage on the estate. Guinness had asked her to manage the 350-acre farm with its fifty head of cattle. The farm hands called her 'Miss Pam', and it was not long before John was calling her 'Miss Pam' too. 'He was mad on kite-flying at the time,' Pamela (now Mrs Jackson) recalled. 'He used to bring his kite down for the week-end. I was in my cottage and on Sunday mornings he'd ring me up and say, "Is that you, Miss Pam?" "Oh, yes, it is." "Well, are you going to matins?" "Yes, I'm going to matins." So then we'd go off on bicycles to the little village church of Appleshaw, Hants.'[106]

Meals in the big house with the Guinnesses usually ended with lusty hymn-singing. 'The parlour-maid, May Amende, was highly religious,' Pamela Jackson said. 'She slightly objected to the hymn singing, because she thought we were scoffing.'[107] John remembered the hymns, too, when he was interviewed by David Pryce-Jones (Alan's son) for a biography of Pamela's Nazi-sympathizing sister, Unity Valkyrie:

> Bryan had just finished a book of poems, he used to do conjuring tricks, and we sang rounds, the old favourites like, Here I go sure and slow, Sang the Turtle down below. There was a piano in the room where we dined, as I remember. We also sang evangelical hymns, Unity Valkyrie was very fond of them. Like the Moody and Sankey one,
>
> > There were ninety [and] nine that safely lay
> > in the shelter of the fold,
> > but one was out on the hills away,
> > far off from the gates of gold.
>
> May Amende was terribly shocked by the way we sang hymns. We sang them in the car too, going to look at old churches, a whole group of us, and attending evensong too if we could find it . . . We very much enjoyed communal games, Grandmother's Footsteps. Once we went to Lytton Strachey at Ham Spray and played statues there . . . It was a sort of Oxford set, we used to see things as an endless party.[108]

Lady Pansy Lamb (née Pakenham) and her husband Henry Lamb, the artist, lived not far away, at Coombe Bissett, and sometimes visited Biddesden when John was there. 'One of John's fantasies,' she told Pryce-Jones, 'was about Henry as a doctor in the First War, and he wrote a poem, which has since been lost:

> I too could be arty, I too could get on
> with the Guinnesses, Gertler, Sickert and John . . .'[109]

At Biddesden, John was within striking distance of Marlborough. He took Pamela there and showed her round the college – 'the classrooms and places where he had suffered'.[110] They also visited the deserted and ruined village of Snape, in the downs, which had been the destination of a gruelling college run.[111] One day, John said he would like to go riding.

So we put him on the mowing-machine pony [Pamela Jackson said] and sent him off into the Collingbourne Woods behind the house, thinking he'd be completely safe, because it was a rather slow old thing. And he hadn't been long gone when (this is his description) 'a whole lot of colonels in red came galloping past' and his pony took to its heels and galloped too, whereupon of course Betj fell off. So then he stopped one of the colonels in red and said, 'Hey! Would you just bring my pony back?' – and it was the Master of Hounds. It was a private pack of hounds which belonged to old Major Scarlett, his son is Peter Scarlett.[112] It was *too* wonderful! And the pony was eventually found a week later. Those woods are very thick, and nobody saw it.[113]

It was generally believed that John had become engaged to Pamela Mitford; though as Osbert Lancaster said, 'There is little doubt that her father, Lord Redesdale, would have regarded John as a "sewer".'[114] Lady Chetwode, John's future mother-in-law, referred to the alleged engagement in a letter warning her daughter that John was fickle.[115] But Pamela Jackson says that she never considered marrying John, though she now thinks he may have been in love with her for a while. 'He was essentially metropolitan, while I was rural,' she said.[116] That is the word John used to describe her in a poem dated 1932:

SONG IN HONOUR OF
THE MITFORD GIRLS
BUT ESPECIALLY
IN HONOUR OF
MISS PAMELA

The Mitford Girls! The Mitford Girls
I love them for their sins
The Young ones all like 'Cavalcade'[117]
The old like 'Maskelyns'.[118]

SOPHISTICATION Blessed dame
Sure they have heard her call
Yes even Gentle Pamela
Most rural of them all.[119]

John's romantic feelings for Pamela were at their height in February 1932, when he wrote to her sister Diana from the Salutation Hotel, Topsham, Devon:

My dear Diana,

Alone in the cold Commercial Room, with a smelly & ancient dog looking at me & a child practicing [*sic*] scales next door, my thoughts are still with Miss Pam. I have been seeing whether a little absence makes the heart grow fonder and my God, it does. Does Miss Pam's heart warm towards that ghastly Czechoslovakian Count?[120] I came down to this eighteenth-century town, alone, for a rest . . . It is built entirely in the Dutch manner except for a few Regency terraces & closes. It subsists on smuggling & in one pub you can buy Brandy for 3/9d a bottle.

I do want to see you when I return – which will be to-morrow – & hear whether this severe test has improved my chances and done down my rival . . .[121]

In 1932 John wrote to Nancy, whom he regarded as 'the warmest' of the sisters: 'If Pamela Mitford refuses me finally, *you* might marry me – I'm rich, handsome and aristocratic.'[122] Nancy drew on John's character for the hero of her 1932 novel *Christmas Pudding*.[123] Paul Fotheringay is an eccentric young man who flits from girl to girl. He has written a book which he intends to be serious but which all the reviewers and most of his friends think hilarious. He is a member of the Buchanite sect, founded by Mrs Elspeth Buchan, a Scottish prototype of Mrs Eddy and Mrs Besant. He earns £300 a year (exactly John's salary on *The Architectural Review*) as private tutor to an Etonian. Terrified of riding, he is thrown from a borrowed horse.

At the beginning of the story, Fotheringay is 'unofficially engaged' to Marcella (Camilla), who dabbles in art and is going to the Slade. Later he proposes to Philadelphia (Pamela), but in the end he loses both women. Amabelle, a former call-girl who has been absorbed into the aristocracy, says of Paul and Philadelphia: 'He has far too weak a character to marry a girl of her sort. He needs something very hard-boiled.'[124]

By the time she wrote those words, Nancy Mitford was well aware that John had fallen in love with Penelope Chetwode, a general's daughter, strong in body and in mind.

15

PAKENHAM HALL[1]

[Edward and Christine Longford] opened their house and extended its
traditional hospitality to the friends of the younger Pakenhams. Oxford
was in general the common bond between the guests. Dons then young
and in uproarious spirits, writers then little known to the public, ori-
ginated escapades and impostures to *épater* the neighbours. Many
courtships were conducted there. I had the impression that, when the
last of us left, Edward and Christine watched us with something of the
relief with which fond parents wave their obstreperous children back to
school.

Evelyn Waugh, obituary of Edward, Earl of Longford, *The Observer*,
2 December 1961

Although John was at loggerheads with his father by 1930, his
mother was still a faithful ally, cluckingly anxious about his health
and his love-life. On 3 April 1931 she wrote to him at Sezincote. She
said she had not slept the night after they had lunched together, not
long before, as she had felt worried about him. 'We are so alike that
I realized exactly how you were feeling, so on edge that you
couldn't bear to stop and really think out your position, you've got
into a sort of maelstrom of social and business affairs & you can't
stop. What you would like would be to get out of it all into a quiet
country cottage, surrounded by your books with Gibbs [the Betjemanns' man-of-all-work] to look after you & a bicycle so that
you could amble round to see churches, isn't that right?'[2] That was
Bess's idea of what would make John happy; it was not necessarily
John's.

He confided in her, but with caution: it was always possible she
might relay to Ernest what he said. In August 1931 he wrote to her
that he was engaged to be married, without divulging Camilla
Russell's name. Bess replied that she was not really surprised. 'I

know the modern idea is that parents are the natural enemies of their progeny, but such is not the case with you and me, we are very closely allies.'³ She added an aggrieved postscript: 'My dear, I think you ought to tell *me* who the girl is, is it Mary Erskine or one of the Pakenham girls?'

Bess was off-target, but 'warm'. John had been seeing a lot of the Pakenhams. In the summer of 1930, Frank Pakenham (the present Earl of Longford) had invited him to Pakenham Hall, the family home in Ireland. It was a battlemented Gothic mansion of 1806 by Francis Johnston, an architect on whom John was to publish the first comprehensive article in 1946.⁴ The land on which it stood in County Westmeath had been a reward to Captain Henry Pakenham by 'the brute Cromwell', as John called him. It now belonged to Frank's elder brother Edward, who in 1915 as a thirteen-year-old schoolboy had become sixth Earl of Longford when their father had been killed at Gallipoli.

Edward and his wife Christine knew that Frank had invited a friend to Ireland, but could not decipher his name or his day of arrival. The Longfords had to leave for Dublin on business and could only ask Edward's sisters Lady Violet and Lady Julia 'to welcome an *innominato* in their absence'.⁵ It was, for summer in Westmeath, an unusually fine evening when the mysterious guest arrived. The Pakenham sisters took him to the roof, and up an iron ladder that led over the top of a battlement to the flag tower. Then they walked him downhill to the kitchen garden to pick up fallen fruit in the hothouses. He began to quote Marvell – 'The nectarine and curious peach,/Into my hands themselves do reach . . .' Back in the house, they asked him to write down his name, 'but he saw through this stratagem, and used Irish letters, which left us none the wiser,' Lady Violet recalled.⁶ It was not until the next day, when Frank arrived, that they learned John's name.

John already knew the Pakenhams' names, having primed himself for the visit by studying *Burke's Peerage*. He knew that after Edward, who was twenty-eight, came Lady Pansy. She was twenty-six and had married Henry Lamb two years before. 'Pansy was a blonde angel,' Christine wrote, 'her eyes lakes of blue, and her "tints", as the Victorians would have called them, . . . like wild roses.'⁷ Next came Francis (Frank), twenty-five. Then Lady Mary (later Lady Mary Clive), twenty-three, with long, pale gold hair and an ironic look that made Christine suspect her of genius. The youngest of the Pakenhams were Lady Violet, eighteen, who married the novelist Anthony Powell in 1934, and Lady Julia, to Christine a 'calm and detached' schoolgirl,[8] to Powell 'a plump, blonde beauty'.[9]

Everything about Pakenham interested John, from the Coade stone sphinxes of 1780 in the garden, which the Irish called 'merrymaids' (mermaids) and the 'River Sham' (a pond curved to look like a river), to the great hall with its wheezy organ by Henry Bevington of Greek Street, London, and the Victorian kitchen with its big iron range, its butter-maker and marmalade-cutter. The billiard-room downstairs was reached by a tower-room; and it may have been of Pakenham especially that John was thinking when he wrote, years later: '. . . in a country house I do not like to see the state rooms only, but the passage to the billiard-room, where the Spy cartoons are, and the bedrooms where I note the hair-brushes of the owner and the sort of hair-oil he uses.'[10] Lady Violet remembered something else that caught his whimsical fancy at Pakenham – some gramophone records of Orange songs which Edward had bought in Northern Ireland. '[John's] favourite was, I think, "the Old Orange Flute", whose only tune was "The Protestant Boys". Its owner "married a Papist called Bridget Maginn" and flew to the "Province of Connaught", where he was obliged to play his flute at the Mass. The flute, more staunch than its master, continued to play "The Protestant Boys", even when "it was taken and burned at the stake as heretic".'[11]

It was as Frank's friend that John arrived at Pakenham, but after Edward and Christine Longford returned from Dublin, it became clear that he had more in common with Edward. The two brothers were markedly unalike. Frank was athletic, with a shock of curly black hair, and was headed for the Labour Party (after brief service with the Conservatives) and a political career in England. Edward had a big blond head and was already inclining to the fat which would make him a caricature Stout Party by his thirties. He was an Irish nationalist.

He had met his future wife, Christine Trew, when both were Oxford undergraduates. Christine, whose mother ran a tea-shop in Oxford,[12] was two years older than Edward, and *jolie laide*: Henry Lamb thought she looked, with her severely cropped hair, like an Aztec.[13] Edward's sense of humour and his religious tastes appealed to John. The young Earl, who had twice won the Wilder

Divinity Prize at Eton, was distinctly 'High'. He was loyal to the Church of Ireland, although his friend Martin MacLoughlin said it 'smelt of the Saxon and guilt'.[14] Edward also wrote poetry. In 1920, when he was seventeen, his adoring mother had had his schoolboy verse privately printed by Bumpus, *A Book of Poems by L. Dedicated with kind permission to my oldest sister*. Some of his poetry was 'Celtic Twilight'. (Yeats had stayed with the Longfords in July 1930, a month before John's visit.) But Edward had also been influenced by Harold Acton and the Sitwells; one of his poems began 'Night is a sweating negro over London . . .'

Edward Longford had come into his inheritance in December 1923: Pakenham and its demesne; the town of Longford; and half of Dun Laoghaire (Kingstown), a seaside suburb of Dublin. His wealth enabled the couple to redecorate Pakenham in the Chinese taste, with a blaze of red in the entrance-hall, inspired by Lady Ottoline Morrell's interiors at Garsington Manor. They littered the rooms with Japanese and Chinese jars bought in the junk shops of the Dublin quays.

Outside the estate, Edward's main interests were the theatre and folk-weaving. In 1930 he became chairman of the Gate Theatre, Dublin, two years after it was founded by Micheál MacLiammóir and Hilton Edwards – 'the Boys', as the Longfords called them. (According to Orson Welles, who arrived in Dublin in 1931, they were less delicately known in Dublin as 'Sodom and Begorrah'.[15]) In 1931 the Gate Company performed Edward's first play, *The Melians*. He also dramatized Greek tragedies and wrote *Yahoo*, a play based on the life of Dean Swift. In 1936 Longford abandoned MacLiammóir and Edwards and formed his own company, the Longford Players, for which John designed some sets. So resentment probably colours the pen-portrait of Edward in MacLiammóir's memoirs: ' "Oh, *jolly, jolly tuck shop*," one thought inevitably after the manner of John Betjeman or *Tom Brown's Schooldays* as he came striding into the theatre with his sudden infectious cackle of laughter, his magnificent expanse of grey flannel trousers and dazzling pullover, and billowing breast where an orchid curled incongruously on the gingerbread homespun . . .'[16]

The Longfords took John to the Gate Theatre. 'He was a very good critic,' Christine Longford said. 'I think his knowledge was wider than we knew, about *everything*. He would come to the Gate

and made very sensible comments on the plays. We all would occasionally whisper; but I remember there was one performance of *She
Stoops to Conquer* in which John whispered (and it pleased us very
much) that our girl playing the principal part, and two boys, were
as good as you could find anywhere; and while I was whispering in
reply I was thumped on the back by a really well-behaved and
devoted theatre-goer, who told me not to talk.'[17] The actress was
Cathleen Delaney, an attractive girl with 'dark, clustering curls'.
John flirted with her and rowed her on Loch Derravaragh while she
sang Moore's Melodies. When she married John O'Dea, an engi-
neer, John Betjeman celebrated the event in a poem, 'The Colleen
and the Eigenherr'.

Edward Longford's father had been known as 'the worst-dressed
man in England' in spite of hot competition from the then Duke of
Devonshire. Edward not only took more care over his own dress;
he was keenly interested in encouraging the Irish clothing industry.
He both wore local tweeds and sold them in shops, first in Rath-
mines, later in central Dublin. His manager, a Plymouth Brother
called Thomas Copithorne, told John how some tweeds were given
an 'authentic Irish smell' for tourists by holding them over a turf
fire. John suggested as a suitable motto for the business two lines
from Thomas Gray's 'The Bard':

> Weave the warp and weave the woof,
> The winding-sheet of Edward's race.

Though Edward and Christine splashed out on the decor of Pakenham and lost money both in the theatre and in their tweed shops,
they were economical in their staff arrangements. Mr White, the
chauffeur, also managed the dynamo for the electric light. Three
Protestant housemaids were replaced by two Roman Catholic girls
from the neighbourhood. Previously, local girls had been banned as
they might 'talk in the town', but, as Christine later wrote, 'We had
no secrets.'[18] A butler accustomed to castles was needed. The Longfords engaged T.P. Andrews who had been footman to Edward's
Aunt Markie (Lady Dynevor) at Dynevor Castle in Wales. In addition, there were footmen, kitchen-maids and Mrs Cruikshanks the
housekeeper. But, to her mother-in-law's astonishment, Christine
declined to have a lady's maid.

The servants might have no scandals to spread in the town, but they had to get used to their master's eccentricities. 'I have seen at Pakenham what I have seen nowhere else,' Evelyn Waugh wrote, 'an entirely sober host literally rolling about the carpet with merriment. Edward soon became uncommonly stout, a condition which caused him no self-consciousness, and which, I think, he never took any steps to relieve. His butler and attendant footmen would gravely bestride the spherical form in its velvet smoking-suit as they carried their trays.'[19]

In his collins to Christine (19 September) John thanked her for 'weeks and weeks' of hospitality.[20] But in fact, as the Pakenham visitors' book shows, he stayed a little over two weeks – 30 August to 15 September.[21] On 1 September he wrote to Patrick Balfour, telling him that 'Bess actually gave me the money for my fare over here on condition that I returned to Cornwall on the 9th.'[22] (He did not keep the bargain: on 13 September he again wrote to Balfour from Pakenham – 'now I must go back to Bess in Cornwall who is getting reproachful.')[23] When Evelyn Waugh arrived at Pakenham with his close friend Alastair Graham on 3 September, he recorded in his diary that the guests already there were John Betjeman and Elizabeth Harman[24] – whom Frank Pakenham had invited to Ireland after dreaming about her in his Oxford lodgings in June.[25] Waugh and Graham stayed for about ten days. Christine later recalled that Waugh, already famous as the author of *Decline and Fall* and *Vile Bodies*, was 'still the same little faun as at Oxford'.[26] He would come down to breakfast with a determined face and demand, 'Who's got any funny letters this morning?' Christine wrote: 'That was the professional writer keen on the scent and we handed them over at once, as a solemn duty. He read rapidly and handed them back. The material was stored for the future.'[27]

'John B. became a bore rather with Irish peers and revivalist hymns and his enthusiasm for every sort of architecture,' Waugh wrote in his diary.[28] In spite of this grumpy comment, he seems to have enjoyed the singing as much as anyone. Christine recalled:

Evelyn organized John's dramatic performances and called on Edward for ballads and rebel songs and encouraged all visitors to join in 'Men of the West', 'Bold Fenian Men', 'Boys of Wexford', 'Felons for Ireland' and 'Paddies Evermore'. 'Now, Edward, who is Ireland's enemy?' Not Austria or Spain, we knew the answer, it was England, cruel England . . . Then, to be quite fair, Edward gave us

'Derry's Walls', 'The Old Orange Flute', 'The Orange Lily-O' and 'The Protestant Boys' ('Slitter, slaughter, Holy Water, scatter the Papishes every one!') 'The Battle of the Boyne' was a particular favourite. There was great drama in

A bullet from the Irish came and grazed King William's arm;
We thought His Majesty was slain, but it did him little harm . . .[29]

Edward and John also liked the rollicking Moody and Sankey hymns at the back of the Church of Ireland hymnbook – 'There were ninety and nine that safely lay in the shelter of the fold', 'Shall we gather at the river?' and

Dare to be a Daniel! dare to stand alone!
Dare to have a purpose firm! dare to make it known![30]

The house-party would stand round the piano or the wheezy organ, with Edward roughly playing the tune with his right hand 'and any old thing with the left hand'.[31] In the evenings, in the great hall, John entertained the company with ghost stories by M.R. James and Sheridan Le Fanu, recitals of Vachel Lindsay's 'Congo', Gothic descriptions of 'basketings' at Marlborough, and parodies of Shakespeare. Elizabeth Longford recalled: 'Practically every evening John would be called on to do a Shakespearean dialogue, sort of "*Enter First Murderer*. 'Hast seen the light?'" and he'd go through the whole thing for about ten minutes. It was fantastic, you could not tell it wasn't some kind of Shakespearean discovery.'[32] The Pakenhams made their own entertainments. These included charades, in which John excelled; 'the marking game', with marks awarded for beauty, brains and other qualities; and a practical-joking game called 'Fish'. One or other of the party would lean out of the car window, as they passed somebody, and call out 'Hello, Mr Fish!' or 'Hello, Mrs Fish!' Marks were scored for the alacrity and warmth of the response: fifteen points for a wave back with extra points if the victim were a clergyman or the driver of a hearse. 'A woman holding a baby and a milk churn still managed to wave back,' Lady Mary Clive remembers.[33]

On Sundays, most of the house-party attended the Strawberry Hill Gothick Church of Ireland church at Castlepollard. At the west end of the church were two box pews, one for the Pakenhams, the other for the Pollard-Urquhart family which owned the village.

Edward Longford read the lessons and roared his favourite hymns, such as 'Will your anchor hold in the storms of life?', to the accompaniment of a small, woodwormed harmonium.[34] Christine Longford recalled:

> John regularly attended our parish church in Castlepollard and he made up a rhyme which I cannot remember accurately in which he showed that he knew that parishes are practically never called after the places that they serve but have some older name; and this one was known as Rathgraffe. John would recite, in a rather good stage Irish accent, a hymn about Rathgraffe and Mayne and Foyren, which were the three parishes amalgamated with churches in the past. We went to Rathgraffe where the clergyman was called Mr Mouritz – a descendant of a foreign evangelist called Mouritz who had come to the town of Drogheda and started a family. The present Mr Mouritz, who had an orange-coloured beard, was considered rather Low Church by John and Edward. They became more friendly with the local Catholic priest, Father Kelly. I once asked John if he was dying and wanted a priest in a hurry, would he send for Father Kelly or Mr Mouritz. And, after one of those pregnant pauses, John said: 'Mouritz, Mouritz' – the Protestant.[35]

When they had explored the Hall, new guests at Pakenham were turned loose in the demesne for walks or for boating on Loch Derravaragh, the lake invoked by John in his poem 'The Attempt'. Edward drove his guests through the Westmeath countryside, stopping to look at some of the Protestant churches. 'They were usually locked,' Christine remembered, 'but John was extremely clever at finding out who had the key. There would be a notice on the door saying, key at a certain cottage, and the man would be out herding his cattle somewhere, but John would in the end get in.'[36] John recalled how Edward would raise his wideawake hat when passing the Protestant churches, in emulation of the Irish who raised their hats or crossed themselves when going past a Roman Catholic church.[37] Edward and Christine also drove John to the Celtic crosses of Clonmacnois and Monasterboice, 'scripture-lessons in stone', as the guide-book called them. They quoted to him T.W. Rolleston's poem about Clonmacnois, 'In a quiet watered land, a land of roses . . .' Rolleston was minor enough to attract John, who later paid him the tribute of pastiche in 'Variation on a Theme by T.W. Rolleston'.

With pride, Edward introduced John to the lakeland of Westmeath. Loch Derravaragh was only one of thirty-two lakes in this central county of Ireland. Lochs Ennel and Owel were named after two of the beautiful daughters of the seer and necromancer Mannin. (John's poem 'The Exile' begins: 'On Mannin's rough coast-line the twilight descending . . .') On the bank of Loch Owel was Portloman, formerly the home of the De Blacquiere family (pronounced 'De Blacker'). John De Blacquiere, who had been Secretary of State, was created Baron De Blacquiere in 1799 for work which helped bring about the Union of England and Ireland in 1800.[38] He bought Portloman, part of the estate of the Earl of Belvedere, built a mansion and laid out magnificent gardens. He supplied Dublin Castle with 'the choicest and the most exquisite fruit from his hot-houses'.[39] In John's poem 'The Return', Sir John Piers says

> I'll nail the wall with Irish peaches,
> Portloman cuttings warmed in silver suns . . .

At Baronstown on Loch Sunderlin had lived the first Baron Sunderlin and the second Baron before the title became extinct in 1816. They were of the Malone family to which belonged Edmond 'Shakespeare' Malone, the eighteenth-century Shakespearean scholar. In 'The Return', Sir John Piers warns:

> And from the North, lest you, Malone, should spy me,
> You, Sunderlin of Baronstown, the peer,
> I'll fill your eye with all the stone that's by me
> And live four-square protected by my fear.

'Dim peers' were what interested John most in Westmeath — obscure peers, not necessarily dim-witted ones. In 'An Impoverished Irish Peer' he mentions Lord Trimlestown. The quest for Lord Trimlestown took up so much of his time on that first Pakenham visit, that even Evelyn Waugh, whose tolerance of peers was high, felt the joke had been carried too far. Near the hamlet of Trim, on the way from Pakenham to Dublin, were the ruins of Trim Castle, where King John Lackland had lived for a time (John was photographed in the ruins), and Bloomsbury, the seat of Lord Trimlestown. John wrote to Patrick Balfour on 1 September:

Lord Trimblestown's [sic] seat is called Bloomsbury near Kells and near this very remote place [Pakenham Hall], as you know. We devised a very clever scheme for calling on him. We made out a petition to prevent the demolition of Dublin Places of Worship – which, by the way, are of course, not going to be destroyed – and took it for him to sign. Bloomsbury is very difficult to find and when you do reach [it], it is very small. We asked about Lord Trimblestown in the district and no one had heard of him. Then we found Bloomsbury, an unpretentious William IVth structure in the Roman Manner and painted light mauve and brown. We learned at a lodge near the grass-grown drive and ruined gates that Lord Trimblestown had left it fourteen years ago – 'those were grand days' the old man said. His eldest daughter is a Mrs Ratcliffe who lives in an even smaller Georgian house near Kells. That is all. Four of his nine sisters are nuns and the rest have not married very well. I am so sorry.

On the way back, heartbroken and stricken, we found an interesting sight on the roadside – An old man who lived in a wheel barrow with a mackintosh and umbrella over the top, all the year round. He was deaf and dumb but not dotty. I think he is the brother of Lord Trimblestown.[40]

John referred to Lord Trimlestown ('whose peerage was created in 1461') in his article 'Peers without Tears' in the *Evening Standard* of 19 December 1933: 'Though over seventy, he is still, thanks to a hard early life before the mast, keen on dancing and racing.'

In a letter of 13 September John told Balfour how he had been to the Cavan Tennis Tournament, which was organized by another 'dim peer', Lord Farnham, 'who did the umpiring, carried a bucket of sand to the place where the competitors serve and arranged that a subscription dance should take place in his house.' The house, too, was called Farnham, 'and as he has had to sell most of his furniture it is a little bare but the acetyline gas makes a brave show, so do Lady Farnham (who has an unfortunate habit of winking) and his two daughters Verbena and Verbosa. They all told us it was very sporting of us to come several times . . . Verbena and Verbosa are so pretty. I fell in love with Verbena and danced with her. She is very London.'[41] (Lord Farnham did have two daughters, but one was *Verena* and the other was Marjory.) Evelyn Waugh also attended the Cavan tournament, and noted in his diary that

Lord Farnham lived 'by staying at Lunn's Swiss resorts all winter. There was an agent of Lunn's there to see how well he organized things.'[42]

John and Waugh were taken to lunch with Lord Dunsany, the author, who was a nephew of John's recent employer, Sir Horace Plunkett, and was married to Edward's Aunt Beatrice, sister of the dowager Lady Longford. Waugh was not impressed by him. 'Lord Dunsany thinks his very nice eighteenth-century Gothic house is genuinely medieval. He was rude to the servants and grossly boastful. He makes odious little faces of plaster.'[43] John, showing off his architectural knowledge, said quite the wrong thing. 'What I chiefly liked about Dunsany Castle, he remembered, 'was the Strawberry Hill Gothic, because that's what it mainly was. I was a complete failure with Lord Dunsany as I asked: "What date is this, sort of 1810?" "*Eleven hundred and six.*" '[44]

As a well-known writer, Lord Dunsany could not be considered a 'dim peer'. Neither could the Earl of Granard, a friend of the Pakenham family who was an Irish senator and lived in some splendour at Castle Forbes, eight miles from Pakenham in County Longford. A daughter of Granard married John's Oxford friend Lord Dumfries, son of the Marquess of Bute, in 1932, and John reported to Christine: 'the Pope (so Edward Stanley[45] says) sent a message beginning "Dear brothers in God, Bute and Grandad . . ." '[46] But Lord Kilmaine of the Neale, whose ancestor is mentioned in John's poem 'The Fête Champêtre' ('And a tower of blancmange from the Baron Kilmaine') was obscure enough to qualify.

Near Trim was another vacated mansion, besides Lord Trimlestown's Bloomsbury—Dangan Castle, once the home of Lord Mornington, whose son, the first Duke of Wellington, had married a Pakenham. John wrote of it in his late poem 'The Small Towns of Ireland':

> But where is his lordship, who once in a phaeton
> Drove out 'twixt his lodges and into the town?
> Oh his tragic misfortunes I will not dilate on,
> His mansion's a ruin, his woods are cut down.
>
> His impoverished descendant is living in Reading,
> His daughters must type for their bread and their board,
> O'er the graves of his forbears the nettle is spreading
> And few will remember the sad Irish lord.

When this first appeared in the *Telegraph* colour magazine in 1966, it gave mild offence to the then Duke of Wellington, who indeed lived near Reading, at Stratfield Saye House. Republishing the poem in his *Collected Poems*, John tactfully altered 'Reading' to 'Ealing', which meant that the nettle now had to be 'stealing', not 'spreading'.

Of the untitled gentry in the neighbourhood, those who interested John most were the Edgeworths of Edgeworthstown and the Misses Chapman of South Hill. Edgeworthstown had been the home of the novelist Maria Edgeworth, who had often visited Pakenham, six miles away, in spite of 'a vast Serbonian bog between us'.[47] And Oscar Wilde's sister Isola had died in Edgeworthstown Rectory at the age of nine – the tragedy which inspired Wilde's poem 'Requiescat'. South Hill had been the seat of Sir Thomas Chapman, the father of T.E. Lawrence. The Longfords exchanged calls with Lady Chapman, whom Sir Thomas had deserted. 'She moved stiffly, encased in a stiff black dress,' Christine recalled, 'Her conversation was about Aldershot and Biarritz.'[48] John was eager to meet Lady Chapman's daughters, Lawrence's half-sisters, but had not yet been introduced to them by 1933, when he wrote to Christine, 'It is my ambition to meet the Miss Chapmans.'[49]

Evelyn Waugh wrote that Edward Longford 'had the gracious habit of tipping his guests on their departure by making bets which he knew he would lose so that he bore the expense of our visits.'[50] Whether John benefited from this largesse is not known; but on 16 September 1930 he at last yielded to his mother's entreaties and left for England. On that day he wrote to Christine from the T.S.S. *Lady Leinster*: 'It is beyond the power . . . of human tongue & pen to express my utter dejection. The boat is crowded with what sweaty priests & pugnacious footballers, with what prim protestants & none too cleanly Catholics – with so many that I cannot get a single cabin, bribe tho' I may and cajole though I can.'[51]

On 19 September, back in Cornwall again, he wrote Christine a long thank-you letter, in which he described a 'rather nasty jar' he had had on the boat to Liverpool:

I left you in the Art Smoking Room of the Leinster or whatever she was called. I had secured for myself the least unpleasant berth in my four-berth cabin. I returned later on to see, lying on the berth I had secured, A LARGE SOILED FOOT. It was attached to an unshaven

& ghastly young man who was picking at a blister on the sole of it. 'Ah,' he said, as I came in, 'Ah've neerlye gawt this blister aowt.' I said that I thought I had put my things on the berth he was occupying. 'Yew did,' he replied, 'But one berth is as gewd as another.'[52]

John returned to Pakenham in June 1931, when he signed the visitors' book 'John Drogo[53] Betjeman'. He was there again in August, when Maurice Bowra wrote to Pierce Synnott from the Hall: 'A very large party here – Rachel [MacCarthy] not yet arrived, but Betj singing revivalist hymns with Edward. At any moment I expect them to fall dead in a religious ecstasy.'[54] Evelyn Waugh and Lord David Cecil were also of the party.

In September 1932 John brought his fiancée, Penelope Chetwode, to Pakenham, where Waugh was again among the guests. Penelope went riding with Waugh, who was grateful to her for not telling the others that he had got caught in a tree.[55] John browsed happily in the library, the handsomest room at Pakenham. Its shelves were lined with leather-bound books and it also contained first editions of Jane Austen, bought by the second Earl when they were published. In this room, on the 1930 visit, Waugh had planned his October journey to Abyssinia which inspired both the travel book *Remote People* (1931) and the novel *Black Mischief* (1932).[56] John worked his way through the volumes published by the Irish Georgian Society. He also read *An Irish Peer on the Continent (1801–03). Being a narrative of the tour of Stephen, 2nd Earl Mount Cashell, through France, Italy etc. as related by Catherine Wilmot*; John sat Lady Mount Cashel next to Lord Belvedere in the bridal skiff at the wedding of Lord Cloncurry in 'The Fête Champêtre'.

In *Annals of Westmeath, Ancient and Modern* by James Woods, John found the story of Sir John Piers's trial on a charge of criminal conspiracy for making a 'diabolical wager' to seduce Lord Cloncurry's wife. Edward and Christine drove him to see the ruins of Piers's Tristernagh Abbey, and the story became the basis of his 'Sir John Piers' cycle, published in the offices of the *Westmeath Examiner*, Mullingar, in 1937. Another book which inspired the Piers cycle was the two-volume *The Grand Juries of the County of Westmeath* printed by John Lyons in 1853. The Historical Appendix in volume two gave a gossipy account of Westmeath families, including an anecdote about Lord De Blacquiere and

Admiral Thomas Pakenham at a Portloman party which got memorably out of hand.

The book John enjoyed most in the Pakenham library was the bound record of the probate trial in Dublin (1877) which followed the death of Adolphus Cooke of Cookesborough, an estate bordering on the Pakenham demesne. Cooke had believed that he would be turned into a screech-owl after his death, or possibly into a fox which would be hunted down by the then Earl of Longford and the Westmeath Hunt. Christine Longford turned the Cooke saga into a comic novel, *Mr Jiggins of Jigginstown* (1934). By then she had already published two well-received novels, *Making Conversation* (1931) – 'the first novel that anybody can write, stories of my past life,' as she modestly put it – and *Country Places* (1932).

The success of Christine Longford and of Evelyn Waugh as novelists may have revived John's ambition to write a novel; but the fragments of a *novella*, written by him on Pakenham Hall writing paper in 1932, suggest a parody of the Longford/Waugh society novel, rather than any serious attempt to write one himself.[57] Titled *Standish Mount Pleasant* (alternatively, *Standish O'Grady*) and purportedly by 'Lord Belmont', it is an even more 'camp' exercise than his Cornish 'novel'. The hero, Standish, has 'yellow hair, blue eyes, yellow eyebrows and long tantalizing yellow lashes' and sometimes paints his lips. When an official letter arrives for him, his sister Emily ('who was always her brother's favourite since she was the most boyish of his sisters yet a woman at the same time') asks him what it is.

> 'Well, I think I ought to tell you, Emily, that it is a warrant for my arrest for being detected in unnatural vice on the loop line between Westland Row and the Broadstone Station on the 21st of August 1932.'
>
> 'Then we had better send for a doctor at once, Standish: I will go and tell mother. Meanwhile, have some of Angela's prawns as I feel sure she will not want any more . . .'[58]

The *novella* fragment ends with a scene which anticipates the end of John's poem 'The Arrest of Oscar Wilde at the Cadogan Hotel' (first published in the next year) – the arrival of two policemen to arrest Standish. ' "If only I could be sure that he was going away a Protestant," said Lady Guillamore between her tears.'[59]

John continued to see much of the Longfords throughout the

1930s, both in Ireland and in London. The visits to Pakenham inspired some of his best poems and his most sustained piece of architectural research, into the life and work of Francis Johnston. And his weeks in the Irish heartland prepared him for his wartime service as press attaché to the British Representative in Dublin. They gave him an understanding of the Irish temper; some good names to drop; insights into the Irish theatre and Irish handicrafts; and a convenient bolt-hole in Westmeath when he needed respite from his duties.

Christine Longford later wrote: 'If friends could be marked in arithmetic in a marking game, as we used to do in the evenings, I would mark John up as the greatest: he gave Edward the most and longest pleasure, either by his company or by letters and books for thirty years.'[60]

16

LATER INFLUENCES

I would not care to read that book again.
It so exactly mingled with the mood
Of those impressionable years, that now
I might be disillusioned. There were laughs
At public schools, at chapel services,
At masters who were still 'big boys at heart' –
While all the time the author's hero knew
A Secret Glory in the hills of Wales:
Caverns of light revealed the Holy Grail
Exhaling gold upon the mountain tops;
At 'Holy! Holy! Holy!' in the Mass
King Brychan's sainted children crowded round,
And past and present were enwrapped in one.

John Betjeman, *Summoned by Bells*, 1960

Of all the books John read as a youth, none affected him more than Arthur Machen's *The Secret Glory* (1922), the novel which the rector of St Ervan lent him. He was bound to identify himself with the hero, Ambrose Meyrick, who at fifteen was about his own age and whose surname[1] was the most illustrious that John could claim (or so he liked to think) among his ancestors. Meyrick was beaten at his philistine public school, 'Lupton', for shirking games and going off to look at a Norman abbey. He was also interested in Victorian architecture ('Then came the Free Library, an admirable instance, as the *Lupton Mercury* declared, of the adaptation of Gothic to modern requirements.'[2]). He was humorous and quizzical: the description of him by his housemaster could well have been given of John by an exasperated Marlborough master – 'To use the musical term, he seems in the wrong key . . . The lad reminds me of those very objectionable persons who are said to have a joke up their sleeve.'³ Meyrick detested the way Greek and Latin were taught, and was made the butt of sarcasm by the classics master, as John was by Gidney. He also despised the pedantic teaching of English literature by which the boys were told that 'Lyonesse = the Scilly Isles'. And for Ambrose Meyrick, the Celtic West of Gwent was a refuge from the brutish reality of school, as the Celtic West of Cornwall was for John.

As a literary model *The Secret Glory* cannot be recommended. It is a strange hybrid between fiction and mystical polemics. The narrative, such as it is, is interlarded with rambling theories about religion, education and Life. It is as if Rousseau's *Contrat Social, Emile* and *Nouvelle Héloïse* were jumbled up, mixed into a school story by Talbot Baines Reed and handed over to Madame Blavatsky for sub-editing. Luckily, John did not imitate Machen's incantatory prose style. But there were redeeming aspects to the book. Like John, Machen could not keep his wit in check for long. The two were amused by the same things: architectural follies, landladies' taste, High Church pomposity (contrasted with the simple piety of the Celtic saints) and Low Church fundamentalism.

John read *The Secret Glory* several times over, and phrases from it lodged in his head like shrapnel, surfacing years later. Describing the chapel of Meyrick's public school, Machen wrote: 'There was a stained-glass window in memory of the Old Luptonians who fell in the Crimea . . . The colouring was like that used in very common, cheap sweets.'⁴ John twice drew an analogy between Victorian architecture and sweets: first in his *Isis* article 'Our Lovely Lodging-Houses' of 1926 ('The upper brackets, supported on pillars like stretched sweets'⁵) and again in *The Architectural Review* in 1930 ('. . . the yellow woods glisten through their varnish like barley-sugar'⁶).

These are only possibly echoes of Machen, but there was to be one direct borrowing from *The Secret Glory*. When John met Myfanwy Piper for the first time, in 1937, he must have recalled one of the 'Welsh poems' in the novel:

> . . . For one day, as I walked by Caer-rhiu in the principal forest
> of Gwent,
> I saw golden Myfanwy, as she bathed in the brook Tarogli.

Her hair flowed about her . . .
When I embraced Myfanwy a moment became immortality!

In his poem 'Myfanwy', John wrote:

Golden the light on the locks of Myfanwy,
    Golden the light on the book on her knee . . .

and in 'Myfanwy at Oxford':

Gold Myfanwy, kisses and art . . .
Gold Myfanwy blesses us all . . .

More significant than any particular derivations was the effect of Machen's views on John's impressionable mind. Machen's reverence for the early Celtic saints was something John was free to indulge in Cornwall, where also there were Celtic saints and holy wells. Machen was an enthusiast for trains and for omnibuses – 'lumbering heavily along to strange regions, such as Turnham Green and Castelnau, Cricklewood and Stoke Newington – why, they were as unknown as cities in Cathay!' Though dogmatic and intolerant in so many things, he argued for a catholicity of taste: one should not despise 'a plain old-fashioned meeting-house because it was not in the least like Lincoln Cathedral'. In *The Secret Glory* he called St Pancras Station a 'masterpiece', fifty years before John used the same word to describe it in *London's Historic Railway Stations* (1972).[7] Towards the end of the novel, Machen indicated the rich material awaiting the writer who would choose the suburbs as his subject, 'who has the insight to see behind those Venetian blinds and white curtains, who has the word that can give him entrance through the polished door by the encaustic porch!' What was needed, Machen considered, was a writer able 'to tell the London suburbs the truth about themselves in their own tongue'. In his later years, Machen moved into the suburbs – to Amersham, on the edge of Metroland. There John visited him and heard stories of Oscar Wilde, who had told Machen he could not *stand* the taste of absinthe.[8]

Another book John read as a youth in Cornwall was Sabine Baring-Gould's novel *In the Roar of the Sea*, set in and around St Enodoc Church. One phrase in it seems to have attracted him so much that he later used it in a poem about Trebetherick. In Chapter XLVII Baring-Gould writes: 'Judith went out on the cliffs. All at once she came upon Mr Desiderius Mules, walking in an opposite direction, engaged in wiping the foam flakes out of his eyes.' John's poem 'Trebetherick', written in 1939, begins:

> We used to picnic where the thrift
> Grew deep and tufted to the edge;
> We saw the yellow foam-flakes drift
> In trembling sponges on the ledge
> Below us . . .

Almost certainly John picked up the phrase 'foam-flakes' from Baring-Gould; although twenty years before *In the Roar of the Sea* was published, 'I.G.S.' (Isaac Gregory Smith) published a book of verse entitled *Foam Flakes* (1872) which contains the line 'But the foam-flakes which fell from our oars in the spray . . .'

According to the novelist John Fowles, '*In the Roar of the Sea* owes a strong debt to Hawker.'[9] John Betjeman was naturally interested in the parson-poet Robert Stephen Hawker, who from 1834 to 1875 was Vicar of Morwenstowe, up the Cornish coast from Trebetherick. Parson Hawker was as notorious in north Cornwall as the Rev. Jack Russell, the hunting parson, was in north Devon. He fascinated John as a Tractarian, an amateur architect, a poet, an eccentric and founder of the Harvest Festival. (John gave a talk about Hawker on BBC radio in 1939.[10]) Hawker's 'Song of the Western Men' ('And have they fixed the where and when? *And shall Trelawny die?*'), which has remained part of the unison repertoire of British boys' schools, is pastiched in the rhetorical question of John's 1952 verses appealing for funds to save Chiselhampton Church, Oxfordshire ('And must that plaintive bell in vain/Plead loud along the dripping lane?/And must the building fall?'[11]).

John owned the 1908 edition of Hawker's *Cornish Ballads and Other Poems* of which the binding was stamped with a floral pattern from old carved oak in the churches of Morwenstowe and Wellcombe. The 'physique' of books always mattered to him. In the Marlborough school library he found the beautiful Kelmscott edition of the Old Marlburian William Morris. We know he admired Morris's poetry, from a tribute he paid him in *The Architectural Review*. John is sometimes capable – half in spoof – of the same kind of luscious sensuality (Morris: 'Her full lips being made to kiss';[12] Betjeman: 'Her sulky lips were shaped for sin'[13]). And though Morris's socialism woke little response in him, he enjoyed the Pre-Raphaelite's escapist medievalism and the archaic language of *The Earthly Paradise* – 'meads', 'perchance', 'eld', 'smote' and 'garth' (just the word John needed, forty years later, to rhyme with 'hearth' in 'Narcissus', a poem which also mentions pottery tiles by Morris's disciple William De Morgan).

The other well-known Marlborough poets were Charles Sorley and Siegfried Sassoon, who had both made their reputations in the Great War; but Sorley was damned in John's eyes as a close friend of Gidney, and Sassoon's denunciation of the war and his anti-war poems had made him suspect reading for members of the OTC. John was more exposed to the poetry of James Elroy Flecker, whose brother Oswald taught John English. John did not fall for Flecker's voluptuous exoticism, but Flecker could write about London suburbs[14] as well as Samarkand, and about English clerks as well as Arabian princes and wazirs. The opening stanza of his 'No Coward's Song' raises a question which was to exercise John too:

> I am afraid to think about my death,
> When it shall be, and whether in great pain
> I shall rise up and fight the air for breath,
> Or calmly wait the bursting of my brain.

That is strikingly similar to John's lines in 'The Cottage Hospital':

> And say shall I groan in dying,
>   as I twist the sweaty sheet?
> Or gasp for breath uncrying,
>   as I feel my senses drown'd? . . .

An Old Marlburian poet John admired was John Meade Falkner (1858–1932), though at first he knew him only as a prose writer, author of the novels *Moonfleet*, *The Lost Stradivarius* and *The Nebuly Coat*. Falkner's poems were not published until the 1930s, and even then only in hard-to-obtain, privately-printed editions. In his anthology *Library Looking Glass* (1975) Lord David Cecil quoted Falkner's poem 'After Trinity', of which a typical stanza is

Post pugnam pausa fiet;
  Lord, we have made our choice;
In the stillness of autumn quiet,
  We have heard the still, small voice,
We have sung *Oh where shall Wisdom?*
  Thick paper, folio, Boyce.

Lord David commented:

> This agreeable poem was written at least sixty years ago. But, alike
> in subject and spirit and manner it is so like the work of Sir John
> Betjeman that any literary historian might take it for granted that its
> author had had a direct and major influence on it. In fact Sir John
> has only come across Meade Falkner's poems in later life and long
> after his own work had achieved its characteristic form. This should
> teach literary historians to beware of laying down the law about
> influences.[15]

There is no reason to doubt John's statement that he did not know
Falkner's poems until his later years. When he gave a brief description of him as an alumnus of Hertford College in *An Oxford University Chest* (1938), he did not mention his poetry. He knew *of* the
poems by 1946[16] and praised them in *The Spectator* in 1956.[17] He
included 'After Trinity' in *Altar and Pew* (1959), his anthology of
'Church of England verses'. In the same year he lent Neville Braybrooke his own copy of Falkner's poems, for use in preparing an
Easter anthology.[18] He had known Falkner's prose since his
Dragon School days, when 'Hum' Lynam had read *Moonfleet*
aloud. In 1937 John ordered *The Nebuly Coat* from Foyle's
Bookshop, London, and in the same year he corresponded about
Falkner with 'Skipper' Lynam, who had been an exact contemporary of Falkner's at Hertford College in the 1870s. (Lynam
revealed that Falkner had been expelled from Marlborough under
the school rule 'One kiss and you go!'[19]) The influence of Falkner's
prose, which was of the Gothic mystery school of Poe and Sheridan
Le Fanu, is seen in John's short story 'Lord Mount Prospect', his
first contribution (1929) to *The London Mercury*.[20]
    Little as John enjoyed his tutorials with C.S. Lewis, the English
Literature course at Oxford introduced him to early English poets
whom he might otherwise have neglected in favour of the Victorians. Chaucer's friend John Gower was among the set authors.

In the mid-1380s, King Richard II – whom Gower had criticized in his *Vox Clamantis* – invited the poet on to his barge on the Thames and encouraged him to write something more palatable. Gower proudly referred to the royal commission in the prologue to his *Confessio Amantis* (completed 1390):

> He hath this charge upon me leid
> And bad me doo my besynesse
> That to his hihe worthinesse
> Some newe thing I scholde boke,
> That he himself it mihte loke
> After the forme of my writynge.

Almost six centuries later, when Prince Charles asked John to write a poem celebrating his approaching investiture as Prince of Wales, John remembered Gower's lines and decided to introduce into the poem ('A Ballad of the Investiture, 1969') an account of how the charge had been laid upon him:

> Then, sir, you said what shook me through
>   So that my courage almost fails:
> 'I want a poem out of you
>   On my Investiture in Wales.'
> Leaving, you slightly raised your hand –
> 'And that,' you said, 'is a command.'

Undergraduates reading English Literature were also required to read the poems of Edmund Spenser and the plays of Christopher Marlowe. A line from Spenser's 'Epithalamium' is paraphrased in John's 'Monody on the Death of Aldersgate Street Station'. The desperate last words of Marlowe's Dr Faustus before devils carry him off – 'I'll burn my books!' – may have been a model for the blustering promises of Sir John Piers as he too faces death in John's 'The Return':

> I'll build against the vista and the duns . . .
> I'll build a mighty wall against the rain . . .
> I'll fill your eyes with all the stone that's by me . . .

The undergraduate poets John met at Oxford had little influence on his poetry. Harold Acton had already published his first book of verse, *Aquarium*, before John arrived at the university; and Acton's second book, *An Indian Ass*, appeared in 1925. For the most part, Acton's verse was Sitwellism *in excelsis*. It was exotic and sexy – just the thing to appeal to adolescents who had been immured in monastic public schools for five or six years. In it were to be found centaurs, eunuchs, tiptoeing fauns, viols, peacocks, birds of paradise, iridescent fireflies, agate chalices, 'lips like currants', 'chartreuse-tinted threnodies' and 'arms/Sticky with strange narcotics'. Rare words were added to give mystique: Mephitic, genethliacs, hispid, fuliginous, systole, lazaret, lupanars. John did not share Acton's taste for the exotic. But in one of Acton's poems, 'The Prodigal Son', a character shows something of John's enthusiasm for well-built girls:

> He'd hum or whistle: 'Gosh, she looks immense,
> You never met a girl like sweet Hortense.'

There, in Acton's poem of 1925, is the first of all those 'goshes' and 'gollys' that have proved so irresistible to parodists of John's verse.

Cyril Connolly's famous parody *Where Engels Fears to Tread* archly suggested that Brian Howard might have introduced John to architectural appreciation. It was not so; but John took some interest in Howard's verse. One Howard line which he never forgot was 'A little furtive music like the rubbing together of biscuits' – an image of which Howard was so proud that he used it, to Harold Acton's derisive amusement, in *two* poems in *Oxford Poetry*, 1924.[21]

At Oxford, Graham Greene was better known as a poet than as a prose writer – rather as Evelyn Waugh, in his undergraduate days, was better known as a magazine illustrator than as a writer. Greene's long poem 'Sad Cure: The Life and Death of John Perry-Perkins' was published in the *Cherwell* in three instalments, on 20 February, 27 February and 6 March 1926. Part I suggests a parallel with one of John's earliest poems, 'Death in Leamington', though Lord David Cecil's warning must apply:

Greene: A maid brought in hot water in a can,
        rolled up the blind, let in a blaze of sun,
        flower beds and trees, the rattle of a hoe.

Somewhere a mowing machine unrolled its whirr,
beyond the trim white lines of tennis court . . .

Betjeman: And Nurse came in with the tea-things . . .
She bolted the big round window,
She let the blinds unroll,
She set a match to the mantle,
She covered the fire with coal.

Bryan Guinness, whose blank verse was also published in the *Cherwell*, influenced John indirectly by showing him the works of his ancestor George Darley, which John admired. 'He particularly liked the "Sea Ritual" group of poems,' Guinness recalled. 'When they were published as a book in 1979 he wrote me an enthusiastic letter about them.'[22] Guinness contended that the metre of Meredith's 'Love in a Valley' (imitated by John in *his* 'Love in a Valley') had been used before Meredith by Darley in his 'Song', which begins:

Sweet in green dell the flower of beauty slumbers,
Lull'd by the faint breezes sighing through her hair;
Sleeps she and hears not the melancholy numbers
Breathed to my sad lute 'mid the lonely air.

John's line 'Bindweed, weave me an emerald rope' ('South London Sketch, 1844') may have owed something to Darley's 'Ah! where the woodbines with sleeping arms weave round her' ('Song').

The undergraduate writer who influenced John most lastingly was not a poet, but a prose writer – Robert Byron, who with *The Road to Oxiana* (1937) was to become the best-known travel-writer of his generation before his early death in the Second World War. (His reputation has outdistanced that of Peter Fleming, who temporarily enjoyed more *réclame* through his *Brazilian Adventure* of 1933 about his quest for the missing Colonel Fawcett.) In 1926 Byron was still at the stage of undergraduate clever-cleverness; but John, breaking loose from the restraints of Marlborough, was at the same stage, and found the show-off style an appealing model for his own literary exhibitionism. To the *Cherwell* of 4 December 1926 Byron contributed an article headed 'Paddington: an Invitation to Oxford', which both encouraged his readers to explore the off-the-beaten-track parts of London, and treated the whole subject with the picturesque irony which became characteristic of John's prose. The article began with a spirited attack on the writers of Bloomsbury ('The intellectual development of England is being stunted, corked, smothered like a moth in a poison bottle, by this group of physically and mentally cobwebbed men and women.'). Byron offered his readers an alternative:

> It is when the modern generation, fresh from the universities or even at them, emulates the example of Bloomsbury that the time is come for protest and alarm.
>
> And so we say, Come to Paddington! Paddington is the symbol of all that Bloomsbury is not. In place of the refined peace of those mausolean streets, here are public-houses, fun-fairs, busses [sic], tubes and vulgar posters. Also here are small brick houses, Gothic mews and great tapering tenements in which to live.

The 'withered lactaries of Bloomsbury', Byron concluded, must be abandoned in favour of the territory west of the Langham Hotel. Here was a game that John would often play: to choose some less well-known quarter of London and to discover in it, or to invest it with, a special character.

A good example of John's later use of the (Robert) Byronic banter, half-mocking, half-affectionate, is a talk he gave on William Butterfield's great London church, All Saints, Margaret Street:

> Here it is – wedged between Bourne and Hollingsworth's and the BBC, near Oxford Circus, in a land of wholesale dress shops where alarm bells constantly ring as though the district were full of burglars – here it is, All Saints, Margaret Street . . . Some it offends. Me it delights. Butterfield thought, 'This is a brick age and a brick town. You can't carve brick, so I'll have patterned bricks and tiles,' and, by Jove, he has . . . There is nothing mean anywhere and a lot that is surprising. Prebendary Mackay, one of the famous vicars of All Saints, said that the red, blue and yellow stained glass windows in the South Aisle reminded him of a good hand of bridge.[23]

When John joined the staff of *The Architectural Review*, the example of Robert Byron was reinforced by that of P. Morton Shand, whose writings on architecture had the same mixture of wide-ranging knowledge, passionate enthusiasms and equally passionate hatreds, a winning picturesque style and a sense of irony bordering on the flippant. Shand's philosophy of architectural history was stated on the first page of his book *The Architecture of Pleasure: Modern Theatres and Cinemas* (1930): 'We want to be amused and not instructed, intrigued but not edified. The pedagogue was never more unpopular. Culture must wear her laurels not only lightly, but jauntily. To command respect she has to prove herself a good, even a racy, *raconteuse*. Academicism is as much taboo as are taboos themselves.'[24] No doubt what David Atwell says about Morton Shand in his 1980 book *Cathedrals of the Movies* is true: that he was 'highly subjective' and that he was guilty of 'arrogant self-gratification as a man who knows a well-turned phrase when he writes it'.[25] To Morton Shand, the Empire Theatre, Leicester Square, was 'one of the most supremely parvenu buildings in the world'. The Marble Arch Regal was damned for its 'strident bedizenment' — 'it looks as if it had been dressed for its part as a flash gigolo by some "Alexander the Great" of the Edgware Road.' But people took note of what was written so strikingly, with all its hyperbole, theatrical ill temper and mischievous asides.

John hero-worshipped Shand and learned more about prose-writing from him than from anybody else. He treasured his irascible letters, which execrated the kind of architecture both men disliked. Even towards the end of Shand's long life, his polemics had lost none of their bite. 'He took great exception to Public Relations Officers, "executives" and all the jargon of advertising,' John recalled. 'He saw in newly coined words like "cladding", "floorscape" and phrases like "blueprint for betterment", the unseeing slickness of those who follow a fashion merely to get for themselves power or money.'[26] In 1958 Shand wrote to John: 'The coolies' compound which is to be built round the amputated stump of the old Imperial Institute is, I am informed, considered an outstandingly progressive advance in contemporary design. There can be no question of monotony or bareness about it because "richness will be imparted throughout by ingenious variety in the 'cladding'."' John too would do his best to ridicule and outlaw those words or phrases which were used to smuggle harmful ideas into public thinking. 'Liaison man', 'viable' and 'development' were all special bugbears, and he brought them devastatingly together in his poem 'Executive'.

One other art he learned from Morton Shand: the composition

of arresting captions to photographs. This minor but valuable literary skill demands the poet's ability to concentrate a description or an idea, often in fewer words than the Japanese *haiku* writer is allowed. Shand was adept at captioning. An example from *The Architecture of Pleasure*: 'Greta Garbo Talks! A rather lymphatic crowd awaits the hundred-dollar-a-syllable voice.' In caption-writing, John was to outstrip his master. The Betjeman caption which John Piper and others of his friends always remembered was that to the photograph of a multi-flanged signpost in the *Shell Guide to Oxfordshire*. It read simply: 'A tree of knowledge'. A photograph of a fine Cotswold stone building was captioned: 'Site for Super Cinema'.

With most of the works mentioned already as possible influences on John, one is reduced to saying, 'This *may* have influenced him' – and Lord David Cecil's example shows how risky such speculation can be. But in the case of *Mary Lee*, the novel by Geoffrey Dennis which John lent Paul Miller at Heddon Court to make him feel less self-conscious about his Plymouth Brethren background, there can be no doubt: the borrowing, though venial, is incontestable. Chapter IV of the novel is headed 'I Go to a Meeting'.

Up rose Brother Browning. 'Let us sing together to the glory of the Lord hymn number one-four-two: *'We praise Thee, O Jehovah!'* There was a turning of leaves, for at this time most of us possessed hymn-books, though a few of the older generation, including Aunt Jael, viewed all hymn-books as snares of the Devil, and bore witness against the fleshly innovation by still singing always from memory. Brother Browning read aloud the whole hymn . . .

> We praise Thee, O Jehovah!
>   We know, whate'er betide,
> Thy name, *'Jehovah Jireh'*,
>   Secures 'Thou wilt provide.'
>
> We praise Thee, O Jehovah!
>   Our banner gladly raise;
> *'Jehovah Nissi!'* rally us
>   For conflict, victory, praise . . .
>
> We praise Thee, O Jehovah!
>   And, clothed in righteousness,
> *'Jehovah'* great *'Tskidkenu!'*
>   Complete, we gladly bless . . .

We sang sitting. O inharmonious howl! . . .[27]

John drew directly on this hymn in his early poem 'Suicide on Junction Road Station after Abstention from Evening Communion in North London':

> With the roar of the gas my heart gives a shout –
> To Jehovah Tsidkenu the praise!
> Bracket and bracket go blazon it out
> In this Evangelical haze!
>
> Jehovah Jireh! the arches ring,
> The Mintons glisten, and grand
> Are the surpliced boys as they sweetly sing
> On the threshold of glory land.
>
> Jehovah Nisi! from Tufnell Park,
> Five minutes to Junction Road,
> Through grey brick Gothic and London dark,
> And my sins, a fearful load . . .

Sir John Addis, another Heddon Court pupil, recalled that on one of the London outings to which John treated him and his brother, John bought him a copy of the verse-story *The Wild Party*, by Joseph Moncure March. The book was published by Martin Secker in 1928 in an edition of 2,000. Of all John's naughty acts of 'irresponsibility' at Heddon Court – lying down in front of buses, organizing conker fights, clambering through windows, driving across the cricket pitch – none would have shocked the boys' parents more, had they known about it, than his presenting this book to a pupil. It described, with nonchalant salacity, the embraces of both male homosexuals and lesbians; and even a scene of straightforward fornication was introduced by this subversive couplet:

> Some love is fire: some love is rust:
> But the fiercest, cleanest love is lust.

And the lust of the two parties concerned was

> A lust so strong, they could have wrenched
> The flesh from bone, and not have blenched.

The author and publisher were lucky not to be prosecuted by the Home Secretary, Sir William Joynson-Hicks ('Jix'), who said of Radclyffe Hall's lesbian novel *The Well of Loneliness*, which was published in the same year as *The Wild Party* (and which did provoke a prosecution) that he would 'sooner put a phial of cyanide in a young girl's hand'.

To John, March's book is likely to have been liberating in two ways. First, its explicit treatment of sex, in a book which was on sale to the public and not just to collectors with secret cabinets of erotica, may have made him feel less inhibited about committing to print his own more restrained references to sex. ('Clash went the billiard balls', published in the 1930s, ends: 'Get on the bed there and start.') And second, March's verse, in which there was plenty of rhyme but less scansion than scandal, may have shown John that it was possible to find a *via media* between the weary conventions of the Georgians and the free verse of Eliot.

The dénouement of March's verse narrative may have had a direct influence on that of John's 'The Arrest of Oscar Wilde at the Cadogan Hotel'.

The Wild Party:
> ... The door sprang open
> And the cops rushed in.

'The Arrest of Oscar Wilde':
> ... As the door of the bedroom swung open
> And TWO PLAIN CLOTHES POLICEMEN came in.

The Wild Party:
> ... He cocked his head to one side,
> Quaintly.
> Suddenly he staggered ...

'The Arrest of Oscar Wilde':
> ... He staggered – and, terrible-eyed,
> He brushed past the palms on the staircase
> And was helped to a hansom outside.

In its modish jazziness and its self-conscious shockingness, *The Wild Party* is almost stereotypically 'twentyish', like Scott Fitzgerald's short stories, shingled haircuts and the Charleston. But there was a wide range of other poetic voices to choose as models in the 1920s, the period most formative of John's style. Douglas Goldring, a minor poet who became a friend of John's in the 1930s, sardonically surveyed the field in his 'Post-Georgian Poet in Search of a Master':

> Now all is chaos, all confusion.
> Bolshies have cast E.M.[28] from his high throne.
> Wild women have rushed in, and savage Yanks
> Blather of Booth and Heaven: and T.S.E.[29]
> Uses great words that are as Greek to me.
> Tell me the truth, and ah, forgo those pranks –
> Whom must I imitate? Who's really It?
> On whose embroidered footstool should I sit? . . .
>
> Are Sitwells really safe? Is Iris Tree
> A certain guide to higher poesy?
> Can Nichols[30] be relied on, for a lead;
> Or should I thump it with Sassoon[31] and Read?[32]
> Or would it not be vastly better fun
> To write of Nymphs, with Richard Aldington?
> To join with Edward Shanks and J.C. Squire
> – A modern 'chorus' in a well-paid choir?
>
> I've thought of J.M. Murry and Sturge Moore,
> I've thought of Yeats (I thought of him before).
> I've toyed with Aldous Huxley and Monro[33] –
> I don't know where I am, or where to go.

This was the predicament which faced John Betjeman and other young poets who found their poetic voice in the 1920s.[34] Today, Eliot seems the central and commanding figure of that decade's poetry; but to a large body of critics he was anathema ('a gash at the root of our poetry,' wrote G.M. Young[35]). To the more reactionary, the very phrase 'free verse' was a red rag. 'You might as well call sleeping in a ditch "free architecture",' G.K. Chesterton snorted.[36] Auden and his contemporaries did not begin to count for much until the 1930s.

Most of the poets and critics of the 1920s were Victorians. With a few exceptions, such as the precocious Peter Quennell, or Edmund Blunden, who was only ten years older than John, they had spent their youth in the High Victorian period. Victorian thought was marked by a willing submission to oracular voices, and Victorian literature reflected Victorian certainty, with a few doubters – the Tennyson of 'In Memoriam', George Eliot, Thomas Hardy, Samuel Butler and A.E. Housman among them. Victorian certainty was undermined by the *fin-de-siècle* decadence of Wilde and his circle, who insisted that morality had nothing to do with art. Poetic imagery became more nebulous through the influence of the 'Celtic Twilight' school, led by W.B. Yeats. The Georgian poets[37] were affected by this numinizing tendency. Their vision was moonlit rather than sunlit,[38] and peopled by mythological creatures. Walter de la Mare was the poet most ensnared by the fey Georgian dreamworld. Georgian poetry contained much restraint and 'good taste', but little in the way of passion, poetic licence, archaisms, tumpty-tum rhythms, obscurities or Christian themes.

The First World War eroded both the Victorian certainty of thought and the Georgian vagueness of language. It reminded everybody that poetry was the natural language of life and death, not just of whimsical idylls. Poets who had trafficked in dreams and heroic idealizations were shocked into realism. After his first sight of corpses Richard Aldington wrote:

> But – the way they wobble! –
> God! that makes one sick.
> Dead men should be so still, austere,
> And beautiful,
> Not wobbling carrion roped upon a cart . . .[39]

The move towards a more precise poetry had begun before the Great War with the Imagists, led by Ezra Pound and F.S. Flint. In 1912 they published a manifesto in *Poetry* magazine which advised: 'Go in fear of "abstractions"; that is, use concrete images having the hardness as of cut-stone.'

So by the 1920s a new tradition was approaching maturity, but the old traditions were not dead. Thomas Hardy, born in 1840, was alive until 1928. John admired his poems, wrote about him in his strange metaphysical poem 'The Heart of Thomas Hardy', and pastiched Hardy's 'Friends Beyond' in his 'Dorset'. (He kept Hardy's Tranter Reuben in the cast of those buried in Mellstock churchyard, but added – allegedly 'not out of malice or satire but merely for euphony' – the names of friends such as T.S. Eliot, Edith Sitwell, Harold Acton, Brian Howard and Mary Borden, as well as the name of Gordon Selfridge, against whose Oxford Street clock *The Architectural Review* was campaigning at the time.) Hardy's poem 'The Last Chrysanthemum' may have suggested the title of John's 1954 collection *A Few Late Chrysanthemums*.

Robert Bridges (born in 1844), who had been the contemporary and friend of Gerard Manley Hopkins, lived until 1930. In 1929 he confounded those who had called him 'the dumb Laureate' by publishing *The Testament of Beauty*, a book-length poem in loose alexandrines. John preferred Bridges's shorter poems. When Lord David Cecil published his *Library Looking Glass* in 1975, John wrote to him: 'The great revelation to me has been Bridges.' The lateness of this eye-opening means that Bridges can have had little influence on John's own poetry.

Some thought that Rudyard Kipling should have been made Laureate instead of Bridges. He survived until 1936, but the carnage of the Great War made the public unsympathetic to his imperialism; and John was less attracted by Kipling than by the poet closest to Kipling in his patriotic themes and poetic virility, Sir Henry Newbolt. As with Hardy, John showed his affection for Newbolt's poetry in parody. He took off Newbolt's 'Admiral Death' (including Newbolt's favourite trick of using italicized lines, often within parentheses, as a kind of chorus or 'offstage') in 'The Old Land Dog' –

> Old General Artichoke lay bloated on his bed,
>   *Just like the Fighting Téméraire.*
> Twelve responsive daughters were gathered round his head
>   *And each of them was ten foot square.*[40]

Newbolt also inspired one of John's most moving poems, 'Variation on a Theme by Newbolt'. John met Sir Henry, as he told Patric Dickinson in a letter of 1969:

a Phádraig, a Chara,
                    There is delight on me at your writing a book about Newbolt . . . I think his poetry is so much better than people realize. It isn't really in any way comparable with Kipling's *Barrack Room Ballads*, but is a bit comparable with Kipling's *Country Poems*. I went to call on Newbolt when Penelope and I stayed with

Edith Olivier[41] at the Daye House. I was expecting to find a breezy rather journalistic sort of man, with an I Zingari hatband round his straw boater. Instead I found this quiet, silver-haired, elegant, literary man with a great interest in 18th century pastoral poetry, or at least so it seemed to me at the time, as that was all I ever talked about in those days. We went up to an enormous room at the top of that charming Manor House where he lived at Netherhampton, it was surrounded by books and looked across the Avon. The house was Morrisey inside, and there was much talk of the Duckworths at Orchard Leigh, and of Mary Coleridge, and of Walter de la Mare, whom Newbolt had originally promoted. He also spoke of Peter Quennell's poetry, which was, you remember, very good, and which he only published in youth and seems never to have written since. He liked Eliot's poetry, and I think you should have a look at that anthology he made, called something like 'The Slopes of Parnassus'.[42] It is a most discriminating choice.[43]

John made a further tribute to Newbolt's poetry when he chose his lines inscribed on Sir Ninian Comper's Welsh [First World] War Memorial in Cardiff, for a Second World War Memorial in Uffington church.

He was also to meet John Masefield who, like Newbolt, was best known to the public by his sea poems. He did not, apparently, see him when Masefield visited Marlborough to give a talk in 1923, but met him when Masefield came to give a poetry-reading in Faringdon church, Oxfordshire. 'When I saw this blood and thunder poet,' John recalled, 'he was not the tweedy, breezy sea-salt I had expected. He was spare, quiet and with luminous blue eyes.'[44] John had known Masefield's work from childhood. In a 1978 preface to a selection of Masefield's poems, he wrote:

My father who, despite his affection for me, was not given to reading poetry, certainly read all Masefield's long poems. When they had swear words in them, my father thought they proved how down to earth Masefield was. In his morning bath my father used to sing a Masefield lyric which had in it the lines 'Underneath her topsails, she trembled like a stag'.[45]

Masefield was approved reading at Marlborough: John remembered how 'the large blue volume of Masefield's *Collected Poems*, first published in 1923, loaded the tables in school halls at prize giving.' And in a few of John's poems one catches what may be a reminiscence of his early exposure to Masefield. For example, 'Bells are booming down the bohreens' – the first line of John's 'Ireland with Emily' – might be a chime of Masefield's 'bells/Come booming into music' of 'St Mary's Bells'. (Masefield's 'Harbour-Bar' also contains surf 'booming down the beach'.) But Masefield's brisk shanties and long narrative poems had less to offer John than the pastoral poetry of Edmund Blunden.

An emotional response to the English countryside was part of the reaction against the Great War and the terrible embroilments on the Continent. However, the post-war pastoral writing could also be seen as continuing a tradition established in the late nineteenth-century prose works of Richard Jefferies, W.H. Hudson and 'George Bourne' (George Sturt), and in the poetry of Edward Thomas (killed in the Great War), for which John expressed admiration in a radio talk of 1940.[46] Blunden himself became somewhat irritated at being branded a 'nature poet' – 'a useful rustic, or perhaps not so useful'. John mentions him twice in poems. In *Summoned by Bells* he lists his poetry among the works he had in his apple-green rooms at Magdalen. And his poem 'An Archaeological Picnic' begins

> In this high pasturage, this Blunden time,
> With Lady's Finger, Smokewort, Lovers' Loss . . .

The two poets became friends and corresponded.[47] Few direct borrowings from Blunden are detectable in John's poetry, though perhaps Blunden's 'This muddy water chuckling in its run', in 'Zillebke Brook', suggested 'waste pipes chuckle into runnels' in John's 'Business Girls'. But Blunden's eclogues, in spite of their admitted debt to John Clare, showed John that it was possible to write pastoral verse in the twentieth century without lapsing into mere archaism. The same lesson could be drawn from the poetry of W.H. Davies, the 'Super-Tramp', and from the rural verse of the journalist-poets G.K. Chesterton and Hilaire Belloc, whose wit and technical virtuosity saved them from the more maundering hedgerow-reveries of the lesser Georgians.

It is as instructive to note the 1920s poets who did *not* influence John, as those who did. One of the most prolific and commercially successful poets of the period – in those respects he was the John Betjeman of his day – was Humbert Wolfe, a fringe Georgian and a flamboyant Civil Servant. Apart from one much-quoted squib about the bribeability of the British journalist, Wolfe is virtually forgotten today. No questions about him are asked in English literature examinations at the universities. But when John was at Oxford, Wolfe was celebrated enough to be accorded a page of fawning praise by Stephen Spender in the *Cherwell*.[48] For a time he was a strong influence on C. Day Lewis.[49] When Geoffrey Grigson first came to London he made a beeline for Wolfe and, as usual, was agreeably unimpressed.[50]

Admittedly, too many of Wolfe's poems are marred by a fatiguing cleverness, by technical exhibitionism and by what would now be called 'high camp'. Even the best have a fluting, precious note. But he was capable of mounting a brilliantly sophistical defence of a perverse premise. For example, the burden of his poem 'Iliad' is that love is meaningless until it is immortalized in poetry:

> Not Helen's wonder
> nor Paris stirs,
> but the bright untender
> hexameters.
> And thus, all passion
> is nothing made,
> but a star to flash in
> an Iliad.
> Mad heart, you were wrong!
> No love of yours,
> but only what is sung
> when love's over, endures.

John was to have good reason to be grateful to Wolfe, who, at the beginning of the Second World War went to great trouble to get him off the Schedule of Reserved Occupations, interceding with the Air Ministry on his behalf. When Wolfe died in 1940, John wrote to his widow saying how kind he had been, and added: 'I was always an admirer of Mr Wolfe's poetry, but only once met him.'[51] But he was immune to Wolfe's debonair artifice, so representative of the 1920s *Zeitgeist* ('Mad heart, you were wrong!' sounds like one of the more perfervid lines from a Noël Coward play.) Wolfe was writing cocktail-party verse for Bright Young People. John's response was to smile, accept it, and tip it behind an aspidistra.

The other outstandingly popular poet of the 1920s, A.E. Housman – another Georgian – did influence John. If Humbert Wolfe's poems appealed to those who wanted to forget the Great War, Housman's ministered to those who could not forget it. *A Shropshire Lad*, Housman's lyrically morbid poem-sequence, in fact appeared in 1896, eighteen years before the outbreak of the war. Like a politician who lives to see the unpalatable views of his youth vindicated, Housman found a generation as wounded and unfulfilled as himself ready to receive his message, his imprint; but where a politician might have disguised his cynicism as sentimentality, Housman disguised his sentimentality as cynicism:

> Yes, lad, I lie easy,
> I lie as lads would choose;
> I cheer a dead man's sweetheart,
> Never ask me whose.[52]

Colonel Kolkhorst remembered John's chanting Housman on the way home from an undergraduate trip to Gloucester. John teasingly gave the title 'A Shropshire Lad' to his poem about the cross-Channel swimmer Captain Webb. Most of his poems are in the simple quatrain measure favoured by Housman, and the similarity of the two poets' rhyme-patterns sometimes suggests more than coincidence.[53] Housman's play on alliterative Shropshire place-names ('Clunton and Clunbury,/Clungunford and Clun/Are the quietest places/Under the sun') may have given John the idea for his play on place-names in 'Dorset'. Housman was almost as susceptible as John to the music of church bells; the insensibility to bells of the doctor's intellectual wife in John's 'Exeter' ('The Cathedral bells pealed over the wall/But never a bell heard she') reminds one of the heedlessness of the girl – alive or dead – in Housman's 'In summertime on Bredon' ('The bells would ring to call her/In valleys far away/. . . But here my love would stay.').

John took little from other Georgian poets, in spite of his friendship in the 1930s with their impresario, Edward Marsh. With all his Tennysonian chimes, he has more in common with Eliot and Auden, in the concreteness and particularity of his poetry, than with the silvery idylls of the Georgians; though indeed there were Georgians who did not succumb to the Georgian vision, such as Wilfrid Gibson, who wrote narrative poems with a north-country industrial setting; D.H. Lawrence, who just qualifies as a Georgian by his inclusion in some of Marsh's anthologies – 'a black sheep let into the fold';[54] and Harold Monro, of whom Henry Newbolt chaffingly remarked: 'Monro is not "at home" to the Muses.'

Monro wrote unmannered poems about ordinary people. ('On Sunday night we hardly laugh or speak;/Week-end begins to merge itself in Week.'[55]) His social realism was a rarity in the escapist 1920s. But there was a tradition of social realism in English poetry which had only recently gone underground and which surfaced again in John. A succession of poets from the mid-nineteenth century to the First World War had already done what Machen, in 1922, suggested English writers should do – had written about London and its suburbs with a Zola-like candour. Frederick Locker-Lampson, a poet of whom John was particularly fond, had published a book of *London Lyrics* in 1857. Hugh Owen Meredith, who became Professor of Economics at Queen's University, Belfast, and was a friend and lover of E.M. Forster, published *Week-Day Poems* in 1911, with verses about Primrose Hill and other districts of London. His 'Seen at a Railway Station' begins with the Betjemanesque lines

> I saw to-day a lovely daughter
> Of England's peerage at a station
> Attended by a railway porter . . .

Herbert Palmer, a critic best known as one of the leading Eliot-bashers, suggested, in a book of 1938, that John's poetry 'has some dim affinities with Douglas Goldring's pre-War volume, *Streets*; while it is also probable that John Betjeman has read the shorter poems of F.O. Mann'.[56] The affinities with Goldring are far from dim. The very titles of his poems are Betjemanesque: 'Living-in (Brixton Rise)'; 'East Sheen'; 'Highbrow Hill'; 'Daisymead'; 'Outside Charing Cross'; and 'The Subaltern Soliloquies'. Like John, Goldring is sympathetic to the problems of ordinary folk and some-times expresses his sympathy through Browning-like monologues, as in 'Malise-Robes' ('The address is good – 10A, North Molton Street –/I'm clever at the trade, and doing well . . .'[57]). Goldring also satirizes arty-crafty people, such as Mrs Murgatroyd Martin, who longs to 'open the door of culture' to the poor:

She tells them of Pater, and Pankhurst, of Tagore and Wilde;
Of 'Man-made-laws' and the virtues of proteid peas;
Of Folk-Song, and Art and of sterilized milk for the child;
Of the joys of the Morris Dance, and of poetry teas.[58]

After Herbert Palmer's book appeared, Goldring wrote to John to
say he could not imagine how the idea had got about that he,
Goldring, had influenced him, though it is clear from the letter that
he thought he had.[59] The two men knew each other quite well in the
1930s through their membership of the Georgian Group (a society
for conserving old buildings, nothing to do with the Georgian
poets). John liked and 'got on' with Goldring in spite of the older
man's prickliness and swollen *amour-propre*; he also enjoyed
Goldring's poems. But Herbert Palmer's word 'affinities' is probably a fair summary of their relationship as poets. It would also
seem to cover John's relation to F.O. Mann, the other poet Palmer
linked with his name. Born in 1885, Mann, like Matthew Arnold,
was a Balliol-educated Inspector of Schools. In common with John
and Goldring, he appreciated the special *timbre* of the London
suburbs. One of his books of verse, published in 1925, was titled
London and Suburban. Mann and his family lived in Dulwich
Village, London SE21 – the 'Valley Fields' loved and satirized by
P.G. Wodehouse.

Like John, Mann feels pangs for those who do not find love. He is
sensitive to the plight of the lonely and the misfits of society: the
blushful gas-meter-reader frightened away by the amorous lady of
the house who breast-feeds her baby in his presence;[60] Uncle Dick
ogling the barmaids in the Connaught bar;[61] the drudge typist;[62] or
the old comedian whose occupation's gone as the cinema has put
the music-hall out of business:

'Then managers were honey;
   The houses fought to hear;
I'd bags o' friends and money,
   Girls and cars and beer.

'But now it's all the movies;
   The managers are hell;
Where's friend or girl or money,
   Bedamned if I can tell.'

He gulped the grounds in silence;
  He sucked the empty spoon;
Vacuous-eyed a moment
  Murdered bits of tune.

Then started up and postured
  In absurd salute,
Cried 'Must be going! Chauffeur!
  Show us home! Toot-toot!'[63]

Though technically inferior to Betjeman, these stanzas are full of analogies with his verse – the nostalgia for the Good Old Days expressed by the ageing night-club proprietress ('Skittles', of Maidenhead) in John's 'Sun and Fun'; the old interior decorator who rehearses his past triumphs and 'solemnly pretends to think';[64] Wilde having his last hock-and-seltzer in the Cadogan Hotel; or the dated testiness of John's Old Poet in 'On Seeing an Old Poet in the Café Royal' –

'Devilled chicken. Devilled whitebait.
  Devil if I understand.'

If John did read Mann's poetry in the 1920s or 30s, it would have shown him that poetry did not have to be about moonlit idylls or wild west winds, but that it could also touch on train journeys, typists, gas meters and Southend Pier. And Mann's poems, like Goldring's, are evidence that John was neither *sui generis* nor a sudden strange throw-back – a Newbolt from the blue, as it were – but part of an identifiable *recent* tradition.

Another poet who belonged to it was Arthur Sabin, whose *East London Poems and Others* appeared in 1931, the year of John's *Mount Zion*. Sabin (1879–1959) was at the time the officer in charge of the Bethnal Green Museum, London; in the same year he published, under the museum's imprint, a learned booklet on *The Silk Weavers of Spitalfields and Bethnal Green*. His *East London Poems* contains verses on furniture makers, silk weavers and costers. A book with such a title would have been likely to attract John's notice, and it is possible that he filched a word from the first poem in Sabin's book, 'The Old Salvationist', for his own poem 'City' published not long afterwards:

Sabin:	Each morning, though the fog hangs dark
	Among the trees, or rain falls thick,
	He toddles through Victoria Park,
	To Hackney Road from Hackney Wick.

Betjeman:	. . . I SIT DOWN
	In St Botolph Bishopsgate Churchyard
	And wait for the spirit of my grandfather
	Toddling along from the Barbican.

Goldring, Mann, Sabin and John Betjeman would all have agreed with Yeats that poetry should be 'a dance in chains' – that to subject meaning to metre and rhyme challenges, as much as it limits, the poet's powers. They understood the virtues of being 'minor'. The subjects they chose would not have been served by passion and transcendentalism. Their poetry answered Machen's plea for a literature which would 'tell the London suburbs the truth about themselves in their own tongue'.

It did not answer the needs of young poets of the 1930s, who wanted to break with the past and to give verse a modernity comparable with that which had transformed painting. They were influenced by Eliot, and, largely through his proselytizing, by the flaying vision, virtuoso word-play, metaphors and paradoxes of the Metaphysical poets. The other tradition they acknowledged began with the publication, in 1918, of an anthology of Gerard Manley Hopkins's poems, chosen and edited by his friend Robert Bridges. (A second edition was published in 1930.) They liked Hopkins's quest for 'inscape' or the inner essence of things, his rejection of stale Latinate words for fresh Anglo-Saxon ones, and the 'liberties' he took with rhythm – though, as Hopkins had explained, the principle of his 'Sprung Rhythm' was nothing more revolutionary than that of the old nursery rhyme 'Díng, dóng, béll, Pússy's ín the wéll' – accents being assigned only to the syllables stressed in ordinary speech. Hopkins was chosen to be the first poet in Michael Roberts's *Faber Book of Modern Verse* (1931). F.R. Leavis, following the lead of I.A. Richards, gave further momentum to Hopkins's reputation in *New Bearings in English Poetry* (1932).

John confessed to C.S. Lewis that he did not understand Hopkins's greatest poem, 'The Wreck of the Deutschland'. He respected the Jesuit poet enough to quote his lines about the Plain,

Oxford, in *An Oxford University Chest* and to allow a Hopkinsian mannerism – 'the weed-waving brook' – into his poem 'Wantage Bells'. But in general his inclination was – as Hopkins said of himself and 'studying masterpieces' – to 'admire and do otherwise'.[65] To poets and critics of the 1930s, Hopkins might well seem the exact opposite of John Betjeman: a Victorian modern.

17

STEPS TO MOUNT ZION[1]

Here's the precious little work.·

John Betjeman to Tom Driberg, November 1931

By November 1928 Alan Pryce-Jones was working for *The London Mercury*. 'He and Mr Squire are great friends now,' the *Cherwell* reported on 3 November, 'and the London Mercury's getting ever so good.'[2] This was John's entrée to 'the Squirearchy', the most powerful literary network of inter-war London. John Squire not only edited *The London Mercury* and until 1933 wrote regular reviews for *The Observer*; he knew everybody, and a word from him could set a young writer on the reviewing circuit or gain a publisher's sympathetic consideration of his first book. He was an adjudicator of the Hawthornden Prize. He persuaded Longman's to publish Thornton Wilder's *The Bridge of San Luis Rey* and Stella Gibbons's *Cold Comfort Farm*. He was a friend of the Prime Minister, Baldwin, who listened to his advice on Civil List pensions for writers. He even gave Paul Robeson advice on how to play Othello.[3]

Not all the literary aspirants who called on Squire came away clutching review copies. Geoffrey Grigson, who visited the *Mercury* office at 229 Strand when he arrived in London in 1931, was not one of the lucky ones:

> [Squire] lifted his head from his waistcoat, unreviewed and I suppose unsaleable books and bulging folders in that hutch seeming likely to topple on him and bury him prematurely, and . . . asked 'Are you interested – in politics?'
> Oafish altogether at my own futility, I told him I was not; which seemed to him (H'm. A pity) to decide me and the matter . . .[4]

With an enthusiastic introduction from Alan Pryce-Jones, John found Squire more welcoming. In 1975 he wrote to John Jensen, who was writing a life of the Australian cartoonist Will Dyson, a friend of Squire's:

> Squire was a jewel of an editor to a literary adventurer like yours truly. He was always to be found during the week around noon at the bar of the Temple Bar Restaurant in the Strand below the office of the *London Mercury*. There he held his court ... Squire liked people to read out their poems to him. He was generous, tolerant and without a trace of malice. The side of him which appealed to me was his passion for architecture, London architecture in particular. This he defended with his pen and [he] wrote some spirited lines against the proposal made by the Bishop of London (Winnington Ingram) to destroy 19 City churches. He was great fun as a parodist – in fact, to a young man coming to London and wanting to write, Squire was a Godsend, though his bodyguard did their best to protect him ... His face was round and red and he had a halo of grey hair and I think he and most of his friends wore tweed.[5]

John told Squire's biographer, Patrick Howarth, that on meeting Squire he was not conscious of the gap in age and that it seemed natural to address him almost at once by his Christian name.[6] Squire was then about forty-five. In 1913 he had become literary editor of the newly founded *New Statesman*. In 1919 he was invited to become the editor of a new magazine, *The London Mercury*, which was so well fanfared that thousands of people agreed to subscribe for a year without seeing a copy. It was to be apolitical, devoted to literature and the arts. The first issue included contributions by Thomas Hardy, Walter de la Mare and Aldous Huxley. The third number contained Belloc's poem 'Tarantella', and in October 1921 there was an incongruous juxtaposition of D.H. Lawrence's 'Snake' and Squire's own poem 'The Rugger Match'. The lack of a consistent policy could give the *Mercury* the appearance of an uncontrolled hodge-podge. A.G. Macdonell, a drinking companion of Squire's and a frequent contributor, affectionately satirized it as such in his novel *England, Their England* (1933). But Squire did have one consistent policy: 'to give youth its opportunity'.[7]

It is perhaps surprising that John took to him as warmly as he did – as surprising as his friendship with Bowra. Squire appeared a bluff, hearty clubman. The passion of his life was cricket, a baleful mystery to John. It was politic for John to hit it off with Squire, but two things made it easier for him to do so: Squire's sense of humour and John's enjoyment of his poetry.[8] John often attended Squire's lunch-time 'court' in the Temple Bar Restaurant. Hilaire Belloc was sometimes there; so was his biographer J.B. Morton ('Beach-comber' of the *Daily Express*). Others who might join the party were the Georgian poet Edward Shanks; 'Archie' Macdonell; F.L. Griggs, the line artist;[9] Anthony Hope, an Old Marlburian; Gerald Barry, another Old Marlburian, who was to give John work when editor of the *Week-end Review*;[10] Lance Sieveking, with whom John was associated in his early BBC broadcasts; the young historian Joan Haslip; and Dudley Carew, who had been at Lancing with Evelyn Waugh.[11]

John first stumbled into the untidy room that Squire liked to call 'the Editor's sanctum' in 1929, the year in which the magazine's tenth anniversary was celebrated. The hundredth issue had appeared in February 1928. In 1933 Squire was to be knighted for his services to literature. But there were disturbing portents. He was drinking heavily and was in debt. Contributors sued over late payments. The typographic errors in the magazine were a Fleet Street joke. T.S. Eliot's *Criterion* magazine (founded in 1922), with its bright lemon and red cover, had upstaged the *Mercury*, made it look old-fashioned and amateurish. The *Mercury* was regarded as a rather intellectual 'society' magazine, something to leave lying around in country houses with the *Tatler*. Robert Nichols wrote in his verse satire *Fisbo* (1934):

> Lo where, recumbent by the fire, His Grace,
> An orange magazine before his face,
> Forgets awhile the all-too-present wraith
> Of Barnes'[12] odd doubts or Inge's[13] yet odder faith.
>
> The fire was welcome, so were tea and toast,
> But the new *Mercury* was welcome most.[14]

In 1970 John sentimentally recalled that Squire was 'the first person to publish a poem by me'.[15] It was not strictly true. Betjeman poems were printed in the *Cherwell* and the *Isis* some years before they began appearing in the *Mercury*. Squire was not even the first editor to bring John's poetry before the general public: de Cronin Hastings published 'Hymn' ('The Church's Restoration . . .') – which had already appeared in the *Cherwell* – in *The Architectural Review* in March 1930, two months before the first Betjeman poem ('Death in Leamington') appeared in the *Mercury*.

John's first contribution to the *Mercury* (in December 1929) was a whimsical short story entitled 'Lord Mount Prospect'. A polished, if eccentric, performance, it owes much to the ghost stories of M.R. James and the novels of John Meade Falkner. It concerns a Society for the Discovery of Obscure Peers which attempts to track down the Irish peer Lord Mount Prospect. He is a member of the Ember Day Bryanites, 'that obscure sect founded by William Bryan, a tailor of Paternoster Row, and William Reeve, a chandler in the city of Exeter . . . They believe in a bodily resurrection and the sleep of the soul. They declare that the sun is four miles from the earth.'[16] Here are traces of John's quest for Lord Trimlestown, the story of Lord Mount Cashell which he read in the library at Pakenham, and his interest in recherché Nonconformist sects, especially the Muggletonians.[17] Touches of extravagant fantasy are reminiscent of the early Evelyn Waugh, such as the obsession of Lord Octagon, one of the Irish peers hunted down by the Society, who breeds electric eels with the intention of harnessing their energies to light his house. Lord Octagon is 'surrounded by Indian relics collected by his ancestors and by himself' – an obvious reminiscence of Clandeboye. And when the Society finally arrives at Lord Mount Prospect's mansion, it has an unmistakable resemblance to Sezincote:

> Now and then we went up backwaters and had to turn, and once we were confronted with a broken bridge in a style formerly Indian, now decayed beyond repair. Here and there, swans, more wild than the wildest of song and story, rushed hissing and flapping on our little party from the dark deep bends of the stream, possibly angered by the community singing. The lights were long among some tattered beech trees when we moored our boat beside the Taj Mahal.
>
> But is the Taj Mahal covered with pink stucco? And are there curious Gothic pinnacles behind it? Has the central dome collapsed so that it looks like a diseased onion? Is there grass along the avenues? and if there are beech trees and box hedges around the Taj Mahal, are they overgrown and straggling?[18]

When the Society discovers Lord Mount Prospect, he is a black-

32 Frank Pakenham (*seated*) and Basil Dufferin in 1932 at
Stairways, the home of Frank and Elizabeth Pakenham (now
Lord and Lady Longford).

33 John at Dumbleton, Gloucestershire (the home of Sir Bolton Monsell), in 1933. Referring to his new book, *Ghastly Good Taste*, he captioned the picture: The author – an example of good taste if ever there was one'.

34 Sir Henry d'Avigdor-Goldsmid was one of the richest men at
Oxford in John's time. He held lavish parties on his steam
yacht. After Oxford, friends such as John were often invited for
the weekend to his home, Somerhill, Kent.
This Somerhill house-party of 1930 includes several of John's
friends: *back row, left to right*: Basil Burton, Randolph
Churchill, Mrs d'Avigdor Goldsmid, Nancy Goldsmid, ?, Julian
Goldsmid, Osmond d'A. Goldsmid; *middle row, left to right*:
Christopher Hobhouse, Pamela Nathan, Clarissa Goldsmid,
Elizabeth Harman (now Lady Longford), J. d'A. Goldsmid;
front row, left to right: Rosamund Fisher, Patrick Balfour (later
Lord Kinross), Dianna Churchill, John Spencer-Churchill (who
was 'unofficially engaged' to John's future wife Penelope
Chetwode), Henry d'A. Goldsmid, Tony Goldsmid.

35 Camilla Russell. Her father was Sir John Russell (Russell Pasha), head of the Cairo police. In 1931 (the date of this photograph) she became John's fiancée but the engagement was broken off when he sent her an allegedly 'pornographic' book.

36 John in 1931: a photograph by Camilla Russell.

37 (*above*) Penelope Chetwode.
38 (*below*) Wilhelmine Cresswell. In 1938 'Billa' married Roy
Harrod, the economist and Oxford don.

39 Field-Marshal Sir Philip (later Lord) Chetwode: a portrait by Oswald Birley. Chetwode, Commander-in-Chief of the Army in India, was fiercely opposed to his daughter's marriage to John.

40 Lady Chetwode.

THE ARCHITECTURAL REVIEW
9,Queen Anne's Gate,Westminster,S.W.1

PROPRIETORS

THE ARCHITECTURAL PRESS
LIMITED

TELEPHONE VICTORIA 6936

28. 4. 33

Dearest General,

I am seeing Honor Guinness quite soon & Chumley, I hope, though. Philitt (Penelope) is back looking hideous like an irritated spider & I shall be marrying her quite soon. Thank you very much for the pamphlets most of them shall be used. Richard Rosse said in a letter to me, that he was going to see you when he came up to Dublin & would like your house. Perhaps he has by now. Love to the General's wife.

yours
John B.

41 Letter of 28 April 1933 from John to Dermott MacManus,
an Irish writer whom he had met through the Longfords.
Penelope had just returned to England from India. MacManus,
who had served in the British and Irish Free State armies, was a
keen Blueshirt (Irish fascist) and a friend of W. B. Yeats.

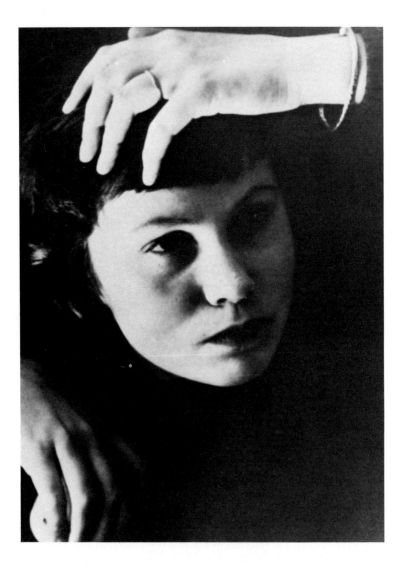

42 Penelope Chetwode: a photograph taken by the Hungarian
designer L. Moholy-Nagy in 1933 shortly after Penelope's
clandestine marriage to John.

gowned skeleton lolling in the pulpit of his chapel. He has been bodily resurrected with the Ember Day Bryanites.

A more glamorous fate awaited this early exercise than any of John's later works enjoyed: in 1946 it was considered by Warner Brothers for possible adaptation into a feature film. When Dorothy L. Sayers, who had become a friend of John's in the Catholic Writers' Guild, asked him for a short story to include in her third *Omnibus of Crime*, he offered 'Lord Mount Prospect', which with some latitude was admitted. In July 1946 an 'analysis' (précis) of the stories in the book was prepared by V. Volland of Warner Brothers, who began his thirteen-line summary of 'Lord Mount Prospect': '*A nonsense story . . .*'[19] In October of the same year the analysis was rudely rubber-stamped 'REJECTED'.[20] Lord Mount Prospect and Lord Octagon's electric eels never came to the silver screen.

'Death in Leamington' was published in the *Mercury* in May 1930: 'Dorset' (as 'Dorset Poem') in December 1932. John's next contribution was a review in the issue of May 1933 which provoked an angry letter. The book he reviewed was *A Pitman Looks at Oxford* by Roger Dataller, a miner from the north who was a research fellow at Oxford from 1928 to 1931. John criticized it with heavy irony. Commenting on a passage in which Dataller records his failure to engage Dean Inge in conversation at a New College luncheon party, John wrote: 'That is not the way to get on in Society, Mr Dataller. Even the broadest-minded of us observe social conventions. The Warden won't ask you again.'[21] The point John was making here and throughout the review was that Oxford's failure to encourage Dataller was an indictment of Oxford. Near the end of the review, he said so explicitly: 'his book is the best condemnation of the University I have read.'[22] But a New College undergraduate, J.M. Bertram (a Rhodes Scholar from New Zealand) took the review as literally as the authorities who put Daniel Defoe in the pillory for *The Shortest Way with Dissenters* (1702) took that ironic pamphlet. He wrote to John on 1 May 1933: 'Don't you think your review was quite as class-conscious as Dataller's book? This, of course, won't worry you; but it is pretty obvious. And I do think it was an unpleasant way to review a courageous book by a young man – a book with plenty of chinks where the knowing could get a dig in; but would a generous critic have used them?'[23]

She died in the Upstairs bed room
  By the light of the ev'ning star
That shone through the plate-glass window
  From over Leamington Spa.

Beside her the lonely crochet
  Lay patiently and unstirred
But the fingers that would have work'd it
  Were dead as the spoken word.

And Nurse came in with the tea things
  Breast high 'mid the stands and chairs —
But Nurse was alone with her own little soul
  And the things were alone with theirs.

She bolted the big round window,
  She let the blinds unroll
She set a match to the mantel,
  She covered the fire with coal.

And "Tea!" she said in a tiny voice,
  "Wake up! It's nearly five"
Oh! Chintzy, chintzy cheeriness
  Half dead & half alive!

Do you know that the stucco is peeling?
  Do you know that the heart will stop?
From those yellow Italianate arches
  Do you hear the plaster drop?

Nurse looked at the silent bedstead
  At the grey, decaying face
As the calm of a Leamington ev'ning
  Drifted into the place;

She moved the table of bottles
Away from the bed to the wall;
And tip-toeing gently over the stairs
Turned down the gas in the hall.

Manuscript of 'Death in Leamington'.

350

John's next contribution to the *Mercury* was a sketch of people lunching in a big London store ('Lunch at the Stores', August 1933). The repetitive banality of their talk is caught with Pinter-like precision:

'Will you have a Craven A? Of course generally I smoke Ardath because I'm saving the coupons. A girl friend runs a little tea-shop near us and I buy them there to help her. It keeps her in pin money. Yes, you see, generally I smoke Ardath because of the coupons. The girl who runs the little shop – Artifex Garth, you remember Dr Garth, don't you? – collected quite a lot from customers who are helping her, you know, and who didn't want the coupons. Yes, she saved two hundred and fifty I think it was, no, two hundred and seventy-five, anyhow I know it was two hundred and something and she got a divine little bag from the Ardath people. I mean one in quite good taste. So you see I generally smoke Ardath because of the coupons . . .'[24]

The sketch ends with one of John's mischievous in-jokes – a cluster of names of his acquaintance.

'I didn't know you were artistic, too, Mrs Crossman.' . . .
'Is Schurhoff alive?'
'Dead.'
'And are the Kittiwakes still at "Treetops"?'[25]
'Both dead – and the boy has gone to the bad.'
'How's Clonmore?'
'Dead.'
'And Etchell?'[26]
'You won't recognize him now.'[27]

A more serious article, simply headed 'Architecture', appeared in the issue of November 1933. In it, John at his most punishing showed his growing disenchantment with his work on *The Architectural Review*.

I am fully aware that even the average reader of the LONDON MERCURY will have passed over these boring looking pages on which I am about to spread myself. But I do not care, because years of unremunerative and heartbreaking work have brought me beyond caring . . . I remember recently a flannel bagged architect, wearing an arty tie, but possessing a shrewd business sense, saying to me between puffs at the foulest pipe I have ever been near, 'Well, it's through us that you get your living.' Apart from the fact that this truth is often the other way about, I felt obliged to burst out, 'Do you think it's any pleasure to me, to come round to offices and be patronized by art school students who crib Renaissance details and stuff them on to steel buildings? . . . Do you even realize that it is through people like you that the word 'modern', connected with building, has become synonymous with ugly . . . ?'[28]

John freelanced for other London publications. Late in 1928, just down from Oxford, he was already acting as a 'stringer' for the *Daily Express*. Among his papers is a docket which shows that he received 10s. for 'Pets' in the issue of 17 November 1928. This appeared in the paper's gossip column, 'The Talk of London', under the heading 'What to Look for in Pets'; and while the gossip columnist and sub-editors no doubt 'knocked into shape' John's text, it must be counted his first appearance in the popular press. It was the kind of story for which there is a perennial market, about decadent youth at the universities.

A friend who has been visiting Oxford tells me that this term's influx of freshmen has brought with it a revival of that exotic 'aestheticism' which had been dormant for a year or two.

Oxford will probably never be without periodical outbursts of the state of mind which produced, many years ago, the classic spectacle of an undergraduate leading a lobster down the High by a pale blue ribbon.

A stranger asked him why he had chosen so unusual a pet. He replied that it knew all the secrets of the deep and did not bark . . .

On 3 January 1930, Patrick Balfour wrote to his mother, Lady Kinross: 'I'm hoping John may get a job on the *Architectural Review*. He is writing a good deal for it. His papers, for which he writes, are heterogeneous enough: *Methodist Recorder, London Mercury, Arch: Rev:*, and *Motor Cycling*. He met the Editor in a train, & is going to do architectural articles!'[29] There is no evidence that John ever wrote for *Motor Cycling*. His views on parish churches would have had little appeal for youths whose interest was in speed trials and in new side-cars shaped and striped like bullseyes. And his 'by-line' never appeared in the *Methodist Recorder*, though he may have contributed under a pseudonym or perhaps anonymously to the 'Notes' column.

If he was a regular reader of the *Recorder*, he may have seen in the issue of 2 January 1930 a review of a book by Gwendolen Greene,[30] to whom the Roman Catholic theologian Baron von Hügel wrote his *Letters to a Niece*. The book's title was *Mount Zion*. There is no copyright in book titles. Did Gwen Greene's book give John the idea for the title of his *Mount Zion*, published in 1931? We know from a paragraph which Patrick Balfour wrote in the *Daily Sketch* gossip column in May 1929 that at that time John's 'first book, a witty volume of verse', was going to be called *Chapel and Spa*.[31] Something must have caused John to change his mind, and it may have been the *Recorder* review. However, he may also have known Gwen Greene and her book through Evelyn Waugh, who first met her in 1925. (The sub-title of John's *Mount Zion*, 'In Touch with the Infinite', was presumably adapted from Ralph Waldo Trine's book *In Tune with the Infinite*, a collection of essays about the spiritual and practical power of 'positive thinking', published in New York in 1898.[32])

In May 1931 Edward James told John that he would like to finance the publication of a book of his poems. John gave James a neatly written manuscript of each of the poems, in some cases adding written or sketched suggestions for illustrations.[33] James had already had a book of his own poems published by the Curwen Press – *Twenty Sonnets to Mary* (1930). But he decided to have John's book printed by the Westminster Press, then in Henrietta Street, Covent Garden. He wrote to John on 11 May, before taking the boat train *en route* for New York, to say that he had been round to the Press and had discussed John's book with Mr Lowe, who was in charge of the office. 'He is awfully slow on the uptake . . . but he is infinitely well-meaning and obliging.'[34]

The Westminster Press had undertaken to print the book in James's absence, with the imprint 'The James Press' on the title page. James had explained to Lowe that for John's poems 'the type most suitable would be a type in awfully bad taste – possibly an abortive Gothic'.[35] But after reflection he had realized that this would only be suitable for about sixty to seventy per cent of the poems. The remaining poems would be altogether wrongly represented by such a type. 'For instance, "the bluish eyeballs of my love" would look far better in graceful 18th or 19th century type.' He had concluded that either the types must be varied from page to page, 'which would be extremely amusing if successfully carried out', or that 'one dull, sober, non-committal type' would have to be used throughout. James had told Lowe to leave these matters to John's judgement, but not to print the book without first sending James proofs in New York. James further suggested that the paper be fairly good and the cover nicely executed, 'so that while the book may present an epitome of everything that is the worst taste in type and decoration, yet there be an underlying feeling that the whole is well-produced. We must not allow the outside world one moment to doubt the deep intensity of our sophistication.'[36]

At the height of John's infatuation with Camilla Russell, he asked her to design a cover for the book. She sent it to him on 10 September, with a note: 'It somehow hasn't turned out quite what I meant it to be like, the church au milieu is very bad – I must admit I think the villa is pretty good! but apart from that I think it is HELL. Of course I went and smudged the R of Ebenezer like a damn fool, I hope it's not too messy . . . I did it in green ink first because I happened to have a large bottle of it – what do you think about that?'[37] Whatever he may have thought, John wrote back:

The cover is a bit of all right, only Edward James considers the idea of removing the central portion & having a sort of cut-out with the illustrations showing through – which is on the inside cover – and perhaps some of that transparent paper such as one sees on bills when they can't bother to address an envelope but spend ages folding the notepaper so that an address shows through.

. . . For God's sake don't think it's much of an honour to decorate the cover of such a precious & boring & slender little volume. I'm fed up with my blasted poetry.[38]

In the event, Camilla's cover design was not used. Instead, an old engraving of a woman using a telephone was chosen – a joke on 'In Touch with the Infinite'. Randolph Churchill corrected the galley proofs. The book was published on 11 November 1931; copies were stacked high in the hallway of 3 Culross Street. It was almost as eccentric a production as James had proposed. While it was printed throughout in the same Victorian type, two different colours of paper were used inside ('God, how it smacks of Cecil Beaton!' John wrote to Camilla[39]), and the cover was bound in paper obtained from Brock's, the firework manufacturers.

Among John's papers is a review, from the *Draconian* of 1948, of his *Selected Poems*. The reviewer, C. de C. Mellor (then a master at the Dragon School) began with a reminiscence of the impression *Mount Zion* had made on him when it was published:

> I can still recall the delight with which I came upon John Betjeman's *Mount Zion* when browsing one afternoon in Blackwell's nearly twenty years ago. It was the cover that first caught my eye. Superimposed on a pattern of golden quatrefoil encircling azure stars was the figure of an amply busted and wasp-waisted lady, holding to her mouth and ear (or where her ear might be supposed to be, for it was entirely concealed beneath a monumental coiffure) what at first appeared to be the two handles of a skipping-rope, but what a closer scrutiny disclosed to be the mouth and ear-piece of an extremely antiquated telephone. Beneath this lady was the revealing legend: 'In Tune [*sic*] with the Infinite'. But if the façade intrigued, the interior fascinated. Pages of shell-pink and duck's egg blue presented an enthralling picture of stucco and pitch-pine; of Victorian whimsy and Edwardian fantasy; of the Anglo-Indian and the arty-crafty; of gabled suburban villas and pinnacled mock-Gothic fanes. And how delicately pointed the wit, how startlingly clear the observation, how telling the sensitive phrase! And as if it were not enough to have discovered a new poet of rare talent, there were enchanting illustrations too. Old steel engravings of spindly gothic steeples, glimpsed through elms on a winter's afternoon; waspish drawings of prickly nonconformist chapels and Ruskinian villas adorned with spiky dormers and turrets; and one page entirely covered with a gruesome collection of eyes, to serve as a pendant to a pastiche of the wilder seventeenth-century Metaphysicals. 'In Tune [*sic*] with the Infinite'? Well, at least with the infinitely amusing.

One of the first copies went to John's parents. Relations between John and his father had improved since 1930, partly because of John's steady job on *The Architectural Review*, but Ernest Betjemann could still be relied on for a candid opinion. In a letter of 15 November he took exception to a phrase in the book's dedication to Ethel Dugdale. Referring to Sezincote, John had written: 'Constantly under these minarets I have been raised from the deepest depression and spent the happiest days of my life.' Ernest thought the dedication 'would have lost nothing by the insertion of the two words "some of" before "happiest days" & would have been more complimentary to Mother & I.'[40] Apart from that, he thought the book excellent: '. . . its chief charm is its obvious spontaneity.' But he added: 'Some of your verse reads a little hurried and loose &

seems to want binding together a bit, & is not always sustained to the end . . . I feel all the time you can do much better. I expect that you feel the same.' He hoped John's royalties would soon equal those of Noël Coward (reported by the *Daily Mail* to be £40,000 a year) 'and then you can financially assist your parents . . .'

Entranced with the novelty of being a published author, John sent out dozens of complimentary copies. Five years later, when he asked Edward James's permission to reprint some of the *Mount Zion* poems in the John Murray collection *Continual Dew*, James complained, from his suite in the Waldorf-Astoria, New York: 'Although the book is entirely sold out, I *lost* quite a lot of money on it – principally because you must have got a bit scared lest it wouldn't sell at first, and so, right at the beginning started by giving so many copies of it away free that there were *literally* only about 45 per cent of the copies left for me to sell. Now, ever since it has been out of print there have been so many demands for it that I could really have sold the whole of that first edition twice without giving any of the copies away.'[41]

John wrote to Tom Driberg at the *Daily Express* on 10 November 1931: 'Here's the precious little work. I beg the favour of a notice. De Cronin Hastings did the drawings (many of them) he is editor of the Archy Rev as the printers call it.'[42] *Mount Zion* was duly given a mention in Driberg's 'Talk of London' column on 12 November: 'Mr Betjeman, of whose wit I have spoken before, has a curious complex about the monstrous architecture of the mid-Victorian temples of Nonconformity (that strange, mongrel Gothic), and about such kindred subjects as the art-and-craft garden cities and Camberley.'[43] As a good gossip columnist, Driberg did not neglect to say that the book's publisher was Edward James – 'husband of Miss Tilly Losch, brother of Mrs Marshall Field, son of the late Mrs Willie James, godson of the late King Edward VII'.

Randolph Churchill did the book equally proud in the December issue of *The Architectural Review*: as John was assistant editor and Churchill was his friend and flat-mate, it was an outrageously partisan choice of reviewer. Further, one of the poems in the book, 'The Wykehamist', was dedicated to Churchill; though Churchill was worried that the dedication, 'To R.S.C.', might lead people to suppose the poem was *about* him (it was actually about Richard Crossman), and in later collections of his poems John changed the dedication: 'To Randolph Churchill, but not about him.' In his review, Churchill wrote:

> If you like the genuine sublimation of the ridiculous you should read these poems. All the ugliness of the suburbs, all the vulgarity of human nature, are transmuted into golden beauty when touched upon by Mr Betjeman's pen. This book contains some of the wittiest satires that have been produced for some time. The very beautifying of the grotesque in life and architecture with which these poems are principally concerned, brings a heightened sense of the ridiculous . . . [44]

Alan Pryce-Jones's praise, in the December issue of *The London Mercury*, was more barbed.

> 'This precious, hyper-sophisticated book,' Mr Betjeman calls *Mount Zion* in his dedication, and thereby he disarms objection. For Mr Betjeman has invented a completely new attitude of mind, and therefore he cannot hope to escape objections . . .
>
> The sophistication . . . is that the poems are deliberately not better. Whereas most poets, especially comic ones, polish their verses, Mr Betjeman unpolishes his so as to make them scratch more horribly on the reader. The ideal reader will be as tortured as the author, and as abruptly amused . . .
>
> Mr Betjeman is not innocent of having read Mr Osbert Sitwell, but otherwise his inspiration seems to have no parents at all. This book is worth buying because it could never happen again. Even Mr Betjeman could not be so eccentric twice running. [45]

John's friends, then, conspired to greet his book as a good joke. But the anonymous reviewer in the *New Statesman* of 5 December regarded it as a bad joke: 'Mr Betjeman is too good to be true. If Mrs Ros[46] had known what she was doing, or had Cornelius Whur[47] tried to parody himself seriously – no, even then *Mount Zion* could not have been produced.'[48]

For a few months, the book was a conversation-piece in smart society. Early in December 1931, Evelyn Waugh sat next to Emerald, Lady Cunard at a dinner party. Later he relayed his conversation with her to Patrick Balfour:

> Me Have you seen a very amusing book of poems by a man called John Betjeman?
>
> E.   Yes, I think so, what are they about?

Me Satires.

E. O yes like Pope.

Me No not like Pope.

E. What did they satirize?

Me Religion chiefly.

E. Oh I shouldn't like that at all. Of course I don't agree with it but we must admit religion is a great thing.

Me Mr Betjeman is a Quaker.

E. Oh they're much the worst.[49]

In 1932 John was too busy at *The Architectural Review* to contribute much to other periodicals. (He was also writing his book *Ghastly Good Taste*.) But through Gilbert Armitage, an Oxford contemporary, he submitted some poems 'grubbily written in pencil on torn bits of paper'[50] to Geoffrey Grigson, who was preparing the first issue of the magazine *New Verse*, published in January 1933. One of the poems was 'The Arrest of Oscar Wilde at the Cadogan Hotel'. Grigson, whose taste was for bone-dry modernism, not for *fin-de-siècle* revival, rejected the poem as 'smart and frivolous'.[51] This repulse, though it came in the form of a polite note, offended John so much, Grigson was told, that later, when John lived at Uffington, he stood on the backside of the White Horse above the Vale and 'gravely cursed' Grigson.[52] The episode added Grigson ('Griggers') to John's demonology, and Grigson did not change his opinion of John's poetry. In a book published six months after John's death in 1984, he wrote: 'I detested and still detest his verses, or most of them.'[53]

New Verse might spurn him, but John could still find a welcome for his poems in the *Cherwell*. Derek Hudson, who was then editor, recalls: 'He sent in a poem which we gladly published on 30 April 1932 as "A Hike with a First; or, Wykehamist Redivivus"; it appears in the *Collected Poems* as "A Hike on the Downs", with only a few minor alterations.'[54] By September John was correcting the proofs of his contribution to *Little Innocents*, the collection of schooldays reminiscences edited by Alan Pryce-Jones and published by Cobden-Sanderson at the end of the year.

In May 1933 Randolph Churchill became assistant editor of the racy society magazine *Oxford and Cambridge*, which had been revived in that year after being founded in 1927 and going out of production in 1928. (This time it lasted until 1934.) A full-page picture of Churchill's classical profile appeared above a caption announcing the appointment. Almost immediately, Churchill must have asked John to contribute, since on 4 May John wrote to him from *The Architectural Review*:

> My dear Randolph,
> The poem will not be long. I have been seized with a perpetual headache for 2 days which has made all forms of concentration impossible. But only wait.
> I am starting a new poem with the lines
>
> 'I knocked out my pipe on my old flannel bags
> I lay back and thought about Kant.'[55]
>
> This paper[56] which I enclose may be of great use to you for your paragraphs in Oxford and Cambridge. It is run by a man who left the Times for Political Reasons; he is a friend of mine. He is called Claud Cockburn.
> Yors till death
> John Betjeman.[57]

On 18 May he sent Churchill two of his poems, with a story by Mary Erskine. Only one of the poems was published: the one Grigson had turned down. It appeared as 'The Arrest of Oscar Wilde' in the Summer Number (June 1933) with a full-page Art Deco illustration in colour by R.S. Sherriffs, showing the haggard Wilde being escorted from the Cadogan Hotel by two policemen. Hilaire Belloc's 'An Heroic Poem in Praise of Wine' appeared in the same issue. So did a 'Head and Shoulders' profile of Edward James by 'Roger de Tyrifin', accompanied by a caricature of him by Mark Ogilvie-Grant. The profile mentioned *Mount Zion* among the works published by the James Press – 'delicious extravaganzas by the irresistible John Betjeman'.[58]

In November, John himself contributed one of the 'Head and Shoulders' profiles. His subject was Evelyn Waugh.

> This is the most terrifying task I have ever undertaken. Supposing you, reader, were asked to write about somebody who saw through you and could do you down, if he were so minded; supposing, too, that you also liked the person you were going to write about. What the hell would you do? Not write about him of course. But then I am a hack journalist who MUST MAKE MONEY . . . Whatever I say, whatever I write, I can see Evelyn, with his fierce eyes reading it,

criticizing it, objecting to it or ignoring it. I am terrified. He hates praise . . .[59]

In the same year John was contributing to the *Financial News*, where his Marlborough and Oxford friend Philip Harding had a contact. (Harding was to join the staff of the *Financial News* in 1935.) Another friend commissioned John to write an article on 'Town Planning – or Jerry Building?' for *Scottish Country Life*. It was published in October 1933 with articles by de Cronin Hastings ('Bogus Architecture') and F.R.S. Yorke ('Modern Design'). John's contribution was an early attack on 'developers':

> Once upon a time the word estate meant an improvement to the landscape. It stood for a decent eighteenth-century house on an eminence, park-like surroundings, a lodge-gate at one end, stables a little further off, and simple model cottages dotted about the domain. Now the word 'estate' means *land for development*, but not for development in the eighteenth-century sense. 'The Baronial Halls Estate', 'The Tudor Estate', 'Hill Rise Estate' are words which reek of the speculative builder, and what the speculative builder does is this. He buys some virgin fields, he measures them out to get as many houses into them as possible, he buys a few hundred front doors and a few hundred stained glass panels to fit into the front doors, a few hundred window frames and some bricks. He hurriedly puts them up, nails some beams on the outside to give what he calls character to the house, regardless of the local characteristics, with the result – long pink strips like Euthymol toothpaste smeared across a field which becomes known as a high-class residential neighbourhood.[60]

On 18 October 1933 John began a long association with the *Daily Herald*. The article he contributed, 'Travelling on Paper', was about one of his favourite subjects, *Bradshaw's Railway Guide*. The 'peg' for the article was that *The Times* had recently announced – in error, as it happened – the *Guide*'s centenary. John wrote:

> At the name of Bradshaw there is always someone in any assembly who will start forward with an exclamation; someone whose pallid features will become animate; someone who is no good at tennis, no good at cricket or football, bicycling, or tricycling, badminton or polo who will, nevertheless, have a surprising knowledge of Bradshaw.

He will be able to understand it and find a convenient train when no one has an A.B.C. I am such a man . . .

'Didcot, Upton and Blewbury, Churn, Compton, Hampstead Norris, Hermitage, Newbury.' When one is sitting in an over-heated office in London, driven silly by the noise of typewriters, motor horns, bicycle bells, gear-changing, stifled by petrol fumes, disconsolate and ill-tempered, how refreshing it is to think, on referring to the notes in Bradshaw, that trains stop at Churn, 'to take up or set down on notice being given to the station-master at Didcot. Evening trains call during daylight only.'[61]

John suggested a parlour game for 'Bradshavians' who were also lovers of detective fiction:

Have you ever tried to find your way from Besses-o'-the-Barn (L.M.S.) to, say, Poison Cross Halt (East Kent Railway) by train? It is quite easy . . . (Several people may play this game.) The distance to go is several hundred miles, so that it probably cannot be done in a day.

As the alternative routes increase, the plot thickens. The winner is the player who can work out a route which takes the shortest time, exclusive of changes. Taxicabs, buses, or walks between stations disqualify.[62]

By the 1970s, when *Bradshaw's Railway Guide* was discontinued, it was so natural to think of it — and Victorian railways — in association with John Betjeman that a *New Statesman* 'Weekend Competition' asked for poems in his manner on its demise.

A writer whose books are privately printed is usually one who cannot get his work published any other way. (Hence the term 'vanity publishing'.) This was not the case with John, and for his first prose work, *Ghastly Good Taste*, he was able to find a commercial publisher, Chapman & Hall, who had been Dickens's main publisher. John was a friend of one of the firm's editors, Eric Gillett, who had returned to the Squirearchy in 1932 after five years as an English literature professor in Singapore. It was Gillett who suggested the book's title.[63]

Evelyn Waugh's father Arthur, who had an aura for John because he had contributed to *The Yellow Book*, had retired as chairman of Chapman & Hall, but was still their literary adviser. The proofs of *Ghastly Good Taste* were sent to him in April 1933. He suggested several changes in punctuation. He thought John should modify an 'unnecessarily impolite' reference to the architect Sir Reginald Blomfield, whose New Regent Street John detested.[64] 'After all,' Waugh wrote, 'he is a distinguished and respected man.' And John's description of James Douglas, a *Sunday Express* columnist, as 'a queer old freak' seemed to Waugh 'rather risky and a bit offensive'. When John agreed to the changes, Waugh wrote to him:

> It is very good of you to be so indulgent to an old man's fussiness; but I liked your book so exceeding much that I was anxious to see it go out as flawless as possible.
>
> I am sure it is a very good book. I love the turns of your humour, and the swift sallies of your wit, and I am sure that you are absolutely right in the principles of your criticism. It only remains for us to sell the book as it deserves, and I hope we shall not fail in our part.[65]

Like *Mount Zion, Ghastly Good Taste* was given a presentation of Gothic eccentricity. When Anthony Blond said he would like to reprint the book, in the late 1960s, John re-read it, and was 'appalled by its sententiousness, arrogance and the sweeping generalizations in which it abounds'.[66] One of the best things about it, he now considered, was the fancy cover designed by himself from display types found in the nineteenth-century premises of Stevens, Shanks & Sons at 89 Southwark Street, type founders. In their collection they found for him the block of the little railway train – which John first reproduced in *The Architectural Review* of June 1933 – and the founts which in descending order were Ultra Bodoni, Argentine, Bodoni and Rustic.

The 'real point of the book', John thought in retrospect, was Peter Fleetwood-Hesketh's pull-out illustration of the 'Street of Taste, or the March of English Art down the Ages', with traffic to match each phase of the debasement of architecture. The pull-out 'was also an old-fashioned thing to do, and the style of architectural caricature was deliberately based on Pugin's caricatures in his book *Contrasts* (1836). This pull-out was what caused people to buy the book, and looking back at it, I regard it as far less modish and much more balanced than the rest.'[67]

John had met Fleetwood-Hesketh through John Summerson. Hesketh and Summerson had been at neighbouring drawing-boards in the studio of the Bartlett School of Architecture, where they had studied under Professor Albert Richardson. The two had become friends and had explored London together. Like Summerson, Hesketh and his brother Roger both went on to the Architectural Association. One day Summerson said, 'You must meet my friend John Betjeman: you have so much in common.' John came to the house Hesketh's mother had in Wyndham Place at the top end of Bryanston Square. (It was destroyed by bombing during the war.) 'I remember John was impressed by the silence of that house,' said Hesketh. 'All you could hear was the ticking of the clock. And that – I am sure quite unconsciously – came out in a poem he wrote forty years later when he was staying with me in my house in Lancashire –

> In early twilight I can hear
> A faintly-ticking clock,
> While near and far and far and near
> Is Liverpool baroque.'[68]

At Wyndham Place John had a learned discussion about architecture with Peter and Roger Hesketh. 'And almost immediately afterwards – a matter of days,' Peter Hesketh recalled, 'my brother and I went with the Mitfords to a party in Mecklenburgh Square, and there was John. I've never seen anybody look so surprised. Having met us in a serious architectural atmosphere less than a week before, he could not associate us with this *milieu* – the Mitfords, Mark Ogilvie-Grant, with whom I had been at school, John Sutro and so on.'[69]

It was delightful for John to find somebody of his own age who not only shared his architectural interests but could speak of some of the great houses of England with an insider's knowledge.[70] Peter Hesketh was equally charmed by John. 'He was very *simpatisch*; seemed to be amused by one's jokes and made some very good ones himself. And the interests we had in common weren't shared by many other people in those days. Architecture was then a very obscure subject. When people asked me what I was interested in and I said "architecture", they'd back away.'[71] Hesketh showed John some of his architectural drawings. He was amused by them, and decided Hesketh was just the man to illustrate *Ghastly Good Taste*. The fold-out illustration, three feet four inches long, began with 'A Genuine Tudor House' and ended with a 'super cinema'

('Jazz-Modern. A misinterpretation of simplicity . . .'). For the 1970 re-issue of the book, Hesketh brought the story up to date in a further pull-out (the total length of the illustration was now nine feet), ending with tower blocks and city centres. He included a scene of the Euston Arch being demolished in 1961 – an outrage which he and John, with the Victorian Society, had vainly tried to prevent.

The reviews of *Ghastly Good Taste* were generally good, though several of the reviewers, understandably, remained puzzled as to what John's own taste in architecture might be. 'Can it be,' asked 'Ribax', 'that he dislikes anything and everything admired by other people?'[72] *Country Life* on 8 July spoke of the 'sad and ironic little book . . . It would be intensely funny were not the decadence represented so horribly true.' The anonymous reviewer added:

> Behind the persiflage is his conviction that good architecture is the expression of a faith, and herein lies the originality of his approach to the old story of architecture's history. He does not mind what the faith may be – mystical, rational or intellectual; chapel, church or State – but he believes fervently in the need for it. When it becomes self-conscious, art declines, and when it disappears, beauty vanishes with it, he declares. It was the nature of English faith, he believes, that prevented the Continental rococo ever striking root here. Cromwell and after him the chapel folk and solid Protestantism, nipped the bud of theatricalism. 'Architecture can only be made alive again,' he concludes, 'by a new order and another Christendom.'[73]

The *Daily Mirror*, a paper more cultural then than now (its literary editor could use French quotations without translating them) was equally enthusiastic:

> *Ghastly Good Taste*, by John Betjeman, is an eminently original book or tractate around and partly about architecture; for the author 'brings in' all the mental symptoms that can be accused of contributing, indirectly, to the monstrosities of stone and brick that represent the taste of an age. Enthusiasts are like that. *Que de choses dans un menuet?* But what is Mr Betjeman's own taste? It appears to be capricious; but favours the vital (vague word) and the unselfconscious.[74]

As with *Mount Zion*, John managed to recruit a small *claque* of his friends to review the book in magazines where he had some influence. 'This is an important little book,' wrote Frederick Etchells in *The Listener* of 30 August, 'written with a disarming candour and a certain Puckishness which is attractive. But more than this, it deals in a fearless and simple way with questions which affect all of us and which are certain to do so still more as time goes on.' The prospective reader was not to be misled by the amusing title and cover into thinking the book an essay in playfulness, 'for behind Mr Betjeman's wit and fancy there lies a fund of common sense.'[75]

Robert Byron reviewed the book for Gerald Barry's *Week-end Review*. The article was headed 'Architectural Revue'.

> The author is in circus-mood and as a circus he presents the architectural vagaries of his countrymen throughout the ages. Thus his exposition has a lack of closely reasoned form which may disconcert those who expect a lesson for the universe from every writer on the arts. Others may welcome, for once, a gayer and more discursive vein; we cannot all be Geoffrey Scotts, and Mr Betjeman, thank heaven, does not try.[76]

Byron called Fleetwood-Hesketh's illustration 'an appalling parody of those drawings technically known as "elevations" . . . The book is primarily an entertainment, to which Mr Hesketh's drawing adds a fitting epilogue. Yet it is an entertainment drawn from solid evidence and reinforced with many apt quotations from contemporary sources.' As a severe critic of Sir Herbert Baker's South Africa House in Trafalgar Square, Byron warmly approved John's comparison of that building with Nash's Coutts Bank building (later itself mutilated by Sir Frederick Gibberd).

The *Times Literary Supplement* of 7 September coupled *Ghastly Good Taste* with Robert Byron's *The Appreciation of Architecture*, giving much more prominence to John's book which the reviewer found 'learned, despondent, but lively'.

> Mr Betjeman does not find it difficult to distinguish the precise proportion of iniquity between the vulgar mistakes of the genuine Victorian school and the timid and pretentious refinement of a later time. He is indulgent to the former, but vicious about the latter. It is natural to be more sore about a recent than a remote ugliness, but Mr Betjeman does not really give sufficient support to his point. It is the defect of the essay that, while all his digressions are amusing and display both knowledge and an original sensibility, the main theme is not stated in a sufficiently orderly or tenacious manner.[77]

Osbert Burdett, a fringe figure of both the Squirearchy and Bloomsbury who was on dining terms with John, reviewed the book not only for *The London Mercury* in September, but also for *The Architectural Review* in October – a breach of critical ethics. Both reviews were eulogies. Perhaps for the sake of form, as John was still on the staff, the notice in *The Architectural Review* was toned down slightly with a few hints of adverse criticism. 'Mr Betjeman does not, I think, define what he means by Ghastly Good Taste . . . One rejoices in the author's divining power, though some of his historical generalities are more open to question.'[78] But the *Mercury* review was a straight 'rave', the kind any young writer would be happy to quote on the back jacket of a second edition.

> . . . graceful and very grave is *Ghastly Good Taste* by Mr Betjeman: the most illuminating essay on English architecture published so far this year . . . The first chapter . . . might have been written by a novelist of much promise . . . This bald summary is admirably filled out, enlivened by unhackneyed quotations, seasoned by good humour, lit by flashes of wit. It is astonishing how mellow the mind of this young author seems to be . . . His pages appeal to tastes so various that I cannot conceive any type of discriminating reader who will not enjoy this book. It is a book to read, to master, to keep, to give to one's friends, and it shows so much talent that, remembering how disappointing precocity quickly rewarded has often proved, if this receives the success that it deserves I shall tremble for his literary future.[79]

18

MARRIAGE

The Forest Officer . . . kept bringing the conversation round to sex by which he appeared to be obsessed. He told me that he was thirty-one and his father had been pressing him to marry for years . . . Did I think that marriage was essential to happiness? Did women like sex? . . .

I asked what he thought of the goddess Durga and he said 'She is a very powerful goddess.'

'Well,' I said, 'she is married under her various forms to Lord Shiva under his various forms so I suppose you too as a good Hindu should follow the example of your gods and get married . . . President Radhakrishnan made a very wise remark: "He who runs back from marriage is in the same boat with one who runs away from battle." '

Penelope Chetwode, *Kulu*, 1972

John Betjeman was fascinated by people's full Christian names and used them promiscuously. 'Nobody ever called me "John Edward" before he did; but then it caught on among all my friends,' John Edward Bowle complained.[1] In the foreword to *Summoned by Bells* John wrote: 'The author . . . is particularly grateful to his friends John Hanbury Angus Sparrow and Thomas Edward Neil Driberg for going through the manuscript and proofs . . .'

Possibly the habit stemmed from early reading of William Brighty Rands ('Godfrey Gordon Gustavus Gore . . ./Was a boy who never would shut a door.'). Or perhaps it was compensation for a resentment that his parents had given him only one Christian name, and that the commonest in England. Or it may have been a kind of 'sympathetic magic': knowing a person's full name – or his school – gave one an obscure power over him, like possessing a swatch of an enemy's hair.

When John was admitted to *Who's Who* in 1940 (giving as his hobby 'dirt track racing') he listed all three Christian names of his wife, the daughter of Field-Marshal Sir Philip Chetwode. Her first name was Penelope, though she was the reverse of Ulysses' Penelope: it was John who stayed at home while Penelope travelled the world. Her second name was Valentine, because she was born on that saint's day, 14 February, in 1910. Her third name (her mother's second) was Hester: Penelope was to have much in common with Lady Hester Stanhope, whom A.W. Kinglake described, in *Eothen*, as 'cool, decisive in manner . . . full of audacious fun, and saying the downright things that the sheepish society around her is afraid to utter.'[2]

Penelope Chetwode was not a serene *Tatler* beauty, like Camilla Russell. She was shortish and coltish. Later, John unkindly referred to her legs as 'Mr and Mrs Broadwood';[3] but she was proud of her full breasts; Lady Rachel Billington remembers her, in 1977, posing jut-chested in front of a voluptuous Indian statue of the goddess Durga in New Delhi and exclaiming: 'Look! *Just* like mine!'[4] Penelope wore her hair in a Shetland pony fringe. Her eyes had the curious property of looking cold but conveying warmth. Her nose was *'retroussé'*, 'button' or 'snub' according to the sympathy of the beholder. Her mouth had a natural droop which wrongly suggested sulkiness. Her voice was irresistibly imitable. At times of pitched emotion, it had an almost ventriloquial *timbre*, like that of a Punch-and-Judy man using his swazzle. Though she had picked up some cockneyisms ('Right you are' was her most frequent remark on the telephone) and in later years was prepared to muck along with drugged vagabonds on the hippie trail in India, she never forgot, or never escaped, her patrician caste. She could replicate, when it was needed, her mother's freezing stare, or quell a dissenting friend with the tally-ho tones of the hunting shires.

When John met her, in 1931, Penelope had a reputation as one of the more truculent debutantes of her year. Like her contemporary and friend Lady Mary Pakenham, who satirized 'the Season' in her 1938 book *Brought Up and Brought Out*, she rebelled against the vapid round of dances and parties where eligible young women were put on show, lightly chaperoned and heavily decked out in their mother's jewellery, in the hope that they would attract some eligible young men. Acceptably, she was interested in horses and loved riding; less acceptably, she was clever. She had already made herself as good a judge of Indian temple sculptures as of horseflesh. The writhings of Krishna and Kali were as intently studied and analysed as the Lippizaner curvetting of Moti, her Arab horse.

Mary Pakenham recalled what a handicap cleverness was in a debutante. She learned 'to palm [herself] off as a no-brow'.[5] But even that modest degree of dissimulation was quite beyond Penelope, who was notoriously candid. (Lunching at Faringdon House, Berkshire, in the 1930s, she reduced H.G. Wells to rare and respectful silence by an exhaustive recital of the history and techniques of the Caesarian operation. 'If I were married to that girl,' Wells told their host, Lord Berners, 'I would throw away my encyclopaedia!'[6])

But though some might regard her as too brainy – a bluestocking in a riding boot, as it were – she was an attractive girl, and to the arbiters of 'Society' she was 'eligible'. The Chetwode family had been established in Staffordshire from at least the fifteenth century, and had held a baronetcy since 1700. The family history, *Chetwode of Chetwode* (1884) by Stephen Tucker, Somerset Herald in Ordinary, recorded of Penelope's grandmother: 'Alice Lady Chetwode through her mother Eliza Jane, daughter of Major Arden of Longcrofts, is derived from a common ancestor with Shakespeare, Cromwell, Hampden and Waller.'[7]

Penelope's father, who was gazetted Field-Marshal in 1933, the year she and John were married, was Commander-in-Chief of the Army in India. His service record was that of a *Boy's Own Paper* hero. He had served in the Chin Hills Expedition of 1892–93 and in the South African War: he was present at the Siege of Ladysmith. By the outbreak of the First World War he was a brigadier-general, and he was the first British officer to be mentioned in dispatches in that war. The action which made him a national hero took place on John Betjeman's eighth birthday, 28 August 1914. 'Sir Philip's is the first reputation of the war,' the *Sketch* declared on 9 September. Under his command the 5th British Cavalry Brigade engaged the German Cavalry in the Battle of Moy, in which the 12th Lancers and the Royal Scots Greys routed the enemy. 'We went through the Uhlans[8] like brown paper,' Chetwode told *The Times*.[9]

Photographs of Chetwode's rather set, intense face now appeared frequently in the Press. They were often accompanied by portraits of his elegantly dressed wife. In 1899 he had married Alice Hester Camilla, daughter of Colonel the Hon. Richard Stapleton-Cotton, a son of Lord Combermere. Their only son Roger was sent to Eton (where his great friend was Frank Pakenham) and to Oxford; and Penelope, their only daughter, went to Queen's College, London, and to St Margaret's, Bushey, Herts., a fashionable girls' school. Lord Vivian's daughter Daphne – later Marchioness of Bath – wrote:

> The shape of Penelope Chetwoode [*sic*], the shrill whine of her schoolgirl voice, highlights my short career at Queen's College. Whenever I see her now I feel she should still be in a gym-tunic, and I imagine her as the hoyden with the bean-bag, standing in the middle of a circle during 'break', viciously swinging that bag filled with dry beans which struck one so painfully on the ankles if one did not jump high enough to clear it.[10]

At St Margaret's, Bushey, Penelope's best friends were her cousin Audrey Talbot, daughter of Lord Ingestre, and Silvia Coke (now Lady Silvia Combe), daughter of Lord Coke, later Earl of Leicester. Another early friend was the comedienne Joyce Grenfell, who was in the Brownies with Penelope – acutely observing the idiosyncrasies of Brown Owl for future skits – and joined the Girl Guides on the same day in 1921. To her, Penelope seemed at that time somewhat affected: 'She had a tremendous drawl and she was so lazy that when she saluted, instead of bringing her two fingers up to her head, she drooped her head down to her hand.'[11]

Penelope was not affected. Affectation is the grafting on to one's natural character, appearance or accent of assumed traits designed to impress. She never did that. She was brought up to talk in a certain way by her parents and her expensive schools: it would have been affectation in her to speak with a different accent. She moved in the grandest society: when her father had the Aldershot command (1923–27) the King sometimes came to luncheon or dinner and Penelope had to help entertain him. The Chetwodes often spent weekends with the royal family. (Lady Chetwode *did* rather enjoy writing to her friends on headed Windsor Castle or Sandringham paper.) A later caricature of Penelope by John[12] shows her in an ornate throne-room asking Queen Mary 'Do you know the work of Gropius, Ma'am?'; the Queen sits baffled and unsmiling under her toque. After Sir Philip became Commander-in-Chief in India (1930), Penelope herself lived the life of a princess, with luxurious quarters, a Christian *ayah*, and a limousine always at her service.

The stately tenor of the Chetwodes' life in India was described by Lady Mary Pakenham in a series of letters written to her sister, Lady Violet, in 1933 when she and Lavender Christie-Miller, another friend of Penelope's, were staying at the Commander-in-Chief's house in Delhi. 'It's like a pantomime palace and we live a kind of pantomime existence,' she wrote. The house was so big that 'everything is done by chits; if you want to talk to someone at the other end of the room you call a bearer and write a note and have it taken across on a silver salver.'[13]

Among the diversions were a ball ('eight hundred men too many'), film shows in a subterranean cinema, and the visiting maharajahs and their ADCs. The Maharajah of Kapurthala arrived with 'a divine little ADC' who thought Lady Mary was two sisters who resembled each other strikingly, 'and talked about obscene rites to Penelope at lunch in great detail to her heart's content . . .'[14] Penelope organized archaeological expeditions, which not all her friends found as enthralling as she did. On 1 March 1933 Lady Mary wrote to Lady Violet: 'This morning we had one of Penelope's specials. Starting at eight we walked across dust and rocks with two extremely fat, black little archaeologists till our tongues hung out to see the remains of a tomb, getting back by twelve . . .'[15] And in mid-March Lady Mary wrote to her sister:

Last night I lost marks by refusing to turn out at ten at night to go to have a farewell gloat at a tomb by midnight, as I was afraid of snakes, ghosts, assassins, rapers and (far worse) being caught by Lady Chetwode. Randal [the Hon. Randal Plunkett, now Lord Dunsany, then ADC to Chetwode] was deputed to sit with her in the drawing-room and when she heard the car coming round to the door and exclaimed 'Hist! What's that?' to reply ''Tis but the wind.' Apparently he was convincing (I funked and went to bed early) as there is no rumpus this morning.[16]

Visits by friends from England made welcome breaks in the social routine. Basil Dufferin and his bride, Maureen Guinness, stayed with the Chetwodes for six weeks on their honeymoon in 1931. Dufferin, whose grandfather had been Viceroy of India, wanted to go to Ava in Burma where the battle which added its name to the title had been fought. 'Our ADCs arranged their tours in Burma and their shooting in Gwalior,' Penelope remembered, 'and then we all spent Christmas together as guests of the Maharajah of

Mysore.'[17] Even in the jungle, Raj formality was not relaxed. Evening dress was worn in the mess tent and strict rules of precedence were observed when going in to dinner.

Another friend of John's who stayed with the Chetwodes in India was Robert Byron, who went out in 1929 to research the special issue of *The Architectural Review* devoted to New Delhi which was published in January 1931 to mark the Indian Round Table Conference in London. (The new capital of India was officially opened in February of that year.) On Boxing Day 1929 Byron and Penelope were given a guided tour of the new Viceroy's House by the architect, Sir Edwin Lutyens, whose daughter, Mary, had been at Queen's College with Penelope.

Robert Byron was the first young man Penelope had met who understood and shared her passion for Indian architecture. In many ways the two could not have been more unalike. Byron was ceremonious, with a literary style of which 'mandarin' might seem too flighty a description. Penelope was informal, take-me-as-you-find-me, and usually wrote as she spoke, not dressing her observations and ideas in fancy imagery. But the two became firm friends during Byron's stay in Delhi and continued to see each other in England. Penelope stayed with him and his 'Queen of the Women's Institute' mother in their Victorian house in Savernake Forest, near Marlborough, and the two went riding together, though Byron's style of riding was not to Penelope's taste. 'His idea was to gallop, which is very bad style when you're hacking. So we used to gallop through the Forest together, because I couldn't do good-style riding if he wanted to do bad-style.'[18]

It was through Robert Byron that Penelope met John. In 1931 she had completed an article on the cave temples of Ellora in the Deccan. She showed it to Byron, who suggested she should take it to de Cronin Hastings at *The Architectural Review*. With his usual disinclination to see 'new people', Hastings refused to meet Penelope and she was shown into John's office instead. John was in the middle of a long telephone conversation with Pamela Mitford, but eventually Penelope was able to show him her article. 'We both got down on the floor on our hands and knees and I showed him all the photographs I had taken of Ellora,' she remembered. 'He wasn't the least bit interested in Indian art. Anyway, the long and short of it was that he did publish it, and that's how we met. And I was suddenly very attracted to him and started falling for him.'[19]

Penelope's article, 'The Paradise of Siva', appeared in the issue of October 1932.

By September 1932, Penelope and John were already writing to each other in the mock Irish brogue, interlarded with English passages in Greek characters, that they were to use for even the most serious correspondence for the rest of John's life. His nicknames for her were 'Ugly' (οογλι), 'Filth' (φιλθ) and 'Beastliness' (βεαστλινεσς), and she frequently signed letters or postcards with one of these sobriquets. She was just as playfully offensive about John, addressing him as 'Dung' (Δυγγ or Δοογγ) or 'Poofy' (ποοφυ), short for 'Puffball', a fungus supposed to resemble his already balding head. (Unfortunately none of John's love-letters to Penelope has survived, because Lady Chetwode had advised her daughter always to destroy love-letters addressed to her – which advice she took.) Lady Longford, who had married Frank Pakenham in 1931, recalls that when Penelope visited their home, 'Stairways', near Aylesbury, Bucks., shortly after she had met John, and was asked what it was that she liked about him, she replied, 'He has green teeth.'[20] When staying with her great-uncle, Lord Methuen, at Corsham Court early in 1933, Penelope wrote to John:

> You are a silly little boy to go on as you do about me not lovin you. You seem to have complexes about yourself and whatnot. You certainly do smell very bad & are as yellow as a quattrocento Florentine, & you have earwigs in your nose which would revolt many people, but you must surely know by now that these defects only serve to enhance your charms in my sight, you στινκιν γελλοω τρεασυρε [stinkin yellow treasure].[21]

James Richards, who joined *The Architectural Review* in 1933, remembered that 'Betjeman was at this time courting Penelope Chetwode, their courtship being conducted, or so it seemed to us, through exchanges of badinage between John, leaning out of his office window, and Penelope standing in the street below calling up in her penetrating upper-class cockney voice.'[22] Penelope began asking John to her home in St John's Wood, London. The Chetwodes lived in the house in Grove End Road which had once belonged to Sir Lawrence Alma-Tadema, the painter of Grecian and Roman scenes. John called the house 'Tadema Towers'. A brass staircase led to Alma-Tadema's studio, which was painted silver, with a gallery lettered 'AS THE SUN COLOURS

FLOWERS, SO ART COLOURS LIFE.' An impluvium (which Penelope's brother Roger called 'the vomitorium') contained a marble sunken bath used by Alma-Tadema to stage tableaux of naked women in his 'five o'clock tea antiquity'. The house had a pleasant garden and the Chetwodes built a tennis-court.

Penelope's sitting-room was a replica of a parlour in the Ship Inn at Greenwich, which Alma-Tadema had had copied. 'It had a very pretty bow window, and I'd done it up in what I suppose you'd now call Art Deco,' Penelope said. 'My mother was mad on that sort of style. She always used to have black walls and very violently coloured cushions in her sitting-room.' Penelope's walls were white, 'but I too had the most extraordinarily coloured cushions, bright orange and gold and pink, and bright blue curtains – every sort of clashing colour – and John sort of hummed and hawed at it and thought it was rather awful. I was a bit upset. I considered my taste was impeccable.'[23]

To the Field-Marshal and Lady Chetwode, John was not a welcome suitor. He was a journalist and had neither land nor capital. He usually looked rather scruffy; though he possessed a few expensive suits, they were lacking in trouser creases. 'We ask people like that to our houses,' Lady Chetwode told Penelope, 'but we don't marry them.'[24] The Chetwodes wanted for their only daughter a lord, an eldest son or at the very least 'somebody with a pheasant shoot', as Penelope later put it. In 1976 Sir Osbert Lancaster recalled:

Old 'Star' Chetwode, Penelope's mother, went round saying 'My daughter's got entangled with a little middle-class Dutchman' – she was a roaring old snob. And John, who never lies down under insults, took *instant* revenge. He wrote to the *Morning Post*: 'Dear Sir, It is often suggested that the British are a xenophobic nation, unwelcoming to foreigners. As a middle-class Dutchman myself, I am happy to state that this is a completely fallacious idea. I have met with nothing but kindness during my stay in London.' And then John bought up several copies of the newspaper and sent cuttings of the letter to Lady Chetwode's friends.[25]

Parental opposition was not the only obstacle to a romance between John and Penelope. She was 'sort of unofficially engaged' to the artist John Spencer-Churchill, Winston Churchill's nephew. Johnnie Churchill had matinée-idol good looks and came from the kind of family Sir Philip and Lady Chetwode approved of; but the path of true love did not run smooth for him and Penelope. 'They quarrelled like Kilkenny cats,' said Osbert Lancaster.[26]

Penelope's love-life was further complicated by an attachment she had formed in India. 'I was madly in love with Sir John Marshall, who was director-general of archaeology in India. He had been taken out by Lord Curzon in the early years of the century to organize the archaeology. He was a very distinguished scholar and he was, I'm afraid, rather one with the girls. Very good-looking.'[27] Penelope had fallen in love with him in 1931 in the one summer she spent in Simla, and later he had come to England and asked her to go off with him and live on a Greek island. Marshall was fifty-five and Penelope was twenty-one.

Then she found herself falling in love with John Betjeman. 'So at that time I was really in love with three Johns, and didn't know which one I wanted to marry. Thank God I settled against Sir John Marshall, because I realized afterwards it is a terrible thing to break up a marriage with two children, I wouldn't have done it for the world.' Her ardour for Johnnie Churchill was cooling. 'He was very very fascinating and attractive, but I realized he wouldn't be an easy person to marry.'

Penelope's romantic vacillations caused John distress. His misery is mentioned in letters to Patrick Balfour from Balfour's friend Mary Sheridan, who was with her French husband Guy de René-ville in Biskra, Algeria. On 15 October 1932 she wrote: 'How are Hester and Etchells and poor, poor Bech [sic]?'[28] And on 2 November: 'Who is Penelope engaged to now? And is the poor Bedj [sic] taking his defeat philosophically?'[29] Etchells, whom John saw often at this time, thought John took a poetic relish in his heartache. After giving a dinner party attended by John, Mary Pakenham and Billy Clonmore, among others, he wrote to Balfour on 4 February 1933, 'Betj. is greatly immersed in all his woes, which give him great pleasure.'[30] One of Etchells's advantages as a confidant was that he was also on good terms with Penelope. 'I was trotted round the Park in great style by Penelope Chetwode last week in a phaeton,' he wrote to Balfour, 'which I found to be delicious, particularly to look on the Park from above, which is very grand.'[31]

Penelope's feelings for John were intensified when he took her to Kew Gardens one day and they made daisy chains together. Her final choice between her three suitors was literally dramatic. She went with Johnnie Churchill to a performance of *The Merchant of Venice*. 'There are about twenty-two scenes in it. [In fact, there are twenty.] Each scene I decided on marrying a different John. And in the last scene of all I decided on John Betjeman. So then I stuck to that.' Penelope's choice mimicked that of Bassanio, who rejected the gold and silver caskets and chose the lead one. She declined the archaeological knight and the artistic scion of a ducal family, and chose the penniless poet.

John had already decided that Penelope was the girl for him. She was not quite the overpowering amazon of his poems, but she had the dominant quality that appealed to him:

> She stands in strong, athletic pose
> And wrinkles her *retroussé* nose.
> Is it distaste that makes her frown,
> So furious and freckled, down
> On an unhealthy worm like me?
> Or am I what she likes to see?
> I do not know, though much I care.
> εἰθε γενοίμην . . . would I were
> (Forgive me, shade of Rupert Brooke)
> An object fit to claim her look.[32]

Penelope's 'frown' (or rather, the semblance of a frown caused by a naturally down-turned mouth) was part of her charm for John. In a letter of 13 February (the year is not stated but is probably *c*. 1955) he wrote:

Feb 13th
Moi darlin Plymmi,[33]
Many appy returns of the day. [Her birthday was on the 14th.] When oi first married your 'air was quoite straight & yew ad a fringe but yew looked joost as angry & ad the same very voolgar beads . . .

Penelope could have given satisfactory answers to the questionnaire in 'Myfanwy':

> Were you a prefect and head of your dormit'ry?
> Were you a hockey girl, tennis or gym?

Who was your favourite? who had a crush on you?
Which were the baths where they taught you to swim?

Hers were the 'firm hand, fond hand' of 'Love in a Valley', the 'bountiful body' of Pam in 'Pot Pourri from a Surrey Garden', the 'uncouth mechanic slacks' of Thelma's sister Pearl in 'Agricultural Caress'. Like Miss Joan Hunter Dunn she had 'the speed of a swallow, the grace of a boy'. John had fantasies of submitting to masterful women. Once, when visiting the Turner Gallery at Somerset House with John Guest, he indicated a strapping woman on the other side of the room and sighed, 'Oh I say, wouldn't you like to be pushed in a pram by her round Hyde Park?'[34] Penelope satisfied John's need to be dominated:

> O love! for love I could not speak,
> It left me winded, wilting, weak . . .[35]

Penelope had two other attractions for John: she was the daughter of a baronet; and she had a brain to rival his own. In her copy of *Mount Zion* he wrote:

Penelope Chetwode, I always think, is not only tastefully dressed despite the hours she wears out her clothes in the Reading Room of the British Museum, but as also the possessor of unique social charm that has made her the cynosure of all eyes – whether surrounded by the horn rims of Bloomsbury spectacle frames or the paint and powder of a high class drawing room. So compelling is her character that I am obliged to write for her this facetious dedication. I am that clever chap John Betjeman.

In keeping with his role for her, Penelope sat on John's knee and proposed to him in her sitting-room, the one modelled on the Ship Inn parlour at Greenwich.

Twenty years later, when asked by the BBC to choose and talk about music which 'evoked special memories' for him, John chose, among other pieces, 'My Heart Stood Still'.

This tune seemed terribly modern to me and rather difficult, but the words said exactly what we all meant, and still mean, when we fall in love. To that tune I became engaged to be married . . . It goes with jogging round in smoky, crowded night-clubs.

'Hullo . . oo . . oo . . oo . . Wanda. Devine to see you my deah. Are you going on to the Blue Lantern? We'll join you there later.' It is the tune that was thumped out by pale men with cigarettes in their mouths and another dry martini waiting for them on the piano.[36]

Penelope commented on this: 'What nonsense! I was never a night-club gel. I only went to a night-club once, with Patrick Balfour – and someone mistook him for the Prince of Wales, goodness knows how.'[37]

When Penelope told her parents that she wanted to marry John, they were predictably upset. However, they decided they must make an attempt to get to know John better, and invited him to a white-tie dinner at the Savoy. 'John went to amazing pains to get a made-up tie sewn on elastic,' said Osbert Lancaster. In those days, only waiters wore such ties. 'Throughout dinner he plucked the bow forward six or seven inches and let it snap back – purely to annoy his future mother-in-law.'[38]

After this unpromising encounter, the Chetwodes insisted that Penelope should go back to India with them. She complied. John came to see her off at the station and gave her a copy of the children's comic paper *Rainbow*. A photograph of Penelope standing wistfully on the platform and holding the copy of *Rainbow* survives. She joined her parents in Government House in Delhi, which later became the Nehru Museum. She and John exchanged long love-letters in Irish-Greek.

Penelope was once again in the dangerous ambit of Sir John Marshall; but it was John who first proved fickle. He wrote and told her that he was engaged to one of her best friends, Wilhelmine Cresswell – 'Billa', who later married [Sir] Roy Harrod. Penelope had known Billa since both were children. Billa's father was killed in the First World War, but her stepfather was a general at Aldershot when Chetwode was commanding there. 'I was absolutely furious and I wrote and told John where he got off,' Penelope recalled. 'Then he broke off the engagement with Billa and she said it would never have worked.'[39]

In spite of this contretemps, the two were on good terms again by the time Penelope made the homeward journey in April 1933. She wrote to John from the British Embassy, Constantinople, on 2 April:

My very own λιττλε κυρλυ ἐαδεδ ἀκωλυτε φρομ στ μιλδρεδ'ς βρεαδ στρεετ [little curly 'eaded acolyte from St Mildred's Bread Street],

I ain't written to you sooner from ere bekorse hoi was ha-waiting your letter which Archie wired to say was followin. H.L. [Her Ladyship = Lady Chetwode] opened the latter's wire so she must have been very mystified. Perhaps she thought it was Archie Norfolk.

Oi AM so appy to think that you is appy & oi am appy & we all are appy. Oh darlin isn't it excoiting. I get into perfectly orrible states of thrill thinkin of you: oi wroithe & wriggle in bed & nearly broke my berth on the Tamus hexpress . . .'[40]

But the lovers were not to be reunited for at least another two weeks. Lady Chetwode had suddenly discovered that Easter was on 16 April and had said there was no point in their going home until after it. ('I suppose she thinks there would be no time to secure an invitation to Wilton or Corsham,' Penelope sourly speculated.) In the meantime, Penelope was to accompany her to Greece.

Penelope had been to Greece before. She had spent three weeks in Athens when she was seventeen, and was not looking forward to revisiting it with her mother. 'H.L. is terribly difficult to sightsee with as you feel all the time that she's bored and wants to go to the cinema. As you know, I like sightseeing in a very pedantic and systematic way, especially places which I probably shan't see again, so it is all extremely trying and I wish to God we were cutting out Greece & coming straight home. But darlin you won't lose your temper & run off with another girl in those 10 days will you? Please please don't because I should go off my head. I love you so much . . .'[41] Evidently the lesson of the Billa Cresswell episode had been taken to heart.

In the letter, Penelope said that (an unspecified) joke John was playing on John Sparrow was extremely funny, but wouldn't he have difficulty in forging the manuscript? 'I suppose it's quite easy to get eighteenth-century paper but old ink must be harder.' Talking of Sparrow reminded her that she had found 'an extremely beautiful poem in the Ox. Bk. of Eng. Mystical Verse by his favourite man J. Donne. It's a sonnet about God & the last 3 lines are:

> Take mee to you, imprison mee, for I
> Except you enthrall mee, never shall be free,
> For ever chast, except you ravish mee.'

She asked John to write to her at the Hotel Grande Bretagne, Athens. They would marry, she promised, as soon as her father came home in early June (he was due to arrive on the 3rd) or, if John preferred, as soon as she returned in April. 'We can't marry in May because it's bad luck and I have the great misfortune to be super-stitious . . .'

Penelope arrived home on 19 April to a rapturous welcome from John. Her father wrote from Simla on 6 May to say that he was laid up with dysentery and had not been on a horse for twenty days. 'I am thinking always so much about you, sweetheart,' he wrote, 'and I pray so hard every day that you may make a wise choice in this great crisis in your life.'[42] On 14 May he wrote again:

Dearest Penelope,
                    I have just got your letter of May 4th in which you say you have made up your mind to marry John Betjeman. I cannot pretend to be pleased, but you are a grown woman with more than the usual share of brains, and if after all this time you have had for reflection you are not certain of your feelings you never will be.

I have told you the risks you are running and it is useless to repeat everything I have said or written – I love you more than I can say & hope & pray you may have chosen right, & that you will be happy.

I know nothing about the proper time for the announcement – so you must consult with your mother. I am writing to Upton [the family solicitor] to go & see her & begin making arrangements, but from the letter John B's father wrote to me I fear they can only be very unsatisfactory ones. Bless you darling.
        Your own daddy,
                    Philip W. Chetwode.[43]

But when her father came home in June, Penelope changed her mind about marrying John. The reason she gave John was that she could not bear to sink herself in married domesticity before she had fully developed her mind. She wanted to become an Indologist and study with the archaeologist Giuseppe Tucci at the University of Rome. John and his friends thought that this was merely an excuse and that Penelope had given in to the objections of her strong-willed parents. On Sir Philip's return to England, John had written to him (6 June) formally asking for the hand of his daughter in mar-riage. On 8 June the Field-Marshal replied that he could only

380

reiterate that if the marriage to Penelope took place, it was against his desire and his advice to her – 'I cannot conceive that you can support her properly on the income you have or will have between you.'[44] If the couple persisted in their intentions, Chetwode added, he could bring nothing into settlement unless John or his father brought a sum equal to or greater than £5,000 into settlement, 'in my daughter's absolute favour'. The phrase smacks of legal advice. Sir Philip was making it insultingly clear to John that, if he were a gold-digger hoping for a dowry, he could think again. 'I regret to have to say this,' Chetwode concluded, 'but I consider it is madness to marry on, what are, in case of illness or death, no prospects at all.'

Penelope was full of guilt and perplexity. So she went to the most worldly-wise man she knew, her mother's youngest brother Colonel Robert Stapleton-Cotton, 'Uncle Bertie'. He had been the black sheep of the family, but had made good: banished to South Africa at fifteen for getting a housemaid with child, he had made a fortune in gold-mining. Uncle Bertie saw that Penelope needed time to work things out, away from John and away from parental pressure. He paid for her to travel to France by train and stay with his sister Polly at Opio, near Grasse, Alpes Maritimes. Penelope had stayed there before with her parents and was fond of Polly. 'She was absolutely divine, a maiden aunt, and we all adored her.'[45]

John was distraught. Penelope wrote to him on 14 June:

My darling,
          After getting your most moving wire I cannot refrain from writing to you, although you asked me not to, and I fully intended to obey you.

It is useless for me to attempt to say 'I am sorry for what I have done' I might as well say to someone, 'I am sorry I murdered your son', one cannot apologise in such tame words, in any words, for committing crime, & I have committed the very worst and most brutal sort of crime . . . That I should make you suffer so terribly is unforgiveable. You have always had an unhappy & squalid life & that on top of all this unhappiness I should do this to you, I should fail at the eleventh hour, is a crime which I don't think even God can ever forgive.[46]

She denied that she had left him 'out of any noble feelings towards my parents . . . because I loved them, or thought I owed them more.

Actually, the only good that has come of this is that I have at last broken away from my parents. I could never live with them again.' Her great mistake, she now considered, had been made in 1932: the minute she had decided to marry John, she should have suppressed her interest in the East and become wholly absorbed in England, thrown herself wholeheartedly into the study of Saxon art or Norman fonts. As it was, she had 'overfed' her interest in India to such an extent that it now irritated her to be a dilettante – '& I suddenly realized that if I married you at the moment & lived in the country (or even in London – it was wonderful of you to say you would live there for me) my appetite would never be satisfied, the longing for Inja would bubble to the surface like the lava of a volcano & I should get irritated & discontented & extremely difficult, selfish & unpleasant to live with.' Her 'great crime', she felt, lay in not having realized this before, in having made John love her and then having left him.

She wondered whether the trouble did not go further back. Perhaps she should have gone to Oxford after leaving school and then taken up some really hard pedantic work. 'I was born to be a little pedant & I cannot be wholly happy until I am.' She was not rejecting John for ever. 'Once I have learnt this blasted bloody Sanskrit . . . & attained a certain mastery over my subject, there is no earthly reason, as Cracky [Clonmore] pointed out, why we should not marry.' One did not need to live in India to be an Orientalist; one need only go out occasionally to write a book on some particular aspect '& one day you might come out with me and write a book about 18th century remains there.' She had found out that Uncle Bertie was going to leave her some money, 'so we should not have a penniless old age, & one can go to India very cheaply & live there very cheaply if one's prepared to put up with a certain amount of discomfort.' She added:

Even if we didn't marry for 5 years I would only be 28 and you 32. But meanwhile we must not be under any fixed obligations to one another, & I suppose we oughtn't to write. If you find somebody else, don't hesitate to marry. I intend to put men out of my head now but I suppose one cannot do that for always so I may end by marrying an archaeologist as pedantic & boring as myself. But to love again as I have loved, & still do love (though you probably can't believe it) is impossible.

It was quite different with Johnnie [Churchill], just young adolescents being in love with love & all mixed up with that awful Wagnerianism. Then Sir John [Marshall] was pure physical passion although I tried, at the time, to think it was archaeology. I was never in love with him after I returned from India & only sorry for him.

But for you I have a love which can never exist for anyone else, I don't want it to & I know it cannot . . .

After this manifesto, the letter tailed off. Penelope would not be coming to England, except to have her wisdom teeth out, 'the associations are much too painful.' She intended going to Rome for two years to study and then to India for two or three years. 'After that, if we marry, it is wonderful to think there will be no parents to interfere, we will just walk off one morning & marry.' She wondered whether John might not be happy as a schoolmaster again. 'You could see a lot of your friends in the holidays & during the term you could write poetry & novels each evening.' She would write to 'Cracky' Clonmore from time to time to learn what John was doing. The letter ended: 'P.S. Dear old Archie must be a tremendous comfort.'

Ernest Betjemann had to be told of Penelope's action – if for no other reason, because of the financial arrangements he had been trying to negotiate with Sir Philip Chetwode. On 14 June he wrote John as sympathetic a letter as he ever sent him. He hoped John was not 'cut up'. He thought the break was all for the best – 'you know my opinion of military brass-hats and the family seemed to me to look upon their daughter's marriage too much from the cash point of view'. He suggested that the situation would have been difficult for John: 'you would either have had to cut yourselves off altogether or accept the position of being looked down upon, a position not warranted and most unjust but created to some extent by the unusual outlook you have on life, an outlook which is not understood by very practical people like these.' Ernest added that he thought all would have gone smoothly 'if you had brought your father into the picture at the beginning, but, as it turns out, I am *decidedly relieved*.' He said he would take John out for a bottle of wine and advised him that 'the best thing to do is to get on with your interesting work.'[47]

John meanwhile had taken refuge with Pamela Mitford at Biddesden. All the Mitfords were full of sympathy for him and indignation over Penelope's behaviour. On 18 June, Bryan

Guinness (who was still married to Diana Mitford, though the next year was to bring divorce) wrote Penelope a stern letter. He admitted he had no right to interfere in her life or John's. But John 'is obviously very miserable. He says you have broken off your engagement to him because you cannot give up your travelling.'[48] Guinness suggested that there could be only two possible reasons for her breaking off the engagement. One was that she did not love John any more. 'It is a pity, if so, that you did not examine your feelings at an earlier stage in your relationship: but the excuse about foreign travel is quite a sensible kind of reason to give so as to hurt John's feelings as little as possible by your incompetence at gauging your own . . .' The other possibility was that she had broken off the engagement because of parental pressure. 'If so I cannot sufficiently express how much I deprecate your cowardice.' He continued:

> John is a very great person. He is eccentric and needs looking after: but he has a genius of a very unusual kind . . . Such a person, endowed as he is for your service, with great emotional capacity, is not lightly to be cast on one side because your parents were not at the same public school as his. If you are ever to live a life of your own unhedged by the false barriers of snobbery you must stand fast . . . I can't bear to see John so unhappy – that is why I have been so impertinent as to write . . .

Penelope had probably not received this letter by the time she wrote to John on 22 June – the day *Ghastly Good Taste* was published:

> My own darlin,
>   Forgive me sending wires every other day – & rather ambiguous ones at that – but I have been so emotionée (!) since coming here that I keep finding I've not been so clear as I thought I was in my successive letters to you & Cracky. There's been a mistral (hot wind) blowing hard & continuously for the last four days which drove me almost to the point of madness (there's a law in Spain to the effect that if someone does a murder during a mistral he shall not be condemned to death). That, coupled with indigestion, liver & insomnia, did not help me to think very clearly & reasonably, though throughout everything I have never doubted my love for you.
>   But now the wind has stopped & a violent thunderstorm cleared

the air early this morning. It is raining & damp & the air is fresher & I feel quieter & better.

I think what made me come here was everything combined. I felt I should go insane if I didn't get away from home. And Roger is coming back on top of it all, with Mummy trying to make me go to dances with him, cocktail parties, all those horrors. And then there was this awful terror that if I settled in the country at once I'd have to suppress all my Indian things & they'd bubble up & get the better of me & make me irritable. And I had awful pangs of conscience that if I married you I oughtn't really to go abroad any more, that you hated it so much that it would be genuinely wrong to take you out of England (& Ireland) ever. And a woman, if she marries a man, should sink her interests in his I thought. And when you used to say over & over again 'I hate it abroad' & 'you mustn't marry me if you can't do this or won't do that', I suddenly got terrified & thought that p'raps it was wrong, that p'raps your friends were right last winter when they told you we were both 'positives' & could never fit in. But I loved you so much that I couldn't bring myself to break. Then that last week was a nightmare, when I couldn't stop croiyin. Oh . . . oi was so weak & silly but I do not think I was quite moiself. And I tried so hard to fight down my desires to indulge my selfish interests & I failed – they kept welling up & waking me in the night & I used to rush to the bathroom & tickle my throat to make myself sick – hoping it would relieve the pressure. Then on Monday (oh how I loved you Sunday down at Etchells'!) I came to the conclusion that I must go right away from everything for a while to try to get clear again. I was so hopelessly confused & unhappy that I knew it would be fatal to marry in that state of mind – although I felt at the same time it was criminal to leave you. – & it *was* – oh darling! it was & I am so so sorry to have brought all this misery upon you.

But now, in spite of this, we both find we still love each other; it would, as you say, be wicked to throw away such a Holy & wonderful thing. And *we mustn't*. I am so thankful to think that I am at any rate free now & can live apart from my mother, & that when we marry it will be independently of my parents. That is a great thing accomplished. It's so awful to think that my own mother should have caused you as much suffering as she has, & humiliated you so – but that is done with now.

The only blot, then, on our landscape, remains the fact that we *are* both 'positives' & that our own temperaments may in some ways be incompatible. But great love should be able to overcome this and ultimately triumph. But I do know now that it is useless for either of us to try & suppress ourselves as we're both too energetic & dynamic to be able to stand successfully the test of prolonged repression. Therefore if we don't marry at once I will go & do my Indian stuff & once I'm advanced enough then I can come & live permanently with you in lawful wedlock & we'll both fit ourselves in & be blissful ... After all, people like H. Nicolson & V. Sackville-West both do their own things, and yet adore each other & get on frightfully well. There's no earthly reason why we shouldn't. And I shouldn't need additional sexual outlets like V.S. West because I'm not at all promiscuous by nature but fundamentally faithful. And if I searched high & low throughout the East & the West among man woman or beast I'd never find anyone to suit me physically so well as you, of that I am utterly certain!

You see, once I'm independent then I can see you as often as I can get away from Rome – no one need ever know I'm in England – or at any rate my relations needn't. I'll just come & live with you wherever you are & sometimes you can come out to me. It's useless my trying to go to the school of oriental studies in London: I've got to get right away from everybody I know if I really want to learn anything. I've got to throw myself right into it then it will all come much quicker & we'll be able to marry. (I suppose you can't tell Cracky I want to live with you as it's against all the tenets of his religion.) Oh my darlin darlin boy is it all impossible for you? You won't get the peaceful background you long for – I wish to Hell I could give it you now at once: I wish to hell I'd never been abroad & had, like you, no desire to go. But owing to bloody circumstances I cannot settle quietly in England at the moment. 'God hateth him who roams', & He has certainly every right to hate me. I hate myself, I cannot understand myself, I only know I am a despicable character, I couldn't have believed I could be so unkind. I love the English country so much & seeing it with you is a revelation – but I've got these other longings & I know the time has not yet come for me to settle permanently in England, I've got to do something first, though I'm not so very clear myself as to what it is ...

But my sweet we still love: can't we adapt our love to our lives? You know that my nature is faithful & that if I'm away from you for long stretches at a time you need never fear my being attracted to anyone else. When I come back to have my [wisdom] teeth out at the end of July, couldn't we go to that Inn in Essex for the first week in

August (I could tell my parents – I shan't be completely independent till they've gone to India – I'm staying with the Ede's[49] or someone?) I do so want to be quite quite alone with you. I'm never so happy with you when other people are around as when we're completely alone together.

Your book comes out to-day. I hope it will go very well – it is amazingly good & clear & I have read it right through again out here. – Talking about pattern in life, it's odd that I met you just when your first book came out & have left you on the appearance of your 2nd. I hope to God that I'll marry you when the third is ready. Polly adores your book & understood every word which proves how clear it is as she knows nothing about architecture. I've ordered 5 copies for pals.

My darlin darlin . . . I am so sorry, Oh God I am sorry – but can't we work it? Because we love, we love . . .[50]

This letter, with its mention of uncontrollable weeping, indigestion and insomnia, suggests that Penelope had suffered a minor nervous breakdown, caused far more by the conflict of loyalties between her parents and John than by that between married domesticity and the continuance of her studies. The mention of 'that Inn in Essex', of physical compatibility and of the subterfuge that was to be practised on her parents gives the hint that John and Penelope had spent some nights together; and this is confirmed by her next letter from Opio:

The actual facts of the case are as follows: we both love each other very very much, with a love that (should we part) will never come to either of us again, the φυσικαλ στοοφ [physical stoof] is ideal & although it's of only secondary importance it is a thing which only comes once in a lifetime as perfectly as it has to us (I believe extremely few women get complete physical satisfaction from any man); we'll have enough money to live fairly comfortably, but, owing to capricious circumstances we each have very strong interests at opposite ends of the world. It's out of the question for you to give up yours (we'd have no money if you did!) & I'm too weak & SELFISH (that's what it comes to) to give up mine. *Can we effect a compromise?*[51]

In the same letter, Penelope said that her plan was either to marry soon, secretly, or to live with John on and off for the next two or three years, at the end of which she would have the necessary knowledge to work on her own. If they were to marry soon, it would have to be secretly, or her allowance from her parents would be cut off and she would be unable to go to Rome. She suggested that only Billy Clonmore should be let into the secret.

In his reply, John evidently insisted that they should marry rather than 'live in sin'. In her next letter, of 25 June, Penelope wrote:

> You are absolutely right about the necessity of marrying as opposed to living together. The latter would be impossible for you: it would mean living for years in a state of uncertainty & would hamper your nerves, general health & work terribly. It would be much better to break away altogether & finally than that.
>
> I meanwhile cannot help having a conscience about marrying you on the terms dictated in my last two letters . . . I love you allright, you needn't fear that, *BUT* just stop & think for a moment (think for a very long time before you ultimately decide) what it will mean for *you* . . . You are the sort of person who ought to have a comfortable ('cosy'!!) home, preferably in the country, which would be an agreeable and peaceful background to your somewhat hectic life. If you marry me now, I probably won't be able to give you that for 4 or 5 years & even after that time I may go off periodically for several months at a time. This means that you've got another few years ahead of noisy smelly London & you'll get the same nerves & headaches & sick feelings as you've had in the past – & your extra money will go mostly in taxis & entertaining. The alternative to this, of course, is to get a bachelor chum to share a small house in the country, get an old woman to 'do' for you & come to London every day for your work.[52]

Penelope added that John's suggestion of their living in Dorset did not appeal to her because she would get 'completely out of touch with all my Injun things'. She herself would prefer Ireland to anywhere, because it was so quiet and restful and ideal for work, '& also the people are so free & easy & independent . . .' Much of the letter (even down to the living in Ireland) is an all too prescient forecast of their marriage, and of some of the reasons for its eventual breakdown:

> Our love has had wonderful moments, moments (minutes, hours sometimes) as you say, of complete understanding, but it's been terribly tempestuous & at times unhappy. Great love is of this nature I suppose. And our love has been great & passionate (& will

continue to be so if we marry) but hardly calm & domestic. When you first saw me you said 'One shouldn't marry for love as much as for friendship.' Well we are tremendous friends but do we fit in quite harmoniously enough for our love to turn domestic and calm?

At first the Chetwodes were pleased that Penelope had allowed herself to be packed off to the south of France, even though she had been put up to it by the disreputable Uncle Bertie. In Opio, Lady Chetwode thought, Penelope might come to her senses. But later some less advantageous aspects of the voluntary exile occurred to her, and she began to write long hectoring letters both to Penelope and to Polly, who left hers lying around for Penelope to read because she thought they were so funny. Penelope reported their contents to John:

Letter to Polly received on same day as I got your last:–
'There is no question of Penelope marrying Mr B., ever. He won't. He's been engaged 5 times already & everyone says he looks upon it as a joke. He is very angry with her writing to him suggesting marriage in a few years, he says why should he wait. He never minds anything very much & I hear is already looking out for someone else. People say he intends to propose to Pam Mitford again at once & he's announced his intention of going out as much as possible. You might tell part of this to P., it will hurt but she had much better know the truth.'

Letter to me received to-day:–
'I hope you will come back soon as J.B. tells everyone it is all quite at an end between you. They say he was upset for two days & has now quite recovered, therefore it is rather humiliating for you to stay abroad because you are miserable when he isn't at all. I wish you would come back & face the music & pretend you don't care even if you do, it would be much more dignified, women never understand that a man may change & after all this is the 5th time he has been engaged, so what may seem a tragedy to you is not one to him, & I fancy he is one of those people with whom nothing goes very deep & he treats life as a joke.'

Letter to Polly received to-day:–
'Do try & make P. come back, people are certain to say she's going to have a baby & that John B. will not marry her, she's so terribly ignorant of the world & you know what people are.(!!!!!!)
'I wish she would come back for the Eton & Harrow [cricket match]. She would have to leave July 12th then she could go to

Honor & Beryl's weddings[53] – it really does look too extraordinary her going off like this, especially when Roger comes home.

'I wish to God Bertie hadn't told her he was going to leave her any money.'[54]

Penelope might represent her mother's comments as a big joke when writing to John, but inevitably some of the darts went at least half-way home. She commented on the extracts:

Well, there are some plums for you there allright & I shall certainly arrive in London at the end of July with a large cushion stuffed in my stomach so as to appear in an advanced state of pregnancy.

I suppose R. Chetwode has told you a great part of this & your semi-friends like Frank Pakenham & others. I dare say you did say you meant to go out as much as possible & I know you were annoyed when I first wrote & suggested marrying in a few years, but when it comes to being engaged *5 times* (actually it's only once besides me isn't it? & then only for 2 days to Billa!) & saying you take everything as a joke & have no depth of feeling it really makes one's blood boil. I wrote to her & said: 'as a matter of fact John is capable of far deeper & finer feelings than you have ever dreamed of or can ever hope to conceive – surely I should know.' If your friends (or rather 'semi-friends', your real pals like Cracky & Etchells would never do it) are really going about saying that you treat life entirely as a joke & never take anything seriously, then Nancy Mitford's novel 'Xmas Pudding' was indeed prophetic – when you appear as a character who longs to be taken seriously but whose every action & production is taken as a joke & thought to be intended as such. In her book, your novel (meant to be deep & serious) was thought to be your funniest joke; in life your engagement to me is perhaps thought to be your funniest joke.[55]

It was Nancy Mitford who goaded John into the action which won Penelope back. She said to him: 'Well, *go after her and get her*, don't just let it go like that. You must go out to the south of France and win her back.'[56] And he did so, even though, as Penelope was so well aware, he hated 'abroad'. Penelope recalled:

He came out on the Blue Train and suddenly turned up at my aunt's house. My aunt didn't quite know what to do. At that time, I remember, I was reading a lot of [Thomas] Hood, because John had been reading Hood to me when we parted. There was one very moving poem that I kept reading over and over again. It begins:

Love, dearest Lady, such as I would speak,
Lives not within the humour of the eye. . .

So I was in a way pleased that he'd come out and in a way upset.
But then he was so insistent. He stayed with my aunt's friend Mrs
Starr, a marvellous American woman, did a lot of good works for
children in the south of France in the war – she lived in a big villa,
very good self-taught painter; my aunt lived in her gardener's
cottage. John stayed in her house for two or three days. And I said,
'All right, I will marry you, but I do want to get my qualifications
first: then I'll be able to go on with a career after I'm married.' And
he said, yes, I could do all that, it was perfectly all right.[57]

John returned to England on 5 July, taking with him a piece of
string which had been tied round Penelope's finger as measurement
for a ring. Apparently the two had had a tiff just before he left, for
she wrote to him the next day:

> I was so unhappy & worried last night thinking of you going off like
> that, hardly out of your tantrum, & all full of remorse about it. I
> wanted to woire [wire] to you on the puff puff at Paris but thought it
> would never catch you . . .
> You know I wasn't really angry with you or loved you less
> because of your tantrum. I just thought you a very silly little boy.
> Perhaps one day you will grow out of those tantrums.
> Darlin I can never never tell you how pleased I am you came out,
> nor how excoited I was at seeing you. It made all the difference, &
> now I feel all clear & happy – before I was all muddled &
> conscience-stricken.[58]

Aunt Polly, certain that Lady Chetwode would hear about John's
visit from the Mitfords, had decided to write to her. Penelope, who
had been shown the letter and thought it 'very sensible', paraphrased it for John: it said he had come to France 'to ease your and
my minds & that she thought it a very good thing & that last night I
slept properly for the first time since I'd been here (which was quite
true).'[59] John was not to worry, but Penelope asked him not to tell
everyone, 'as H.L. will be humiliated if other people get to know in
large quantities . . .' Penelope asked John to find out about
'obscure register offices' and wondered whether the wedding
should be postponed until September when the Chetwodes would
be safely back in India. She had heard from Patrick Balfour that her

brother Roger was in love with Lady Mary Lygon. 'I hope he marries her. H.L. would be so pleased.'

Her two days in Opio with John, she wrote, had been 'bliss'. 'I know that it's inevitable we should marry, & I swear not to let you down.' She was sure that once they were married it would be easy for them to see each other, 'but we MUST keep it all secret for the next year or two' so that she would not lose her £250 a year allowance from her parents.

In her elation, Penelope wrote John another letter later in the day:

> I have been feeling so different to-day to what I felt before you came. I love you so much, moi own akolyte . . . We'll both be very happy together & one day we'll settle down & oi'll produce some offspring clad in grey flannel shorts, & oi'll wroite soom borin books which you'll help me to produce, in fact in every way you're indispensable to me.[60]

Before she had gone to bed the previous night, she told him, she had walked into the garden and stood where she and John had stood. 'The moon was nearly full & the fireflies was fillin the olives with dancing lights.' And she had thought to herself: 'No I am too young to think of giving up love just yet' and had thanked God for bringing John back to her.

Penelope was sleeping well again. She felt such universal benevolence now John had put her mind at rest, that she was even prepared to go to 'that bloody dance' her parents continued to make such a fuss about. 'I really don't mind what I do now you've come back.' The next week, she, Polly and Elizabeth Starr were going to motor to Arles, Les Baux and Avignon. She felt so much better that now she would also be able to go and look at the churches in Opio and Châteauneuf – 'I couldn't bear to think of a church before.' She would also go to Grasse Cathedral again 'as I was too unhappy to pay much attention to it last time'. She would be boarding the Blue Train at Avignon on 16 July; would arrive in London on the 19th; on the 20th she would put her name in the marriage register; in the evening of that day she would attend 'that bloody dance'; on the 21st she would be in a nursing home to have her teeth out. The letter ended: 'Must write to P.M. Shand now. All my love forever . . .'

With 'Cracky' Clonmore, P. Morton Shand, John's *Architectural Review* friend, was a sympathetic adviser to both Penelope and

John at this crisis in their lives. In her letter of 25 June Penelope told John, 'P. Morton Shand is the best person you could have confided in. Discuss all the points of this letter over with him & reason it all out. I shall probably write to him as well tomorrow.'[61]

On 8 July, Penelope wrote to John:

My darlin',
                    Just got yours of July 6th. I think you are quite right. We'd much better marry in August, then my parents (if they find out, which pray God they don't) won't be able to say 'How deceitful! they waited till we went away & did it the moment we got out of England.' But I think it'd be much easier & nicer to have our honeymoon in Sept. when you get your proper holiday. Can't we marry on *Sat. July 29* & go to Essex for that wk-end, then I'll go up to N.B.* July 1st & we'll go off for a proper spree the 2nd week in Sept . . .

I thought of a very good scheme for letters, as Mummy always wants to know my address to forward them to. I'll say I'm going to stay with the Ede's & give them the address of your friend Paul Nash [the artist] who will forward the letters to our inn (you needn't tell him we're married but just on a jolly spree.)[62]

A postscript read: 'A most helpful & delightful letter from P. Morton Shand this morning.' This was probably the letter which Shand wrote on 5 July. In it, he said, 'I very much doubt whether I am wise – after all, wise people don't marry four times – but I may be mildly practical in some way.'[63] He thought Penelope had done well to leave England when she did. 'Such an abrupt transition is often the only way to gain a proper perspective.' He offered a practical compromise as a solution of the young couple's difficulties. Penelope, he felt, should surrender to her longing to go to the Oriental School in Rome. 'I believe everyone who feels he or she has got anything to express or do, ought to have the best opportunity for doing so. Then there can be no subsequent grievances about that silly catchphrase "repression".'

He felt John should travel more, too. 'This xenophobia of his will do him positive harm unless he checks it.' Unless John could see England from outside and compare it with other countries, he would be in danger of 'writing himself out'; or he would 'deliberately starve himself as a writer at the very outset of his career'.

* North Britain, ie Scotland.

Personally I think the further you took him the better it would be for him. I rather suspect there's a certain 'snobisme' about his 'I hate being abroad' attitude. All his little friends are globe-trotters, Evelyn Waugh, Pryce-Jones, etc., so he has to be different – especially as we live in an age of cruising and journalistic exploration. (For this reason I think it will be quite good for him to have to work – for a bit – for even such an incredibly ordinary and stupid young man as Randolph Churchill.)

Shand told Penelope that she should not suppress anything in, or about herself. Let her go to the Oriental School in Rome; only, if she wanted to marry John, 'marry him first – the sooner the better. Then you can both make careers for two to three years.' Penelope should also go to the East – 'only don't leave him for too many months at a stretch. He's got to settle himself. He has not got a real "element" yet. Like you, he's got to find it. That "setness" of tastes is a confession of youthful weakness, not strength.'

Unlike Bryan Guinness, Shand did not take sides between the two. He was able to tell Penelope that John 'is quite sure he wants to marry you; and I think sees now there can't be "terms" about it.' He added: 'I utterly fail to see that you're being selfish at all, as I've told him.' John had been talking to him, 'and was clearly very unhappy and confused in mind', but 'he does – I think really desperately, and sincerely – want to marry you.' Telling Penelope she was in the right, and at the same time playing on her sympathy and love for John, was a tactic far more likely to win her over than Guinness's lecturing, if well-meaning, approach – though by the time Shand's letter arrived at Opio, the end to which it was a means was a *fait accompli*.

The letter shows that Shand had given John the same advice as Nancy Mitford had given him – to hotfoot it to the south of France.

By the way I am, I suppose, partly responsible for the fact that the poor boy is now kicking his heels in a (naturally!) expensive hotel in Grasse waiting for you to come back from a motor-tour. I can't bear inaction or inertia. I advised him to go and see you – partly as a 'gesture' to show he was not afraid of going to foreign parts for your sake; partly because he was so tormented in his mind that I knew only talking to you would be any good, your letters were just progressively obscuring the situation. Only I urged him – if he was going – to go much earlier than he did in the end!

Finally, Shand advised Penelope, if she married John, to keep the marriage secret for some time. The years of secrecy might help her parents to get accustomed to John – 'either as a "faithful" or an "ami de coeur" '. He returned to this theme in a letter of 12 July written after he had received Penelope's letter and had talked with John, now back in England. ('I was amused but scarcely surprised to hear of John's return in the Blue Train, the next best inoculation against travelling on the Continent after a "Cook's Conducted".'[64])

Both Shand and his wife Sybil had thought John in 'an encouragingly practical and energetic mood'; but Shand had warned him of the dangers ahead: chattersome friends and acquaintances, professional and otherwise; indiscreet office telephone conversations; leaving letters about. 'I consider this the major one, because John has no idea of reticence, like most of his younger friends.' Then there was the problem that parents' names and fathers' professions had to be stated to the registrar on giving formal notice. 'How to get round title and rank in your case I hardly know. John's part-time profession, gossip-writing, has so corrupted all classes of the community that it would indeed be a callow registrar's clerk who didn't think of passing on such a tit-bit of information ("for a slight consideration") to our unspeakable press.' And with her passport, Penelope would have to take one of two risks. Either not to have it changed, for which there might be heavy penalties; or to comply with the law and never dare to leave her passport about or travel with relations or 'dubiously reliable friends'. Shand had impressed on John that both ought to be prepared for sudden discovery and to know what each was going to say. Also, John had better make a list of the various people he had told at one time or another, classifying them into 'their proper degrees of garrulousness and the chances of their garrulousness getting "home" '.

Shand thought that marriage to Penelope would give John the 'backbone' he lacked.

I hope John will start to write when he marries. 'Being amusing' which I fancy (though no doubt I'm wrong) is a phase drawing to its close, is his great danger. Marriage should cure it. Many imbeciles only know him in that light, and John usually does nothing to open their eyes. In fact the contrary. Travel, sustained, persistent travel, is the thing he needs above all. Plus a window into another language.[65]

By 13 July the date of the marriage had been fixed: 29 July. The place was to be Edmonton Register Office – because Edmonton was sufficiently remote, and because it was near Heddon Court, where John was temporarily lodging with John Humphrey Hope. (When John first told her he was staying with the Hopes, Penelope jumped to the conclusion that he meant Anthony Hope, author of *The Prisoner of Zenda*, and his wife.[66])

Penelope wrote again from Opio on 17 July:

I got another letter to-day & one on Sat. Why Evelyn's[67] suddenly taken me under his protection & defends me from persecution I'm at a loss to understand!

Another very helpful letter from P.M. Shand, too. He emphasizes the danger of leaving letters about. I very nearly destroyed all the ones received from you since you left here but couldn't, the drawin's is so clever, so I've hidden them away in an envelope.

Don't forget I'll ring you up on Thurs. morning at 10.30, & don't mention μαρριαγε [marriage] down the 'phone, only tell me where we are to meet at tea-time.[68]

Penelope had her wisdom teeth out on 21 July, having stoically endured a worse ordeal – 'that bloody dance' – on the previous evening. She recovered quickly, and the wedding took place at Edmonton Register Office on 29 July, with Isabel Hope and H. de C. Hastings (for once, not elusive) as witnesses. Under 'Rank or profession of father', John entered 'Art Manufacturer'. Penelope wrote: 'Baronet. Field Marshal. Army Commander in Chief.'

Ernest and Bess Betjemann attended the ceremony. Ernest's views on 'brasshats' and his resentment about the slights to which his son might be exposed were no doubt counterbalanced by relief that he himself would not now be expected to haggle over a legal contract with the Field-Marshal's solicitors; elopement has its own etiquette. Perhaps, too, the Betjemanns were pleased that at last, after all his romantic tergiversations, John was showing himself ready to 'settle down'.

John, with his love of Cowper, must have been put in mind of John Gilpin:

> Said John, it is my wedding-day,
> And all the world would stare,
> If wife should dine at Edmonton,
> And I should dine at Ware.

Penelope, who disliked any kind of formality, was quite happy to get the thing over with quickly. But how far short of John's ideal the suburban form-filling must have been! He would probably have preferred a wedding like that imagined in 'Pot Pourri from a Surrey Garden':

> Over the redolent pinewoods, in at the bathroom casement,
>   One fine Saturday, Windlesham bells shall call:
> Up the Butterfield aisle rich with Gothic enlacement,
>   Licensed now for embracement,
>   Pam and I, as the organ
> Thunders over you all.

And afterwards, he would perhaps have envisaged a reception like that he described in 'Fête Champêtre' (the wedding of Lord Cloncurry):

> The grotto is reached and the parties alight,
> The feast is spread out, and begob! what a sight,
> Pagodas of jelly in bowls of champagne,
> And a tower of blancmange from the Baron Kilmaine.

Instead, there was roast beef and Yorkshire pudding with a few friends at the Great Eastern Hotel, by Liverpool Street Station. Not that the Great Eastern Hotel was a place lacking in romance for John. As Max Beerbohm said of Oxford, the very name was fraught for him with the most actual magic. The Great Eastern was and remained John's favourite London hotel,[69] even though it was the Charing Cross Hotel which in 1977 honoured him by renaming its opulent Victorian dining-room after him.

After the 'hurried little affair'[70] in the register office, the marriage was blessed in St Anselm's, Davies Street, an Edwardian church (now demolished) designed by Michael Dugdale's grandfather Eustace Balfour and Thackeray Turner.[71] The church was opposite Frederick Etchells's office, 52 Davies Street, which was one of John's London *pieds-à-terre*. (Part of *Ghastly Good Taste* had been written there.)[72]

As planned, the couple spent a few days in the Essex inn; their main honeymoon was to be a bicycle tour of East Anglian churches in September. Then Penelope went back to live with her parents –

'because, for all they knew, I wasn't married'.[73] In the weeks that followed, John and Penelope played mouse and cat with the Chetwodes. Penelope wrote to John from 44 Grove End Road:

> I roong oop this afternoon to tell you that I loove you very mooch but you was ooot (4 P.M.)
>
> Also I can't ring you up from my sitting-room any more as father is in bed next door & can hear every word.
>
> Will you take afternoon tea with me tomorrow at 5 P.M. Tuesday. I have to be back here at 6.30 so if you can come at 5 it will be very nice. Will you ring up 1852 from [Etchells's office in] Davies St. at 9.30 tomorrow morning & I will answer. Then I needn't say your name out loud ... But you can say whether you will be able to manage afternoon tea or not & where. Shall we risk Davies St.?
>
> Ooooo I did enjoy Essex. Don't forget to write to Mrs Zachariah Petty ...[74]

Sir Philip Chetwode was convalescing from a stomach complaint. Penelope trailed round with him on a circuit of grand houses. On 18 August they were at Garrowby, York, as guests of Lord Irwin, the former Viceroy of India. They moved on to Innes House, Elgin, Morayshire, the home of Colonel Edward Tennant. A piper played round the house every evening at eight and again at eight in the morning, which, Penelope told John, made her ''orrible kross'. The couple were making elaborate plans for their East Anglian honeymoon. The architect M.H. Baillie-Scott – not the Edes, Paul Nash or P. Morton Shand – was to cover up for them: 'Ascertain that Baillie-Scott will be at Ockhams when we go on our East Anglian tour,' Penelope wrote, '& you might ask him to send you a few sheets of his writing paper (if they have the address on) so that I can write home on them.'[75]

On 24 August, she wrote to John:

> You poor little boy feelin' sad & depressed ... Yew moostn't get worried about our E. Anglian tour, as I think I can save about £10 on this month's allowance to pay for my journeys & pubs. We'd better just go to Cambridge for 2 days & on to Ely for the rest of the time as staying in one place will be cheaper than always moving. We might hire cycles (very M.C.* word) at Ely & cycle to nearby churches.

* Middle Class.

She was beginning to take John in hand:

> Mr Tennant (proprietor of Innes) has found a wonderful tailor in Bond St., a retired army officer who 'knows what a gentleman wants'. He is called Major Daniel Ltd. & makes suits of the best cloth for 8 guineas, his only stipulation being that you pay on the nail. That's an improvement on your £14 tailor, isn't it? . . . Is your light brown suit nice now it's been cleaned? And promise to ask Mrs Munn to take that *Revolting* blue one to Selfridge's please.[76]

In her next letter she made it clear that she was still as intent as ever on continuing her Indian studies: 'I do not feel I can ever be spiritually at rest until I have done it . . .' She was bored by the constant talk of golf and fishing at Innes, but 'Father is much better in health & this atmosphere & these surroundings are evidently his idea of Paradise. I've never seen him so bright.'[77]

In a further letter, she returned to the subject of her studies abroad. She had decided that if, as was likely, Giuseppe Tucci – 'my Italian professor' – did not come back to Rome until Christmas, she would go to Germany for two months, 'as I have to learn German sometime & the only way to do it quickly is to go to the country.'[78] Three-quarters of the books on Indian art and religion were in German and had not been translated, '& even if no more are written in future owing to the Nazis I've got to read some of the already existing ones.' She knew of a family in Stuttgart with whom she could stay. She would go about 12 October and return to England on 20 December to spend a fortnight with John at Christmas. She supposed that he would be resuming work on 9 October after a three-week holiday. 'So we will be able to do some 'orrible things together for 3 days before I go to Stuttgart.'

Her next letter came from Clarendon Park, Salisbury, the home of her friend Lavender Christie-Miller. ('I'm not staying here but just passing the afternoon.') It again discussed arrangements for the East Anglian holiday, which was now imminent: 'Darlin' . . . it will be lovely next week & we'll get boicycles . . . Don't forget to fix everything with Baillie-Scott & ask him for some writing paper with Ockhams written on it. I am sure it will be very nice staying in Lynn.'[79]

The newly-wed pair also stayed with John Humphrey Hope, who had just sold Heddon Court as building land.[80] He had joined the remnants of the school with Horton School at Ickwell Bury in

Bedfordshire, and had settled with his wife and their daughter Ann in a cottage nearby. Ann, who by now was eight, remembers the Betjemans' visit as by no means all billing and cooing:

> My mother told me that John Betjeman had eloped with Penelope and they were hiding with my parents to escape the wrath of her father. I have a vivid memory of JB pouring a full watering-can of water down the back of Penelope's neck, and she screamed and he screamed and they shouted at length and they threw things. So this, I noted, is how newly-married couples behave. The next village was Old Warden, about two miles from the cottage. JB had used letters from Old Warden in *Ghastly Good Taste* without knowing, or even bothering to check, whether the place really existed.[81] I remember going to Old Warden church with JB and my parents. Screams of laughter – why, look, the place actually exists, and what a coincidence, with us living now so near.[82]

When the couple returned to London, Penelope learnt that her parents would be going back to India in late September. 'Then I thought, I must tell them about our marriage before they go back. I had the most terrible guilt about it. And I did tell them, and of course it was the most terrible shock. They were very upset. I had been going to Angkor Wat and all sorts of marvellous places that autumn, but of course I'd married so I couldn't.'[83] A story went the rounds about how Penelope had broken the news to her parents. It suggested that she had waited until they were all three being ushered into a reception at Buckingham Palace. When the flunkey announced: 'Miss Penelope Chetwode', she squawked: 'No, I'm Mrs John Betjeman!' (Lady Betjeman said this was not true: 'I told my mother in her sitting-room at "Tadema Towers".'[84])

Shyly and sometimes slyly she broke the news to her friends. Mrs Elizabeth Thesiger, daughter of the humorous versifier Harry Graham, recalled: 'I was staying with Lavender Christie-Miller and Penelope was there too. She asked us, "Should I marry John Betjeman?" And we said, "No! He's a horrible little white slug!" And then it turned out she'd already been married to him for a month.'[85] On 27 September the news was at last made public, in the *Daily Telegraph*: 'SIR P. CHETWODE'S DAUGHTER. MARRIED AFTER BROKEN ENGAGEMENT.' Penelope's aunt, Lady Birch, had given the paper the story. 'My niece and Mr John Betjeman became engaged quite a long time ago, but the engagement was later broken off,' she told the reporter. 'This wedding was a complete surprise to all her relatives. Not even her parents knew anything about this marriage until after it was over. It took place very quietly indeed on July 29.'[86] Lady Birch dismissively described John as 'the author of a volume of burlesque poems'. Nancy Mitford wrote to Mark Ogilvie-Grant on 3 October: 'Betjeman was married to Filth in July and announced it three days ago. They intend to live apart permanently – so wise.'[87]

In fact, Penelope and John had set up house together – 'a really slummy sort of existence,' as Penelope later described it. First they rented a small flat, one room and a kitchenette in Museum Street, London, by the British Museum. John was still on *The Architectural Review* earning £300 a year, and Penelope's marriage settlement had not yet been agreed. They then moved to what she considered a worse flat, near her parents' home in Grove End Road.

> It was in a new block of flats [Penelope recalled] and there you were under the impression that you were living in slightly more luxury than in Museum Street because it was new, but we had one room and a kitchenette again, and we were just next to the lift shaft, so all night the lift used to go up and down, and, being modern, everything came to bits all the time, cupboards came off the walls and everything. I simply hated all that side of it. I don't mind when I'm travelling staying in squalor if I'm seeing wonderful things, but that was terribly squalid, and St John's Wood is short on scenic wonders. John was out most of the day at *The Architectural Review* and when I was by myself I used to get rather depressed by the squalor of it.
>
> Then we got a flat in a tiny street off the Strand. It was pretty slummy but not so bad as the others. That had two rooms, and we had to share a bathroom on the landing with a lady whom John called 'Mrs Turveydrop'.[88]

In October, Penelope went to Germany for three months. Silvia Coke's father, Lord Coke, whose main interest was in music, was able to arrange for her to lodge in the Barbarossastrasse, Berlin, with Gerda Busoni, widow of the composer and pianist Ferruccio Busoni. She took a *Kursus für Ausländer* (course for foreigners). 'I saw Hitler going about in his car and soldiers doing the goose-step,' Penelope recalled, '– it was just after the burning of the Reichstag. But I've never taken much interest in politics, I'm afraid. I wasn't besotted by Hitler and I wasn't particularly horrified at that time. I was immersed in my studies.'[89]

At this time John sent Penelope two illustrated fables. The first, typewritten and titled *The Life and Miracles of Beata Mrs Δοογγ* [Doong] was dated 1933. In the story, Penelope is canonized, acquiring a golden halo and the power to work miracles. She changes an International Style building in the Unter den Linden into 'a Dravijjian buildin', and decides to 'beautify the flat of dear old Frau Busoni' by turning all her ornaments into 'exquisite little bits of broken Vedic (853 B.C.–831 B.C.) pottery' and the sofa into 'a lovely lump of sandstone with possible traces of Moghul scoolpture on it'. She also changes dog turds into bread and *Apfelkuchen* into dog turds. 'In the end, as a reward for her kindness she met the man of her dreams, an extremely cooltured and highly spiritually developed Vedic professor, whom she married and shared half her halo with. Her first husband returned to the English soil from which he supposed he had originally sprung.'[90] (Here John drew a toadstool springing from the ground – a puffball.)

The other fable, hand-written, is entitled *SS Centipeda & Giomonsella, Martyrs* ('The Catholic Truth Society. Price 1d.') In this both Penelope and Joan Eyres-Monsell are given haloes. The farcical story, in which Penelope is related to Julius Caesar and is the daughter of a Spartan general, oddly anticipates Evelyn Waugh's *Helena* in which she is the daughter of the British King Coel. Joan Eyres-Monsell's brother appears as 'St Graham Hermaphrodite'.

Penelope had intended to stay six months in Germany, 'but after three John was making a fuss and wanted me to come back'.[91] He told her that Christian Barman, the nominal editor of *The Architectural Review*, who lived in Uffington, Berkshire, had found them a farmhouse there at £36 a year rent. By the time Penelope returned from Germany, the Chetwodes had decided to make the best of a bad job. Lady Chetwode, so implacable before the marriage, was the first to give in: she was more of an opportunist than Sir Philip, the rigid military disciplinarian. Within a few months of the wedding, Osbert Lancaster went round to the Chetwodes' house in St John's Wood. He had to wait a while for John to come downstairs. He looked for a clock, but all the clocks were wrong. 'Oh yes,' Lady Chetwode said, 'we've had to stop all the clocks in the house. The ticking keeps dear John awake.' Lancaster thought that 'Star Chetwode and John got on very well afterwards: she was an extremely intelligent woman, though utterly ruthless. John, also, finally got on quite well with the old Field-Marshal. Chetwode was always saying, "Tell me, John, I don't drop me 'g's', do I?" '[92]

But it was a long time before even that degree of *rapprochement* was achieved. To begin with, the Field-Marshal found it difficult to remember John's surname. As Maurice Bowra commented, it was 'not the kind of name to be found in a cavalry regiment'.[93] Not long after her marriage, Penelope said something to the Chetwodes' butler, who replied, 'Yes, Miss Penelope.' The Field-Marshal snorted: 'She's not Miss Penelope. She's Mrs Bargeman.'[94] Bowra recalled the difficulty Chetwode had in deciding how John should address him. ' "Sir" might be all right, but did not seem intimate enough. So he sought for a solution. "You can't call me Philip, that wouldn't do. You can't call me Father – I'm not your father. You'd better call me Field-Marshal." So that was settled.'[95]

The Chetwodes sailed for India in early October 1933. Chetwode wrote to Penelope *en route* on 6 October, from Marseilles:

I *just hated* saying goodbye to my own darling. It would have been just the same whoever you had married. It is such a break when the young birds one has watched growing, leave the nest.

I am happier now about you. I can never say I like your choice – but I feel that you are so quite sure you are right, & have mapped out your life so thoroughly, that it will be the worst luck if it is not a success. It is your life, not ours, and you have chosen for yourself . . . Remember always if you are unhappy or in trouble there are always your old daddy's arms to fly to, always open & always ready as long as I live.

Mother I think is more reconciled now, & her great love for you is conquering her disappointment . . .[96]

Penelope's brother Roger, who had sided with his parents in their opposition to the match, continued to stir up trouble. When Lady Chetwode offered to buy the couple a large new car, he wrote sharply to tell her it was '*quite* unnecessary'. He also reported to his parents that he had heard John had been doing comic imitations of them. On 20 November the Field-Marshal wrote to Penelope (who was by then in Germany):

Penelope darling, Your John must be a very stupid man. We have had quite a lot of letters from people who are cross with him

because he mimics and mocks at me & mother – & imitates interviews with us. People all think it is in such bad taste. We have
smothered our feelings & done all we can for both of you & it is so
common & rude to mock at any older people let alone those who
have done all they can for you. Several people have said they won't
have you again because of it. Even Roger has heard of it in America.
It is not only rude & common but it is surely very foolish if nothing
else, & leaves a nasty taste in the mouth my dear, & makes us think
we were right in our objection to the marriage. Try and stop him
doing it.[97]

John immediately wrote to the Field-Marshal denying that he had
imitated him. It is plain that Chetwode was not convinced (and
Lady Chetwode wrote to Penelope: 'I believe it and always shall'[98])
but he replied with stiff courtesy on 10 December: 'I naturally
accept your denial at once, & can only suppose it must be enemies
of yours who have sown these tares . . .'[99] To Penelope he wrote
(17 December): '. . . as he is your husband I have accepted his word
at once. Someone must be maligning you as it is curious how many
people have written about it.'[100]

Chetwode became more cordial towards John when the Betjemans' first child, Paul, was born in 1937. But Lord Longford
thinks that John's kindness and sympathy after Roger Chetwode
committed suicide in 1940 (when John called on the Field-Marshal
and wisely insisted he continue to go in to work to take his mind off
the tragedy) finally ended the animosity.[101]

Christopher Sykes, Evelyn Waugh's friend and biographer, was
not so sure. He recalled meeting John in late 1945. John told him,
half angry and half amused, that Lord Chetwode* had just given
him a lift in his car. The Field-Marshal had told his chauffeur:
'Drop me at the House of Lords – and then take Mr Thingummy
wherever it is he wants to go.'[102] If Chetwode indeed said these
words (the story has a whiff of the apocryphal) John must have
added them to his litany of slights – the snubs and rebuffs that he
had hoarded, almost treasured, since childhood. They were his precious bane. Fermenting in him, they precipitated some of his best
poetry. 'Why did I mind so much?' he asked of the 'common little
boy' sneer. 'Heaven knows. But I still do . . .'[103] Why did he sustain
with such animus the vendettas against Jack Shakespeare, Kelly,

---

* Sir Philip was raised to the peerage as Baron Chetwode in July 1945.

Gidney and C.S. Lewis? Perhaps it was the response of injured innocence to a world where virtue was not rewarded, as it is in fairy tales. With rare exceptions, John was kind and well-intentioned towards others. Why, then, must they be 'beastly' to him, victimize and insult him? His was the desolation of the Romantic whose vision of the world is eroded by the world's reality.

Rather as a Proustian invalid cosseting his ailments can outlive a fit man unprepared for sudden illness, John, by nursing the fleers and jeers, learnt how to withstand them and how to hit back. Chetwode had gone through the Uhlans 'like brown paper' at the Battle of Moy, and John was the despair of the Marlborough OTC; but the Field-Marshal met his match in his son-in-law. When Susan Barnes profiled John for the *Sunday Times* in 1972, a 'lifelong friend' of his told her: 'What the Chetwodes . . . didn't realize, toughies that they were, was that this shabby, shambling figure was tougher than they. John doesn't realize it himself.'[104]

A NOTE ON THE NOTES

John Betjeman himself coined the enjoyable phrase 'the rash of foot and note disease', and I know that some readers regard the little numerals bobbing above the text as signs of a pedantic approach. (I have seen a book irascibly reviewed as 'footnoted up to the hilt'.)

In this book, the notes serve three purposes. Some of them amplify passages in the chapters. For example, when John was at the Dragon School, Oxford, during the First World War, he and his friends wondered why the Government wanted them to collect horse chestnuts. The Imperial War Museum gave me the answer, which is summarized in note 25 to Chapter 3. Notes of this sort save the narrative from getting snagged on digressions.

Other notes identify the oral sources, usually with the date of an interview. A third group of notes gives reference to written sources. I have spent ten years in the research for this book, and it would be sadistic to make future writers toil through the same papers to find out something they can learn painlessly from a reference note.

To those who persist in their hostility to 'footnotes' even after these winning arguments, I would say: like television programmes, the notes can be looked at or not looked at; there is no coercion.

B.H.

ABBREVIATIONS USED IN
THE NOTES

AR   *The Architectural Review*.

BBCWA   BBC Written Archives Centre, Caversham Park, Reading.

FLL   John Betjeman, *First and Last Loves*, John Murray, London 1952 (1969 edn.).

GGT   John Betjeman, *Ghastly Good Taste*, Chapman & Hall, London 1933 and 1970 edition published by Anthony Blond, London.

Huntington   The Huntington Library, San Marino, California.

interview   This denotes a tape-recorded interview with the author, conducted at the stated date.

JB   John Betjeman.

JBP   John Betjeman's papers.

PB   Penelope Betjeman.

PBP   Penelope Betjeman's papers.

PC   Penelope Chetwode.

S by B   John Betjeman, *Summoned by Bells*, John Murray, London 1960.

UP   John Betjeman, *Uncollected Poems*, John Murray, London 1982.

Victoria   The McPherson Library of the University of Victoria, British Columbia, Canada.

Whenever a poem by Sir John Betjeman is referred to by its title only, it will be found in *John Betjeman's Collected Poems*, John Murray, London (4th edition, 1987).

NOTES

Chapter 1: Family

1 JB, 'English Schoolgirl Makes First Steps Towards Stardom', *Evening Standard*, 25 August 1934, p.8.
2 *Loc. cit.*
3 'And quarrelling downstairs until
   Doors slammed at Thirty One West Hill.'
   ('Archibald', *UP*, p.25.) See also *S by B*, pp.82 and 83–84.
4 Joan Kunzer, interview, 1977. On Joan Kunzer (*née* Larkworthy), see Chapter 6.
5 'The Epic'. See Preface. *Mr and Mrs John Piper*.
6 On the popularity of German products in England during the late nineteenth century, see Ernest Edwin Williams, *'Made in Germany'*, Heinemann, London 1896.
7 *S by B*, p.4.
8 *Ibid*, p.8.
9 Robert Hurd to JB, 20 December 1960. *Victoria*.
10 Ernest Betjemann to JB, 26 October 1927. *JBP*.
11 *Radio Times*, 28 August–3 September 1976.
12 JB preserved among his papers a report by J. Meier Schwencke claiming that one Joost Betjeman lived in Dordrecht, Holland, from 1493 to 1541 and that he was 'pensionaris van Dordrecht' (pensionary, or governor) from 1514 to 1537. Schwencke added that the States of Holland, in gratitude for Joost Betjeman's services, had voted him one hundred pieces of wainscot for the panelling of his house, and that he died as Stadhouder of the Margraviate of Bergen-op-Zoom, a city in the south of Holland, in 1541. No confirmation of these claims has been found in the records of Dordrecht or of Bergen-op-Zoom.
13 One theory suggests that Betjeman(n) means 'little praying man' and that it has the same root as the English word 'beadsman', as in Keats's 'The Eve of St Agnes' or in the opening chapter of Trollope's *The Warden*. This interpretation is rejected by most modern authorities on German names. They believe that Betjeman(n) is of Frisian derivation; a diminutive or pet form of the personal name of Bertold or Bertram. (Bertram originally meant 'the bright raven', from *Beraht*, bright, shining; *Hraban*, raven [Wotan's bird].) The Instituut voor Naamkunde in Leuven, Belgium, while agreeing that the name is of Frisian origin, think that it may be either a 'metronymicum' of a mother's name (a name derived from a female Christian name) or that, more probably, it was derived from the male 'Bette', to which the diminutive suffix '-ke' was added – Betke, which in the Frisian pronunciation becomes 'Betse' . . . 'Betsje' . . . 'Betje'.
14 Rebecca Excelsior Merrick to JB, 1927. *JBP*.
15 George Betjemann and Eleanor Smith were married at St George's-in-the-East on 1 March 1797.
16 John Merrick and Rebecca Betjemann were married at St Martin-in-the-Fields, London, on 20 May 1846.
17 JB to David E.R. Bateman, 10 November 1953. *Victoria*.
18 Although no Betjemanns lived in Bremen itself in the eighteenth century, a number of families of that name lived in the neighbouring area known as *Die Heide* (the Heath), in Lower Saxony.
19 In the early nineteenth century, Carsten Betjemann, from Die Heide, took employment in the English sugar industry. Possibly this was a continuation of an earlier connexion between Betjemanns of Die Heide and the English sugar trade.
   Carsten Betjemann was one of four brothers born in Bokel, about twenty miles

from Bremen and ten from Bremerhaven. In 1841 he married, at St John's Church, Wapping, east London, Sophia Maria Dettmar (1818–86) whose father David (also described as 'sugar baker' on the marriage certificate) and mother had come to England from Hesse-Darmstadt. Carsten's and Sophia's first five children were born in England. Then the family moved back to Germany and the sixth and seventh children were born (in 1851 and 1853) in Cologne. Carsten's younger brother Johann (b. 1825) was employed in Cologne by the same sugar manufacturer as Carsten.

Carsten and Sophia finally moved with their family from Cologne to Tauh in Sweden where their last child Lucy was born in 1857; most of their descendants have lived there ever since. Because all the Betjemann brothers had gone abroad, the Betjemann farm in Bokel, with its half-timbering and horse-head gable, was taken over by their older sister Margaretha (1816–65) and her husband Ludwig Rugen.

Carsten's great-granddaughter, Marie-Louise Thümmel (*née* Betjemann, b. 1954) who lives in Hamburg, was told by her grandfather John Betjemann (1888–1978) that the British Poet Laureate was related to them, but it has not been possible to confirm this.

The 1851 census returns of Bethnal Green in east London contain further evidence of Betjeman(n)s coming to England from Germany: 'Head of House at 39 Culworth Street . . . John Betjeman aged 53 a Gunmaker being a Brit. Subject but born in Germany . . .' (This information was sent to JB on 6 November 1968 by Mr Richard Austin-Cooper of Ancestry Researchers, Rayleigh, Essex. Letter in *Victoria.*)

Two further pieces of evidence point to German origins for the Betjeman(n) family. First, the middle name given to Catherine Alheit Betjemann (daughter of George Betjemann) who was baptized at St Botolph without Aldersgate on 28 July 1805. Second, the marriage of a Mary Ann Betjemann to Carsten Adolph Schafer at Christ Church, Spitalfields, on 4 February 1844. A woman of Dutch extraction *could* have married a man of German family; but it is far more likely that Mary Ann Betjemann married within a German community to which she belonged.

20 Washington Irving, *The Sketch Book of Geoffrey Crayon, Gent.*, Everyman, J.M. Dent, 1944 edn., p.237.
21 Rebecca Excelsior Merrick to JB, 1927. *JBP.*
22 *Ibid.* Celsie Merrick alleged that the two boys were 'left in the care of guardians of the name of Fuller' but were sent to London. The elder was apprenticed to a jeweller and was the father of Alfred Merrick, the jeweller at Eton. The younger, JB's great-great-grandfather, was apprenticed to a cabinet-maker.

The Fullers, Celsie claimed, had taken possession of Bodorgan (House) and had called themselves Fuller-Merrick (*sic*, for Fuller-Meyrick). 'It was known all round that they were not the rightful owners,' she wrote. The two boys prospered and did not bring the matter to the courts, although, Celsie told JB in 1927, 'even in your time a solicitor from that part came to Uncle Alfred at Slough . . . and wanted him to take it up.' She gave JB a melodramatic account of visits she had made to Bodorgan and to the solicitors of its owners. ('Never in my life had I been treated so rudely.')

In a letter to the author dated 29 March 1987, Sir George Tapps-Gervis-Meyrick, the present owner of Bodorgan, said that he had never heard of any of the 'Merricks', and denied that Celsie Merrick had ever visited Bodorgan.
23 Bodorgan, a mansion designed by James Defferd about 1800, is in the parish of Llangadwaladr, Anglesey. Nearby are the ruins of Bodowen (formerly known as Bodeon), the seat of the Owen family with whom the Meyricks intermarried.

The Meyrick family, descended from Cadafel, lord of Cedewain in Powys, came to prominence under the Tudors, a Welsh dynasty. Llewelyn ap Heilyn fought under Henry Tudor (King Henry VII) at the Battle of Bosworth Field. His son Meurig ap Llewelyn served under Henry VIII and was promoted captain of the bodyguard. The parish church of St Cadwaladr in Llangadwaladr contains stained-glass portraits of the armoured figures of Owen ap Meyric, a great-great-grandson of Dafydd ap Iorwerth, and of Meurig ap Llewelyn, who is shown in civilian clothes kneeling at a *prie-dieu*.

24   Rebecca Excelsior Merrick to JB, 1927. *JBP.*

Bodorgan passed from the male line of the Meyrick family in 1825 on the death of Owen Putland Meyrick (1752–1825), who had married in 1774 a considerable heiress, Clara, daughter of Richard Garth of Morden Park, Surrey. The Bodorgan property went to his daughter Clara (1775–1857) who in 1801 had married Augustus Eliott Fuller (1777–1857) of Ashdown House, Sussex. Their son, Owen John Augustus Fuller, who was Sheriff of Anglesey in 1827 and adopted the name Meyrick (under the conditions of Owen Putland Meyrick's will), died unmarried in 1876 and left the Bodorgan and Ashdown properties to Sir George Eliott Meyrick Tapps-Gervis (1827–96) who in 1825 had married Fuller [-Meyrick]'s elder sister Clara (1802–31) and who also adopted the name Meyrick: Bodorgan now belongs to Sir George's grandson, Sir George Eliott Tapps-Gervis-Meyrick (b. 1915).

To this extent, then, Celsie Merrick's story is confirmed: Bodorgan House did pass from the Meyrick family to a family called Fuller which (quite legally) assumed the name Meyrick. Celsie's story suggests that her grandfather (John Betjeman's great-great-grandfather) William Merrick or Meyrick was a younger brother of Clara Meyrick, and that he and his brother were packed off to London by her and her husband, Augustus Fuller, and done out of their inheritance. If William's descendants believed that, they might well feel aggrieved: when Sir George Tapps-Gervis-Meyrick died at Bodorgan on 12 May 1928, the gross value of his property was £1,105,059.

A monument in St Cadwaladr's Church, Llangadwaladr, Anglesey, is engraved: 'In Memory of Owen Putland, the son of Owen Meyrick Esq. of Bodorgan; who died March 24th 1825, aged 72 years. A truly honest man: whose delight was to do good and "to own affliction".' A further inscription below reads: 'He married Clara, daughter of Richard Garth Esq. of Morden Surry [*sic*], with whom he lived in happy union 50 years; and by her has left two only surviving children, Clara, the wife of Augustus Eliott Fuller, and Lucy Elizabeth now the widow of Isaac Hartman Esq. His only son, Owen Garth, was born August the 16th 1776 and died 12 September 1783 aged 7 years.'

Is there a suspicious defensiveness in that 'two *only* surviving children'? Did Augustus and Clara Fuller falsify the record? Were there two further Meyrick sons, banished to London by a manoeuvre of Uncle Silas-like dastardliness? No sons are mentioned in Owen Putland Meyrick's will; but it is just possible that William Meyrick (Merrick) and his brother were *illegitimate* sons, an embarrassment resolved by their removal to London. However, this is mere hypothesis; there is no hard evidence to support Celsie Merrick's statements.

25   'In 1836 a local landlord, Sir George Tapps of Westover and Hinton Admiral, built on the eastern bank of the Bourne Stream. Adding Gervis to his name, he went on building and called in Benjamin Ferrey, the Gothic church architect and friend of Pugin, to lay out the estate. Thus Gervis Place arose with its stucco Tudor-style villas ... The name Tapps-Gervis is increased to Tapps-Gervis-Meyrick, hence Meyrick Avenue, Meyrick Park, Meyrick Road.' ('Bournemouth', *FLL*, p.12.)

26 Rebecca Excelsior Merrick to JB, 1927. *JBP.*
27 Minutes of the meetings of the Select Vestry of St George-the-Martyr in the County of Middlesex (now in Camden). *Greater London Record Office.* The author is grateful to Miss Doris Baum for the research which led to the discovery of this record.
28 The verses were not published, but JB preserved some of them, in manuscript, among his papers.
29 On 7 June 1957 Mr H. Jack Hayden of the *County Express and Dudley Mercury,* Stourbridge, Worcs., wrote to JB: 'Looking through some old files in this office today, in the 8 April 1871 issue of the *Stourbridge Observer* I came across a reference to a Stanley Betjeman [*sic*], a member of a touring opera company . . . In the issue of 1 April 1871 there appeared an advertisement of a visit of the Isidore de Solla London Opera Co. to the Corn Exchange, Stourbridge, on the 3, 4 and 5 April. On the first night, the 3rd, Balfe's *Rose of Castile,* followed by the "laughable farce" *The Quaker* were to be performed for the benefit of Mr Stanley Betjeman. The short report of the entertainment in the issue of 8 April stated that Mr Betjeman took the part of Manuel in *The Rose.* There was no comment except that with the other principals he came in for a good share of applause and was repeatedly encored.' (*Victoria.*)

JB replied on 19 June: 'Stanley Betjeman [*sic*] was, I believe, quite a well-known singer and a brother of the violinist Gilbert Betjeman [*sic*]. He left England for America in the 80s. He was I should think my father's second cousin. My greatgrandfather, who must have been Stanley Betjeman's uncle, invented the tantalus which founded our family fortunes. These have subsequently been lost . . .' (*Victoria.*)
30 The cantata, which was in the Novello catalogue, was specially composed for the Highbury Athenaeum. It was based on the Rev. Robert Stephen Hawker's poem of the same title.
31 Michael Parkinson Show, BBC Television, 1977.
32 The mention of Hillmarton Road in *S by B* (p.15) prompted a letter to JB from the composer and conductor Julius Harrison – then seventy-five – who had known Gilbert Betjemann well between 1909 and 1914, and who gave JB amusing examples of Gilbert's autocratic manner. (Harrison to JB, 26 December 1960. *Victoria.*)
33 In an outburst recorded in *S by B* (p.84), Ernest Betjemann called JB:
Bone lazy, like my eldest brother Jack,
A rotten, low, deceitful, little snob.
34 JB may have been wrong in suggesting that his grandfather *invented* the tantalus. See W.J.L. Bertollé to JB, 27 December 1959 (*Victoria*); also tantalus patent No. 7414 taken out by Alfred Watson on 8 May 1884.
35 JB to John Dade, 15 September 1976. Copy in *JBP.*
36 In *S by B,* these two lines are compressed into one: 'Bradshaw and Pettit of the lathe and plane . . .'
37 Dan Leno (1860–1904). Real name George Galvin. One of the best-known stars of the English music halls.
38 Charles Coborn (1852–1945). Real name Colin McCallum. Music-hall comedian who had his greatest successes with the songs 'Two Lovely Black Eyes' and 'The Man Who Broke the Bank at Monte Carlo'.
39 'The Epic'. See Preface. Mr and Mrs John Piper.
40 The friend, who signed herself 'Evelyn' [perhaps Evelyn Bowman], wrote to JB from Lynton, Devon, on 19 December 1952. *Victoria.*
41 JB, 'St Saviour's Aberdeen Park, Highbury, London, N.'

42 *Op. cit.*

43 JB to Terence O'Neil, 1 October 1976. *Victoria.*

Chapter 2: Highgate

1 Valerie Jenkins (now Valerie Grove), *Evening Standard*, 29 June 1974.

2 *S by B*, p.5.

3 JB, 'Parliament Hill Fields'.

4 *S by B*, pp.79–80.

5 Queenie Avril to JB, 16 December 1952. *Victoria.*

6 Against this must be set JB's portrait of her in his 1927 playlet *The Artsenkrafts* (*Oxford Outlook*). When Jim (John Betjeman) shows his mother a copy of *Greek Revival in London Ecclesiastical Architecture* which he has just bought, she 'looks at it stupidly, without the faintest idea what it is about because she has not been listening, even if she had she would not have understood.'

7 There are four main sources for Bess Betjemann's character: *S by B*; JB's portrait of her in 'The Artsenkrafts', *Oxford Outlook*, 1927; letters written by her to JB from the early 1930s to 1952 (*Victoria*); and letters written to JB by others after her death in 1952 (*Victoria*). Vasey Adams, who had spent childhood holidays in Cornwall near the Betjemanns, wrote to JB on 16 December 1952: 'I remember her singing duets with my mother at the piano . . . the "Belle of New York" and "Little Grey Home in the West". I remember particularly how glad I always was to see her in the lane, or at St Enodoc View, always friendly, with very trim ankles and always a gay scarf . . . I never heard her make an unkind comment on anyone . . .' (*Victoria.*)

8 See her letters to JB, *Victoria.*

9 *S by B*, p.80.

10 All these expressions are found in Bess Betjemann's letters to JB. *Victoria.*

11 *S by B*, p.81.

12 Mary Bouman, interview, 1978.

13 Winston Churchill, *Savrola*, 1900. Quoted by Randolph Churchill, *Winston S. Churchill*, Heinemann, London 1966, i, 35.

14 JB, 'Christmas Nostalgia', BBC radio talk, 25 December 1947. *BBCWA.*

15 *Ibid.*

16 *Ibid.*

17 In fact, Hannah Wallis was 87 and still alive in 1947. She died in 1949 aged 89. (Hilda Moore to JB, 22 July 1950. *Victoria.*)

18 JB, 'Christmas Nostalgia', BBC radio talk, 25 December 1947. *BBCWA.*

19 *S by B*, p.88.

20 When people write stories for children, they often reveal their subconscious, almost as in a dream. JB wrote a story for children which he described in a letter of 19 September 1969 to Harry Moore of the BBC (*Victoria*): '. . . it was published in Sweden . . . it was about somebody getting out at an underground station and finding it was shut, and that he couldn't reach the street . . .' This image might perhaps represent a child being born but being denied life. (JB's story, 'South Kentish Town', was also published in *The Cynthia Asquith Book*, Macdonald & Co., London 1948.)

In one of his early radio broadcasts, JB invented a sister, 'Miss Jessie Betjeman', to whom he ascribed a poem, 'The Most Popular Girl in the School'. (See Lance

Sieveking, *John Betjeman and Dorset*, Dorset Natural History and Archaeological Society, Dorchester 1963, p.7.)

21 JB, 'Childhood Days: or Old Friends and Young Bullies', BBC radio talk, 16 July 1950. *BBCWA*.

22 After JB's radio broadcast about his childhood, Hilda Moore wrote to him: 'I knew you at just the age you talked most about – seven – eight – and was one of the little girls you so delighted to lock in lavatories . . . You really were a hateful little boy – I detested you, mainly, I suppose, because you teased me so.' (Hilda Moore to JB, 22 July 1950. *Victoria*.)

23 JB, 'Childhood Days . . .', BBC radio talk, 16 July 1950. *BBCWA*.
(*cf*. JB, 'Huxley Hall': 'Barry smashes Shirley's dolly, Shirley's eyes are crossed with hate . . .')

24 *Ibid*.

25 *Ibid*.

26 *Ibid*.

27 For an account of the fire, see *Evening Standard*, 27 August 1976, p.7.

28 JB to Iain Hamilton, 1976. *JBP*. JB also referred to the squirrels and hornbeams in *S by B*, p.3.

29 *S by B*, p.19.

30 Deborah Pearson to JB, 4 June 1961. *Victoria*.

31 Anne Lee Michell to JB, 7 November 1960. *Victoria*.

32 Marjorie Bond to JB, 6 November 1960. *Victoria*.

33 Robert Hurd to JB, 26 September 1960. *Victoria*.

34 Anne Lee Michell to JB, 7 November 1960. *Victoria*.

35 *S by B*, p.5.

36 On 8 April 1953, Philip Donnellan, then general programme assistant in the Midland Region of the BBC, wrote to ask JB if he would take part in a 'short and slightly satirical programme on the disappearance of the last tram from the streets of Birmingham'. JB replied with unusual sharpness: 'I don't like the idea of writing satirically about trams, or taking part in anything satirical about their disappearance, because I like trams, and regard their disappearance as a disaster.' (Both letters in *Victoria*.)

37 On JB's memories of Charrington's shop in the Kentish Town Road, see his letter to Mrs P. Alger, 3 February 1976. *JBP*.

38 Quoted, Valerie Jenkins, *Evening Standard*, 29 June 1974.

39 JB, foreword to the catalogue of the Highgate Literary and Scientific Institution's exhibition of portraits of 'Some Highgate Celebrities', March 1960.

40 *S by B*, p.3.

41 *Ibid*, pp.3–4.

42 This and other information about the Bouman family was obtained in an interview with Miss Mary Bouman, 1978.

43 Mary Bouman, interview, 1978.

44 *Ibid*.

45 JB, 'Childhood Days . . .', BBC radio talk, 16 July 1950. *BBCWA*.

46 Letter in the possession of Miss Mary Bouman.

47 JB, 'Childhood Days . . .', BBC radio talk, 16 July 1950. *BBCWA*. When Bill Bouman died in 1979 JB wrote Mary a letter of condolence in which he said, 'I associate the happiest moments of childhood with him.' *Miss Mary Bouman*. In a profile of JB, 'The Bard of the Railway Gas-Lamp' (*The Observer*, 15 October 1972), Michael Davie wrote: 'An acute physical sense of his childhood circumstances has never left him; nor have its scars and humiliations healed. In late middle-age, he wrote three poems about childhood: one about being thought a

common little boy by the mother of one of his friends; one about his nanny – a Puritan and a prig – giving him a fear of death; and a third about his mother reproving him for what he was doing with a friend called Bobby.'

48 Allan Cunningham (1784–1842), Scottish man of letters.

49 Ethelwynne Bouman to JB, 'Xmas 1956'. *Victoria*.

50 George MacDonald (1824–1905). W.H. Auden, who was six months younger than JB, and whose childhood reading diet was similar, thought that Mac-Donald's *The Princess and the Goblin* was 'the only English children's book in the same class as the Alice books'. (Quoted, Humphrey Carpenter, *W.H. Auden: A Biography*, Allen & Unwin, London 1981, p.9.)

51 JB to Ethelwynne Bouman, 27 December 1956. *Miss Mary Bouman*.

52 Mary Bouman, interview, 1978.

53 JB, 'Childhood Days . . .', BBC radio talk, 16 July 1950. *BBCWA*.

54 Letter in the possession of Miss Mary Bouman.

55 *Ibid*.

56 See Arthur Hayden to JB, 29 September 1943 and 23 June 1945. *Victoria*.

57 Valerie Jenkins, *Evening Standard*, 29 June 1974.

58 *Loc. cit.*

59 *S by B*, p.25.

60 *Loc. cit.*

61 *Loc. cit.*

62 JB, *op. cit.*, p.26. The book which JB calls *House of the Sleeping Winds* was almost certainly *Four Winds Farm* by Mrs (Mary Louisa) Molesworth, illustrated by Walter Crane, Macmillan, London 1887 – though JB may have had a later edition, perhaps that of 1903. The book contains this passage: 'I wish I could make you *feel* what I can fancy I feel myself when I think of it – the wonder-ful fresh breath on one's face even on a calm day standing at the door of the farm-house, the sense of life and mischief and wild force about you, though held in check for the moment, the knowledge that the wind – the winds rather, all four of them, are there somewhere, hidden or pretending to be asleep, maybe, but ready all the same to burst out at a moment's notice.' (p.2 of 1887 edn.) JB no doubt changed the book's title, and made the illustrations 'Walter Crane-ish' rather than 'by Walter Crane', for the sake of the metre. The author is grateful to his mother, Mary Hillier, for the information in this note.

63 *S by B*, p.26.

64 Another episode, though JB set it in Cornwall, is so similar that the London party incident may have been transposed to a Cornish setting – or vice versa. The second recollection occurs in *S by B*. JB and his friends in Cornwall were told that Miss Usher was coming. She was very nice to his friends Audrey and Joc Lynam, Biddy Walsham and Joan Larkworthy, '. . . but somehow, somehow, not so nice to me'. When Miss Usher had gone home to Frant, Miss Tunstall, a neighbour of the Betjemanns in Cornwall, took him quietly to the hedge:

> 'Now shall I tell you what Miss Usher said
> About you, John?' 'Oh, please, Miss Tunstall, do!'
> 'She said you were a common little boy.'

In his radio talk 'Childhood Days . . .' (16 July 1950. *BBCWA*) JB gave a version of the same story, using the names 'Miss Tunstead' and 'Miss Fisher'. Miss Tunstead is identified as 'a governess down in Cornwall'. Miss Fisher was alleged to have said he was 'rather a common little boy'. Betjeman added: 'Why did I mind? Heaven knows. But I still do and I bet you would too. Silly, unimaginative Miss Tunstead, that wasn't the way to make me improve my manners!'

65 A method of teaching children aged 3 to 6, based on individual activity and free expression, named after Maria Montessori (1870–1952), Italian educator and physician.

66 Mary Chubb, 'In the Morning Sow Thy Seed', BBC radio talk, 24 August 1953. *BBCWA*.

67 *Ibid*.

68 Miss Thompson's recollections were written for Mrs Gwynnydd Gosling of the Highgate Literary and Scientific Institution, where they are lodged. Extracts were printed in the *Hampstead and Highgate Express*, 9 November 1984.

69 Miss D.G. Doubleday to JB, 30 April 1964. *Victoria*.

70 Miss Winifred Macdonald, interview, 1980.

71 Mrs Nancy Richardson, interview, 1980.

72 Mary Chubb, 'In the Morning Sow Thy Seed,' BBC radio talk, 24 August 1953. *BBCWA*.

73 *Ibid*.

74 *Ibid*.

75 *Ex inf*. Mrs Margaret Darlington and Miss Winifred Macdonald, interview, 1980.

76 JB, 'Childhood Days . . .', BBC radio talk, 16 July 1950. *BBCWA*.
   In later years, JB appears to have become confused about the participants in the punching incident, and even about the school he was attending when it occurred. In 1954, in reply to Harold Langley who had sent him a poem about the head-master of Highgate Junior School, JB wrote: 'Of course I remember you very well and you were something to do with printing. You lived in Muswell Hill, you had freckles and your red coat had furry knobs on it and was more expensive than the kind that I wore . . . I remember you as a friendly person and I remember a nice boy called Jelly who I think was a friend of yours. The most horrible one was Jack Shakespeare. You will find an account of life at Highgate Junior School in my last book of verses called *A Few Late Chrysanthemums*, but I have changed the name to the south coast of England.' (*Victoria*.)
   The poem, 'Original Sin on the Sussex Coast', alleges that Jack Shakespeare ('Jack Drayton' – one Tudor poet's name being substituted for another's) gave a whistle as a signal for attack; but the attackers are identified as Andrew Knox and Willie Buchanan.
   Andrew Knox, though he was with JB at Byron House, left that school in 1914 at the age of eight to go to a preparatory school in Hertfordshire, and never saw him again. When 'Original Sin on the Sussex Coast' appeared, Knox was indignant about the use of his name, and even thought of writing to JB 'to tell him [the reference] was libellous and to request a donation to a charity to call it quits'. (Andrew Knox, letter to the author, 5 April 1985.)
   In *S by B* (p.26) the story changed slightly again. It seems likely that the version given in the radio talk of 1950 – the earliest version – is the most accurate.

77 JB, 'Childhood Days . . .', BBC radio talk, 16 July 1950 (*BBCWA*) and *S by B*, p.28.

78 *S by B*, p.26.

79 Henry Matthew Brock, RI (1875–1960), book illustrator and landscape painter.

80 *S by B*, p.27.

81 *Ex inf*. Mr R.C. Giles, headmaster of Highgate School, letter to Mrs Gwynnydd Gosling of the Highgate Literary and Scientific Institution, 15 June 1979. JB's own recollection that 'In 1914–15 I spent two unsuccessful terms at Highgate Junior School' (*T.S. Eliot*, ed. Tambimuttu and Richard March, Frank Cass, London 1965 edn., p.89) is erroneous.

82 *S by B*, p.27.
83 Sir Anthony Plowman, letter to the author, 16 January 1985.
84 *Ibid.* The line of asterisks indicates a passage that Sir Anthony could not remember.
85 *Victoria.*
86 *T.S. Eliot*, ed. Tambimuttu and Richard March, Frank Cass, London 1965 edn., p.89.
87 JB to Harold Langley, 6 August 1954. *Victoria.*
88 JB, 'Childhood Days . . .', BBC radio talk, 16 July 1950. *BBCWA.*
89 *S by B*, p.28.
90 Frank Delaney, *Betjeman Country*, Hodder & Stoughton/John Murray, London 1983, p.28.
91 *S by B*, p.29.
92 Valerie Jenkins, *Evening Standard*, 29 June 1974.
93 Sir Anthony Plowman, letter to the author, 16 January 1985.
94 JB to Harold Langley, 6 August 1954. *Victoria.*
95 N.C. Selway to JB, 1960. *Victoria.* (In a letter to Robert Sencourt, 19 January 1967, in *Victoria*, JB mentions N.C. Selway, 'who was the son of the superintendent of the Great Northern [Railway] and who recently wrote a book about coaches and coaching'.
96 Robert Hurd to JB, 26 September 1960. *Victoria.*
97 JB, 'Childhood Days . . .', BBC radio talk, 16 July 1950. *BBCWA.*
98 *T.S. Eliot*, ed. Tambimuttu and Richard March, Frank & Cass, London 1965 edn., p.89; and *S by B*, p.29.
99 Of JB's fellow-pupils at Highgate Junior School, Harold Langley came from Muswell Hill (see note 76); and in a letter JB wrote to Sir Anthony Plowman on 20 July 1946 he listed 'Christie-Miller (sultry-looking Muswell Hill)' among those of their schoolfellows whom he could remember. *Sir Anthony Plowman.*
100 *T.S. Eliot*, ed. Tambimuttu and Richard March, Frank & Cass, London 1965 edn., p.89.
101 *S by B*, pp.29–30.
102 *Ibid*, p.16.
103 *Ibid*, p.18.
104 *Victoria.*
105 *Victoria.*
106 JB, 'Childhood Days . . .', BBC radio talk, 16 July 1950. *BBCWA.*

Chapter 3: The Dragon School

1 JB to J.B. Brown, nd but July 1965. *Victoria.*
2 *Ibid.*
3 For information about the Dragon School in this and several other paragraphs in this chapter, I am indebted to the late Martin Higham.
4 Martin Higham, letter to the author, 23 July 1979.
5 John Vassall (b. 1915), a civil servant at the Admiralty, was convicted of spying for the Russians in 1962 and sentenced to 18 years' imprisonment.
6 J.P.W. (later Sir William) Mallalieu (1908–1980). Labour MP for Huddersfield, 1945–50, and for the east division of Huddersfield, 1950–79. Knighted 1979.
7 J.P.W. Mallalieu, *On Larkhill*, Alison & Busby, London 1983, p.38.

8 *Loc. cit.*
9 *S by B*, pp.48–49.
10 JB to J.B. Brown, nd but July 1965. *Victoria.*
11 *Ibid.*
12 Mallalieu, *op. cit.*, pp.30–31.
13 JB to J.B. Brown, nd but July 1965. *Victoria.*
14 *Ibid.*
15 Mallalieu, *op. cit.*, p.42.
16 JB to J.B. Brown, nd but July 1965. *Victoria.*
17 *Ibid.*
18 Mallalieu, *op. cit.*, pp.41–42.
19 Quoted to the late Martin Higham by Tony Bushell and reported to the author by Higham.
20 Audrey Lynam to JB, 1976. *JBP.*
21 JB to Audrey Lynam, 1976. *JBP.*
22 Mrs Kenneth Crookshank, interview, 1984.
23 Mallalieu, *op. cit.*, p.48.
24 *S by B*, pp.44–45.
25 Mallalieu, *op. cit.* The Imperial War Museum's Information Sheet No. 7, 'The Collection of Horse Chestnuts, 1917', reveals that the horse chestnuts were needed to produce the acetone that was used, with ether-alcohol, as a solvent for manufacturing cordite, the basic propellant for shells. The fact sheet adds: 'Nobody really knew exactly why they were collecting horse chestnuts. The Government was, naturally, reticent to reveal the motive behind its scheme since the Germans could very well copy this novel form of acetone production.'
26 John Oxenham: pseudonym of William Arthur Dunkerley (1852–1941), novelist and poet. His book of verses *Bees in Amber* (1913) had sold 286,000 copies by 1942. Eight small volumes of his verse were issued in the First World War. 'The little books . . . went out to all the Fronts, and were carried in pockets and haversacks, and read in tents and trenches and on the ships.' (Erica Oxenham, *'J.O.'*, Longmans Green, London 1942, p.167.)
27 *S by B*, p.45.
28 Mallalieu, *op. cit.*, p.30.
29 *S by B*, p.44.
30 Arthur G. Lanham to JB, 1976. *JBP.*
31 JB to Arthur Lanham, 1976. *JBP.*
32 J.B. Brown, letter to the author, 27 February 1976.
33 JB to Alan Wood, 1951. *Victoria.*
34 Quoted, Alan Wood to JB, 8 February 1951. *Victoria.*
35 Mallalieu, *op. cit.*, p.45.
36 *S by B*, p.43. JB identified his challenger as Mallalieu in his BBC radio talk 'Christmas Nostalgia', 25 December 1947, in which he said that the reason Mallalieu wanted to fight him was that he thought JB had been bullying another boy.
37 Mallalieu, *op. cit.*, pp.36–37.
38 *Ibid*, p.47.
39 *Loc. cit.*
40 *The Draconian*, December 1918, p.5117.
41 *The Draconian*, April 1920, p.5260.
42 Quoted *ibid*, p.5263.
43 *Ibid*, p.5262. Rosa Filippi (1866–1930) made her first appearance on the stage at the Gaiety, 1883, as Mary Moleseye in *Doctor Davey*. In 1895 she played Madame Vinard in *Trilby* at the Haymarket; in 1901 she played Mrs Bennett in her own

play, *The Bennetts*, at the Adelphi. In 1914 she attempted to found a 'People's Theatre' at the Royal Victoria Hall. She continued to appear on the West End stage until 1929.

44 Martin Higham, who was the son of T.F. Higham, Fellow of Trinity College, Oxford (Dean, 1919–33, Senior Tutor, 1938–39 and 1945–48) wrote (letter to the author, 23 July 1979): 'I have long maintained that the line "The toothbrush too is airing in this new North Oxford air" referred to my parents' bathroom in Northmoor Road. The window was always opened wide (except when bathing) and our toothbrushes stood in a tumbler on the window-sill, easily visible across the hard tennis court of the house on the corner of Northmoor and Belbroughton Roads. In *Oxford University Chest* (1938) JB refers to North Oxford as the area full of airing toothbrushes.' JB was a friend of T.F. Higham (see their correspondence in the Bodleian Library, Oxford).

45 *S by B*, p.45.

46 JB, in *My Oxford*, ed. Ann Thwaite, Robson, London 1977, pp.61–62.

47 'Anglo-Jackson': term derived from the name of the Oxford architect Sir Thomas Jackson (1835–1924), who designed the Examination Schools (foundations laid 1876), the chapel (finished 1908) of Hertford College and its 'Bridge of Sighs' (1913). Betjeman's poem 'Myfanwy at Oxford' begins: 'Pink may, double may, dead laburnum/Shedding an Anglo-Jackson shade . . .'

48 JB, in Thwaite, *op. cit.*, p.62.

49 On the church of St Philip and St James, see JB, *An Oxford University Chest*, John Miles, London 1938, p.161n, in which Ronald Knox's limerick about the incumbent is quoted.

50 JB, in Thwaite, *op. cit.*, p.62.

51 *S by B*, p.46.

52 JB, in Thwaite, *op. cit.*, p.62.

53 JB and David Vaisey, *Victorian and Edwardian Oxford from Old Photographs*, Batsford, London 1971, under Plate 6.

54 *Ibid*, pp.v–vi.

55 Thwaite, *op. cit.*, Introduction.

56 *S by B*, p.46.

57 JB, in Thwaite, *op. cit.*, p.46.

58 *Loc. cit.*

59 'Fr. Ronald Wright, OSB', obituary in *The Ampleforth Journal*, Summer 1969.

60 Norman, Early English and Decorated.

61 Perpendicular.

62 *S by B*, p.48.

63 *Ibid*, p.49.

64 JB, in Thwaite, *op. cit.*, p.63.

65 *S by B*, p.49.

66 *Ibid*, p.57.

67 *Ibid*, p.59.

68 Holograph manuscript of JB's introduction to the 1970 edn. of *GGT (Victoria)*. He omitted these words from the published version.

69 *S by B*, p.56.

70 *Ibid*, p.60.

71 *Loc. cit.* A similar sentence is spoken by the character who represents JB's mother in his playlet 'The Artsenkrafts', *Oxford Outlook*, 1927, p.221: 'When I'm dead, Jim, you'll be sorry for all the things you've said to me.'

72 JB, 'The Artsenkrafts', *Oxford Outlook*, 1927, p.219.

73 *S by B*, p.81.

Chapter 4: Father and Son

1 See B. Hillier, *Asprey of Bond Street, 1781–1981*, Quartet Books, London 1981, p.59.
2 Eric Asprey, interview, 1978. On the brothers Philip and Eric Asprey, their New Bond Street shop and their association with Ernest Betjemann, see Hillier, *op. cit.*
3 See *The Times*, 18 January 1933.
4 *S by B*, p.16.
5 F.P[ercy] Threadgill, interview, 1978. (Threadgill, b.1909, joined Betjemann's in 1924 as an office-boy in the drawing office of the managing director, Horace Andrew. Later he was the firm's chief travelling salesman.)
6 William Hammond, interview, 1978.
7 George Jones, interview, 1978. (Jones was fourteen when he joined Betjemann's in 1916.)
8 Albert Dubery, interview, 1978. (Dubery began a six-year apprenticeship with Betjemann's in 1916. He graduated from tea-boy to working on the tantaluses.)
9 JB recalled these days in his poem 'Norfolk'.
10 George Jones, interview, 1978.
11 William Hammond, interview, 1978.
12 On Epping Forest as a playground for Londoners, a 'cockney paradise', see Bernard Ward, *The Retreats of Epping Forest*, Conservators of Epping Forest (Corporation of the City of London), 1978.
13 Albert Dubery, interview, 1978.
14 William Hammond, interview, 1978.
15 G. Betjemann & Sons made the trays; the china was made, to Ernest Betjemann's design, by Charles J. Noke of the Royal Doulton Potteries, on whom see Desmond Eyles, *Royal Doulton Character and Toby Jugs*, Royal Doulton, Stoke-on-Trent 1979, pp.33–34.
16 F.P. Threadgill, interview, 1978.
17 Boddy's remarks were quoted in a letter to JB from Carol Lobb, 1974. *JBP*.
18 JB refers to this habit of Allwright's in *S by B*, p.15.
19 JB to Carol Lobb, 1974. Copy in *JBP*.
20 F.P. Threadgill, interview, 1978.
21 The Betjemanns' family doctor, who appears in *S by B* as 'Dr Macmillan'.
22 *JBP*.
23 *Ibid.*
24 *S by B*, p.11.
25 Michael Parkinson Show, BBC Television, 1973.
26 *S by B*, p.11.
27 Valerie Jenkins, *Evening Standard*, 29 June 1974.
28 The premises are still (1988) occupied by the Medici Society.
29 Valerie Jenkins, *Evening Standard*, 29 June 1974.
30 *S by B*, p.12.
31 *Ibid*, p.13.
32 *Loc. cit.*
33 *Ibid*, p.14.
34 *Ibid*, p.15.
35 *Ibid*, p.20.
36 On 24 October 1960, Mr R.E. Hawker of Mousehole, Cornwall, wrote to John to recall how he (Hawker) had once had a share in a shoot at Buntingford, of which one of the other members was Ernest Betjemann – 'a cheery companion, but very

deaf'. Hawker added: 'He brought with him a young son of school age (knicker-bockers and possibly socks) and while we had our lunches he was given a gun – to see if he could get a rabbit . . . We were in fear and trembling lest the rabbit should run our way.' *(Victoria.)*

37 Eric Asprey, interview, 1978.
38 Philip Asprey, interview, 1978.
39 *S by B*, p.17.
40 *Ibid*, p.20.

Chapter 5: Early Influences

1 Lord David Cecil, interview, 1978.
2 JB, 'The Usher of Highgate Junior School', in *T.S. Eliot*, ed. Tambimuttu and Richard Marsh, Frank Cass, London 1965 edn., p.89.
3 Quoted *ibid*, p.90. (T.S. Eliot, *Four Quartets*.)
4 *Ibid*, p.92.
5 *Ibid*, p.91.
6 Quoted *loc. cit.* (T.S. Eliot, 'The Fire Sermon'.)
7 *Loc. cit.*
8 According to *S by B*, p.29.
9 One of the Dumbleton poems is quoted in Chapter 9; the other is printed in *UP*, pp.34–35.
10 According to *S by B*, p.29.
11 JB to Randolph Churchill, June 1946. Copy in *JBP*.
12 *S by B*, p.4.
13 *Loc. cit.*
14 PB, interview, 1976.
15 *S by B*, p.25.
16 *Ibid*, p.29. On 6 November 1960, Alban Blakelock wrote to JB: '. . . I was at Highgate Junior School until I was 13; I left at the end of the Summer Term in 1910. I was very fond of Miss Long. I have never forgotten her reading to us, once a week, about the early life . . . of Michael Angelo; and the feeling of peace and happiness which that story, read by Miss Long, gave to me. I rather feared the rough and tumble of school life and Miss Long somehow stood for quietness and serenity, and for a life which I would have loved to have had, where fear and dread of the next day had no existence.' *(Victoria.)*
17 *Ibid*, p.18.
18 In the late 1920s or early 1930s, Mark Ogilvie-Grant sent Patrick Balfour an early version of the poem, which was then titled simply 'A Calvinistic Hymn' and had the sub-title 'The Pleasure of Pain'. *(Huntington.)* The last line of the poem also differed from the later published version. Underneath the title was the explanation, clearly from JB: 'Modelled on "Gadsby's Collection" still used by the PARTICULAR BAPTISTS and sung unaccompanied'.

JB meant Gadsby's *Selections: A Selection of Hymns for Public Worship* compiled by William Gadsby and first published in 1814. (Extra 'supplements' were added later in the century.) Gadsby (1773–1844), a labourer's son, became a stocking weaver. In 1799 he went to see a man hanged: the experience turned his mind toward religion and he became a Nonconformist minister. The hymns in the *Selections* which most closely resemble JB's 'An Eighteenth-Century Calvinist Hymn' were by Joseph Hart (1712–68), for example:

> Poor wretched worthless worm!
> In what sad plight I stand!
> When good I would perform
> Then evil is at hand.
> My leprous soul is all unclean,
> My heart obscene, my nature foul . . .

19 Sir Walter Sendall, preface to C.S. Calverley, *Collected Works*, George Bell & Sons, London 1901.
20 *Loc. cit.*
21 JB, 'Bristol and Clifton'.
22 JB, interview, 1976.
23 *S by B*, p.17.
24 Letter from J.B. Brown to the author, 27 February 1976.
25 'The number of bad influences, some of them good writers, that Betjeman can digest or parody defeats belief: Locker-Lampson, Father Prout, Dibdin, the Rev. E.E. Bradford, *Hymns Ancient and Modern*, Felicia Hemans, Thomas Ingoldsby, Poe, Dowson, Calverley, Newbolt, Lionel Johnson, Campbell, Dobson, Scott, Longfellow – ignoring for the moment Crabbe, Hardy, Tennyson, Praed – this incomplete list of under-vitaminized fodder might stretch to the crack of eructation.' Herbert Lomas, 'Standing up for failure', *London Magazine*, December 1984–January 1985.
26 *S by B*, p.4.
27 Alfred, Lord Tennyson, 'The Princess'.
28 JB, 'St Barnabas, Oxford'.
29 JB, 'English Gentleman', *The New English Weekly*, 14 September 1939, p. 285.

Chapter 6: Cornwall

1 Mr Rosevear's house, much enlarged, is now the Beaudaire Hotel.
2 See Sir Arthur Keith, *An Autobiography*, Watts & Co., London 1950, p.367.
3 JB describes the fly 'With red transparent body' in *S by B*, p.34.
4 Undertown, which is still standing, though it has been altered, was built for Ernest Betjemann in 1928 to the design of Robert Atkinson FRIBA.
5 Mrs Joan Kunzer, interview, 1977.
6 JB, 'Remembering Summer', a television programme on Cornwall, BBC Television, January 1960. *BBCWA*.
7 *Ibid.*
8 *Ibid.*
9 Nell Oakley and her husband Ernest, who had retired from the Calcutta jute trade, lived in St Enodoc Cottage. They had two children, Joan (now Mrs Hechle), who still lives in Trebetherick, and Roland, who died in 1967. Roland is mentioned in JB's poem 'Old Friends'. ('Where's Roland, easing his most unwieldy car,/With its load of golf-clubs, backwards into the lane?')
10 Trebetherick is in the chapelry of St Enodoc, parish of St Minver.
11 Mrs Joan Kunzer, interview, 1977.
12 *Ibid.*
13 *Ibid.*
14 Rhoda Poulden is mentioned in JB's poem 'Sunday Afternoon Service in St Enodoc Church, Cornwall'.
15 Mrs Joan Kunzer, interview, 1977.

16 *Ex inf.* Mrs Kunzer.
17 *S by B*, p.37.
18 'One of the things that makes Cornwall so different from England is the vegetation. These hedges built of upturned slates. They are called hedges in Cornwall and they are stuffed with wild flowers and wild ferns. You can stop anywhere looking into a Cornish hedge and see about 15 different sorts of plants, while everything around you clicks with grasshoppers and hums with insects.' (JB, 'Remembering Summer', BBC Television, January 1960. *BBCWA*. In the same film, JB spoke of the 'lush streams' of Cornwall, 'heavy with the scent of mint and yellow in the spring with iris'.)
19 In an article entitled 'Verse writing: some advice – practical and cautionary – to beginners' (*English, the Magazine of the English Association*, Spring 1947, p.189), Cicely Boas wrote that roses, lilies and violets should be 'taboo in beginners' verse ... but a discreet reference to the escholtzia, the gloxinia, or the devil's-bit scabious would suggest authenticity.' Mrs Boas's article appeared when many of JB's best poems had already been published, but he instinctively followed her precept. He wrote of lady's finger, smokewort, kingcups and lovers' loss in 'An Archaeological Picnic'; of saffron in 'Ireland with Emily'; of fritillaries in 'St Barnabas, Oxford', knapweed in 'The Return', ribbonweed in 'Old Friends', blue squills in 'A Bay in Anglesey', sorrel in 'Norfolk', and scabious in 'Felixstowe'. It was left to Edith Sitwell to hymn gloxinias, but JB worked mesembreanthemums into one poem.
20 JB, 'Sunday Afternoon Service in St Enodoc Church, Cornwall'.
21 *FLL*, p.180.
22 *Loc. cit.*
23 *Ibid*, p.218.
24 *Loc. cit.*
25 *Loc. cit.*
26 *Ibid*, p.220.
27 *Ibid*, pp.218–19.
28 *Ibid*, p.223.
29 *Ibid*, pp.223–24.
30 See the last stanza of 'Seaside Golf'; also the description of the links in 'The Hon. Sec.' – a poem commemorating Ned Burden, Honorary Secretary of the St Enodoc Golf Club.
31 'A glorious, sailing, bounding drive/That made me glad I was alive'. JB, 'Seaside Golf'.

Chapter 7: Marlborough

1 Arthur Byron, 'A lesson from the shy loner', *The Times*, 22 May 1984.
2 Derek Hill, telephone conversation with the author, 1985.
3 On 'barnes' and 'kishes', see poem by Charles Sorley, *The Marlburian*, 11 November 1912; also, *The Marlburian*, 29 May 1924.
4 See Beverley Nichols, *Prelude*, London 1920, p.29.
5 See Louis MacNeice, *The Strings Are False*, ed. E.R. Dodds, Faber, London 1965, pp.80–81.
6 Professor J.E. Bowle, interview, 1976.
7 For etymological explanations of this word, see *A History of Marlborough College* by A.G. Bradley, A.C. Champneys and J.W. Baines, revised and

continued by J.R. Taylor, H.C. Brentnall and G.C. Turner (1923), p.159; and H.C. Brentnall in *Marlborough College, 1843–1943*, Cambridge University Press, 1943, p.17. See also *The Marlburian* of 22 February 1921 for the school song 'Bolly!'

8 Charles D'Costa to JB, 20 January 1967. *Victoria.*

9 Nichols, *op. cit.*, p.56.

10 *Loc. cit.*

11 See Wilfrid Blunt, *Married to a Single Life*, Michael Russell, London 1983, p.60. JB's contemporary John Parker (who became a Member of Parliament and Father of the House) confirmed that both tortures were still practised in their time at Marlborough. (*Ex inf.* Mr Tony Barker of the University of Essex.)

12 Charles D'Costa (b.1910) entered Marlborough in 1924 and left in 1926. He told JB that he had left early because he had been temporarily blinded in a rugby accident. However, the young Cyril Connolly, who later tutored D'Costa in Jamaica, wrote to Noel Blakiston on 20 January 1927: 'Benji [Charles D'Costa] . . . confided that the blow on the head which had occasioned his six months rest and the prohibition to use his eyes had been a pure invention as he had concocted it the day after the match in order to "stay out" the week end. . . ' (Noel Blakiston [ed.] *A Romantic Friendship: The Letters of Cyril Connolly to Noel Blakiston*, Constable, London 1975, p. 217.)

13 Charles D'Costa to JB, 20 January 1967. *Victoria.*

14 *Marlborough College, 1843–1943*, Cambridge University Press, 1943, p.22.

15 Professor J.E. Bowle, interview, 1976.

16 Bowra's actual phrase was: 'Cyril Norwood, who looked like a policeman in an early Chaplin film . . .' (*Memories 1898–1939*, Weidenfeld & Nicolson, London 1966, p.165.)

17 Professor J.E. Bowle, interview, 1976.

18 *Ibid.*

19 Beverley Nichols, *The Unforgiving Minute*, W.H. Allen, London 1978, p.1.

20 Professor J.E. Bowle, interview, 1976.

21 JB, 'Dead from the Waist Down', *Spectator*, 14 March 1958, pp.320–21.

22 *Spectator*, 21 March 1958, p.362.

23 George White to JB, 2 April 1958. *Victoria.*

24 *Daily Mail*, 20 December 1958.

25 JB to Gerald Murray, 1 April 1971. Shown to the author by the late Mr Murray. The Old Marlburian First World War poet Charles Sorley (1885–1915) was a cousin of R.A. Butler.

26 *Ibid*, 26 January 1976.

27 A.R. Gidney, interview, 1977.

28 *S by B*, p.67.

29 *A History of Marlborough College* (1923 edn., see note 7).

30 MacNeice, *op. cit.*, p.86.

31 J.E. Bowle's diary, quoted in his unpublished memoirs. Shown to the author by the late Professor Bowle.

32 *Ibid.*

33 *Ex inf.* JB and Professor J.E. Bowle, conversations with the author.

34 MacNeice, *op. cit.*, p.83.

35 *S by B*, pp. 67–68.

36 See MacNeice, *op. cit.*, p.84, and *S by B*, p.68.

37 According to Charles D'Costa to JB, 20 January 1967. *Victoria.*

38 *S by B*, p.69.

39 MacNeice, *op. cit.*, pp.84–85.

40 *S by B*, p.70.

41 *Little Innocents*, ed. Alan Pryce-Jones, Cobden-Sanderson, London 1932, pp.86–87.
42 Elizabeth, Countess of Longford, interview, 1976.
43 *S by B*, p.71.
44 T.C. Worsley, *Flannelled Fool*, Alan Ross, London 1967, p.45.
45 Professor J.E. Bowle, interview, 1976.
46 Anthony Blunt, interview, 1977.
47 In his unpublished thesis *Athleticism: a comparative study of the emergence and consolidation of an educational ideology* (1976) – shown to the author by the late Gerald Murray, archivist of Marlborough College – James A. Mangan shows how a succession of Marlborough headmasters pitted themselves against the dominance of sport. See also Bruce Haley, *The Healthy Body and Victorian Culture*, Harvard University Press, Cambridge, Mass., 1978, pp.161–62.
48 Professor J.E. Bowle, interview, 1976.
49 JB, preface to *GGT*, 1970 edn., p.xvi.
50 *Ibid*, p.xvii.
51 Quoted by Anthony Blunt, interview, 1977.
52 *Ibid*.
53 *Ibid*.
54 Hilton's diary is quoted in Louis MacNeice, *op. cit.*, p.24.
55 J.E. Bowle's diary (see note 31).
56 Anthony Blunt, 'From Bloomsbury to Marxism', *Studio International*, November 1973, p.164.
57 J.E. Bowle's diary (see note 31).
58 *Ibid*.
59 *Ibid*.
60 Quoted, *ibid*.
61 Sir Ellis Waterhouse, interview, 1978.
62 Sir Ellis Waterhouse said (interview, 1978): 'My father was at Christ's, Cambridge, with Calverley, and I was brought up on Calverley quotations. It is possible that John Betjeman knew about that, and that his first line is a reference to it.'
63 J.E. Bowle's diary (see note 31).
64 An artificial cone of chalk. It has been compared with Silbury Hill, which lies five miles west of it.
65 The quotation is from Pope's *Rape of the Lock*.
66 MacNeice, *op. cit.*, pp.94–95.
67 JB to Patrick Balfour, dated 'Lord's Day 1930'. *Huntington*.
68 Arthur Byron, 'A lesson from the shy loner', *The Times*, 22 May 1984.
69 *Ibid*.
70 *Ex inf.* the late Philip Harding, who was the author's colleague on *The Times* in the early 1960s.
71 Professor J.E. Bowle, interview, 1976.
72 J.E. Bowle's diary (see note 31).
73 *Ibid*.
74 J.E. Bowle to Mrs Edward Bowle, 12 May 1924. Quoted in Bowle's unpublished memoirs.
75 Professor J.E. Bowle, interview, 1976.
76 Quoted, *North Somerset Mercury*, 5 February 1975.
77 J.E. Bowle's diary (see note 31).
78 *Ibid*.
79 Frederic William Farrar (1831–1903), Master of Marlborough 1871–76, Dean of

Canterbury 1895. Wrote the school novels *Eric, or Little by Little* (1858) and *St Winifred's* (1862).

80 JB to Kingsley Amis, 5 April 1973. Copy in *JBP*.

81 Anthony Blunt, interview, 1977.

82 Professor J.E. Bowle, interview, 1976. The quotation is from 'Jonquil and the Fleur-de-Lys', *The Complete Poems of Lord Alfred Douglas*, Martin Secker, London 1928, p.32.

83 Churchill was present at the Old Bailey, London, for the opening of criminal libel proceedings against Douglas on 10 December 1923. (See Martin Gilbert, *Winston S. Churchill*, Heinemann, London 1976, v, p. 21. Also H. Montgomery Hyde, *Lord Alfred Douglas*, Methuen, London 1984, Chapter VI.)

84 William Sharp (1855–1905). Wrote verse and lives of poets under his own name but in 1893 began to write mystical prose and verse under the pseudonym 'Fiona McLeod'. *The Immortal Hour* (1900) was turned into a 'musical drama' by Rutland Boughton.

85 *The Complete Poems of Lord Alfred Douglas*, Martin Secker, London 1928.

86 Evan Morgan did not write a book on Douglas. Percy Colson, with the Marquess of Queensberry, wrote *Oscar Wilde and the Black Douglas* (Hutchinson, London 1949).

87 JB, interview, 1976.

88 *S by B*, p.67.

89 *Ibid*, p.72.

90 *Ibid*, p.73.

91 *Loc. cit.*

92 *Ibid*, pp.73–74.

93 G.K. White, *The Last Word*, Allen Figgis, Dublin 1977, p.47.

94 Anthony Blunt, interview, 1977.

95 JB, in *Marlborough College: The Corps, 1860–1960*, ed. W.P. Harling, Marlborough College, Wilts., 1960, p.13.

96 Arthur Byron, 'A lesson from the shy loner', *The Times*, 22 May 1984.

97 G.K. White, *op. cit.*, pp.47–48. For those unfamiliar with army terminology, the point of the story is that John was given the honour of starting the Corps marching. Instead, being flustered, he ordered the Corps to halt.

98 JB, in *Marlborough College: The Corps, 1860–1960*, ed. W.P. Harling, Marlborough College, Wilts., 1960, p.13.

99 T.C.G.S. Sandford, housemaster of Preshute House.

100 Richard F. Fairbairn to JB, 18 October 1960. *Victoria*.

101 *S by B*, p.67.

102 JB was asked to make the broadcast by Miss Sunday Wilshin of the BBC's 'London Calling Asia' service (letter of 24 March 1954, *Victoria*). A copy of his script is also in *Victoria*.

Chapter 8: The Secret Glory

1 For JB's almost Japanese preoccupation with teatime, see the following poems: 'Death in Leamington', 'Myfanwy', 'On an Old-Fashioned Water-Colour of Oxford', 'Margate 1940', 'In a Bath Teashop', 'Indoor Games near Newbury', 'House of Rest', 'How to Get On in Society', 'Felixstowe or The Last of Her Order', 'Kegans' and *S by B*, pp.5, 25, 36, 83 and 85.

Lord David Cecil (interview, 1978) remembered that JB composed the following ditty, which was sung to the tune of 'Three Blind Mice' on country car rides:

Home-made cakes,
Home-made cakes;
Dainty buttered scones,
Dainty buttered scones;
But all of them served by gentlefolk
On rickety tables of unstained oak,
Wherever we went we always spoke
For home-made cakes.

2 Wilfrid Johnson wrote to JB on 28 April 1949 *(Victoria)*: 'Until I had your letter I had never connected the John Betjeman whom I have heard of in later times with the lad who came over here such a long time ago . . .'
3 *S by B*, p.86.
4 *Ibid*, pp.86–87.
5 Professor J.E. Bowle, interview, 1976.
6 Arthur Machen, *The Secret Glory*, Martin Secker, London 1922, pp.291–92.
7 See JB's letter of 5 April 1973 to Kingsley Amis, quoted in Chapter 7.
8 *S by B*, p.89.
9 *Loc. cit.*
10 *Ibid*, p.90.
11 *Ex inf.* Mrs Joan Kunzer, interview, 1977.
12 *Ibid*.
13 The manuscript is in *Victoria*.
14 Mrs Kenneth Crookshank, interview, 1984.
15 A reproduction of Tuke's painting 'August Blue' is mentioned in JB's poem 'Monody on the Death of a Platonist Bank Clerk'.
   Patrick Leigh Fermor (nd, *Victoria*) sent John this rhyme:

      You, my dear, are Prime Minister;
      He, my dear, is a duke;
      But I, in my day, I'm ecstatic to say,
      Posed in Polperro for *Tuke*.

16 Samuel John Lamorna Birch, R.A. (1869–1955). Landscape painter in oil and water-colour. From 1889 he regularly visited Cornwall, and in 1902 he settled at Lamorna. Born Samuel John Birch, he took the name 'Lamorna Birch' to distinguish himself from an artist called Lionel Birch living at Newlyn.
17 *FLL*, p.217.

Chapter 9: Oxford

1 JB, conversation with the author, 1971.
2 Ernest Betjemann to JB, 13 May 1925. *JBP*.
3 Sir Herbert Warren to Ernest Betjemann, 19 August 1925. *JBP*.
4 Sir Herbert Warren to JB, 21 August 1925. *JBP*.
5 Ernest Betjemann to JB, 16 October 1925. *JBP*.
6 Bryan Guinness, letter to the editor, *Cherwell*, 28 November 1925.
7 John Fernald (interview, 1977) accompanied JB to *The Co-Optimists*. He remembered that JB thought the show terrible; though later 'Melville Gideon on the gramophone' became a nostalgic memory for JB (*S by B*, p.88).
8 See Philip Harding's review of Pickford, *Isis*, 6 November 1926.
9 *Isis*, 20 December 1926.

10 JB, 'The Silver Age of Aesthetes: A Picture of Oxford during the Twenties', *Parson's Pleasure*, Oxford, 15 October 1958.
11 Martyn Skinner, interview, 1979.
12 Humphrey Ellis, letter to the author, 7 July 1978.
13 JB to Ernest Betjemann, October 1925. *JBP.*
14 Ernest Betjemann to JB, 7 November 1925. *JBP.*
15 Ernest Betjemann to JB, 13 May 1926. *JBP.*
16 JB, 'The Silver Age of Aesthetes . . .', *Parson's Pleasure*, Oxford, 15 October 1958.
17 *Ibid.*
18 John Fernald, interview, 1977. JB also recalled this jape in his 1958 *Parson's Pleasure* article (see note 10).
19 Quoted, JB, in *My Oxford*, ed. Ann Thwaite, Robson, London 1977, p.69.
20 C.S. Lewis, *Surprised by Joy*, Geoffrey Bles, London 1955, p.215.
21 Lord David Cecil, interview, 1978.
22 C.S. Lewis, *Diary*, 27 May 1926. *Wheaton College, Illinois.*
23 JB was staying with John Dugdale at Sezincote, Moreton-in-Marsh, Glos.
24 C.S. Lewis, *Diary*, 19 January 1927. *Wheaton College, Illinois.*
25 *S by B*, p.93.
26 Lord David Cecil, interview, 1978.
27 C.S. Lewis, *Diary*, 24 January 1927. *Wheaton College, Illinois.*
28 *JBP.*
29 JB, 'The Silver Age of Aesthetes . . .', *Parson's Pleasure*, 15 October 1958.
30 J.M. Thompson, *My Apologia*, Alden Press, June 1940.
31 Dr N. Hampson, in Albert Goodwin, *Reverend James Matthew Thompson 1878–1956, Proceedings of the British Academy*, vol. xliii, p.284.
32 Martyn Skinner, interview, 1979.
33 JB to Martyn Skinner. *Skinner papers, Bodleian Library, Oxford.*
34 JB, 'St Barnabas, Oxford'.
35 JB, 'The Silver Age of Aesthetes . . .', *Parson's Pleasure*, 15 October 1958.
36 Alan Pryce-Jones recalls the joke as '. . . no public virtues and no private parts' but I prefer the version that I was first told at Oxford in 1960 when Bowra was Warden of Wadham and Boase was President of Magdalen.
37 JB sent the lecture notes to Martyn Skinner, and they are among the *Skinner papers, Bodleian Library, Oxford.*
38 *Ibid.*
39 Kenneth Clark, *Another Part of the Wood*, John Murray, London 1974, p.99.
40 John Sparrow, 'C.M.B.', *Times Literary Supplement*, 23 June 1972.
41 *S by B*, p.103.
42 Osbert Lancaster, *With an Eye to the Future*, John Murray, London 1967, p.71.
43 Kenneth Clark, *op. cit.*, p.100.
44 *S by B*, p.101.
45 C.M. Bowra, *Memories, 1898–1939*, Weidenfeld & Nicolson, London 1966, p.56.
46 Anthony Powell, *Infants of the Spring*, Heinemann, London 1976, p.178.
47 A.L. Rowse, *A Cornishman Abroad*, Jonathan Cape, London 1976, p.201.
48 Lord Birkenhead, introduction to *John Betjeman's Collected Poems*, John Murray, London 1958, p.xiii.
49 From Bowra's taste for untrivial writers, Kenneth Clark called him 'Big Stuff Bowra'. (Clark, *op. cit.*, p.100.)
50 Bowra, *op. cit.*, p.165.
51 *S by B*, p.102.
52 Lord David Cecil, interview, 1978.

53 Elizabeth, Countess of Longford, interview, 1976.
54 *Ibid.*
55 Lancaster, *op. cit.*, p.73.
56 *S by B*, p.96.
57 *Ibid*, p.97.
58 Lancaster, *op. cit.*, p.74.
59 *Ibid*, p.75.
60 Paul Wilson was a scholar at Trinity College, Oxford, 1922–25.
61 George Kolkhorst to JB, 1956. *Rev. Prebendary Gerard Irvine.*
62 George Kolkhorst to JB, 1957. *Rev. Prebendary Gerard Irvine.*
63 Quoted, *S by B*, p.97.
64 Lancaster, *op. cit.*, p.76.
65 JB, in *My Oxford*, ed. Ann Thwaite, Robson, London 1977, p.66.
66 Lancaster, *op. cit.*, p.76.
67 Martyn Skinner, interview, 1979.
68 Lionel Perry, interview, 1979.
69 Bowra, *op. cit.*, p.165.
70 Henry Green, *Pack My Bag*, Hogarth Press, London 1940, p.222.
71 *Loc. cit.*
72 Alan Pryce-Jones, interview, 1976.
73 Vere Pryce-Jones to JB, 1927. *Victoria.*
74 Vere Pryce-Jones to JB, 1927. *Victoria.*
75 See Alan Pryce-Jones, *The Bonus of Laughter*, Hamish Hamilton, London 1986, pp. 51–52.
76 Vere Pryce-Jones to JB, 1928. *Victoria.*
77 Professor J.E. Bowle, interview, 1976.
78 Evelyn Waugh, *A Little Learning*, Chapman & Hall, London 1964, p.200.
79 JB to Lionel Perry, 9 April 1978. In Lionel Perry's possession in 1979.
80 Brian Howard, *New English Review*, January 1947.
81 Lionel Perry, interview, 1979.
82 A typewritten copy of the Gilbertian verse was in the possession of the late Lionel Perry in 1979.
83 JB, 'Dumbleton Hall', *UP*, p.43.
84 Recalled for the author, from memory, by JB in 1976.
85 *S by B*, p.99.
86 *Ibid*, p.98.
87 *Ibid*, p.100.
88 JB, in *Hugh Gaitskell 1906–63*, ed. W.T. Rodgers, London 1964, p.16.
89 *Loc. cit.*
90 Henry Green, *Pack My Bag*, Hogarth Press, London 1940, p.235.
91 Geoffrey Grigson, *The Crest on the Silver*, Cresset Press, London 1950, p.99.
92 Anthony Powell, *Infants of the Spring*, Heinemann, London 1976, pp.195–96.
93 Emlyn Williams, *George*, Hamish Hamilton, London 1961, pp. 401–2.
94 Ernest Betjemann to JB, 13 May 1926. *JBP*. 'Drage' was a large London furniture store, which offered hire-purchase arrangements under the slogan 'Pay the easy way, the Drage way'. *Cf.* JB, 'The Outer Suburbs', *Mount Zion* (1931):

> A stained-glass window, red and green,
> Shines, hiding what should not be seen,
> While wifey knits through hubby's gloom,
> Safe in the Drage-way drawing room.

95 Bede Griffiths OSB, *The Golden String*, Harvill Press, London 1954, pp.28–29.

96 Sean Day-Lewis, *C. Day-Lewis: An English Literary Life*, Weidenfeld & Nicolson, London 1980, p.39. C. Day-Lewis incorporated some of his General Strike experiences into his novel *Starting Point*, Collins, London 1937.

97 Tom Driberg, *Ruling Passions*, Jonathan Cape, London 1977, p.72.

98 Humphrey Carpenter, *W.H. Auden: A Biography*, Allen & Unwin, London 1981, p.52.

99 JB, in *Hugh Gaitskell 1906–63*, ed. W.T. Rodgers, London 1964, p.16.

100 Bryan Guinness, *Dairy* [sic] *Not Kept*, Compton Press, Compton Chamberlayne, Salisbury 1975, p.159.

101 Martyn Skinner, interview, 1979.

102 See Chapter 13.

103 Lionel D.R. Edwards, RI (1878–1966), painter of breezy hunting scenes in watercolour sometimes varied with coloured chalk. See Simon Houfe, *The Dictionary of British Book Illustrators and Caricaturists*, Antique Collectors' Club, Woodbridge, Suffolk, 1978, p.294. JB also mentioned Lionel Edwards in his poem 'Hertfordshire'.

104 *Cf. S by B*: 'Then what, by God was this –
　　　　　　This tender, humble, unrequited love
　　　　　　For Biddy Walsham? What the worshipping
　　　　　　That put me off my supper, fixed my hair
　　　　　　Thick with Anzora for the dance tonight?'

105 *Cherwell*, 5 November 1927.

106 A Gaude (or Gaudy) is a celebration dinner for *alumni* of a college.

107 Ernest Betjemann to JB, 28 September 1928. *JBP*.

108 Emlyn Williams, *George*, Hamish Hamilton, London 1961, p.378.

109 *Ibid*, p.379.

110 The photograph appeared in the issue of 19 February 1927. The caption – hardly ribald – was 'A Last Minute Rehearsal of the O.U.D.S.' JB was assistant editor, not editor, at the time.

111 Lancaster, *op. cit.*, p.66.

112 Quoted by JB, conversation with the author, 1976.

113 JB, quoted by Derek Stanford, *John Betjeman*, Neville Spearman, London 1961, p.25.

114 The development of JB's religious views will be treated in Volume Two. His persisting – but not overwhelming – doubts are evident from his poems, for example:
　　　　'"*I am the Resurrection and the Life*":
　　　　　Strong, deep and painful, doubt inserts the knife.'
　　　　　('Aldershot Crematorium')

115 Quoted by Stanford, *loc. cit.*

116 *Loc. cit.*

117 See Lancaster, *op. cit.*, p.83.

118 Pusey House, founded in 1884 in memory of E.B. Pusey (d.1882), is a theological centre with close links to the University. The architect of its Gothic-style buildings, erected in 1911–14, was Temple Moore.

119 JB may have been referring to the Rev. Colin Gill, later Rector of St Magnus-the-Martyr, City of London, and the Rev. William Favell, later Vicar of St Paul's, Oxford, St Paul's, Brighton, and St Thomas's, Hove.

120 *S by B*, p.95.

121 'Travers' baroque: Martin Travers (1886–1948), stained-glass window artist and architect, started as a disciple of Ninian Comper but broke away and developed a theatrical 'baroque' style using cheap materials. His characteristic reddish gilding was achieved with coloured silver-gilt foil. His most noted works were the altarpiece at St Augustine's, Queen's Gate, and the sanctuary of St Mary, Bourne Street, Pimlico.

NOTES

122 Quoted by the Rev. Prebendary Gerard Irvine, letter to the author, 12 January 1986.
123 Frederick Hood to JB, nd. *Victoria*.
124 The Catholic Apostolic Church ('Irvingites') was a nineteenth-century foundation which owed much to the preaching of the Scots speaker Edward Irving (1792–1834). Though it was a charismatic and eschatological body, its supporters were mainly wealthy and Tory. See Dr Gordon Strachan, *The Pentecostal Theology of Edward Irving*, Darton, Longman & Todd, London 1973, and Andrew Walker, 'Will no one stand up for Edward Irving?', *The Listener*, 6 December 1984.

   JB continued to be interested in the Irvingites throughout his life. In 1961 he began corresponding with a schoolboy, William Norton (see *Daily Herald*, 24 August 1961), who in 1979 became Metropolitan of Glastonbury and VIIth British Patriarch in the Catholic Apostolic Church. In 1975 he persuaded JB to lend his name for support to the 'Irvingite' Albury Society. (JB to William Norton, 7 March 1975. *Metropolitan Seraphim*.) When JB took the actress Prunella Scales (a Cornish neighbour whose Christian name was immortalized in JB's poem 'Hunter Trials') on a tour of London, he showed her the Irvingite church in Gordon Square which serves as the Anglican chaplaincy for London University.
125 F.L. Cross to JB, 13 October 1928. *Victoria*.
126 *Isis*, 17 November 1928.
127 JB, in *My Oxford*, ed. Ann Thwaite, Robson, London 1977, p.65.
128 Sir Harold Acton, letter to the author, 1977.
129 Eric Walter White, interview, 1981.
130 See for example White's 'Min', *Cherwell*, 18 June 1927.
131 The poem, entitled 'Cheltenham', begins 'Eric Walter White/Walter Thursby Pelham . . .' It was published anonymously, and White did not realize that JB was the author until twenty years later when JB came up to him at a party in a Hampstead cellar and recited the whole poem at him. (Eric Walter White, interview, 1981.)
132 Geoffrey Grigson, *The Crest on the Silver*, Cresset Press, London 1950, p.115.
133 *S by B*, p.106.
134 JB, 'The Silver Age of Aesthetes . . .', *Parson's Pleasure*, Oxford, 15 October 1958.
135 Lord Clonmore to JB, 16 August 1927. *Victoria*.
136 Quoted, Sir Osbert Lancaster, interview, 1976.
137 The manuscript of this poem is in *Victoria*. It begins: 'Up! leap up! then *down* and into the alder'd surface . . .'
138 The manuscript of Bowra's poem is bound into a volume of Bowra's satirical verses, now in the possession of John Sparrow.
139 *Ex. inf.* Anthony Powell, letter to the author, 22 August 1976.
140 Quoted by Professor J.E. Bowle, interview, 1976.
141 *Ibid.*
142 On 19 December 1980, when JB was writing an introduction to a posthumous collection of Michael Dugdale's verse, *An Omelette of Vultures' Eggs*, he wrote to Dugdale's sister, Frances, Lady Fergusson of Kilkerran: 'I have an idea that your mother and Edgar [Dugdale's father], in the background [at Roland Gardens], typing away the letters of Bismarck with two fingers, were my introduction to a hopeful world beyond commerce.' (*Lady Fergusson*.)
143 *Cherwell*, 26 November 1927.
144 Ernest Betjemann to JB, 19 October 1926. *JBP*.
145 *S by B*, p.104.

431

146 Lionel Perry, interview, 1979.
147 Edward James, interview, 1981.
148 *S by B*, p.108.
149 Edward James, interview, 1981.
150 *Ibid.*
151 Christopher Sykes, interview, 1977.
152 Christopher Sykes to JB, nd. *Victoria.*
153 Christopher Sykes, interview, 1977.
154 Edward James, interview, 1981.
155 Randolph Churchill, *Twenty-One Years*, Weidenfeld & Nicolson, London 1965, p.97.
156 Edward James, interview, 1981.
157 Elizabeth, Countess of Longford, interview, 1976.
158 JB, 'In Memory of Basil, Marquess of Dufferin and Ava'.
159 JB to Kay Halle, 8 April 1969. *Victoria.*
160 Randolph Churchill, *loc. cit.*
161 JB, 'Oxford', in *W.H. Auden: a Tribute*, ed. Stephen Spender, Weidenfeld & Nicolson, London 1975, p.44.
162 *Loc. cit.*
163 *Ibid*, p.45.
164 See JB to the Rev. Austin Lee, 13 February 1957 *(Victoria)* on this visit and on JB's correspondence with Bradford.
165 *Ibid.*
166 Humphrey Carpenter (author of *W.H. Auden: A Biography*, Allen & Unwin, London 1981), letter to the author, 6 October 1987.
167 J.M. Thompson, *Lectures in Foreign History*, Oxford University Press, 1925, p.330.
168 A.J.P. Taylor, *A Personal History*, Hamish Hamilton, London 1983, pp.82–83.
169 C.M. Bowra, in *Hugh Gaitskell, 1906–63*, ed. W.T. Rodgers, London 1964, p.20.
170 Quoted Emlyn Williams, *George*, Hamish Hamilton, London 1961, p.384.
171 Lancaster, *op. cit.*, p.69.
172 When Elizabeth Longford asked JB how she had got into a party he held for Lord Alfred Douglas in Oscar Wilde's old rooms at Magdalen, he replied: 'Oh, you were one of the aesthetes' molls . . .' (Elizabeth Longford, *The Pebbled Shore*, Weidenfeld & Nicolson, London 1986, p.68.)
173 A.J.P. Taylor, *English History 1914–1945*, Oxford University Press, 1965, p.260.
174 See A.J.P. Taylor, *A Personal History*, Hamish Hamilton, London 1983, p.140, on his Magdalen colleague K.B. McFarlane: '. . . like most homosexuals he was neurotic, easily involved with his pupils, for or against, and often emotional over college business.'
175 Lionel Perry, interview, 1979.
176 Professor J.E. Bowle, interview, 1976.
177 *Victoria.*
178 *Victoria.*
179 Michael Davie, 'The Bard of the Railway Gas-Lamp', *The Observer*, 15 October 1972.
180 *Ibid.*
181 JB to Pierce Synnott, 6 September 1927. *Pierce Synnott papers, Furness, Naas, Co. Kildare, Mr David Synnott.*
182 JB conversation with the author, 1974.
183 Alan Pryce-Jones, interview, 1976.
184 Ernest Betjemann to JB, 22 January 1928. *JBP.*

185 Ernest Betjemann to JB, 2 February 1928. *JBP*.
186 C.M. Bowra, *Memories 1898–1939*, Weidenfeld & Nicolson, London 1966, p.168.
187 JB, conversation with the author, 1976.
188 The document relating to this offer is in *Victoria*.
189 C.S. Lewis to JB, 18 September [1928]. *Duncan Andrews Collection*.
190 Sir Osbert Lancaster, interview, 1976.
191 JB to C.S. Lewis, 13 December 1939. *Victoria*.
192 *Ibid*.
193 G.R. Barcley-Smith, telephone conversation with the author, 23 April 1985.
194 A.H. Windrum to JB, 1928. *Victoria*.
195 A.H. Windrum to JB, September 1928. *Victoria*.
196 JB to J.E. Bowle, 17 May 1928. *Victoria*.
197 Edward James to JB, 31 May 1928. *JBP*.
198 Alan Pryce-Jones gives a less detailed account of the piano recitals in *The Bonus of Laughter*, Hamish Hamilton, London 1986, p.232.
199 Alan Pryce-Jones, interview, 1976.
200 'Business man' was a term that JB continued to use pejoratively – for example, in his early poem 'The City':

> Business men with awkward hips
> And dirty jokes upon their lips . . .

201 JB, 'The Artsenkrafts', *Oxford Outlook*, 1927.
202 Ernest Betjemann to JB, 9 March 1928. *JBP*.
203 Manager of Westminster Bank, Oxford, to Ernest Betjemann, 14 May 1928. *JBP*.
204 Ernest Betjemann to JB, nd but May 1928. *JBP*.
205 Ernest Betjemann to JB, 20 May 1928. *JBP*.
206 Ernest Betjemann to JB, 22 June 1928. *JBP*.
207 Ernest Betjemann to JB, 27 September 1928. *JBP*.
208 Ernest Betjemann to JB, 29 July 1928. *JBP*.
209 G.C. Lee to JB, 19 September 1928. *JBP*.
210 Lancaster, *op. cit.*, p.93.
211 Christopher Hobhouse (1910–1940), writer on architecture.

Chapter 10: The Stately Homes of Ireland

1 See for example Maurice Bowra to Pierce Synnott, 14 December 1925; and the poem he sent him on 3 April 1928. Both among *Pierce Synnott papers*.
2 *Ex inf.* Cyril Connolly to Patrick Balfour, January 1925. *Huntington*.
3 See *ibid*, in which Connolly asks Balfour: 'Would you mind awfully if I slept with Synnott . . . ? He must have a marvellous body.'
4 Pierce Synnott to Patrick Balfour, nd but from Balliol College, Oxford. *Huntington*.
5 See Mark Bence-Jones, *Burke's Guide to Country Houses*, vol. i, Ireland, Burke's Peerage, London 1978, p.129. I am also grateful to Mr David Synnott for his kind hospitality at Furness.
6 See Katharine Tynan, *Memories*, Everleigh, Nash & Grayson, London 1924, p.155.
7 Pierce Synnott to F.F. Urquhart, nd but written during the period of John's visit to Furness, ie June 1926. *Pierce Synnott papers*.
8 Bence-Jones, *op. cit.*, p.250.
9 Katharine Tynan's article survives in a cutting in the possession of Mr David Synnott at Furness, Naas, Co. Wicklow, Ireland. It was contributed to a paper called the . . . *Star*, 11 August 1926. (The first part of the paper's name is missing.)

10 Pierce Synnott to Lord Clonmore, nd but written during the period of JB's visit to Furness, ie June 1926. *Huntington*. (Clonmore had sent Synnott's letter on to Patrick Balfour.)

11 JB, interview, 1976.

12 Pierce Synnott to Lord Clonmore (see note 10).

13 Alan Pryce-Jones suggests in *The Bonus of Laughter* (Hamish Hamilton, London 1987, p.231) that not only did Ernest Betjemann have mistresses; he also contracted a bigamous marriage. '[John's] funeral was less sensational than that of his father, which took place in Chelsea Old Church. John was an only child, and while he and his mother were waiting for the ceremony to begin a scene occurred like that in the second act of *Der Rosenkavalier*. A second, unknown, Mrs Betjeman[n] suddenly irrupted with a second family, and it turned out that for many years Mr Betjeman[n] had lived a second and hitherto secret life.' If true, this might account for the bitter ending to John's 'Variation on a Theme by Newbolt', a poem about the death of an Ernest-like figure with a yacht and a shoot:

> ... my mind sees one thing only,
> A luxurious bedroom looking on miles of fir
> From a Surrey height where his widow sits silent and lonely
> For the man whose love seemed wholly given to her.

14 Pierce Synnott to Lord Clonmore (see note 10).

15 *Ibid*.

16 Pierce Synnott to Patrick Balfour, nd (but June 1926). *Huntington*.

17 Sir Hugh Lane was drowned in the *Lusitania* on 7 May 1915. A dispute followed as to whether he had intended to leave his paintings – mainly French nineteenth-century works – to the National Gallery, London (as in his will) or to the National Gallery of Ireland, Dublin (as in an unsigned codicil). In 1959 an agreement was concluded between the National Gallery, London, and the Commissioners of Public Works in Dublin that the Lane Collection should be loaned to Dublin, one half at a time, for successive periods of five years.

18 Pierce Synnott to Lord Clonmore (see note 10).

19 JB to Pierce Synnott, 21 June 1926. *Pierce Synnott papers*.

20 *Ibid*.

21 *Ibid*.

22 *Ex inf*. Maurice Bowra to Pierce Synnott, 25 July 1926. *Pierce Synnott papers*.

23 Rev. Canon Sir (George) Percy Maryon-Wilson, 12th Bart. (1898–1965). Educated Eton and Magdalen College, Oxford. Assistant Magdalen College Missioner 1924–27. Head of Magdalen College Mission 1927–41.

24 Maurice Bowra to Patrick Balfour, 11 January 1927. *Huntington*.

25 *Ibid*.

26 JB, interview, 1976.

27 See James Fox, *White Mischief*, Jonathan Cape, London 1982.

28 Eleanor, Countess of Wicklow, interview, 1978.

29 Quoted *ibid*.

30 Lord Clonmore to JB, September 1928. *Victoria*.

31 Lord Clonmore to JB, nd but probably 1928. *Victoria*.

32 JB to Pierce Synnott, 7 August 1927. *Pierce Synnott papers*.

33 *Ibid*.

34 *Ibid*.

35 Maurice Bowra to Pierce Synnott, 1 October 1927. *Pierce Synnott papers*.

36 JB to Pierce Synnott, 3 October 1927. *Pierce Synnott papers*. The nursing home no longer exists; possibly the operation was for sinus trouble.

37 *Ibid.*
38 *Ibid.*
39 Lord Clonmore to JB, 14 November 1927. *Victoria.*
40 See Mark Bence-Jones, *Burke's Guide to Country Houses*, vol. i, Ireland, Burke's Peerage, London 1978, p.83. I am also grateful to the Marquess and Marchioness of Dufferin and Ava for their kind hospitality at Clandeboye.
41 Harold Nicolson, *Helen's Tower*, Constable & Co., London 1937, p.56.
42 *Ibid*, p.76.
43 Caroline Blackwood, *Great Granny Webster*, Picador edn., London 1977, p.56.
44 *Ibid*, pp.64 and 70.
45 Edward James, interview, 1981.
46 Blackwood, *op. cit.*, p.77. Lady Caroline Blackwood has confirmed (telephone message to the author's sister, 1984) that her novel gives an accurate portrait of Brenda, Marchioness of Dufferin and Ava.
47 *Ibid*, p.79.
48 *Ibid*, p.75.
49 Edward James, interview, 1981.
50 JB to Lord Clonmore, September 1928. *Huntington.*
51 *Ibid.*

Chapter 11: 'H.P.'

1 Patrick Balfour to Lady Kinross, nd but March or April 1929. *National Library of Scotland.*
2 JB gave this information to Senator Trevor West of Dublin, author of the most recent book on Plunkett, *Horace Plunkett, Co-operation and Politics: an Irish Biography*, Colin Smythe 1986 (and Catholic University of America Press, Washington DC).
3 Balfour's letter does not necessarily contradict JB's recollection. Like the Dufferins, Heard was an Ulsterman. They moved in the same kind of society and it is possible that Lady Dufferin learnt from Heard that Plunkett was in need of a new secretary and put in a word for her son's friend.
4 Diary of Sir Horace Plunkett. *Plunkett Foundation, Oxford.*
5 Derek Stanford, *John Betjeman: a Study*, Neville Spearman, London 1961, p.22.
6 Quoted, *loc. cit.*
7 Plunkett is shown with the motor-car in the illustration opposite p.227 of Lady Fingall's *Seventy Years Young*, Collins, London 1937.
8 Professor J.E. Bowle, interview, 1981.
9 On cooperative creameries, see Margaret Digby, *Horace Plunkett*, Basil Blackwell, Oxford 1949.
10 Quoted West, *op. cit.*, respectively pp.101, 217 and again 217.
11 Quoted *ibid*, p.184.
12 Augusta, Lady Gregory (1852–1932), friend and patron of W.B. Yeats; author of plays and stories founded on Irish mythology.
13 Quoted West, *op. cit.*, p.91.
14 Robert Erskine Childers (1870–1922), Irish politician and author of *The Riddle of the Sands.*
15 Quoted West, *op. cit.*, p.200.
16 G.B. Shaw to Margaret Digby, 16 June 1948. *Plunkett Foundation.*
17 Sir Horace Plunkett to Charlotte Shaw, 14 March 1928. *Plunkett Foundation.*

18 George Moore (1852–1933), Irish novelist.
19 Quoted West, *op. cit.*, p.93.
20 George Moore, *Vale*, Heinemann, London 1937 edn., pp.148–49.
21 Lord Dunsany, *The Story of Mona Sheehy*, Heinemann, London 1929, p.317.
22 Quoted Digby, *op. cit.*, p.141.
23 Quoted *ibid*, p.96.
24 Professor J.E. Bowle, interview, 1981.
25 On the burning of Kilteragh, see Digby, *op. cit.*, p.255; Fingall, *op. cit.*, pp.417–18, and West, *op. cit.*, pp.203–6.
26 See Fingall, *op. cit.*, pp.423–24.
27 On Plunkett's roof shelter, or 'sleeping shed', see Clive Aslet, *The Last Country Houses*, Yale University Press, New Haven and London, 1982, pp.72–73.
28 JB's poem 'Camberley', about an Anglo-Indian colonel's bungalow, was published in *Mount Zion* (1931).
29 JB to Patrick Balfour, 10 February 1929. *Huntington*.
30 On the Countess of Huntingdon's Connection, see Basil Williams, *The Whig Supremacy, 1714–1760*, Oxford 1962 edn., p.96.
31 Diary of Sir Horace Plunkett. *Plunkett Foundation.*
32 Evelyn Waugh mentioned 'Birchington, where visitors who wish to may, with some difficulty, find his grave'. (*Rossetti, His Life and Works*, Duckworth, London 1928, p.220.)
33 On the person and character of Gerald Heard, see Sybille Bedford, *Aldous Huxley: a Biography*, Chatto & Windus, London 1973, i, pp.367–68 and ii, p.123; P.N. Furbank, *E.M. Forster: a Life*, Secker & Warburg, London 1978, ii, 136; Christopher Isherwood, *Down There on a Visit*, London 1979, Magnum edn., pp.190–91; and Christopher Isherwood, *My Guru and His Disciple*, Eyre Methuen, London 1980, Magnum edn., pp.76, 168 and 296.
34 See Sybille Bedford, *op. cit.*, i, p.367.
35 Humphrey Carpenter, *W.H. Auden: a Biography*, Allen & Unwin, London 1981, p.136.
36 Professor J.E. Bowle, interview, 1981.
37 Quoted, *ibid*.
38 Quoted, Christopher Isherwood, *My Guru and His Disciple*, Eyre Methuen, London 1980, Magnum edn., p.88.
39 *The Diaries of Evelyn Waugh*, ed. Michael Davie, Weidenfeld & Nicolson, London 1976, p.321. (The diary entry is for 8 July 1930.)
40 JB, 'Which Shall Die?', *Evening Standard*, 27 July 1935.
41 Horace Plunkett, *Ireland in the New Century*, John Murray, London 1904, p.26.
42 Digby, *op. cit.*, p.271.
43 *UP*, pp.39–40.
44 Digby, *op. cit.*, p.96.
45 Diary of Sir Horace Plunkett. *Plunkett Foundation.*
46 *Ibid.*
47 *Ibid.*
48 *Ibid.*
49 *Ibid.*
50 *Ibid*, 7 March 1929.
51 Sir Horace Plunkett to JB, 19 March 1929. *JBP.*
52 Professor J.E. Bowle, interview, 1981.
53 Diary of Sir Horace Plunkett. *Plunkett Foundation.*
54 JB had failed to pay the fine levied for a driving offence.
55 On 13 February 1929 JB and Plunkett took the night sleeper to Newcastle-upon-

Tyne, where there was snow on the ground. They returned to London on 15 February, then drove down to The Crest House, Weybridge, 'in biting cold weather'. (Diary of Sir Horace Plunkett. *Plunkett Foundation*.)

56 Ernest Betjemann to JB, 16 February 1929. *JBP*.
57 Ernest Betjemann to JB, 22 February 1929. *JBP*.
58 JB to Ernest Betjemann *(not sent)*, 25 February 1929. *JBP*.
59 Ernest Betjemann to JB, 8 March 1929. *JBP*.
60 *Ibid*.
61 Diary of Sir Horace Plunkett. *Plunkett Foundation*.
62 Sir Horace Plunkett to JB, 19 March 1929. *JBP*.
63 On Lionel Edwards, watercolourist, see Chapter 9, note 103.
64 JB, 'Hertfordshire'.

Chapter 12: Heddon Court

1 The card was returned to him and is among his papers.
2 Michael Parkinson Show, BBC Television, 17 February 1983.
3 JB published a long quotation from 'L.E.L.' on 'Manchester' in *AR*, July 1931, p.29.
4 Ashmole wrote in his diary (11 July 1635): 'I came to live at Mount Pleasant, neere Barnet, & staied the rest of the summer.' (*Elias Ashmole 1617–1692. His Autobiographical and Historical Notes, etc.*, ed. C.H. Iosten, Oxford 1966, ii, p.319.)
5 Gavin Maxwell, *The House of Elrig*, Longman, London 1965, p.65.
6 Sir John Addis, interview, 1981.
7 David Soltau, interview, 1981.
8 Introduction to *GGT*, p.xxiv.
9 *Loc. cit.*
10 *Loc. cit.*
11 Kenric Rice, interview, 1981.
12 David Soltau, interview, 1981.
13 Canon Paul Miller, interview, 1981.
14 *Ibid*.
15 James Orr, interview, 1981.
16 Canon Paul Miller, interview, 1981.
17 Ann Wolff, *The Grand Master Plan*, Marion Boyars, London 1985.
18 JB inscribed these catcalls in the copy of *Mount Zion* which he presented to J.H. Hope ('from James Joyce and the author') in 1931. The copy is now in Ann Wolff's possession.
19 Ann Wolff, letter to the author, 18 January 1985.
20 Ann Wolff, letter to the author, 6 February 1985.
21 James Orr, interview, 1981.
22 Mrs Walter Moule, interview, 1981.
23 Kenric Rice, interview, 1981.
24 Quoted by Dr George Gomez (a Betjeman pupil at Heddon Court), interview, 1981. A description of Mr Summers's boxing matches is given in Ann Wolff, *op. cit.*
25 Mrs Walter Moule, interview, 1981.
26 *Ibid*.
27 JB to Patrick Balfour, 9 December 1929. *Huntington*.
28 *Mr Perrin and Mr Traill* is a novel of 1911 by Hugh Walpole. It concerns the bitter rivalry of two prep-school masters, one of whom tries to kill the other but is himself drowned. JB again mentioned the book in *AR*, April 1931 (writing under the pseudonym 'Lionel Cuffe').

29 JB to Patrick Balfour, 10 February 1930. *Huntington*.
30 Mrs Walter Moule, interview, 1981.
31 *Ibid*. On Jack Malden, see Gavin Maxwell, *The House of Elrig*, Longman, London 1965, p.62.
32 *Ibid*.
33 Shown to the author by Mrs Walter Moule, 1981.
34 Walter Moule had been a schoolboy at Lancing with Tom Driberg, Roger Fulford and Evelyn Waugh. He was the same age as Waugh. 'I couldn't stand him,' Mr Moule said. (Interview, 1981.)
35 Shown to the author by Mrs Walter Moule, 1981.
36 *Ibid*.
37 Mrs Walter Moule, interview, 1981.
38 Shown to the author by Mrs Walter Moule, 1981.
39 *Ibid*.
40 Miss Zeglio was matron of the Sir John Lister Nursing Home, where Walter Moule's father was a patient.
41 Shown to the author by Mrs Walter Moule, 1981.
42 Mrs Walter Moule, interview, 1981.
43 *Ibid*.
44 Shown to the author by Mrs Walter Moule, 1981.
45 *Ibid*.
46 *Ibid*.
47 Mrs Walter Moule, interview, 1981.
48 Sir Jasper Hollom, interview, 1981.
49 *Ibid*.
50 Sir John Addis, interview, 1981.
51 Dr George Gomez, interview, 1981.
52 Sir John Addis, interview, 1981.
53 Evelyn Waugh, *A Little Learning*, Chapman & Hall, London 1964, p.225.
54 Christopher Sykes, *Evelyn Waugh*, Collins, London 1975, p.69.
55 Sir Jasper Hollom, interview, 1981.
56 Canon Paul Miller, interview, 1981.
57 David Soltau to his parents, 13 October 1929. *Mr Soltau*.
58 Dr George Gomez, interview, 1981.
59 Sir Jasper Hollom, interview, 1981.
60 Robert Vernon Harcourt to JB, 20 May 1959. *Victoria*.
61 James Orr, interview, 1981.
62 Bryans was an American. On 9 June 1929 David Soltau wrote to his parents: 'Yesterday was Bryans's birthday. He was ten. He had a very big cake.' *(Mr Soltau.)*
63 David Soltau to his parents, nd but Summer Term 1929. *Mr Soltau*.
64 Vincent Hollom, letter to the author, 18 August 1981.
65 Alan Nightingale, interview, 1981.
66 Canon Paul Miller, interview, 1981.
67 *Ibid*.
68 Vachel Lindsay, *The Congo and Other Poems*, The Macmillan Company, New York, 1915, pp. 3–4.
69 Edith Sitwell's book *Alexander Pope* was published by the Chiswick Press in 1930.

70 Canon Paul Miller, interview, 1981.
71 James Orr, interview, 1981.
72 Mrs Walter Moule, interview, 1981.
73 Robert Hunter to JB, 1 June 1944. *Victoria.*
74 Roger Roughton to JB, nd. *Victoria.*
75 Robert Vernon Harcourt to JB, 20 May 1959. *Victoria.*
76 Dr George Gomez, interview, 1981.
77 James Orr, interview, 1981.
78 *Ibid.*
79 David Soltau to his parents, 27 June 1929. *Mr Soltau.*
80 Kenric Rice, interview, 1981.
81 *Ibid.*
82 Words by Bud de Sylva, music by Ray Henderson (1928).
83 JB to Kenric Rice, 31 March 1981. *Mr Rice.*
84 Canon Paul Miller, interview, 1981.
85 *Ibid.*
86 *Ibid.*
87 *Mary Lee* by Geoffrey Dennis was published by Heinemann in 1922. One passage in it influenced JB's poetry. (See Chapter 16.)
88 Canon Paul Miller, interview, 1981.
89 In 1969 JB replied to Miller's congratulations on his knighthood with a letter which began:
'Dear and Saintly Canon,
I am so glad you *are* a canon.

'Knight = Canon
Bart = Residentiary Canon
Baron = Archdeacon
Viscount = Dean
Earl = Suffragan
Marquess = Bishop
Duke = Archbishop.
'You are above me: you are residentiary. Quite right, too . . .'
(Canon Miller.)
90 On 16 November 1930 David Soltau told his parents that Mr Hunter Blair (a master who had arrived at the school in September 1929) 'has bought a very large 8-cylinder 27hp Hupmobile. It is painted blue and has central heating under the back seat.' *(Mr Soltau.)* JB had left the school by then, but he made a number of return visits to the Hopes and no doubt heard about or saw the Hupmobile. He mentioned that make of car in his later poem 'Indoor Games near Newbury'.
91 Manuscript in *Victoria.*
92 Alan Nightingale, interview, 1981.
93 David Soltau to his parents, 30 March 1930. *Mr Soltau.*
94 Jasper Hollom to Alan Nightingale, 2 January 1930. *Mr Nightingale.*
95 Quoted by Sir Jasper Hollom, interview, 1981.
96 David Soltau to his parents, 30 March 1930. *Mr Soltau.*
97 Vincent Hollom, letter to the author, 18 August 1981. The film *Mädchen in Uniform* (1931), directed by Leontine Sagan for Deutsche Film-Gemeinschaft, was based on a story by Baroness Havatny (Christa Winsloe) about a schoolgirl, Manuela, who falls in love with one of her women teachers and ultimately commits suicide by plunging down a stairwell. As film critic of the *Evening Standard* in 1934, JB praised *Mädchen in Uniform* in the issues of 10 February and 22 August.
98 Nancy Price (1880–1970) played the part of Mrs Jones in Galsworthy's *The Silver Box*

(first London performance 1906) for 114 performances from 24 January 1931 at the Fortune Theatre, London, and again in October 1932 at the Little Theatre, London.
99 Sir John Addis, interview, 1981.
100 *Ibid*. Joseph Moncure March's *The Wild Party*, published by Martin Secker in 1928, was a book-length poem. Its possible influence on JB's poetry is discussed in Chapter 16.
101 *Ibid*.
102 Vincent Hollom, letter to the author, 18 August 1981.

Chapter 13: Archie Rev

1 James Lees-Milne, *Another Self*, Hamish Hamilton, London 1970, p.93.
2 *Ibid*, p.94.
3 *Loc. cit.*
4 See C.M. Bowra, *Memories 1898–1939*, Weidenfeld & Nicolson, London 1966, p.211.
5 Rosemary Crane, whose family were paper manufacturers in Massachusetts.
6 Alan Pryce-Jones, interview, 1976.
7 Lees-Milne, *op. cit.*, p.95.
8 Alan Pryce-Jones, interview, 1976.
9 JB, 'H. de C.: Betjeman recalls', *AR*, vol.155, February 1974, p.120.
10 'I start work on October 1st . . .' JB to Patrick Balfour, 21 September 1930. *Huntington*.
11 Sir Hugh Casson, 'The Elusive H. de C.', *RIBA Journal*, February 1971, p.58.
12 See Sir Percy Hastings, letter to the editor of *AR*, December 1932, p.305.
13 Sir Hugh Casson, 'The Elusive H. de C.', *RIBA Journal*, February 1971, p.58.
14 J.M. Richards, *Memoirs of an Unjust Fella*, Weidenfeld & Nicolson, London 1980, p.90.
15 John Piper, interview, 1982.
16 *Ibid*.
17 Sir John Summerson, interview, 1984.
18 Sir James Richards, interview, 1982.
19 Sir Hugh Casson, 'The Elusive H. de C.', *RIBA Journal*, February 1971, p.58.
20 *Loc. cit.*
21 *Ibid*, pp.58–59.
22 JB to Edward Carter, 7 March 1932, reproduced in David Dean, *The Thirties: Recalling the English Architectural Scene*, Trefoil Books, London 1983, p.80.
23 Sir James Richards, interview, 1982.
24 John Piper, interview, 1982.
25 Richard Holmes, conversation with the author, 1982.
26 *Ibid*.
27 Richard Holmes later became China Correspondent of *The Times*, London.
28 Richard Holmes, letter to the author, 27 March 1981.
29 Sir James Richards, interview, 1982.
30 'Jaggers was simply Hastings's adaptation – admittedly rather a far-fetched one – of the name "John Betjeman", the ending of course being that commonly employed for the ending of cant words in the 1920s and 1930s, e.g. "champers" [for champagne].' Sir James Richards to the author, 26 January 1985.
31 H. de Cronin Hastings to JB, 14 March 1938. *Victoria*.
32 Sir James Richards, interview, 1982. John did not in fact leave the Society of Friends until March 1937; but he may have been going through an 'extreme Anglo-Catholic . . . phase' well before that.

33 Sir James Pennethorne (1801–71). English architect and government planner.
34 J.M. Richards, *op. cit.*, p.91.
35 Alan Pryce-Jones, 'Museum Piece', *The London Mercury*, vol. xxviii, no.163, May 1933, pp.46–48.
36 James Lees-Milne also remembered 'planting' exhibits with John. See his *Prophesying Peace*, Chatto & Windus, London 1977, p.5.
37 Christian Barman died on 5 October 1980. See his obituary in *The Times*, 11 October 1980, p.14.
38 Sir James Richards, interview, 1982. Richards's recollection of Hastings 'shouting around the building' might seem to contradict JB's view of him as 'Obscurity' Hastings, but it was only strangers Hastings fought shy of; to his colleagues, he was sometimes an aggressive presence.
39 *Ibid.*
40 JB, 'H. de C.: Betjeman recalls', *AR*, vol. 155, February 1974, p.120.
41 A.E. Doyle to JB, 27 September 1932. *Victoria*.
42 JB to Patrick Balfour, 8 December 1931. *Huntington*.
43 Sir James Richards, interview, 1982.
44 Peter Quennell, 'Picture of a Poet', *Sunday Telegraph*, 28 October 1984.
45 Quoted, Susan Barnes (Crosland), ' "Betjeman, I bet your racket brings you in a pretty packet" ', *Sunday Times Magazine*, 30 January 1972, p.13.
46 *Loc. cit.*
47 *AR*, vol. 66, December 1929, p.297.
48 Quoted in Jonathan Glancy's obituary of JB, *Architect's Journal*, 30 May 1984, p.28. I am grateful to Mr Simon Garwood for drawing this to my attention.
49 JB, 'Mackay Hugh Baillie Scott', *The Journal of the Manx Museum*, vol. vii, no. 84, 1968, p.77.
50 Mackay Hugh Baillie Scott (1865–1945), British architect associated with the Arts and Crafts Movement.
51 This is confirmed by JB's article in *AR*, May 1930, p.240.
52 JB, 'Mackay Hugh Baillie Scott', *The Journal of the Manx Museum*, vol. vii, no. 84, 1968, p.77.
53 Verse shown to the author by John Gloag, 1980.
54 J.M. Richards, *op. cit.*, pp.123–24.
55 A caption JB wrote for two illustrations of buildings by Voysey and Walton, as accompaniment to an article by Clough Williams-Ellis in *AR*, May 1934, claimed Walton and Voysey as 'pioneers of what, in architecture and design generally, we consider "Modern" . . .'
56 In his *AR* article of May 1930, JB wrote of Morris's 'lovely poem, "The Message of the March Wind",' and quoted from it.
57 Lady Betjeman gave the author the catalogue of this sale, in which JB had marked bids against certain lots.
58 JB, 'Mackay Hugh Baillie Scott,' *The Journal of the Manx Museum*, vol. vii, no. 84, 1968, p.77.
59 *Ibid*, p.78.
60 *Loc. cit.*
61 JB, 'Charles Francis Annesley Voysey: The Architect of Individualism', *AR*, vol. 70, October 1931, p.96.
62 C.F.A. Voysey, '1874 and After', *AR*, vol. 70, October 1931, p.92.
63 Sir Edwin Lutyens, Foreword, *AR*, vol. 70, October 1931, p.91.
64 JB, 'Mackay Hugh Baillie Scott', *The Journal of the Manx Museum*, vol. vii, no. 84, 1968, p.77.
65 Introduction to *GGT*, 1970 edn., p.xxvi.

66 JB, 'A preservationist's progress', in *The Future of the Past*, ed. Jane Fawcett, Thames & Hudson, London 1976, p.57.

67 JB, 'Mackay Hugh Baillie Scott', *The Journal of the Manx Museum*, vol. vii, no. 84, 1968, p.78.

68 *Loc. cit.*

69 *Loc. cit.*

70 *Loc. cit.*

71 *Loc. cit.*

72 *Loc. cit.*

73 JB, 'Baillie Scott and Beresford', *AR*, vol. 73, May 1933, p.206.

74 Edward Walton to the author, 4 October 1982.

75 *Ibid.*

76 See papers filed under 'George Walton'. *Victoria.*

77 The obituary is on p.36 of the January 1934 issue.

78 JB to Canon Peter Bourne, 29 October 1975. Copy in *JBP.*

79 JB, obituary of Frederick Etchells, *AR*, vol. 154, October 1973, p.271.

80 On the impact made by the translation, see John Brandon-Jones, interviewed by Gavin Stamp, *Architectural Design*, vol. 49, nos. 10–11, 1979, p.97.

81 J.M. Richards (*op. cit.*, p.122) considers Etchells's office building for Crawford's the first English building of the Modern Movement 'if we except a few small houses that were not part of any concerted movement, and if we except Sir Owen Williams's concrete and glass factory at Nottingham, which was unseen by the public and hardly regarded as a work of architecture.'

82 JB, 'A preservationist's progress', in *The Future of the Past*, ed. Jane Fawcett, Thames & Hudson, London 1976, p.57.

83 See introduction to *GGT*, 1970 edn., p.xxvi.

84 *AR*, vol. 72, July 1932, p.40.

85 JB, obituary of Frederick Etchells, *AR*, vol. 154, October 1973, p.271.

86 Quoted C.M. Bowra, *Memories 1898–1939*, Weidenfeld & Nicolson, London 1966, p.165.

87 On his life and career see Alan Powers, 'Goodhart-Rendel: the Appropriateness of Style', *Architectural Design*, vol. 49, nos. 10–11, 1979, p.44.

88 Quoted *ibid*, p.44.

89 JB, conversation with the author, 1971.

90 As John Summerson confirmed to Gavin Stamp, *Architectural Design*, vol. 49, nos. 10–11, p.101, note 4.

91 *AA Journal*, vol. 54, p.67.

92 Sir John Summerson, interview, 1984.

93 Summerson's earliest correspondence with JB was about Nash. See Summerson's letter to JB of 3 May 1933. *Victoria.*

94 Coolmore was the seat of Summerson's mother's family, the Newenhams, in Co. Cork, Ireland.

95 F.R. Yerbury, photographer and author of books on modern architecture such as *Modern European Buildings*, Victor Gollancz, London 1928.

96 JB to Michael Dugdale, 17 December 1931. *Victoria.*

97 *AR*, February 1974, p.120.

98 Quoted, David Dean, *The Thirties: Recalling the English Architectural Scene*, Trefoil Books, London 1983, p.113.

99 *Architectural Design*, vol. 49, nos. 10–11, p.98.

100 *Loc. cit.*

101 JB, 'Dictating to the Railways', *AR*, vol. 74, September 1933, p.84.

102 *Loc. cit.*

103 *AR*, vol. 74, September 1933, opposite p.105.
104 Brian Howard, 'Anglo-German Art', *AR*, vol. 68, November 1930, p.219.
105 R.H. Wilenski, letter to the editor of *AR*, vol. 68, December 1930, p.270.
106 *AR*, vol. 70, November 1931, opposite p.140.
107 *AR*, vol. 74, no. 444, November 1933, p.209.
108 *Loc. cit.*
109 *Ibid*, p.210.
110 JB, 'Architecture', *The London Mercury*, November 1933.
111 R. Morris to JB, 1960. *Victoria*.
112 Sir James Richards, interview, 1982.
113 *FLL*, p.141.
114 *AR*, vol. 72, September 1932, p.106.
115 From Stephen Spender, 'The Pylons', *Poems 1933*, quoted in *AR*, vol. 74, October 1933, opposite p.158.
116 *AR*, vol. 74, October 1933, opposite p.190.
117 JB, 'Inexpensive Progress'.
118 George Mansell to JB, nd. *Victoria*.
119 JB to George Mansell, 8 January 1957. *Victoria*.
120 *GGT*, p.58.
121 JB, *Antiquarian Prejudice*, Hogarth Press, London 1939, pp.16–17.
122 Sir John Summerson, introduction to Trevor Dannatt, *Modern Architecture in Britain*, Batsford, London 1959, p.15.
123 P. Morton Shand to JB, 21 October 1958. *Major Bruce Shand*.
124 *Ibid*.
125 JB to H. de Cronin Hastings, nd. *Victoria*.

Chapter 14: With the Bright Young People

1 Quoted by Lionel Perry, interview, 1979.
2 Lord Kinross: 'The Years with Kinross: 4. Youth', *Punch*, 16 August 1961, p.246.
3 Quoted, *loc. cit.*
4 i.e. the area around Brompton Road, in which the Victoria and Albert Museum stands.
5 Lord Kinross, 'The Years with Kinross: 4. Youth', *Punch*, 16 August 1961, p.246.
6 Cyril Connolly to Patrick Balfour, nd but datable to about June 1928. *Huntington*.
7 Cyril Connolly, *The Evening Colonnade*, David Bruce & Watson, London 1973, p.240.
8 Connolly's first signed appearance in print was an article on a seven-volume edition of Sterne's works, in the *New Statesman* of 25 June 1927. On 31 July 1927 he wrote to tell Patrick Balfour (*Huntington*) that Desmond MacCarthy, the magazine's literary editor, had invited him to become a regular reviewer of novels. 'A signed review once a fortnight . . . It means I shall have at least £10 a week.'
9 Bess Betjemann to Patrick Balfour, 7 February (?1930). *Huntington*.
10 Patrick Balfour to Lady Kinross, nd but March or April 1929. *National Library of Scotland*.
11 Roger Roughton to Patrick Balfour, 14 February 1932. *Huntington*.
12 Pseudonyms have been used for both 'Sheldon' brothers.
13 JB to Patrick Balfour, 2 December 1929. *Huntington*.
14 'Marcus Sheldon' to Patrick Balfour, 10 February 1930. *Huntington*.

15 JB to Lord Kinross, 22 November 1949. *Huntington*.
16 Elizabeth, Countess of Longford, interview, 1976.
17 Claude Allin Shepperson (1867–1921), *Punch* artist, book illustrator, water-colourist and Associate of the Royal Academy.
18 JB to Patrick Balfour, August 1929. *Huntington*.
19 JB to Patrick Balfour, 10 February 1929. *Huntington*.
20 Lady Mary Dunn, interview, 1984.
21 *Ibid.*
22 *Ibid.*
23 Harold Acton, *Nancy Mitford*, Hamish Hamilton, London 1975, p.28.
24 Sir (Charles) Michael (Robert Vivian) Duff, the 3rd baronet, who succeeded to his title in 1914 when he was seven.
25 John de Forest, later Count John de Bendern. Amateur golf champion in 1930 and 1931.
26 Daphne Fielding, *Mercury Presides*, Eyre & Spottiswoode, London 1954, p.160.
27 Sir (Mark Tatton) Richard Sykes, the 7th baronet.
28 Fielding, *loc. cit.*
29 *Loc. cit.*
30 Lady Mary St Clair-Erskine to JB, nd but 1929. *JBP*.
31 Lady Mary Dunn, interview, 1984.
32 Angela Brazil (1869–1947), author of novels about life in girls' boarding schools.
33 The copy of *Mount Zion* is in Lady Mary Dunn's possession and was shown by her to the author, 1984.
34 Lady Mary Dunn, interview, 1984.
35 The photograph of Lady Mary by Lord Rothschild is reproduced at Plate 29.
36 JB to Lady Mary Dunn, 1978. *Lady Mary Dunn*.
37 JB to Patrick Balfour, 31 July 1929. *Huntington*.
38 JB to Patrick Balfour, 5 August 1929. *Huntington*.
39 Sir John Addis, interview, 1981.
40 *Ibid.*
41 In 1981 the visitors' book was in the possession of Sir John Addis.
42 *Cf.* JB's poem 'Thoughts in a Train' (*UP*, p.37):

> But why, if she's somebody's mistress,
>   Is she travelling up in a third?
> Her luggage is leather, not plastic,
>   Her jewelry rich and absurd . . .

43 JB to Patrick Balfour, 17 August 1929. *Huntington*.
44 Mrs M. Geddes, interview, 1983.
45 JB to Lady Kinross, 16 September 1929. *National Library of Scotland*.
46 *Ibid.*
47 Pierce Synnott to Patrick Balfour, 25 September 1929. *Huntington*.
48 Patrick Balfour to Lady Kinross, 29 October 1929. *National Library of Scotland*.
49 Patrick Balfour to Lady Kinross, 3 January 1930. *National Library of Scotland*.
50 JB to Patrick Balfour, 9 December 1929. *Huntington*.
51 *Ex inf.* Professor J.E. Bowle, letter to the author, 29 August 1978.
52 Sir Angus Wilson, conversation with the author, 1977.
53 JB was a friend of Harold Nicolson's by 23 December 1931, when Nicolson wrote him a letter on the headed writing-paper of *Action*, the magazine of Sir Oswald Mosley's New Movement: 'My dear Betj, It was very polite of you to send me a Collins and a poem. I like good manners in the young. Hobvilla [Christopher Hobhouse], for instance, is a polite young man – though not, as

you may have gained from the telephone, lavish in his politeness. I did not observe that you were drunk on Monday – yet otherwise how could you have celebrated the auspicious return of [Christopher] Sykes? . . . I loved your poem. But was it in the best of taste? Yours ever, Harold. PS. I was at Wellington College.' *(Victoria)* JB may have sent Nicolson one of his 'indecent poems'.

54 Quoted by Professor J.E. Bowle, conversation, 1981.
55 *Ibid.*
56 Quoted by Edward James, interview, 1981.
57 Sir Osbert Lancaster, interview, 1976.
58 JB to Patrick Balfour, 15 April 1930. *Huntington.*
59 Introduction to *GGT*, 1970 edn., p.xxv.
60 *The Diaries of Evelyn Waugh*, ed. Michael Davie, Weidenfeld & Nicolson, London 1976, p.311.
61 *Ibid*, p.316.
62 *Loc. cit.*
63 See the example quoted by Waugh, *loc. cit.*
64 Camilla Sykes, interview, 1978.
65 *Ibid.*
66 JB to Camilla Russell, 6 August 1930. *Victoria.*
67 JB to Camilla Russell, 12 August 1930. *Victoria.*
68 JB to Patrick Balfour, 18 August 1930. *Huntington.*
69 Alan Pryce-Jones to Patrick Balfour, 7 August 1930. *Huntington.*
70 JB to Camilla Russell, 23 August 1930. *Victoria.*
71 Maurice Bowra to Patrick Balfour, 23 August 1930. *Huntington.*
72 Camilla Russell to JB, 1931. *Victoria.*
73 JB to Camilla Russell, August 1931. *Victoria.*
74 JB to Camilla Russell, 2 September 1931. *Victoria.*
75 JB to Camilla Russell, 1931. *Victoria.*
76 See Chapter 15, Pakenham Hall.
77 JB to Camilla Russell, 23 August 1931. *Victoria.*
78 *Ibid.*
79 JB to Camilla Russell, 26 August 1931. *Victoria.*
80 JB to Camilla Russell, 29 August 1931. *Victoria.*
81 JB to Camilla Russell, 26 August 1931. *Victoria.*
82 *Ibid.*
83 *Ibid.*
84 JB to Camilla Russell, 21 December 1931. *Victoria.*
85 JB to Camilla Russell, 2 October 1931. *Victoria.*
86 *Ibid.*
87 JB to Camilla Russell, 17 October 1931. *Victoria.*
88 JB to Camilla Russell, 2 October 1931. *Victoria.*
89 JB to Camilla Russell, 29 September 1931. *Victoria.*
90 Sir Osbert Lancaster, interview, 1976.
91 On Peter Watson, see Hugo Vickers, *Cecil Beaton*, Weidenfeld & Nicolson, London 1985, Chapter 12, 'I Love You, Mr Watson'.
92 Camilla Sykes, interview, 1978.
93 Camilla Russell to JB, 23 October 1931. *Victoria.*
94 Camilla Russell to JB, 1 November 1931. *Victoria.*
95 *Ibid.*
96 *Ibid.*
97 JB to Camilla Russell, 22 November 1931. *Victoria.*
98 *Ibid.*

99 JB to Camilla Russell, August 1931. *Victoria.*
100 JB to Camilla Russell, 4 September 1931. *Victoria.*
101 JB to Camilla Russell, 22 November 1931. *Victoria.*
102 Camilla Russell to JB, 4 December 1931. *Victoria.*
103 *Ex inf.* Camilla Sykes, interview, 1978.
104 *Ibid.*
105 *Ibid.*
106 Pamela Jackson (*née* Mitford), interview, 1983.
107 *Ibid.*
108 David Pryce-Jones, *Unity Mitford: A Quest*, Weidenfeld & Nicolson, London 1976, p.47.
109 Quoted *ibid*, p.48.
110 Pamela Jackson, interview, 1983.
111 *Ex inf.* Pamela Jackson.
112 Sir Peter Scarlett (1905–88), son of William James Yorke Scarlett of Fyfield House, Andover. British Ambassador to Norway (1955) and HM Minister to the Holy See (1960–65).
113 Pamela Jackson, interview, 1983.
114 Sir Osbert Lancaster, interview, 1976. Selina Hastings writes of Lord Redesdale (*Nancy Mitford*, Hamish Hamilton, London 1985, p.59): 'He despised and disliked . . . effeminate young men who didn't know one end of a gun from the other, and he made no effort to conceal his dislike. "Sewer" was his favourite epithet when referring to them: "Damned sewers!".'
115 Lady Chetwode to PC, quoted by the latter in a letter to JB, nd but June 1933. *PBP.*
116 Pamela Jackson, interview, 1983.
117 Noël Coward's patriotic play of 1932, which celebrated British history during the first thirty years of the century.
118 Maskelyne & Devant's Magic Show. Pamela's father and her uncle George Bowles were keen amateur conjurors and members of the Magic Circle, and attended 'Maskelyne's' every week in the Christmas season, often taking Nancy and Pamela.
119 In the possession of Pamela Jackson.
120 Pamela Jackson commented on this sentence: 'He was Russian, not Czech – Serge Orloff, who joined the "Wavy Navy" during the [Second World] War and married an English girl. I was very fond of him – not, again, from the marrying point of view.' (Wavy Navy: slang term for the former Royal Naval Volunteer Reserve whose officers wore gold distinction lace in wavy lines instead of straight, as worn on the sleeves of regular officers in the 'Straight Navy'.)
121 JB to Diana Mitford, 27 February 1932. *Pamela Jackson.*
122 JB to Nancy Mitford, 19 April 1932. *Deborah, Duchess of Devonshire.*
123 Nancy Mitford wrote to Mark Ogilvie-Grant in 1931: 'My new book *[Christmas Pudding]* is jolly good, all about Hamish [Erskine] at Eton. "All father's sisters married well thank God" is his opening remark. Betjeman is co-hero.' *Deborah, Duchess of Devonshire.* The author is indebted to Lady Selina Hastings for drawing his attention to this reference.
124 Nancy Mitford, *Christmas Pudding*, Hamish Hamilton, London 1975 edn., p.172.

Chapter 15: Pakenham Hall

1 Pakenham Hall is now called Tullynally Castle. Mr Thomas Pakenham, who lives there with his family, felt that the house should be known by its original Irish name.

2 Bess Betjemann to JB, 3 April 1931. *JBP.*
3 Bess Betjemann to JB, August 1931. *JBP.*
4 JB, 'Francis Johnston, Irish Architect', *The Pavilion*, ed. Myfanwy Evans, I.T. Publications, London 1946, pp.21–38.
5 Violet Powell, *Five out of Six*, Heinemann, London 1960, p.234.
6 *Ibid*, p.235.
7 Christine, Countess of Longford, unpublished memoirs. *Lady Mary Clive.*
8 *Ibid.*
9 Anthony Powell, *To Keep the Ball Rolling*, vol. iii, 'Faces in My Time', Heinemann, London 1980, p.15.
10 JB, *The English Town in the Last Hundred Years*, Cambridge University Press, 1956, p.4.
11 Violet Powell, *op. cit.*, pp.235–36.
12 See Elizabeth Longford, *The Pebbled Shore*, Weidenfeld & Nicolson, London 1986, p.102.
13 Quoted Anthony Powell, *op. cit.*, p.7.
14 Quoted, Christine Longford, unpublished memoirs.
15 See Barbara Leaming, *Orson Welles*, Viking, New York 1985, p.42.
16 Micheál MacLiammóir, *All for Hecuba*, Branden Press, Boston, Mass., 1967, p.123. (The book was originally published by Methuen, London, in 1961; the American edn. of 1967 was revised, with extra material.)
17 Christine Longford, unpublished memoirs.
18 *Ibid.*
19 Evelyn Waugh, obituary of Edward, Earl of Longford, *The Observer*, London, 2 December 1961.
20 JB to Christine, Countess of Longford, 19 September 1930. *Lady Mary Clive.*
21 Mr Thomas Pakenham kindly transcribed the relevant entries in the Pakenham visitors' book in a letter to the author, 15 October 1985.
22 JB to Patrick Balfour, 1 September 1930. *Huntington.*
23 JB to Patrick Balfour, 13 September 1930. *Huntington.*
24 *The Diaries of Evelyn Waugh*, ed. Michael Davie, Weidenfeld & Nicolson, London 1976, p.328.
25 Lord Pakenham, *Born to Believe*, Jonathan Cape, London 1953, p.62.
26 Christine Longford, unpublished memoirs.
27 *Ibid.*
28 *The Diaries of Evelyn Waugh*, ed. Michael Davie, Weidenfeld & Nicolson, London 1976, p.328.
29 Christine Longford, unpublished memoirs. I have taken the liberty of combining her recollections of the singing as recorded in the original manuscript of her memoirs (shown to me by Mr Thomas Pakenham) and the slightly different typewritten version shown to me by Lady Mary Clive.
30 Recalled by JB, interview, 1976.
31 *Ibid.*
32 Elizabeth, Countess of Longford, interview, 1976.
33 Lady Mary Clive, conversation with the author, 1980.
34 Christine Longford, unpublished memoirs.
35 Christine Longford, interview, 1979.
36 *Ibid.*
37 JB, interview, 1976.
38 In the spring of 1800 the Irish parliament voted away its own existence and England and Ireland were united under one legislature at Westminster.
39 *The Grand Juries of the County of Westmeath*, John Charles Lyons, Ledestown,

Ireland 1853, ii, p.60.

40 JB to Patrick Balfour, 1 September 1930. *Huntington.*

41 JB to Patrick Balfour, 13 September 1930. *Huntington.*

42 *The Diaries of Evelyn Waugh*, ed. Michael Davie, Weidenfeld & Nicolson, London 1976, p.328.

43 *Loc. cit.*

44 JB, interview, 1976.

45 Lord Stanley of Alderley, 1907–1971. On 3 March 1932 he married Penelope Chetwode's cousin Lady Audrey Talbot.

46 JB to Christine Longford, 29 September 1930. *Lady Mary Clive.*

47 Maria Edgeworth, quoted in Marilyn Butler, *Maria Edgeworth: A Literary Biography*, Oxford University Press, 1972, p.97.

48 Christine Longford, unpublished memoirs.

49 JB to Christine Longford, 1933. *Lady Mary Clive.*

50 Evelyn Waugh, obituary of Edward, Earl of Longford, *The Observer*, London, 2 December 1961.

51 JB to Christine Longford, 16 September 1930. *Lady Mary Clive.*

52 JB to Christine Longford, 19 September 1930. *Lady Mary Clive.*

53 Castle Drogo, Devon, designed by Sir Edwin Lutyens for Julius Drew, co-founder of the Home and Colonial Stores, was completed in 1930 – as John, on *The Architectural Review*, would have been aware.

54 Maurice Bowra to Pierce Synnott, August 1931. *Pierce Synnott papers.*

55 See Penelope Chetwode, 'Recollections', in *Evelyn Waugh and His World*, ed. David Pryce-Jones, Weidenfeld & Nicolson, London 1973, pp.98–99.

56 'Six weeks before I had barely heard Ras Tafari's name,' Waugh wrote in *Remote People* (Duckworth, London 1931). 'I was in Ireland, staying in a house where chinoiserie and Victorian Gothic contend for mastery over a Georgian structure. We were in the library discussing over an atlas a journey I proposed to make to China and Japan. We began talking of other journeys, and so of Abyssinia . . . A fortnight later I was back in London and had booked my passage to Djibouti.'

57 The manuscript of JB's 'novel' is now in the possession of Lady Mary Clive.

58 JB, manuscript novel.

59 *Ibid.*

60 Christine Longford, unpublished memoirs.

Chapter 16: Later Influences

1 Machen was born (in 1863) in Caerleon-on-Usk in Gwent. Of the three large houses there, one, Lansoar, was owned by a man descended in the female line from the Meyricks. He told Machen: 'The Meyricks always get white with love or hate.' (Arthur Machen, *Autobiography*, The Richards Press, London 1951, p.25.)

2 Arthur Machen, *The Secret Glory*, Martin Secker, London 1922, p.2.

3 *Ibid*, p.6.

4 *Ibid*, p.117.

5 *Isis*, 27 October 1926.

6 *AR*, vol. 67, May 1930, p.236.

7 JB and John Gay, *London's Historic Railway Stations*, John Murray, London 1972, p.15.

8 Machen repeats the Wilde story in his *Autobiography* (The Richards Press, London 1951, p.205). JB introduced the journalist and author Anthony Lejeune to Machen, and Lejeune gives his reminiscences of Machen in *Arthur Machen: a*

Miscellany, ed. Father Brocard Sewell, St Albert's Press, Llandeilo, 1960, pp.33–38.

9 John Fowles, foreword to Piers Brendon's *Hawker of Morwenstowe*, Jonathan Cape, London 1975, p.16.

10 A brief extract from the talk was published in *The Listener*, 23 February 1939.

11 JB, 'Verses Turned in aid of a Public Subscription (1952) towards the restoration of the Church of St Katherine, Chiselhampton, Oxon'.

12 William Morris, *Pre-Raphaelite Ballads*, A. Wessels Co., New York City 1900, verse 11.

13 JB, 'The Licorice Fields at Pontefract.'

14 See, for example, his 'The Ballad of Hampstead Heath' and his 'The Ballad of Camden Town'.

15 Lord David Cecil, *Library Looking Glass*, Constable, London 1975, p.135.

16 In 1946 Geoffrey Grigson, who was preparing a radio talk on Falkner, wrote to JB that Falkner's sister-in-law was sending him (Grigson) Falkner's privately-printed poems. *Victoria.*

17 *The Spectator*, 1 June 1956.

18 See Neville Braybrooke to JB, 9 June 1956. *Victoria.*

19 C.C. Lynam to JB, 6 April 1937. *Victoria.*

20 See Chapter 17.

21 See *Brian Howard: Portrait of a Failure*, ed. Marie-Jaqueline Lancaster, Anthony Blond, London 1968, p.140.

22 Lord Moyne (Bryan Guinness), interview, 1979.

23 JB, 'All Saints, Margaret Street' (typescript). *Victoria.*

24 P. Morton Shand, *The Architecture of Pleasure: Modern Theatres and Cinemas*, B.T. Batsford, London 1930, p.1.

25 David Atwell, *Cathedrals of the Movies*, The Architectural Press, London 1980, p.51.

26 JB, obituary of P. Morton Shand, *AR*, no. 128, November 1960, p.327.

27 Geoffrey Dennis, *Mary Lee*, William Heinemann, London 1922, p.43.

28 Edward Marsh (1872–1953), friend and biographer of Rupert Brooke and editor of a series of anthologies of Georgian Poetry.

29 T.S. Eliot (1888–1965), poet.

30 Robert Nichols (1893–1944), writer and editor.

31 Siegfried Sassoon (1886–1967), poet and prose writer.

32 (Sir) Herbert Read (1893–1984), poet and critic.

33 Harold Monro (1879–1932), a Georgian poet who ran the Poetry Bookshop in Bloomsbury.

34 It was not a new predicament for English poets. At the beginning of Sonnet 76, Shakespeare responded to taunts about his stylistic conservatism amid the changing verse techniques of the 1590s:

> Why is my verse so barren of new pride,
> So far from variation or quick change?
> Why with the time do I not glance aside
> To new-found methods and to compounds strange?

35 G.M. Young, *Daylight and Champaign*, Jonathan Cape, London 1937, p.202.

36 Quoted by Alfred Noyes, *Some Aspects of Modern Poetry*, Hodder & Stoughton, London 1934, p.267.

37 The Georgian poets were defined by publication of their works in a series of anthologies edited by Edward Marsh, beginning with *Georgian Poetry 1911–12*.

38 Herbert Palmer drew attention to the large number of 'Georgian' poems about the moon or moonlight, in *Post-Victorian Poetry*, Dent, London 1938, pp.184–96.

39 Richard Aldington, 'Soliloquy-1', in *Images of War*, Beaumont Press, London 1919.
40 JB, 'The Old Land Dog', *UP*, p.54.
41 On Edith Olivier, writer and *saloniste*, see Hugo Vickers, *Cecil Beaton*, Weidenfeld & Nicolson, London 1985, p.96. She was one of the ten children of the Rector of Wilton, Wiltshire, and a first cousin of Laurence Olivier's father. She lived in the Daye House, the former dairy house of the Wilton estate.
42 Newbolt's anthology was in fact entitled *New Paths on Helicon* (Nelson & Sons, London 1927).
43 JB to Patric Dickinson, 19 September 1969. *Victoria*.
44 JB, foreword to *Selected Poems of John Masefield*, Heinemann, London 1978, p.vii.
45 *Loc. cit.* The actual line (which begins Masefield's 'Posted as Missing') is 'Under all her topsails she trembled like a stag'.
46 'I think of Edward Thomas's lovely poem on Adelstrop, a station in the Cotswolds.' JB, *The Listener*, 28 March 1940.
47 See, for example, Blunden's letters to JB dated 24 May 1939 and 20 September 1964. *Victoria*.
48 Stephen Spender, 'Homage to Mr Wolfe', *Cherwell*, 19 November 1927, p.160.
49 See Sean F. Day-Lewis, *C. Day-Lewis: An English Literary Life*, Weidenfeld & Nicolson, London 1980, p.38. But W.H. Auden, in his 'Verse-letter to C. Day-Lewis' (quoted on p.310 of the same biography) wrote:

> While Wolfe, the typists' poet, made us sick
> Whose thoughts are dapper and whose lines are slick.

50 See Geoffrey Grigson, 'Coming to London – VII', *The London Magazine*, June 1956, vol. 3, no. 6, p.43.
51 JB to Mrs Humbert Wolfe, 7 January 1940. *Victoria*.
52 'Bredon Hill', XXVII, *A Shropshire Lad*, in *Collected Poems of A.E. Housman*, Jonathan Cape, London 1939, p.32.
53 For example, Housman ('The Merry Guide', *A Shropshire Lad*):

> Once in the wind of morning
> I ranged the thymy wold;
> The world-wide air was azure
> And all the brooks ran gold.

Betjeman ('A Lincolnshire Church'):

> Greyly tremulous the thunder
> Hung over the width of the wold
> But here the green marsh was alight
> In a huge cloud cavern of gold.

54 Herbert Palmer, *Post-Victorian Poetry*, Dent, London 1938, p.94.
55 Harold Monro, Sonnet IX of 'Weekend', *Collected Poems*, Cobden-Sanderson, London 1933.
56 Herbert Palmer, *op. cit.*, p.364.
57 Douglas Goldring, 'Malise-Robes', from *In The Town: A Book of London Verses*, Selwyn & Blount, London 1921, p.70.
58 Douglas Goldring, 'Mrs Murgatroyd Martin', from *Streets and Other Verses*, Selwyn & Blount, London 1916, p.49.
59 Douglas Goldring to JB, 8 June 1941. *Victoria*.
60 F.O. Mann, 'The Gas Collector', in *St James's Park and Other Poems*, Hogarth Press, London 1930, p.64.

61 F.O. Mann, 'The Habitué', *ibid*, p.55.
62 F.O. Mann, 'The Typist', in *London and Suburban*, G. Bell & Sons, London 1925, p.56.
63 F.O. Mann, 'The Comedian', in *St James's Park and Other Poems*, Hogarth Press, London 1930, p.65.
64 JB, 'Interior Decorator', *UP*, p.19.
65 Quoted, W.H. Gardner, Introduction to the Fourth Edition, *The Poems of Gerard Manley Hopkins*, ed. W.H. Gardner and N.H. MacKenzie, Oxford University Press 1967, p.xxxviii.

Chapter 17: Steps to Mount Zion

1 The chapter heading has been chosen in pastiche of *Gradus ad Parnassum*, but the chapter takes JB's literary progress somewhat beyond the publication of *Mount Zion* in 1931, to the appearance of *Ghastly Good Taste* in 1933. In fact, it covers his published work up to 31 December 1933, except for his contributions to school and university magazines, which are mentioned in the relevant chapters; his work for *The Architectural Review*, to which Chapter 13 is devoted; his contributions to *The Listener*, with which I shall deal in Volume II in a chapter on John's radio and television broadcasting; and his article 'Peers without Tears' (*Evening Standard*, 19 December 1933) which will also be treated in Volume II.
2 Alan Pryce-Jones gives an account of Squire, and of what it was like to work for him, in *The Bonus of Laughter*, Hamish Hamilton, London 1987, pp.53–58.
3 Patrick Howarth, *Squire: Most Generous of Men*, Hutchinson, London 1963, p.231.
4 Geoffrey Grigson, 'Coming to London – VII', *The London Magazine*, June 1956, vol. 3, no. 6, p.44.
5 JB to John Jensen, nd but in reply to Jensen's letter of 3 September 1975. *JBP*.
6 Howarth, *op. cit.*, p.218.
7 Quoted *ibid*, p.123.
8 See JB's remarks about Squire's poetry in his preface to *Collected Poems by J.C. Squire*, Macmillan, London 1959, p.viii. The poet Roy Campbell was less charitable about Squire's poems in *The Georgiad*, Boriswood Ltd., London 1931, p.22.
9 On 19 January 1958 the artist's daughter, Mia Griggs, wrote to JB to say how pleased she was by his reference to her father in connexion with Barnsley, Gimson and Morris. JB replied, on 22 January: 'I have long admired the beautiful drawings done by your father . . . I once met him at the Temple Bar Restaurant with Jack Squire.' (Both letters in *Victoria*.)
10 See, for example, JB's review (*Week-end Review*, 30 September 1930) of Dudley Harbron's *Amphion – or the Nineteenth Century*.
11 See Dudley Carew, *The House is Gone: A Personal Retrospect*, Robert Hale, London 1949, p.205.
12 Ernest William Barnes (1874–1953), Bishop of Birmingham, attacked the doctrine of Real Presence and belief in miracles. Many churchmen regarded him as an atheist.
13 William Ralph Inge (1860–1954), Dean of St Paul's. He became known as 'the gloomy Dean' for his weekly jeremiads in the *Evening Standard*, 1921–46.
14 Robert Nichols, *Fisbo*, William Heinemann, London 1934, p.26.
15 Introduction to *GGT*, 1970 edn., p.xxvii.
16 JB, 'Lord Mount Prospect', *The London Mercury*, vol. xxi, no. 122, December 1929, p.115.

17 It is clear that JB's 'Ember Day Bryanites' were based partly on the Muggletonian sect, followers of Lodowicke Muggleton (1609–98) and of John Reeve (1608–51), a journeyman tailor. The members of the sect, which existed until c.1865, believed that their two founders, Muggleton and Reeve, were the 'two witnesses' spoken of in Revelation, xi, 3. (DNB and Brewer's *Dictionary of Phrase and Fable*, revised Ivor H. Evans, 1981 edn., p.762.) The hymn of the Old sect of the Muggletonians began:

> I do believe in God alone
> Likewise in Reeve and Muggleton.
> This is the God which we believe;
> None salvation-knowledge hath
> But those of Muggleton and Reeve ...
>> (*Verse and Worse*, ed. Arnold Silcock, Faber & Faber, London 1973 edn., p.252.)

JB mentions Muggleton and a 'Muggletonian blacksmith' in *GGT*, 1970 edn., pp.2 and 4 respectively.

18 JB, 'Lord Mount Prospect', *The London Mercury*, vol. xxi, no. 122, December 1929, p.114.

19 *Warner Brothers Archives, Burbank, California.*

20 *Ibid.*

21 *The London Mercury*, vol. xxviii, no. 163, May 1933, p.85.

22 *Loc. cit.*

23 J.M. Bertram to JB, 1 May 1933. *Victoria.*

24 JB, 'Lunch at the Stores', *The London Mercury*, vol. xxviii, no. 166, August 1933, p.344.

25 The Kittiwakes turn up again in JB's early poem 'Camberley', though rehoused in 'Coolgrena'.

26 JB and his friends teased Frederick Etchells by calling him 'Etchell', after he had been irritated at receiving a letter in which he was so addressed.

27 JB, 'Lunch at the Stores', *The London Mercury*, vol. xxviii, no. 166, August 1933, p.347.

28 JB, 'Architecture', *The London Mercury*, vol. xxix, no. 169, November 1933, pp.65–66.

29 Patrick Balfour to Lady Kinross, 3 January 1930. *National Library of Scotland.*

30 Gwendolen Plunket Greene. She was a daughter of Sir Hubert Parry, the musician, whose wife, Lady Maud Parry, was the sister-in-law of Baron von Hügel. The Baron died in 1925 and Gwen Greene edited his letters to her for publication in 1928.

31 'A Man of Promise', *Daily Sketch*, 2 May 1929. On the title page of the holograph manuscript of *Mount Zion*, which is preserved among Edward James's papers, JB first wrote the word 'CHAPEL' and then crossed it out before writing 'MOUNT ZION'. (*Edward James Foundation.*)

32 Trine's book was very popular during the early years of the twentieth century. In an article in the Fall, 1901 issue of *Metropolitan Magazine* (New York), the American interior decorator Elsie de Wolfe (later Lady Mendl) wrote: 'I hope I shall not be considered pedantic if I confess that no book has helped me more personally than Ralph Waldo Trine's *In Tune with the Infinite*. I am sure I must have given away at least fifty copies, for I am always finding people who need it.' (Quoted, Jane S. Smith, *Elsie de Wolfe*, Atheneum, New York 1982, pp.82–83.)

33 The manuscript is among Edward James's papers. *Edward James Foundation.*

34 Edward James to JB, 11 May 1933. *Victoria.*

35 *Ibid.*

36 *Ibid.*
37 Camilla Russell to JB, 10 September 1931. *Victoria.*
38 JB to Camilla Russell, 29 September 1931. *Victoria.*
39 JB to Camilla Russell, 2 October 1931. *Victoria.*
40 Ernest Betjemann to JB, 15 November 1931. *JBP.*
41 Edward James to JB, 18 December 1936. *Victoria.*
42 JB to Thomas Driberg, 10 November 1931. *Driberg papers, Christ Church, Oxford.*
43 'The Talk of London', *Daily Express*, 12 November 1931, p.11.
44 *AR*, vol. LXX, December 1931, p.184.
45 *The London Mercury*, vol. xxv, no. 146, December 1931, pp.202–3.
46 Amanda M'Kittrick Ros, 1861–1939, novelist renowned for the absurd inflation of her style. Her visiting-card was printed: 'Mrs Amanda M. Ros, Authoress. At Home always to the honourable.'
47 Cornelius Whur, author of *Village Musings on moral and religious subjects by a Villager* (1837) and *Gratitude's Offering* (1845).
48 *New Statesman*, 5 December 1931, p.726.
49 Quoted, Evelyn Waugh to Patrick Balfour, 3 December 1931. *Huntington.*
50 Geoffrey Grigson, *Recollections Mainly of Artists and Writers*, The Hogarth Press, London 1984, p.7.
51 *Loc. cit.*
52 Grigson, *op. cit.*, pp.7 and 169.
53 *Ibid*, p.169.
54 Derek Hudson, letter to the author, 27 August 1984.
55 The poem, 'The Wykehamist at Home', appeared in *Continual Dew*, John Murray, London 1937, p.21.
56 *The Week*, the left-wing, anti-Nazi paper edited by Claud Cockburn, who wrote to JB in May 1933. (See letter in *Victoria.*)
57 JB to Randolph Churchill, 4 May 1933. (In the 1960s Churchill sent JB a copy of this letter for his records. *JBP.*)
58 *Oxford and Cambridge*, June 1933, pp.194–95.
59 *Ibid*, November 1933, p.222.
60 JB, 'Town Planning – or Jerry Building', *Scottish Country Life*, vol. xxii, no. 10, October 1933.
61 JB, 'Travelling on Paper', *Daily Herald*, 18 October 1933.
62 *Ibid.*
63 According to the introduction to *GGT*, 1970 edn., p.xiii.
64 Arthur Waugh's suggestions were passed on to JB in a letter of 26 April 1933 from John Bale of Chapman & Hall. *Victoria.* JB wrote a poem attacking Blomfield ('1930 Commercial Style') which was published in *The Times*, 14 December 1932. It is reprinted in *UP*, p.44.
65 Arthur Waugh to JB, 29 April 1933. *Victoria.* By 31 December 1933, Chapman & Hall had sold 1,145 copies of *Ghastly Good Taste* at 5s. a copy. JB received a 12 per cent royalty. (Chapman & Hall statement to JB. *Victoria.*)
66 Introduction to *GGT*, 1970 edn., p.xiii.
67 *Loc. cit.*
68 Peter Fleetwood-Hesketh, interview, 1976. The quotation is from JB's poem 'The Manor House, Hale, near Liverpool'.
69 Peter Fleetwood-Hesketh, interview, 1976.
70 A year older than JB, Fleetwood-Hesketh had grown up at Stocken Hall, Rutland, on an estate of 3,000 acres. His father's friends included the Duke of Rutland at nearby Beauvoir Castle, 'but what we knew much better was Grimsthorpe, by

Vanbrugh, as we were friends of the Ancasters, the family of Lord Willoughby de Eresby.' (Peter Fleetwood-Hesketh, interview, 1976.)

71 *Ibid.*

72 The cutting from a review signed 'Ribax' is in the *Victoria* collection. It has not been possible to establish in what magazine or newspaper the review appeared.

73 *Country Life*, vol. lxxiv, no. 1903, 8 July 1933, p.21.

74 *Daily Mirror*, 17 July 1933.

75 Frederick Etchells, 'Architecture and the Average Man', *The Listener*, 30 August 1933, p.316.

76 Robert Byron, 'Architectural Revue', *Week-end Review*, 15 July 1933, p.66.

77 *Times Literary Supplement*, 7 September 1933.

78 Osbert Burdett, 'Christendom to Capital', *AR*, vol. lxxiv, no. 443, October 1933, p.142.

79 Osbert Burdett, 'Belles-Lettres', *The London Mercury*, vol. xxviii, no. 167, September 1933, p.467.

Chapter 18: Marriage

1 Professor J.E. Bowle, interview, 1976.

2 A.W. Kinglake, *Eothen*, Blackwood, London 1896 edn., pp.122–23.

3 *Ex inf.* John Piper, 1983.

4 Quoted by Lady Rachel Billington, conversation with the author, 1987.

5 Mary Pakenham (later Clive), *Brought Up and Brought Out*, Cobden-Sanderson, London 1938, p.174.

6 Quoted by PB, interview, 1977.

7 The book was privately printed for Sir George Chetwode, Bart., by Mitchell & Hughes, printers, London.

8 'Uhlans'; the Preussisches Ulanen Regiment, a crack cavalry regiment.

9 *The Times*, 5 September 1914.

10 Daphne Fielding, *Mercury Presides*, Eyre & Spottiswoode, London 1954, pp.53–54.

11 Joyce Grenfell, conversation with the author, 1978.

12 The caricature is reproduced in Bevis Hillier, *John Betjeman: A Life in Pictures*, John Murray, London 1984, p.106.

13 Lady Mary Pakenham to Lady Violet Pakenham, 8 February 1933.

14 Lady Mary Pakenham to Lady Violet Pakenham, 15 February 1933.

15 Lady Mary Pakenham to Lady Violet Pakenham, 1 March 1933.

16 Lady Mary Pakenham to Lady Violet Pakenham, dated 'Middle of March, 1933'.

17 PB, interview, 1977.

18 *Ibid.*

19 *Ibid.*

20 Elizabeth, Countess of Longford, interview, 1976.

21 PC to JB, nd but early 1933. *PBP.*

22 J.M. Richards, *Memoirs of an Unjust Fella*, Weidenfeld & Nicolson, London 1980, p.91.

23 PB, interview, 1977.

24 Quoted by C.M. Bowra, *Memories 1898–1939*, Weidenfeld & Nicolson, London 1966, p.169.

25 Sir Osbert Lancaster, interview, 1976. Alan Pryce-Jones gives a slightly different

version of this story in *The Bonus of Laughter*, Hamish Hamilton, London 1986, p.231.

26 Sir Osbert Lancaster, interview, 1976.
27 PB, interview, 1977.
28 Mary Sheridan de Renéville to Patrick Balfour, 15 October 1932. *Huntington*.
29 Mary Sheridan de Renéville to Patrick Balfour, 2 November 1932. *Huntington*.
30 Frederick Etchells to Patrick Balfour, 4 February 1933. *Huntington*.
31 Frederick Etchells to Patrick Balfour, nd but probably 1933. *Huntington*.
32 JB, 'The Olympic Girl'.
33 PB thought that JB had given her this nickname from the River Plym, which separates Cornwall from Devon and flows into Plymouth Sound, but she could not remember why. (Interview, 1977.)
34 John Guest, conversation with the author, 1977. John Guest edited *The Best of Betjeman*, published by John Murray in association with Penguin Books, Harmondsworth 1978.
35 JB, 'The Licorice Fields at Pontefract'.
36 JB was asked to make this broadcast by Miss Sunday Wilshin of the BBC's 'London Calling Asia' service (letter of 24 March 1954, *Victoria*). A copy of his script is also in *Victoria*.
37 PB, interview, 1983.
38 Quoted by Susan Barnes (Crosland), ' "Betjeman, I bet your racket brings you in a pretty packet" ', *Sunday Times Magazine*, 30 January 1972.
39 PB, interview, 1977.
40 PC to JB, 2 April 1933. *PBP*.
41 *Ibid.*
42 Field-Marshal Sir Philip Chetwode to PC, 6 May 1933. *PBP*.
43 Field-Marshal Sir Philip Chetwode to PC, 14 May 1933. *PBP*.
44 Field-Marshal Sir Philip Chetwode to JB, 8 June 1933. *PBP*.
45 PB, interview, 1977.
46 PC to JB, 14 June 1933. *PBP*.
47 Ernest Betjemann to JB, 14 June 1933. *Victoria*.
48 Bryan Guinness to PC, 18 June 1933. *PBP*.
49 James Ede, art historian, author of *Savage Messiah* (Heinemann, London 1931), and his wife Helen.
50 PC to JB, 18 June 1933. *PBP*.
51 PC to JB, June 1933. *PBP*.
52 PC to JB, 25 June 1933. *PBP*.
53 Honor Guinness; Beryl Quilter.
54 Quoted by PC in a letter to JB, nd but June 1933. *PBP*.
55 *Ibid.*
56 Quoted by PB, interview, 1977.
57 *Ibid.*
58 PC to JB, 6 July 1933 (1). *PBP*.
59 *Ibid.*
60 PC to JB, 6 July 1933 (2). *PBP*.
61 PC to JB, 25 June 1933. *PBP*.
62 PC to JB, 8 July 1933. *PBP*.
63 P. Morton Shand to PC, 5 July 1933. *PBP*.
64 P. Morton Shand to PC, 12 July 1933. *PBP*.
65 *Ibid.*
66 PB, interview, 1977.
67 Presumably Evelyn Waugh, who had first met Penelope at Pakenham Hall in 1932

and always liked her. The character of Cordelia in *Brideshead Revisited* is thought to have been partly based on her. Waugh drew on her qualities more extensively in his novel *Helena* (1950), which he dedicated to her.

68 PC to JB, 17 July 1933. *PBP.*

69 For JB's views on the Great Eastern Hotel, see JB and John Gay, *London's Historic Railway Stations*, John Murray, London 1972, pp.32–33.

70 JB thus described the Edmonton wedding in a letter to Frances, Lady Fergusson of Kilkerran, 22 October [?1980]. *Lady Fergusson.*

71 'Michael [Dugdale] and I [in the 1930s] were all for that undiscovered female, Modern Architecture, and thought she must be German and an art historian. We did not realize then, as I do now, that Michael's uncle [*sic*] and his partner Thackeray Turner were very good.' (JB to Frances, Lady Fergusson of Kilkerran, nd but *c.* 1980. *Lady Fergusson.*) In his letter to Lady Fergusson of 22 October [?1980], JB wrote: 'We were not allowed to think your grandfather Eustace good in the solemn twenties and thirties. We were allowed to admire Thackeray Turner because he was Arts and Crafts; but Eustace Balfour was Scottish Aristocratic: like Michael Arthur Stratford [Dugdale] he will be back in fame and favour in 20 years.' *Lady Fergusson.*

72 JB described this period of his life in Chapter III of *GGT* (pp.22–23), in which he called St Anselm's 'St Agatha's': 'I am pleasantly awoken every morning in London by the sound of a church bell at eight o'clock. It sounds above the early lorries and rides triumphant over the roaring engines being warmed up in the garage of the street behind me, before the chauffeurs depart to fetch their precious masters to the office. And every morning as this bell rings, one elderly sexton, two old ladies and a pale youth attend the daily communion – or mass, as it is called among Anglo-Catholics – in St Agatha's . . . That early morning bell is symbolic of the lost age of faith; the symbolism becomes even more pathetic when, twenty minutes after the eight o'clock bell, six strokes on the sanctus tell the people cleaning the gramophone shop and the men at the 'Lex Garage' opposite that the Son of Man died to save the world, and has died again just across the road today.'

73 PB, interview, 1977.

74 PB to JB, August 1933. *PBP.*

75 PB to JB, 18 August 1933. *PBP.*

76 PB to JB, 24 August 1933. *PBP.*

77 PB to JB, August 1933. *PBP.*

78 PB to JB, August 1933. *PBP.*

79 PB to JB, nd but August 1933. *PBP.*

80 Sir Jasper Hollom said: 'Heddon Court was sufficiently open to London suburban development to be worth far too much as building land to be used as a school's playing fields. It made no conceivable economic sense.' (Interview, 1981.) Vera Moule had the impression that Hope moved out because of the new Cockfosters Underground station. 'It was a boarding school. And if there was an Underground station there, people would want their boys to be day boys. And you don't get enough profits out of day boys!' (Interview, 1981.)

81 For JB's use of the name Old Warden, see *GGT*, 1970 edn., p.51.

82 Ann Wolff, letter to the author, 6 February 1985.

83 PB, interview, 1977.

84 *Ibid.*

85 Mrs Elizabeth Thesiger, conversation with the author, 1978.

86 *Daily Telegraph*, 27 September 1933.

87 Ogilvie-Grant gave this quotation from Nancy Mitford's letter in a letter to JB dated 25 February 1961. *Victoria.*

88 PB, interview, 1977.
89 *Ibid.*
90 JB, *The Life and Miracles of Beata Mrs Δοογγ*, 1933. *PBP.*
91 PB, interview, 1977.
92 Sir Osbert Lancaster, interview, 1977.
93 C.M. Bowra, *Memories 1898–1939*, Weidenfeld & Nicolson, London 1966, p.170.
94 *Loc. cit.*
95 *Loc. cit.*
96 Field-Marshal Sir Philip Chetwode to PB, 6 October 1933. *PBP.*
97 Field-Marshal Sir Philip Chetwode to PB, 20 November 1933. *PBP.*
98 Lady Chetwode to PB, 9 December 1933. *PBP.*
99 Field-Marshal Sir Philip Chetwode to JB, 10 December 1933. *PBP.*
100 Field-Marshal Sir Philip Chetwode to PB, 17 December 1933. *PBP.*
101 The Earl of Longford, interview, 1979.
102 Christopher Sykes, interview, 1978.
103 See Chapter 2, 'Highgate', note 64.
104 Quoted by Susan Barnes, ' "Betjeman, I bet your racket brings you in a pretty packet" ', *Sunday Times Magazine*, 30 January 1972.

INDEX

THE CAESARS
Allan Massie

Allan Massie's self-confessed 'enjoyment of the period and characters' certainly shows in this witty account of the lives of the Caesars. As a novelist he is well set to make the imaginative leaps and connections necessary – because of the limited historical documentation surviving from the ancient world – to get to the heart of these remarkable men.

0 7474 0179 9   NON-FICTION   £3.99

THE LIFE AND DEATH OF MOZART
Michael Levey

'Essential reading for all Mozartians' *The Times*

Mozart's reputation as a composer continues in the ascendant, yet, curiously, our understanding of the man has been clouded: his personality has been seen as irreconcilable with the musical genius. This picture is unsatisfactory and unsatisfying. Michael Levey sees behind that darkened varnish the clear image of a man of immense liveliness and great humanity not at all at odds with the genius we acknowledge in the music. Simply, Michael Levey reveals the real Mozart.

0 7474 0150 0   NON-FICTION   £3.99

THE LAST MEDICI
Harold Acton

'*Doomed ornamental beings, mere occupants of a remarkable museum; exotic fish hidden behind seaweed, stirring languidly in a subaqueous current of history . . .*'

Strange fish, indeed, revealed here in all their decaying glory. Cosimo III, pious and profligate, ever devising new draconian taxes and punishments for the dwindling Florentine population, whilst indulging in conspicuous gluttony, grotesque paintings of double-headed calves, monstrous plants and hideous martyrdoms, and freak shows of human deformity. Cosimo's son and successor, Gian Gastone, permanently drunk, encouraging his servants to steal and sell back to him his own curios, living in his nightshirt for the last thirteen years of his reign . . .

With his enthusiastic appetite for the baroque, Harold Acton chronicles every decadent detail of the late 17th century decline of the great Medici dynasty in this classic account

0 7474 0236 1   NON-FICTION   £4.99

FOUR DUBLINERS
Richard Ellmann

Ellmann's four Dubliners are Wilde, Yeats, Joyce and Beckett, and his slim, rich book comes up with new material on each . . . His gift for uniting critical insight with biography is as freshening, as undogmatic and as humane as ever' John Carey, *Sunday Times*

'In Ellmann's best manner' Frank Kermode, *Guardian*

'A skilful and distinguished book' P N Furbank, *Sunday Telegraph*

'This brief, witty book . . . is a model of literary perception' William Trevor, *Observer*

0 7474 0276 0   NON-FICTION   £3.99

CARDINAL

THE AGE OF REVOLUTION
1789–1848
E J Hobsbawm

'A brilliant account of Europe in its revolutionary age . . . No one could ask for more' AJP Taylor

'A harsh, brilliant, powerful, fascinating book.' Peter Laslett, *Guardian*

0 7474 0290 6   NON-FICTION   £5.99

THE AGE OF CAPITAL
1848–1875
E J Hobsbawm

'This brilliant book sparkles on every page . . . With a power of decision that commands a terrified admiration, he selects basic themes, illustrates them with a wealth of reference. European and global . . . What a book! For heaven's sake, and your own, read it.' *Guardian*

'Will undoubtedly be read and valued as widely as the earlier AGE OF REVOLUTION, and that is high praise indeed' *Times Higher Educational Supplement*

'His two great syntheses on the origins of the society we inhabit – THE AGE OF REVOLUTION (1962) and THE AGE OF CAPITAL (1975) – have become part of the mental furniture of educated Englishmen.' *Observer*

0 7474 0291 4   NON-FICTION   £5.99

THE EAGLE AND THE DOVE
V Sackville-West

A Study in contrasts – St Teresa of Avila, St Thérèse of Lisieux

The lives of these two saints with similar names could hardly be more contrasting. St Teresa, reformer of the Carmelites, 'busy woman and great saint', endured the religious mania of sixteenth-century Spain and lived in a state of near perpetual ecstasy. Thérèse, on the other hand, lived the quiet life of a nun in late-nineteenth-century France, was meek, devout and perhaps rather dim. She became a saint of the common people, largely because of the ordinariness of her life (excepting the odd vision).

The lives of many other saints, and the saintly, wind through the lives of these two great women saints: St Christina the Astonishing, for example, who flew from her coffin during her own requiem mass, St Walburga who emitted a pleasant odour for 1,200 years, or Maria Villani, the nun who sizzled when she drank. Levitation, mysterious appearances of blood, manna and perfumes are all worked into what is seen by many as Victoria Sackville-West's finest work, in her best style.

0 7474 0274 4   NON-FICTION   £4.99

E M FORSTER: A LIFE
P N Furbank

'*It is impossible to overpraise Furbank's style and sympathy as a biographer*'
Listener

'A work of the very first rank. The reasons for its excellence are many'
New Yorker

'Mr Furbank is a masterly biographer. He has done what Forster asked his biographer to do: he has told the truth'
TLS

'[Forster] has received the biography that he and his works deserved, one that is just as decent, civil and humane as its subject'
Times Magazine

0 7474 0277 9   NON-FICTION   £6.99

THE MYSTERY OF WILLIAM SHAKESPEARE
Charlton Ogburn

Could Shakespeare have been the man of Stratford who died in 1616, years after writing his last play, leaving no books, and exciting no tributes from his fellow writers? A man who could barely write his own name, but had twice the vocabulary of Milton; a man who was never referred to as a writer; a mediocre actor, forever in trouble and in debt, whose greatest role was the ghost in his own HAMLET: could this man be Ben Jonson's 'soul of the age'?

Why do we know so little about Shakespeare? Is it because we are looking in the wrong place?

Sigmund Freud wrote, 'The man of Stratford seems to have nothing at all to justify his claims, whereas Oxford has almost everything'.

'Oxford' is Edward de Vere, the seventeenth Earl of Oxford, courtier, patron of the arts, classical scholar, poet, dramatist, sportsman, Italophile and favourite of Elizabeth I. In this brilliant detective story Charlton Ogburn presents the strongest case ever against 'Stratford' and for 'Oxford'. His life time's quest has resulted in a work of enthralling historical reconstruction and imagination.

0 7474 0255 8   NON-FICTION   £7.99

COUNTRY LIFE
Howard Newby

'Howard Newby has achieved what has long been needed, a single and authoritative telling of village England's economic tale over the past two centuries' Ronald Blythe, *Guardian*

Every age has mythologised the countryside. Our jealously guarded 'heritage' is almost entirely mythical.

With humanity and clarity Howard Newby tells the real story of country life: from the enclosure of the old strip farms to create fields and the first capitalist industry in the world, the effects of the ensuing competition and changes in the law, machinery and farming techniques, to the Napoleonic Wars and the Corn Law, the First World War and Lloyd George's budget, the Second World War and the EEC. It spans the various attempts at unionization and rioting, changing aesthetic perceptions of country living in architecture, literature and painting, and changing patterns of population and movement of labour. All are worked into an extremely readable and moving account of the real heritage of our countryside.

0 7474 0286 8   SOCIAL HISTORY   £4.99

MY LIFE
Isadora Duncan

Born in 1878, Isadora Duncan was one of the most famous dancers of modern times. Variously described as 'eccentric', 'mad', and 'a genius', she was one of the most original artistic personalities of this century. Defying convention from the moment she was born – when, as she frequently remarked, 'Venus was in the ascendant' – she was always a reckless, courageous and dedicated exponent of freedom and love. Her dancing was freestyle, improvised and unique. Dressed in a simple white tunic, she danced her way across America and Europe, found fame and (fickle) fortune, and courted love, disaster, and ultimately tragedy.

Her writing, like her life and her 'Art', is an extraordinary mixture of grace, inspiration and exquisite exaggeration. If she is to be believed – and sometimes it is difficult – she had a 'religious and awe-inspiring' effect on men, she 'discovered the dance', and her life was 'more interesting than any novel and more adventurous than any cinema'.

Her death was as flamboyant as her life. In 1927, shortly after completing this book, she was strangled by her flowing scarf, which had become caught in the wheels of the car in which she was travelling. *Isadora: My Life* first appeared the following year, and was promptly banned.

0 7474 0377 5   NON-FICTION   £3.99

GUSTAV MAHLER
Alma Mahler

'I lived his life. I had none of my own. He never noticed this surrender of my existence. He was utterly self-centred by nature, and yet he never thought of himself. His work was all in all.'

Both Alma's devotion to Mahler and her own forceful character shine through her recollections of the ten intense years they shared from 1901 to 1911. Her lively account of these last days of the Hapsburg Empire mixes domestic detail with anecdotes of such figures as Richard Strauss, Debussy, Freud and Schoenberg, personal moments with musical analysis – Alma was herself a gifted musician and helped Mahler considerably with his work when he forbade her own. Combined with a large collection of Gustav's letters and sixteen pages of photographs, her memories contribute much to our understanding of one of the most popular composers of recent years.

Edited by the eminent music scholar Donald Mitchell, who also provides the biographical listing, appendix and chronology.

0 7474 0317 1   NON-FICTION   £6.99

CARDINAL

CASANOVA

John Masters

Giacomo Casanova's reputation rests largely on his obsession with 'the mystery of exactly what was lurking between any particular woman's legs'. But he was much more than the Great 18th century Lover: lawyer, mathematician, poet, translator, librarian and fluent in several languages, he was described by one contemporary as 'the most civilised man in Europe'. That he was also a con-man, cabalist, spy, revenge-taker and experienced prisoner only enhances his appeal as one who personified the extreme social and moral contradictions of the time.

In chronicling the life of this bastard son of Venetian actors, John Masters has drawn on Casanova's own highly expansive memoirs, unavailable until the 1960s.

0 7474 0388 0   NON-FICTION   £3.99

HEMINGWAY

Kenneth S. Lynn

'This brilliant biography . . . Hemingway studies will never be the same again'
Daily Telegraph

'Kenneth S. Lynn's magnificent biography . . . Accomplished, revealing and, all in all, profoundly sympathetic'
Times Literary Supplement

Kenneth S. Lynn reveals a man dogged with the fear that he could not support his own myth. Two contemporaries, both female, already sensed this: Zelda Fitzgerald put it tersely – 'No man could be as male as all that' and Gertrude Stein said 'What a book would be the real story of Hemingway, not those he writes, but the confessions of the real Ernest Hemingway'. This is that book; a detective story which tracks down Hemingway's real debts and obsessions. This brilliant biography may appear to be the case against Hemingway, but Hemingway finally emerges as a genuine hero. As Norman Mailer put it: 'he carried a weight of anxiety with him which would have suffocated any man smaller than himself.'

0 7474 0320 1   NON-FICTION   £7.99

CHAOS

MAKING A NEW SCIENCE

JAMES GLEICK

'An awe-inspiring book. Reading it gave me the sensation that someone had just found the light switch.'
Douglas Adams

'An exceedingly readable introduction to a new intellectual world . . . Attractive and accessible to a lay audience.'
John Naughton *Observer*

'Unlike relativity and quantum mechanics, chaos is a science of everyday things – of art and economics, of biological rhythms and traffic jams, of waterfalls and weather. Curiously, the very familiarity of these phenomena makes the new discoveries more difficult to comprehend and absorb. Almost every one of Mr Gleick's paragraphs contains a jolt, and the urge to reread them is strong. The questions they instil in the reader do not arise from lack of understanding or clarity; rather, they spring from the revolutionary nature of the material – can I believe what I just read? Can this really be true?'
The New York Times

0 7474 0413 5   NON FICTION   £5.99

CARDINAL

WHAT IS REMEMBERED

Alice B. Toklas

WHAT IS REMEMBERED really *is* Alice B Toklas's autobiography, not to be confused with *The Autobiography of Alice B Toklas*, which was written by Gertrude Stein in 1933. At that time Toklas refused to write her autobiography, so Stein did it for her. It was not until 1963, seventeen years after Stein's death, that Toklas was prepared to give her own account of her extraordinary life. The book resounds with names of the famous, and is rich in accounts of celebrated friendships and encounters with such people as Apollinaire, Henri Rousseau, Lytton Strachey, Clive Bell and the Sitwells. Yet its true distinction derives from the dry, humorous, perceptive and ultimately moving voice of Alice B Toklas.

0 7474 0439 9   AUTOBIOGRAPHY   £4.99

Recollections of
VIRGINIA WOOLF
by her contemporaries
Edited by Joan Russell Noble

The 28 contributors to this volume – many of whom are literary legends in themselves – were either friends, relations or contemporaries of Virginia Woolf. T S Eliot, E M Forster, Stephen Spender, Christopher Isherwood, Vita Sackville-West, Rose Macaulay and many others write frankly of their impressions of their friend. Louie Mayer, the Woolf's cook for 30 years, recalls that she talked to herself in the bath and baked perfect bread. Elizabeth Bowen remembers her beauty, Rebecca West remembers that she looked as if she had been dragged through a hedge backwards. E M Forster remembers her curiosity and her honesty, William Plomer her teasing, and John Lehmann speaks of her gnawing uncertainty about the quality of her work.

0 7474 0429 1   NON-FICTION   £4.50

CARDINAL

CHRISTOPHER COLUMBUS
John Stewart Collis

'He has the gift of translating prose into magic'
Arthur Calder-Marshall

Cristobal Colon, otherwise known as Christopher Columbus, refused all his life to believe that he had discovered America. He had the greatest objection to discovering any continent except Asia, and insisted that he had confirmed the world view of the Middle Ages – that there was only one land mass on the earth's surface, with Spain at one end and Asia at the other. A difficult man, Columbus was something of a religious maniac, and crazy for power and wealth. Part of his mission to discover the East was to recover the Holy Sepulchre and to meet the much talked of Grand Khan (who had, in fact, been dead for over 200 years). The man who in 1492 became 'The Very Magnificent Lord Don Cristobal Colon, High Admiral of the Ocean Sea' was brought back to Spain in chains after his third voyage, was in command again for a fourth expedition, and died in disgrace and poverty.

0 7474 0532 8   BIOGRAPHY   £3.99

THE VISION OF GLORY
John Stewart Collis

The Vision of Glory is a unique examination of natural phenomena, of the interconnectedness of things, and a poetic study of the relationship between man and his environment.
'John Stewart Collis' divine gift is to explain the *extraordinary nature of the ordinary*. He has faithfully and gladly pursued a quest which, starting with physics, ends quite naturally with metaphysics'
Sunday Times

'*The Vision of Glory* conveys a quite unsentimental impression of the holiness which man has found in the natural order'
Philip Toynbee, Observer

'He is the poet among modern ecologists, a natural philosopher who, whether he is writing about trees or rainbows, an iceberg or a piece of chalk, never takes a fact without linking it to an idea, or an idea without connecting it to a fact. His book dispenses information in the language of the imagination, and by peeling back the film by which everything appears dully familiar, reveals a vision of the world miraculously transfigured'
Michael Holroyd, The Times

0 7474 0534 4   NON-FICTION   £4.99